gilbert
LAW SUMMARIES

BANKRUPTCY

Fourth Edition

Ned W. Waxman, B.S., J.D.
Professor, Graduate School of Business Administration
College of William and Mary

THE **barbri** GROUP

1999 Supplement in Back of Book

BOARD OF EDITORS

RICHARD J. CONVISER
Professor of Law, IIT/Kent
MICHAEL R. ASIMOW
Professor of Law, U.C.L.A.
JOHN A. BAUMAN
Professor of Law, U.C.L.A.
PAUL D. CARRINGTON
Professor of Law, Duke University
JESSE H. CHOPER
Professor of Law, U.C. Berkeley
GEORGE E. DIX
Professor of Law, University of Texas
JESSE DUKEMINIER
Professor of Law, U.C.L.A.
MELVIN A. EISENBERG
Professor of Law, U.C. Berkeley
WILLIAM A. FLETCHER
Professor of Law, U.C. Berkeley
MARC A. FRANKLIN
Professor of Law, Stanford University
EDWARD C. HALBACH, JR.
Professor of Law, U.C. Berkeley
GEOFFREY C. HAZARD, JR.
Professor of Law, University of Pennsylvania
STANLEY M. JOHANSON
Professor of Law, University of Texas
THOMAS M. JORDE
Professor of Law, U.C. Berkeley
HERMA HILL KAY
Dean and Professor of Law, U.C. Berkeley
JOHN H. McCORD
Professor of Law, University of Illinois
PAUL MARCUS
Professor of Law, College of William and Mary
RICHARD L. MARCUS
Professor of Law, U.C. Hastings
ROBERT H. MNOOKIN
Professor of Law, Harvard University
THOMAS D. MORGAN
Professor of Law, George Washington University
JARRET C. OELTJEN
Professor of Law, Florida State University
JAMES C. OLDHAM
Professor of Law, Georgetown University
ROGER C. PARK
Professor of Law, U.C. Hastings
WILLIAM A. REPPY, JR.
Professor of Law, Duke University
THOMAS D. ROWE, JR.
Professor of Law, Duke University
JON R. WALTZ
Professor of Law, Northwestern University
DOUGLAS J. WHALEY
Professor of Law, Ohio State University
CHARLES H. WHITEBREAD
Professor of Law, U.S.C.
KENNETH H. YORK
Professor of Law, Pepperdine University

HARCOURT BRACE LEGAL AND PROFESSIONAL PUBLICATIONS, INC.
EDITORIAL OFFICES: 111 W. Jackson Blvd., 7th Floor, Chicago, IL 60604

gilbert
LAW SUMMARIES

REGIONAL OFFICES: Chicago, Dallas, Los Angeles, New York, Washington, D.C.
Distributed by: **Harcourt Brace & Company** 6277 Sea Harbor Drive, Orlando, FL 32887 (800)787-8717

PROJECT EDITOR
Steven Levin, B.A., J.D.
Attorney At Law

QUALITY CONTROL EDITOR
Blythe C. Smith, B.A.

Copyright © 1997 by Harcourt Brace Legal and Professional Publications, Inc. All rights reserved. No part of this publication may be reproduced or transmitted in any form or by any means, electronic or mechanical, including photocopy, recording, or any information storage and retrieval system, without permission in writing from the publisher. Printed in the United States of America.

ACKNOWLEDGEMENT

The preparation of this manuscript has been facilitated by the efforts of the following individuals to whom I wish to express my sincere appreciation: Honorable W. Homer Drake, Jr., who has encouraged me to study, teach, and write about the United States Bankruptcy Code; and Grant Stein, William Trencher, Richard H. W. Maloy, and John Howard, whose many hours of consultation have assisted me in clarifying complex and unsettled legal issues.

Ned W. Waxman

gilbert
LAW SUMMARIES

Titles Available

Administrative Law
Agency & Partnership
Antitrust
Bankruptcy
Basic Accounting for Lawyers
Business Law
California Bar Performance
  Test Skills
Civil Procedure
Commercial Paper &
  Payment Law
Community Property
Conflict of Laws
Constitutional Law
Contracts
Corporations
Criminal Law
Criminal Procedure
Dictionary of Legal Terms
Estate & Gift Tax
Evidence

Family Law
Federal Courts
First Year Questions & Answers
Future Interests
Income Tax I (Individual)
Income Tax II (Corporate)
Labor Law
Legal Ethics (Prof. Responsibility)
Legal Research, Writing,
  & Analysis
Multistate Bar Exam
Personal Property
Property
Remedies
Sales & Lease of Goods
Securities Regulation
Secured Transactions
Torts
Trusts
Wills

Also Available:
First Year Program
Pocket Size Law Dictionary
The Eight Secrets Of Top Exam Performance In Law School

All Titles Available at Your Law School Bookstore,
or Call to Order: 1-800-787-8717

Harcourt Brace Legal and Professional Publications, Inc.
176 West Adams, Suite 2100
Chicago, IL 60603

First We Get You Through Law School...

gilbert LAW SUMMARIES

Gilbert Law Summaries —
America's Best Selling Legal Outlines

Legalines

Legalines Case Briefs —
Detailed Briefs of Every Major Case

Law School Legends Audio Tape Series.

Law School Legends
America's Greatest Law Professors On Audio Cassette

Over 4 Million Copies Sold

Call or write for free product catalog:

Gilbert Law Summaries
176 West Adams • Suite 2100 • Chicago, IL 60603 • 1-800-787-8717

...Then We Get You Through The Bar Exam!

barbri **BAR/BRI Bar Review—**
The Country's Leading Bar Review Provider

Over 500,000 Students Have Used BAR/BRI
To Prepare For The Bar Exam During The Past 25+ Years

Call or write for free product catalog:

BAR/BRI Bar Review
176 West Adams • Suite 2100 • Chicago, IL 60603 • 1-800-621-0498

THE barbri GROUP

Our Only Mission Is Test Preparation

Refer to the catalog in the back of this book for a complete title list.

SUMMARY OF CONTENTS

Page

BANKRUPTCY CAPSULE SUMMARY I

TEXT CORRELATION CHART i

APPROACH TO EXAMS .... (i)

I. **INTRODUCTION** 1
   Chapter Approach 1
   A. Goals of the Federal Bankruptcy Laws 1
   B. Legislative History 1
   C. Organization of the Bankruptcy Code 2
   D. Rules of Construction 3
   E. Participants in the Bankruptcy Case 4
   F. Terminology 5

II. **JURISDICTION AND PROCEDURE** 7
   Chapter Approach 7
   A. Bankruptcy Court 7
   B. Personal Jurisdiction 9
   C. Subject Matter Jurisdiction 9
   D. Core/Non-Core Proceedings 11
   E. Jury Trials 13
   F. Withdrawal 14
   G. Abstention 15
   H. Removal 16
   I. Venue 16
   J. Appeals 18

III. **COMMENCEMENT AND ADMINISTRATION OF THE CASE** 22
   Chapter Approach 22
   A. Eligibility 23
   B. Voluntary Case 26
   C. Involuntary Case 28
   D. Case Ancillary to Foreign Proceeding 32
   E. Abstention 33
   F. Section 341 Meeting of Creditors 33
   G. Debtor's Duties 36
   H. Conversion 37
   I. Dismissal 38

IV. **OFFICERS OF THE ESTATE** 40
   Chapter Approach 40
   A. Trustee 40
   B. Examiner 46
   C. Professional Persons 47
   D. Compensation of Officers 50
   E. United States Trustee 53

V. THE BANKRUPTCY ESTATE AND THE TRUSTEE'S AVOIDING POWERS 56
Chapter Approach 56
- A. The Bankruptcy Estate 56
- B. Turnover of Property to Trustee 60
- C. Creditor's Right of Setoff 63
- D. Trustee's Avoidance of Statutory Liens 66
- E. Trustee's Avoiding Powers as Hypothetical Creditor or Purchaser, and as Successor to Certain Actual Creditors 67
- F. Trustee's Power to Avoid Preferences 69
- G. Trustee's Power to Avoid Fraudulent Transfers 77
- H. Post-Petition Transactions 81
- I. Limitations on Trustee's Avoiding Powers 82
- J. Transferee's Liability to Estate for Avoided Transfer 85
- K. Post-Petition Effect of Security Interest 87
- L. Abandonment of Estate Property 88
- M. Sovereign Immunity 89

VI. CLAIMS OF CREDITORS 91
Chapter Approach 91
- A. Filing Proofs of Claims 91
- B. Allowance of Claims 96
- C. Secured Claims 99
- D. Administrative Expenses 102
- E. Priority Claims 104
- F. Tax Claims 109
- G. Subrogation Claims 111
- H. Subordination of Claims 112
- I. Distribution Outside of Bankruptcy Code 113

VII. DEBTOR'S EXEMPTIONS AND DISCHARGE OF INDEBTEDNESS 115
Chapter Approach 115
- A. Exemptions 115
- B. Nondischargeable Debts 127
- C. Effects of Discharge 137
- D. Reaffirmation Agreements 138
- E. Redemption—Chapter 7 Cases Only 140
- F. Protection Against Discrimination 141

VIII. ADMINISTRATIVE POWERS 143
Chapter Approach 143
- A. Adequate Protection 144
- B. Automatic Stay 146
- C. Use, Sale, or Lease of Property 158
- D. Obtaining Credit 163
- E. Executory Contracts and Unexpired Leases 165
- F. Utility Service 176

IX. CHAPTER 7—LIQUIDATION 178
Chapter Approach 178
- A. Introduction 178
- B. Distribution of Property of Estate 180
- C. Treatment of Certain Liens in Chapter 7 Case 182

	D.	Partnership Trustee's Claim Against General Partners	183
	E.	Chapter 7 Discharge	184
	F.	Conversion	187
	G.	Dismissal	187

X.	**CHAPTER 11—REORGANIZATION**	189
	Chapter Approach	189
	A. Eligibility for Relief	189
	B. Administration of Chapter 11 Case	190
	C. Rejection of Collective Bargaining Agreements	199
	D. Chapter 11 Plan	200
	E. Confirmation of Plan	209
	F. Post-Confirmation Matters	215
	G. Small Businesses	218
	H. *Manville*-Type Trust/Injunction	218

XI.	**CHAPTER 13—INDIVIDUAL WITH REGULAR INCOME**	220
	Chapter Approach	220
	A. Eligibility for Relief	220
	B. Co-Debtor Stay	221
	C. Administration of Chapter 13 Case	222
	D. Chapter 13 Plan	226
	E. Confirmation of Plan	230
	F. Payments	232
	G. Post-Confirmation Matters	233

XII.	**CHAPTER 12—FAMILY FARMER WITH REGULAR ANNUAL INCOME**	236
	Chapter Approach	236
	A. Eligibility for Relief	236
	B. Similarities to Chapter 13	238
	C. Differences from Chapter 13	239
	D. Differences from Chapter 11	241
	E. Secured Creditors	242
	F. Unsecured Creditors	243
	G. Conversion or Dismissal	244
	H. Sunset Provision	245

REVIEW QUESTIONS AND ANSWERS ... 247

SAMPLE EXAM QUESTIONS AND ANSWERS ... 267

TABLE OF CITATIONS TO BANKRUPTCY CODE ... 281

TABLE OF CITATIONS TO FEDERAL RULES OF BANKRUPTCY PROCEDURE ... 293

TABLE OF CASES ... 295

INDEX ... 305

gilbert
capsule summary
bankruptcy

Text Section

I. INTRODUCTION

A. GOALS OF THE FEDERAL BANKRUPTCY LAWS
One of the main purposes of bankruptcy is to relieve an honest debtor of debts, thereby providing an opportunity for a *fresh start.* The bankruptcy laws also benefit creditors by (i) providing a forum for either an orderly liquidation of a debtor's estate or a judicially confirmed plan for full or partial repayment of creditors, (ii) protecting unsecured creditors from preferential or fraudulent transfers of the debtor's property, and (iii) requiring adequate protection of secured creditors' interests in collateral under certain circumstances .... [1]

B. RULES OF CONSTRUCTION
1. **"After Notice and a Hearing":** This statutory language requires notice and an opportunity for a hearing. However, the statutory language authorizes an act without an actual hearing if proper notice is given and: (i) no hearing is requested by a party in interest; or (ii) there is insufficient time for a hearing and the court authorizes the act .... [14]
2. **"Order for Relief":** Entry of an order for relief occurs automatically by the filing of a voluntary petition or upon court determination in an involuntary case that the debtor is generally not paying his debts as they become due. Entry of an order for relief merely means that the case can proceed .... [17]

C. TERMINOLOGY
1. **Person:** Individuals, corporations, and partnerships are persons; governmental units are not (with one exception for eligibility of certain governmental units to serve on a Chapter 11 creditors' committee) .... [28]
2. **Entity:** This term includes persons, trusts, estates, governmental units, and the United States trustee .... [29]
3. **Insider:** An insider is defined in terms of whether the debtor is an individual, a corporation, or a partnership, and generally includes the debtor's relatives and persons such as directors, officers, control persons, partners, and relatives thereof .... [30]
4. **Claim:** A claim is a right to payment, even if it is unliquidated, unmatured, disputed, or contingent. It also includes the right to an equitable remedy for breach of performance if the breach gives rise to a right to payment. Congress intended a broad definition of "claim" .... [34]
5. **Debt:** This is a liability on a claim. A consumer debt is one incurred by an individual for a personal, family, or household purpose .... [35]
6. **Insolvent:** An entity is insolvent when its debts total more than the aggregate value of all of its property, excluding property fraudulently transferred and exempt property .... [37]
7. **Transfer:** This is any voluntary *or* involuntary disposition of property or interest therein .... [38]

II. JURISDICTION AND PROCEDURE

Copyright © 1996 Harcourt Brace Legal and Professional Publications, Inc.

Bankruptcy—I

A. BANKRUPTCY COURT

In each federal judicial district, the bankruptcy court constitutes a unit of the respective district court and receives its authority to hear cases and proceedings *by referral* from the district court. Bankruptcy judges are appointed by the U.S. courts of appeals to 14-year terms. To implement provisions of the Bankruptcy Code, bankruptcy judges can issue any necessary or appropriate order, judgment, or process, and are expressly authorized to take sua sponte actions where necessary or appropriate to enforce court orders or prevent an abuse of process. The court also may hold *status conferences* and issue orders to expedite the case .... [39]

1. **Contempt:** Although expressly authorized by Bankruptcy Rule 9020, there is much disagreement as to whether a bankruptcy judge can enter contempt orders. Under this rule, such orders must be *reviewed de novo* by the district court if timely objection is made .... [45]
2. **Sanctions:** A bankruptcy judge may impose sanctions on attorneys and/or litigants who file pleadings or other documents (i) not supported by fact or law or (ii) for an improper purpose .... [48]

B. PERSONAL JURISDICTION

Service of process in a bankruptcy case or proceeding may be had anywhere in the United States by first class prepaid mail (except certified mail generally is required to serve an insured depository institution). Minimum contacts with the forum are *not* necessary .... [50]

C. SUBJECT MATTER JURISDICTION

1. **District Courts:** District courts have *original and exclusive* jurisdiction over all cases under the Code; *original but not exclusive* jurisdiction over all civil proceedings (controversies arising under the Code, or in or related to a bankruptcy case); and *original and exclusive in rem* jurisdiction over all of the debtor's property, wherever located, and over estate property .... [52]
2. **Referral to Bankruptcy Courts:** Almost all cases and proceedings (with the exception of *trials* of personal injury tort and wrongful death claims) have been referred by district courts to the bankruptcy courts. Bankruptcy judges can hear and decide all referred *cases and core proceedings* and can issue final orders and judgments, which are appealable to the appropriate district courts. However, in *non-core matters*, bankruptcy judges may hear the proceedings and then must submit proposed findings of fact and conclusions of law to the district court for final disposition, and if objection is filed, de novo review ...... [56]
    a. **Exception—consent:** If all parties consent, a bankruptcy court may enter *final* orders and judgments in a non-core proceeding .... [60]
3. **Personal Injury Tort and Wrongful Death Claims:** These claims must be tried in the *district court,* not in the bankruptcy court .... [62]

D. CORE/NON-CORE PROCEEDINGS

1. **Core Proceedings:** These include matters regarding administration of the debtor's estate, allowance or disallowance of property exemptions and creditors' claims, counterclaims by the estate against claimants, the automatic stay, fraudulent transfers, preferences, use or sale or lease of estate property, and other matters listed in 28 U.S.C. section 157(b)(2). Core matters also include proceedings affecting liquidation of estate assets or debtor-creditor adjustments (other than personal injury tort or wrongful death claims) .... [63]
2. **Non-Core Proceedings—Majority View:** Also known as related matters, non-core matters include causes of action that the debtor could have brought in state or federal court had there been no bankruptcy case (*e.g.,* pre-petition breaches of contract and collection of pre-petition accounts receivable). Non-core proceedings also include controversies between nondebtor litigants where the

		Text Section
	outcome affects the bankruptcy estate, and the estimation or liquidation of personal injury tort or wrongful death claims for ***purposes of distribution***	[65]
3.	**Bankruptcy Judge Determines Status:** Whether a proceeding is core or non-core is determined by the bankruptcy judge, and the decision is appealable. A matter may not be ruled non-core solely because state law is involved	[71]
4.	**Comment:** Opinions differ substantially as to core and non-core status. However, except for (i) trials of personal injury tort or wrongful death claims, (ii) proceedings withdrawn by the district court, or (iii) proceedings abstained from in favor of resolution in state court, the bankruptcy judge hears both core and non-core proceedings but, absent consent, enters final orders only in core proceedings	[72]

E. JURY TRIALS

The Supreme Court has held that a party is constitutionally entitled to a jury trial of a bankruptcy proceeding if (i) the action would have been brought at law prior to the merger of law and equity courts, (ii) the remedy sought is legal in nature, and (iii) the proceeding involves a private right. Where the right exists, Congress has authorized bankruptcy judges to conduct jury trials if the district court has specially designated this jurisdiction and ***all parties expressly consent.*** A party will lose any right to a jury trial by filing a claim in the case .... [73]

F. WITHDRAWAL

On its own motion or upon timely motion of a party, the district court may for cause withdraw a case or proceeding it had referred to the bankruptcy court. Upon timely motion, the district court ***must*** withdraw the proceeding (under the majority view) if its resolution requires consideration of the Bankruptcy Code ***and*** substantial and material consideration of a federal nonbankruptcy statute "regulating organizations or activities affecting interstate commerce." Although not all authorities agree, the better rule is that district court orders withdrawing a case from the bankruptcy court are not appealable .... [81]

G. ABSTENTION

1. **Permissive Abstention:** The district court may abstain from hearing ***a particular core or non-core proceeding*** if justice, comity, or respect for state law favors resolution in state court .... [86]
2. **Mandatory Abstention:** Upon timely motion, a district court must abstain from hearing a ***non-core*** proceeding if it is based on a state-law cause of action ***related to the bankruptcy case*** (but ***not arising in the bankruptcy case or under the Code***) that: (i) could not have been brought in federal court without bankruptcy jurisdiction; (ii) has already been filed in state court; and (iii) is capable of being timely adjudicated in that forum. However, personal injury tort and wrongful death claim proceedings are not subject to mandatory abstention. [87]
3. **Appeal:** A bankruptcy court's order in favor of or against abstention from hearing a particular proceeding is reviewable by the district court, but an abstention decision by the district court (other than a decision ***not*** to abstain mandatorily) is not reviewable by the court of appeals or the Supreme Court .... [89]

H. REMOVAL

1. **Civil Actions:** If there is proper jurisdiction, a claim or cause of action in a civil proceeding may be removed from a nonbankruptcy court to the appropriate federal district court (and, generally, by automatic reference to the bankruptcy court). *But note:* Tax court proceedings and civil actions by governmental units to enforce police or regulatory powers are ***not*** subject to removal .... [90]
2. **Remand:** After removal, the court, depending on the equities, may remand the action to the forum where it was pending. A bankruptcy court's order to remand or not to remand a removed proceeding is reviewable by the district court, but

		Text Section
	a remand decision by the district court is not reviewable by the court of appeals or the Supreme Court	[92]

I. VENUE
1. **Bankruptcy Case:** Venue for the filing of a bankruptcy petition is in the federal district where the debtor has maintained her *residence, domicile, or principal place of business or assets* in the United States during or for the longest portion of the 180 days immediately prior to filing. Venue also lies where a bankruptcy case concerning a general partner, partnership, or affiliate of the debtor is pending . . . . [94]
2. **Bankruptcy Proceeding:** For bankruptcy proceedings, venue lies in the district where the case is pending . . . . [95]
    a. **Exceptions:** Proceedings by a bankruptcy trustee to recover money or property worth *less than $1,000* or a consumer debt *under $5,000* must be filed where the defendant *resides*. A proceeding by a trustee based on a cause of action arising post-petition from the *operation of the debtor's business* can be filed only where the action could have been filed under applicable nonbankruptcy venue law . . . . [96]
    b. **Post-petition claims against estate:** A proceeding against the trustee based on a claim arising post-petition from the operation of debtor's business may be brought in the district where the case is pending *or* where the action could have been brought under applicable nonbankruptcy venue law . . . . [98]
3. **Venue in District Court:** Venue of cases and proceedings lies in the district court for the appropriate district . . . . [100]
4. **Change of Venue:** A district court may transfer a case or proceeding to another district court for reasons of justice or convenience of the parties. Motions to change venue are treated as core proceedings, thus giving the bankruptcy court the power to order transfers . . . . [101]
    a. **Improper venue:** Where a case or proceeding is filed in a district of improper venue, upon timely objection it may be either *dismissed* or *transferred* to a district where venue is proper, but it cannot be retained . [103]

J. APPEALS
1. **Appeals from Bankruptcy Court:** An appeal can be made from the bankruptcy court to the district court or (with the consent of all parties) to a bankruptcy appellate panel. Appellate jurisdiction of the district court and bankruptcy appellate panels includes appeals from final orders and judgments of the bankruptcy court and optional review of interlocutory orders (except that interlocutory orders reducing or increasing a Chapter II debtor's exclusivity period are appealable as a matter of right). An appeal may not be taken from the bankruptcy court directly to the circuit court, even with the parties' consent . . . . [104]
    a. **Standard:** The district court applies the *clearly erroneous* standard for review of final orders or judgments . . . . [109]
    b. **Interlocutory orders:** The district court has discretion to review interlocutory orders of the bankruptcy court. Some district courts will review such orders only where (i) there is a controlling question of law with substantial ground for variance of opinion, and (ii) an immediate appeal may materially advance the final outcome of the case or proceeding . . . . [110]
    c. **Time for appeal:** A party must file notice of appeal with the clerk of the bankruptcy court within 10 days after entry of the order or judgment . . . . . [111]
2. **Appeal from District Court:** One may appeal to the circuit court from *final* decisions, orders, or judgments of the district court in its appellate capacity or of the bankruptcy appellate panel. Appeals from *interlocutory orders* of the district court in its appellate capacity are governed by the general appellate standard (*see* above). Where the district court functions as a court of original

jurisdiction (*e.g.,* non-core or withdrawn proceedings), final decisions (and interlocutory orders in *exceptional circumstances,* described above) may be appealed to the circuit court under the general appellate standard of 28 U.S.C. sections 1291, 1292. "Finality" is interpreted liberally in bankruptcy law . . . . [112]

3. **Orders Concerning Automatic Stay:** Automatic stay rulings are final and appealable. Note that if relief from the stay is granted but the debtor does not obtain a *stay pending appeal,* the appeal generally becomes moot once a foreclosure sale has occurred . . . . [118]

III. COMMENCEMENT AND ADMINISTRATION OF THE CASE

A. ELIGIBILITY

1. **Person:** Only a person (individual, corporation, or partnership) who resides or has a domicile, place of business, or property in the United States can be a debtor under the Code. (A municipality also may be eligible under Chapter 9.) Insolvency is *not* required, and "corporation" includes business trusts and most companies or associations with corporate attributes, except limited partnerships . . . . [120]

2. **Chapter 7—"Liquidation":** Chapter 7 relief is available to persons meeting the criteria above *except* for: railroads, domestic savings institutions and insurance companies, foreign savings and insurance companies engaged in business in the United States, and certain small business investment companies. Stockbrokers and commodity brokers may be debtors under special provisions of Chapter 7 . . . . [123]

3. **Chapter 11—"Reorganization":** Only individuals, partnerships, and corporations eligible for Chapter 7 relief can be debtors under Chapter 11. However, under Chapter 11, stockbrokers and commodity brokers *cannot* be debtors, but *railroads* are eligible for relief under special provisions . . . . [130]

    a. **Business or consumer debtors:** Designed mainly for business reorganizations, Chapter 11 may also provide relief for consumer debtors. Relief usually entails debtor reorganization by means of a confirmable plan, but provisions also provide for a liquidating plan . . . . [134]

4. **Chapter 13—"Adjustment of Debts of Individuals with Regular Income":** Chapter 13 relief is available only to an *individual* who has regular income from any legitimate source, whose noncontingent, liquidated, unsecured debts total less than $250,000 and whose noncontingent liquidated, secured debts total less than $750,000. An individual with regular income and his spouse may file a joint petition if their *aggregate* unsecured and secured debts are less than the totals above. Stockbrokers and commodity brokers do *not* qualify for Chapter 13 relief. A Chapter 13 case can be commenced only by the debtor's *voluntary* petition . . . . [136]

5. **Chapter 12—"Family Farmer with Regular Annual Income":** Family farmers—including certain individuals (and their spouses), corporations, and partnerships with regular yearly income can file a *voluntary* petition under Chapter 12 . . . . [142]

6. **Ineligibility—Multiple Petitions:** An *individual or family farmer* cannot file a petition under any chapter if he was a debtor in a case dismissed within the *preceding 180 days* because he willfully failed to obey court orders or to appear and properly prosecute the case, *or* because he requested a voluntary dismissal after a party's request for relief from the automatic stay . . . . [143]

B. VOLUNTARY CASE

1. **Filing the Petition:** A voluntary case commences upon an eligible debtor's filing the petition under Chapter 7, 11, 12, or 13. At that time, the filing fee must be paid unless the court has approved installment payments. The clerk of the court must notify an individual with primarily *consumer debts* of the chapters

	Text Section
under which he may file. Commencement of a voluntary case automatically constitutes an ***order for relief***	[144]
a. **Notice:** Notice of the order for relief is sent to all parties in interest	[146]
b. **Joint case:** Spouses can ***voluntarily*** file jointly, thus avoiding another filing fee	[147]
c. **Corporation:** The filing of a voluntary petition must first be approved by the board of directors	[151]
d. **Partnership:** One or more general partners can file a voluntary petition with the ***consent of all*** the general partners. If unanimous consent is not obtained, the petition will be treated as an involuntary one	[152]
2. **Schedules to be Filed:** In addition to the petition, a debtor under Chapter 7, 11, 12, or 13 must timely file a list of creditors and addresses, a schedule of assets and liabilities, a schedule of current income and expenditures, a schedule of executory contracts and unexpired leases, and a statement of debtor's financial affairs. Additional documents are required, depending on the chapter of the particular case	[153]
3. **Automatic Stay:** Once a voluntary or involuntary petition is filed, the automatic stay becomes effective against ***all entities*** to protect the debtor, his property, and the estate property	[160]

C. INVOLUNTARY CASE

1. **Eligibility:** An involuntary petition can be filed only under Chapter 7 or 11 against a qualifying debtor. However, it ***cannot*** be filed against a farmer, family farmer, or nonprofit or charitable organization	[161]
2. **Filing the Petition**	
a. **Petitioning entities:** Involuntary bankruptcy petitions may be filed against a debtor by the following	[162]
(1) **Three or more creditors:** If there are ***at least 12 creditors*** with noncontingent, undisputed claims against the debtor, then three or more entities with at least $10,000 in aggregated ***unsecured***, noncontingent, and undisputed claims can file	[163]
(2) **One or more creditors:** If there are ***fewer than 12 creditors*** with noncontingent, undisputed claims, one or more may file a petition if their aggregated unsecured, noncontingent, and undisputed claims total at least $10,000. After filing, but before the court enters an order for relief or dismisses the case, additional unsecured creditors may be joined to cure a defective filing by one creditor who in ***good faith*** believed there were fewer then 12 creditors; but if the filing was in bad faith, it should be dismissed	[164]
(3) **General partner:** Fewer than all the general partners may file an involuntary petition against the partnership. If relief has been ordered concerning all general partners, an involuntary petition against the partnership may be filed by a general partner, her trustee, or a creditor of the partnership	[166]
(4) **Foreign representative:** A foreign representative (*e.g.,* trustee or administrator) of the bankruptcy estate named in a foreign proceeding concerning the debtor can file an involuntary petition to administer the debtor's property located in the United States	[167]
b. **Indemnity bond:** The court may require petitioners to file a bond to indemnify the debtor for any damages awarded if the petition is dismissed. Notice and a hearing are required, and sufficient cause must be shown	[168]
3. **Answer:** Only the debtor (or a nonpetitioning general partner) can file an answer to an involuntary petition	[169]
4. **Entry of an Order for Relief:** The court will enter an order for relief against the debtor if a timely answer is not filed, or if the court finds that the debtor	

	Text Section

is ***generally not paying undisputed debts as they become due*** or that a custodian was appointed within 120 days before the petition was filed . . . . [170]

5. **Gap Period:** Between the filing of the petition and the entry of an order for relief (the "gap period"), the debtor can remain in possession of his property, continue business operations, and use, acquire, or dispose of assets unless these rights are denied by the court or an interim trustee is appointed . . . . [174]

    a. **Transfers during gap period:** A debtor's transfer during the gap period is not subject to the trustee's avoiding powers to the extent of post-petition value given in exchange by the transferee. The purpose of the transfer must not be to satisfy or secure a pre-petition debt . . . . [175]

    b. **Priority for gap creditors:** Unsecured claims arising in the ordinary course of the debtor's business during the gap period, before the earlier of the appointment of a trustee or the entry of an order for relief, are entitled to ***second priority status*** . . . . [176]

    c. **Interim trustee:** During the gap period, the court may direct the United States trustee to appoint an interim trustee if necessary to preserve estate property. In a Chapter 7 case, the debtor may be permitted to retake possession of his property prior to the order for relief by filing a bond . . . . [177]

6. **Dismissal of Involuntary Petition:** Upon dismissal of an involuntary petition other than on consent of all petitioners and the debtor, the court may award the debtor costs and/or reasonable attorney's fees. If the petition was filed in bad faith, damages proximately caused by the involuntary petition and/or ***punitive*** damages may also be awarded. An involuntary petition may be dismissed only after notice and opportunity for a hearing are given to all creditors . . . . [178]

7. **Schedules to be Filed:** If an order for relief is entered, the debtor must timely file the required lists, schedules, and statements (*see supra*) . . . . [181]

D. ABSTENTION
The court may abstain from hearing ***an entire case*** by dismissing it or suspending all proceedings if: (i) abstention would better serve the interests of the creditors and debtor or (ii) a foreign proceeding is pending and abstention would facilitate an economical and expeditious administration of the estate. Notice and hearing are required. Abstention decisions are reviewable by the district court, but not by the court of appeals or the Supreme Court . . . . [188]

E. SECTION 341 MEETING OF CREDITORS
Shortly after the order for relief (20-40 days under Chapter 7 or 11, 20-35 days under Chapter 12, and 20-50 days under Chapter 13), a meeting of creditors is held. The debtor must personally attend the meeting, and the United States trustee (or an assistant) presides. The United States trustee may also convene a meeting of the debtor's equity security holders if appropriate . . . . [191]

1. **Notice:** The clerk of the court provides by mail at least 20 days' notice to the debtor, the trustee, all secured and unsecured creditors, indenture trustees, taxing authorities, and holders of community claims. If mailed notice is impracticable, notice may be by publication. The notice usually includes notice of the order for relief, the automatic stay, and final dates for filing proofs of claims, complaints to determine dischargeability of certain debts, objections to a Chapter 7 debtor's entire discharge, and objections to debtor's exemptions . . . . [193]

2. **Purpose of Section 341 Meeting:** The primary function is to allow creditors, the trustee (or an examiner), any indenture trustee, or the United States trustee to examine the debtor under oath about issues related to the case . . . . [197]

F. DEBTOR'S DUTIES
In addition to filing the required schedules, etc., the debtor must cooperate with the trustee and relinquish estate property and relevant records, keep her address current, and appear at the discharge hearing (individuals only) if one is held. Also, in a Chapter 7 case, an ***individual debtor with secured consumer debts*** must file a

statement of intention to retain or surrender (and if applicable, to exempt, redeem, or reaffirm debts secured by) collateral and must perform such intention in a timely manner .... [204]

G. CONVERSION
Chapters 7, 11, 12, and 13 provide rules for conversion of a case from one chapter to another chapter under which the debtor is eligible for relief. Note that the debtor must request conversion to Chapter 12 or 13. Conversion operates as an order for relief under the new chapter, but as a general rule does not change the *date* of the filing of the bankruptcy petition, the commencement of the case, or the order for relief. However, there are many exceptions to this rule, where the *date of the order for relief* is deemed to be the date the case was converted. Any claims in a Chapter 11, 12, or 13 case (except administrative expenses) arising after the order for relief but before conversion are considered pre-petition claims for all purposes. Conversion terminates a trustee's or examiner's service. Where a case is converted from Chapter 13 to another chapter, *property of the estate* in the converted case consists of property of the estate *on the date of the Chapter 13 filing* that remains in the debtor's possession or control on the date of conversion. However, if the debtor converts in bad faith, property of the estate consists of the estate property on the date of conversion .... [211]

H. DISMISSAL
Each chapter provides varying rules regarding matters such as who may move for dismissal and when it may or must be granted. Dismissal usually is *without prejudice* (*i.e.,* debtor may file a subsequent petition) unless, for cause, the court orders otherwise. However, dismissal is *with prejudice* to the extent that the debtor is ineligible to file again within 180 days due to Code section 109(g). The court has inherent authority to dismiss a petition not filed in good faith or intended to abuse the opportunity for a fresh start .... [217]

IV. OFFICERS OF THE ESTATE

A. TRUSTEE
The trustee is the official representative of the estate and in this capacity can sue or be sued. The trustee has numerous administrative powers and specific duties, which vary according to the chapter under which he is serving .... [220]

1. **Eligibility:** A *disinterested* individual who is competent or a disinterested corporation authorized by its charter or bylaws may serve as trustee. In Chapter 7, 12, or 13 cases, the trustee must reside or have an office in the judicial district where the case is pending or in the adjacent district. If necessary, the United States trustee for the district may serve in a Chapter 7, 12, or 13 case, but not in a Chapter 11 case .... [221]

    a. **"Disinterested person":** This important term *excludes* the debtor's creditors, equity security holders, insiders, directors, officers, employees, and investment bankers (for securities), and any person with a *materially adverse* interest .... [222]

2. **Qualification:** Within five days after appointment or election, and before beginning service, a trustee must file a bond with the court in an amount set by the United States trustee .... [225]

3. **Selection of Trustee**

    a. **Chapter 7:** All Chapter 7 cases require a trustee chosen from a panel of private trustees maintained by the United States trustee to serve in a particular region. Immediately after entry of the order for relief, the United States trustee appoints a disinterested panel member to serve as the *interim trustee* until the section 341 meeting, at which the interim trustee will become the permanent trustee unless another person is elected ..... [227]

b. **Chapter 11:** Generally, a Chapter 11 debtor remains in possession of estate property and continues to manage the business so that a trustee's appointment is *not necessary.* However for cause *or* in the interest of creditors, equity security holders, and the estate, the court may order the United States trustee to appoint a disinterested person (other than himself), to act as trustee, subject to court approval. If appointment of a trustee is ordered, a party in interest may request an election of the trustee, instead .... [234]

c. **Chapters 13 and 12:** In a region with many Chapter 13 cases, the United States trustee usually appoints a *standing trustee* for all of those cases; otherwise a distinterested person is appointed or the United States trustee himself serves. The same procedure applies to Chapter 12 cases. Under both chapters, the debtor usually retains possession of estate property .. [238]

4. **Duties of Trustee**
   a. **Chapter 7:** The primary duties are to: (i) *locate and take possession* of property; (ii) *convert* the property to cash; (iii) *make distributions* to claimants in the prescribed order; and (iv) expeditiously *close* the estate. A Chapter 7 trustee also has other important statutory duties .... [239]
   b. **Chapter 11:** A trustee who replaces the debtor in possession is usually authorized to *operate the debtor's business* and is charged with certain of the duties of a Chapter 7 trustee, as well as other duties that relate specifically to a Chapter 11 case (*e.g.,* investigating and filing a report on the debtors conduct, financial condition, and business operations and the advisability of continuing the business; filing a Chapter 11 plan; etc.) ..... [242]
   c. **Chapter 13:** A Chapter 13 trustee must perform certain of the duties of a Chapter 7 trustee and must: *testify* at any hearing concerning (i) valuation of liened property, (ii) confirmation of a plan, or (iii) post-confirmation modification of a plan; *furnish nonlegal advice* to the debtor; *ensure that the debtor begins making payments* within 30 days after the plan is filed; *disburse payments* to creditors under a confirmed plan; and (if the debtor is engaged in business), *investigate* the debtor's conduct, financial condition, business operations, and the advisability of continuing the business and file a report of the investigation .... [243]
   d. **Chapter 12:** Duties are similar to those of a Chapter 13 trustee as long as the debtor remains a debtor in possession; if the debtor is removed, the trustee's duties include many of those of a Chapter 11 trustee and operation of the debtor's farm .... [244]

5. **Liability of Trustee:** A trustee, as fiduciary of the estate, may be *personally liable* for breach of duties based on an *intentional or* (in some jurisdictions) *negligent* violation .... [245]

6. **Powers of Trustee:** As the representative of the estate, the trustee is granted many administrative powers, including the power to *file a proof of claim* on behalf of a creditor; *operate the debtor's business* (in a Chapter 11 case and sometimes in Chapter 7 or 12 cases); *deposit or invest money; employ* professional persons; *avoid* certain transfers and liens; *use, sell, or lease property; obtain credit; assume or reject executory contracts or unexpired leases;* demand utility services; abandon property; and waive a debtor corporation's attorney-client privilege .... [247]

7. **Removal of Trustee:** A trustee (other than the United States trustee) or an examiner may be removed by the court *for cause* (*e.g.,* misconduct, incompetence, conflict of interest) .... [248]

B. **EXAMINER**
1. **Role and Capacity:** If appointment of a trustee has not been ordered in a Chapter 11 case, the court sometimes will order the appointment of an examiner to investigate charges of fraud, dishonesty, incompetence, or mismanagement

regarding past or present management of debtor's business. The debtor in possession retains her property and continues to operate the business. A disinterested person other than the United States trustee may serve as examiner .... [251]

2. **Reasons for Appointment:** Upon request by a party in interest or the United States trustee, the court, after notice and hearing, ***must order*** the appointment if the debtor's fixed, liquidated, unsecured debts exceed $5 million (excluding debts for goods, services, taxes, or any debts owed to an insider). Appointment is also ordered if it is in the best interests of creditors, equity security holders, and the estate .... [253]

3. **Duties:** Duties include investigating the debtor's conduct, financial condition, and business operations, as well as the advisability of continuing the business; filing a report of the investigation; and any other trustee responsibilities that the court directs the debtor in possession not to perform. Note that an ***examiner may not serve as a trustee or professional person*** in the same case he has served as examiner .... [254]

C. **PROFESSIONAL PERSONS**
A trustee or a debtor in possession may, with court approval, hire professional persons (*e.g.,* attorneys, accountants) to perform services with respect to the estate. Professional persons must be ***disinterested*** persons with ***no interest adverse*** to the estate. Prior to beginning performance, they ***must be approved by the court;*** otherwise, compensation to the professional may be denied .... [256]

1. **Special Purpose Attorney:** The court may approve the employment by the trustee or debtor in possession of a former attorney of the debtor for a special purpose if the hiring is in the estate's best interest and the lawyer has no adverse interest in the subject matter. The purpose may not be to represent the trustee in administering the case .... [265]

2. **Creditor's Representative:** In Chapters 7, 11, and 12 cases, a professional person is not disqualified from employment by a trustee solely because of her employment by or representation of a creditor, unless there is objection from another creditor or the United States trustee ***and*** the court finds an actual conflict of interest .... [266]

3. **Trustee as Professional Person:** The court may permit a trustee to also serve as an attorney or accountant if it is in the estate's best interest .... [267]

4. **Creditors' Committee May Hire Professional Persons:** In a Chapter 11 case, a creditors' or equity security holders' committee may hire professional persons to serve the committee. While representing or employed by the committee, the professional person may not represent an entity with an ***adverse interest,*** but representing a creditor of the same class as the committee is not adverse per se .... [268]

D. **COMPENSATION OF OFFICERS**
Officers of the estate (trustee; examiner; Chapter 12 or 13 individual debtor's attorney; professionals employed by a trustee, debtor in possession, or creditor's committee) may be awarded ***reasonable fees*** for actual and necessary services and ***reimbursement*** for actual and necessary expenses .... [269]

1. **Reasonable Compensation for Professional Services:** Fee applications must comply with Bankruptcy Rule 2016(a), the procedural guidelines issued by the Executive Office for United States Trustees, and any applicable local rules. The criteria for awarding reasonable compensation (section 330) include: time spent, rates charged, the necessity and benefit to the administration of the case, the reasonableness of the time spent considering the complexity and importance of the work, and comparable fees in nonbankruptcy cases. Any agreed-upon compensation may be ***modified by the court*** because of unanticipated developments. The court may also ***deny compensation*** if at any time during

employment a professional person is *not disinterested* or has an *adverse interest.* Note that fees for a trustee who also serves as a professional are *bifurcated; i.e.,* professional fees do not include trustee compensation, which is accounted for separately .... [272]

2. **Interim Compensation:** A trustee, examiner, debtor's attorney, or other professional may apply for interim compensation or reimbursement of expenses once every 120 days after the order for relief. Any amount awarded must be deducted from an award under section 330 (above) .... [284]

3. **Debtor's Transactions with Attorneys:** The debtor's attorney must file a statement of any fees paid or any fee agreement made within a year prior to bankruptcy for legal services related to the case, and also the source of the payment. The court can cancel unreasonable fee agreements or order return of any portion that is excessive .... [286]

4. **Sharing of Fees Prohibited:** Estate officers cannot share fees or reimbursements with another person *except* (i) where they are members of the same professional firm or (ii) where a creditor's attorney filing an involuntary petition shares her fee with another attorney contributing to her services or expenses . [287]

E. UNITED STATES TRUSTEE

1. **Administrative Duties:** Under supervision of the Attorney General, the United States trustee functions as an administrator of the bankruptcy system in his region and, as such, has various duties; *e.g.,* establishes a panel of private trustees for Chapter 7 cases; appoints interim trustees in Chapter 7 cases, a trustee or an examiner (if the court orders) in Chapter 11 cases, and a standing trustee (or one for the particular case) in Chapter 12 and 13 cases; convenes and presides at section 341 meetings; supervises the administration of bankruptcy cases and trustees; monitors applications for employment of professional persons; and reviews fee applications of trustees, examiners, attorneys, and other professional persons .... [292]

2. **Standing:** The Code grants a United States trustee standing to appear and be heard as to any issue in a bankruptcy case. However, he cannot file a plan in a Chapter 11 case .... [293]

V. THE BANKRUPTCY ESTATE AND THE TRUSTEE'S AVOIDING POWERS

A. THE BANKRUPTCY ESTATE

The bankruptcy estate is created automatically on the filing of a petition and consists of a comprehensive range of rights and property interests, including *all legal and equitable interests* of the debtor at the time the petition is filed (*e.g.,* bank deposits, product liability insurance, compensation rights for *pre-petition* services, causes of action, beneficial interest in corpus of nonspendthrift trust). Also included are community property (subject to certain limitations); property recovered by the trustee; certain property acquired within *six months* after the date of bankruptcy (*e.g.,* by inheritance, life insurance, or property settlement); proceeds, rents, profits, product, or offspring of estate property; and property acquired by the estate after bankruptcy. An individual's post-petition earnings for services rendered *after* filing are excluded from the estate .... [294]

1. **Ipso Facto or "Bankruptcy" Clauses:** Clauses in a contract, deed, or nonbankruptcy law that restrict or condition a debtor's transfer of property or that cause a forfeiture, termination, or modification of the debtor's property interest because of the debtor's insolvency or financial condition, or because of the filing of a bankruptcy case or appointment of a bankruptcy trustee or nonbankruptcy custodian, do not prevent the property from being included in the bankruptcy estate. *Exception:* Debtor's beneficial interest in a traditional spendthrift trust is excluded from the estate if the spendthrift restriction is enforceable under applicable nonbankruptcy law .... [306]

			Text Section
	2.	**Property Excluded from Estate:** The following property is excluded: (i) an individual's post-petition earnings (but not in a Chapter 12 or 13 case); (ii) spendthrift trusts enforceable under nonbankruptcy law and ERISA-qualified pension plans; (iii) a power exercisable by the debtor solely for the benefit of another entity; (iv) a debtor's interest as a *lessee* in an expired lease of nonresidential real estate; (v) certain property of educational institutions; (vi) certain interests transferred under a farmout agreement; (vii) certain gas and oil production payments; and (viii) certain proceeds of money orders	[309]
B.	**TURNOVER OF PROPERTY TO TRUSTEE**		
	1.	**Turnover by Entity Other than Custodian:** Property that may be used, sold, or leased by the trustee or that may be exempted by the debtor must be delivered to the trustee and accounted for by any entity **in possession or control** who is not a custodian. *"Entity"* can include a governmental unit or trust	[317]
		a. **Note:** A *secured creditor* who repossessed property before a bankruptcy petition was filed but who has not yet sold the collateral to a bona fide purchaser must turn over the collateral to the trustee or debtor in possession; however, the secured creditor is entitled to adequate protection of its interest	[319]
	2.	**Payment of indebtedness to Estate:** An entity (such as a bank) owing a matured debt or debt payable on demand or order (and constituting estate property) must pay the amount of the debt less any setoff allowable under Code section 553 to the trustee or to the payee of a check drawn by the trustee	[320]
	3.	**Exceptions to Turnover:** Turnover is not required for property of *inconsequential value* or property (or a debt owing to debtor) that has been *transferred (or paid) in good faith* and without actual notice or knowledge of the bankruptcy. *Note:* The payee or transferee is *not* protected under this provision and may be subject to the trustee's avoiding power	[322]
	4.	**Turnover of Property by Custodian:** A custodian who knows of the bankruptcy cannot disburse or administer any of the debtor's property (or proceeds thereof) or any estate property in her possession, custody, or control. She must turn it over to the trustee and file an accounting	[327]
		a. **"Custodian":** A custodian may be a receiver or nonbankruptcy trustee, an assignee for benefit of the debtor's creditors, or a nonbankruptcy trustee, receiver, or agent authorized to take possession of the debtor's property to enforce a lien or administer the property for creditors' benefit. A custodian is often a public official (*e.g.,* a sheriff)	[328]
		b. **Exceptions to custodian's turnover:** A custodian's turnover duty *may* be excused if in the best interests of the creditors (and, if debtor is solvent, of equity security holders); and it *must* be excused, unless necessary to avoid fraud or injustice, where the custodian is an assignee for benefit of creditors who was appointed or took possession of the property more than 120 days before the bankruptcy petition was filed	[329]
		c. **Compensation or surcharge:** The court may award reasonable compensation to a custodian for services and actual expenses. A custodian may be liable for wrongful or excessive disbursements	[330]
	5.	**Turnover of Books and Records:** Absent assertion of a valid privilege, an attorney or other person may be ordered to turn over to the trustee books records, or documents concerning the debtor's finances or property. Note that the trustee can **waive a corporation's attorney-client privilege** concerning prebankruptcy communications. Also, there is **no accountant-client privilege** under the Code	[331]
C.	**CREDITOR'S RIGHT OF SETOFF** A creditor with a state law setoff right may set off a debt owed to the debtor against his claim against the debtor if both the debt and claim are **mutual** and arose **prior** to bankruptcy		[334]

	Text Section
1. **Exceptions to Right of Setoff:** Setoff is not available for:	[335]
a. ***A disallowed claim;***	
b. ***Claims transferred to the creditor by a nondebtor*** party after the filing of the bankruptcy petition or within 90 days before bankruptcy when the debtor was insolvent. (*Note:* for purposes of the Code section on setoffs, there is a statutory presumption of debtor's insolvency during the 90 days before bankruptcy);	
c. ***Debts created by the creditor for setoff purposes*** within 90 days before bankruptcy when debtor was insolvent;	
d. ***Creditor's improved position due to pre-bankruptcy setoff.*** (*Note:* For this exception, the setoff must have occurred within 90 days before bankruptcy, but debtor's insolvency is *not* required); and	
e. ***Creditor's inequitable or bad faith conduct.***	
2. **Automatic Stay:** The automatic stay enjoins setoff of a pre-petition debt (owed to debtor) against a creditor's claim, thereby requiring the creditor to ***obtain relief from the stay*** before exercising a setoff. (Compare ***recoupment***, which has been held not to be subject to the automatic stay)	[345]
a. **Post-petition freeze of debtor's bank account:** A bank's temporary post-petition administrative freeze of the debtor's bank account (while seeking relief from the stay and a judicial determination of its right to setoff) does not violate the automatic stay but rather protects the bank's setoff rights	[346]
3. **Secured Status of Claim Subject to Setoff:** A claim that may be set off is deemed ***secured*** as to the amount subject to setoff. Thus, a creditor is entitled to ***adequate protection*** unless the court lifts the stay and permits exercise of the setoff	[350]

D. TRUSTEE'S AVOIDANCE OF STATUTORY LIENS

A trustee may avoid certain statutory, nonconsensual liens on the debtor's property: [351]

1. ***Liens arising automatically due to the debtor's financial condition*** (*e.g.*, liens triggered by the filing of a bankruptcy petition or the debtor's insolvency);
2. ***Liens not perfected or enforceable against a bona fide purchaser at the time of bankruptcy*** (*e.g.*, unfiled federal tax lien)—note that the avoiding power is subject to any retroactive perfection permitted under nonbankruptcy law; and
3. ***Liens for rent.***

E. TRUSTEE'S AVOIDING POWERS AS HYPOTHETICAL CREDITOR OR PURCHASER AND AS SUCCESSOR TO CERTAIN ACTUAL CREDITORS

1. **Strong Arm Provision:** When a bankruptcy case is commenced, the trustee has the ***hypothetical*** status and the rights and powers of (i) a judicial lien creditor, (ii) a creditor with an unsatisfied execution, and (iii) a bona fide purchaser of real property. Thus, the trustee can avoid any transfer of debtor's property that any of these entities could avoid ... [357]
2. **Trustee's Avoiding Power Based on Actual Unsecured Creditors:** If at the time of bankruptcy there exists an ***actual,*** unsecured creditor with an allowable claim who has the right under applicable nonbankruptcy law to avoid a transfer of the debtor's property, the trustee can avoid the whole transfer ***for the estate's benefit,*** even if its value exceeds the amount of the creditor's claim ... [363]

F. TRUSTEE'S POWER TO AVOID PREFERENCES

The trustee can avoid pre-petition preferential transfers, thereby enlarging the estate for the benefit of creditors ... [364]

1. **Elements of Preference:** A voidable preference occurs when there is a ***transfer*** of debtor's interest in property, made ***to or for the benefit of a creditor*** concerning an ***antecedent debt*** of the debtor, at a time when the debtor is ***insolvent,*** and within ***90 days before filing*** the bankruptcy petition (or up to one year if the creditor is an insider), which results in a ***larger distribution***

	Text Section
than the creditor would have received in a Chapter 7 liquidation had the transfer not occurred	[365]
a. **Presumption of insolvency:** For purposes of preferences, there is a rebuttable, statutory presumption that the debtor was insolvent during the 90 days prior to the filing of the petition	[373]
b. **Secured creditors:** Payments of fully secured creditors' allowed claims are not preferences since such transfers do not result in a greater distribution	[378]
2. **Exceptions to Preference Rule:** The following transfers are not avoidable:	[379]

    a. *Substantially contemporaneous exchanges for new value;*
    b. *"Ordinary course of business"* transfers;
    c. *Purchase money security interests* securing *new value* (given and used to buy the property described) and *perfected within 20 days* after debtor receives possession of the collateral;
    d. *Subsequent advances of new unsecured value* (*i.e.*, after the transfer);
    e. *Security interests in inventory and receivables* (voidable only to the extent that the creditor's position has improved, to the prejudice of the estate, during specified period);
    f. *Statutory liens* (*e.g.*, tax liens, mechanic's liens) that cannot be avoided under section 545;
    g. Alimony, and spousal or child support, payments; and
    h. *Consumer payments under $600.*

3. **Burden of Proof:** The trustee must prove the elements of a voidable preference, but the creditor bears the burden regarding asserted exceptions	[408]

G. TRUSTEE'S POWER TO AVOID FRAUDULENT TRANSFERS

The trustee can avoid fraudulent transfers or the fraudulent incurring of obligations, done voluntarily or involuntarily by the debtor within *one year* prior to bankruptcy. For purposes of this section, a *transfer* is deemed to have been made when it is sufficiently perfected to preclude a bona fide purchaser from acquiring a superior interest in the property or, if not perfected before commencement of the case, then immediately before the bankruptcy petition was filed	[409]
1. **"Fraudulent" Transfer:** A transfer of the debtor's property is fraudulent if:	[412]

    a. *Made with the actual intent to hinder, delay, or defraud* a creditor. Note that sometimes the debtor's actual intent may be inferred circumstantially by certain *"badges of fraud"*, or
    b. *Debtor receives less than reasonably equivalent value and* (i) was insolvent at the time of the transfer or became insolvent because of it; (ii) had *"unreasonably small capital"* remaining after the transfer for his business operations; or (iii) intends to incur debts that he will be *unable to repay* as they mature.

2. **Good Faith Transferee:** A good faith transferee for value (of a transfer voidable under this section) may retain or receive a lien on any property conveyed to her *to the extent of value* given by her to the debtor, except to the extent that the transfer is also voidable under Code section 544 (strongarm clause and trustee's avoiding power as successor to certain actual creditors), 545 (statutory liens), or 547 (preferences)	[424]

H. POST-PETITION TRANSACTIONS

The trustee may *avoid* transfers of estate property occurring after the filing of the petition unless the transfer comes within an exception below, is authorized by the Code, or is approved by the court	[427]
1. **Transferor Without Notice or Knowledge:** If the transferor has no actual notice or knowledge of the bankruptcy case, it is not liable for a good faith post-petition transfer (such as a bank honoring debtor's check), although the transferee may be subject to the trustee's avoiding power	[428]

			Text Section
	2.	**Exceptions to Trustee's Avoidance:** The trustee may avoid a transfer made during the *gap period* in an involuntary case *except to the extent of post-petition value* (including services) *given* (but this exception does not include payment or securing of a pre-petition debt). Also, the trustee may not avoid a transfer to a *bona fide purchaser of real property* who does not know of the bankruptcy case and who has *paid present fair equivalent value,* if notice of the bankruptcy case has not yet been filed in the recording office of the county where the land is located	[429]

I. LIMITATIONS ON TRUSTEE'S AVOIDING POWERS

1. **Statute of Limitations:** Most of the trustee's avoiding powers are subject to the limitation that he file an action to avoid a transfer before the *earlier* of (i) the later of *two years* after the entry of the order for relief or *one year* after the appointment or election of the first trustee if the appointment or election occurs before the expiration of the two-year period or (ii) the time of the *closing or dismissal of the case.* This statute of limitations applies to actions to avoid a setoff, certain statutory liens, transfers avoidable under the strongarm clause or avoidable by the trustee as successor to certain actual creditors, a preference, or a fraudulent transfer .... [434]

2. **Retroactive Perfection; Continuation Statements:** A trustee's avoiding powers (i) under the strongarm clause, (ii) where trustee acts as successor to certain actual creditors, or (iii) concerning certain statutory liens and (iv) concerning post-petition transactions are subject to any applicable nonbankruptcy law that permits retroactive perfection of a security interest, or the filing of a continuation statement (*e.g.,* Uniform Commercial Code provisions) .... [438]

3. **Seller's Reclamation of Goods:** The Code recognizes a seller's statutory or common law right to reclaim goods from an insolvent buyer if all of the following elements are present: (i) the property sought to be reclaimed is *goods;* (ii) the sale was in the *ordinary course of the seller's business;* (iii) the debtor received the goods while *insolvent;* and (iv) the seller made *written demand* for reclamation *within 10 days* after debtor received the goods (unless the 10-day period expires after the commencement of the case—then the rule is 20 days after receipt). This right prevails over a trustee's power to avoid transfers avoidable under the strongarm clause, statutory liens, preferences, or post-petition transfers .... [441]

    a. **Denial of reclamation:** Even if all elements are satisfied, the court may deny reclamation, but if so, must grant the seller either a lien securing his claim or an administrative expense priority .... [451]

    b. **Right to stop goods in transit:** Courts have held that the Code's reclamation provision also recognizes a seller's state law right to stop goods in transit upon discovering the debtor's insolvency .... [452]

4. **Return of Goods:** A Chapter 11 debtor may, with the creditor's consent, return goods shipped by the creditor before bankruptcy, and the creditor may offset the purchase price against any pre-petition claim .... [454]

J. TRANSFEREE'S LIABILITY TO ESTATE FOR AVOIDED TRANSFERS

Any avoided transfer or lien void under Code section 506(d) is automatically preserved *for the benefit of the estate.* The trustee may recover either the transferred property *or* (if ordered by the court) its value. Recovery may be had from (i) the initial transferee; (ii) the entity the initial transfer was designed to benefit; or (iii) any future transferee after the first transfer (except the trustee may *not* recover from a *good faith future transferee* who gave value and did not know the transfer was voidable). (*But note:* a trustee who has avoided a transfer is permitted only *one satisfaction* in the case.) The trustee must bring the action to recover property (or its value) before the earlier of (i) one year after the corresponding transfer was avoided or (ii) the time of closing or dismissal of the case .... [455]

Text Section

K. POST-PETITION EFFECT OF SECURITY INTEREST
An **after-acquired property clause** in a pre-petition security agreement does **not** create a security interest in property acquired by the debtor or the estate **after** the filing of the bankruptcy petition. An **exception** provides that if the security interest includes collateral the debtor acquired **prior** to bankruptcy and also the proceeds, profits, products, or offspring of the collateral, then the security interest is valid as to any such proceeds, etc. that the estate obtains post-petition. Another **exception** provides that if an assignment of rents or hotel/motel room revenues is specified in a mortgage, they will be treated as secured, and as cash collateral. The court, after notice and a hearing, may decide not to apply these exceptions, depending on the equities .... [465]

L. ABANDONMENT OF ESTATE PROPERTY
The trustee may abandon property that is burdensome or of inconsequential value to the estate. However, estate property that violates environmental laws may **not** be abandoned if public health or safety will thereby be threatened by "imminent and identifiable harm." Generally, abandonment results in the property being abandoned **to the debtor**, although it does not affect the continuing validity of a lien on the property .... [469]

M. SOVEREIGN IMMUNITY
Sovereign immunity of governmental units has been abrogated with respect to many Code sections, to the extent provided in section 106. Thus, monetary recoveries (other than punitive damages), as well as declaratory and injunctive relief against governmental units, can be ordered. (*Note:* The Supreme Court has questioned the constitutionality of section 106) .... [474]

VI. CLAIMS OF CREDITORS

A. FILING PROOFS OF CLAIMS
1. **Claim:** A claim is a **right to payment,** whether "reduced to judgment, liquidated, unliquidated, fixed, contingent, matured, unmatured, disputed, undisputed, legal, equitable, secured, or unsecured." Also, the right to an **equitable remedy** for breach of performance is a claim if the breach gives rise to a right to payment. In addition, a claim **against debtor's property** is considered to be a claim against the debtor. "Claim" is given a broad definition in bankruptcy ..... [478]
2. **Claimants**
   a. **Who must file:** Generally, for a claim or interest to be allowed, an **unsecured creditor** must file a proof of claim and an **equity security holder** must file a proof of interest .... [484]
   b. **Who may file:** In addition to those above, a secured creditor or an indenture trustee (trustee under a mortgage, deed of trust, or indenture contract relating to an outstanding security of the debtor) may file a proof of claim. If a creditor does not file, a co-debtor, surety, guarantor, the debtor, or the trustee may file for the creditor .... [485]
      (1) **Creditor:** A creditor is an entity holding a claim against the debtor or the estate that arose (or is deemed to have arisen) **at or prior to the order for relief,** or an entity holding a community claim .... [486]
      (2) **Equity security holder:** An equity security holder is a holder of a share in a corporation, an interest in a limited partnership interest, or a warrant to buy or sell an equity security .... [488]
      (3) **Class action:** There is a split of authority concerning whether a proof of claim may be filed for a class of creditors, but the trend at the appellate level appears to allow it .... [489]
3. **Time to File**
   a. **Chapters 7, 12, and 13:** A proof of claim must ordinarily be filed **within 90 days** after the first date set for the section 341 meeting .... [492]

		Text Section
b.	**Chapter 11:** All proofs of claims or interests must be filed by the *bar date* set by the court (unless a late filing is permitted for excusable neglect). Any claim or interest in the debtor's schedules is deemed *automatically filed* (for the amount scheduled) unless it is scheduled as contingent, unliquidated, or disputed..	[494]
c.	**Conversion to Chapter 7:** In a converted Chapter 11, 12, or 13 case, all claims *actually* filed in the superseded case are considered automatically filed in the Chapter 7 case...	[500]
d.	**Governmental claims:** These may be filed up to 180 days after the order for relief unless the Bankruptcy Rules provide a longer time.........	[501]

4. **Claims Deemed Pre-Petition:** The following post-petition claims are treated as pre-petition claims for filing purposes:............................... [502]
   a. *A co-debtor's or surety's claim for reimbursement or contribution* that became fixed after the filing of the bankruptcy petition;
   b. *A claim arising in the ordinary course of the debtor's business* after the filing of an *involuntary petition* but before the earlier of the order for relief or appointment of a trustee;
   c. *A claim arising from rejection of an executory contract or an unexpired lease* that the trustee or debtor in possession has not assumed;
   d. *A claim arising from recovery of property* by the trustee or debtor;
   e. *A post-petition tax claim entitled to eighth priority;* and
   f. *A claim* (other than for administrative expenses) arising *after the order for relief* in a Chapter 11, 12, or 13 case, but *before conversion to another chapter.*

5. **Secured Claims:** If a secured creditor does not file a proof of claim, her lien on the collateral usually remains intact; she may, however, prefer to file a claim. [503]

B. **ALLOWANCE OF CLAIMS**
Unless a party in interest objects, a filed claim or interest will be allowed and serves as the basis for distribution. If an objection is raised, the court (after notice and hearing) determines the amount of the claim as of *the date of the filing of the petition* and allows it unless it is within an exception................................ [504]

1. **Exceptions to Allowance:** The following claims are not allowable:......... [507]
   a. *A claim unenforceable because the debtor has a valid defense;*
   b. *A claim for post-petition (or unmatured) interest on an unsecured claim;*
   c. *A claim for an unsecured property tax in excess of debtor's equity;*
   d. *An unreasonable claim for an insider's or attorney's services;*
   e. *Nondischargeable alimony, maintenance, or spousal or child support that is unmatured* as of date of bankruptcy;
   f. *Lessor's excessive claim for damages for a terminated lease;*
   g. *Employee's excessive claim for employer's breach of contract;*
   h. *Claim for disallowance of a federal employment tax credit* resulting from late payment of state unemployment insurance taxes;
   i. *Claims by possessor of recoverable estate property or transferee of an avoidable transfer* (unless the property is returned or its value paid); and
   j. *Tardy claims* (with certain exceptions).

2. **Estimation of Claims:** If the fixing or liquidation of a *contingent or unliquidated* claim would cause undue delay in the case's administration, the court must estimate the claim *solely for allowance* purposes. Similarly, if a right to an *equitable remedy* for breach of performance gives rise to a right to payment, the court must estimate the claim for the purpose of allowance......... [518]

3. **Claim for Reimbursement or Contribution:** A co-debtor's, surety's, or guarantor's claim for reimbursement or contribution will be *disallowed* if: (i) the claim is *contingent* (*i.e.*, surety has not yet paid the principal creditor); (ii)

Bankruptcy—XVII

			Text Section
		the ***principal creditor's claim*** is disallowed; or (iii) the ***surety elects subrogation*** to the principal creditor's rights	[520]
	4.	**Claims Deemed Pre-Petition:** Claims considered pre-petition for the purpose of allowance are the same claims treated as pre-petition for filing purposes (*supra*, §502)	[522]

C. SECURED CLAIMS

In bankruptcy, a secured claim is one that has been allowed and is either ***secured by a lien*** on estate property or is subject to ***setoff.*** Under the Code, it is secured ***only to the extent of the value of the creditor's collateral*** or up to the amount subject to setoff .... [523]

1. **Undersecured Claims—Bifurcation:** If a creditor's claim exceeds the value of the collateral, the claim is undersecured and is divided into two separate ones; (i) a ***secured claim*** equal to the collateral's value, and (ii) ***an unsecured claim*** equal to the amount by which the claim exceeds the collateral's value .. [524]

2. **Valuation of Collateral:** In determining the value of collateral, the court considers both the ***purpose of the valuation*** and the ***intended disposition or use*** of the collateral .... [525]

3. **Oversecured Claims:** To the extent that the collateral's value exceeds the creditor's claim it secures (plus any surcharges), the creditor is entitled to the allowance of ***post-petition interest*** (whether the creditor's lien is consensual or nonconsensual), and if the lien is consensual, to reasonable fees, costs, or other charges specified in the agreement. Note that an oversecured creditor is entitled to the ***accrual*** of post-petition interest, but this allowance does not require present payments .... [529]

4. **Surcharge against Collateral:** To the extent that a creditor ***benefits directly,*** the trustee or debtor in possession may recover from the collateral necessary and reasonable costs of preserving or disposing of the collateral, and this recovery ranks ahead of post-petition interest, fees, or charges awarded to an oversecured creditor .... [532]

5. **Liens Deemed Void:** Generally, a valid lien survives bankruptcy even if the secured creditor does not file a proof of claim. However, for a reason other than (i) failure to file a proof of claim; (ii) disallowance of a claim for nondischargeable alimony, maintenance, or spousal or child support that is unmatured at the date of bankruptcy; or (iii) disallowance of a claim for reimbursement or contribution on the grounds in Code section 502(e), a lien is void to the extent that it secures a claim that is ***not an allowed secured claim*** .... [533]

6. **Treatment of Secured Claims:** Prior to final distribution to unsecured creditors in a Chapter 7 case, a secured creditor usually receives cash equal to the total amount of her allowed secured claim, or alternatively, a return of the property securing the claim. There are special provisions regarding secured creditors that must be satisfied for a court to confirm a plan under Chapters 11, 12, and 13 .... [535]

7. **Adequate Protection:** A secured creditor is entitled to adequate protection of her interest in the collateral; failure to provide it is cause for granting her relief from the automatic stay .... [536]

D. ADMINISTRATIVE EXPENSES

1. **Priority:** After payment of secured claims from property constituting collateral, entities holding claims for administrative expenses are usually entitled to the highest priority in distribution of the estate's assets .... [537]

2. **Allowable Administrative Expenses:** Allowable administrative expenses include actual and necessary post-petition costs of preserving the estate; post-petition taxes (and related tax penalties and interest) incurred by the estate; compensation and reimbursement to officers of the estate; a creditor's expenses for the filing of an involuntary petition, recovering concealed or

transferred property, or participating in a criminal prosecution related to the bankruptcy case: expenses of certain substantial contributors in Chapter 11 cases; expenses and compensation of a superseded pre-petition custodian; actual and necessary expenses (but not compensation) of an official Chapter 11 creditors' committee; certain reasonable attorney's or accountant's fees and actual and necessary expenses; compensation of an indenture trustee; witnesses' fees; and pre-confirmation retiree benefit payments in a Chapter 11 case .... [538]

3. **Exception—Gap Creditors:** In an *involuntary* case, post-petition claims arising in the ordinary course of the debtor's business or financial affairs before the earlier of the appointment of a trustee and the order for relief are *not* considered administrative expense claims. They are given **second priority** .... [552]

E. **PRIORITY CLAIMS**
Priority claims are usually the first *unsecured claims* paid following distribution to secured creditors. The eight tiers for payment of *allowed* priority claims are, in order: .... [554]

(i) *First priority—administrative expenses,* including filing and other fees;
(ii) *Second priority—involuntary case gap claims;*
(iii) *Third priority—wages, salaries, or commissions* earned by an *individual* (or by certain independent corporate sales representatives with only one employee) within 90 days before bankruptcy or the cessation of debtor's business, whichever is earlier (subject to $4,000 limit for each claimant);
(iv) *Fourth priority—contributions to employee benefit plans* for services rendered within 180 days before either bankruptcy or cessation of debtor's business, whichever is earlier (subject to monetary limitations);
(v) *Fifth priority—claims of grain farmers and U.S. fishermen* against debtors who own/operate grain storage facilities or who operate fish produce storage or processing facilities ($4,000 limit per claimant);
(vi) *Sixth priority—consumer claims* ("layaway" priority) arising from an individual's pre-petition deposit of money with the debtor for the purchase, lease, or rental of property, *or* the purchase of services that have not been delivered or provided and were intended for personal, family, or household use of claimant ($1,800 limit per individual);
(vii) *Seventh priority—alimony, and spousal or child support claims;*
(viii) *Eighth priority—unsecured pre-petition tax claims,* including income taxes (for three years prior to bankruptcy), property tax, trust fund tax (*e.g.,* employees' withholding taxes), employment tax, excise tax, customs duties, and penalties on eighth priority tax claims (if in compensation for actual pecuniary loss); and
(ix) *Ninth priority—failure to maintain capital requirements of an insured depository institution:* This priority is for unsecured claims of certain federal regulators for any deficiency under the debtor's agreement to maintain the capital of an insured depository institution.

1. **Insufficient Funds—Pro Rata Distribution Within Priority:** In a Chapter 7 case, distribution on all claims of a particular priority must be made on a pro rata basis. *Exception:* In a case **converted to Chapter 7** from Chapter 11, 12, or 13, the Chapter 7 administrative expense claims **after conversion** have priority over administrative expenses incurred prior to conversion .... [577]

2. **Superpriority—Inadequately Protected Secured Creditor:** If *adequate protection* furnished to a creditor whose claim is secured by a lien on debtor's property **proves to be deficient,** the creditor will receive an administrative expense claim with priority over all other administrative expenses .... [579]

3. **Super-Superpriority—Post Petition Credit:** If the trustee or debtor in possession cannot obtain unsecured post-petition credit through an administrative expense priority, the court may approve new credit or debt with priority over all administrative expense claims, including superpriority claims .... [580]

			Text Section
	4.	**Subrogation:** A third party (*e.g.,* co-debtor or surety) who becomes subrogated to the rights of a holder of a claim entitled to a third through ninth priority does ***not*** become subrogated to that holder's priority right. Thus, the subrogated claim is treated as a nonpriority claim. However subrogees to administrative expense claims and involuntary case gap claims do become subrogated to the respective priorities of those claims	[581]

F. TAX CLAIMS

The bankruptcy court has jurisdiction to determine the amount or legality of any tax, fine, penalty, or addition to tax that has not been contested and adjudicated in a judicial or administrative court ***prior to bankruptcy,*** regardless of whether the tax has been assessed or paid. The bankruptcy court may also determine the ***estate's*** right to a tax refund, but only after 120 days after the trustee's proper request to the appropriate governmental unit for the refund ***or*** an actual determination by that unit of the request, whichever occurs earlier .... [584]

1. **Tax Liability of Estate:** A trustee may request (accompanied by a tax return) that the appropriate taxing authority determine any unpaid tax liability of the ***estate*** incurred during administration of the case. Once this request has been made, a discharge from liability for the tax on the part of the trustee, debtor, or successor to the debtor will occur when there is payment of the tax indicated on the return (if the taxing authority fails to act timely) or the tax determined by the taxing authority or the court. No discharge occurs if the return is ***fraudulent*** or contains a material misrepresentation .... [587]

2. **Assessment:** After a court determination of tax liability, the taxing authority may assess the tax amount against the estate, the debtor, or a successor to the debtor, notwithstanding the automatic stay provisions .... [590]

G. SUBROGATION CLAIMS

A subrogee is an entity that ***has paid*** a creditor's claim because it either had secured the claim or was liable with the debtor on the claim (*e.g.,* as co-debtor or surety). Generally, a subrogee ***succeeds to the rights of the creditor*** whose claim it paid to the extent of the payment; however, there are several exceptions to this rule. A co-debtor's claim, either by way of subrogation or for reimbursement or contribution, will be subordinated to the principal creditor's claim until that claim is fully satisfied . [591]

H. SUBORDINATION OF CLAIMS

1. **Subordination Agreement:** A contract to subordinate a claim to the payment of other claims is valid if enforceable under nonbankruptcy law .... [599]

2. **Defrauded Security Holders:** Claims for damages, rescission, or contribution or reimbursement arising from the purchase or sale of a security of the debtor or its affiliate ***must*** be subordinated to all claims or interests ***senior or equal*** to that which the security represents. *Exception:* If the security is common stock, the claim will be subordinated to the same priority as common stock .... [600]

3. **Equitable Subordination:** The court also has equitable power to subordinate all or part of an allowed secured or unsecured claim (or interest) to another allowed claim (or interest). Equitable subordination generally requires a showing of some fault on the claimant's part (*e.g.,* fraud, undercapitalization, use of the debtor as an alter ego). Establishment of fault requires proof: (i) of claimant's ***inequitable conduct;*** (ii) of ***injury to the debtor's creditors*** or an ***unfair advantage*** to the claimant due to the misconduct; and (iii) that equitable subordination is consistent with Code provisions .... [602]

   a. **Insiders and fiduciaries:** Courts usually examine with strict scrutiny the dealings of insiders and fiduciaries (when they are claimants) ***for good faith and fairness,*** but a claimant's status as an insider or fiduciary should not, in the absence of misconduct, result in equitable subordination of his claim .... [606]

VII. DEBTOR'S EXEMPTIONS AND DISCHARGE OF INDEBTEDNESS

A. EXEMPTIONS

1. **Fresh Start—Exempt Property:** An *individual* debtor is entitled to certain exemptions, either under the Code or pursuant to applicable state and federal nonbankruptcy law. Thirty-five states have opted out of the federal bankruptcy scheme, thereby restricting their domiciliaries to exemptions permitted under state and federal nonbankruptcy law. In states not opting out, the debtor may choose *either* the federal bankruptcy exemptions or state (and federal nonbankruptcy) law exemptions .... [609]

2. **Federal Bankruptcy Exemptions**
   a. *Homestead*—up to $15,000 in real or personal property used by the debtor or a dependent as a *residence* .... [614]
   b. *Motor vehicle*—up to $2,400 for one motor vehicle .... [615]
   c. *Household goods, crops, animals*—up to $400 in any item of household furnishings or goods (for personal, family, or household use). *Note:* The exemption cannot exceed $8,000 in total value .... [616]
   d. *Jewelry*—up to $1,000 in personal, family, or household jewelry .... [617]
   e. *Wildcard exemption*—up to $800 plus up to $7,500 of any unused portion of the homestead exemption, *in any property. Note:* This exemption benefits primarily nonhomeowner debtors .... [618]
   f. *Other exemptions—professional books or tools of the trade* (up to $1,500); *unmatured life insurance* contract owned by debtor; *loan value or accrued interest or dividends* of any debtor-owned unmatured life insurance contract (up to $8,000); prescribed **health aids; certain government benefits; alimony, support, or maintenance** to the extent reasonably necessary to support debtor and any dependent; rights to payments under eligible **pension plans;** awards to **crime victims; wrongful death** award to dependent-debtor (with limitations); **personal injury** award (up to $15,000), not including compensation for pain and suffering or for actual pecuniary loss; and loss of **future earnings** (with limitations) ..... [619]

3. **State Exemptions and Nonbankruptcy Federal Exemptions**
   a. **State law exemptions:** Allowable state law exemptions are those in effect on the date of the filing of the bankruptcy petition in the state where the debtor has been domiciled for the 180 days before bankruptcy or for the longest part of such period. Exemptions very widely among the states . [631]
   b. **Nonbankruptcy federal law:** Federal nonbankruptcy laws sometimes provide for exemptions (*e.g.*, social security payments) .... [633]
   c. **Tenancy by the entirety or joint tenancy:** A debtor using the state alternative also may exempt any interest in property he held in this manner immediately prior to bankruptcy, to the extent that applicable nonbankruptcy law (usually state property law) exempts such property from process .... [634]

4. **Joint Case:** In a joint case, *each debtor* is entitled to a separate claim of any allowable exemptions. *Both debtors* must elect the same exemption plan (either federal or state) since the stacking of federal and state exemptions is prohibited .... [640]
   a. **Federal exemptions:** Joint debtors who elect the federal exemptions may stack their exemptions (*e.g.*, up to $30,000 in a homestead) .... [641]
   b. **State exemptions:** Courts are split on whether the Code provision allowing joint debtors separate exemptions applies to states that have opted out of the federal bankruptcy exemption scheme .... [642]

5. **Effect of Exemptions:** Generally, property exempted by the debtor is not liable *during or after the case* for any pre-petition debts or those deemed to have arisen before bankruptcy. *Exceptions:* nondischargeable taxes; nondischargeable alimony, maintenance, or child support; a debt secured by a lien that is not void under section 506(d) and has not been avoided under another

Code provision; a debt secured by a tax lien if notice of the lien has been filed properly; and certain debts owed by an institution-affiliated party of an insured depository institution .... [647]

6. **Avoidance of Liens:** The debtor may avoid the fixing of the following liens when they *impair an exemption* that she could claim: (i) *judicial liens* (except when they secure alimony or child support) and (ii) *nonpossessory, nonpurchase-money security interests* in *household goods* and certain other items held primarily for personal, family, or household use, professional books or tools of the trade, and prescribed health aids .... [649]

7. **Property Recovered by Trustee:** The debtor may *exempt* transferred property that, absent the transfer, could have been properly exempted and that is in the estate due to recovery by the trustee if (i) the debtor *did not voluntarily* transfer or conceal the property or (ii) the transfer *could have been avoided* under section 522(f)(2) by the debtor. Such property can be exempted only to the extent that the maximum amount permitted for the relevant category has not already been claimed .... [670]

8. **Avoidance by Debtor:** A debtor can *avoid* a transfer or *recover* a setoff if the trustee has the power to do so, but does not exercise it, to the extent that the property could have been exempted under Code section 522(g)(1) (*i.e.,* not voluntarily transferred or concealed by debtor) had the trustee avoided the transfer .... [672]

9. **Recovery and Exemption:** A debtor who avoids a transfer or recovers a setoff (*see supra,* §§649, 672) may *recover* the property or setoff in accordance with Code section 550 (*see supra,* §§456-464) and may *exempt* it subject to the applicable exemption scheme .... [673]

B. **NONDISCHARGEABLE DEBTS**
1. **Exceptions to Discharge:** Certain debts of an *individual debtor* survive the granting of a discharge under Chapter 7, 11, or 12, or under Chapter 13 for a debtor who has received a hardship discharge. A nondischargeable debt permits that creditor to pursue recovery from the debtor after the debtor's discharge in bankruptcy .... [675]

2. **Taxes:** Certain tax claims are nondischargeable: taxes entitled to *second priority* (unsecured tax claims—gap period) or *eighth priority* (various unsecured pre-petition tax claims); those for which a *return* was *not filed* or was *filed late* and within two years of bankruptcy; and taxes for which debtor filed a *fraudulent return* or that debtor *intentionally tried to evade* .... [679]

3. **Fraud:** Debts for money, property, services, or credit obtained by false representation or fraud are nondischargeable. *But note:* Nondischargeability based on a false statement about the financial condition of debtor or an insider requires proof of the five elements of Code section 523(a)(2)(B) .... [680]

4. **Failure to Schedule Debts:** The debtor's failure to list or schedule a debt will render the debt nondischargeable where it precludes a creditor without notice or actual knowledge of the bankruptcy case from filing a proof of claim (or under Code section 523(a)(2), (a)(4), or (a)(6), a proof of claim and a complaint to determine dischargeability of a debt) .... [686]

5. **Fiduciary Fraud or Defalcation:** Debts for fraud or defalcation *while acting in a fiduciary capacity* are nondischargeable, as are debts for embezzlement or larceny (no fiduciary capacity required) .... [689]

6. **Alimony, Maintenance, and Spousal or Child Support:** Such debts are nondischargeable (unless assigned to an entity other than the government) .... [691]

7. **Property Settlements and "Hold Harmless" Obligations Arising out of a Separation Agreement or Divorce Decree:** These debts are nondischargeable *unless* (i) the debtor does not have the ability to pay, or (ii) discharging the debt would produce a greater benefit to the debtor than the harm to the spouse, ex-spouse, or child .... [693]

		Text Section
8.	**Willful and Malicious Injury:** Debts for willful and malicious injury by the debtor to another entity or its property are nondischargeable	[695]
9.	**Fines and Penalties; Court Costs:** A fine, penalty, or forfeiture owed to a governmental unit (including state court-ordered criminal restitution) is nondischargeable *if it is not compensation* for actual pecuniary loss. Court costs and fees are also nondischargeable.	[699]
10.	**Student Loans:** These are nondischargeable unless (i) the loan first became due (usually, the first payment) more than *seven years* before the filing of the bankruptcy petition or (ii) there will be *undue hardship* on the debtor and her dependents	[703]
11.	**Liability for Drunk Driving:** Any debt for personal injury or death caused by the debtor's drunk or drugged driving is nondischargeable	[709]
12.	**Fiduciary Fraud of Officers and Directors of Financial Institutions:** A debt for fraud or defalcation while acting in a fiduciary capacity concerning any depository institution or insured credit union is nondischargeable if provided for in a judgment, consent decree, or settlement agreement	[710]
13.	**Failure to Maintain Capital Commitment Concerning Insured Depository Institutions:** A debt for *malicious or reckless* failure to maintain the capital of an insured depository institution in breach of an agreement with a federal depository institutions regulatory agency is nondischargeable	[711]
14.	**Federal Criminal Restitution:** The payment of an order of restitution for most federal crimes is nondischargeable	[712]
15.	**Debts Incurred to Pay Federal Taxes:** Debts incurred (*e.g.,* by use of credit cards) to pay nondischargeable federal taxes are nondischargeable	[713]
16.	**Condominium and Cooperative Housing Fees:** Such debts that become due and payable *after the order for relief* are nondischargeable if they cover a period when the debtor either physically occupied or rented the unit	[714]
17.	**Prior Bankruptcy:** A debt is nondischargeable if it was or could have been listed by the debtor in a prior bankruptcy case in which she either waived discharge or was denied a discharge under Chapter 7 for any reason except the bar against receiving a discharge in a subsequent bankruptcy case filed within six years	[715]
18.	**Proof:** The standard of proof for the exceptions to discharge described above is the *preponderance of the evidence* standard	[717]
19.	**Prior State Court Judgments:** In determining dischargeability of a debt, the bankruptcy court is not bound by a prior state court judgment on the basis of *res judicata.* However, the doctrine of *collateral estoppel* applies to preclude retrial of issues of fact "actually litigated and determined" in an earlier action in a nonbankruptcy court	[718]
20.	**Debts under Code Section 523(a)(2), (a)(4), (a)(6), and (a)(15):** A complaint requesting determination of dischargeability of any of these kinds of debts generally must be filed by the creditor within *60 days* after the first date set for the section 341 meeting. Otherwise, these debts are discharged	[723]

C. EFFECTS OF DISCHARGE

A debtor is relieved of *personal* liability for all discharged debts. A discharge automatically *voids any judgment* against the debtor for personal liability on a debt included in the discharge and also acts as a *permanent statutory injunction* prohibiting creditors from acting to recover the discharged debt from the debtor personally . . [726]

1. **Co-Debtor or Surety—No Discharge:** The discharge of a debt does *not* affect the liability of any entity other than the debtor (*e.g.,* a surety) or of the property of another; exception exists, under certain circumstances, for community property acquired post-petition . . . . [731]
2. **Voluntary Repayment:** The Code expressly permits the debtor to voluntarily repay any debt, although she is not legally obligated to repay a discharged debt absent an enforceable reaffirmation agreement . . . . [732]

	Text Section

D. REAFFIRMATION AGREEMENTS
A reaffirmation agreement is a voluntary contract between the debtor and the holder of a dischargeable claim whereby debtor promises to repay all or part of the debt after bankruptcy . . . . [733]

1. **Requirements for Enforceability:** To be enforceable, a reaffirmation agreement must: (i) be enforceable under nonbankruptcy law; (ii) be made before discharge; (iii) contain a clear, conspicuous statement advising the debtor that she lawfully ***may rescind*** any time before discharge or within 60 days after filing of the agreement, whichever is later, and also a clear, conspicuous statement advising the debtor that a reaffirmation is completely ***voluntary;*** (iv) be filed with the court along with debtor's attorney's affidavit; (v) if the debtor is an individual who was not represented by an attorney when the agreement was negotiated, it must be approved by the court and found to be in the debtor's best interest and not causing undue hardship (unless it is a consumer debt secured by real estate); and (vi) not have been timely rescinded by the debtor. The requirements concerning a discharge hearing must also have been fulfilled . . . . [734]

2. **Creditor Pressure Forbidden:** The automatic stay prohibits creditor coercion of the debtor to reaffirm pre-petition debts . . . . [744]

3. **Discharge Hearing:** A discharge hearing is required if the debtor reaffirms a debt and was not represented by an attorney when the reaffirmation was negotiated. Otherwise, a discharge hearing is discretionary with the court. At a discharge hearing, the court informs an individual debtor whether her discharge has been granted, or if it is denied explains the reasons therefor; and, when required (*see* (v) above), approves or disapproves proposed reaffirmation agreements and informs debtor of the voluntary nature and legal effect of such agreements. If a discharge hearing is scheduled, debtor must personally attend . . . . [745]

E. REDEMPTION—CHAPTER 7 CASES ONLY
An individual debtor in Chapter 7 cases may redeem tangible personal property intended for personal, family, or household use from a lien securing a dischargeable consumer debt if the property was exempted by the debtor or abandoned by the trustee. The debtor may retain such collateral by paying the secured party the ***amount of the allowed secured claim*** (*i.e.,* the collateral's market value) ***in a lump sum*** . . [752]

F. PROTECTION AGAINST DISCRIMINATION
In addition to a discharge of debts, the law enhances a debtor's fresh start by expressly prohibiting discriminatory treatment of one who has been a debtor under the Bankruptcy Code or a bankrupt under the Bankruptcy Act. This prohibition applies to discrimination by ***governmental units*** against a person (individual, corporation, or partnership) and to discrimination by ***private employers*** with respect to an individual's employment or termination. The prohibition also applies to discrimination by governmental units and lenders engaged in a ***guaranteed student loan program.*** Note that consideration of an applicant's future financial responsibility with respect to a post-bankruptcy credit application is not discriminatory if there is no discrimination against bankruptcy debtors . . . . [756]

VIII. ADMINISTRATIVE POWERS

A. ADEQUATE PROTECTION
1. **Interest in Property:** Adequate protection of an entity's interest in property is required if (i) the interest is subject to the ***automatic stay*** and relief from the stay has not been granted; (ii) the ***property is used, sold, or leased*** by the trustee or debtor in possession; and (iii) the debt was incurred or credit obtained (with court approval) secured by a lien on estate property ***equal or senior to the entity's lien*** on the same property . . . . [761]

		Text Section
2.	**Methods of Providing Adequate Protection:** Three ways of providing adequate protection are set forth in the Code: (i) ***periodic cash payments*** by the trustee (or debtor in possession) to the extent the entity's interest in the property has decreased (or will decrease) in value; (ii) the furnishing of an ***additional or replacement lien*** to cover any decrease in value; and (iii) granting relief constituting the ***indubitable equivalent*** of the entity's interest (catchall provision). Adequate protection may be provided in other ways as well, but *not* by giving an entity an administrative expense	[765]
3.	**Equity Cushion:** An ***oversecured*** creditor may be adequately protected if the value of the collateral substantially exceeds the debt owed to the creditor	[770]
4.	**Rejection of *American Mariner*:** Adequate protection does *not* entitle an undersecured creditor to receive compensation (*i.e.,* interest) for the delay caused by the automatic stay in foreclosing on the collateral and reinvesting the proceeds. Rather, adequate protection protects against depreciation in the value of the collateral and does not protect a secured party's right to immediate foreclosure	[774]
5.	**Valuation of Collateral:** In determining what constitutes adequate protection, the court ascertains the collateral's value, generally using either a liquidation standard or a going concern approach, depending on the circumstances surrounding the intended use or disposition of the collateral and the probability of an effective reorganization	[775]
6.	**Failure of Adequate Protection:** If the adequate protection provided proves to be deficient, the secured creditor will receive an administrative expense claim with priority over all other allowed administrative expenses	[776]
7.	**Chapter 12 Cases:** The adequate protection provisions of Code section 361 are inapplicable in a Chapter 12 case concerning a family farmer; such cases are governed by Code section 1205	[777]

B. AUTOMATIC STAY

The automatic stay, applicable to ***all entities,*** takes effect ***when the bankruptcy petition is filed*** and protects the debtor, his property, the estate property from certain creditors' actions. It provides a respite for the debtor and promotes an orderly case administration . . . [778]

1. **Acts Enjoined**
   a. **Proceedings against debtor:** The commencement or continuation (including issuance or service of process) of a judicial, administrative, or other action against the debtor is stayed if its purpose is to recover a ***pre-petition claim,*** or if the action was, or could have been, commenced before the filing of the bankruptcy petition . . . [780]
   b. **Pre-petition judgments:** Also enjoined is enforcement of ***pre-petition judgments*** against the debtor or estate property . . . [783]
   c. **Acts against estate property:** Any act to obtain possession of property of the estate or in its possession, or to exert control over estate property, is prohibited. Similarly, any act to create, perfect, or enforce a lien against estate property is enjoined . . . [784]
   d. **Liens against debtor's property:** An act to create, perfect, or enforce a lien against the debtor's property is barred ***to the extent the lien secures a pre-petition claim*** . . . [786]
   e. **Collection efforts:** Acts to collect, recover, or assess a claim against the debtor that arose prior to the filing of the bankruptcy petition are forbidden . [787]
   f. **Tax Court proceedings:** The commencement or continuation of a case in the United States Tax concerning the debtor is stayed . . . [788]
   g. **Setoffs:** The automatic stay also enjoins the post-petition setoff of a pre-petition debt owing to the debtor against any claim against the debtor . . . [789]
2. **Exceptions to Automatic Stay**
   a. The commencement or continuation of a ***criminal action*** against the debtor . [792]

			Text Section
	b.	***Collection of alimony, maintenance, or spousal or child support*** is not enjoined if obtained from non-estate property (*e.g.,* exempt property) .	[793]
	c.	The commencement or continuation of a ***paternity suit*** or of an action seeking ***modification*** of an order for alimony, maintenance, or support . .	[794]
	d.	***Perfection of an interest in property,*** if accomplished within the 10 (or 20, for purchase-money transactions) day grace period allowed by section 547(e)(2)(A) or if it would prevail over the trustee's avoiding powers pursuant to section 546(b). The filing of a ***continuation statement*** also is excepted	[795]
	e.	The commencement or continuation of a governmental proceeding to enforce its ***police or regulatory powers***	[796]
	f.	***Enforcement of judgments by governmental units*** to implement police or regulatory powers, if the judgment is ***other than a money judgment*** . .	[797]
	g.	***Certain securities, repo, and swap setoffs***	[798]
	h.	***Commencement of certain HUD mortgage foreclosures***	[799]
	i.	A ***tax audit,*** an ***issuance of notice of tax deficiency,*** a ***demand for tax returns,*** or a ***tax assessment*** and issuance of notice and demand for payment	[800]
	j.	***Recovery of nonresidential real property by a lessor*** when the lease terminated by ***the expiration of its stated term*** prior to the filing of the bankruptcy petition or during the case	[802]
	k.	***Presentment of negotiable instrument,*** notice of dishonor, and protesting dishonor	[803]
	l.	***Certain actions against educational institutions***	[804]
	m.	***Repossession of certain aircrafts, aircraft equipment, and vessels*** by lessors, conditional vendors, or secured parties (whether or not they have a purchase-money security interest) in a ***Chapter 11 case*** (subject to certain limitations)	[805]
	n.	***Creation or perfection of statutory liens*** for ad valorem property taxes becoming due post-petition	[806]
3.	**Expiration of Stay:** Absent a grant of relief, the stay remains operative from the filing of the bankruptcy petition until it statutorily terminates as follows:		[807]
	(i)	***An act against estate property*** is stayed until the property no longer constitutes property of the estate; and	
	(ii)	***Any other enjoined act*** (*supra,* §§779 *et seq.*) Is subject to the stay until a discharge is granted or denied, the case is dismissed, or it is closed, whichever occurs first.	
4.	**Relief from Stay:** Upon request, relief (*e.g.,* termination, annulment, modification, conditioning of stay) from the automatic stay may be granted to a party in interest after notice and a hearing		[809]
	a.	**Grounds for relief:** For *cause,* the court will grant relief from the stay of *any act* enjoined. The stay will also be lifted for *an act against property* where (i) the *debtor lacks equity* in the property and (ii) the property is *not necessary for an effective reorganization* (*i.e.,* debtor does not have a reasonable possibility of successfully reorganizing within a reasonable time)	[811]
	(1)	**"Cause":** The bankruptcy court, as an equity court, has broad discretion to determine what constitutes cause for granting relief from the stay. One basis for relief is *lack of adequate protection,* but there may be other reasons for relief (*e.g.,* debtor's lack of good faith in filing the bankruptcy petition). Thus, courts generally follow a case-by-case approach	[812]
	(2)	**Single asset real estate:** Under certain specified conditions, the Code provides relief from the automatic stay for an act against single asset real estate not exceeding $4 million in value	[823]
5.	**Willful Violation of Stay:** Individuals injured by a willful violation may recover		

XXVI—Bankruptcy

actual damages, costs, attorney's fees and, if warranted, punitive damages. The courts are split as to whether this Code provision applies to corporations and partnerships harmed, or is limited to natural persons .... [831]

C. USE, SALE, OR LEASE OF PROPERTY
The use, sale, or lease of estate property, both in and out of the ordinary course of the debtor's business, is an integral part of the bankruptcy process .... [832]

1. **Out of Ordinary Course of Business:** After *notice and a hearing,* a trustee or debtor in possession may use, sell, or lease estate property out of the ordinary course of the debtor's business. Action may be taken *without* an actual hearing if, after appropriate notice is given, no party in interest timely requests one .... [835]
2. **In Ordinary Course of Business:** A trustee or debtor in possession may generally use, sell, or lease estate property in the ordinary course of business *without notice or a hearing* .... [840]
    a. **Exception—cash collateral:** The trustee or debtor in possession may use, sell, or lease cash collateral in the ordinary course of business only if she obtains either *court authorization* (after notice and a hearing) or the *consent* of all entities having an interest in the cash collateral .... [844]
3. **Automatic Stay:** Any use, sale, or lease of the property by the trustee must not conflict with any relief granted from the automatic stay .... [848]
4. **Adequate Protection:** Upon request by an entity having an interest in the property to be used, sold, or leased, the court will *prohibit or condition* the use, sale, or lease so as to provide adequate protection of the entity's interest. For lessors of personal property, this remedy is to the exclusion of relief from the automatic stay .... [849]
5. **Ipso Facto or "Bankruptcy" Clauses:** Clauses in a contract or lease (or nonbankruptcy law provision) that would cause a forfeiture, modification, or termination of the debtor's interest in property upon the occurrence of insolvency, bankruptcy, or other similar events do *not* affect the right of a trustee or debtor in possession to use, sell, or lease the property in or out of the ordinary course of business or under a Chapter 11, 12, or 13 plan .... [852]
6. **Sale Free and Clear:** When the trustee or debtor in possession sells estate property, either in or out of the ordinary course of business, the sale may be transacted free and clear of any lien or other interest if one or more of the following elements is present: .... [853]
    (i) *Applicable state or other nonbankruptcy law permits* a free and clear sale;
    (ii) *There is consent* by the entity holding the interest;
    (iii) *If the interest is a lien, the selling price is greater than the total value of all liens* on the property;
    (iv) *There is a bona fide dispute* concerning the entity's interest; or
    (v) *The entity holding the interest could be required to accept a money satisfaction* in a legal or equitable action.
7. **Sales and Use Taxes Permitted:** A bankruptcy liquidation sale is not immune from a nondiscriminatory state sales or use tax .... [862]

D. OBTAINING CREDIT
A trustee, debtor in possession, or debtor engaged in business under Chapter 13 may need to obtain credit or incur debt. Generally, *unsecured* credit or debt may be obtained *in the ordinary course of business* without notice and a hearing, and is allowable as an administrative expense. Unsecured credit or debt *out of the ordinary course of business* may be obtained as an allowable administrative expense only after notice and hearing and court approval .... [863]

1. **Priority or Security:** If the trustee or debtor in possession is unable to obtain unsecured credit with an administrative expense priority, the court, after notice

and a hearing, may authorize obtaining credit or incurring debt (i) with a ***super-superpriority*** ahead of all administrative expense claims and of any superpriority expense claims resulting from the failure of adequate protection; (ii) secured by a ***lien on unencumbered estate property;*** or (iii) secured by a ***junior lien*** on already encumbered property . . . . [867]

    2. **Priming Lien:** Also, if post-petition credit ***cannot be obtained*** other than by a senior or equal lien on encumbered property, the court may, after notice and a hearing, approve new credit or debt secured by a lien on estate property that will be ***senior or equal*** to any lien already held by an entity on that same property. Adequate protection for the original lienholder must be provided . . . . [871]

E. EXECUTORY CONTRACTS AND UNEXPIRED LEASES

The trustee or debtor in possession may assume or reject an executory contract or unexpired lease ***with court approval.*** In determining whether a contract is ***executory,*** many courts look to see if there is substantial performance left to be done by both the debtor and the nondebtor party. An unexpired lease must be a ***true lease,*** not intended as a secured transaction . . . . [875]

    1. **Business Judgment Rule:** When considering a request to assume or reject an executory contract or unexpired lease, courts generally apply the ***business judgment rule*** and approve the trustee's decision unless there is bad faith or gross abuse of discretion. Generally, rejection operates as a breach of the contract or lease . . . . [880]

    2. **Assumption of Contracts and Leases in Default:** An executory contract or unexpired lease in default may be assumed only if at the time of assumption the trustee or debtor in possession: (i) ***cures*** the default or provides adequate assurance of a prompt cure (at the nondefault rate); (ii) ***compensates*** (or provides adequate assurance of prompt redress to) the nondebtor party for any monetary loss caused by the default; and (iii) furnishes ***adequate assurance of future performance*** of the contract or lease . . . . [885]

    3. **Agreements Not Assumable or Assignable:** The following are ***not*** assumable or assignable: personal service contracts and government contracts where the nondebtor party does not consent; contracts to loan money to debtor, grant other debt financing or financial accommodations, or issue its securities; and leases of nonresidential real estate validly terminated under nonbankruptcy law before the order for relief . . . . [896]

    4. **Time Limitations for Assumption or Rejection:** Generally, in a ***Chapter 7*** case, assumption or rejection of executory contracts or unexpired leases of ***personal property or residential real property*** must occur within 60 days after the order for relief or, in a ***Chapter 11, 12, or 13*** case, at any time before confirmation of a plan. In a ***Chapter 11*** case, the trustee or debtor in possession must timely perform all obligations in a lease of ***nonconsumer personal property*** (except those in Code section 365(b)(2)), first arising from 60 days after the order for relief until the lease is assumed or rejected. This includes payment of the amount of rent specified in the lease. Assumption or rejection of an unexpired lease of ***nonresidential real property,*** where the debtor is the lessee, under ***any chapter*** generally must occur within 60 days after the order for relief, and the trustee or debtor in possession must timely perform all duties (except those found in Code section 365(b)(2)) arising after the order for relief and until assumption or rejection . . . . [900]

    5. **Assignment:** An executory contract or unexpired lease may be assigned by the trustee or debtor in possession only if it has been properly assumed and adequate assurance of the assignee's future performance is provided (regardless of whether there has been a default) . . . . [915]

F. UTILITY SERVICE

The debtor's utility services may not be discontinued, altered, or refused solely

	Text Section
because of the filing of the bankruptcy case or the failure to timely pay a utility bill for services furnished before the order for relief. However, services may be discontinued, etc., if within *20 days* after the order for relief the debtor or trustee does not provide a deposit or other security constituting adequate assurance that the utility will be paid for services rendered after the order for relief	[937]

IX. CHAPTER 7—LIQUIDATION

A. INTRODUCTION

1. **Eligibility for Relief:** A person (individual, partnership, corporation) that resides or has a domicile, a place of business, or property in the United States may be a debtor under Chapter 7 unless specifically excepted .... [939]
    a. **Exceptions:** Not eligible to be a Chapter 7 debtor are railroads; domestic banks, insurance companies, savings institutions, etc.; foreign banks, insurance companies, etc., doing business in the United States; and an individual or family farmer who was a debtor in a case *dismissed in the preceding 180 days* because the debtor intentionally failed to obey court orders or to appear before the court, or because he requested a voluntary dismissal of the case following a party's request for relief from the automatic stay........ [940]
2. **Chapter 7 Trustee:** Immediately after the order for relief, the U.S. trustee appoints an interim trustee to serve until the section 341 meeting, at which time the interim trustee will become the permanent trustee unless another person is elected. Some of the trustee's principal duties are to locate and collect estate property and convert it to cash, make distributions, and to expeditiously close the estate......... [941]
3. **Meeting of Creditors:** Within 20 to 40 days after the order for relief, the U.S. trustee convenes and presides at the section 341 meeting, *supra*........... [944]

B. DISTRIBUTION OF PROPERTY OF ESTATE

1. **Order of Payment**
    a. *Secured claims*—allowed secured claims are the first to be paid, and they are paid from the collateral securing the respective claim. A claim is secured only to the extent of the value of the collateral. Recall that to the extent that a claim is *oversecured,* allowed post-petition interest and allowed fees, costs, or charges generally accrue until the time of distribution in a Chapter 7 case........ [946]
    b. *Priority claims*—these *unsecured* claims are paid before the general unsecured claims, in the following order: (i) administrative expenses; (ii) involuntary case gap claims; (iii) wages, salaries, or commissions; (iv) contributions to employee benefit plans; (v) claims of grain farmers and U.S. fishermen; (vi) consumer layaway claims; (vii) alimony, and spousal or child support; (viii) unsecured pre-petition taxes; and (ix) capital requirements of an insured depository institution. They must either be timely filed, or tardily filed before the trustee begins distribution .... [948]
    c. *General unsecured claims*—paid if timely filed and allowed. Also paid at this time are *justifiably* tardy claims (*e.g.,* lack of notice) if filed in time for distribution .... [949]
    d. *Unexcused tardy claims* .... [951]
    e. *Penalty claims*—secured or unsecured, for punitive, exemplary, or multiple damages, or for fines, penalties, or forfeitures not constituting compensation for actual pecuniary loss .... [952]
    f. *Interest*—if the estate is solvent, then after payment of all of the above claims, post-petition interest is paid on unsecured claims and on secured or unsecured penalty claims .... [953]
    g. *Payment to debtor*—if any estate property is left over .... [954]

			Text Section
	2.	**Pro Rata Payment:** Claims within any tier of priority or any level of distribution share pro rata in the property distributed to that particular category of claims. *Exception:* Administrative expenses allowed in a Chapter 7 case **after conversion** from Chapter 11, 12, or 13 have priority over any administrative expenses incurred prior to conversion	[955]
	3.	**Community Property:** Any community property in the estate or its proceeds must be segregated from other estate property and is distributed under special rules	[957]
	4.	**Exception—Subordination of Claims:** The order of distribution (above) may differ when a claim is subordinated to a lower rank (*e.g.,* when there is a subordination agreement, there are claims of defrauded security holders, or the principles of equitable subordination apply)	[958]

C. **TREATMENT OF CERTAIN LIENS IN CHAPTER 7 CASE**

1. **Avoidance of Liens Securing Penalties:** The trustee may avoid a lien securing the type of claim described in Code section 726(a)(4) for a fine, penalty, punitive damages, etc., not constituting compensation for actual pecuniary loss . [960]

2. **Subordination of Tax Liens:** If an allowed tax claim is secured by a nonavoidable lien on estate property, distribution of the property or its proceeds is in the following order: [961]

   (i) *To any lienholder* possessing an allowed claim secured by a nonavoidable lien on the collateral that is *senior to the tax lien;*

   (ii) *To the holders of any priority claims* in the first seven priority levels, with the aggregate of such distributions not to exceed the amount of the allowed secured tax claim;

   (iii) *To the tax lienholder* to the extent the allowed secured tax claim is *greater* than the total of all distributions made under (ii), above, to priority claimants;

   (iv) *To any lienholder* possessing an allowed claim secured by a nonavoidable lien on the collateral that is *junior to the tax lien;*

   (v) *To the tax lienholder* to the extent the allowed secured tax claim is *not satisfied* under (iii), above; and

   (vi) *To the Chapter 7 estate.*

3. **Similar Statutory Liens:** Statutory liens (*e.g.,* ERISA lien) with priority determined in the same way as prescribed under 28 U.S.C. section 6323 for priority of tax liens are treated exactly like tax liens, and are subordinated accordingly . [963]

D. **PARTNERSHIP TRUSTEE'S CLAIM AGAINST GENERAL PARTNERS**
   If the estate of a Chapter 7 partnership debtor lacks sufficient property to fully satisfy all claims against the partnership, the **trustee** is entitled to a claim for the **deficiency** against any general partner who is personally liable, but only to the extent that the general partner is personally liable under applicable nonbankruptcy law. The trustee, where practicable, must first pursue nondebtor general partners to recover the deficiency. The trustee's claim against the estate of each debtor general partner equals the total of all allowed claims of creditors in the partnership's bankruptcy case [964]

   1. **Excess Recovery by Trustee:** Property recovered from the estates of the debtor general partners in excess of a deficiency remaining after payment by the nondebtor general partners is returned to the estates of the debtor general partners in an equitable manner [968]

E. **CHAPTER 7 DISCHARGE**
   An individual Chapter 7 debtor must be granted a discharge, unless any of the 10 independent statutory grounds for denial of a discharge applies. A discharge relieves a debtor of all debts that arose prior to the order for relief under Chapter 7, as well as debts that are treated as pre-petition debts under Code section 502 [969]

		Text Section
1.	**Exception—Nondischargeable Debts:** The discharge does not include particular debts that are nondischargeable under Code section 523 (*see supra*, §§675 *et seq.*). One must distinguish between a **denial of the entire discharge** and a determination that a **specific debt is nondischargeable**	[970]
2.	**Objection to Discharge:** A creditor, the trustee, or the U.S. trustee may object to the discharge. Also, when a party in interest requests, the court may order the trustee to investigate the debtor's conduct to determine if there is a basis for denying the discharge	[971]
3.	**Grounds for Denial of Discharge:** A Chapter 7 discharge may be denied for any of the following reasons:	[972]

    (i) The debtor is **not an individual;**
    (ii) The debtor **transferred, concealed, or destroyed property with an intent to hinder, delay, or defraud a creditor** or officer of the estate entitled to possession;
    (iii) The debtor **destroyed, concealed, or failed to keep books or records;**
    (iv) The debtor knowingly and fraudulently **committed perjury, bribery, extortion,** etc.;
    (v) The debtor **failed to satisfactorily explain any loss of assets or deficiency of assets** to meet liabilities;
    (vi) The debtor **refused to obey a valid court order or to testify;**
    (vii) The debtor **committed an act** described in Code section 727(a)(2)-(6), within one year before bankruptcy or during the case, in connection with a separate bankruptcy case **regarding an insider;**
    (viii) The debtor **obtained a prior discharge** in a Chapter 7 or 11 case **commenced within six years** before the filing of the petition in the present case;
    (ix) The debtor **obtained a prior discharge** in a Chapter 12 or 13 case **commenced within six years** before the filing of the petition in the present case **unless:** (i) all allowed unsecured claims in the earlier case were **paid in full** or (ii) payments in the earlier case totaled **at least 70%** of the allowed unsecured claims and the plan was proposed in **good faith** and represented her **best effort;**
    (x) The debtor **executed a court-approved written waiver** of discharge after the Chapter 7 order for relief.

| 4. | **Revocation of Discharge:** After notice and a hearing, the debtor's discharge may be revoked if the debtor **obtained the discharge fraudulently, acquired** or became entitled to acquire what would be property of the estate **and knowingly and fraudulently failed to disclose** this fact or **turn over** that property to the trustee, or **committed an act** delineated in Code section 727(a)(6) | [984] |

F. CONVERSION

1.	**Voluntary Conversion:** If a Chapter 7 case has not been converted from Chapter 11, 12, or 13, the debtor has an **absolute nonwaivable right** to convert the case from Chapter 7 to any of such other chapters at any time	[986]
2.	**Involuntary Conversion:** Absent a request by the debtor, the court may **not** convert a Chapter 7 case to one under Chapter 12 or 13, but may convert it to Chapter 11 upon request by a party in interest, after notice and a hearing	[987]
3.	**Eligibility:** Conversion of a Chapter 7 case requires that the debtor be eligible for relief under the chapter to which it is being converted	[988]

G. DISMISSAL

After notice and a hearing, the court may dismiss a Chapter 7 case **for cause** (*e.g.*, debtor guilty of unreasonable delay prejudicing creditors). A case may also be dismissed if it was filed by an individual debtor with **primarily consumer debts** under circumstances constituting substantial abuse of relief under Chapter 7, but note that

	Text Section
there is a statutory presumption in the debtor's favor regarding whether granting relief would be a substantial abuse of Chapter 7. Dismissal for substantial abuse can be initiated only by the U.S. trustee's or the court's own motion—not by motion or suggestion of a party in interest..	[989]

X. CHAPTER 11—REORGANIZATION

A. ELIGIBILITY FOR RELIEF

Chapter 11 relief is available to any person qualifying as a debtor under chapter 7 except for stockbrokers or commodity brokers. *Note:* Railroads are eligible for relief under special provisions of Chapter 11. Designed primarily for business reorganizations, Chapter 11 also may provide relief for consumer debtors .... [993]

B. ADMINISTRATION OF CHAPTER 11 CASE

1. **Creditors' Committees:** Shortly after the order for relief, the U.S. trustee appoints a committee of unsecured creditors, usually consisting of those willing creditors holding the ***seven largest unsecured claims*** against the debtor. (*Exception:* If the debtor elects to be treated as a "small business," a creditors' committee is not always required). Additional committees of creditors or equity security holders may be appointed by the U.S. trustee. A creditors' or equity security holders' committee may engage in the following: consultation with the debtor in possession or the trustee; investigation of debtor's conduct, finances, etc.; participation in the preparation of a reorganization plan; advising the creditors or equity security holders it represents about the committee's judgment or conclusions about a plan; collection and filing of acceptances or rejections of a plan; and requesting appointment of a trustee or examiner. The committee may also hire professionals (*e.g.,* attorneys) with court approval .... [995]

2. **Debtor in Possession:** Unless a trustee is appointed, the debtor remains in possession of the estate property and generally continues to operate the business. The debtor in possession has all the rights, powers, and duties of a trustee, ***except*** the right to compensation and the duty to investigate the debtor. He has authority to make reasonable business judgments about the ordinary affairs of the debtor and may employ professionals, who must be disinterested persons not holding or representing an adverse interest .... [1006]

3. **Appointment of Trustee:** It is viewed as an exception rather than the rule for appointment of a trustee to be ordered in a Chapter 11 case, since the debtor in possession is usually the most appropriate person to operate the business. In fact, there is a presumption that the debtor should remain in possession .... [1009]

   a. **Cause for appointment:** Cause for an order to appoint a trustee exists when ***current management*** (before or after the filing of the bankruptcy petition) has committed acts showing, *e.g.,* fraud, dishonesty, incompetence, or gross mismanagement. Appointment is made by the U.S. trustee, unless an election is timely requested .... [1010]

   b. **Duties of trustee:** The duties of a Chapter 11 trustee are to: account for property received; examine proofs of claims and object to improper ones; provide information requested by parties in interest; file periodic reports on the operation of debtor's business; prepare and file a final report and account; file documents required under Code section 521(1) and not filed by the debtor; investigate debtor's conduct, financial condition, and business operations, and the advisability of continuing the business; file a report of the investigation; file a Chapter 11 plan; give information to taxing authorities about any year for which debtor failed to file a required return; and after a plan has been confirmed, file any required reports. The trustee is also authorized to operate the debtor's business unless the court rules otherwise. .... [1013]

				Text Section

4. **Appointment of Examiner:** The court will sometimes order appointment of an examiner rather than a trustee, before confirmation of a plan, to investigate charges of fraud, dishonesty, misconduct, incompetence, or mismanagement by debtor's present or former management. If requested by a party interest or the U.S. trustee, the court *must order* appointment of an examiner if the debtor's fixed, liquidated, unsecured debts exceed $5 million, excluding debts for goods, services, taxes, or those owed to insiders. Appointment is made by the U.S. trustee . . . . [1016]

5. **Claims and Interests—Special Rules for Chapter 11**
   a. **Proofs of claims or interests:** In Chapter 11 cases, the court fixes a *bar date* for filing a proof of claim or interest. However, if listed in the schedules filed by the debtor, a claim or interest is deemed filed unless it is scheduled as disputed, contingent, or unliquidated . . . . [1023]
   b. **Secured claims:** For purposes of allowance, both recourse and nonrecourse secured claims are treated as recourse claims. Thus, an undersecured creditor holding a nonrecourse claim will not have her unsecured claim for a deficiency disallowed. There are several exceptions to this rule . [1024]
   c. **Section 1111(b) election:** Under Chapter 11, a partially secured creditor may elect to have her claim treated as *secured to the full extent that the claim is allowed* (instead of secured only up to the value of the collateral) . . . . [1026]
      (1) **Exceptions:** Election cannot be made if the *creditor's interest in the property is of inconsequential value* or *the creditor has recourse and the collateral is sold* under the plan or under section 363 . . . . [1027]
      (2) **Waiver of deficiency:** If election is made, the secured party *forfeits her unsecured claim for any deficiency* . . . . [1028]
      (3) **Time of election:** Election may be exercised any time before the end of the hearing on the disclosure statement, or later as set by the court . . . . [1031]

6. **Conversion or Dismissal:** A Chapter 11 case may be dismissed or converted to another chapter as follows: . . . . [1032]
   a. **Voluntary conversion to Chapter 7:** The debtor may convert to Chapter 7 if a trustee has not been appointed under Chapter 11, the case originally was not an involuntary Chapter 11 case, and it was not converted involuntarily to Chapter 11. No notice or hearing is required . . . . [1033]
   b. **Discretionary conversion to Chapter 7 or dismissal:** Upon request by the U.S. trustee, the bankruptcy administrator, or a party in interest (including the debtor), or sua sponte when appropriate, the court *for cause* (*e.g.,* lack of good faith, continuing loss to the estate and no reasonable probability of rehabilitation, inability to effectuate a Chapter 11 plan) may dismiss the case or convert it to Chapter 7, whichever is better for creditors and the estate. Notice and a hearing are required . . . . [1034]
   c. **Exceptions:** If the debtor is a *farmer or nonbusiness corporation,* conversion to Chapter 7 is prohibited unless the debtor requests the conversion . [1037]
   d. **Conversion to Chapter 12 or 13:** The court may convert a Chapter 11 case to Chapter 12 or 13 only if the *debtor requests* it, he has *not received a Chapter 11 discharge,* and, if the conversion sought is to Chapter 12, the court finds that it is *equitable* . . . . [1038]

C. **REJECTION OF COLLECTIVE BARGAINING AGREEMENTS**
Rejection of a collective bargaining agreement may be an important factor in the debtor's effort to reorganize and is governed by a different standard than other kinds of executory contracts. Court approval of an application to reject a collective bargaining agreement requires proof by the debtor in possession (or trustee if one has been appointed) of the nine elements of Code section 1113 . . . . [1039]

D. **CHAPTER 11 PLAN**
1. **Filing a Plan:** A debtor may file a plan of reorganization with the petition or at any other time in a voluntary case. In an involuntary case, he may file a plan at any time. If no trustee has been appointed, the **debtor has the exclusive right** to file a plan for the first **120 days** after the order for relief . . . . [1044]
   a. **Other proponents:** A plan may be filed by **any party in interest** (but not the U.S. trustee) if: (i) a Chapter 11 **trustee has been appointed;** (ii) **the debtor has not filed a plan within 120 days** after the order for relief; or (iii) **the debtor has not filed a plan and obtained the acceptances** of every impaired class of claims or interests within **180 days** after the order for relief . . . . [1046]
   b. **Extension or reduction of time:** For cause, the court may shorten or lengthen the 120-day or 180-day period . . . . [1047]
2. **Classification of Claims or Interests:** A Chapter 11 plan must classify claims as well as equity interests. A claim or interest **may** be placed in a particular class only if it is **substantially similar** to the other claims or interests in that class. Most courts construe this provision so as not to compel the classification of all substantially similar claims together in one class (but each class must be homogeneous and there must be a reasonable and bona fide purpose for separate classification). Gerrymandering is not a proper purpose . . . . [1048]
   a. **Specific types of claims or interests**
      (1) **Secured claims:** Where secured creditors' liens are in different property or are entitled to different priorities in the same property, each secured claim should be placed alone in a separate class . . . . [1053]
      (2) **Priority claims:** Administrative expenses, involuntary case gap claims, and eighth priority tax claims are excepted from classification requirements. However, all other priority claims should be placed in separate classes with claims of equal priority . . . . [1054]
      (3) **Administrative convenience class:** The Code permits the plan to designate a separate class of small claims comprised of all unsecured claims that are less than, or by consent decreased to, an amount approved by the court as **reasonable and necessary** . . . . [1055]
      (4) **Interests:** Equity interests in a sole proprietorship, partnership, or a corporation must be classified separately from creditors' claims; common and preferred stock interests should also be placed in separated classes . . . . [1056]
3. **Contents of Plan**
   a. **Mandatory provisions:** A Chapter 11 plan must: . . . . [1058]
      (i) **Classify all claims and interests,** other than the excepted priority claims;
      (ii) **Specify any class that is not impaired;**
      (iii) **Describe the treatment to be accorded any impaired class;**
      (iv) **Treat every claim or interest within a particular class identically** unless a holder consents to a less favorable treatment;
      (v) **Establish adequate ways to implement the plan,** e.g., transfer of estate property to another entity, merger, or consolidation;
      (vi) **Include in the charter of a corporate debtor a provision prohibiting the issuance of nonvoting equity securities** and certain other voting power provisions; and
      (vii) **Provide for the selection of officers and directors** in a manner consistent with public policy and the interests of creditors and equity security holders.
   b. **Permissive provisions:** In addition to the mandatory items, a plan **may** provide for other measures (e.g., the assumption, rejection, or assignment of executory contracts or unexpired leases; the liquidation of all or substantially all of the estate property; the modification of the rights of secured

or unsecured creditors, *except* where the creditor's claim is secured *solely* by real property constituting the debtor's principal residence; or the allocation of tax payments to trust fund taxes where necessary for success of a reorganization plan) .... [1059]

    c. **Exempt property:** If the debtor is an individual, any plan proposed by another entity may not provide for the use, sale, or lease of exempt property without the debtor's consent .... [1060]

    d. **Interest on arrearages:** If the plan proposes to cure a default, the amount necessary to cure is determined by the underlying contract and applicable nonbankruptcy law .... [1061]

4. **Impairment of Classes:** Whether a class is impaired under a plan is significant because if a class is *not* impaired, there is a *conclusive presumption* that the plan has been accepted by that class and by each holder of a claim or interest in the class; the proponent need not solicit their acceptances. A class is *deemed to be impaired unless* the plan provides for all claims or interests of that class to be treated in accordance with either of two methods .... [1062]

    a. **Rights unmodified:** A class is unimpaired if the plan does *not alter* the legal, equitable, or contractual rights of the claim or interest holders ..... [1063]

    b. **Cure and deacceleration:** A class is unimpaired if, regardless of any contractual or other legal right to accelerate payment upon default, the plan proposes to *cure any default* (other than one under Code section 365(b)(2); see §894), *reinstate the original maturity date, pay for any damages* caused by the claimant's or interest holder's *reasonable reliance* on the right to accelerate, and *not otherwise alter* the legal, equitable, or contractual rights of the clamant or interest holder .... [1064]

5. **Solicitation and Disclosure:** Post-petition solicitation for acceptances or rejections of a plan may be conducted only at or after the plan (or summary) and a *written court-approved disclosure statement* have been sent to the relevant holders of claims or interests. If there is an objection to a proposed disclosure statement, the court conducts a hearing to determine whether it contains *adequate information* (*i.e.,* sufficient under the circumstances to enable a reasonable investor typical of holders of claims or interests of the relevant class to make an informed decision to accept or reject the plan) .... [1066]

    a. **Safe harbor provision:** Chapter 11 contains a provision that insulates from liability, for violation of a securities law, rule or regulation, a person who in good faith and in compliance with the Code solicits acceptances or rejections of a plan or participates in the offer, issuance, purchase, or sale of a security under the plan .... [1069]

    b. **Pre-petition solicitation:** Acceptances or rejections may be solicited before the filing of a Chapter 11 petition only if solicitation meets the disclosure requirements of any applicable securities or other nonbankruptcy law or regulation, or in the absence of any such law or regulation, is preceded by disclosure of adequate information (as defined in Code section 1125(a)) . [1070]

6. **Acceptance of Plan:** Any creditor or equity security holder whose claim or interest has been allowed may accept or reject a Chapter 11 plan by a signed writing identifying the plan and conforming to the appropriate official form. If made before commencement of the case, an acceptance or rejection is valid if: (i) it was solicited in accordance with the requirements for pre-petition solicitation; (ii) the plan was sent to substantially all creditors and equity security holders of the same class within a reasonable time to accept or reject it; and (iii) where the claim was based on a security of record, the creditor or equity security holder was the holder of record on the date specified in the solicitation .... [1071]

    a. **Classes of claims:** Acceptance by creditors holding at least *two-thirds in amount and more than half in number of the allowed claims* actually being voted is necessary for acceptance of the plan .... [1072]

    b. **Classes of interests:** Acceptance of a plan requires acceptance by equity

		Text Section
	security holders having at least *two-thirds in amount* of the allowed interests actually being voted	[1073]
c.	**Unimpaired classes:** If a class is not impaired under a plan, there is a conclusive presumption that the class and each holder of a claim or interest in that class has accepted it	[1075]
d.	**Classes receiving no property:** A class that receives or retains no property under a plan is deemed to have rejected it	[1076]
7.	**Modifying a Plan:** Prior to confirmation, a plan may be modified only by its proponent. After confirmation and before substantial consummation, it may be modified, if warranted, by the proponent *or* the reorganized debtor	[1077]

E. **CONFIRMATION OF PLAN**
 1. **Requirements for Confirmation:** To be confirmed, a plan must satisfy the following requirements. A hearing is required . . . . [1079]
    - (i) *Plan must comply with relevant Code provisions* (*e.g.,* mandatory contents of plan);
    - (ii) *Plan's proponent must comply with Code provisions* (*e.g.,* disclosure and solicitation of acceptances);
    - (iii) *Plan must be proposed in good faith;*
    - (iv) *All payments* by the proponent, debtor, or a person issuing securities or receiving property under the plan *for services or expenses must be approved* by the court;
    - (v) *All officers, directors, voting trustees, and insiders* of the reorganized debtor (or successor) *must be disclosed,* as well as proposed compensation for insiders;
    - (vi) *Debtor's rate changes must be approved* by the appropriate governmental regulatory commission;
    - (vii) *"Best interests of creditors test" must be met* concerning each *holder* of a claim or interest of an impaired class;
    - (viii) *All impaired classes must have accepted the plan;*
    - (ix) *At least one impaired class of claims has accepted the plan* (excluding acceptances by insiders of the consenting class);
    - (x) *All administrative expenses and involuntary gap claims must be paid completely in cash* on the effective date of the plan, unless a particular claim holder consents to a different treatment;
    - (xi) *Third, fourth, fifth, sixth, and seventh priority claims must be provided* for as required by the Code;
    - (xii) *Each eighth priority tax claimant must receive deferred cash payments* having a present value, as of the effective date of the plan, equal to the allowed amount of the claim, unless it consents to different treatment (note that the payout period may not exceed six years after the date the tax was assessed);
    - (xiii) *Plan must be feasible;*
    - (xiv) *All bankruptcy fees must have been paid* or will be paid on or before the effective date of the plan; and
    - (xv) *Plan must provide for continued payment of retiree benefits,* unless modified by agreement or court order.
 2. **Cram Down:** If all of the requirements have been satisfied *except* that which requires that every class of claims or interests either has accepted the plan or is unimpaired under the plan, the court, upon request by the plan proponent, will confirm the plan if it is *not unfairly discriminatory and is fair and equitable* with respect to any dissenting impaired classes . . . . [1097]
    - a. **Secured claims:** To be considered fair and equitable, the plan must propose one of three methods with respect to secured claims: (i) the secured party *retains her lien for the allowed amount of the claim and receives payment in deferred cash installments* totaling at least the allowed

				Text Section
			amount of the secured claim and having a present value, as of the effective date of the plan, of at least the value of the collateral; (ii) the secured creditor *receives the indubitable equivalent* of her secured claim; or (iii) *the collateral is sold* free and clear, but the creditor's *lien attaches to the proceeds* of the sale and is treated as in (i) and (ii)	[1100]
		b.	**Unsecured claims:** To be considered fair and equitable, a plan must propose one of two methods of treating a class of unsecured claims: (i) *each creditor receives property,* having a present value as of the effective date of the plan *equal to the allowed amount of her claim* or (ii) *no creditor or holder of an interest that is junior* to the class receives or retains any property at all (*absolute priority rule*). The courts are split concerning the validity of the "new value exception"	[1107]
		c.	**Equity interests:** For a plan to be fair and equitable with regard to a class of equity interests, it must propose one of two methods of treatment: (i) each interest holder *receives or retains property,* having a present value as of the effective date of the plan *equal to any fixed liquidation preference, fixed redemption price, or the holder's equity interest,* whichever is greatest; or (ii) no interest holder junior to the class receives or retains any property at all	[1111]
F.	**POST-CONFIRMATION MATTERS**			
	1.	**Effect of Confirmation:** Upon confirmation, a plan's provisions are binding on all creditors and equity security holders, the debtor, any general partner in the debtor, and any entity that issues securities or acquires property under the plan, whether or not they have accepted the plan or are impaired under the plan		[1117]
		a.	**On property:** Unless otherwise provided, confirmation causes all estate property to vest in the debtor and all property dealt with in the plan to be free and clear of all claims and interests. *Note:* There is conflicting authority regarding a secured creditor who fails to file a proof of claim in a Chapter 11 case; some courts hold that he does not lose his pre-petition lien if no action was brought to avoid the lien; other courts may require filing a claim and/or including a provision in the plan expressly preserving the creditor's lien	[1118]
		b.	**Discharge of debts:** Generally, confirmation discharges the debtor from *all pre-confirmation debts* as well as certain other debts (*e.g.,* those arising from the rejection of executory contracts or unexpired leases not assumed by the trustee or debtor in possession). Individuals, corporations, and partnerships may be discharged under Chapter 11 (except as indicated below)	[1119]
			(1) **Exceptions to discharge:** Confirmation does not discharge *an individual's nondischargeable debts.* Also, if the plan provides for all or substantially *all of the estate property to be liquidated,* the debtor does *not continue in business,* and the debtor *would not be granted a discharge in a Chapter 7 case,* there will be no discharge	[1120]
	2.	**Implementation of Plan:** The debtor and any successor are required to implement the plan and comply with all court orders. The court also has authority to order the debtor and any other necessary party to execute or deliver instruments required for property transfers under the plan and to perform whatever else is needed to consummate the plan		[1126]
	3.	**Revocation of Confirmation Order:** Within 180 days after entry of the order confirming a Chapter 11 plan, a party in interest may request the court to revoke the order, but only on the ground that it was procured by *fraud.* Notice and a hearing are required		[1128]
G.	**SMALL BUSINESSES**			
	The reorganization of an electing small business (whose aggregate secured and			

unsecured debts do not exceed $2 million) can be expedited by Code provisions authorizing: (i) that a creditors' committee not be appointed, (ii) that the debtor's exclusivity period for filing a plan to be the first 100 days after the order for relief, (iii) that the deadline for filing all other plans be 160 days after the order for relief, (iv) court approval of a conditional disclosure statement which, under certain conditions, may be used to solicit acceptances and rejections, and (v) a combined hearing on the disclosure statement and confirmation of the plan .... [1131]

H. "*MANVILLE*-TYPE" TRUST/INJUNCTION
The Code contains a provision authorizing the court to order the type of trust/injunction used in the *Johns-Manville* case. It applies only to cases in Chapter 11 involving **asbestos-related liabilities** of the debtor, where an indeterminable number of substantial future demands for payment necessitate use of the trust to deal equitably with claims and future demands. This provision permits the court, after notice and a hearing, to enjoin suits against the debtor; officers, directors, affiliates, and insurance companies of the debtor; and successors to the debtor. Instead of suits being brought against the debtor (or such other entities), **present and future claims and demands will be brought against the trust,** which will be established under the plan of reorganization and will be funded by securities of the debtor and future payments to be made by the debtor. The requirements for the trust/injunction are found in Code section 524(g) .... [1134]

XI. CHAPTER 13—INDIVIDUAL WITH REGULAR INCOME

A. ELIGIBILITY FOR RELIEF
Chapter 13 relief is available to an **individual with regular income** (and her spouse), whose **unsecured debts** total less than $250,000 and whose **secured debts** total less than $750,000. "Regular income" means income that is sufficiently stable and regular to allow the individual to make payments under a plan. Stockbrokers and commodity brokers are **not** entitled to Chapter 13 relief, nor are individuals whose case was dismissed in the preceding 180 days due to intentional failure to obey court orders or appear or by voluntary dismissal following a party's request for relief from the automatic stay. A Chapter 13 case can be commenced only by a voluntary petition .... [1138]

B. CO-DEBTOR STAY
The filing of a Chapter 13 petition invokes not only the automatic stay but also a stay against any civil action or other act by a creditor to collect **a consumer debt from an individual who has guaranteed or secured a liability** of the debtor or who is otherwise **liable with the debtor.** A consumer debt is one incurred primarily for personal, family, or household purposes .... [1143]
1. **Exceptions:** The co-debtor stay does not apply if the Chapter 13 case has been closed, dismissed, or converted to Chapter 7 or 11, or if the co-debtor's liability was incurred in the ordinary course of *his* business .... [1145]
2. **Grounds for Relief:** A creditor may be granted relief from the co-debtor stay to the extent that the co-debtor **actually received the consideration** for the claim, the **creditor's claim will not be paid** under the debtor's proposed plan, or the **creditor will be irreparably harmed** if the stay remains in effect ...... [1146]

C. ADMINISTRATION OF CHAPTER 13 CASE
1. **Appointment of Chapter 13 Trustee:** In regions where many Chapter 13 cases are filed, the U.S. trustee ordinarily appoints a **standing trustee.** Otherwise, he may appoint a trustee for a particular case or serve himself. A Chapter 13 trustee performs certain of the duties of a Chapter 7 trustee (not including liquidation of the estate property). Additional duties include testifying at any hearing

regarding valuation of property subject to a lien, or confirmation (or post-confirmation modification) of a Chapter 13 plan; furnishing nonlegal advice to the debtor; ensuring that the debtor timely begins making payments; investigating the conduct, financial condition, and advisability of continuing the business of a debtor engaged in business; and ordinarily, disbursement of payments to creditors .... [1150]

2. **Rights and Powers of Debtor:** The debtor has the *exclusive right* to use, sell, or lease estate property under Code section 363(b), (d), (e), (f), or (l). A *debtor engaged in business* (*i.e.,* a *self-employed* individual who incurs *trade credit* in producing income from her business) may operate the business *unless the court orders otherwise* and usually has the exclusive right to use, sell, or lease property in the ordinary course of business and to obtain credit. These rights are subject to any applicable Code provisions and court-imposed restrictions. A debtor engaged in business must also file periodic financial reports with the court, U.S. trustee, and appropriate taxing authorities .... [1152]

3. **Post-Petition Claims:** Post-petition claims for *taxes* that become due during pendency of the case and for *consumer debts necessary* for the debtor's performance under the plan are determined as of the date they arise, but are treated as *pre-petition claims* for purposes of *allowance, except* a post-petition claim for a necessary consumer debt will be disallowed if the claimant knew or should have known that prior approval of the debt by the trustee was practicable and was not procured .... [1155]

4. **Property of Estate:** Debtor retains estate property unless a confirmed plan or confirmation order provides otherwise. The Chapter 13 estate consists of: (i) all "section 541 property"; (ii) all "section 541 property" acquired by the debtor post-petition, but before the earliest of the closing, dismissal, or conversion of the case; and (iii) all of the *debtor's earnings* from services performed post-petition, but before the earliest of the closing, dismissal, or conversion of the case . [1158]

5. **Conversion or Dismissal**
    a. **Voluntary conversion to Chapter 7 or dismissal:** The debtor has an absolute, nonwaivable right to *convert* the case to Chapter 7, and also has the nonwaivable right to *dismiss* the case if it has not already been converted from Chapter 7, 11, or 12 .... [1160]
    b. **Discretionary dismissal or conversion to Chapter 7:** Upon request by a party in interest or the U.S. trustee, and after notice and a hearing, the court *for cause* may dismiss the case or convert it to Chapter 7, whichever is better for the creditors and the estate. Such dismissal or conversion is discretionary .... [1162]
    c. **Conversion to Chapter 11 or 12:** Before confirmation of a Chapter 13 plan, upon request by a party in interest (including debtor) or the U.S. trustee, the court may convert the case to Chapter 11 or 12, after notice and a hearing. Debtor must be eligible for relief under the alternative chapter .... [1164]
    d. **Exception:** If the debtor is a *farmer,* a Chapter 13 case cannot be converted to Chapter 7, 11, or 12 *unless* the debtor so requests .... [1165]
    e. **Property of estate in converted case:** If a case is converted from Chapter 13 to another chapter, property of the estate in the converted case consists of property of the estate on the date of the Chapter 13 filing that remains in the debtor's possession or control on the date of conversion. However, if the debtor converts in bad faith, property of the estate will consist of the estate property on the date of conversion .... [1166]

D. **CHAPTER 13 PLAN**
   1. **Filing:** Only the *debtor* may file a Chapter 13 plan, which must be filed with the petition or within 15 days thereafter, unless an extension for cause is granted . [1167]

	Text Section

2. **Mandatory Provisions:** A Chapter 13 plan must include provisions that *sufficient future income to implement the plan will be turned over to the trustee; all priority claims will be paid fully* in deferred cash payments (unless a creditor consents to different treatment); and, if classes of claims are designated, *claims in a single class must receive identical treatment* . . . . [1168]

3. **Permissive Provisions:** The plan may include: . . . . [1172]
   (i) *Specification of various classes of unsecured claims,* in accordance with Code section 1122, if it does not discriminate unfairly against any particular class; however, different treatment is allowed for a consumer debt on which an individual co-debtor is also liable than for other unsecured claims;
   (ii) *Modification of the rights of secured creditors or unsecured creditors, except* where the creditor's claim is secured *solely* by a security interest in real property constituting debtor's principal residence;
   (iii) *Cure or waiver of any default;*
   (iv) *Payment of a general unsecured claim concurrently with payment of a secured or priority claim;*
   (v) *Curing of any default* within a reasonable time and the *maintenance of payments* during the case on any *long-term* secured or unsecured debt for which final payment is due *after* the final payment required by the plan (notwithstanding (ii), above;
   (vi) *Payment of any allowed post-petition tax claims or necessary consumer debts;*
   (vii) *Assumption, rejection or assignment of executory contracts or unexpired leases;*
   (viii) *Payment of particular claims from estate property or debtor's property;*
   (ix) *Vesting of property* in the debtor or other entity; and
   (x) *Any other provisions* appropriate and consistent with the Code (*e.g.,* a provision to pay a mortgage under the plan, where the underlying personal debt that the mortgaged property secures has been discharged in an earlier Chapter 7 case.)

4. **Duration of Plan:** Payments under a plan may not extend beyond **three years,** unless, for cause, the court approves a longer period, up to a maximum of **five years** . . . . [1191]

5. **Modification of Plan:** The debtor has the exclusive right to modify a plan **prior to confirmation** . . . . [1192]

E. **CONFIRMATION OF PLAN**
After notice, the court holds a hearing to determine whether a proposed plan satisfies the necessary elements for confirmation. Any party in interest may file an objection. A plan must *comply with Code provisions,* and *all fees* must have been paid. The plan must be proposed in *good faith;* provide that *each unsecured creditor* holding an allowed claim will receive property having a present value as of the effective date of the plan of not less than the amount he would receive in a Chapter 7 liquidation on that date ("best interests of creditors test" met); and provide that *each secured creditor has accepted the plan,* or *collateral is surrendered* by the debtor to the creditor, or the plan must *preserve the creditor's* lien on the collateral and provide him with a distribution of *cash installments or other property* having a present value as of the effective date of the plan of at least the amount of his allowed secured claim. The *plan must be feasible* . . . . [1193]

1. **Best Efforts of Debtor:** If an objection is filed by an unsecured creditor or the Chapter 13 trustee, the plan may not be confirmed *unless;* (i) it proposes to pay the objecting creditor the *total amount* of his allowed claim; or (ii) all of the debtor's *"projected disposable income"* for three years from the due date of the first payment will be used to make payments under the plan . . . . [1203]

XL—Bankruptcy

2. **Payment Orders:** After confirmation, the court may order the debtor's employer or other entities providing income to the debtor to make direct payments to the Chapter 13 trustee. *Exception:* Social Security payments .... [1205]

F. PAYMENTS
Generally, debtor's payments under a proposed plan must begin within **30 days** after the plan is filed. After confirmation of the plan, payments are sent to creditors by the trustee as soon as practicable, unless the plan or confirmation order provides otherwise (*e.g.,* where debtor engaged in business is allowed to perform this function) .... [1206]

G. POST-CONFIRMATION MATTERS
1. **Effects of Confirmation:** A confirmed plan binds the debtor **and every creditor,** regardless of whether he has accepted, rejected, or objected to the plan, or whether his claim is provided for by the plan .... [1210]
    a. **Property:** Unless the Chapter 13 plan or confirmation order provides otherwise, confirmation causes all estate property to vest in the debtor free and clear of any claim or interest of any creditor provided for by the plan. Thus, if the plan provides for a secured creditor's claim, the creditor may more effectively protect his **lien** by filing a claim and requiring that the plan expressly provide for the retention of the lien .... [1212]
    b. **Debts:** Confirmation does *not* operate as a discharge of the debtor's debts .... [1213]
2. **Chapter 13 Discharge:** Discharge is granted to the debtor **after she has made all payments under the plan** unless, subsequent to the order for relief, she has executed a court-approved written waiver of discharge .... [1214]
    a. **Debts discharged:** A standard discharge includes all debts provided for in the plan or disallowed under Code section 502, **except** for (i) **long-term debts** provided for under Code section 1322(b)(5) (*i.e.,* curing any default within a reasonable time and maintaining payments during the case, etc.); (ii) **alimony, maintenance, and spousal or child support;** (iii) **student loans** (with two possible exceptions); (iv) Health Education Assistance Loans ("HEAL") if the three conditions for discharge under the federal nonbankruptcy statute have not been met; (v) liability for **drunk or drugged driving** that caused personal injury or death; (vi) **criminal restitution** and criminal fines; and (vii) post-petition claims allowed for necessary consumer debts not approved in advance by the trustee, where approval was practicable .... [1215]
    b. **Hardship discharge:** After notice and a hearing, a hardship discharge may be awarded (where debtor has not made all payments under the plan) where the **reason for the debtor's failure** to complete payments is, in fairness, one for which she should not be held accountable; the **"best interests of creditors test"** has been met with respect to **each unsecured claim;** and **modification of the plan is not practicable** .... [1217]
        (1) **Debts discharged:** A hardship discharge includes the unsecured debts that would ordinarily be discharged in a Chapter 13 case, **except** it does not discharge any debts that would be nondischargeable under section 523(a) (*see supra,* §675) or any long-term debts provided for under the cure provision of section 1322(b)(5) .... [1218]
3. **Post-Confirmation Modification:** The debtor, trustee, or an unsecured creditor may request a modification of a plan any time after confirmation but before all payments have been made .... [1220]
4. **Revocation of Confirmation Order:** Within 180 days after entry of a confirmation order, a party in interest may request revocation of the order on fraud grounds. Revocation is discretionary. If, after notice and a hearing, it is revoked, the court may grant the debtor time to propose and obtain confirmation of a modified plan; otherwise it must convert or dismiss the case .... [1221]

Bankruptcy—XLI

Text Section

XII. CHAPTER 12—FAMILY FARMER WITH REGULAR ANNUAL INCOME

A. ELIGIBILITY FOR RELIEF
Chapter 12 relief is available only to a *family farmer with regular annual income* (*i.e.*, annual income sufficiently stable and regular to enable him to make payments under a plan). In addition to certain individuals (or individuals and their spouses), certain corporations and partnerships may be eligible for Chapter 12 relief. A family farmer is *ineligible* for relief if he was a debtor in a case dismissed within the preceding 180 days for intentional failure to obey court orders or appear or by voluntary dismissal following a party's request for relief from the automatic stay. A Chapter 12 case may be commenced only by the filing of a voluntary petition .... [1223]

B. SIMILARITIES AND DIFFERENCES—CHAPTERS 12 AND 13
Many of the provisions of Chapter 12 are identical or bear great resemblance to their counterparts in Chapter 13. The major *differences* between these chapters include: .... [1232]

1. **Eligibility for Relief:** The debt ceiling in Chapter 12 is significantly higher ($1.5 million) .... [1245]
2. **Filing Plan:** A Chapter 12 debtor has a longer period in which to file the plan (90 days after the order for relief) .... [1246]
3. **Commencement of Payments:** There is no specific period in which a Chapter 12 debtor must begin making payments .... [1247]
4. **Debtor's Rights and Duties:** In addition to continuing to operate the farm, a Chapter 12 debtor in possession has all of the rights and duties of a Chapter 11 trustee except for the right to compensation and the duty to investigate the debtor .... [1248]
5. **Adequate Protection:** Bankruptcy Code section 361 does not apply to Chapter 12; however, a separate section concerning adequate protection has been enacted for Chapter 12. It specifies that adequate protection is designed to protect against a decline in the value of the *property* securing the claim (rather than against a decrease in the value of an entity's interest in the property). It also sets forth several nonexclusive methods of providing adequate protection in a Chapter 12 case .... [1249]
6. **Sales Free and Clear:** A Chapter 12 *trustee* may sell farmland or farm equipment free and clear of liens (or other interests) if proceeds from the sale become subject to the secured creditor's interest. Notice and a hearing are required ... [1250]
7. **Permissive Provisions of Chapter 12 Plan:** The power of a Chapter 12 debtor to *modify* rights of creditors is not subject to the Chapter 13 exception regarding a claim secured solely by a security interest in real property constituting the debtor's principal residence. A Chapter 12 plan may provide for *sale* of estate property *or distribution* of it among entities having an interest in the property. The plan may also allow payments to secured creditors to be made over a *longer period* than the three or five years in Code section 1222(c) (but must be consistent with confirmation requirements in section 1225(a)(5)) .... [1251]
8. **Confirmation Hearing:** The court must conclude the confirmation hearing within 45 days after the plan is filed, except for cause .... [1255]
9. **Best Efforts:** If an unsecured creditor or the trustee objects to a plan that does not propose full repayment, the "best efforts" test is not always limited to three years' projected disposable income; the court may approve a longer period up to five years .... [1256]
10. **Discharge:** A standard discharge under Chapter 12 does not discharge debts that are nondischargeable under section 523(a) .... [1257]

C. DIFFERENCES FROM CHAPTER 11
Some of the ways in which Chapter 12 differs from Chapter 11 include Chapter 12 provisions for: only voluntary petitions, mandatory trustee appointment (although a

family farmer remains a debtor in possession unless removed by the court), application of the co-debtor stay, "adequate protection" determined under section 1205, no creditors' committees, filing of plan only by debtor, no solicitations of acceptance or rejection of the plan, earlier confirmation, no absolute priority rule, no discharge by confirmation of the plan, no section 1111(b)-type election by partially secured creditors, and payment to creditors by Chapter 12 trustee .... [1258]

D. SECURED CREDITORS
1. **Requirement for Confirmation:** Each allowed secured claim must be treated by one of the following methods: (i) the secured creditor **accepts the plan;** (ii) the debtor **surrenders the collateral** to the secured creditor; or (iii) the plan **preserves the creditor's lien** on the collateral and provides him with distribution of **cash installments or other property** having a present value as of the effective date of the plan of at least the amount of his allowed secured claim .. [1271]
2. **Permissive Plan Provisions:** If there has been a large decline in the value of debtor's farm, Chapter 12 may allow a "write down" of a secured claim to the collateral's market value, and payments may extend over a longer time and be at a lower (reasonable) interest rate (but must be consistent with confirmation requirements) .... [1272]

E. UNSECURED CREDITORS
Each unsecured creditor holding an allowed claim must receive property having a present value as of the effective date of the plan of not less than the amount he would receive for his claim under Chapter 7 if the estate were liquidated on that date, considering the debtor's exemptions (**"best interest of creditors test"**). If an unsecured creditor or the trustee objects to confirmation of a plan not proposing full payment, confirmation will be denied unless the **"best efforts" test** is met .... [1273]

F. CONVERSION OR DISMISSAL
The debtor has an absolute, nonwaivable right to **convert** the case to Chapter 7, and a nonwaivable right to **dismiss** the case **if** it has not already been converted from Chapter 7 or 11. Upon request by a party in interest, the court may (i) convert a case to Chapter 7 or dismiss it **where the debtor has committed fraud** concerning the case or (ii) dismiss the case for cause other than fraud. Notice and a hearing are required .... [1276]

G. SUNSET PROVISION
Chapter 12 will automatically be repealed on October 1, 1998 (unless extended), but will remain in effect and be applicable for cases filed before that date .... [1281]

TEXT CORRELATION CHART

Gilbert Law Summary Bankruptcy	Alces, Howard Bankruptcy 1995	Baird, Jackson Bankruptcy 1990 (2nd ed.) 1994 Supp.	Eisenberg Bankruptcy and Debtor-Creditor Law 1988 (2nd ed.)	Epstein, Nickles Debt, Bankruptcy, Article 9 and Related Laws 1994	Jorden, Warren Bankruptcy 1995 (4th ed.)	White, Nimmer Bankruptcy 1992 (2nd ed.)
I. INTRODUCTION						
A. Goals of the Federal Bankruptcy Laws	10-11	22-23, 65-68, 749-762	455		22-23	52-54
B. Legislative History	9-10, 14-15	26-37, 1195-1219	452-456, 897-898	719-721, 1016-1019	19-22, 923-926	54-57
C. Organization of the Bankruptcy Code	11-14	36-38	455-456	720, 722	23-25	57-60
D. Rules of Construction		86, 665-666				
E. Participants in the Bankruptcy Case	2, 6, 8, 11-12	60-64, 132	12, 687-688, 814-815	721-722	23-25	60-66
F. Terminology	110-112, 153	3, 66, 105-107, 136-141, 432	583, 713-714	721-722		66-68
II. JURISDICTION AND PROCEDURE						
A. Bankruptcy Court	15, 96-97, 590	740-748, 1191-1195, 1207-1219, 1241-1254; Supp. 187	895-909	734, 782-785, 1018-1019, 1020-1021	23, 921-923	61
B. Personal Jurisdiction		1254	909-915			98
C. Subject Matter Jurisdiction	14-15	1206-1219, 1241-1254	898-909	1019-1020	923-939	93-105
D. Core/Non-Core Proceedings	15	36-37, 1193-1194, 1209-1219; Supp. 187	915-940	1021	926-939	96-105
E. Jury Trials	17-21	1220-1241; Supp. 187-188	460, 946-954	1023-1029	947-963	111-121
F. Withdrawal		1193, 1240	899, 931-932	1022	939	
G. Abstention	15		899-907	1022-1023	939-940	97-98
H. Removal		1255-1264	940-946	1023	944-947	
I. Venue	15-17	1254-1266	915		940-943	106-111
J. Appeals		1266-1270; Supp. 188-190	946	1029		
III. COMMENCEMENT AND ADMINISTRATION OF THE CASE						
A. Eligibility	11-14, 25-32, 45	68-81; Supp. 1	459-460	722, 723, 726-729, 731, 742-743	25-26	58, 70, 634-635, 640-641
B. Voluntary Case	23-32, 88	81-87; Supp. 2-4	455-456	723, 731-732, 735-748, 762	26	69, 72-91
C. Involuntary Case	32-64, 88	87-110	458-467	723, 732-748, 762	272-299, 300-302	69-70
D. Case Ancillary to Foreign Proceeding						
E. Abstention	13, 590-604	114, 1253	907	735, 1022-1023	28-29	58
F. Section 341 Meeting of Creditors		62-63, 950-951, 1280-1281; Supp. 191	814-822	722, 1047-1051		63, 69
G. Debtor's Duties		61-62				
H. Conversion	63	56, 104	455	748	26	72-91
I. Dismissal	39-64	111-129; Supp. 5-7		735-748		
IV. OFFICERS OF THE ESTATE						
A. Trustee	11-13, 195-196, 429-430, 437-438, 590-597	60-61, 197, 210-211, 275-293, 308-356, 647-656, 1127-1129, 1270-1275; Supp. 41-42, 190-191	687-688, 814-822	721-722, 724-725, 727, 1040-1046	26-28, 748-750	61-63, 639, 682

TEXT CORRELATION CHART—continued

Gilbert Law Summary Bankruptcy		Alces, Howard Bankruptcy 1995	Baird, Jackson Bankruptcy 1990 (2nd ed.) 1994 Supp.	Eisenberg Bankruptcy and Debtor-Creditor Law 1988 (2nd ed.)	Epstein, Nickles Debt, Bankruptcy, Article 9 and Related Laws 1994	Jorden, Warren Bankruptcy 1995 (4th ed.)	White, Nimmer Bankruptcy 1992 (2nd ed.)
B.	Examiner		62, 683-688, 948, 951 950, 1274-1279	820, 822	1041-1042	751-753	58
C.	Professional Persons			814		27-28	682-683
D.	Compensation of Officers		1273-1280	821		27, 752	63-64
E.	United States Trustee		63, 950-951	932-933	722, 1035-1037	748-750	
V.	**THE BANKRUPTCY ESTATE AND THE TRUSTEE'S AVOIDING POWERS**						
A.	The Bankruptcy Estate	64-76, 469	189-306, 851-894; Supp. 25-40, 129-137	467-480	750-757, 758-759	32-54	124-134
B.	Turnover of Property to Trustee		636-646	502-510	894-899, 1010-1012		127, 131-132
C.	Creditor's Right of Setoff	197, 426-437	510-531, 646-653	691-693, 767-772	994-998	501-516	351-361
D.	Trustee's Avoidance of Statutory Liens	248-249, 408, 437-438	218-223, 401-416; Supp. 61-74	459, 750-767	1009	631-633	292-304, 344-345
E.	Trustee's Avoiding Powers as Hypothetical Creditor or Purchaser, and as Successor to Certain Actual Creditors	276-277, 294, 404-409	336-357; Supp. 41-42	18-19, 689-706	998-1004	610-630	293-306
F.	Trustee's Power to Avoid Preferences	330-368, 438	417-510; Supp. 75-89	711-750	954-994, 1004-1007, 1008-1009	430-501	306-351
G.	Trustee's Power to Avoid Fraudulent Transfers	275-329	357-401; Supp. 42-61	689-694, 706-711	947-954, 998, 1007-1008	516-610	370-424
H.	Post-Petition Transactions	438-439	272, 531-533, 536-537, 653-657	601, 698	823, 1010-1013		424-427
I.	Limitations on Trustee's Avoiding Powers	7-8, 330, 439-441	328-332, 453-454, 510-511, 532-533; Supp. 41-42	452-453, 487-493, 511-523, 698-706, 757-767	1004, 1006-1007, 1009, 1012-1013		
J.	Transferee's Liability to Estate for Avoided Transfer	369-403	308-309, 321-327, 447-453, 497-510, 531	711	945-947, 966-973	600-609	
K.	Post-Petition Effect of Security Interest		230-232, 330-331	737-740			
L.	Abandonment of Estate Property	195-196	474-478, 480-481, 634	650-651, 662-663	780-876	33, 470-485	463-472, 632-633
M.	Sovereign Immunity	402-403	234-235, 573-593 510-511	425-433			
VI.	**CLAIMS OF CREDITORS**						
A.	Filing Proofs of Claims	32, 110-134, 158-164, 484	95-103, 131-165, 472, 599-600, 784-785, 948, 1017-1037; Supp. 9-24	583, 597-599	723, 726, 728, 731-732, 822, 831-843	104-128	67, 69-71, 428-432, 439-441, 488-503
B.	Allowance of Claims	110-111, 150-158, 164	165-188, 715	525-532, 583, 592-599, 601-602	725, 831-843, 872, 1061, 1126	109-143	202, 455, 488-509
C.	Secured Claims	111, 195-197, 249-273, 608-612	224-232, 450-451, 511, 561, 618-636, 655-656, 693-694, 725	583-591, 601, 611-617, 644, 719-720, 729-735, 845-855, 865-866	872-876, 903-913	212-248	163-171, 428, 433-448
D.	Administrative Expenses	165-174	275, 693-705	602-618	844-847	249-252	
E.	Priority Claims	124-125, 165-180, 512-514, 551, 619-628	224-231, 321-327, 576-577, 590-592, 693-727	408-425, 431-433, 583-591, 602-630	843-851, 859	248-249, 252-260, 632-633	448-456, 463-488 173, 193, 448-488, 633
F.	Tax Claims	166-172, 248-249	957				
G.	Subrogation Claims	164-165	719-723, 726-727				

ii—Bankruptcy

TEXT CORRELATION CHART—continued

	Gilbert Law Summary Bankruptcy	Alces, Howard Bankruptcy 1995	Baird, Jackson Bankruptcy 1990 (2nd ed.) 1994 Supp.	Eisenberg Bankruptcy and Debtor-Creditor Law 1988 (2nd ed.)	Epstein, Nickles Debt, Bankruptcy, Article 9 and Related Laws 1994	Jorden, Warren Bankruptcy 1995 (4th ed.)	White, Nimmer Bankruptcy 1992 (2nd ed.)
H.	Subordination of Claims	180-187	724-726, 728-740	618-633	851-858	634-661	361-370
I.	Distribution Outside of Bankruptcy Code						
VII.	**DEBTOR'S EXEMPTIONS AND DISCHARGE OF INDEBTEDNESS**						
A.	Exemptions	76-88, 222-223, 410-426, 551	13-16, 33, 190-203, 490-494, 874-881, 894-946, 1164-1173; Supp. 133-134, 136-155	398-406, 480-502	724, 757-761, 823	54-103	708-759
B.	Nondischargeable Debts	531-566	784-786, 795-796, 803, 810-837, 1132-1145; Supp. 179 762-803; Supp. 111-127	493-502, 663-675, 773-781	726, 759, 799-813	148-201, 260-271	632-652
C.	Effects of Discharge	566-567	803-807	643-657, 677, 798-801	813-818	143-145	632
D.	Reaffirmation Agreements	567-568	644-646, 808-809	675-677	818-819	260-271	671-678
E.	Redemption—Chapter 7 Cases Only	229-237	786-801	647-653	899-903	261-270	671-678
F.	Protection Against Discrimination	568-581		677-686, 784-792	819	201-212	653-671
VIII.	**ADMINISTRATIVE POWERS**						
A.	Adequate Protection	197-213, 249-256, 604-612, 618-628, 634-641	297-305, 535-536, 618-636, 645-646	536-549, 611-618, 888-894	876-894, 1062-1069	730-748, 905-906	145-163
B.	Automatic Stay	88-109, 197-213, 551, 583-590	535-653; Supp. 91-102	486, 511, 524-536, 547-549, 805-806	761-785	303-342, 684-685	58, 71, 122-171
C.	Use, Sale, or Lease of Property	195-213, 508-514, 604-612, 629-634	535-536, 538-544, 560-563, 647-656, 890-891, 948, 1092-1105	509, 548-549, 688, 819	1060-1061, 1087-1107, 1159-1198	739-740, 756-763, 777-791	70-71, 172-201
D.	Obtaining Credit	612-618	653-683, 705-708, 1241; Supp. 102-110	888-894	1061-1087	764-777	201-223
E.	Executory Contracts and Unexpired Leases	442-514	233-306; Supp. 39-40	439-452, 472-473, 511-523, 549-582	916-941	343-429	224-269
F.	Utility Service					207-212	
IX.	**CHAPTER 7—LIQUIDATION**						
A.	Introduction	11-12, 26-32	60-63, 79-81, 88		724-725, 726	44-45	69-72
B.	Distribution of Property of Estate	134-135, 195-196, 229-249	58, 224-231, 693-748, 784-786, 890-894; Supp. 25-37, 124-127	583-603	822-823, 843-847, 859, 875	30, 248	433-434, 448, 456, 639-678
C.	Treatment of Certain Liens in Chapter 7 Case	248-249	717, 724-725, 784-786	408-425, 431-433, 601, 610-611, 750-767		182-185, 259, 632-633	633
D.	Partnership Trustee's Claim Against General Partners		453			334-338	
E.	Chapter 7 Discharge	63, 294, 531-534, 537-538	750-751, 795-796, 810-827, 832-833, 889-890	644, 677	720-721, 725-726, 788-789, 793-810, 813	30-31, 143-148	633-636, 639-641
F.	Conversion		56	455	748		
G.	Dismissal	52-59, 61, 62-63	111-113, 749-751, 837-848		735-739	300-302	

Bankruptcy—iii

TEXT CORRELATION CHART—continued

Gilbert Law Summary Bankruptcy	Alces, Howard Bankruptcy 1995	Baird, Jackson Bankruptcy 1990 (2nd ed.) 1994 Supp.	Eisenberg Bankruptcy and Debtor-Creditor Law 1988 (2nd ed.)	Epstein, Nickles Debt, Bankruptcy, Article 9 and Related Laws 1994	Jorden, Warren Bankruptcy 1995 (4th ed.)	White, Nimmer Bankruptcy 1992 (2nd ed.)
X. CHAPTER 11—REORGANIZATION						
A. Eligibility for Relief	25-32	80-81	811-814	742-743, 1032-1034, 1052, 1117	25-26, 723-726, 728-729	63-66, 510-512, 613-616
B. Administration of Chapter 11 Case	110-111, 590-604, 641-655	58-59, 124-129, 226, 947-952, 999-1001, 1073-1091, 1124-1129	809-822, 830-833, 880-894	735-748, 1034-1107, 1155-1156	748-756, 839-849	70-72, 523-525, 613-631
C. Rejection of Collective Bargaining Agreements		57, 265-271	564-582	1108-1116		269-290
D. Chapter 11 Plan	165, 187-188, 194, 641-656	952, 1001-1040, 1048-1055, 1116-1129	822-830, 833-845, 866, 870, 887-888	859, 865-870, 907, 913, 1117-1139, 1157, 1159-1198, 1201-1213	792-833, 890-893	523-524, 527-554, 576-612
E. Confirmation of Plan	194, 272-273, 643-648, 656-689	950, 957-999, 1024, 1041-1092, 1105-1116; Supp. 157-170	845-888	831, 844, 1139-1157	833-885	554-565, 567-575
F. Post-Confirmation Matters	537		879-880, 888	813, 1156-1157	885-890	612-613
G. Small Businesses	641					
H. *Manville*-Type Trust/Injunction	158-164, 583-590				729-730, 821-823 124-128	488-501
XI. CHAPTER 13—INDIVIDUAL WITH REGULAR INCOME						
A. Eligibility for Relief	12, 253-255	1131-1132	773-784	726-727	24	679-681
B. Co-Debtor Stay	197	1133	802-806	762-764	24	692-693
C. Administration of Chapter 13 Case	76, 604, 612, 629	60-61, 63, 257-258, 1132-1134, 1151	687-689, 773-784, 802-806, 932-933	748, 750-751, 762	24	69-70, 682-692
D. Chapter 13 Plan	165, 187-194, 223-228, 267-272, 457-470, 484, 489-492, 497-502, 508-514	1026, 1132-1137, 1155-1173; Supp. 179-185	773-797	789-791, 793, 799, 810-813	24	681-696
E. Confirmation of Plan	135-150, 256-272	1134-1155, 1171-1173; Supp. 179	775-784, 797-802	823-831, 844, 859-865, 872-880, 894-899	24	681, 698-708
F. Payments	187-188, 249-272					
G. Post-Confirmation Matters	534-537, 547-551, 564-565	1133-1137, 1151, 1173	806	810-819	24	693-697
XII. CHAPTER 12—FAMILY FARMER WITH REGULAR ANNUAL INCOME						
A. Eligibility for Relief	13-14	1174	455	728-729	896-905	60
B. Similarities to Chapter 13	13, 187-188	81-82, 1174	455-456	728	895-896, 907-908, 917-920	555, 682
C. Differences from Chapter 13	212-213, 537	1174-1181	455-456	728-729	905-906	
D. Differences from Chapter 11	32, 212-213	1174-1176	455-456	729	895	
E. Secured Creditors	197	1174-1187			908-917	
F. Unsecured Creditors	135	1175-1180			895	
G. Conversion or Dismissal	63-64	1187-1190				
H. Sunset Provision		1181			896	

approach to exams

A bankruptcy law examination is likely to involve your consideration of many of the issues below. In analyzing and writing your answers, ask yourself the following questions:

A. Is the debtor *eligible for relief* under a particular chapter of the Bankruptcy Code? [B.C. §109]

   1. May an *involuntary petition* (when applicable) be filed under that chapter, and is the debtor a person against whom an involuntary petition may be filed?

B. After the filing of a bankruptcy petition, has any act been committed that violates the *automatic stay*? [B.C. §362(a)]

   1. Does the act come within one of the *exceptions* to the stay? [B.C. §362(b)]

C. What *property* comprises the bankruptcy *estate*?

   1. Is there any property in the possession of third parties that is subject to *turnover*?

   2. Are there any transactions that can be *avoided* by the trustee or the debtor in possession, as a result of which additional property can be *recovered* to enlarge the estate for the benefit of creditors?

   3. Is there any property that is burdensome or of inconsequential value to the estate and that may be *abandoned* by the trustee?

D. From the *debtor's* perspective:

   1. Has the debtor filed all *lists, schedules, and statements* that are required?

   2. What *exemptions* are available to an individual debtor under the Code or under applicable nonbankruptcy law? Has the applicable state law opted out of the federal exemption scheme?

   3. Does the debtor desire to *reaffirm* any debts?

   4. Does an individual Chapter 7 debtor desire to *redeem* any property?

   5. Is the debtor entitled to a *discharge* under the applicable chapter?

   6. If the debtor is an individual, are there any *particular debts that will be nondischargeable*? [B.C. §523(a)]

E. What *claims or interests* have been filed in the case? Are they (i) secured claims, (ii) unsecured priority claims, (iii) general unsecured claims, (iv) subordinated claims, or (v) owners' interests?

   1. Is there any basis for objecting to the *allowance* of a claim or interest that has been filed?

   2. Is a particular claim *fully secured*? If not, remember that an undersecured claim generally is *bifurcated*, resulting in two claims—one that is secured up to the value of the collateral and the other that is unsecured for the amount of the deficiency.

3. Have any secured creditors requested *relief from the automatic stay*, and should such relief be granted?

   a. Has *adequate protection* been provided as required by the Code?

   b. Does the debtor have equity in the collateral, and is the property necessary for an effective reorganization?

4. How much will the holder of each claim or interest be paid on *final distribution* in a Chapter 7 case or pursuant to a *confirmed plan* in a case under Chapter 11, 12, or 13?

F. Under *which chapter* of the Code has the case been filed?

1. If it is a *Chapter 7 case*:

   a. Under the circumstances, are there any reasons to consider *converting* the case to another chapter of the Code (if the debtor is eligible) or *dismissing* the case entirely?

   b. Is there any ground for *denial of the debtor's discharge* under Bankruptcy Code section 727(a)?

2. If it is a *Chapter 11 case*:

   a. Are there questions to be considered concerning: (i) *relief from the automatic stay*; (ii) the *use, sale, or lease of estate property*; (iii) the *obtaining of credit*; or (iv) the *assumption or rejection of executory contracts or unexpired leases*? (While these issues are not limited to Chapter 11 cases, they frequently arise in this context.)

      (1) Has *adequate protection* been provided when required by the Code? [B.C. §§362(d)(1); 363(e); 364(d)(1)(B)]

   b. Is there a ground to request the *appointment of a trustee* to replace the debtor in possession? If not, is it appropriate to request the *appointment of an examiner*?

   c. If a trustee has not been appointed, has the debtor filed a plan within the *exclusivity period*?

   d. Does a proposed *plan* include the mandatory Chapter 11 plan provisions? Which permissive provisions are appropriate to include in the plan?

   e. How are the claims and interests *classified*?

   f. Which classes are *impaired or unimpaired*?

   g. Has the *disclosure statement* concerning a proposed plan been approved by the court?

   h. Which classes of claims or interests have *accepted or rejected* the plan?

   i. Can the plan be *confirmed*?

(1) Are all of the requirements of Bankruptcy Code section 1129(a) satisfied?

(2) If all of the requirements of section 1129(a) are met *except* section 1129(a)(8), can the plan be confirmed by a *cramdown* under section 1129(b)—*i.e.*, is the plan (i) *not unfairly discriminatory* and (ii) *fair and equitable* with respect to any dissenting impaired classes?

3. If it is a *Chapter 13 case*:

   a. Have any creditors sought relief from the *co-debtor stay*, and should such relief be granted?

   b. Does the debtor's proposed *plan* include the mandatory Chapter 13 plan provisions? Which permissive provisions are appropriate to include in the plan?

   c. Are the six requirements for *confirmation* satisfied? [B.C. §1325(a)]

      (1) If an objection to confirmation is filed by an unsecured creditor whose claim the plan does not propose to pay in full, has the debtor committed all of his projected *disposable income* for the next three years to be used to make payments under the plan? [B.C. §1325(b)]

   d. Has the debtor begun making payments within 30 days after the plan is filed?

   e. Which debts are dischargeable under Chapter 13, and which ones are not?

4. If it is a *Chapter 12 case*:

   a. Does the debtor come within the Code's definition of a *family farmer*? [B.C. §101(18)]

   b. Is the debtor continuing to operate the farm? Is there a ground for *removal* of the debtor in possession and replacement by the Chapter 12 trustee?

   c. Where *adequate protection* is required, does it satisfy section 1205?

   d. Does the debtor's proposed *plan* include the mandatory Chapter 12 plan provisions? Which permissive provisions are appropriate to include in the plan?

   e. Have the six requirements for *confirmation* been met? [B.C. §1225(a)]

      (1) Where an objection to confirmation has been filed by an unsecured creditor whose claim the plan does not propose to pay in full, is the *projected disposable income* test of Bankruptcy Code section 1225(b) satisfied by the plan?

G. If *professional persons*, such as attorneys or accountants, have been employed in the case, has their employment been approved by the court *before* the rendering of professional services? Are they *disinterested persons* who do *not have an interest adverse* to the estate?

I. INTRODUCTION

chapter approach

Success on your bankruptcy law examination requires a thorough understanding of the provisions of the Bankruptcy Code in light of the interests that the statute was designed to protect. It is important for you to study the Code language in its bankruptcy context, keeping in mind the definitions in section 101 of the Code as well as certain rules of construction. In addition, you must develop a perspective of the organizational structure of the Code, the kinds of relief available under the various chapters, and the manner in which the sections of different chapters interrelate.

A. GOALS OF THE FEDERAL BANKRUPTCY LAWS

1. **Fresh Start:** [§1] Bankruptcy is designed to relieve the honest debtor of his debts and to provide him the opportunity for a fresh start financially.

    a. **Example:** Debtor worked in a manufacturing plant. Recently, he lost his job due to the closing of the factory. Shortly thereafter, he contracted cancer and, after a long bout, recovered. His medical expenses totaled $500,000, he had limited assets and no health insurance, and his only savings account was exhausted. Judgments were obtained against Debtor for $500,000. Debtor then filed a voluntary bankruptcy petition.

    b. **Comment:** Were it not for the protection of the bankruptcy laws, Debtor probably would be burdened for the rest of his life by these debts. The Bankruptcy Code, however, allows him to discharge his indebtedness and to void the judgments without harassment by creditors and without fear of being subjected to future actions to collect the amounts owed.

2. **Forum for Creditors:** [§2] Creditors also benefit from the establishment of a forum in which there will be either an orderly liquidation of the debtor's estate or a judicially scrutinized plan to repay creditors partially or fully over a period of time. Unsecured creditors are protected from acts such as selective repayment of particular creditors shortly before bankruptcy and fraudulent transfers of the debtor's property; secured creditors are ensured that their interest in collateral will be adequately protected under statutorily defined circumstances.

B. LEGISLATIVE HISTORY

1. **Bankruptcy Act:** [§3] Article 1, Section 8 of the United States Constitution empowers Congress to enact uniform laws on bankruptcy. Under this grant of authority, Congress passed the Bankruptcy Act of 1898, which was amended substantially by the Chandler Act of 1938. [Pub. L. No. 76-242 (1939)] The bankruptcy court's jurisdiction, called *summary jurisdiction*, was limited to the debtor, his property, and the administration of the bankruptcy case. Therefore, the bankruptcy court had no jurisdiction over property in the possession of a third person who had an adverse claim to the property unless the third party *consented* to the bankruptcy

court's jurisdiction. Thus, much litigation involving property outside of the bankruptcy court's in rem jurisdiction could occur only in the United States district court, under its *plenary jurisdiction*, or in the various state courts. [1 L. King, Collier on Bankruptcy ¶3.01(1)(b)(iv) (15th ed. 1995) (hereafter "Collier")] Consequently, the potential number of forums with jurisdiction over issues arising in or related to any single bankruptcy case generally proved to be unduly burdensome and expensive and, as a practical matter, often precluded a trustee's actions to recover property for the benefit of the estate and ultimately for creditors. Moreover, unnecessary and costly litigation regarding which court had proper jurisdiction frequently delayed the efficient administration of bankruptcy cases.

2. **Bankruptcy Code:** [§4] The 1978 Bankruptcy Reform Act repealed the Bankruptcy Act of 1898, and it created the Bankruptcy Code, which became effective on October 1, 1979. [11 U.S.C. §§101 *et seq.* (hereafter "B.C.")] The Bankruptcy Code made sweeping substantive revisions to the bankruptcy laws that had developed under the Bankruptcy Act. In addition, the bankruptcy court's jurisdiction was substantially expanded to enable the bankruptcy judge to hear practically all matters arising in or related to the bankruptcy case, thereby eliminating some of the logistical problems of litigation under the Bankruptcy Act. (Thus, under the Bankruptcy Code, the distinction between summary and plenary jurisdiction is an obsolete concept.) Furthermore, changes were made to separate the bankruptcy judge's judicial functions from those relating purely to administration of the case. Note that the laws concerning jurisdictional issues are contained in the Judicial Code [28 U.S.C.] rather than the Bankruptcy Code.

3. **The *Marathon* Case:** [§5] In 1982, the United States Supreme Court ruled that the comprehensive grant of jurisdiction to the bankruptcy courts under the Bankruptcy Reform Act of 1978 was unconstitutional. [Northern Pipeline Construction Co. v. Marathon Pipe Line Co., 458 U.S. 50 (1982)] The Court held that such a broad grant of jurisdiction could be vested only in an Article III court, and the bankruptcy courts do not qualify as Article III courts because bankruptcy judges do not have the protections of Article III judges (life tenure and a guarantee against diminution of salary). This decision thrust the entire bankruptcy system into a state of turmoil for the next two years, and a temporary Emergency Rule was adopted in each federal district to refer bankruptcy cases and proceedings to the bankruptcy courts.

4. **Bankruptcy Amendments and Federal Judgeship Act of 1984:** [§6] In 1984, Congress adopted legislation amending the bankruptcy laws. The legislation did not grant Article III status to bankruptcy judges, but it did correct the jurisdictional defects and certain substantive problems that had arisen under the 1978 Bankruptcy Reform Act.

5. **Subsequent Legislation:** [§7] Congress again made significant changes to the bankruptcy laws in 1986, when it added Chapter 12 (relief for family farmers with regular income; *see infra*, §§1223 *et seq.*) and established a permanent United States trustee system (*see infra*, §§290 *et seq.*). Major amendments also were made to the Bankruptcy Code and Judicial Code by legislation in 1990 and by the Bankruptcy Reform Act of 1994.

C. ORGANIZATION OF THE BANKRUPTCY CODE

1. **Chapters 1, 3, and 5:** [§8]   Chapters 1, 3, and 5 of the Bankruptcy Code contain general rules, definitions, and eligibility requirements for bankruptcy relief, as well as provisions about the commencement of a case, the administration of cases, the debtor, the estate and its officers, the trustee's powers to avoid certain transfers and recover property for the estate's benefit, creditors, claims, the automatic stay, adequate protection, and certain administrative powers of a trustee or a debtor in possession. All three chapters apply to cases under Chapters 7, 11, 12, and 13. [B.C. §103(a)]

2. **Chapter 7:** [§9]   The *liquidation* provisions of the Bankruptcy Code are contained in Chapter 7, which contemplates an orderly procedure by which the trustee collects the assets of the debtor's estate, reduces them to cash, and makes distributions to creditors, subject to the debtor's right to retain certain (exempt) property and the rights of secured parties in their collateral. [B.C. §§701 *et seq.*; *and see infra*, §§939 *et seq.*]

3. **Chapter 9:** [§10]   Chapter 9 involves adjustments of debts of a municipality and is beyond the scope of this summary.

4. **Chapter 11:** [§11]   Chapter 11 is entitled *"reorganization"* and ordinarily concerns a commercial debtor who desires to continue operating a business and to repay creditors concurrently through an acceptable plan of reorganization confirmed by the court. [B.C. §§1101 *et seq.*; *and see infra*, §§993 *et seq.*] *Note*: The Supreme Court has held that a consumer debtor also may qualify for Chapter 11 relief. [Toibb v. Radloff, 501 U.S. 157 (1991)]

5. **Chapter 12:** [§12]   Chapter 12 provides relief for debtors who are *family farmers* with regular annual income, allowing them to continue to operate their farms. It allows the family farmer access to the bankruptcy court through a speedier, simpler, and less expensive procedure than under Chapter 11, and with higher debt limitations than those of Chapter 13. [B.C. §§1201 *et seq.*; *and see infra*, §§1223 *et seq.*]

6. **Chapter 13:** [§13]   Chapter 13 provides a method by which an *individual with regular income* may repay all or a portion of her indebtedness over a period of time, pursuant to a plan proposed by the debtor and confirmed by the court. [B.C. §§1301 *et seq.*; *and see infra*, §§1138 *et seq.*]

D. RULES OF CONSTRUCTION

1. **"After Notice and a Hearing":** [§14]   When the language "after notice and a hearing" appears in the Bankruptcy Code, it means notice appropriate under the specific circumstances and an *opportunity for a hearing* appropriate under those circumstances. However, such language authorizes an act without an actual hearing if proper notice is given and (i) no hearing is requested by a party in interest or (ii) there is not enough time for a hearing before the act must be done and the court authorizes the act. [B.C. §102(1)]

    a. **Example:** Trustee desires to sell an asset of the estate outside the ordinary course of business and provides proper notice, with a description of the asset, to all creditors. If no creditor objects, Trustee may proceed to conduct the sale without an actual hearing and without obtaining the judge's approval. [B.C. §§102(1), 363(b)(1); *and see infra*, §835]

2. **"Claim Against the Debtor":** [§15] The phrase "claim against the debtor" is construed to include a claim against the debtor's property. [B.C. §102(2)]

3. **"Including":** [§16] Where the language of the Code uses the word "including" or "includes," it is not meant to be limiting or exclusive [B.C. §102(3)] (*i.e.*, items need not be listed to fall within the section).

4. **"Order for Relief":** [§17] The entry of an order for relief in a bankruptcy case occurs automatically by the filing of a *voluntary* petition or a *joint* petition. (Note that there is no corporeal paper or action by a clerk or a bankruptcy judge; rather, the commencement of a voluntary or joint case constitutes the order for relief.) It occurs in an *involuntary* case when the court determines (after a trial) that the debtor is generally not paying his debts as they become due. [B.C. §§102(6), 301, 302(a), 303(h)] The order for relief is a term that appears throughout the Code as a point of reference in time and which means simply that the bankruptcy case may go forward unless otherwise ordered by the court.

E. PARTICIPANTS IN THE BANKRUPTCY CASE

1. **Bankruptcy Judge:** [§18] For many years, under the Bankruptcy Act, the judicial officer in the case was called the "referee"; however, this terminology is now obsolete. The judicial officer is referred to as the "bankruptcy judge."

2. **Debtor:** [§19] Under the Bankruptcy Act, the person about whom a bankruptcy case was commenced was called the "bankrupt." That term is not used under the Bankruptcy Code; such a person is called a "debtor." [B.C. §101(13)]

3. **Debtor in Possession:** [§20] In a Chapter 11 case, the debtor is called a "debtor in possession" *unless a trustee has been appointed*. [B.C. §1101(1)]

4. **Trustee:** [§21] The trustee is the official representative of the estate and, as such, exercises statutory powers principally for the benefit of the *unsecured creditors*. [B.C. §323(a)]

5. **United States Trustee:** [§22] The United States trustee assumes many of the administrative responsibilities previously performed by the court, including the *appointment and supervision of bankruptcy trustees*, thereby helping to separate the administrative and judicial functions in bankruptcy cases. The United States trustee is appointed by the Attorney General to a term of five years. [28 U.S.C. §§581 *et seq.*; *and see infra*, §§290 *et seq.*]

6. **Unsecured Creditor:** [§23] An unsecured creditor is an entity holding a claim against the debtor that is not secured by collateral.

7. **Secured Creditor:** [§24] A secured creditor is an entity holding a claim against the debtor that is *secured by a lien* on property of the estate or that is *subject to setoff*. [B.C. §506(a)] Frequently, bankruptcy litigation involves a contest between a secured creditor and the trustee (as the champion of the unsecured creditors) concerning the validity, extent, or priority of an alleged security interest.

8. **Creditors' Committee:** [§25] In a Chapter 11 case, a committee of unsecured creditors is appointed by the United States trustee. The committee usually consists

of those willing persons holding the *seven largest unsecured claims* against the debtor (although there may be additional committees of creditors or equity security holders appointed). A creditors' committee can be particularly helpful in consulting with the debtor in possession or with a trustee, and also in participating in the formulation of an acceptable plan of reorganization. [B.C. §§1102, 1103(c)] Sometimes, in a large Chapter 7 case, the unsecured creditors will elect a creditors' committee consisting of between three and 11 unsecured creditors to consult with the trustee about the administration of the estate. [B.C. §705]

9. **Equity Security Holder:** [§26] An equity security holder is a holder of a share or similar security in a debtor corporation, a holder of a warrant or a right to buy or sell a security in a debtor corporation (but not a right to convert), or a limited partner holding an interest in a limited partnership debtor. [B.C. §101(16), (17)]

10. **Professional Persons:** [§27] Professional persons (*e.g.*, attorneys, accountants, appraisers, and auctioneers) often are hired by a trustee, a debtor in possession, or a creditors' or equity security holders' committee. Their expertise usually plays an important role in a bankruptcy case, and their employment and compensation must be approved by the court. [B.C. §§327-331; *and see infra*, §§256-289]

F. TERMINOLOGY

There are a number of terms that appear frequently throughout the Code; an understanding of their bankruptcy definition is helpful.

1. **Person:** [§28] Individuals, corporations, and partnerships are "persons," but governmental units (with one exception; *see infra*, §998) are not. [B.C. §101(41)]

2. **Entity:** [§29] "Entity" is a more comprehensive term than "person" and includes, *additionally*, trusts, estates, governmental units, and the United States trustee. [B.C. §101(15)]

3. **Insider:** [§30] An "insider" is defined in terms of whether the debtor is an individual, a corporation, or a partnership. [B.C. §101(31)]

    a. **Individual debtor:** [§31] With respect to an individual debtor, the following persons are insiders: relatives [B.C. §101(45)], general partners, relatives of general partners, a partnership if the debtor is a general partner, and a corporation if the debtor is an officer, a director, or a person in control [B.C. §101(31)(A)].

    b. **Corporate debtor:** [§32] With respect to a corporate debtor, the following persons are insiders: directors, officers, *persons in control*, general partners of the debtor, relatives of any of the above, and a partnership if the debtor is a general partner. [B.C. §101(31)(B)]

    c. **Partnership debtor:** [§33] With respect to a partnership debtor, the following persons are insiders: general partners in or of the debtor, *persons in control*, relatives of any of the above, and a partnership if the debtor is a general partner. [B.C. §101(31)(C)]

4. **Claim:** [§34] A "claim" is a *right to payment*, even if it is unliquidated, unmatured, disputed, or contingent. It also includes the "right to an equitable remedy for

breach of performance if such breach gives rise to a right to payment." The concept of a claim is significant in determining which debts are discharged and who shares in distribution. [B.C. §101(5); *and see infra*, §§478 *et seq.*]

    a. **Example:** Debtor was ordered by a state court to clean up a hazardous waste disposal site. After Debtor failed to comply, the state court appointed a receiver and ordered the receiver to carry out the mandatory injunction while taking possession of Debtor's property, including the disposal site. Debtor then filed a bankruptcy petition. The performance that the receiver sought from Debtor was limited to the payment of money to cover the expense of removal of the wastes. The receiver's *right to payment of money was a claim*, and the liability on that claim was a *debt* capable of being discharged. [Ohio v. Kovacs, 469 U.S. 274 (1985)]

    b. **Note:** In the example above, Debtor was dispossessed of his property because of the state-court receivership and, thus, was precluded from implementing the injunction himself. Therefore, Debtor's only obligation was the *payment of money*.

    c. **Comment:** The Supreme Court has emphasized the legislative intent to ascribe the broadest possible definition to "claim." The Court stated: "The plain meaning of a 'right to payment' is nothing more nor less than an enforceable obligation. . . ." [Pennsylvania Department of Public Welfare v. Davenport, 493 U.S. 808 (1990)]

5. **Debt:** [§35] "Debt" is defined as a "liability on a claim" [B.C. §101(12)], and the discharge of debts in bankruptcy is the legal means of providing the debtor with a fresh start.

6. **Consumer Debt:** [§36] A "consumer debt" is one "incurred by an *individual* primarily for a personal, family, or household purpose." [B.C. §101(8)]

7. **Insolvent:** [§37] An entity is "insolvent" when its debts total more than the aggregate value of all of its property, excluding property fraudulently transferred and exempt property. In the case of a partnership, the excess of the nonexempt personal assets of each general partner over his nonpartnership debts is included. [B.C. §101(32)]

8. **Transfer:** [§38] A "transfer" is any *voluntary or involuntary* disposition of property or an interest in property, including, for example, the debtor's conveyance of a security interest or a mortgage, the fixing of a lien on property of the debtor by judicial process, or even a foreclosure sale of collateral securing a debt. [B.C. §101(54)]

II. JURISDICTION AND PROCEDURE

chapter approach

An exam question about bankruptcy jurisdiction and procedure will often focus on one or more of the following issues:

1. Is the pending matter a *core* or a *non-core* proceeding? Your answer should show an understanding of the designated core areas under 28 U.S.C. section 157(b)(2), as well as the kinds of actions that would appear to be non-core following the United States Supreme Court's decision in the *Marathon* case. Remember that although the bankruptcy judge hears both core and non-core matters, final orders in non-core matters (absent the consent of all of the parties) can be made only by the district court.

2. Does a particular proceeding involve the trial of a *personal injury tort or wrongful death claim* for the purpose of distribution? If so, the trial must be conducted in the district court.

3. If requested, is there a right to a *jury trial* in a particular bankruptcy proceeding?

4. Should the case or proceeding be *withdrawn* by the district court from the bankruptcy court? Is withdrawal of a particular proceeding mandatory?

5. Is *abstention* from hearing a particular proceeding required or appropriate under the circumstances? The core/non-core distinction may be important here, as well as state law concerns.

6. Is *venue* of the bankruptcy case or proceeding proper? If a change of venue is requested, what are the criteria for transfer?

7. If an order or judgment is *appealed*, consider the court from which it is appealed, the court to which it is appealed, and whether the order *is final or interlocutory* in the context of bankruptcy.

A. BANKRUPTCY COURT

1. **Unit of a District Court:** [§39] The bankruptcy court in each federal judicial district constitutes a unit of the respective district court, and it receives its authority to hear cases and proceedings by *referral* from the district court. [28 U.S.C. §§151, 157(a)]

2. **Appointment of Bankruptcy Judges:** [§40] Bankruptcy judges are appointed by the United States court of appeals for a term of 14 years. [28 U.S.C. §152(a)(1)]

3. **Clerk of the Bankruptcy Court:** [§41] If there is a sufficient number of bankruptcy cases and proceedings within a particular jurisdiction, the bankruptcy judges for that district may be authorized by the Director of the Administrative Office of the United States Courts to appoint a clerk of the court. [28 U.S.C. §156(b)]

4. **Power of Court:** [§42] The bankruptcy judge is authorized to implement the provisions of the Bankruptcy Code by issuing *any necessary or appropriate order, judgment, or process*. [B.C. §105(a)] For example, the bankruptcy court may enjoin an action in a nonbankruptcy forum if the injunction is necessary to prevent substantial interference with the bankruptcy proceedings or to prevent the frustration of a debtor's reorganization. [*In re* Johns-Manville Corp., 57 B.R. 680 (Bankr. S.D.N.Y. 1986); Celotex Corporation v. Edwards, 115 S. Ct. 1493 (1995)—injunction prohibiting creditors from executing on supersedeas bond posted by surety in another court; 2 Collier ¶105.02] The court, however, does not have the authority to appoint a receiver (a Bankruptcy Act concept similar to an interim trustee under the Code). [B.C. §105(b)]

   a. **Sua sponte action by court:** [§43] The court is expressly authorized to take any necessary or appropriate action, *on its own motion*, to enforce its orders or to prevent an abuse of process—even where the Code provides for such action to be requested by a party in interest (*e.g.*, the dismissal of a Chapter 11 case). [B.C. §§105(a), 1112(b); *In re* Daily Corp., 72 B.R. 489 (Bankr. E.D. Pa. 1987)]

   b. **Status conferences:** [§44] The court, on its own motion or on the request of a party in interest (and after notice) may hold status conferences and issue orders to expedite the case, such as setting a deadline for the trustee to assume or reject an executory contract or unexpired lease; or, in a Chapter 11 case: (i) setting a deadline for the debtor (or trustee) to file a disclosure statement and plan or to solicit acceptances of a plan, (ii) setting a deadline for other parties in interest to file a plan or solicit acceptances, (iii) fixing the scope and format of the notice of the hearing on the disclosure statement, or (iv) combining the disclosure statement hearing with the confirmation hearing. [B.C. §105(d)]

   c. **Contempt:** [§45] There is much disagreement about the power of a bankruptcy judge to issue civil or criminal contempt orders despite the authorization contained in Federal Rule of Bankruptcy Procedure ("Bankruptcy Rule") 9020, which states: "The order shall be effective 10 days after service . . . and shall have the same force and effect as an order of contempt entered by the district court. . . ." However, Bankruptcy Rule 9020 requires a bankruptcy judge's contempt order to be reviewed de novo by the district court if an objection is made within 10 days after service.

      (1) **Civil contempt:** [§46] Most courts have ruled that the bankruptcy court has the inherent power "to cite and punish for civil contempt" and that Bankruptcy Rule 9020 merely confirms the bankruptcy court's authority. [*In re* Miller, 81 B.R. 669 (Bankr. M.D. Fla. 1988); *see* 2 Collier ¶105.06(1)] Even if there is no inherent power, it has been held that civil contempt power is authorized by the plain meaning of Bankruptcy Code section 105(a) (*see supra*, §42). [*In re* Skinner, 917 F.2d 444 (10th Cir. 1990)] However, some authorities have held that a bankruptcy judge lacks civil contempt power and must certify findings to the district judge for de novo review, issuance of the contempt order, and appropriate sanctions. [*In re* Sequoia Auto Brokers, Ltd., 827 F.2d 1281 (9th Cir. 1987)]

      (2) **Criminal contempt:** [§47] As to criminal contempt, one circuit has ruled "that bankruptcy courts do not have inherent *criminal* contempt

powers, at least with respect to the criminal contempts not committed in (or near) their presence." [*In re* Hipp, 895 F.2d 1503 (5th Cir. 1990)] However, another circuit has held that section 105(a) authorizes the bankruptcy court to enter criminal contempt orders, subject to district court review if an objection is filed within 10 days after service. [*In re* Ragar, 3 F.3d 1174 (8th Cir. 1993)]

d. **Sanctions:** [§48] The bankruptcy court may impose sanctions on attorneys and/or litigants who sign and file pleadings or other documents that (i) are not well-grounded in fact or in law (allowing good faith arguments for change of existing law) or (ii) are filed for any improper purpose. [Bankruptcy Rule 9011; *In re* Marsch, 36 F.3d 825 (9th Cir. 1994)]

e. **Substantive consolidation:** [§49] In appropriate circumstances, the court may order the substantive consolidation of debtors' estates, *i.e.*, the pooling of their assets, debts, and causes of action. The factors to be considered are: "(1) the necessity of consolidation due to the interrelationship among the debtors; (2) whether the benefits of consolidation outweigh the harm to creditors; and (3) prejudice resulting from not consolidating the debtors." [*In re* Giller, 962 F.2d 796 (8th Cir. 1992)—substantive consolidation of six interrelated corporations and their majority shareholder, where the corporate form had been abused and there might exist preferential and fraudulent transfers] (Contrast *procedural consolidation*, which is done solely for administrative purposes—such as the appointment of a single trustee to administer related cases, maintenance of a single case file for related cases, and the combining of notices concerning the estate—but which does not result in a pooling of the debtors' assets, debts, and causes of action. [*See In re* Parkway Calabasas, Ltd., 89 B.R. 832 (Bankr. C.D. Cal. 1988), *aff'd*, 949 F.2d 1058 (9th Cir. 1991)] Substantive consolidation is imposed much less frequently than procedural consolidation, but it can be an invaluable tool in certain circumstances.)

B. PERSONAL JURISDICTION [§50]

Service of process in a bankruptcy case or proceeding may be accomplished by first class prepaid mail *anywhere in the United States*. The entity served need not have any minimum contacts with the state in which the bankruptcy case or proceeding is being heard. [Bankruptcy Rule 7004; Diamond Mortgage Corp. of Illinois v. Sugar, 913 F.2d 1233 (7th Cir. 1990)]

1. **Insured Depository Institutions:** [§51] Service of process on an insured depository institution requires certified mail, rather than simply first class mail, unless (i) the institution has appeared by its attorney, (ii) the institution has waived this entitlement, or (iii) the court orders otherwise after service by certified mail of an application to permit service by first class mail. [Bankruptcy Rule 7004(h)]

C. SUBJECT MATTER JURISDICTION

1. **District Courts:** [§52] The United States district courts have original jurisdiction over all *cases* under the Bankruptcy Code; over all *civil proceedings* arising under the Code or arising in or related to a case under the Code; and over the *debtor's property* (as of the filing of the petition) and *property of the estate*, wherever located. [28 U.S.C. §1334]

a. **Cases:** [§53] The jurisdiction of the district courts over cases under the Bankruptcy Code is both *original and exclusive*. Therefore, district court jurisdiction completely preempts any state court jurisdiction. [28 U.S.C. §133(4)(a)]

b. **Civil proceedings:** [§54] The controversies that arise under the Bankruptcy Code, or in or related to a bankruptcy case, after the petition has been filed are called "proceedings," and the district court has *original but not exclusive* jurisdiction over them. Such proceedings are designated as either *core* or *non-core*. [28 U.S.C. §§1334(b), 157(b)(2); *see infra*, §§63-72; *In re* Time Construction, Inc., 43 F.3d 1041 (6th Cir. 1995)—court had jurisdiction over removed state court action involving debtor's largest asset (good discussion of "related" proceedings)]

c. **Debtor's property:** [§55] The district courts are vested with *exclusive in rem jurisdiction* over all of the debtor's property, regardless of its location, as of the filing of a bankruptcy petition under one of the appropriate chapters. In addition, this jurisdiction includes property that the estate subsequently acquires during the pendency of the case. [28 U.S.C. §1334(d)]

2. **Referral to Bankruptcy Courts:** [§56] Almost all cases and proceedings (with the exception of *trials* of personal injury tort and wrongful death claims; *see infra*, §62) have been referred by the district court to the bankruptcy court in all federal districts, and such referral has been held to be constitutional. [28 U.S.C. §157(a); *In re* Production Steel, Inc., 48 B.R. 841 (M.D. Tenn. 1985)]

    a. **Final orders and judgments:** [§57] Bankruptcy judges may hear and decide all *cases and core proceedings* referred to them, and have authority to issue final orders and judgments appealable to the appropriate district court. [28 U.S.C. §157(b)(1)]

    b. **Proposed findings and rulings:** [§58] In *non-core* matters, however, bankruptcy judges may hear the proceedings and must submit *proposed findings of fact and conclusions of law* to the district court for final disposition and for de novo review of these issues to which there has been timely and specific objection. [28 U.S.C. §157(c)(1)]

        (1) **De novo review:** [§59] De novo review of a non-core proceeding is *not an appeal* from a final order or judgment. It requires the district judge, without the necessity of a new trial, to examine independently the record before making a final ruling. The ruling may adopt (but does not rubber-stamp) the bankruptcy court's opinion. [Moody v. Amoco Oil Co., 734 F.2d 1200 (7th Cir. 1984)]

        (2) **Exception—consent:** [§60] If all of the parties to a non-core proceeding consent, the bankruptcy court may enter *final orders and judgments*, which have the same effect as those in core proceedings. [28 U.S.C. §157(c)(2)]

    c. **Interlocutory orders:** [§61] Bankruptcy judges may issue interlocutory orders in both core and non-core proceedings. [28 U.S.C. §157(b)(l), (c)(1); *In re* Lion Capital Group, 46 B.R. 850 (Bankr. S.D.N.Y. 1985)]

3. **Personal Injury Tort and Wrongful Death Claims:** [§62]   Personal injury tort and wrongful death claims must be tried in the *district court*, not in the bankruptcy court. [28 U.S.C. §157(b)(5)]

D. CORE/NON-CORE PROCEEDINGS

1. **Core Proceedings:** [§63]   Core matters are civil proceedings arising under the Bankruptcy Code or in a bankruptcy case (*see supra*, §54). They include, but are not limited to, proceedings concerning the administration of the debtor's estate, allowance or disallowance of creditors' claims, estimation of claims or interests for the purpose of confirmation of a Chapter 11, 12, or 13 plan (*but not* the estimation or liquidation of personal injury tort or wrongful death claims for the purpose of *distribution*; *see* above), allowance of property exemptions, counterclaims asserted by the estate against claimants in the case, obtaining of credit, turnover of property, preferences, the automatic stay, fraudulent transfers, dischargeability of particular debts, objections to the debtor's discharge, validity and priority of liens, confirmation of plans, use of estate property (including cash collateral), and sale or lease of estate property. [28 U.S.C. §157(b)(2)]

    a. **Catchall provision:** [§64]   Core matters also include any proceedings that *affect the liquidation* of the estate's assets or the adjustment of the *debtor-creditor (or equity security holder) relationship*, other than claims for personal injury tort or wrongful death. [28 U.S.C. §157(b)(2)(O)]

2. **Non-Core Proceedings—Majority View:** [§65]   Non-core proceedings, also known as *"related matters,"* include the *debtor's causes of action* that could have been brought in state court or in federal district court had there been no bankruptcy case, such as pre-petition breaches of contract, pre-petition breaches of warranty, and collection of pre-petition accounts receivable. [*In re* Castlerock Properties, 781 F.2d 159 (9th Cir. 1986); *In re* Atlas Automation, Inc., 42 B.R. 246 (Bankr. E.D. Mich. 1984)]

    a. **Criteria:** [§66]   The following characteristics have been used to identify a non-core proceeding:

    (i) It is *not specifically identified* as a core proceeding under section 157(b)(2) (B) through (N);

    (ii) It *existed prior to the filing* of the bankruptcy case;

    (iii) It *would continue to exist independent of the Bankruptcy Code*; and

    (iv) The parties' *rights and/or obligations are not significantly affected* as a result of filing the bankruptcy case.

    [*In re* Commercial Heat Treating of Dayton, Inc., 80 B.R. 880 (Bankr. S.D. Ohio 1987)]

    b. **Example:** Debtor brings an action in the bankruptcy court against his supplier for damages caused by an alleged pre-petition breach of warranty in the sale of certain (nonconforming) zippers used in tents that Debtor had contracted to furnish for the United States government. This civil proceeding, which is related to Debtor's bankruptcy case, is *non-core* and is the kind of state-law cause of action for which the *Marathon* case ***requires final adjudication in an Article III court***. [Mohawk Industries, Inc. v. Robinson Industries, Inc., 46 B.R. 464 (D. Mass. 1985); *see supra*, §5]

    c. **Minority view:** [§67] There is some authority for treating the collection of pre-petition accounts receivable and similar actions as core proceedings, on the basis that they concern the administration of the estate, involve turnover of property of the estate, or are includable under the catchall provision (*see supra*, §64). [28 U.S.C. §157(b)(2)(A), (E), (O)] However, this view has been criticized as being in conflict with the *Marathon* decision. [1 Collier ¶3.01(2)(b)(iv)]

    d. **Compare—post-petition accounts receivable:** [§68] Where the action concerns accounts receivable that arise post-petition, the authorities are divided, but the better view considers the proceeding as core. [*In re* Arnold Print Works, Inc., 815 F.2d 165 (1st Cir. 1987); 1 Collier ¶3.01(2)(b)(iv)]

    e. **Other non-core matters**

        (1) **Controversies between nondebtor litigants:** [§69] Actions that are related to the bankruptcy case (*e.g.*, because of the effect of their outcome on property or debts of the bankruptcy estate) but that involve nondebtor parties are generally considered to be non-core proceedings. [*In re* Destron, Inc., 38 B.R. 310 (Bankr. N.D. Ill. 1984)]

            (a) **Example:** An action in the bankruptcy court by Debtor's creditor against Debtor's bank for breach of a contract to provide Debtor with working capital was held to be non-core. [*In re* Destron, Inc., *supra*]

        (2) **Personal injury tort and wrongful death claims:** [§70] Proceedings concerning the estimation or liquidation of personal injury tort or wrongful death claims, *for purposes of distribution*, are non-core and must be tried in the district court. [28 U.S.C. §157(b)(2)(B), (5); *see supra*, §§62-63]

            (a) **Compare:** If the purpose of proceedings to estimate personal injury tort or wrongful death claims is not distribution (*e.g.*, proceedings to estimate unliquidated asbestos tort claims for the purpose of developing or confirming a Chapter 11 plan), the proceedings are *core matters*, and the bankruptcy judge may estimate the claims even though the claims ultimately must be litigated in the district court for the purpose of distribution. [*In re* UNR Industries, Inc., 45 B.R. 322 (N.D. Ill. 1984)]

3. **Bankruptcy Judge Determines Core/Non-Core Status:** [§71] The bankruptcy judge decides, subject to appeal, whether a proceeding is core or non-core, but she may not determine that it is non-core solely because state law is involved. [28 U.S.C. §157(b)(3)]

    a. **Partially core and non-core:** [§72] If a proceeding is predominantly core, it may be considered a core matter even if there is an insignificant non-core aspect to it. [*In re* Blackman, 55 B.R. 437 (Bankr. D.D.C. 1985)]

4. **Comment:** There is a substantial difference of opinion about what constitutes a core or non-core proceeding. However, unless (i) a proceeding is the trial of a personal injury tort or a wrongful death claim (*see supra*, §62), (ii) the proceeding is withdrawn by the district court (*see infra*, §§81-85), or (iii) abstention is exercised in favor of resolution in a state court (*see infra*, §§86-89), the bankruptcy judge *hears* both core and non-core matters. The only practical difference is which court enters the *final order*, the bankruptcy judge or the district judge (*see supra*, §§57-60).

E. JURY TRIALS

1. **Right to Jury Trial:** [§73]   The United States Supreme Court has held that the Seventh Amendment to the Constitution entitles a party to a jury trial of a bankruptcy proceeding where: (i) the cause of action would have been brought *at law* (in 18th Century England) "prior to the merger of the courts of law and equity"; (ii) the remedy requested is *legal* in nature; and (iii) the proceeding does not involve a public right that may be and has been assigned to an Article I court without a jury (*i.e.*, the proceeding concerns a private right). [Granfinanciera, S.A. v. Nordberg, 492 U.S. 33 (1989)] However, a party will lose any right to a jury trial if he files a claim in the bankruptcy case. [Lagenkamp v. Culp, 498 U.S. 42 (1990); Katchen v. Landy, 382 U.S. 323 (1966); *and see infra*, §77] (*Note:* The only relevant federal statute [28 U.S.C. §1411(a)] indicates that a right to a jury trial exists for an individual who would have that right under applicable nonbankruptcy law in a *personal injury tort or wrongful death* case, which must be tried in the district court; *see supra*, §62.)

   a. **Example—fraudulent transfer:** [§74]   Trustee brings an action for money damages against Transferee based on an alleged fraudulent transfer made by Debtor prior to bankruptcy. Since an action to recover a fraudulent transfer would have been brought at law prior to the merger of the courts of law and equity, and since the remedy sought is legal in nature, Transferee is entitled to a jury trial under the Seventh Amendment. [Granfinanciera, S.A. v. Nordberg, *supra*]

      (1) **Compare—equitable remedy:** [§75]   Insurer sought an accounting and the imposition of a constructive trust on insurance proceeds paid to Debtors, commercial fishermen, following the sinking of Debtors' boat. Insurer alleged that the boat had been intentionally sunk by Debtors to defraud Insurer. Since Insurer's demand for relief was equitable in nature, the court held that there was no right to a trial by jury. [American Universal Insurance Co. v. Pugh, 821 F.2d 1352 (9th Cir. 1987)]

   b. **Example—preference:** [§76]   Trustee brings an action for a money judgment against Creditor, who allegedly received a preferential transfer from Debtor shortly before the filing of the bankruptcy petition. Creditor has not filed a claim in the bankruptcy case. Since an action to recover a preferential transfer would have been brought at law prior to the merger of the courts of law and equity, and since the remedy sought is legal in nature, Creditor is entitled to a jury trial. [*See* Schoenthal v. Irving Trust Co., 287 U.S. 92 (1932)]

      (1) **Compare—creditor files a claim:** [§77]   If Creditor files a claim in the bankruptcy case, and Trustee responds with a preference action against

Creditor for money damages, Creditor is *not* entitled to a jury trial because the preference issue arose in the context of a proceeding to determine the allowance of a claim against the bankruptcy estate, which is an action in equity. [Lagenkamp v. Culp, *supra*, §73; Katchen v. Landy, *supra*, §73; *and see In re* Silver Mill Frozen Foods, Inc., 80 B.R. 848 (Bankr. W.D. Mich. 1987)—certain recipients of alleged preferential transfers were entitled to jury trial since they had not filed claims, but other recipients who had filed claims were not entitled to jury trial; *but see* Smith v. Dowden, 47 F.3d 940 (8th Cir. 1995)—creditor, who withdrew claim prior to trustee's filing action to avoid fraudulent transfer, entitled to jury trial]

    c. **Example—tortious interference:** [§78] Trustee brings an action for money damages against Creditor, alleging "(1) tortious interference with the debtor's business, (2) coercion and duress, (3) breach of the contractual duty of good faith, (4) unfair or deceptive trade practices, and (5) misrepresentation." The court found that the action concerns private rights and is "not *integrally* related to any substantive bankruptcy provisions," that some of the claims (including tortious interference) could have been tried in common law courts, and that Trustee is seeking money damages. Therefore, the court held that Trustee is entitled to a jury trial. [Germain v. Connecticut National Bank, 988 F.2d 1323 (2d Cir. 1993)]

    d. **Example—dischargeability of debts:** [§79] Creditor brings an action to determine the dischargeability of a particular debt, and Debtor requests a jury trial. Since a proceeding concerning the dischargeability of a debt is an equitable action that would not have been tried by a jury prior to the merger of the courts of law and equity, and a declaration that a debt is dischargeable or nondischargeable constitutes equitable relief, it has been held that Debtor is *not* entitled to a jury trial under the *Granfinanciera* test (*see supra*, §73). [*In re* Hallahan, 936 F.2d 1496 (7th Cir. 1991)]

2. **Power of Bankruptcy Judges to Try Jury Cases:** [§80] Where the right to a jury trial exists, the Bankruptcy Reform Act of 1994 authorizes bankruptcy judges to conduct jury trials, provided that the district court specially designates the exercise of this jurisdiction and all parties expressly consent. [28 U.S.C. §157(e)] Whether this practice is constitutional remains an open question.

F. WITHDRAWAL

1. **Permissive Withdrawal:** [§81] A case or proceeding that has been referred to the bankruptcy court may be withdrawn by the district court on its own motion or on the timely motion of a party, for cause. [28 U.S.C. §157(d)]

2. **Mandatory Withdrawal:** [§82] On a timely motion, the district court must withdraw a proceeding from the bankruptcy court if *its resolution* requires consideration of the Bankruptcy Code *and* substantial and material consideration of a *federal nonbankruptcy statute* "regulating organizations or activities affecting interstate commerce." [28 U.S.C. §157(d); *In re* Texaco, Inc., 84 B.R. 911 (S.D.N.Y. 1988)]

    a. **"Substantial and material consideration":** [§83] A *minority view* requires that "substantial and material consideration" of *both* the nonbankruptcy federal law and the Bankruptcy Code be necessary to resolve the proceeding for mandatory withdrawal to be proper. [*In re* Carolina Produce Distributors, Inc., 110 B.R. 207 (W.D.N.C. 1990)] Under this view, a proceeding concerning a claim in the bankruptcy case, the resolution of which requires substantial and material consideration of a federal nonbankruptcy statute, but which does not entail interpretation or application of the Bankruptcy Code, need *not* be withdrawn. [1 Collier ¶3.01(2)(e)(ii)] The *majority view*, however, holds that "it is enough for mandatory withdrawal if the resolution of the proceeding requires consideration of bankruptcy law and the substantial and material consideration of [a] non-bankruptcy federal statute." [Franklin Savings v. Office of Thrift Supervision, 150 B.R. 976 (D. Kan. 1993)]

    b. **Interstate commerce:** [§84] The nonbankruptcy federal statute must have "more than a de minimis effect on interstate commerce." [*In re* Anthony Tammaro, Inc., 56 B.R. 999 (D.N.J. 1986)]

3. **No Appeal:** [§85] While not all authorities agree, the better rule is that an order by the district court withdrawing a case or proceeding from the bankruptcy court is not appealable. [*In re* Kemble, 776 F.2d 802 (9th Cir. 1985)]

G. ABSTENTION

1. **Permissive Abstention:** [§86] The district court may abstain from hearing *a particular core or non-core proceeding* in a bankruptcy case when justice, comity with state courts, or respect for state law favors resolution of the matter in a state forum. [28 U.S.C. §1334(c)(1); 1 Collier ¶3.01(3)(a); Carver v. Carver, 954 F.2d 1573 (11th Cir. 1992)—domestic relations]

    a. **Example:** Debtor was a co-defendant in numerous products liability actions in various state courts. To avoid inconsistent decisions and duplicity of judicial resources, the district court abstained from hearing the contingent personal injury tort cases. [*In re* White Motor Credit, 761 F.2d 270 (6th Cir. 1985)]

2. **Mandatory Abstention:** [§87] On a timely motion, the district court must abstain from hearing *a particular non-core proceeding* if it is based on a state-law cause of action *related to the bankruptcy case* (but not arising in the bankruptcy case or under the Code) that: (i) could not have been brought in a federal court without bankruptcy jurisdiction; (ii) already has been filed in an appropriate state court; and (iii) is capable of being timely adjudicated in that forum. [28 U.S.C. §1334(c)(2); State Bank of Lombard v. Chart House, 46 B.R. 468 (N.D. Ill. 1985)]

    a. **Personal injury tort and wrongful death:** [§88] Proceedings based on personal injury tort or wrongful death claims are not subject to mandatory abstention. [28 U.S.C. §157(b)(4)]

    b. **Appeal:** [§89] A bankruptcy court's order in favor of or against abstention from hearing a particular proceeding is reviewable by the district court, but an abstention decision by the district court is not reviewable by the court of appeals or the Supreme Court. One exception permits an appeal of a decision *not* to abstain mandatorily (*see supra*, §87) to be taken to the court of appeals and the Supreme Court. [28 U.S.C. §1334(d)]

H. REMOVAL

1. **Civil Actions:** [§90] A claim or a cause of action in a civil proceeding may be removed from a nonbankruptcy court to the federal district court (and generally, to the bankruptcy court by automatic reference) for the district where the civil action is pending, if there is proper jurisdiction under 28 U.S.C. section 1334 (*see supra*, §52). [28 U.S.C. §1452(a)] The notice of removal is filed in the *bankruptcy court*. [Bankruptcy Rules 9027(a)(1), 9001(3)]

    a. **Exceptions:** [§91] Proceedings in the United States Tax Court or civil actions by governmental units to enforce their police or regulatory powers are not subject to removal. [28 U.S.C. §1452(a)]

2. **Remand:** [§92] The court to which a claim or cause of action has been removed has the power, based on the equities, to remand the action to the forum where it was pending. [28 U.S.C. §1452(b)]

    a. **Appeal:** [§93] A bankruptcy court's order to remand or not to remand a removed proceeding is reviewable by the district court, but a remand decision by the district court is not reviewable by the court of appeals or the Supreme Court. [28 U.S.C. §1452(b); Things Remembered, Inc. v. Petrarca, 115 S. Ct. 1821 (1995)—remand on jurisdictional, as opposed to equitable, basis held nonreviewable by court of appeals]

I. VENUE

1. **Bankruptcy Case:** [§94] The appropriate venue for the *filing of a bankruptcy petition* is in the federal district where the debtor has maintained her *residence, domicile, principal place of business* in the United States, or *principal assets* in the United States during or for the longest portion of the 180-day period immediately before commencement of the case. Venue is also proper in a district where a bankruptcy case concerning a general partner, partnership, or affiliate of the debtor is pending. [28 U.S.C. §1408]

2. **Bankruptcy Proceedings:** [§95] The general rule for a proceeding arising under the Code, or arising in or related to a bankruptcy case, is that venue lies in the *district in which the case is pending*. [28 U.S.C. §1409(a)]

    a. **Exception—proceedings under specified dollar amounts:** [§96] A proceeding by a bankruptcy trustee to recover money or property worth less than $1,000, or to recover a consumer debt under $5,000, must be filed in the district where the defendant resides. [28 U.S.C. §1409(b)]

    b. **Exception—certain post-petition claims of trustee:** [§97] A proceeding by a trustee based on a cause of action that arises post-petition *from the operation of the debtor's business* can be filed only in the district where the action could have been filed (by the debtor) under applicable nonbankruptcy venue law. [28 U.S.C. §1409(d)] This rule applies even if the trustee's claim is for a small amount that, otherwise, would qualify for the exception contained in 28 U.S.C. section 1409(b), above.

c. **Post-petition claims against estate:** [§98] A proceeding *against the trustee* based on a cause of action that arises post-petition from the operation of the debtor's business may be brought either in the district where the case is pending (*see supra*, §95) *or* in the district where the action could have been commenced under applicable nonbankruptcy venue law. [28 U.S.C. §1409(e)]

d. **Trustee as statutory successor:** [§99] A seldom-used *permissive* venue provision provides the trustee, as the statutory successor to the debtor or to creditors under Code sections 541 (*see infra*, §§294 *et seq.*) or 544(b) (*see infra*, §363), the option of commencing the action in the district where the case is pending *or* in the district where it could have been brought by the debtor or such creditors under applicable nonbankruptcy venue law if the bankruptcy case had not been filed. [28 U.S.C. §1409(c)] This provision, however, is subject to the exception noted above for proceedings under specified dollar amounts. [28 U.S.C. §1409(b); *see supra*, §96]

3. **Venue in District Court:** [§100] Venue of both cases and proceedings lies in the district court for the appropriate district. [28 U.S.C. §§1408, 1409]

4. **Change of Venue:** [§101] A case or a proceeding may be transferred by one district court to another "in the interest of justice or for the convenience of the parties." [28 U.S.C. §1412] As to the "interest of justice," the courts have adopted a flexible case-by-case approach based on the following factors: "(i) efficient administration of the bankruptcy estate; (ii) judicial economy; (iii) timeliness; and (iv) fairness." [*In re* Manville Forest Products Corp., 896 F.2d 1384 (2d Cir. 1990)] *Note:* The **bankruptcy court** can order a transfer, since motions to change venue generally are treated as core proceedings. [*In re* Oceanquest Feeder Service, Inc., 56 B.R. 715 (Bankr. D. Conn. 1986); 1 Collier ¶3.02(4)(a)]

   a. **Criteria when venue is proper:** [§102] When a case or a proceeding has been filed in a district of proper venue, the court usually considers the following factors in ruling on a request to change the venue to another district [*In re* Old Delmar Corp., 45 B.R. 883 (S.D.N.Y. 1985)]:

   (1) The *location of the debtor's estate*;

   (2) The *economic and efficient administration* of the debtor's estate;

   (3) The *proximity of the debtor*;

   (4) The *proximity of the creditors*;

   (5) The *proximity of witnesses*; and

   (6) The *probability that a liquidation will be ordered*.

   b. **Improper venue:** [§103] If a case or a proceeding has been filed in a district of improper venue and if a timely objection has been made, the case or proceeding may be *transferred* to a district where venue is proper *or* it may be *dismissed*. [28 U.S.C. §1406; Bankruptcy Rule 1014(a)(2)] It appears that the bankruptcy court lacks the authority to retain a case filed in the wrong venue. [*In re* Pick, 95 B.R. 712 (Bankr. D.S.D. 1989)]

J. APPEALS

1. **Appeal from Bankruptcy Court:** [§104] An appeal may be taken from the bankruptcy court to the federal district court or to a bankruptcy appellate panel, if there exists such a panel in the particular jurisdiction. [28 U.S.C. §158; *see infra*, §107]

    a. **District court:** [§105] The appellate jurisdiction of the district court (and the bankruptcy appellate panel) includes appeals from final orders and judgments of the bankruptcy court. Appellate jurisdiction over interlocutory orders generally is discretionary. However, appeal of interlocutory orders extending or shortening a Chapter 11 debtor's exclusivity period to file a plan, or to file a plan and obtain acceptances (*see infra*, §1047), is as of right. [28 U.S.C. §158(a); 1 Collier ¶3.03(6)(a)]

        (1) **Compare—recommendations from bankruptcy court:** [§106] Proposed findings of fact and conclusions of law submitted by the bankruptcy court to the district court in a ***non-core matter*** are ***not issues on appeal***, but merely recommendations to the district court for: (i) its consideration; (ii) de novo review of matters objected to; and (iii) final order or judgment. [28 U.S.C. §157(c)(1); *see supra*, §§58-59]

    b. **Bankruptcy appellate panel:** [§107] Prior to the Bankruptcy Reform Act of 1994, the Ninth Circuit was the only circuit utilizing bankruptcy appellate panels (instead of the district court) to hear appeals from the bankruptcy court. However, the 1994 legislation requires the judicial council of each circuit to establish a bankruptcy appellate panel, comprised of bankruptcy judges from that circuit, unless (i) there are insufficient judicial resources or (ii) the procedure would cause undue delay or increased cost to parties in bankruptcy cases. Each appeal is to be heard by three members of the bankruptcy appellate panel who are not from the district where the appeal arises. Additionally, bankruptcy panels may hear appeals only if:

        (i) A ***majority of the district judges*** for the district in which the appeal arises have authorized the use of bankruptcy appellate panels; and

        (ii) ***All parties consent*** (the appellant or any other party may elect to have the appeal heard by the district court instead of the bankruptcy appellate panel).

        [28 U.S.C. §158(b), (c)] *Note:* A joint bankruptcy appellate panel may be established by the judicial councils of two or more circuits if authorized by the Judicial Conference of the United States. [28 U.S.C. §158(b)(2)]

    c. **No direct appeal to circuit court:** [§108] An appeal may not be taken from the bankruptcy court directly to the circuit court, even with the parties' consent. [*In re* Exclusive Industries Corp., 751 F.2d 806 (5th Cir. 1985)]

    d. **"Clearly erroneous" standard:** [§109] When a final order or judgment of the bankruptcy court is appealed, the district court or the bankruptcy appellate panel must use the "clearly erroneous" standard of appellate review. [Gaslight Club v. Official Creditors Committee, 46 B.R. 209 (N.D. Ill. 1985)] Under the "clearly erroneous" standard, the district court may not perform additional fact finding, but must either accept the findings of the bankruptcy judge or, if the findings are clearly erroneous, reject them. This is not a de novo review. [*In re Neis*, 723 F.2d 584 (7th Cir. 1983)]

e. **Interlocutory orders:** [§110] The district court has discretion to hear appeals from interlocutory orders of the bankruptcy court (*see supra*, §105). Some district courts have adopted the general standard for review of interlocutory orders, which requires *exceptional circumstances*—*i.e.*, when (i) there is a controlling question of law with substantial ground for variance of opinion, and (ii) an immediate appeal may materially advance the final outcome of the case or proceeding. [28 U.S.C. §1292(b)]

   (1) **Example:** Where the bankruptcy judge issued an interlocutory order providing for the appointment of a legal representative for future asbestos tort claimants, the district court permitted an interlocutory appeal because there was substantial disagreement about the novel legal issue and deferral of consideration of the issue could have resulted in jeopardizing the entire reorganization plan. [*In re Johns-Manville Corp.*, 45 B.R. 833 (S.D.N.Y. 1984)]

   (2) **Compare:** Suppose, in the example above, the bankruptcy judge issued an interlocutory order denying a request to *disqualify the attorney* for the legal representative of the future tort claimants. An interlocutory appeal of just such an order has been denied because it did not involve a controlling question of law and an immediate appeal would not have materially advanced the termination of the lawsuit. [*In re Johns-Manville Corp.*, 47 B.R. 957 (S.D.N.Y. 1985)]

f. **Time for appeal:** [§111] A party is allowed *10 days*, from the date of the entry of the bankruptcy judge's order or judgment, to appeal to the district court or to the bankruptcy appellate panel. The notice of appeal must be filed with the clerk of the *bankruptcy court*. [28 U.S.C. §158(c); Bankruptcy Rules 8002(a), 8001(a)]

2. **Appeal from District Court**

   a. **Sitting as court of appeals:** [§112] An appeal may be taken to the circuit court from a *final decision, order, or judgment* of the district court in its *appellate capacity* or of the bankruptcy appellate panel. [28 U.S.C. §158(d); Capitol Credit Plan of Tennessee, Inc. v. Shaffer, 912 F.2d 749 (4th Cir. 1990)]

      (1) **Final Orders:** [§113] Generally, *both* the bankruptcy court's order as well as the district court's appellate order must be final decisions. [*In re Stanton*, 766 F.2d 1283 (9th Cir. 1985)] However, some courts recognize an exception where a nonfinal order of the bankruptcy court is cured by a final order of the district court. [*In re Phillips*, 844 F.2d 230 (5th Cir. 1988)] For example, where the bankruptcy court denies a motion to dismiss for lack of jurisdiction (interlocutory order), but the district court reverses and holds that jurisdiction is not present, the order of the district court constitutes a final order that may be appealed. [*In re Cash Currency*

Exchange, Inc., 762 F.2d 542 (7th Cir. 1985), *cert. denied*, 474 U.S. 904 (1985)]

    (2) **Interlocutory orders:** [§114] The Supreme Court has held that appeals from interlocutory orders of the district court sitting in its appellate capacity are governed by the general standard for review of interlocutory orders (28 U.S.C. section 1292, *supra*, §110). [Connecticut National Bank v. Germain, 503 U.S. 249 (1992)]

b. **Sitting as a court of original jurisdiction:** [§115] When the district court functions as a court of original jurisdiction, rather than as an appellate court (*e.g.*, in proceedings that are *non-core* or that have been *withdrawn*), an appeal to the circuit court is governed by the general appellate standard (28 U.S.C. section 1291). The rule here is similar to the rule where the district court sits as an appellate court (*supra*, §112)—appeals may be taken only from final decisions (except as provided in 28 U.S.C. section 1292; *see supra*, §110). [*In re* Amatex Corp., 755 F.2d 1034 (3d Cir. 1985)]

    (1) **Example:** In *Amatex*, the Third Circuit held that an order of the *district court* (as a court of original jurisdiction) denying the appointment of a legal representative for future asbestos tort claimants was a final decision and thus was appealable under 28 U.S.C. section 1291. *But note*: The Seventh Circuit has ruled that such an order was not final and, therefore, was not appealable. [*In re* UNR Industries, Inc., 725 F.2d 1111 (7th Cir. 1984)]

c. **"Finality"—liberal interpretation:** [§116] The concept of finality of a district court's order or judgment is significant since it will determine whether an appeal may be taken to the circuit court. Courts have developed a liberal definition of finality in the context of bankruptcy by viewing *a proceeding* as the "relevant judicial unit" or as a "discrete dispute within the larger case." [*In re* Saco Local Development Corp., 711 F.2d 441 (1st Cir. 1983)] Factors to be considered are "the extent to which (1) the order leaves the bankruptcy court nothing to do but execute the order; (2) delay in obtaining review would prevent the aggrieved party from obtaining effective relief; and (3) a later reversal on that issue would require recommencement of the entire proceeding." [*In re* Huebner, 986 F.2d 1222 (8th Cir. 1993)—order denying debtor's exemption is final]

    (1) **Example—final order:** An order holding that Insurance Company's claim for Debtor's "employee group life, health, and disability insurance premiums" was entitled to fourth priority status constituted the final disposition of a discrete controversy within the bankruptcy case, and such order could be appealed separately. [*In re* Saco Local Development Corp., *supra*]

    (2) **Example—interlocutory order:** A bankruptcy court's order denying the appointment of an equity security holders' committee to represent the common shareholders was held to be an interlocutory order, which, when affirmed by the district court, was not appealable to the circuit court. [*In re* Johns-Manville Corp., 824 F.2d 176 (2d Cir. 1987)]

d. **District court's remand to bankruptcy court:** [§117] Although there is some disagreement among the circuits, it has been held that if an order of the bankruptcy court has been appealed to the district court, and the district court has remanded the proceeding to the bankruptcy court, an appeal of the remand may be taken to the circuit court only if: (i) the bankruptcy court's order was final, and (ii) the remand does not require "extensive further proceedings." [*In re* Greene County Hospital, 835 F.2d 589 (5th Cir. 1988)]

   (1) **Example:** A bankruptcy judge's final order concerning an objection to the discharge of a certain debt was reversed and remanded by the district court. The circuit court held that the district court's order of remand for significant further proceedings was neither final nor appealable. [*In re* Riggsby, 745 F.2d 1153 (7th Cir. 1984)]

3. **Orders Concerning Automatic Stay:** [§118] Rulings that grant or deny relief from the automatic stay (*see infra*, §809) are considered to be final decisions and may be appealed. [*In re* American Mariner Industries, Inc., 734 F.2d 426 (9th Cir. 1984)]

   a. **Mootness:** [§119] However, if relief from the automatic stay is granted, but the debtor does not obtain a *stay pending appeal*, the appeal generally will be moot once a foreclosure sale has occurred. [Markstein v. Massey Associates, Ltd., 763 F.2d 1325 (11th Cir. 1985)]

III. COMMENCEMENT AND ADMINISTRATION OF THE CASE

chapter approach

In answering an examination question concerning the commencement of a bankruptcy case, be certain to consider all of the items on the following checklist:

1. *Is the debtor a person*, as defined in the Bankruptcy Code—*i.e.*, an individual, a partnership, or a corporation?

2. *Does the debtor have a residence, domicile, place of business,* or **property** in the United States?

3. *What kind of relief* is the most suitable under the debtor's financial circumstances? Of course, the debtor's future expected income will be an important factor in determining whether repayment to creditors under a Chapter 11, 12, or 13 plan is feasible or whether liquidation under Chapter 7 is more appropriate.

4. *Is the debtor eligible* under the desired chapter?

5. *If the debtor is married*, is it advisable to file a *joint* petition?

6. *Is the filing of an involuntary case* against the debtor being considered by creditors? If so,

    a. Will the case be filed under **Chapter 7 or Chapter 11**? (Remember that an involuntary petition cannot be filed under Chapter 12 or Chapter 13.)

    b. Is the debtor *generally not paying his debts as they become due*?

    c. If the debtor has *12 or more creditors* holding noncontingent, undisputed claims, are there *at least three* such creditors who are willing to file an involuntary petition, and does the aggregate of their *noncontingent, undisputed, unsecured claims total at least $10,000*?

    d. If the debtor has *fewer than 12* creditors holding noncontingent, undisputed claims, is there *one* (or more) such creditor(s) willing to file an involuntary petition and does the aggregate of his (their) *noncontingent, undisputed, unsecured claim(s) total at least $10,000*?

7. *Would the court's abstention* from accepting jurisdiction over the case be appropriate under the circumstances, such as in furtherance of a pending out-of-court workout or state court insolvency proceeding?

8. *Is there a ground for dismissal* of the bankruptcy petition? Has the petition been filed in *good faith*?

9. *Do circumstances indicate that conversion* to another chapter would be more appropriate than the chapter under which the case was filed? Is the debtor eligible for relief under the other chapter?

A. ELIGIBILITY

1. **Person:** [§120] Only a *person* (individual, partnership, or corporation) that resides or has a domicile, a place of business, or property in the United States is eligible to be a debtor under the Bankruptcy Code. (*Note:* A municipality also may be eligible under Chapter 9, but that is a topic that is beyond the scope of this book.) [B.C. §109(a)]

   a. **Insolvency not required:** [§121] A person's eligibility to be a debtor under the Code does not require that his financial condition be in a state of insolvency. [B.C. §109; 2 Collier ¶109.02]

   b. **Corporation:** [§122] The bankruptcy definition of the term "corporation" is expansive and includes *business trusts* and most companies or associations with corporate attributes, except limited partnerships. [B.C. §101(9)]

      (1) **Example—Labor Union:** A labor union is treated as a corporation under the Bankruptcy Code and, therefore, is eligible to be a debtor under the Code. [*In re* Lane County Sheriff's Officers Association, Inc., 16 B.R. 190 (Bankr. D. Or. 1981)]

      (2) **Example—business trust:** A family trust operating a mill complex leasing business involving industrial and commercial lessees was considered to be a business trust and thus eligible for relief under the Bankruptcy Code. [B.C. §101(9)(A)(v); *In re* Gonic Realty Trust, 50 B.R. 710 (Bankr. D.N.H. 1985)]

         (a) **Compare:** A family trust that was *not engaged in business* but that was created to preserve assets for the maintenance and support of the grantor's family was found not to be a business trust and thus was ineligible to be a debtor under the Code. [*In re* Mosby, 46 B.R. 175 (Bankr. E.D. Mo. 1985), *aff'd*, 791 F.2d 628 (8th Cir. 1986)] Likewise, it is well-established that a probate estate does not qualify to be a debtor under the statute. [*In re* Estate of Whiteside, 64 B.R. 99 (Bankr. E.D. Cal. 1986)] Similarly, a trust created to facilitate secured financing by enabling "numerous lenders to receive the benefit of a security interest without the need for multiple security agreements and filings" was held to be ineligible for relief. [*In re* Secured Equipment Trust of Eastern Airlines, 38 F.3d 86 (2d Cir. 1994)]

2. **Chapter 7—"Liquidation":** [§123] Chapter 7 relief is available to any person satisfying Bankruptcy Code section 109(a) (*see supra*, §120) except those listed below. [B.C. §109(b)]

   a. **Exceptions:** [§124] The following persons are not eligible debtors under Chapter 7:

      (1) **Railroads:** [§125] Railroads are not eligible for Chapter 7 relief. [B.C. §109(b)(1)]

      (2) **Domestic savings institutions and insurance companies:** [§126] Domestic banks, insurance companies, credit unions, savings and loan asso-

ciations, building and loan associations, homestead associations, cooperative banks, and other similar domestic institutions are not eligible for relief under Chapter 7. [B.C. §109(b)(2); *In re* Estate of Medcare HMO, 998 F.2d 436 (7th Cir. 1993)—HMO, under Illinois law, was a domestic insurance company and was not eligible (Chapter 11 case); *see infra*, §130]

- (a) **Rationale:** These kinds of financial institutions are regulated directly by the banking and insurance industries; thus, they are not eligible for relief under the Bankruptcy Code. [Israel-British Bank (London) Ltd. v. Federal Deposit Insurance Corp., 536 F.2d 509 (2d Cir. 1976)]

- (b) **Compare:** A mortgage and trust company that was *not considered to be a bank under Texas law* was found to be an eligible debtor under section 109 of the Code. [*In re* Central Mortgage & Trust, Inc., 50 B.R. 1010 (S.D. Tex. 1985)] Similarly, a community currency exchange engaged in the business of cashing checks and selling money orders was held not to be the substantial equivalent of a bank because it did not accept deposits. [*In re* Cash Currency Exchange, Inc., *supra*, §113]

(3) **Small business investment companies:** [§127] Small business investment companies licensed by the Small Business Administration under the Small Business Investment Act of 1958 are not eligible for Chapter 7 relief. [B.C. §109(b)(2)]

(4) **Foreign savings institutions and insurance companies:** [§128] Foreign banks, insurance companies, savings and loan associations, and other similar financial institutions that are *engaged in such business in the United States* are not eligible for Chapter 7 relief. [B.C. §109(b)(3)]

- (a) **Note:** Such foreign institutions, however, are eligible if they are *not* engaged in business in the United States but have property in this country. [Israel-British Bank (London) Ltd. v. Federal Deposit Insurance Corp., *supra*]

b. **Stockbrokers and commodity brokers:** [§129] Stockbrokers and commodity brokers may be debtors under special provisions of Chapter 7. [B.C. §§741 *et seq.*, 761 *et seq.*]

3. **Chapter 11—"Reorganization":** [§130] Generally, only an individual, partnership, or corporation that is eligible for relief under Chapter 7 may be a debtor under Chapter 11. [B.C. §109(d)]

a. **Exceptions:** [§131] The following differences exist between eligibility under Chapter 7 and eligibility under Chapter 11:

(1) **Stockbrokers and commodity brokers:** [§132] Stockbrokers and commodity brokers *cannot* be debtors under Chapter 11. [B.C. §109(d)]

(2) **Railroads:** [§133] Railroads *are eligible* for relief under special provisions of Chapter 11. [B.C. §§109(d), 1161 *et seq.*; *and see supra*, §125]

b. **Reorganization of business or consumer debtors:** [§134] Chapter 11 is designed principally for business reorganizations. However, the Supreme Court has held that a consumer debtor (*i.e.*, an individual not engaged in business) also may qualify for relief under this chapter. [Toibb v. Radloff, *supra*, §11]

c. **Liquidating Chapter 11:** [§135] Although the purpose of a Chapter 11 case usually is to reorganize the debtor by means of a confirmable plan, an otherwise eligible debtor seeking to liquidate its assets also may qualify for Chapter 11 relief and may propose a liquidating plan). [B.C. §1123(b)(4)]

4. **Chapter 13—"Adjustment of Debts of Individual with Regular Income":** [§136] Chapter 13 relief is available *only to an individual* (*i.e.*, not to a partnership or a corporation) *who has regular income*, whose unsecured debts total less than $250,000, and whose secured debts total less than $750,000. The indebtedness used for these calculations must be noncontingent and liquidated liabilities, determined as of the date of the filing of the petition. [B.C. §109(e); *In re* Pearson, 773 F.2d 751 (6th Cir. 1985)]

    a. **"Individual with regular income":** [§137] An individual with regular income is defined as an "individual whose income is sufficiently stable and regular to enable such individual to make payments under a plan under Chapter 13." [B.C. §101(30)]

        (1) **Sources of regular income:** [§138] A Chapter 13 debtor's regular income usually is generated from wages or salary, but it may be derived from almost any legitimate source, *e.g.*, interest income, rental income, a pension, a business, a trust, social security, or even Aid to Families with Dependent Children. The key issue is whether it is sufficiently stable and capable of funding the debtor's repayment plan. [*In re* Hammonds, 729 F.2d 1391 (11th Cir. 1984)]

    b. **Voluntary petition:** [§139] A Chapter 13 case must be commenced by the debtor's voluntary petition, never by an involuntary petition. [B.C. §303(a)]

    c. **Joint case:** [§140] An individual with regular income and his spouse may file a joint petition under Chapter 13, provided that their *aggregate* unsecured indebtedness is less than $250,000 and that their aggregate secured indebtedness is less than $750,000. [B.C. §109(e)]

    d. **Exception—stockbrokers and commodity brokers:** [§141] Stockbrokers and commodity brokers do *not* qualify for relief under Chapter 13. [B.C. §109(e)]

5. **Chapter 12—"Family Farmer with Regular Annual Income":** [§142] A family farmer whose yearly income is sufficiently stable and regular to fund a Chapter 12 plan may file a petition under that chapter. [B.C. §§109(f), 101(19); *see infra*, §§1223 *et seq.*] Certain individuals, individuals and their spouses, corporations, or partnerships may qualify as a family farmer. [B.C. §101(18)] A Chapter 12 case may be commenced only by the filing of a *voluntary* bankruptcy petition, never by an involuntary petition. [B.C. §303(a)]

6. **Ineligibility—Multiple Petitions:** [§143] An *individual* or a *family farmer* is not eligible to file a petition under any chapter of the Bankruptcy Code if he has been a debtor in a case that was *dismissed in the preceding 180 days*, either because of the debtor's intentional failure to obey court orders or "to appear before the court in proper prosecution of the case," *or* because he requested a voluntary dismissal of the case following a party's request for relief from the automatic stay. [B.C. §109(g)]

   a. **Rationale:** This provision is intended to curtail abusive and repetitive filings, particularly in consumer bankruptcy cases.

   b. **Example—failure to obey court orders or prosecute case:** Debtor's Chapter 13 petition was dismissed because he (i) did not pay certain mortgage installments while his case was pending, (ii) did not attend the section 341 meeting of creditors, and (iii) failed to file a Chapter 13 plan. On the same day, Debtor's spouse's Chapter 11 petition was dismissed because no plan had been proposed over a two-year period. Five months later, Debtor and his spouse filed a joint Chapter 13 petition. They were not eligible debtors, and therefore their case was dismissed. [B.C. §109(g)(1); *In re* Nelkovski, 46 B.R. 542 (Bankr. N.D. Ill. 1985); *see also In re* Montgomery, 37 F.3d 413 (8th Cir. 1994)—debtor bears burden of proof to show that "failure to obey a court order was not willful"]

   c. **Example—debtor's voluntary dismissal following creditor's request for relief from stay:** Debtor filed a Chapter 13 petition, and Creditor requested relief from the automatic stay. Debtor then obtained a voluntary dismissal of the case. Three months later, Debtor filed another Chapter 13 petition. Debtor was not eligible for relief under the Code, and thus the second petition was dismissed. [B.C. §109(g)(2); *In re* Denson, 56 B.R. 543 (Bankr. N.D. Ala. 1986)]

B. VOLUNTARY CASE

1. **Filing the Petition:** [§144] A voluntary case is *commenced* when an eligible debtor (*see supra*, §§120 *et seq.*) files a petition under Chapter 7, 11, 12, or 13. At that time, the appropriate filing fee should be paid, except under special circumstances where the court approves an individual's application to pay the fee in installments. [Bankruptcy Rule 1006; 28 U.S.C. §1930] The filing of a voluntary petition statutorily constitutes an *order for relief* (*see supra*, §17). [B.C. §301]

   a. **Consumer debtor:** [§145] Before filing a petition, a debtor who is an *individual with primarily consumer debts* must be notified in writing by the clerk of the court of each chapter under which the debtor may commence a case. [B.C. §342(b)]

   b. **Notice:** [§146] The Code requires notice of the order for relief. [B.C. §342(a)] This notice is sent to *all parties in interest*, including the debtor, the trustee, all secured and unsecured creditors, equity security holders in a Chapter 11 case, indenture trustees (*see infra*, §487), and holders of community claims, as well as to the appropriate taxing authorities. [2 Collier ¶342.01] The notice generally is included in the same document as the notice of the section 341 meeting of creditors. (*See infra*, §§193-194.)

c. **Husband and wife—joint case:** [§147] An individual debtor who desires to file a single petition together with his spouse may commence a joint case. [B.C. §302(a)] The debtors must be legally married; a joint petition may not be filed if they merely cohabitate. [*In re* Malone, 50 B.R. 2 (Bankr. E.D. Mich. 1985)] The election of a joint case will result in the debtors' paying only one filing fee, and the filing of a joint petition operates automatically as an order for relief in the case.

  (1) **Only in a voluntary case:** [§148] The option to file a joint petition is available only in a voluntary case, and thus it cannot be used by creditors to commence an involuntary case against both spouses. [*In re* Benny, 842 F.2d 1147 (9th Cir. 1988)]

  (2) **Consolidation:** [§149] In a joint case, the court *may* consolidate the debtors' estates by pooling their assets and liabilities, especially if their property and debts are held jointly. [B.C. §302(b)] Factors to be considered by the court are: "(1) whether there is a substantial identity between the assets, liabilities, and handling of financial affairs between the debtor spouses; and (2) whether harm will result from permitting or denying consolidation." [*In re* Reider, 31 F.3d 1102 (11th Cir. 1994)]

    (a) **Distinguish—joint administration:** [§150] Under certain circumstances (*e.g.*, when there is a joint petition or two or more separate petitions concerning a husband and wife in the same court), the judge may expedite the cases by ordering joint administration regarding matters such as notices to creditors, listing of claims, and other similar functions. [Bankruptcy Rule 1015(b)]

d. **Corporation:** [§151] For a corporation to file a voluntary bankruptcy petition, generally its board of directors must first pass a resolution authorizing the filing. [*In re* Bel-Aire Investments, Inc., 97 B.R. 88 (Bankr. M.D. Fla. 1989)] "The president of a corporation cannot, without authority or ratification of the board of directors, institute voluntary bankruptcy proceedings" on behalf of the corporation. [*In re* Penny Saver, Inc., 15 B.R. 252 (Bankr. E.D. Pa. 1981)]

e. **Partnership:** [§152] While one or more general partners may file a voluntary bankruptcy petition on behalf of a partnership, it is necessary to obtain the *consent of all the general partners*. [Bankruptcy Rule 1004(a)] Otherwise, a petition filed by fewer than all of the general partners will be treated as an involuntary one. [B.C. §303(b)(3)(A); *In re* R.S. Pinellas Motel Partnership, 5 B.R. 269 (Bankr. M.D. Fla. 1980); *see infra*, §166]

2. **Schedules to Be Filed:** [§153] In addition to filing the bankruptcy petition, a debtor under any chapter of the Code must file a list of creditors and their addresses, as well as (except in Chapter 9—Municipality) a schedule of assets and liabilities, a schedule of current income and current expenditures, a statement of the debtor's financial affairs, and a schedule of executory contracts and unexpired leases. [B.C. §521(1); Bankruptcy Rule 1007(a), (b)(l)]

  a. **Chapter 7—consumer debtor:** [§154] An individual debtor who has primarily consumer debts (*see supra*, §36) must include a statement in his Chapter 7 petition that he knows that he may proceed under Chapter 7, 11, 12, or

13; that he understands the type of relief that each chapter provides; and that he elects to commence a case under Chapter 7. Additionally, his attorney must attach to the petition an affidavit or a declaration stating that she has informed the debtor of the eligibility and the relief available under Chapters 7, 11, 12, and 13. [Official Bankruptcy Form No. 1]

b. **Chapter 11:** [§155] In a Chapter 11 case, the debtor also must file a separate list disclosing the names and addresses of the ***creditors holding the 20 largest unsecured claims*** (excluding insiders) and the amounts of their claims [Bankruptcy Rule 1007(d)], as well as a detailed list of the debtor's equity security holders [Bankruptcy Rule 1007(a)(3)].

c. **Chapter 13:** [§156] In addition to filing the schedules specified above (*see supra*, §153), a Chapter 13 debtor is also required to file a proposed plan of repayment with the petition or within 15 days thereafter. [B.C. §1321; Bankruptcy Rule 3015(b)]

d. **Chapter 12:** [§157] In addition to filing the schedules specified above (*see supra*, §153), a Chapter 12 debtor also must file a proposed plan of repayment with the petition or within 90 days after the order for relief. [B.C. §1221; Bankruptcy Rule 3015(a)]

e. **Partnership debtor:** [§158] General partners are required to file the appropriate schedules and statements for a partnership debtor, and the court also may order a general partner to file a statement of personal assets and liabilities. [Bankruptcy Rule 1007(g)]

f. **Time limits:** [§159] The debtor must file the required lists, schedules, and statements within the time limits fixed by Bankruptcy Rule 1007.

3. **Automatic Stay:** [§160] When a ***bankruptcy petition is filed***, commencing a voluntary or an involuntary case, the automatic stay (*see infra*, §§778 *et seq.*) becomes effective against ***all entities*** (including a governmental unit) to protect the debtor, his property, and the property of the bankruptcy estate from creditors, while the debtor is granted a respite. The stay is a statutory injunction and helps to ensure an orderly administration of the case and an evenhanded treatment of creditors so that the creditors' shares in the ultimate distribution will not depend on a race to the courthouse. [B.C. §362(a)]

C. INVOLUNTARY CASE

1. **Eligibility:** [§161] An involuntary petition may be filed only under ***Chapter 7 or Chapter 11*** (not under Chapter 12 or Chapter 13) against a person who qualifies as a debtor under the applicable chapter. [B.C. §303(a)]

    a. **Exceptions:** An involuntary petition may ***not*** be filed against (i) a farmer, (ii) a family farmer, or (iii) a nonprofit or charitable corporation. [B.C. §303(a)]

2. **Filing the Petition**

    a. **Petitioning entities:** [§162] An involuntary case may be commenced against a debtor by the filing of a petition by the following entities (*see supra*, §29) [B.C. §303(b)]:

(1) **Three or more creditors:** [§163]   Where there are *at least 12 creditors* (excluding the debtor's insiders and employees, and transferees of voidable transfers) holding claims against the debtor that are neither contingent as to liability nor the subject of a bona fide dispute, *three or more of these entities* may file an involuntary petition provided that at least $10,000 of their claims, in the aggregate, are *unsecured*, noncontingent, and undisputed. [B.C. §303(b)(1); *see also In re* Sims, 994 F.2d 210 (5th Cir. 1993)—three petitioning corporations with "substantial interrelation" held to be separate entities]

   (a) **Example:** Debtor has 20 creditors, and three of them file an involuntary petition against Debtor. The petitioning creditors hold noncontingent unsecured claims totaling $12,000. However, the claims of two of the petitioning creditors (which total $6,000) are the subject of a *bona fide dispute* arising from Debtor's cross-claims in state court. Therefore, those two creditors do not qualify under section 303(b)(1), and the involuntary petition will be dismissed. [*See In re* Henry, 52 B.R. 8 (Bankr. S.D. Ohio 1985)]

(2) **One or more creditors:** [§164]   Where there are *fewer than 12 creditors* (excluding the debtor's insiders and employees, and transferees of voidable transfers) holding noncontingent, undisputed claims against the debtor, *one or more of these entities* may file an involuntary petition provided that at least $10,000 of their claims, in the aggregate, are *unsecured*, noncontingent, and undisputed. [B.C. §303(b)(2)]

   (a) **Joining additional petitioning creditors:** [§165]   After an involuntary petition has been filed but before the court either has entered an order for relief or has dismissed the case, additional unsecured creditors with noncontingent claims may be joined as petitioning creditors to cure a defective filing by a single creditor who, *in good faith*, erroneously believed that the debtor had fewer than 12 creditors. [B.C. §303(c)] However, if the creditor knows that the debtor has at least 12 creditors, but files an involuntary petition for the purpose of resolving a contract dispute, additional petitioning creditors may not be joined, and the involuntary petition should be dismissed for bad faith. [Basin Electric Power Cooperative v. Midwest Processing Co., 769 F.2d 483 (8th Cir. 1985)]

(3) **General partner:** [§166]   An involuntary case against a partnership debtor may be filed by fewer than all of the general partners (*see supra*, §152). Where relief has been ordered concerning all of the general partners, an involuntary petition against the partnership may be filed by (i) a general partner, (ii) the trustee of a general partner, or (iii) a creditor holding a claim against the partnership. [B.C. §303(b)(3)]

(4) **Foreign representative:** [§167]   An involuntary petition may be filed by a foreign representative (*e.g.*, a trustee or an administrator) of the bankruptcy estate named in a foreign proceeding concerning the debtor. The foreign representative files the petition to administer the debtor's property located in the United States. [B.C. §§303(b)(4), 101(23), (24); 2 Collier ¶303.10]

b. **Indemnity bond:** [§168] The petitioning entities may be ordered by the court to file a bond to indemnify the debtor for any damages that might be awarded if the involuntary petition subsequently is dismissed. Notice and a hearing are required, and sufficient cause must be shown. [B.C. §303(e); *see infra*, §§178-179]

3. **Answer:** [§169] Only the debtor, or in the case of a partnership debtor a nonpetitioning general partner, may file an answer to the involuntary petition. In the answer, the debtor tries to controvert the allegations made in the petition. [B.C. §303(d)]

4. **Entry of an Order for Relief:** [§170] The court will enter an order for relief against the debtor (under the appropriate chapter) for any of the following reasons:

    a. **Untimely answer:** [§171] If the involuntary petition is *not answered within 20 days* after it is served, generally an order for relief will be entered (*see supra*, §17). However, the court may extend the time to respond when service is made by publication outside the state in which the court is located. [B.C. §303(h); Bankruptcy Rules 1011(b), 1013(b)]

    b. **Debtor's general nonpayment of debts as they mature:** [§172] If after a trial, the court finds that the debtor is *generally not paying his (undisputed) debts as they become due*, an order for relief will be entered, irrespective of whether the debtor has the ability to pay. [B.C. §303(h)(1); *In re* Manchester Lakes Associates, 47 B.R. 798 (Bankr. E.D. Va. 1985)] To determine whether a debtor is generally not paying his debts as they become due, the court considers both the amount of the unpaid indebtedness as well as the number of unpaid creditors. Therefore, an order for relief will be entered if the debtor either regularly defaults on "a significant number of payments to creditors," or regularly fails to pay debts constituting a substantial portion of his aggregate liabilities. [*In re* All Media Properties, Inc., 5 B.R. 126 (Bankr. S.D. Tex. 1980), *aff'd*, 646 F.2d 193 (5th Cir. 1981)]

    c. **Appointment of a custodian:** [§173] The court also will enter an order for relief if, after a trial, it finds that within 120 days before the petition was filed, a *custodian* was appointed to take charge of the debtor's property other than for the purpose of enforcing a lien against less than substantially all of such property. [B.C. §§303(h)(2), 101 (11)]

5. **Gap Period:** [§174] During t' e interim between the *filing of an involuntary petition and the entry of an order for relief* (the gap period), the debtor may remain in possession of his property, continue to operate his business, and use, acquire, or dispose of assets unless the court denies these privileges or appoints an interim trustee. [B.C. §303(f)]

    a. **Transfers during gap period:** [§175] If the debtor makes a transfer during the gap period, the transfer is not subject to the trustee's avoiding powers *to the extent of post-petition value given in exchange for the transfer* by the transferee. "Value" includes services (such as those of the debtor's attorney). To be free of the trustee's avoiding power, the purpose of the transfer must not be to satisfy or secure a pre-petition debt. [B.C. §549(b); *and see infra*, §§430-431]

b. **Priority for gap creditors:** [§176] Any creditors whose claims arise in the ordinary course of the debtor's business or financial affairs during the gap period, before a trustee is appointed or an order for relief is entered (whichever is earlier), are entitled to *second priority status* (*see infra*, §557) in the order of distribution to claimants. [B.C. §507(a)(2)]

c. **Interim trustee:** [§177] During the gap period in a Chapter 7 case, on request by a party in interest and after notice to the debtor and a hearing, the court may direct the United States trustee to appoint an interim trustee if the court finds that such an appointment is needed to preserve property of the estate (*see infra*, §§294 *et seq.*) or to avoid loss. If an interim trustee is appointed, she takes possession of property of the estate and, where applicable, operates the debtor's business. [B.C. §303(g)] (For the appointment of a trustee in a Chapter 11 case [B.C. §1104], *see infra*, §§1009 *et seq.*)

   (1) **Note:** The court may permit the debtor, prior to an order for relief, to retake possession of his property from a Chapter 7 interim trustee upon the filing of a bond in an amount set by the court. [B.C. §303(g)]

6. **Dismissal of Involuntary Petition**

   a. **Damages possible:** [§178] If the court dismisses an involuntary petition (*e.g.*, when the petition is filed by fewer than the required number of creditors or the debtor *is* generally paying his debts as they become due) other than on the consent of all the petitioning entities *and the debtor*, and if the debtor has not waived his right to damages, the court may award a judgment to the debtor and against the petitioners for costs and/or reasonable attorney's fees. [B.C. §303(i)(1); *In re* R. Eric Peterson Construction Co., 951 F.2d 1175 (10th Cir. 1991)]

      (1) **Rationale:** This provision is designed to prevent the indiscriminate filing of an involuntary petition by creditors.

      (2) **Punitive damages for bad faith:** [§179] Where an involuntary petition is dismissed as described above, and the court finds that a petitioning entity filed the petition in bad faith, it may grant judgment for the debtor and award damages proximately caused by the involuntary petition and/or punitive damages. [B.C. §303(i)(2)]

         (a) **Example:** Creditor, suspecting that she is Debtor's only creditor, singly files an involuntary petition against Debtor without reasonably investigating how many creditors Debtor has. In actuality, the number of Debtor's creditors greatly exceeds 12. Creditor's petition may be found to have been filed in bad faith, and the court may award both attorney's fees and punitive damages to Debtor. [B.C. §303(i)(1), (2); *In re* Godroy Wholesale Co., 37 B.R. 496 (Bankr. D. Mass. 1984)]

   b. **Notice and hearing:** [§180] The court may dismiss an involuntary petition on the motion of a petitioning creditor, on the consent of all petitioning creditors and the debtor, or for lack of prosecution only after *notice* and an opportunity for a *hearing* is given to *all creditors*. [B.C. §303(j)]

7. **Schedules to Be Filed:** [§181]   If an order for relief is entered in an involuntary case, the debtor must file the required lists, schedules, and statements (*see supra*, §§153, 155, 158) within the time limits fixed by Bankruptcy Rule 1007.

8. **Foreign Bank:** [§182]   An involuntary petition may be filed against a foreign bank *only*: (i) under Chapter 7; (ii) if the bank is ***not engaged in business in the United States***; and (iii) if a foreign proceeding is pending with respect to the bank. [B.C. §§303(k), 101(23)]

D. CASE ANCILLARY TO FOREIGN PROCEEDING

1. **Purpose:** [§183]   Usually, a case that is ancillary to a foreign proceeding is commenced to assist a foreign court in which the debtor's bankruptcy is pending and to protect or marshall property of the debtor located in the United States. [*In re* Goerg, 844 F.2d 1562 (11th Cir. 1988)]

2. **Eligibility:** [§184]   A foreign representative may commence a case ancillary to a foreign proceeding by filing a petition concerning a person who resides or has a domicile, a place of business, or property in the United States. [B.C. §§304(a), 109(a); *but see In re* Goerg, *supra*—court entertained a section 304 petition concerning an insolvent decedent's estate, which was not a person (or consequently a debtor) under the Code]

   a. **Example:** Debtor is a foreign reinsurance company and is the debtor in a bankruptcy case pending in a foreign court. Debtor's principal place of business is in New York. Although Debtor would not be eligible for Chapter 7 or Chapter 11 relief since it is a foreign insurance company engaged in business in the United States [B.C. §109(b)(3), (d)], it may be the subject of a case ancillary to the foreign proceeding if a petition is filed by a foreign representative. [B.C. §304(a); *In re* Gee, 53 B.R. 891 (Bankr. S.D.N.Y. 1985)]

3. **No Automatic Stay:** [§185]   A case filed under Bankruptcy Code section 304 is not a complete bankruptcy case and therefore invokes neither the automatic stay of section 362(a) nor the avoiding powers of a bankruptcy trustee. [*In re* Gee, *supra*]

4. **Relief**

   a. **Forms of relief:** [§186]   The court is authorized to grant any of the following remedies in a case ancillary to a foreign proceeding:

      (1) *An injunction against filing or continuing any action* against the debtor regarding property involved in the foreign proceeding [B.C. §304(b)(1)(A)];

      (2) *An injunction against the enforcement of a judgment* against the debtor regarding property involved in the foreign proceeding, or against filing or continuing any action to place or enforce a lien on property of the foreign estate [B.C. §304(b)(1)(B)];

      (3) *Turnover of property* of the estate, or of proceeds, to the foreign representative [B.C. §304(b)(2); *but see In re* Koreag, Controle Et Revision S.A., 961 F.2d 341 (2d Cir. 1992)—required threshold determination of whether certain funds in a New York bank account were property of the debtor's estate, where the issue was raised by an adverse claimant]; or

(4) *Other suitable relief* [B.C. §304(b)(3)].

b. **Criteria:** [§187] In deciding what kind of relief is appropriate, the court considers the following factors to assure an expeditious and economical administration of the debtor's estate [B.C. §304(c)]:

(1) *Fair treatment of all creditors* of the estate [B.C. §304(c)(1)];

(2) *Potential prejudice and inconvenience to domestic creditors* in prosecution of their claims in the foreign case [B.C. §304(c)(2)];

(3) *Prevention of fraudulent or preferential transfers* [B.C. §304(c)(3)];

(4) *Distribution of proceeds of the estate in a manner consistent with the Bankruptcy Code* [B.C. §304(c)(4)];

(5) *Comity* [B.C. §304(c)(5)]; and

(6) *The debtor's opportunity for a fresh start* [B.C. §304(c)(6)].

E. **ABSTENTION**

1. **Dismissal or Suspension:** [§188] The bankruptcy court may (at any time) abstain from hearing *an entire case* by dismissing it or by suspending all proceedings if it finds that abstention would better serve the interests of creditors and the debtor. Abstention may also be proper if there is a foreign proceeding pending and abstention would facilitate an efficient and economical administration of the estate (*see supra*, §187). Notice and a hearing are required. [B.C. §305(a)]

   a. **Example:** Debtor, an insolvent corporation, is the subject of a state court receivership. The receiver has been granted possession of Debtor's property and is about to conclude a liquidation after four years of administration and the expenditure of hundreds of thousands of dollars by the parties in interest and their attorneys. Even though a significant number of Debtor's creditors will be paid in full if the state court liquidation proceeds, a few adamant creditors file an involuntary Chapter 7 petition against Debtor. Here, abstention and dismissal of the case will be in the best interests of the creditors and Debtor. [*In re* Sun World Broadcasters, Inc., 5 B.R. 719 (Bankr. M.D. Fla. 1980)]

2. **Compare—Abstention from Hearing Proceeding:** [§189] It is important to differentiate between the court's abstention in declining jurisdiction over the whole bankruptcy case [B.C. §305(a)] and its abstention from hearing a single proceeding that is only one component of the bankruptcy case. [28 U.S.C. §1334(c); *see supra*, §§86-89]

3. **Appeal:** [§190] A bankruptcy court's order in favor of or against abstention from hearing a case is reviewable by the district court, but an abstention decision by the district court is not reviewable by the court of appeals or the Supreme Court. [B.C. §305(c); *In re* Axona International Credit Commerce Limited, 924 F.2d 31 (2d Cir. 1991)]

F. **SECTION 341 MEETING OF CREDITORS**

1. **Time and Place:** [§191] In a Chapter 7 or Chapter 11 case, within 20 to 40 days after the order for relief, a meeting of creditors is held at the courthouse or at another location within the district, designated by the United States trustee for the convenience of the parties in interest. This meeting, which had been known under the Bankruptcy Act as the *"first meeting of creditors,"* is referred to under the Code as the *"section 341 meeting* of creditors." (*Note:* In a Chapter 12 case, the meeting is held within 20 to 35 days after the order for relief. In a Chapter 13 case, the meeting is held within 20 to 50 days after the order for relief.) [B.C. §341(a); Bankruptcy Rule 2003(a)]

   a. **Meeting of equity security holders:** [§192] When appropriate, a meeting of the debtor's equity security holders also may be convened by the United States trustee. [B.C. §341(b)]

2. **Notice:** [§193] The clerk of the court provides by mail at least 20 days' notice of the section 341 meeting to the debtor, the trustee, all secured and unsecured creditors, indenture trustees, appropriate taxing authorities, and holders of community claims. If notice by mail is impracticable, the court may order that notice be given by publication. [Bankruptcy Rule 2002(a)(1), (l); 2 Collier ¶342.01] In a reorganization case under Chapter 11, equity security holders must be notified of any section 341 meeting of equity security holders. [Bankruptcy Rule 2002(d)]

   a. **Contents of notice:** [§194] The notice of the section 341 meeting of creditors also includes notice of the order for relief [B.C. §342(a); *see supra*, §§146, 170], notice of the automatic stay [B.C. §362(a), *see infra*, §§778 *et seq.*], and notice of the final dates for: (i) filing proofs of claims [B.C. §501(a); *see infra*, §§478 *et seq.*]; (ii) filing complaints to determine the dischargeability of certain debts [B.C. §523(c); *see infra*, §§723 *et seq.*]; (iii) filing objections to the debtor's entire discharge (in a Chapter 7 case) [B.C. §727(a); *see infra*, §§972-983]; and (iv) filing objections to the debtor's claim of exempt property [B.C. §522; *see infra*, §645]. [Official Bankruptcy Form 9]

3. **United States Trustee Presides:** [§195] The section 341 meeting is not a judicial hearing; thus, the United States trustee (or an assistant United States trustee) convenes and presides at the meeting. This procedure is designed to separate the administrative functions from the judicial functions of the court. Moreover, the judge is prohibited from attending the section 341 meeting, since facts and circumstances concerning issues to be adjudicated by the court in subsequent proceedings in the bankruptcy case are likely to be discussed. [B.C. §341; Bankruptcy Rule 2003(b); 2 Collier ¶341.01(3)] In North Carolina and Alabama (which have not yet elected to be included in the United States Trustee System), the bankruptcy administrator is authorized to preside at the meetings of creditors and examine the debtor. [Bankruptcy Reform Act of 1994, §105, 108 Stat. at 4111]

4. **Debtor Must Attend:** [§196] The debtor must personally attend the section 341 meeting, and the courts are divided concerning excusal under extenuating circumstances. [B.C. §343]

   a. **Example—strict view:** Debtor files a joint Chapter 7 petition with his wife but is unable to appear in person at the section 341 meeting because he is confined to a nursing home following a stroke. Debtor's wife attends the section

341 meeting, and Debtor asks the court either to excuse his appearance or, instead, to use depositions or interrogatories, to conduct the meeting at the nursing home, or to permit his wife to answer questions for him with a power of attorney. Under a strict construction of the statute, the bankruptcy judge denies Debtor's request and dismisses the case on the basis that the Code provides no judicial discretion for excusal. [*In re* Martin, 12 B.R. 319 (Bankr. S.D. Ala. 1981)]

   (1) **Comment:** This result seems harsh, particularly in light of Bankruptcy Rule 2003, which provides that a section 341 meeting may be held " . . . at any other place designated by the United States trustee within the district convenient for the parties in interest" (*see supra*, §191).

   b. **Example—flexible view:** Debtor and her spouse file a joint Chapter 7 petition, but Debtor is unable to appear in person at the section 341 meeting because of a serious and worsening cardiac condition. Debtor's condition has been documented by a cardiologist's written statement. Debtor is unemployed, and all of the unsecured debts that might be discharged in the bankruptcy case were incurred by her husband, who attends the section 341 meeting and provides the same testimony that Debtor would have offered. The judge, acting as a court of equity, waives Debtor's attendance and refuses to dismiss the case. [*In re* Stewart, 14 B.R. 959 (Bankr. N.D. Ohio 1981)]

5. **Purpose of Section 341 Meeting:** [§197] The primary function of the section 341 meeting is to provide an opportunity for creditors, the trustee (or an examiner; *see infra*, §§251-255), any indenture trustee (*see infra*, §487), and the United States trustee (or bankruptcy administrator) *to examine the debtor under oath* about issues related to the bankruptcy case. Typical questions concern the location and condition of a secured creditor's collateral, the exemptions claimed by the debtor, the facts relating to an allegedly nondischargeable debt, the disappearance of assets, the operation of the debtor's business, the reasons for filing, and goals for reorganization. [B.C. §343]

   a. **Compare—examination under Bankruptcy Rule 2004:** [§198] Frequently, there are many parties interested in examining the debtor at the section 341 meeting, and the time allotted to each is limited. Therefore, the debtor also may be questioned at greater length (similar to a deposition) at another time and place. In such case, the party in interest will need to file a motion requesting that the court order the debtor to appear for the examination. [Bankruptcy Rule 2004]

   b. **Examination by trustee:** [§199] In a Chapter 7 case, before the conclusion of the meeting of creditors or equity security holders, the trustee must orally examine the Chapter 7 debtor to ensure his awareness of: (i) the potential effects of seeking a bankruptcy discharge, including those relating to credit history; (ii) his ability to file a petition under a different chapter of the Code; (iii) the effect of receiving a discharge; and (iv) the effect of reaffirming a debt, including the debtor's understanding that a reaffirmation is not required under the Code or under state law, and that the debtor would be personally liable for a subsequent default. [B.C. §341(d)] The legislative history indicates that the trustee also should inform the debtor that he may voluntarily repay any debt without reaffirming. [140 Cong. Rec. H10,766 (daily ed. Oct. 4, 1994)—section-by-section description of Bankruptcy Reform Act of 1994; *see also* B.C. §524(f)]

c. **Debtor's immunity from prosecution:** [§200] If the debtor validly asserts the constitutional privilege against self-incrimination, he may be granted immunity from prosecution *by the district court judge*, and then he may be required to provide information at the section 341 meeting or at a hearing in the case despite the privilege. [B.C. §344; 18 U.S.C. §6003; Kastigar v. United States, 406 U.S. 441 (1972)]

   (1) **Individual's privilege:** [§201] Only an *individual* may avail himself of the constitutional privilege against compulsory self-incrimination. Thus, the privilege cannot be invoked by a corporation. [*In re* Butcher, 10 Collier Bankr. Cas. 2d 200 (Bankr. E.D. Tenn. 1984)]

   (2) **Incarceration of debtor or denial of discharge:** [§202] If the district judge grants immunity to the debtor, who then still refuses to testify in the case, the debtor may be held in contempt and incarcerated. Alternatively, he may be denied a discharge. [B.C. §727(a)(6)(B); *In re* Martin-Trigona, 732 F.2d 170 (2d Cir. 1984); *In re* Younger, 986 F.2d 1376 (11th Cir. 1993)]

6. **Other Business at Section 341 Meeting:** [§203] In addition to examining the debtor, creditors often participate in many of the following matters:

   a. *The election of a trustee*, in a Chapter 7 case, if requested by a sufficient number of unsecured creditors [B.C. §702; *see infra*, §§229-233];

   b. *The election of an unsecured creditors' committee*, in a Chapter 7 case (when desired), to consult with the trustee or with the United States trustee [B.C. §705];

   c. *Discussion about the trustee's abandonment of property* that is burdensome or of inconsequential value to the estate [B.C. §554; *see infra*, §§469-473];

   d. *Discussion about the debtor's reaffirmation of particular debts* [B.C. §524(c); *see infra*, §§733 et seq.]; and

   e. *Discussion, in a Chapter 7 case, about an individual debtor's redemption of tangible personal property* intended primarily for consumer use [B.C. §722; *see infra*, §§752 et seq.].

G. DEBTOR'S DUTIES [§204]

In addition to filing the required lists, schedules, and statements (*see supra*, §§153-159, 181), the debtor must perform certain other duties in the case.

1. **Statement of Intention Regarding Collateral:** [§205] In a Chapter 7 case, an *individual debtor with secured consumer debts* must file a statement of her intention to retain or surrender the collateral securing such debts, and if applicable, to exempt any of the collateral, to redeem any of the property, or to reaffirm any debts secured by the collateral. The declaration must be filed by the earlier of (i) the date of the section 341 meeting or (ii) 30 days after the filing of the petition. [B.C. §521(2)(A)]

a. **Performance within forty-five days:** [§206]   Within 45 days after filing her statement of intent regarding the collateral, the debtor must perform her intention. It is the trustee's duty to monitor this performance. [B.C. §§521(2)(B), 704(3)]

2. **Cooperation and Turnover:** [§207]   If a trustee has been appointed in a case, the debtor must cooperate with him and must relinquish to him all property of the estate and any relevant books, records, and documents (even if immunity has not been granted). [B.C. §521(3), (4)] In a Chapter 12 or Chapter 13 case, however, the debtor usually may remain in possession of estate property. [B.C. §§1207(b), 1306(b)]

3. **Appearance at Discharge Hearing:** [§208]   An *individual debtor*, under any chapter, must attend the discharge hearing if one is held by the court. [B.C. §§521(5), 524(d); *see infra*, §§745-747]

4. **Keep Address Current:** [§209]   The debtor must file a statement of any change of her address. [Bankruptcy Rule 4002]

5. **Notices:** [§210]   Any notice that the debtor is required to give to a creditor must contain the debtor's name, address, and social security number. [B.C. §342(c)]

H. CONVERSION

1. **Authorization:** [§211]   Chapters 7, 11, 12, and 13 provide rules for conversion of a case from one chapter to another when the debtor satisfies the eligibility requirements for the succeeding chapter. However, conversion to Chapter 12 or Chapter 13 may occur *only upon the debtor's request*. [B.C. §§706, 1112, 1208, 1307] If a case is converted to Chapter 13, the debtor must file a plan within 15 days thereafter. [Bankruptcy Rule 3015(b)]

2. **Effects of Conversion:** [§212]   The conversion of a case to another chapter operates as an order for relief under the new chapter but, as a general rule, does not alter the *date* of the filing of the bankruptcy petition, the commencement of the case, or the order for relief. [B.C. §348(a)]

    a. **Example:** Where an entity was granted relief from the automatic stay (*see infra*, §§778 *et seq.*) in a Chapter 11 case that subsequently was converted to Chapter 7, the conversion did not reimpose the stay. [*In re* State Airlines, Inc., 873 F.2d 264 (11th Cir. 1989)]

    b. **Exceptions:** [§213]   There are a number of exceptions to this rule, where the *date of the order for relief* is deemed to be the date that the case was converted. [B.C. §348(b)] In addition to these exceptions, there are two instances where the conversion order is considered to be the order for relief [B.C. §348(c)]: one concerning the required notice of the order for relief [B.C. §342(a), *see supra*, §146], and the other concerning the time allowed under Bankruptcy Code section 365(d) for the trustee to assume or reject an executory contract or an unexpired lease of the debtor (*see infra*, §§900 *et seq.*).

3. **Pre-Conversion Claims:** [§214]   Except for administrative expenses [B.C. §503(b); *see infra*, §§537-553], any claims arising in a Chapter 11, 12, or 13 case after the order for relief but before conversion to another chapter are considered

pre-petition claims for all purposes (*e.g.*, for allowance, distribution, or discharge). [B.C. §348(d); *see infra*, §§504, 945, 969]

4. **Trustee or Examiner:** [§215] The service of a trustee or an examiner in a case that is converted from Chapter 7, 11, 12, or 13 is terminated by the conversion to another chapter. [B.C. §348(e)]

5. **Conversion from Chapter 13—Property of the Estate:** [§216] If a case is converted from Chapter 13 to another chapter of the Code, property of the estate in the converted case consists of property of the estate *on the date of the Chapter 13 filing* that remains in the possession or control of the debtor on the date of conversion. If payments have been made to secured creditors under the Chapter 13 plan, their allowed secured claims will be reduced commensurately. If the debtor converts the case in *bad faith*, however, property of the estate in the converted case will consist of the estate property *on the date of conversion* (including property acquired after the date of the Chapter 13 filing). [B.C. §348(f)]

   a. **Example:** Debtor files a Chapter 13 petition, at which time she owns a home valued at $200,000 and owes a mortgage balance of $200,000. During the Chapter 13 case, Debtor makes $30,000 in payments to Mortgagee in accordance with the Chapter 13 plan. Subsequently, Debtor converts the case to one under Chapter 7, at which time the home is still worth $200,000, resulting in $30,000 equity in the home on the date of conversion. The applicable homestead exemption is $15,000. Under Code section 348(f) (above), property of the estate in the Chapter 7 case will not include the $30,000 equity gained during the Chapter 13 case, unless Debtor converted in bad faith. If the equity were included in property of the Chapter 7 estate, the trustee would seek to sell the home in order to realize $15,000 (the amount by which the equity exceeds the exemption) for the benefit of the general unsecured creditors, and Debtor would lose her home. [*See* 140 Cong. Rec. H10,771 (daily ed. Oct. 4, 1994)—section-by-section description of Bankruptcy Reform Act of 1994]

I. DISMISSAL

1. **Different Rules for Chapters 7, 11, 12, and 13:** [§217] Whether the debtor, a party in interest, the United States trustee, or the court on its own motion may move for the dismissal of a petition, and when the court may or must order a dismissal, are questions that vary according to the chapter of the Code under which the petition was filed. [*See* B.C. §§707, 1112, 1208, 1307] These rules will be discussed more specifically in connection with each chapter.

2. **Effect of Dismissal:** [§218] Generally, the dismissal of a case is *without prejudice* to the debtor's right to file a subsequent petition and obtain a discharge of debts that could have been discharged in the case dismissed. [B.C. §349(a)]

   a. **Exceptions:** The effect of a dismissal is *with prejudice*, however, to the extent that the debtor is ineligible to file again within 180 days due to Bankruptcy Code section 109(g) (*see supra*, §143), or if the court finds *cause* to dismiss the case with prejudice. [B.C. §349(a)]

3. **Dismissal for Bad Faith:** [§219] The bankruptcy court has inherent authority to dismiss a petition that was not filed in good faith or that was intended to abuse the opportunity for a fresh start.

a. **Example—Chapter 7:** Debtor's obligations consist primarily of consumer debts, including a home mortgage, but he also has guaranteed several business debts that he desires to avoid by commencing a bankruptcy case. Debtor's monthly income sufficiently exceeds his monthly expenses to enable him to repay a substantial portion of his debts under a Chapter 13 plan. However, Debtor files a Chapter 7 petition, overstating considerably his family's monthly expenses, intentionally misrepresenting his current financial condition, and omitting to schedule certain debts. Since Debtor seeks to continue "to lead the life of Riley . . . while taking shelter from his creditors under the Bankruptcy provisions," his petition may be dismissed for substantial abuse of Chapter 7. [B.C. §707(b); *In re* Bryant, 47 B.R. 21 (Bankr. W.D.N.C. 1984); *and see infra*, §§990-992]

b. **Example—Chapter 11:** Debtor, a landowner, excavates dirt from his borrow pits to sell to construction companies. The borrow pits, which are located near County's principal source of water, sometimes are filled by Debtor with organic and inorganic materials that County claims are toxic, thus constituting a nuisance to the community. After County obtains an injunction in a state court, Debtor files a Chapter 11 petition for the sole purpose of circumventing County's efforts to protect the environment. This is not an appropriate reason for filing a case under Chapter 11, and therefore, Debtor's petition may be dismissed. [B.C. §1112(b); *In re* Martin, 51 B.R. 490 (Bankr. M.D. Fla. 1985)]

c. **Example—Chapter 13:** Debtor and his spouse, having granted to a large oil company the option to purchase a certain tract of land, now decide that the agreement is not as good a bargain as originally envisioned. Therefore, although in good financial condition and debt-free, they file a joint Chapter 13 petition admittedly for the single purpose of using the bankruptcy laws to reject the option contract. The case may be dismissed for bad faith under the equitable power of the bankruptcy court to consider the motives of the debtors in filing their petition. [B.C. §§1325(a)(3), 1307(c); *In re* Waldron, 785 F.2d 936 (11th Cir. 1986)]

IV. OFFICERS OF THE ESTATE

chapter approach

This chapter discusses the roles and duties of a bankruptcy trustee, an examiner, professional persons, and the United States trustee. Regarding the first of these officers, remember that the nature of relief available varies according to the chapters of the Bankruptcy Code. Thus, appointment of a ***bankruptcy trustee*** is necessary in a Chapter 7 case to collect and liquidate the assets of the estate and to distribute the proceeds to creditors. However, under Chapter 11 (reorganization), appointment of a trustee is the exception, and a ***debtor in possession*** is preferred. In Chapter 13 (individual repayment) cases and in Chapter 12 (family farmer) cases, a trustee's service also is required (often a standing trustee for all such cases), although the debtor usually remains in possession of property of the estate.

In a Chapter 11 case, sometimes an ***examiner*** will be appointed, in which case the debtor remains in possession of his property and his business. The examiner will investigate the debtor's conduct and business operations and help determine the advisability of continuing the debtor's business.

In answering an examination question about the employment of a ***professional person*** (*e.g.*, an attorney) and her compensation, always make certain that ***court approval*** has been obtained ***before*** the professional services are performed; otherwise, the professional may be denied compensation. Furthermore, make sure that a professional hired by a trustee or a debtor in possession is a ***disinterested person*** and that she does not have an interest adverse to the estate.

The main thing to recall about the ***United States trustee*** is that the trustee assumes many of the administrative responsibilities previously performed by the bankruptcy court (including the appointment and supervision of bankruptcy trustees, as well as the review of fee applications of attorneys and other professional persons), thereby helping to separate the administrative and judicial functions in bankruptcy cases.

A. **TRUSTEE**

1. **Role and Capacity:** [§220] The trustee is the official representative of the estate. The trustee's duties are set by statute (*see infra*, §§239-244). Besides various administrative powers (*see infra*, §247), the trustee has the authority to initiate and defend lawsuits. [B.C. §323]

2. **Eligibility:** [§221] A disinterested individual or corporation is eligible to serve as a trustee. An individual must be competent to perform the required responsibilities, and a corporation must be authorized by its charter or bylaws to serve as a trustee. In a Chapter 7, 12, or 13 case, the trustee also must reside or have an office in the judicial district where the bankruptcy case is pending or in the adjacent district. [B.C. §321(a)]

    a. **"Disinterested person":** [§222] The bankruptcy definition of a disinterested person *excludes* the following:

(i) *Creditors, equity security holders, and insiders*;

(ii) *Directors, officers, and employees* of the debtor, currently or within two years prior to the commencement of the case;

(iii) *Investment bankers* (and their employees) for securities of the debtor [*In re* Eagle-Picher Industries, Inc., 999 F.2d 969 (6th Cir. 1993)]; and

(iv) *Any person with a materially adverse interest* to the estate or to any class of creditors or equity security holders.

[B.C. §101(14)]

b. **Examiner precluded:** [§223] Any person who has served as an examiner is prohibited from becoming a trustee in the same case. [B.C. §321(b)]

c. **United States trustee:** [§224] If necessary, the United States trustee for the respective judicial district may serve as the trustee in a Chapter 7, 12, or 13 case, but not in a Chapter 11 case. [B.C. §§321(c), 1104(d)]

3. **Qualification of Trustee—Bond:** [§225] Within five days after appointment or election, and before beginning service, a trustee must file with the court a *bond*, in favor of the United States, in the amount set by the United States trustee. The United States trustee also approves the surety on the bond. [B.C. §322]

4. **Selection of Trustee:** [§226] The chapter of the Bankruptcy Code governing the particular case determines *whether* a trustee is required, and if so, how the trustee is to be chosen.

   a. **Chapter 7:** [§227] All Chapter 7 cases require the services of a trustee, and thus each United States trustee establishes and maintains a panel of private trustees to serve in the Chapter 7 cases for the particular region. There are 21 regions. [28 U.S.C. §§586(a)(1), 581(a)]

      (1) **Interim trustee:** [§228] Immediately after the entry of the order for relief in a Chapter 7 case, the United States trustee appoints a disinterested member of the private panel to serve as the interim trustee until the section 341 meeting (*see supra*, §§191 *et seq.*). At the section 341 meeting, the interim trustee will become the permanent trustee unless another person is elected by creditors. In most cases, no election is held and the interim trustee serves as the permanent trustee in the case. [B.C. §§701(a), 702(d)]

      (2) **Election of trustee:** [§229] If an election is requested by creditors who hold at least 20% in amount of the claims entitled to vote for a trustee, an election is conducted at the section 341 meeting. [B.C. §702(b)]

         (a) **Who may vote:** [§230] A creditor is eligible to vote for a trustee only if: (i) he holds an allowable, *unsecured, nonpriority*, undisputed, fixed, and liquidated claim; (ii) his interest is not materially adverse to other creditors holding such claims; and (iii) he is not an insider (*see supra*, §30). [B.C. §702(a)]

1) **Provisional allowance:** [§231] As a general rule, a claim that appears on its face to be valid will be allowed temporarily, *for voting purposes only*, to expedite the process of electing a trustee and preserving assets of the estate. [*In re* A & J Elastic Mills, Inc., 34 B.R. 977 (S.D.N.Y. 1983)]

2) **Compare—materially adverse interest:** [§232] A creditor who has received a *voidable preference* from the debtor prior to bankruptcy should not be allowed to vote for a trustee, since his claim is materially adverse to the interests of the other unsecured creditors. [*In re* Lang Cartage Corp., 20 B.R. 534 (Bankr. E.D. Wis. 1982); *and see infra*, §§364 *et seq.*]

(b) **Votes needed to be elected:** [§233] Election of a candidate as the permanent trustee requires (i) that creditors aggregately possessing at least 20% in amount of the eligible voting claims actually vote, and (ii) that the candidate receive votes representing a majority *in amount* of the claims that have been voted. [B.C. §702(c)]

b. **Chapter 11:** [§234] In a Chapter 11 case, the debtor generally remains in possession of property of the estate and continues to manage the business, in an effort to reorganize, *without the necessity of a trustee's appointment.* The rationale is that the debtor's current management ordinarily is better acquainted with and more experienced in the particular business operations than an outside trustee. [*In re* Sharon Steel Corp., 871 F.2d 1217 (3d Cir. 1989)] However, the court may order the appointment of a trustee for cause, *or* in the interest of creditors, equity security holders, and the estate. [B.C. §1104(a)] In such circumstances, the United States trustee consults with parties in interest and then appoints a disinterested person, subject to the court's approval. The United States trustee may not serve as the trustee in the case. [B.C. §1104(d)]

(1) **Causes for appointment:** [§235] Reasons for the appointment of a Chapter 11 trustee include one or more of the following acts *of current management*: (i) *fraud*; (ii) *dishonesty*; (iii) *incompetence*; or (iv) *gross mismanagement.* [B.C. §1104(a)(1)]

(2) **Appointment before confirmation:** [§236] The appointment of a Chapter 11 trustee can occur only after the filing of the bankruptcy petition but before confirmation of a Chapter 11 plan. [B.C. §1104(a)]

(3) **Election of trustee:** [§237] If appointment of a trustee is ordered, in cases other than railroad reorganizations, the Code authorizes election of the trustee, rather than appointment, if a party in interest requests an election within 30 days after the court orders the appointment. The election is held at a meeting of the creditors convened by the United States trustee and is conducted in the same manner as the election of a trustee under Chapter 7. The trustee must be a disinterested person. [B.C. §§1104(b), 702; *and see supra*, §§229-233]

c. **Chapters 13 and 12:** [§238] In a region where many Chapter 13 cases are filed, the United States trustee ordinarily appoints a qualified individual to serve as a *standing trustee* for all Chapter 13 cases in that region. Otherwise, the United States trustee appoints a disinterested person as the trustee for a particular case, or the United States trustee may serve as the trustee in the case himself. [B.C. §1302(a); 28 U.S.C. §586(b)] The same procedure applies in cases under Chapter 12. [B.C. §1202(a); 28 U.S.C. §586(b)] Usually, however, the Chapter 13 or 12 debtor remains in possession of property of the estate. [B.C. §§1306(b), 1207(b)]

5. **Duties of Trustee:** [§239] The duties of a trustee vary according to the chapter under which the trustee is serving, although many of the basic functions overlap. [B.C. §§704, 1106(a), 1202(b), 1302(b)]

   a. **Chapter 7:** [§240] The primary responsibilities of a Chapter 7 trustee are to:

   (i) *Locate and take possession* of property of the estate;

   (ii) *Convert* the property to *cash*;

   (iii) *Make distributions* to claimants in the order prescribed by the Code; and

   (iv) *Close* the estate expeditiously.

   [B.C. §§704(1), 725, 726; *and see infra*, §§945 *et seq.*]

   (1) **Other duties:** [§241] Additional duties of a Chapter 7 trustee are to:

   (a) *Account* for all property received [B.C. §704(2)];

   (b) *Monitor* the debtor's performance of his intentions regarding collateral securing consumer debts [B.C. §§704(3), 521(2)(B); *see supra*, §§205-206];

   (c) *Investigate* the debtor's financial affairs [B.C. §704(4)];

   (d) *Examine proofs of claims* and object to the allowance of any improper claims [B.C. §704(5)];

   (e) *Object to the debtor's discharge* if circumstances warrant [B.C. §704(6)];

   (f) *Provide information* requested by parties in interest about the estate and the administration of the estate [B.C. §704(7)];

   (g) *File periodic financial reports*, including a statement of receipts and disbursements with the court, the United States trustee, and the appropriate taxing authorities—if the trustee is operating the debtor's business (*see infra*, §943) [B.C. §704(8)]; and

   (h) *Prepare and file* with the court and the United States trustee, a *final report and account* concerning the case [B.C. §704(9)].

   b. **Chapter 11:** [§242] A Chapter 11 trustee, appointed to replace a debtor in possession, ordinarily is authorized to **operate the debtor's business** [B.C. §1108] and is charged with the following responsibilities [B.C. §1106(a)]:

(1) ***To account*** for all property received, to ***examine proofs of claims*** and object to improper ones, to ***provide information*** to parties in interest about the estate or its administration, to ***file periodic financial reports*** with the court, the United States trustee, and taxing authorities, and to ***prepare and file a final report and account.*** [B.C. §§1106(a)(1), 704(2), (5), (7), (8), (9); *and see supra*, §241];

(2) ***To file any document required under section 521(1)*** (*i.e.*, a list of creditors, schedule of assets and liabilities, schedule of current income and expenditures, and a statement of the debtor's financial affairs) that has not been filed by the debtor [B.C. §§1106(a)(2), 521(1); *and see supra*, §153]

(3) ***To investigate*** the debtor's conduct, financial condition, and business operations, as well as the ***advisability of continuing the debtor's business*** [B.C. §1106(a)(3)];

(4) ***To file a report of the investigation*** relating any facts evidencing fraud, dishonesty, incompetence, misconduct, or mismanagement, and to send a copy of the findings to any creditors' committee or equity security holders' committee [B.C. §1106(a)(4)];

(5) ***To file a Chapter 11 plan*** as soon as feasible, or recommend conversion of the case to another chapter [B.C. §1106(a)(5)];

(6) ***To provide information***, if available, to the taxing authorities concerning any year for which the debtor failed to file a return [B.C. §1106(a)(6)]; and

(7) ***After a plan has been confirmed, to file*** any required reports [B.C. §1106(a)(7)].

c. **Chapter 13:** [§243] A Chapter 13 trustee has the following duties:

(1) ***To account*** for all property received, to ***monitor*** debtor's performance of his intentions regarding collateral securing consumer debts, to ***investigate*** debtor's financial affairs, to ***examine proofs of claims*** and object to improper ones, to ***object*** to debtor's discharge if circumstances warrant, to ***provide information*** to the parties in interest about the estate and its administration, and to ***prepare and file a final report and account.*** [B.C. §§1302(b)(1), 704(2), (3), (4), (5), (6), (7), (9); *and see supra*, §241];

(2) ***To testify*** at any hearing regarding (i) valuation of property on which there is a lien, (ii) confirmation of a Chapter 13 plan, or (iii) post-confirmation modification of a plan [B.C. §1302(b)(2)];

(3) ***To furnish nonlegal advice*** to the debtor, and to assist the debtor in implementing the plan [B.C. §1302(b)(4)];

(4) ***To ensure that the debtor begins making the payments*** proposed by the plan within 30 days after the filing of the plan [B.C. §§1302(b)(5), 1326(a)(1)];

(5) ***If the debtor is engaged in business*** (*see infra*, §1153), to ***investigate*** the debtor's conduct, financial condition, and business operations, as well as the ***advisability of continuing*** the debtor's business [B.C. §§1302(c), 1106(a)(3)]; and to ***file a report of the investigation*** relating any facts evidencing fraud, dishonesty, incompetence, misconduct, or mismanagement [B.C. §§1302(c), 1106(a)(4)]; and

(6) ***Ordinarily, to disburse the payments*** to creditors under a confirmed plan [B.C. §1326(c); *and see infra*, §1208].

d. **Chapter 12:** [§244] The duties of a Chapter 12 trustee are similar to those of a Chapter 13 trustee (*see above*) as long as the debtor continues to be a debtor in possession. However, if a Chapter 12 debtor is removed from possession, the trustee is charged with many of the duties of a Chapter 11 trustee (*see supra*, §242), including operation of the debtor's farm. [B.C. §§1202(b), 1203]

6. **Liability of Trustee:** [§245] As a fiduciary of the estate, a trustee may be held ***personally liable*** for breach of duties. [Mosser v. Darrow, 341 U.S. 267 (1951)]

   a. **Intent:** [§246] Some jurisdictions hold trustees personally liable for ***either*** intentional or negligent violations of their fiduciary duties. [*In re* Cochise College Park, Inc., 703 F.2d 1339 (9th Cir. 1983); *In re* Gorski, 766 F.2d 723 (2d Cir. 1985)] Other jurisdictions impose personal liability only for intentional violations of the trustee's duties. [Yadkin Valley Bank & Trust Co. v. McGee, 819 F.2d 74 (4th Cir. 1987)]

7. **Powers of Trustee:** [§247] The bankruptcy trustee, as the representative of the estate, is entrusted with a variety of administrative powers that he may use when appropriate. Included among them are the powers to:

   a. ***File a proof of claim on behalf of a creditor*** who has not timely filed his claim [B.C. §501(c); *see infra*, §491];

   b. ***Operate the debtor's business*** (i) in a Chapter 11 case, unless ordered otherwise; (ii) sometimes in a Chapter 7 case, for a short period prior to liquidation, if the court permits; or (iii) in a Chapter 12 case where the debtor in possession has been removed by the court. [B.C. §§1108, 721, 1202(b)(5), 1203; *and see infra*, §§943, 1014, 1234];

   c. ***Deposit or invest money*** of the estate [B.C. §345];

   d. ***Employ professional persons***, such as attorneys, accountants, auctioneers, or appraisers [B.C. §327(a); *and see infra*, §§256-268];

   e. ***Avoid certain transfers and liens***, and thereby enlarge the estate for the benefit of creditors [B.C. §§544-551, 553; *and see infra*, §§334-464];

   f. ***Use, sell, or lease property*** of the estate [B.C. §363; *and see infra*, §§832 et seq.];

   g. ***Obtain credit*** [B.C. §364; *and see infra*, §§863 et seq.];

h. *Assume or reject executory contracts or unexpired leases* [B.C. §365; *and see infra*, §§875 *et seq.*];

i. *Demand utility services* for the estate [B.C. §366; *and see infra*, §§937-938];

j. *Abandon property* of the estate [B.C. §554; *and see infra*, §§469-473]; and

k. *Waive a debtor corporation's attorney-client privilege* concerning communications made by former officers and directors to the debtor's attorney before the bankruptcy petition was filed [Commodity Futures Trading Commission v. Weintraub, 471 U.S. 343 (1985); *and see infra*, §332].

8. **Removal of Trustee:** [§248] A trustee (other than the United States trustee) or an examiner may be removed by the court *for cause.* "Cause" generally involves the trustee's misconduct, incompetence, or conflict of interest. Notice and a hearing are required. [B.C. §324]

   a. **Potential malfeasance—actual harm required:** [§249] Most courts have adopted a standard requiring *fraud or actual harm* to the estate before the trustee may be removed where the cause alleged for removal concerns a potential conflict of interest or a potential breach of fiduciary duties. [*In re* Hartley, 50 B.R. 852 (Bankr. N.D. Ohio 1985)]

   b. **Minority view:** [§250] In the absence of fraud or actual harm, some courts have ordered removal where it is in the *best interest of the estate*, such as where discord otherwise is certain to ensue between the trustee and creditors. This line of authority stresses the importance of harmony and efficiency in the administration of the debtor's estate. [*In re* Savoia Macaroni Manufacturing Co., 4 F. Supp. 626 (E.D.N.Y. 1933)] A recent appellate court case ruled that removal should depend on whether the potential for conflict makes the trustee's interest *materially adverse* to the bankruptcy estate. [*In re* BH & P Inc., 949 F.2d 1300 (3d Cir. 1991)]

B. **EXAMINER**

1. **Role and Capacity:** [§251] In a Chapter 11 case in which the court has not ordered the appointment of a trustee, the court sometimes will order the appointment of an examiner. The examiner is appointed prior to confirmation of a plan *to investigate* any charges of fraud, dishonesty, incompetence, or mismanagement on the part of the debtor's present or former management. The debtor in possession retains her property and continues to operate the business. [B.C. §1104(c)]

2. **Eligibility:** [§252] The United States trustee selects a disinterested person other than himself to act as examiner. [B.C. §1104(d)]

3. **Reasons for Appointment:** [§253] When a party in interest or the United States trustee requests appointment of an examiner, the court (after notice and a hearing) *must order* that an examiner be appointed if the debtor's fixed, liquidated, unsecured debts exceed $5 million, excluding debts for goods, services, or taxes, and any debts owed to an insider. The existence of *large debenture debt* is a good example of such a circumstance. [B.C. §1104(c)(2)] Also, the court will order the appointment of an examiner where such action is in the *best interests of creditors, equity security holders, and the estate*. [B.C. §1104(c)(1)] The appointment is then

made by the United States trustee (after consulting with the parties in interest) and is subject to approval by the court. [B.C. §1104(d)]

4. **Duties of Examiner:** [§254] An examiner's duties include the following:

   a. *To investigate the debtor's conduct, financial condition, and business operations,* as well as the *advisability of continuing* the debtor's business [B.C. §1106(b), (a)(3)];

   b. *To file a report of the investigation* relating any facts evidencing fraud, dishonesty, incompetence, misconduct, or mismanagement, and to send a copy of the findings to any creditors' committee or equity security holders' committee [B.C. §1106(b), (a)(4)]; and

   c. *Any other responsibilities of a trustee* that the judge directs the debtor in possession not to perform [B.C. §1106(b)].

5. **Examiner May Not Serve as Trustee or Professional Person:** [§255] An examiner in a particular Chapter 11 case may not serve as the trustee (if one is appointed) or be employed as a professional person by the trustee *in the same case.* [B.C. §§321(b), 327(f)]

C. PROFESSIONAL PERSONS

1. **Role and Capacity:** [§256] A trustee (or a debtor in possession), with court approval, may hire professional persons (*e.g.*, attorneys or accountants) to perform services with respect to the bankruptcy estate. [B.C. §§327(a), 1107(a)]

2. **Eligibility:** [§257] Professional persons must be *disinterested persons* [B.C. §101(14); *and see supra,* §222] who *do not have an interest adverse* to the estate. [B.C. §327(a)] Court approval *must* be obtained *prior to performing services*; otherwise, the professional's application for compensation may be denied by the court.

   a. **Examples—professional persons:** The following persons are examples of those who have been held to be professional persons:

   (1) *Attorneys and accountants* [B.C. §327(a)];

   (2) *Auctioneers* [B.C. §327(a)];

   (3) *Appraisers* [B.C. §327(a); United States *ex rel.* Kraft v. Aetna Casualty & Surety Co., 43 B.R. 119 (M.D. Tenn. 1984)];

   (4) *Executives and officers of the debtor in possession* [*In re* Zerodec Mega Corp., 39 B.R. 932 (Bankr. E.D. Pa. 1984)];

   (5) *Consulting firms* [*In re* Carolina Sales Corp., 45 B.R. 750 (Bankr. E.D.N.C. 1985)]; and

   (6) *Collection agencies* [*In re* Windsor Communications Group, 54 B.R. 844 (Bankr. E.D. Pa. 1985)].

   b. **Approval before hiring:** [§258] It is important that judicial approval to hire a professional be obtained before she begins to perform services, since many courts will not grant approval retroactively unless there are extraordinary circumstances. Therefore, the failure to apply for approval first may result in denial of any compensation to the professional, even if her services have benefited the estate. [*See In re* Land, 943 F.2d 1265 (10th Cir. 1991)—return of attorney's fees ordered; *but see In re* Singson, 41 F.3d 316 (7th Cir. 1994)—excusable neglect standard]

(1) **Example:** A professional broker successfully negotiated the lease of an airplane on behalf of the debtor in possession and was awarded a $450,000 commission by the bankruptcy court *nunc pro tunc*. The court of appeals reversed the retroactive approval of the broker's employment because there was no evidence of extraordinary circumstances. [F/S AirLease II, Inc. v. Simon, 844 F.2d 99 (3d Cir. 1988); *see also In re* Jarvis, 53 F.3d 416 (1st Cir. 1995)—real estate broker's commission denied "because the lack of punctuality . . . was attributable entirely to inadvertence"]

(2) **Extraordinary circumstances:** [§259] The following criteria have been held to be a guide to determine whether particular circumstances are so extraordinary as to justify the court's *nunc pro tunc* approval of a professional's services [*In re* Arkansas Co., 798 F.2d 645 (3d Cir. 1986)]:

(a) Whether the applicant or some other person bore responsibility for applying for approval;

(b) Whether the applicant was under time pressure to begin service without approval;

(c) The amount of delay after the applicant learned that initial approval had not been granted;

(d) The extent to which compensation to the applicant will prejudice innocent third parties; and

(e) Other relevant factors.

c. **"Disinterested":** [§260] Certain persons are deemed to be *not* disinterested. [B.C. §101(14); *see In re* Federated Department Stores, Inc., 44 F.3d 1310 (6th Cir. 1995); *and see supra*, §222]

(1) **Insiders and equity security holders:** [§261] Insiders (*see supra*, §§30-33) and equity security holders are not disinterested persons. [B.C. §101(14)(A); *In re* Middleton Arms Limited Partnership, 934 F.2d 723 (6th Cir. 1991)—insider]

(2) **Officers, directors, and employees:** [§262] Generally a professional person, such as an attorney or an accountant, who is or has been an officer, a director, or an employee of the debtor within two years prior to bankruptcy is not considered to be disinterested and, therefore, may not be employed as a professional person by the trustee or the debtor in possession. Moreover, it would appear that any other attorney or accountant

in the same law or accounting firm is also disqualified. [B.C. §§327(a), 101(14)(D)]

    (a) **Exception—salaried professionals:** [§263] A trustee who is permitted to operate the debtor's business [B.C. §§721, 1108, 1202; *see supra*, §247] may retain or replace essential salaried professionals, such as attorneys and accountants, who have been regularly employed by the debtor. [B.C. §327(b)]

(3) **Creditors:** [§264] A creditor is not a disinterested person. [B.C. §101(14)(A)]

    (a) **Attorneys:** An attorney who is owed a pre-petition debt by the debtor for legal fees might not be considered disinterested and so would be ineligible for employment. Thus, the court could deny compensation for the attorney's fees and costs in connection with her employment by the Chapter 11 debtor in possession. [B.C. §328(c)] There are three views concerning whether an attorney with a pre-petition claim is disqualified from employment (note that the claim should be disclosed in the application for employment filed under Bankruptcy Rule 2014):

        1) **Strict view:** Under the strict, per se rule, if the debtor owes the attorney money, the attorney is a creditor and cannot represent the debtor in possession. [*In re* Pierce, 809 F.2d 1356 (8th Cir. 1987); *see also* United States Trustee v. Price Waterhouse, 19 F.3d 138 (3d Cir. 1994)—accountant] (But note that the attorney or accountant could waive her claim against the debtor.)

        2) ***Roberts* view:** Another approach deems the attorney to be not disinterested if the pre-petition debt for legal fees is *unrelated to the bankruptcy case.* [*In re* Roberts, 75 B.R. 402 (D. Utah 1987)]

        3) **Rule of reason:** A *practical view* is to ascertain whether the amount of the claim really impairs the attorney's ability to be independent and to exercise judgment for the debtor. [*In re* Heatron, Inc., 5 B.R. 703 (Bankr. W.D. Mo. 1980)]

d. **Special purpose attorney:** [§265] The court may authorize a trustee or a debtor in possession to employ a former attorney of the debtor for a special purpose, such as continuing legal expertise in an intricate proceeding, provided that the employment is in the estate's best interest and the lawyer does not have an adverse interest concerning the specific subject matter of the employment. However, the purpose may not be to represent the trustee in administering the bankruptcy case. [B.C. §327(e); 2 Collier ¶327.03(6)]

e. **Creditor's representative:** [§266] In a Chapter 7, 11, or 12 case, a professional person is not disqualified from *employment by a trustee* solely because of her employment by or representation of a creditor, unless another creditor or the United States trustee objects and the court finds an *actual conflict of interest.* [B.C. §327(c)]

(1) **But note:** Ordinarily, there would be an inherent conflict of interest that would preclude a professional person from being employed by or representing *both the debtor in possession and a creditor.* [*In re* Georgetown of Kettering, Ltd., 750 F.2d 536 (6th Cir. 1984)]

 f. **Trustee as a professional person:** [§267] The court may permit the trustee to serve also as an attorney or an accountant for the estate if that employment is in the estate's best interest. [B.C. §327(d)]

3. **Creditors' Committee May Hire Professional Persons:** [§268] In a Chapter 11 case, a creditors' committee or an equity security holders' committee may employ attorneys, accountants, or other professionals to perform services for the committee. [B.C. §1103(a); *and see infra*, §§1003-1005] While representing or in the employ of the committee, the professional person may not represent an entity having an *adverse interest*. However, representation of a creditor or creditors of the same class as the committee represents is not adverse per se. [B.C. §1103(b); *and see infra*, §1004]

D. COMPENSATION OF OFFICERS [§269]

Officers of the estate, including a trustee, an examiner, a Chapter 12 or 13 individual debtor's attorney, and any professional person properly employed (by a trustee, a debtor in possession, or a creditors' committee) may be awarded, by the court, a *reasonable fee* for actual and necessary services, as well as *reimbursement* for actual and necessary expenses. [B.C. §330(a)(1), (a)(4)(B)]

1. **Debtor's Attorney:** [§270] The Bankruptcy Code expressly provides that the court may award reasonable compensation to the attorney of an individual Chapter 12 or Chapter 13 debtor, based on the benefit and necessity of the services to the debtor and the statutory criteria listed below. [B.C. §330(a)(4)(B); *see infra*, §272] It is unclear, however, whether section 330(a), as amended by the Bankruptcy Reform Act of 1994, allows compensation to be awarded to the debtor's attorney in a Chapter 7 case, or in a Chapter 11 case where the debtor is not a debtor in possession. [B.C. §330(a)(1)] The inference is that it does not after the 1994 amendments, especially in light of the express provision (above) allowing compensation for attorneys of individual Chapter 12 and Chapter 13 debtors. [*In re* Kinnemore, 181 B.R. 520 (Bankr. D. Idaho 1995)—compensation denied]

2. **Fee Application:** [§271] An application for compensation for services or reimbursement of necessary expenses must include a *detailed* statement of (i) the services performed, (ii) the time spent, (iii) the expenses incurred, and (iv) the amounts requested. It also must include disclosures concerning (i) payments that have been made or promised, (ii) the source of such payments, (iii) the sharing of, or any agreement to share, compensation previously received or to be received, and (iv) the details concerning any sharing of, or agreement to share, compensation (unless the sharing is with other members of the same firm of attorneys or accountants). A copy of the fee application must be sent to the United States trustee. [Bankruptcy Rule 2016(a)] The application must contain all information required by the *procedural guidelines issued by the Executive Office for United States Trustees*. Also, local bankruptcy rules may require additional information.

 a. **Note:** The rules and details concerning time records are far more stringent than the average nonbankruptcy attorney is accustomed to.

3. **Criteria for Determining Reasonable Compensation:** [§272]   In determining a reasonable fee, the court must consider the nature, extent, and value of the services, taking in account all relevant factors, including the following [B.C. §330(a)(3)]:

   (i)   The *time* spent;

   (ii) The *rates* charged;

   (iii) Whether the *services were necessary or beneficial* for the administration or completion of the case when the services were rendered;

   (iv) Whether the services were performed within a *reasonable time*, considering the nature, complexity, and importance of work; and

   (v)   Whether the *compensation is reasonable* based on the customary fees charged by comparably skilled practitioners in nonbankruptcy cases.

   However, the court cannot allow compensation for services that are (i) unnecessarily duplicative, (ii) not reasonably likely to benefit the estate, or (iii) not necessary to the administration of the case. [B.C. §330(a)(4)(A)]

   a. **Note:** With respect to an out-of-state professional, a recent appellate court held that the correct method starts with the rates in the professional's customary market and then makes any adjustments due to other factors. [Zolfo, Cooper & Co. v. Sunbeam-Oster Company, Inc., 50 F.3d 253 (3d Cir. 1995)]

4. **Limitations on Professionals' Compensation:** [§273]   An award of compensation to a professional person is subject to the following limitations [B.C. §328]:

   a. **Modification by court:** [§274]   A professional person may be hired by a trustee, a debtor in possession, or a creditors' committee on any reasonable basis, including a retainer, an hourly standard, or a contingent fee. However, the compensation ultimately allowed by the court may vary from such terms after the employment has been completed because of developments that could not have been anticipated. [B.C. §328(a)]

   b. **Denial of compensation:** [§275]   If, at any time during employment, a professional person is *not disinterested* or *has an interest adverse to the estate* regarding the subject matter of her employment, the court may deny her compensation for services and reimbursement of expenses. [B.C. §328(c); *In re Prince*, 40 F.3d 356 (11th Cir. 1994)—all attorney's fees and expenses in connection with the case denied because of conflicts of interest; *see also In re Kendavis Industries International, Inc.*, 91 B.R. 742 (Bankr. N.D. Tex. 1988)—debtors' law firm found to have conflict of interest; bankruptcy court reduced interim compensation awards exceeding $4 million by 50%]

      (1) **Exceptions:** [§276]   This rule is subject to the three possible exceptions for (i) a creditor's representative [B.C. §327(c); *see supra*, §266], (ii) a "special purpose" attorney [B.C. §327(e); *see supra*, §265], and (iii) a professional hired by the debtor before the bankruptcy case [B.C. §1107(b); *see infra*, §1008].

c. **Bifurcation of trustee's compensation:** [§277] If a trustee also serves as an attorney or an accountant for the estate, her fee for professional employment may not include compensation for the performance of her duties as trustee. Compensation for services as trustee must be accounted for separately. [B.C. §328(b)]

5. **No-Asset Cases:** [§278] In a case filed under Chapter 7, the trustee is entitled to receive a minimum compensation of $60 (out of the filing fee) when the estate has no property from which to make disbursements to creditors. [B.C. §330(b)]

6. **Trustee's Maximum Compensation:** [§279] The maximum compensation that may be awarded for a *trustee's services* (other than reimbursement for necessary expenses) varies according to the chapter under which the case is filed. [B.C. §326]

   a. **Chapters 7 and 11:** [§280] In a Chapter 7 or Chapter 11 case, a trustee's compensation may not be greater than 25% of the first $5,000 disbursed by the trustee to parties in interest, 10% of the next $45,000, 5% of any amount disbursed in excess of $50,000, but not more than $1 million and reasonable compensation not to exceed 3% of amounts more than $1 million. [B.C. §326(a)]

      (1) **Exclusion of disbursements to debtor:** [§281] Any disbursements by the trustee to the debtor, such as exempt property, are excluded from the computation under Bankruptcy Code section 326(a). [*In re* Dondey, 50 B.R. 12 (Bankr. S.D. Fla. 1985)]

      (2) **Inclusion of disbursements to secured creditors:** [§282] On the other hand, generally the calculation of the trustee's total disbursements includes payments made to holders of secured claims. [B.C. §326(a); 2 Collier ¶326.01(4)(b)] However, there is some authority that if the payments constitute all or substantially all of the proceeds of the sale of a secured party's collateral (*i.e.*, there would be no equity for the unsecured creditors and no benefit to the estate), the trustee should not be entitled to a commission (or expenses) for selling the collateral instead of simply abandoning the property to the debtor. [*In re* Lambert Implement Co., 44 B.R. 860 (Bankr. W.D. Ky. 1984)]

   b. **Chapter 12 and Chapter 13:** [§283] The maximum compensation that a standing Chapter 12 or Chapter 13 trustee may receive is the lesser of 5% of all payments made under the plans that he administered, or the highest yearly basic salary rate for a United States employee at level V of the Executive Schedule plus the cash value of certain employment benefits. [28 U.S.C. §586(e)] The actual annual compensation (not necessarily the maximum) for a particular standing trustee is set by the attorney general, except in Alabama and North Carolina, where it is set by the bankruptcy court. For a nonstanding trustee appointed in a particular case under Chapter 12 or Chapter 13, the maximum compensation is 5% of all payments made under the plan. [B.C. §326(b)]

7. **Interim Compensation:** [§284] A trustee, examiner, debtor's attorney, or other professional person may apply for interim compensation or reimbursement of expenses once every 120 days after the order for relief (or more frequently, if the court allows), instead of waiting until the conclusion of the bankruptcy case to be

paid. [B.C. §331] Any award of interim compensation will cause a reduction, by that amount, in an award of compensation made under section 330 (*see supra*, §269). [B.C. §330(a)(5)]

    a. **Limitations regarding maximum compensation inapplicable:** [§285] Since the limitations on a trustee's compensation [B.C. §326; *see supra*, §§279-283] refer only to the *maximum compensation allowable in an entire case* (rather than to the time of payment), they do not preclude an award of interim compensation. Thus, interim compensation may be granted based on a trustee's services of receiving and administering funds even if disbursements have not yet been made. [*In re* Tom Carter Enterprises, 49 B.R. 243 (Bankr. C.D. Cal. 1985)]

8. **Debtor's Transactions with Attorneys:** [§286] The debtor's attorney (whether or not applying for compensation) is required to file a statement of any fees paid or any fee agreement made within one year before bankruptcy for legal services related to the case. The statement also must indicate the source of payment. If the court determines that the compensation is unreasonable, it may cancel the fee agreement or order that any excessive portion be returned to the estate or to the entity that made the payment. [B.C. §329; *In re* Lee, 884 F.2d 897 (5th Cir. 1989); *see also* Bankruptcy Rules 2016(b), 2017] Also, it has been held that disgorgement of excessive fees paid more than one year before bankruptcy may be ordered as a sanction for nondisclosure if it is shown that the fees were for services performed in contemplation of the case. [*In re* Prudhomme, 43 F.3d 1000 (5th Cir. 1995)]

9. **Sharing of Fees Prohibited:** [§287] A trustee, examiner, attorney, accountant, or other professional person employed in a bankruptcy case is prohibited from sharing any compensation or reimbursement with another person. [B.C. §504(a)] This rule is subject to two exceptions:

    a. **Exception—members of same firm:** [§288] Compensation or reimbursement may be shared with another member, partner, or associate of the same professional firm. [B.C. §504(b)(1)]

    b. **Exception—involuntary case:** [§289] An attorney representing a creditor who files an involuntary petition is permitted to share her fee with any other attorney who contributes to her services or expenses. [B.C. §504(b)(2)]

E. **UNITED STATES TRUSTEE**

1. **Appointment and Term:** [§290] For each of 21 regions throughout the nation, the Attorney General appoints one United States trustee for a five-year term. Where necessary, the Attorney General also may appoint assistant United States trustees. [28 U.S.C. §§581, 582]

    a. **Exceptions:** [§291] The judicial districts for Alabama and North Carolina will not be included in their respective bankruptcy regions until the earlier of the time those districts elect to be included or October 1, 2002. [P.L. 99-554, §302(d)(3) (1986), as amended by P.L. 101-650, §317(a) (1990)] This statutory exception for Alabama and North Carolina has been held to be unconstitutional because it violates the Uniformity Clause of the United States Constitution [art. I, §8]. [St. Angelo v. Victoria Farms, Inc., 38 F.3d 1525 (9th Cir. 1994), *as amended by* 46 F.3d 969 (9th Cir. 1995)]

2. **Administrative Duties:** [§292] The United States trustee performs numerous administrative functions under the supervision of the Attorney General. Some of these duties are as follows:

   a. *To establish and supervise a panel of private trustees* to serve in Chapter 7 cases [28 U.S.C. §586(a)(1)];

   b. *To appoint an interim trustee* from the private panel in a Chapter 7 case [B.C. §701(a)(l)]; *to appoint a trustee or an examiner* in a Chapter 11 case when the court orders such appointment to be made [B.C. §1104(d)], or *to convene a meeting of creditors to elect a trustee* when the court orders a trustee's appointment and a party in interest timely requests an election, instead [B.C. §1104(b)]; and either *to appoint a standing trustee* for Chapter 12 or Chapter 13 cases [28 U.S.C. §586(b)], or, instead, *to appoint a trustee* for a particular case under Chapter 12 or Chapter 13 [B.C. §§1202(a), 1302(a)];

   c. In a Chapter 11 case, *to appoint and monitor creditors' committees and equity security holders' committees* [B.C. §1102(a); 28 U.S.C. §586(a)(3)(E)];

   d. *To convene and preside at the section 341 meeting* of creditors [B.C. §341(a)], and when appropriate, *to examine the debtor* at that meeting [B.C. §343];

   e. *When necessary, to serve as the trustee* in a case under Chapter 7, 12, or 13, but not in a Chapter 11 case [28 U.S.C. §586(a)(2); B.C. §1104(c)];

   f. *To supervise the administration of bankruptcy cases and trustees* [28 U.S.C. §586(a)(3)];

   g. *To monitor applications for the employment of professional persons* and, when appropriate, file comments with the court regarding their approval [28 U.S.C. §586(a)(3)(H)];

   h. *To review fee applications* of trustees, examiners, attorneys, and other professional persons (generally based on uniform application of procedural guidelines adopted by its Executive Office), file comments with the court concerning the applications, and, when appropriate, file objections [28 U.S.C. §586(a)(3)(A)];

   i. *To monitor plans* filed in cases under Chapter 11, 12, and 13, and, when appropriate, to file with the court comments regarding such plans [28 U.S.C. §586(a)(3)(B),(C)];

   j. *To monitor Chapter 11 disclosure statements* and, when appropriate, file comments with the court [28 U.S.C. §586(a)(3)(B)];

   k. *To monitor the progress of bankruptcy cases* and take actions that are necessary to avoid undue delay [28 U.S.C. §586(a)(3)(G)];

   l. To take appropriate action *to ensure that the debtor timely files all necessary reports*, schedules, and fees [28 U.S.C. §586(a)(3)(D)];

   m. *To inform the United States Attorney about crimes* that may have been committed under federal law [28 U.S.C. §586(a)(3)(F)];

n. ***To deposit or invest money*** (as allowed under Code section 345; *see supra*, §247) received as the trustee in bankruptcy cases [28 U.S.C. §586(a)(4)]; and

o. ***To make any reports or to perform other duties*** prescribed by the Attorney General [28 U.S.C. §586(a)(5), (6)].

3. **Standing:** [§293]   The Bankruptcy Code grants the United States trustee the right to appear and be heard with respect to any issue in a bankruptcy case. However, the United States trustee may not file a plan in a case under Chapter 11. [B.C. §307; United States Trustee v. Price Waterhouse, 19 F.3d 138 (3d Cir. 1994)—United States trustee has standing to object to debtors' employment of professional who was not disinterested; *In re* Columbia Gas Systems, Inc., 33 F.3d 294 (3d Cir. 1994)—United States trustee has standing to object to Chapter 11 debtors' investment guidelines]

V. THE BANKRUPTCY ESTATE AND THE TRUSTEE'S AVOIDING POWERS

chapter approach

The bankruptcy estate contains all property described in Bankruptcy Code section 541. In general, "section 541 property" includes all of the debtor's legal and equitable interests in property at the time the bankruptcy petition is filed, certain kinds of property acquired by the debtor within 180 days after the date of bankruptcy, *and* property that the trustee brings into the estate by exercising her *avoiding powers*. As a general rule, any entity that has possession or custody of estate property must *turn over* such property to the trustee. Property that is either burdensome or of inconsequential value to the estate ordinarily may be *abandoned* by the trustee. But note that abandonment of property in violation of state or federal environmental laws will not be permitted if the result will be to threaten the health or safety of the public with imminent and identifiable harm.

One of the most important bankruptcy topics for exam purposes concerns the trustee's avoiding powers. You will undoubtedly see a question that asks you to discuss these powers. Recall that under appropriate circumstances, the trustee may avoid certain *setoffs* [B.C. §553], *statutory liens* [B.C. §545], *preferences* [B.C. §547], *fraudulent transfers* [B.C. §548], *postpetition transactions* [B.C. §549], as well as other transfers that can be defeated because of the *different statuses* conferred upon the trustee by Bankruptcy Code section 544. Remember that, as of the commencement of the bankruptcy case, the trustee has the status of a *hypothetical* (i) judicial lien creditor, (ii) creditor with an unsatisfied execution, or (iii) bona fide purchaser who has perfected the transfer of real property from the debtor. Also, if there is an *actual* unsecured creditor who has the right to avoid a transfer of the debtor's property under nonbankruptcy law, the trustee can step into that creditor's shoes to avoid such a transfer for the benefit of the estate.

With respect to the time periods for the trustee to exercise her avoiding powers, keep in mind that for voidable preferences, the *90 days* prior to the filing of the bankruptcy petition constitutes the preference period, unless the creditor was an insider, in which case, the preference period extends to *one year* before bankruptcy. If a question concerns a fraudulent transfer, remember that the trustee can avoid such a transfer made within *one year* before bankruptcy. Also, sometimes state fraudulent transfer laws may be applied under section 544(b) to avoid transfers that occurred more than one year before bankruptcy.

Finally, you should be aware that in a Chapter 11 case, the trustee's avoiding powers ordinarily may be exercised by the debtor in possession if a trustee has not been appointed *(see infra*, §1006).

A. THE BANKRUPTCY ESTATE

1. **Property Included in Bankruptcy Estate:** [§294] The creation of a bankruptcy estate occurs automatically upon the filing of a petition commencing a voluntary, joint, or involuntary bankruptcy case. The estate consists of a comprehensive range of rights and interests in property (irrespective of the property's location or the

entity in possession), as well as various causes of action and claims held by the debtor. [B.C. §541(a)]

   a. **All legal and equitable interests of debtor:** [§295] The estate includes all of the debtor's legal and equitable interests in property, real or personal, tangible or intangible, *at the time the petition is filed*. [B.C. §541(a)(1)]

      (1) **Legal interests:** [§296] Examples of legal interests in property that may be included in the estate are:

          (a) *Bank deposits* [4 Collier ¶541.11];

          (b) *Stocks, bonds, and instruments*;

          (c) *Product liability insurance* [*In re* Johns-Manville Corp., 40 B.R. 219 (S.D.N.Y. 1984)];

          (d) *Rights to compensation* for *pre-petition* employment services [*In re* Ryerson, 739 F.2d 1423 (9th Cir. 1984)];

          (e) *Executory contracts* (*see infra*, §§875 *et seq.*);

          (f) *Personal injury claims* by the debtor [Tignor v. Parkinson, 729 F.2d 977 (4th Cir. 1984)];

          (g) *Causes of action for damage to property* [4 Collier ¶541.10(6)];

          (h) *Other rights of action*, including a shareholder's derivative action against corporate officers and directors for breach of their fiduciary duties [Mitchell Excavators, Inc. v. Mitchell, 734 F.2d 129 (2d Cir. 1984)];

          (i) *Income tax refunds* based on *pre-petition* earnings or losses [Kokoszka v. Belford, 417 U.S. 642 (1974); United States v. Michaels, 840 F.2d 901 (11th Cir. 1988)];

          (j) *Net operating loss carryovers* [*In re* Prudential Lines, Inc., 928 F.2d 565 (2d Cir. 1991)];

          (k) *Licenses, copyrights, and patents*;

          (l) *A remainder interest in real property* [*In re* Reynolds, 50 B.R. 20 (Bankr. C.D. Ill. 1985); and

          (m) *A right to possession of property* under an unexpired lease [*In re* Tel-A-Communications Consultants, Inc., 50 B.R. 250 (Bankr. D. Conn. 1985)].

      (2) **Equitable interests:** [§297] Examples of equitable interests that may be part of the estate are:

          (a) *A beneficial interest in the corpus of a nonspendthrift trust* [*In re* Dias, 37 B.R. 584 (Bankr. D. Idaho 1984)]; and

(b) *An equitable right to redeem foreclosed property* under state law [*In re* Sapphire Investments, 19 B.R. 492 (Bankr. D. Ariz. 1982)].

(3) **Limitation:** [§298] The estate's interest in property is no greater than the debtor's interest when the bankruptcy petition is filed. [*In re* Sanders, 969 F.2d 591 (7th Cir. 1992)—trustee could not compel turnover of contributions to nonexempt pension that debtor could not reach unless she terminated her employment or died]

b. **Other kinds of estate property:** [§299] In addition to the debtor's legal and equitable interests in property as of the date of bankruptcy, estate property also includes the following:

(1) **Community property:** [§300] All of the debtor and debtor's spouse's community property, as defined under applicable state law, at the time of the filing of the bankruptcy petition becomes property of the estate if the property is under the debtor's sole or joint control or is liable for a claim against the debtor or for a joint claim against the debtor and debtor's spouse. [B.C. §541(a)(2)]

(2) **Property recovered by trustee:** [§301] Any interests in property that the trustee recovers or preserves for the benefit of the estate (*e.g.*, where the trustee has avoided a preferential or fraudulent transfer of the debtor's interest in property) are included in property of the estate. [B.C. §541(a)(3), (4); *In re* First Capital Mortgage Loan Corporation, 917 F.2d 424 (10th Cir. 1990)]

(3) **Certain property acquired post-petition:** [§302] Property obtained by the debtor within *180 days after the date of bankruptcy* from a bequest, devise, inheritance, property settlement, divorce decree, or beneficial interest in a life insurance policy or death benefit plan is considered to be property of the estate. [B.C. §541(a)(5); *In re* Chenoweth, 3 F.3d 1111 (7th Cir. 1993)—inheritance constituted property of the estate where testator died five months after bankruptcy petition was filed, but the will was probated 196 days after date of bankruptcy]

(4) **Proceeds of estate property:** [§303] Proceeds, rents, profits, product, or offspring emanating from estate property also become property of the estate. [B.C. §541(a)(6)]

(a) **Example:** Debtor filed a voluntary bankruptcy petition on September 1, at which time he owned a car. On October 1, Debtor was involved in an accident, resulting in substantial damage to the car. On December 15, Debtor received a check in the amount of $5,000 from his insurance company for the repairs to the car. The insurance check constitutes proceeds of the car and, therefore, is property of the estate. [*See* Bradt v. Woodlawn Auto Workers, 757 F.2d 512 (2d Cir. 1985)]

(b) **Exception—individual debtor's post-petition earnings:** [§304] Other than in a Chapter 12 or Chapter 13 case [B.C. §§1207(a)(2), 1306(a)(2); *see infra* §§1235, 1157], an *individual debtor's earnings* for services rendered *after* the filing of the petition are not included in property of the estate. [B.C. §541(a)(6); *see In re* Clark, 891 F.2d 111 (5th Cir. 1989)—football player's salary corresponding to nine post-petition games excluded from bankruptcy estate]

    (5) **Property acquired by estate after bankruptcy:** [§305] Any property that the *estate* acquires after the filing of the petition becomes property of the estate. [B.C. §541(a)(7)] Thus, under this provision, a post-petition contract made by the trustee or the debtor in possession would constitute property of the estate. [4 Collier ¶541.20]

2. **Ipso Facto or "Bankruptcy" Clauses—Invalid:** [§306] Property of the debtor that becomes part of the bankruptcy estate is not affected by a clause in a contract, deed, or nonbankruptcy law that places restrictions or conditions on the debtor's transfer of the property. Likewise, clauses that purport to cause a forfeiture, termination, or modification of the debtor's interest in the property due to (i) the debtor's insolvency, (ii) the debtor's financial condition, (iii) the filing of a bankruptcy case concerning the debtor, or (iv) the appointment of a bankruptcy trustee or a nonbankruptcy custodian or the seizure of property by such persons will not prevent the property from being included in the bankruptcy estate. Such clauses are *unenforceable* under Bankruptcy Code section 541(c)(1).

    a. **Exception—certain trusts:** [§307] An exception to this principle provides for the enforceability of a restriction on the transfer of the debtor's beneficial interest in a trust if that restriction is enforceable under *applicable nonbankruptcy law*. [B.C. §541(c)(2)] This exception consistently has been held to apply to traditional spendthrift trusts, and the Supreme Court has held that it also covers ERISA-qualified pension plans. [Patterson v. Shumate, 504 U.S. 753 (1992)] The effect of the exception is to exclude the debtor's interest in the trust of the ERISA plan from property of the bankruptcy estate. However, IRA and Keogh annuities that do not contain anti-alienability provisions are included in the estate. [*In re* Walker, 959 F.2d 894 (10th Cir. 1992)]

        (1) **Distinguish—payment of trust income to debtor:** [§308] The income from a testamentary spendthrift trust that is *paid or owing* to a debtor-beneficiary within 180 days after the filing of the bankruptcy petition is included in the estate even though the corpus of the trust is excluded and beyond the trustee's reach. [B.C. §541(a)(5); *In re* Hecht, 54 B.R. 379 (Bankr. S.D.N.Y. 1985), *aff'd*, 69 B.R. 290 (S.D.N.Y. 1987); *and see supra*, §302]

3. **Property Excluded from Estate:** [§309] In addition to the post-petition earnings of an individual debtor (*see supra*, §304) and spendthrift trusts enforceable under applicable nonbankruptcy law (*see supra*, §307), the following items are *not included* in property of the estate:

    a. **Certain powers:** [§310] A power that may be exercised by the debtor solely for the benefit of another entity is not part of the estate. However, if the debtor can exercise the power for his own benefit, this exclusion does not apply. [B.C. §541(b)(1)]

    b. **Expired commercial lease of real property:** [§311] A debtor's interest *as a lessee* of nonresidential real property is excluded from property of the estate if that interest has terminated due to the expiration of the lease's stated term either prior to the filing of the petition or during the case. [B.C. §541(b)(2); *In re* Neville, 118 B.R. 14 (Bankr. E.D.N.Y. 1990)]

    c. **Certain property of educational institutions:** [§312] Also excluded from estate property are the debtor's eligibility to participate in programs under the Higher Education Act of 1965 and the debtor's accreditation status or state licensure as an educational institution. [B.C. §541(b)(3)]

    d. **Farmout agreements:** [§313] Certain interests of the debtor (in liquid or gaseous hydrocarbons) transferred under a farmout agreement are also excluded from the estate. [B.C. §§541(b)(4)(A), 101(21A)]

    e. **Production payments:** [§314] Certain production payments from oil or gas producers are excluded from property of the estate, too. [B.C. §541(b)(4)(B); 101(42)(A), (56)(A)] "A production payment is an interest in [certain reserves] of an oil or gas producer that lasts for a limited period of time and that is not affected by production costs." [140 Cong. Rec. H10,767 (daily ed. Oct. 4, 1994)—section-by-section description of Bankruptcy Reform Act of 1994; *see also* 140 Cong. Rec. S14,462 (daily ed. Oct. 6, 1994)]—statement of Sen. Simpson] For example, when a debtor owns oil or gas wells and finances the drilling by promising to pay (in cash or in kind) a percentage as production occurs, these payments are not included in the property of the estate. [B.C. §541(b)(4)(B)]

    f. **Proceeds of money orders:** [§315] Another exclusion is for proceeds of money orders sold within 14 days of bankruptcy, where there was an agreement between the debtor and the money order issuer not to commingle proceeds with property of the debtor, and the money order issuer took action to require compliance with the prohibition before bankruptcy. Since the proceeds should have been segregated, they are excluded from the bankruptcy estate. [B.C. §541(b)(5)]

4. **Compare—Exemptions:** [§316] An individual debtor is entitled to exempt certain items of estate property. Whether property is exempt is a separate issue. Therefore, first, it must be determined what property is included in the estate of an individual debtor; then it is necessary to consider which estate property qualifies for exemption. [B.C. §522(b); *and see infra*, §§609 *et seq.*]

B. TURNOVER OF PROPERTY TO TRUSTEE

1. **Turnover by Entity Other than Custodian:** [§317] Property that may be used, sold, or leased by the trustee under Bankruptcy Code section 363 (*see infra*, §§832 *et seq.*) or property that may be exempted by the debtor under section 522 (*see infra*, §§609 *et seq.*) must be delivered to the trustee and accounted for ***by any entity who is in possession or control*** of such property and who is not a custodian. [B.C. §542(a)]

    a. **"Entity":** [§318] Since an "entity" is defined more broadly than a "person" (*see supra*, §28), even a governmental unit or a trust (business or nonbusiness) is subject to the turnover provisions. [B.C. §101(15)]

b. **Turnover of property repossessed before bankruptcy:** [§319] A secured creditor who has repossessed property before the filing of a Chapter 11 petition but who has not yet sold such collateral to a bona fide purchaser must turn over such collateral to the trustee or the debtor in possession, since ownership is not transferred until such a sale occurs. [United States v. Whiting Pools, Inc., 462 U.S. 198 (1983); *see also In re* Challenge Air International, Inc., 952 F.2d 384 (11th Cir. 1992)—ordered turnover of cash fund held by credit card company and owed to debtor, where Internal Revenue Service had levied on the fund before debtor's bankruptcy] The secured creditor is entitled to adequate protection of its interest (*see infra*, §§761 *et seq.*); thus, the court will order turnover only if the debtor can prove its ability to provide such protection. [B.C. §§363(e), 361; United States v. Whiting Pools, Inc., *supra*]

(1) **Note:** The *Whiting Pools* doctrine has been extended to a pre-petition repossession by a secured creditor in a Chapter 13 case [*In re* Attinello, 38 B.R. 992 (Bankr. E.D. Pa. 1984)], and to (pledged) property in the possession of a secured creditor in a Chapter 7 liquidation case [*In re* Gerwer, 898 F.2d 730 (9th Cir. 1990)].

2. **Payment of Indebtedness to Estate:** [§320] An entity, such as a bank, that owes a matured debt or a debt payable on demand or order (*e.g.*, the debtor's checking account) which constitutes estate property is required to pay the trustee (or a payee of a check drawn by the trustee) the amount of the debt in excess of any setoff permitted the entity under Bankruptcy Code section 553 (*see infra*, §§334 *et seq.*). [B.C. §542(b)]

a. **Bank's freeze of debtor's account:** [§321] The United States Supreme Court has held that this provision justifies a bank's *temporary hold* on a debtor's checking account (up to the amount allegedly subject to setoff) while the bank seeks relief from the automatic stay and the court's determination of its right to a setoff. Such an administrative freeze pending the court's ruling keeps the debtor from spending the funds in the account and thereby making the bank's setoff rights useless. [Citizens Bank of Maryland v. Strumpf, 116 S. Ct. 286 (1995); *and see infra*, §§346-349]

3. **Exceptions to Turnover:** [§322] In the following situations, an entity will not be obligated to turn over property to the trustee:

a. **Property of inconsequential value:** [§323] If the property in the possession or under the control of a noncustodian "is of inconsequential value or benefit to the estate," turnover is not required. [B.C. §542(a)]

b. **Transfer without actual notice or knowledge of bankruptcy case:** [§324] Turnover is not required where an entity (such as a bank) *in good faith* and without either actual notice or knowledge of the bankruptcy petition transfers property of the estate or pays a debt owing to the debtor (*e.g.*, honors the debtor's check) to an entity other than the trustee. [B.C. §542(c)]

(1) **Example:** On August 1, Debtor, who has a checking account with funds on deposit in Bank, draws a check payable to the order of Payee. On August 2, Debtor files a voluntary bankruptcy petition. On August 3, Bank, with neither actual notice nor knowledge of the commencement of the

bankruptcy case, pays the amount of the check to Payee in good faith. Bank, as payor, is not liable. [B.C. §542(c)]

(2) **Transferee not protected:** [§325] Note that the payee or transferee in such a transaction is not protected by this provision and may be subject to the trustee's avoiding power under section 549 (*see infra*, §§427-428) and to liability under Code section 550 (*see infra*, §§455 *et seq.*). [4 Collier ¶542.04]

(3) **Post-petition setoff not excepted:** [§326] Even if a bank lacks actual notice or knowledge of the bankruptcy petition, it may not set off a pre-petition debt without obtaining judicial relief from the automatic stay. [B.C. §§542(c), 362(a)(7); *and see infra*, §789]

4. **Turnover of Property by Custodian:** [§327] A custodian who has knowledge of the filing of a bankruptcy petition is prohibited from disbursing or administering (other than for preservation) any property of the debtor; any proceeds, rent, profits, product, or offspring of the debtor's property; or any property of the estate in her possession, custody, or control. The custodian must turn over the property to the trustee and file an accounting. [B.C. §543(a), (b); Smitty's Inc. v. Southeast National Bank of Orlando, 1 Collier Bankr. Cas. 2d 366 (Bankr. M.D. Fla. 1979)]

   a. **"Custodian" defined:** [§328] The bankruptcy definition of a custodian is: (i) a receiver or trustee of the debtor's property appointed in a non-Bankruptcy Code action; (ii) an assignee for the benefit of the debtor's creditors; or (iii) a trustee or receiver designated to take control of the debtor's property to enforce a lien or to administer the property for the benefit of creditors. Frequently, a custodian is a public official or quasi-public official, such as a sheriff or a marshal, who is authorized to take charge of the debtor's property. [B.C. §101(11)]

      (1) **Example:** Debtor, a financially distressed cash currency exchange, is placed under a state statutory administrative receivership. As a result, a receiver takes title to all of Debtor's assets, and state liquidation proceedings are commenced against Debtor. One week later, Debtor files a voluntary petition under the Bankruptcy Code. The state administrative receiver is deemed to be a custodian under federal bankruptcy law and must turn over to the trustee all of Debtor's property. [*In re* Cash Currency Exchange, Inc., *supra*, §126]

   b. **Exceptions to custodian's turnover:** [§329] A custodian's duty to deliver the debtor's property to the trustee *may be excused* in the best interests of creditors and (if the debtor is solvent) of equity security holders. It *must be excused*, unless necessary to avoid fraud or injustice, where the custodian is an assignee for the benefit of creditors who was appointed or took possession of the debtor's property more than 120 days before the commencement of the bankruptcy case. [B.C. §543(d)]

   c. **Compensation or surcharge:** [§330] Within the court's discretion, a custodian may be awarded reasonable compensation for her services and actual expenses. On the other hand, a custodian may be liable for wrongful or excessive disbursements. [B.C. §543(c)]

5. **Turnover of Books and Records:** [§331] Unless a valid privilege applies (mainly the attorney-client privilege), an attorney, accountant, or other person, if directed by the court (after notice and a hearing), must turn over to the trustee any books, records, or other documents concerning the debtor's finances or property. [B.C. §542(e)]

   a. **Waiver of corporate attorney-client privilege:** [§332] In the case of a *corporate debtor*, the trustee has the power to waive the corporation's attorney-client privilege concerning *pre-bankruptcy communications* made by former officers and directors to the debtor's attorney. The attorney may then be required to testify. [Commodity Futures Trading Commission v. Weintraub, *supra*, §247] (*Note:* There is authority holding that the trustee cannot waive the attorney-client privilege of an individual debtor. [McClarty v. Gudenau, 166 B.R. 101 (E.D. Mich. 1994)])

      (1) **Rationale:** Upon appointment, the bankruptcy trustee effectively becomes the corporate debtor's new management, and she is expected to investigate the conduct of the corporation's prior officers and directors. Thus, the corporate attorney-client privilege also must pass from former management to the trustee in order to facilitate the trustee's search for any misappropriated corporate assets or insider fraud. [Commodity Futures Trading Commission v. Weintraub, *supra*]

   b. **No accountant-client privilege:** [§333] Where access to information relating to the debtor's financial condition is needed for complete and accurate disclosure, an accountant or an accounting firm will be required to turn over documents and workpapers in its possession. There is no applicable federal privilege, and state evidentiary accountant-client privileges are not recognized in proceedings under the Bankruptcy Code. [*In re* International Horizons, Inc., 689 F.2d 996 (11th Cir. 1982)]

C. CREDITOR'S RIGHT OF SETOFF

1. **Right of Setoff:** [§334] A creditor entitled to a right of setoff under state law may set off a debt he owes to the debtor against a claim he holds against the debtor, if *both the debt and the claim are mutual and arose prior to the filing of the bankruptcy case*. [B.C. §553(a); *In re* Saugus General Hospital, Inc., 698 F.2d 42 (1st Cir. 1983); *In re* Braniff Airways, Inc., 42 B.R. 443 (Bankr. N.D. Tex. 1984)]

   a. **Example:** On March 1, Debtor borrows $5,000 from Bank and executes an unsecured promissory note in Bank's favor. On April 1, Debtor deposits checks totaling $2,500 into his checking account with Bank. On April 2, Debtor files a voluntary bankruptcy petition. The checks are collected by Bank on April 4. Since Bank had not completed its collection process before the petition was filed, the funds deposited on April 2 actually were not contained in Debtor's account at the time of bankruptcy. Therefore, Bank is not entitled to set off the $2,500 deposit against its $5,000 claim because the element of *mutuality is* missing. [*In re* All-Brite Sign Service Co., 11 B.R. 409 (Bankr. W.D. Ky. (1981)]

2. **Exceptions to Right of Setoff:** [§335] A creditor's right of setoff is subject to the following exceptions under the Code:

a. **Disallowed claim:** [§336]   There is no right of setoff to the extent that the court has disallowed the creditor's claim against the debtor. [B.C. §553(a)(1)]

b. **Claim transferred by nondebtor party:** [§337]   There is no right of setoff where an entity other than the debtor transferred the claim to the creditor after the filing of the bankruptcy petition or within 90 days prior to the bankruptcy petition at a time when the debtor was insolvent. [B.C. §553(a)(2)]

   (1) **Presumption of insolvency:** [§338]   For purposes of Code section 553, there is a *statutory presumption* that the debtor was insolvent during the 90 days immediately preceding bankruptcy. [B.C. §553(c)]

c. **Debt created for purpose of setoff:** [§339]   There is no right of setoff where the creditor incurred the debt owed to the debtor within 90 days prior to the bankruptcy petition, at a time when the debtor was insolvent, for the purpose of using that debt as a setoff. [B.C. §553(a)(3)]

   (1) **Example—bank's "build-up":** Debtor owed a balance of $100,000 to Trust Company on a loan guaranteed by Debtor's president and vice president. On September 1, Debtor deposited $10,000 into his checking account with Trust Company. Trust Company was fully aware that Debtor was undergoing serious financial problems at the time of the deposit. On September 3, Trust Company completed its collection of the deposit, then proceeded to set off $30,000 (the entire balance of Debtor's account) against the $100,000 debt owed to Trust Company, and also dishonored several checks that had been drawn on Debtor's account and presented for payment. On October 15, Debtor filed a voluntary bankruptcy petition. Since insolvency is presumed during the 90-day period before bankruptcy, the trustee may avoid Trust Company's setoff *to the extent of $10,000* if the court finds that Trust Company's acceptance of the deposit was not in the ordinary course of business, but rather was for the purpose of acquiring a setoff against Debtor. [B.C. §553(a)(3); *In re* Union Cartage Co., 38 B.R. 134 (Bankr. N.D. Ohio 1984)]

d. **Creditor's improved position due to pre-bankruptcy setoff:** [§340]   The trustee may avoid and recover for the estate a setoff made by a creditor within 90 days prior to the filing of the petition *to the extent that* the creditor (usually a bank) has improved its position. [B.C. §553(b)(1)]

   (1) **Rationale:** This exception is designed to deter lenders from executing pre-petition setoffs, especially since the need for available cash ordinarily is critical during the months immediately before the commencement of a bankruptcy case.

   (2) **Amount recoverable:** [§341]   The trustee may recover the amount by which any insufficiency on the date of the setoff is less than the insufficiency present on the ninetieth day before bankruptcy *or on the first date within the 90-day pre-petition period on which an insufficiency existed*, whichever is later. [B.C. §553(b)(1); *In re* Duncan, 10 B.R. 13 (Bankr. E.D. Tenn. 1980)]

   (a) **"Insufficiency" defined:** An insufficiency is computed by subtracting the amount that the creditor owes to the debtor (*e.g.*, the balance in the debtor's deposit account, where the creditor is a bank) from the amount of the creditor's claim against the debtor. [B.C. §553(b)(2)]

 (b) **Example:** Debtor owed Bank $100,000 on an unsecured loan. On the ninetieth day before the filing of Debtor's bankruptcy petition, Debtor's checking account with Bank had a balance of $100,000. This balance remained unchanged until the sixtieth day before bankruptcy, when the account held $60,000. This was the first date on which an insufficiency existed. On the fiftieth day before bankruptcy, the account balance was $50,000, but on the fortieth day before bankruptcy it was $70,000, at which time Bank set off $70,000 against the unpaid loan. The amount recoverable by the trustee is $10,000, since the insufficiency on the date of setoff ($30,000) constitutes a $10,000 improvement in Bank's position relative to the insufficiency ($40,000) on the first date that one existed during the 90-day period. [B.C. §553(b)(1)]

(3) **Debtor may be solvent:** [§342] The debtor's insolvency is not an element of this exception.

e. **Creditor's bad faith conduct:** [§343] Setoffs are permissive and within the court's equitable discretion. Therefore, a setoff may be denied where the creditor's conduct is inequitable or in bad faith. [*In re* Cascade Roads, Inc., 34 F.3d 756 (9th Cir. 1994)—Government stonewalled on discovery, caused years of litigation by assertion of meritless defenses, and delayed distribution to creditors for eight years]

3. **Compare—Recoupment:** [§344] Setoff should be distinguished from the equitable doctrine of recoupment, which sometimes is used to prevent unjust enrichment. The setoff of mutual debts between two parties involves independent obligations which usually are derived from *separate transactions*. "Recoupment, on the other hand, is the setting up of a demand arising from the *same transaction* as the plaintiff's claim or cause of action strictly for the purpose of abatement or reduction of such claim." [4 Collier ¶553.03] It has been held that recoupment is not subject to the automatic stay (*see infra*, §345). [*In re* Holford, 896 F.2d 176 (5th Cir. 1990)]

 a. **Example:** Purchaser acquired the right to buy crude oil produced by Debtor. Pursuant to the parties' agreement, oil was delivered to Purchaser in June, and Purchaser mistakenly overpaid Debtor $90,000. In September, Debtor filed a voluntary Chapter 11 petition and continued to sell oil to Purchaser in accordance with the provisions of the contract. Purchaser now seeks to recoup its overpayment from the amount it owes Debtor for post-petition purchases. While a creditor may not set off a pre-petition claim against a post-petition debt, the doctrine of recoupment allows Purchaser, under its *single contract* with Debtor, to recoup the amount of the overpayment from the subsequent purchases, rather than unjustly enriching the other creditors in the case. [*In re* B & L Oil Co., 782 F.2d 155 (10th Cir. 1986)]

4. **Automatic Stay:** [§345] Once a bankruptcy petition has been filed, the automatic stay enjoins the post-petition setoff of a pre-petition debt (owed to the

debtor) against a creditor's claim. [B.C. §362(a)(7); *and see infra*, §789] Therefore, a creditor must obtain *relief from the stay* before a setoff may be exercised. Furthermore, the right of setoff may be subject to the trustee's use, sale, or lease of property under Bankruptcy Code section 363, although adequate protection must be provided to the creditor. [B.C. §§553(a), 363(e); *and see infra*, §849]

  a. **Post-petition administrative freeze of debtor's bank account:** [§346] The United States Supreme Court has held that a bank's *temporary hold* on a debtor's deposit account (up to the amount allegedly subject to setoff), while the bank seeks relief from the automatic stay and the court's determination of its right to a setoff, does not violate the automatic stay. [Citizens Bank of Maryland v. Strumpf, *supra*, §321; *and see infra*, §§789-790] It is a permissible response to the bank's dilemma of protecting its right of setoff (if one exists) from the debtor's dissipation of the cash in his deposit account. *Note:* Based on the facts in *Strumpf*, it appears that the bank should *promptly* request relief from the automatic stay and a determination of its right of setoff.

    (1) **First rationale:** [§347] A temporary administrative freeze, pending a judicial determination of the bank's "Motion for Relief from the Automatic Stay and for Setoff," *does not constitute a setoff*, which involves a three-step process: "(i) a decision to effectuate a setoff, (ii) some action accomplishing the setoff, and (iii) a recording of the setoff." [Citizens Bank of Maryland v. Strumpf, *supra*; *see also* Baker v. National City Bank of Cleveland, 511 F.2d 1016 (6th Cir. 1975)]

    (2) **Second rationale:** [§348] Since the Bankruptcy Code *excepts from turnover* funds owed to the debtor that may be used for setoff [B.C. §542(b); *see supra*, §320], a temporary administrative hold on the debtor's account preserves the bank's right of setoff pending a judicial resolution. [Citizens Bank of Maryland v. Strumpf, *supra*]

    (3) **Comment:** [§349] Another important rationale for the result in *Strumpf, supra*, (although not discussed by the Court) is that the debtor's deposit account is included in the definition of *cash collateral* [B.C. §363(a); *see infra*, §350] and thus may not be used by the trustee or debtor in possession without the bank's consent or the court's approval. [B.C. §363(c)(2); *see infra*, §§844-847] "Central to any such authorization is a determination that adequate protection to the secured party would be provided." [B.C. §363(e); Kenney's Franchise Corp. v. Central Fidelity Bank NA, 22 B.R. 747 (W.D. Va. 1982); *and see infra*, §849]

 5. **Secured Status of Claim Subject to Setoff:** [§350] A claim that may be set off *is deemed secured* to the extent of the amount subject to setoff. Therefore, a creditor holding such a claim is entitled to *adequate protection* unless the court lifts the automatic stay and permits the creditor to exercise her right of setoff. [B.C. §§506(a), 362(d)(1); *In re* Braniff Airways, Inc., *supra*, §334; *and see infra*, §§523 *et seq.*]

D. TRUSTEE'S AVOIDANCE OF STATUTORY LIENS

 1. **In General:** [§351] The trustee has several avoiding powers, which may be used to enlarge the bankruptcy estate for the benefit of creditors. One is the trustee's

power to avoid certain types of statutory liens on the debtor's property. These liens are expressly created by statute and are *not consensual*. [B.C. §§545, 101(53)]:

2. **Avoidable Statutory Liens:** [§352] The following kinds of statutory liens may be avoided by the trustee:

   a. **Liens arising automatically due to debtor's financial condition:** [§353] The trustee may avoid a *statutory lien* that is triggered by any of the following events, usually indicating the poor financial condition of the debtor:

      (1) *The filing of a petition* concerning the debtor *under the Bankruptcy Code* [B.C. §545(1)(A)];

      (2) *The filing of an insolvency proceeding* concerning the debtor *outside* of the Bankruptcy Code [B.C. §545(1)(B)];

      (3) *The appointment of a custodian* [B.C. §545(1)(C)];

      (4) *The debtor's insolvency* [B.C. §545(1)(D)];

      (5) *The failure of the debtor's financial condition to satisfy a specified standard* [B.C. §545(1)(E)]; or

      (6) *An execution against the debtor's property by an entity other than the holder of a statutory lien* of this type [B.C. §545(1)(F)].

   b. **Liens not perfected against bona fide purchaser:** [§354] A statutory lien that is not perfected or enforceable against a bona fide purchaser at the time that the bankruptcy petition is filed may also be avoided by the trustee. [B.C. §545(2)]

      (1) **Example—unfiled federal tax lien:** A federal tax lien, notice of which has not been filed by the IRS prior to the commencement of the bankruptcy case, can be avoided since it is not enforceable against a bona fide purchaser. [26 U.S.C. §6323(a); B.C. §545(2)] On the other hand, if notice of the tax lien has been filed, its enforceability against a bona fide purchaser depends on the type of property involved. [26 U.S.C. §6323(b)]

      (2) **Retroactive perfection:** [§355] The trustee's avoiding power under Code section 545(2) is subject to any retroactive perfection permitted under state law or other nonbankruptcy law. [B.C. §546(b); *see infra*, §§438-440]

   c. **Liens for rent:** [§356] Statutory liens for rent or for distress of rent also are avoidable by the trustee. [B.C. §545(3), (4)]

E. **TRUSTEE'S AVOIDING POWERS AS HYPOTHETICAL CREDITOR OR PURCHASER, AND AS SUCCESSOR TO CERTAIN ACTUAL CREDITORS**

   1. **Strong Arm Provision:** [§357] The Bankruptcy Code grants to the trustee, at the commencement of the bankruptcy case, the hypothetical status and the rights and

powers of (i) a judicial lien creditor, (ii) a creditor with an unsatisfied execution, and (iii) a bona fide purchaser of real property. Consequently, the trustee is able to avoid any transfer of the debtor's property that any of these entities—regardless of whether one really exists—could avoid, "without regard to any knowledge of the trustee or any creditor." [B.C. §544(a)]

- a. **Judicial lien creditor:** [§358] The trustee is accorded the rights and powers of a *hypothetical* creditor who furnishes credit to the debtor at the time that the bankruptcy case is commenced, and who simultaneously acquires a judicial lien on as much of the debtor's property as is permitted under applicable state or other nonbankruptcy law. [B.C. §544(a)(1); 4 Collier ¶544.02, footnote 3]

    (1) **Example:** On June 1, Debtor borrows $5,000 from Finance Company, granting a security interest in a famous painting recently inherited by Debtor. On December 1, Debtor files a voluntary bankruptcy petition. At this time, Finance Company has not perfected its security interest in the painting. Since, under the Uniform Commercial Code ("U.C.C."), a judicial lien has priority over an unperfected security interest [U.C.C. §9-301(1)(b)], the trustee's hypothetical judicial lien as of the time the case is commenced will prevail over Finance Company's unperfected security interest in the painting. Hence, the trustee will be able to avoid the security interest and thereby increase the amount available for distribution to the unsecured creditors. [B.C. §544(a)(1)]

    (2) **Compare—where retroactive perfection allowable under state law:** [§359] Bank loans Debtor $10,000 and obtains a *purchase money security interest* in the new office furniture that Debtor purchases with the loan proceeds on June 1 and takes into her possession on the same day. On June 8, Debtor files a voluntary bankruptcy petition. On June 9, Bank perfects its security interest by filing a U.C.C. financing statement. The trustee (as a hypothetical judicial lien creditor as of the commencement of the case) will be *unable* to avoid Bank's security interest in the furniture, since the trustee's powers under Bankruptcy Code section 544 are subject to any retroactive perfection allowable under applicable nonbankruptcy law. Here, such law is the U.C.C.'s 10 (or 20)-day grace period (following Debtor's taking possession of the furniture) for Bank to perfect a purchase money security interest that will have priority over an intervening lien creditor. [B.C. §546(b); U.C.C. §9-301(2); *and see infra*, §§438-440]

- b. **Creditor with unsatisfied execution:** [§360] The trustee also is granted the rights and powers of a *hypothetical* creditor who extends credit to the debtor at the time that the bankruptcy case is filed, and who acquires, at that time, an unsatisfied execution concerning the indebtedness. [B.C. §544(a)(2)]

- c. **Bona fide purchaser of real property:** [§361] In addition, the trustee is given the rights and powers of a *hypothetical* bona fide purchaser *who has perfected the transfer of real property* (exclusive of fixtures) from the debtor at the time of bankruptcy. Thus, the trustee may avoid any transfer voidable by such a bona fide purchaser. [B.C. §544(a)(3)]

(1) **Exception—constructive notice:** [§362] A trustee may not avoid an unrecorded transfer of real property if, under state law, she is charged with constructive notice of the rights of another entity. For example, the trustee had constructive notice where there was open possession of property by a seller to whom a defaulting debtor had voluntarily returned the property before bankruptcy, or open possession by a prior purchaser of the property. [*In re* Flaten, 50 B.R. 186 (Bankr. D.N.D. 1985); McCannon v. Marston, 679 F.2d 13 (3d Cir. 1982)]

(a) **Note:** It is not the trustee's personal knowledge that is important (her own knowledge is disregarded in her capacity as a hypothetical bona fide purchaser); it is the existence of constructive notice under nonbankruptcy law sufficient to defeat the priority of a bona fide purchaser that will nullify the avoiding power of the trustee. [B.C. §544(a)(3); *In re* Flaten, *supra*]

2. **Trustee's Avoiding Power Based on Actual Unsecured Creditors:** [§363] If there exists at the time of bankruptcy an *actual creditor* who possesses an allowable unsecured claim and who has the right, under applicable nonbankruptcy law, to avoid a transfer of the debtor's property, then the trustee is entitled to avoid the whole transfer *for the benefit of the estate*, even if its value exceeds the amount of the creditor's claim. [B.C. §544(b); Moore v. Bay, 284 U.S. 4 (1931); *In re* Acequia, Inc., 34 F.3d 800 (9th Cir. 1994)] Generally, it is state law concerning fraudulent transfers, bulk sales (U.C.C. Article 6), or consignments (U.C.C. section 2-326) that may provide such a right to a creditor who extended credit prior to the transfer sought to be avoided. [*In re* Verco Industries, 704 F.2d 1134 (9th Cir. 1983)]

a. **Example:** On March 1, 1993, Bank made a $10,000 unsecured loan to Debtor. On January 1, 1994, Debtor transferred certain real property, valued at $50,000, to Best Friend for no consideration and with the undisputed intention of defrauding Debtor's creditors. On April 1, 1995, Debtor, who still owed $10,000 to Bank, filed a voluntary bankruptcy petition. All of the events took place in Alabama, which has a 10-year statute of limitations for fraudulent transfers. The trustee cannot avoid Debtor's fraudulent transfer of the property under Bankruptcy Code section 548(a) since it occurred more than one year prior to bankruptcy (*see infra*, §§409 *et seq.*). However, the trustee can find an *actual unsecured creditor* (Bank) that (i) extended credit before January 1, 1994, (ii) may avoid the transfer under Alabama law, and (iii) holds an allowable claim as of April 1, 1995. Thus, under Bankruptcy Code section 544(b), the trustee may use the Alabama fraudulent transfer statute to avoid the transfer and thereby bring the real property or its total value (*see infra*, §456) into the estate *for the benefit of all the unsecured creditors*, including Bank, which then will share pro rata with the others. [*See In re* Bethune, 18 B.R. 418 (Bankr. N.D. Ala. 1982)]

F. TRUSTEE'S POWER TO AVOID PREFERENCES

1. **In General:** [§364] The bankruptcy trustee has the power to avoid pre-petition preferential transfers. Use of this power constitutes another method by which, in appropriate circumstances, the bankruptcy estate may be enlarged for the benefit of creditors. [B.C. §547]

a. **Purpose:** This avoiding power is designed to accomplish an equitable distribution of estate property in the *order established by the Bankruptcy Code* and to prevent the debtor from choosing which creditors to repay.

b. **Example:** Debtor owes $5,000 to Bank and $5,000 to Credit Union. Both creditors are unsecured, and neither is entitled to priority under the Code. On May 1, Debtor, who is insolvent, withdraws the entire balance of $5,000 from her savings account and repays Credit Union in full, while paying nothing to Bank. On June 1, Debtor files a voluntary Chapter 7 petition, and there are no assets available for distribution. The trustee may avoid the preferential transfer to Credit Union and recover the $5,000 payment for the benefit of the estate. After full payment of all priority claims in the case, including administrative expenses, Credit Union and Bank will share pro rata with any other general unsecured creditors. [B.C. §547(b)]

2. **Elements of Preference:** [§365] A voidable preference occurs when there is a *transfer* of the debtor's interest in property made *to or for the benefit of a creditor*, concerning an *antecedent debt* of the debtor, at a time when the *debtor is insolvent*, and *within 90 days prior to the filing of the bankruptcy petition* (or up to one year before bankruptcy if the creditor is an insider), and that results in the creditor receiving a *larger share* than he would have obtained under the Bankruptcy Code if the transfer had not been made and the estate had been liquidated under Chapter 7. [B.C. §547(b)] Each of these elements of a preference is discussed below.

   a. **Transfer:** [§366] A transfer is any *voluntary or involuntary* disposition of property or an interest in property. "Transfer" includes, for example, the debtor's conveyance of a security interest or a mortgage, the fixing of a lien on property of the debtor by judicial process, or even a foreclosure sale of collateral securing a debt. [B.C. §101(54); *see supra*, §38]

   b. **Debtor's interest in property:** [§367] The subject matter of the transfer must be property interest *of the debtor*. [B.C. §547(b)] Therefore, the use of another entity's property to repay a creditor (*e.g.*, the personal funds of a guarantor or of a relative of the debtor) does not constitute a preference where there is no diminution of the debtor's estate. [Brown v. First National Bank of Little Rock, 748 F.2d 490 (8th Cir. 1984)] However, if the debtor grants a security interest to the third party for making the payment, then the payment constitutes a preference, but "only to the extent of the actual value of the collateral given by the debtor. . . ." [*In re* Royal Golf Products Corp., 908 F.2d 91 (6th Cir. 1990)]

      (1) **Trust-fund taxes:** [§368] The Supreme Court has held that a debtor's payments to the IRS of trust-fund taxes *(e.g.*, withheld federal income and FICA taxes) from its general operating accounts are not voidable preferences because they are not transfers of the debtor's property. [Begier v. IRS, 496 U.S. 53 (1990)]

   c. **To or for benefit of creditor:** [§369] The recipient or beneficiary of the transfer must be the *debtor's creditor*. The fact that the creditor is a creditor of another entity closely connected to the debtor (*e.g.*, a corporate debtor's president) is not sufficient to make a transfer preferential. [B.C. §§547(b)(1), 101(10); *see In re* Evans Potato Co., 44 B.R. 191 (Bankr. S.D. Ohio 1984)]

(1) **Indirect preference:** [§370] A transfer may be preferential as to a creditor even if another entity actually received the property transferred. The key is whether the transfer *benefits the creditor.* For example, where the debtor's payment to a first mortgagee increases the value of the second mortgagee's interest in the collateral, where the debtor's payment to a lender relieves a surety or guarantor from liability, or where the debtor pays a third party pursuant to the creditor's instructions, the indirect preference is recoverable by the trustee from the junior mortgagee, the guarantor, or the instructing creditor, respectively, if all of the other elements of a preference are present. [*In re* Prescott, 805 F.2d 719 (7th Cir. 1986); *In re* Compton Corp., 831 F.2d 586 (5th Cir. 1987)—letter of credit issued to secure antecedent unsecured debt]

d. **Pre-existing debt:** [§371] The transfer must concern a debt ("liability on a claim") that was incurred by the debtor before the transfer was executed. [B.C. §§547(b)(2), 101(12); *In re* Perma Pacific Properties, 983 F.2d 964 (10th Cir. 1992)]

e. **Debtor's insolvency:** [§372] The transfer must have occurred when the debtor was insolvent, which generally means that his debts were greater than the aggregate value of his assets, excluding exempt property or property that has been transferred fraudulently. [B.C. §§547(b)(3), 101(32); *In re* Espinoza, 51 B.R. 170 (Bankr. D.N.M. 1985); *and see supra*, §37]

(1) **Presumption of insolvency:** [§373] For the purpose of determining whether a preference has been made, there is a statutory presumption that the debtor was insolvent during the *90 days* immediately prior to the date on which the petition commencing the case was filed. [B.C. §547(f)] This presumption is rebuttable. Thus, the transferee or the beneficiary of a transfer that the trustee seeks to avoid may present evidence to rebut the presumption of the debtor's insolvency at the time of the transfer. The trustee then must prove insolvency to avoid the transfer. [*In re* Koubourlis, 869 F.2d 1319 (9th Cir. 1989); *In re* Almarc Manufacturing, Inc., 60 B.R. 584 (Bankr. N.D. Ill. 1986)]

f. **Preference period—within ninety days before filing:** [§374] To constitute a preference, the transfer must have been made *within 90 days prior to the filing of the bankruptcy petition* unless the creditor was an insider at the time of the transfer, in which case the preference period extends to one year before bankruptcy. [B.C. §§547(b)(4), 101(31); *and see supra*, §§30-33]

(1) **Note—special provisions:** [§375] To ascertain *when* a transfer is deemed to have been made for purposes of Bankruptcy Code section 547, the rules set forth in section 547(e) must be applied (*see infra*, §§397 *et seq.*).

(2) **Presumption of insolvency—limited to ninety days:** [§376] Even where the preference period is one year before bankruptcy because the creditor was an insider, there is no presumption of insolvency beyond the 90-day period prior to bankruptcy. [4 Collier ¶547.07; *see supra*, §373]

g. **Creditor receives greater share in distribution:** [§377] A transfer is preferential only if it enables the creditor to obtain a larger distribution than he would have received in a Chapter 7 case if the transfer had not occurred. This computation is based on a hypothetical liquidation of the estate as of the date of the filing of the bankruptcy petition. [B.C. §547(b)(5); *In re* Tenna Corp., 801 F.2d 819 (6th Cir. 1986); *see also In re* LCO Enterprises, 12 F.3d 938 (9th Cir. 1993)—"hypothetical Chapter 7 analysis must be based on the actual facts of the case"] Thus, a transfer to a nonpriority unsecured creditor is preferential (as to this factor) unless the estate is solvent.

(1) **Secured creditors:** [§378] Payments made to a creditor whose allowed claim is completely secured do not constitute a preference because such transfers do not result in a greater distribution than a Chapter 7 liquidation would provide. [*In re* Flaten, *supra*, §362]

3. **Exceptions to Preference Rule:** [§379] The following transfers are not avoidable by the trustee [B.C. §547(c)]:

   a. **Substantially contemporaneous exchange for new value:** [§380] To the extent that a transfer is a substantially contemporaneous exchange for new value, it is not avoidable. This exception requires two elements: (i) that the debtor and the creditor *intended* the transfer to constitute a contemporaneous exchange *for new value* furnished to the debtor, and (ii) that the transfer *actually was* a substantially contemporaneous exchange. [B.C. §547(c)(1); *In re* Jet Florida Systems, Inc., 861 F.2d 1555 (11th Cir. 1988)]

      (1) **Example:** On June 1, Bank made a $10,000 *secured* cash loan to Debtor, who promised to convey to Bank a mortgage on Debtor's factory as collateral. On June 8, the mortgage was executed, and, on June 9, it was recorded. On June 14, an involuntary bankruptcy petition was filed against Debtor. Since the loan was intended by both Debtor and Bank to have been secured contemporaneously by the mortgage, and since the conveyance of the mortgage was substantially contemporaneous with Debtor's receipt of new value ($10,000), the transfer does not constitute a voidable preference even though it was delayed briefly. [B.C. §547(c)(1); Dean v. Davis, 242 U.S. 438 (1917)]

      (2) **Compare:** At 10:00 a.m. on June 1, Bank loaned Debtor $10,000 on an *unsecured* basis. At 2:00 p.m. on the same day, Bank discovered that Debtor was experiencing unusual monetary problems, and it demanded collateral to secure the debt. Debtor immediately complied by delivering certain securities to Bank as collateral. Two hours later, an involuntary bankruptcy petition was filed against Debtor. The transfer of the securities does not come within this exception since it was *not intended* by Debtor and Bank to be a contemporaneous exchange for new value. Thus, the trustee may avoid it as a preference if all the elements of section 547(b) are present. [National City Bank of New York v. Hotchkiss, 231 U.S. 50 (1913)]

      (3) **"New value" defined:** [§381] The Code defines new value as "money or money's worth in goods, services, or new credit, or release by a transferee of property previously transferred to such transferee in a transaction that is neither void nor voidable by the debtor or the trustee. . . ." [B.C. §547(a)(2)]

(a) **Proof:** [§382]   Appellate courts have held that proof of the *specific dollar amount* of new value given to the debtor (*i.e.*, not merely "some" new value) is required to satisfy this exception. [*In re* Spada, 903 F.2d 971 (3d Cir. 1990)]

b. **Transfer in ordinary course of business:** [§383]   A transfer is not voidable to the extent that it was made (i) in the ordinary course of business of the debtor and the transferee, (ii) according to ordinary business terms, and (iii) for the purpose of repaying a debt that the debtor incurred in the ordinary course of business of the debtor and the transferee. [B.C. §547(c)(2); *In re* Fulghum Construction Corp., 872 F.2d 739 (6th Cir. 1989)]

(1) **Criteria:** [§384]   In determining whether the transfer meets these requirements, the courts are likely to consider the following factors: (i) the prior course of dealing between the debtor and the transferee; (ii) the size of the payment; (iii) the timing of the transfer; and (iv) the circumstances under which the transfer was made. [*In re* White, 58 B.R. 266 (Bankr. E.D. Tenn. 1986)] Also, the trend in the appellate courts is to apply an objective test in determining whether the transfer was made "*according to ordinary business terms*," considering both the norms in the creditor's industry and the length of the relationship between the debtor and the creditor. The longer and more consistent the pre-insolvency relationship, "the more the creditor will be allowed to vary its credit terms from the industry norm" and still be covered by the exception. However, unusual departures are not protected. [*In re* Molded Acoustical Products, Inc., 18 F.3d 217 (3d Cir. 1994); Advo-System, Inc. v. Maxway Corp., 37 F.3d 1044 (4th Cir. 1994)]

(2) **Late payments:** [§385]   While all cases are not in accord, it appears that late payments generally do not come within the "ordinary course of business" exception unless they are consistent with the prior course of dealing between the debtor and transferee, and (in many courts) with the practices of the industry. [*In re* Tolona Pizza Products Corp., 3 F.3d 1029 (7th Cir. 1993)—late payments held to be made in ordinary course of business]

(3) **Long-term debt:** [§386]   The Supreme Court has held that payments on long-term debt, as well as payments on short-term debt, may qualify for the "ordinary course of business" exception. [Union Bank v. Wolas, 502 U.S. 151 (1991)]

c. **Purchase money security interest:** [§387]   A purchase money security interest securing *new value* extended to the debtor for the purpose of acquiring certain property described in the security agreement and actually purchased by the debtor with the funds furnished by the creditor is protected from avoidance by the trustee. [B.C. §547(c)(3)]

(1) **Tracing necessary:** [§388]   For this exception to apply, the debtor actually must use the new value received from the creditor to purchase the collateral. [B.C. §547(c)(3)(A)(iv); 4 Collier ¶547.11]

(2) **Perfection within twenty days after possession:** [§389]   The secured party must perfect his purchase money security interest no later than 20

days after the debtor takes possession of the collateral; failure to perfect within that time will render the transfer voidable. [B.C. §547(c)(3)(B)]

d. **Subsequent advance of new value:** [§390] A transfer is nonavoidable to the extent that, *subsequent to the transfer*, the creditor extended *new* (prepetition) value that is "not secured by an otherwise unavoidable security interest" and that has not been repaid by "an otherwise unavoidable transfer." [B.C. §547(c)(4)] This exception is designed to induce creditors to continue extending credit and doing business with debtors in financial straits. [*In re Meredith Manor, Inc.*, 902 F.2d 257 (4th Cir. 1990)] The exception differs from the "net result" rule (a judge-made doctrine under the old Bankruptcy Act of simply adding all the preferences and subtracting all the advances). "This [former practice] is not allowed . . . , since the advance to be offset must be subsequent to the preference." [*In re Fulghum Construction Corp.*, 706 F.2d 171 (6th Cir. 1983)]

(1) **Comment:** For a creditor to use this exception, most courts have required that the new value remain **unpaid**. [*In re* Kroh Brothers Development Co., 930 F.2d 648 (8th Cir. 1991); *In re* Braniff, Inc., 154 B.R. 773 (Bankr. M.D. Fla. 1993)—good discussion] However, a recent trend allows subsequent advances of new value "to offset prior (although not immediately prior) preferences." Under this approach, "a creditor is permitted to carry forward preferences until they are exhausted by subsequent advances of new value." [*In re* IRFM, Inc., 52 F.3d 228 (9th Cir. 1995), *affirming* 144 B.R. 886 (Bankr. C.D. Cal. 1992)—detailed analysis] The latter method appears to be the better approach because it more accurately accounts for any enhancement or depletion of the estate during the preference period.

(2) **Example:** Within 90 days before bankruptcy, the following transactions occur: On August 1, Debtor makes a $50,000 payment to Creditor that constitutes a preference; on August 5, Creditor ships goods worth $40,000 on credit (new value); on September 1, Debtor makes a $40,000 payment out of the ordinary course of business (for the August 5 shipment) to Creditor that constitutes a preference; and on September 5, Creditor ships goods worth $50,000 on credit (new value). Under the "*Kroh Brothers*" approach (above), the trustee can recover $40,000 ($90,000 minus $50,000) because the August 5 extension of new value was fully repaid. However, under the "IRFM" approach (above), the trustee cannot recover anything because the September 1 payment is not "an otherwise unavoidable transfer" (*i.e.*, it would be avoidable but for this exception), and the September 5 extension of new value (which was subsequent to both preferences) covered the $10,000 not covered by the August 5 extension of new value.

e. **Security interest in inventory and receivables:** [§391] A transfer that creates a perfected security interest in the debtor's inventory, receivables, or proceeds of inventory or receivables is voidable only *to the extent that the creditor's position has improved*, to the prejudice of the estate, during the period beginning on the later of the ninetieth day (or one year, if the secured party was an insider at the time of the transfer) before bankruptcy *or* the first date on which the creditor gave new value pursuant to the security agreement, and ending on the date that the petition was filed. [B.C. §547(c)(5); *In re American Ambulance Service, Inc.*, 46 B.R. 658 (Bankr. S.D. Cal. 1985)]

    (1) **Improvement in position test:** [§392] In determining how much, if any, a creditor has improved her position, the court examines the amount of any insufficiency (*i.e.*, the difference between the outstanding balance of the debt owed and the value of the collateral) existing at ***two specific times:*** the ninetieth day before bankruptcy (or the first date on which new value was extended) and the date that the bankruptcy petition was filed. Thus, regardless of any fluctuations during the preference period, the transfer will be voidable only to the extent that the insufficiency has been reduced between these two dates. [*In re* Savig, 50 B.R. 1003 (D. Minn. 1985)]

        (a) **Note:** The transfer would not be voidable if the creditor's improvement in position did not harm the unsecured creditors, such as if the insufficiency's reduction was caused solely by a seasonal appreciation in the value of collateral consisting of an inventory of swimwear held in storage in New York for 90 days from January until the filing of the petition in April. [4 Collier ¶547.13]

    (2) **"Receivable":** [§393] For purposes of a preference, a receivable is defined as a "right to payment, whether or not such right has been earned by performance." [B.C. §547(a)(3)]

  f. **Statutory lien:** [§394] The sixth exception makes the fixing of a statutory lien, such as a tax lien, a mechanic's lien, or an artisan's lien, nonavoidable as a preference ***if the lien cannot be avoided under Bankruptcy Code section 545*** (*see supra*, §§351 *et seq.*), even if it was perfected within 90 days before bankruptcy. [B.C. §547(c)(6); 4 Collier ¶547.14]

    (1) **Example:** On September 1, Sam's Service Station perfects an artisan's lien against Debtor's automobile for unpaid repairs to the engine. On November 1, Debtor files a Chapter 7 bankruptcy petition. Sam's has remained continuously in possession of the automobile, and under the relevant state statute the lien is enforceable against a bona fide purchaser. Since the lien is not avoidable under Code section 545 (*see supra*, §354), it also is not subject to the trustee's power to avoid preferential transfers.

  g. **Alimony and child support:** [§395] Bona fide payment of alimony, or spousal or child support, is not avoidable by the trustee (unless it has been assigned to another entity). [B.C. §547(c)(7)]

  h. **Consumer payments under $600:** [§396] A transfer of property worth less than $600 by an individual debtor with primarily consumer debts (*see supra*, §36) is not avoidable by the trustee. [B.C. §547(c)(8)]

4. **Special Rules for Preferences:** [§397] For the purpose of preference determination, the Code specifies when certain transfers ***are deemed to have been perfected*** and when certain transfers are ***considered to have been made***. [B.C. §547(e)]

  a. **When perfection occurs:** [§398] A transfer of ***real property*** is deemed perfected when, under state law (*i.e.*, recording statutes), it is superior to the interest of a *subsequent bona fide purchaser*. A transfer of *fixtures or personal property* is deemed perfected when, under state law (*i.e.*, U.C.C. Article 9), it is superior to the interest of a *subsequent judicial lien creditor*. [B.C. §547(e)(1); *In re* Busenlehner, 918 F.2d 928 (11th Cir. 1990)]

b. **When transfer is made:** [§399]   For the purpose of preference analysis, the time a transfer is considered to have been made depends on when the transfer was perfected [B.C. §547(e)(2)], provided that the debtor had acquired rights in the property at the time of the transfer [B.C. §547(e)(3); *and see infra*, §403].

   (1) **Perfection within ten days:** [§400]   A transfer is considered to have been made on the date it became effective between the parties if perfection occurs within the next 10 days (except for perfection of a purchase money security interest, for which the grace period is 20 days after the debtor takes possession of the collateral; *see supra*, §389). [B.C. §547(e)(2)(A)]

   (a) **Example:** Debtor is in default on a debt owed to Bank and secured by Blackacre, which is depreciating greatly in value. On June 1, in an attempt to avoid foreclosure, Debtor conveys to Bank a mortgage on Whiteacre as additional collateral for the same debt. On June 9, Bank records the mortgage properly under state law. On September 4, Debtor files a voluntary bankruptcy petition. Since perfection occurred *within 10 days* after the transfer took effect between the parties, the transfer is deemed to have been made on June 1, which is a date outside the 90-day preference period. Therefore, the transfer may not be avoided by the trustee as a preference. [B.C. §547(e)(2)(A)]

   (2) **Perfection after ten days:** [§401]   A transfer is deemed to have been made on the date that it is perfected if perfection occurs more than 10 days after the transfer originally became effective between the parties (except for perfection of a purchase money security interest as noted above). [B.C. §547(e)(2)(B)]

   (a) **Example:** Assume the same facts as in the preceding example except that Bank did not record the mortgage until September 1. Since perfection occurred more than 10 days after the transfer took effect between the parties, the transfer will be deemed to have been made on September 1 (a date well within the 90-day preference period). If the other elements of a preference are met, the trustee may avoid this transfer. [B.C. §547(e)(2)(B)]

   (3) **No perfection before bankruptcy:** [§402]   A transfer is deemed to have been made immediately prior to bankruptcy if perfection has not occurred by the time the petition is filed or within 10 days after the transfer became effective between the parties, whichever is later. [B.C. §547(e)(2)(C)]

   (4) **Debtor's rights in property:** [§403]   Note that with respect to preferences, a transfer is not deemed to have been made until the debtor has obtained rights in the property transferred. [B.C. §547(e)(3)]

(a) **Exception—inventory and receivables:** [§404] Inventory and receivables are not governed by the above rule but, instead, are treated under the improvement in position test (*see supra*, §§392-393). [B.C. §547(c)(5)]

(b) **Rights in garnished wages:** [§405] Although there is a split of authority, the better rule is that, even where a garnishment lien has been executed more than 90 days before bankruptcy, the amounts of the debtor's wages garnished during the preference period are voidable transfers since the debtor does not acquire rights in wages until he has earned them. [*In re* Taylor, 151 B.R. 772 (Bankr. N.D. Miss. 1993); *compare In re* Coppie, 728 F.2d 951 (7th Cir. 1984)]

1) **Exception—consumer debtor:** [§406] This rule, however, is subject to the exception to preferences concerning a transfer of property having an aggregate value of less than $600 by an individual debtor with primarily consumer debts. [B.C. §547(c)(8); *In re* Newell, 71 B.R. 672 (Bankr. M.D. Ga. 1987); *see supra*, §396]

c. **When transfer occurs if debtor pays by check:** [§407] Where the debtor pays a creditor by check, the transfer is deemed to have occurred, for purposes of the section 547(b) preference period, *at the time the bank honors the check*. [Barnhill v. Johnson, 503 U.S. 393 (1992); *and see supra*, §374] On the other hand, most courts have adopted a date of delivery rule for some of the exceptions to preferences [B.C. §547(c); *see supra*, §§379 *et seq*.], and particularly for the subsequent advance exception (*see supra*, §390) [*In re* Kroh Brothers Development Co., 930 F.2d 648 (8th Cir. 1991)] The Supreme Court expressed no view on this issue. [*See* Barnhill v. Johnson, *supra*]

(1) **Note:** This issue can take on great importance when the debtor's check is delivered to the creditor more than 90 days before bankruptcy but is honored by the bank within the preference period.

5. **Burden of Proof:** [§408] The trustee has the burden of proof concerning the existence of a voidable preference, but the creditor bears the burden of proof concerning any exception that might be asserted. [B.C. §547(g)]

G. TRUSTEE'S POWER TO AVOID FRAUDULENT TRANSFERS

1. **In General:** [§409] The trustee has the power to avoid a fraudulent transfer of the debtor's interest in property or the fraudulent incurring of an obligation if the transfer was made or the obligation was incurred by the debtor, voluntarily or involuntarily, *within one year* prior to bankruptcy. [B.C. §548(a)]

2. **"Transfer":** [§410] A transfer is a *voluntary or involuntary* disposition of property or an interest in property. A transfer includes, for example, the debtor's conveyance of a security interest or mortgage, the fixing of a lien on the debtor's property by judicial process, or even a foreclosure sale of collateral securing a debt. [B.C. §101(54); *see supra*, §38]

a. **When transfer occurs:** [§411] For purposes of Bankruptcy Code section 548, a transfer is deemed to have been made when it is sufficiently perfected to preclude a subsequent bona fide purchaser from acquiring a superior interest in the property. However, if such perfection has not occurred prior to the filing of the petition, the time of the conveyance is deemed to be immediately prior to bankruptcy. [B.C. §548(d)(1)]

3. **"Fraudulent" Transfer:** [§412] A transfer may be considered fraudulent not only when there is *actual intent* to hinder, delay, or defraud a creditor, but also in cases deemed to constitute *constructive fraud* where the debtor did not receive back something of reasonably equivalent value and (i) was insolvent or rendered insolvent, (ii) was undercapitalized after the transfer, or (iii) intended to incur debts beyond his ability to repay. [B.C. §548(a)]

   a. **Actual intent to hinder, delay, or defraud:** [§413] A transfer of the debtor's property is fraudulent if it was made with *actual intent* to hinder, delay, or defraud a creditor. [B.C. §548(a)(1)]

      (1) **Example:** On March 1, Debtor, who was hopelessly in debt, transferred all of his assets into his wife's name for no consideration and for the express purpose of placing them out of the reach of his creditors. On March 3, Debtor filed a voluntary bankruptcy petition. The trustee may avoid the conveyance of Debtor's assets as a fraudulent transfer and may recover them for the benefit of the estate. [B.C. §548(a)(1)]

      (2) **Badges of fraud:** [§414] Since the debtor's actual intent to hinder, delay, or defraud creditors usually is not as obvious as in the example above, the law has developed certain "badges of fraud" which *circumstantially may infer actual intent*. Some of these indicators are [*In re Kaiser,* 722 F.2d 1574 (2d Cir. 1983)]:

         (a) When *inadequate or no consideration* is received for the transfer;

         (b) When the *transferee is a relative or a close friend* of the debtor;

         (c) When the *debtor continues to enjoy the use* of the property for his personal benefit;

         (d) When the *conveyance occurs during or following the debtor's incurrence of financial problems*; and

         (e) When the *debtor transfers his assets to a corporation that he completely controls*.

      (3) **Insolvency not required:** [§415] If actual intent can be proved, the transfer is voidable regardless of whether the debtor was insolvent at the time of the transfer.

   b. **Receipt of less than reasonably equivalent value and debtor's insolvency:** [§416] A transfer also is considered to be fraudulent if the debtor received less than reasonably equivalent value for the transfer and was insolvent (*see supra,* §37) on the date the conveyance occurred or became insolvent as a consequence of it. [B.C. §548(a)(2)(A), (B)(i); *In re* Rodriguez, 895 F.2d 725 (11th Cir. 1990)]

(1) **Example:** On January 1, Debtor Corporation redeemed 100 shares of stock from Shareholder, giving Shareholder, in exchange, a $300,000 promissory note and a security interest in all of its inventory, accounts receivable, and equipment. The redeemed shares were practically worthless to Debtor Corporation, and the additional liability of $300,000 caused it to become insolvent. On December 1 of the same year, an involuntary petition was filed against Debtor Corporation. The transaction with Shareholder was a fraudulent transfer and could be avoided by the bankruptcy trustee. [*See In re* Roco Corp., 701 F.2d 978 (1st Cir. 1983)]

(2) **"Value" defined:** [§417] For purposes of section 548, value includes not only property, but also the "satisfaction or securing of a present or antecedent debt of the debtor." [B.C. §548(d)(2)(A)]

(3) **Foreclosure sales:** [§418] Since a foreclosure sale of the debtor's property constitutes a *transfer* [B.C. §101(54); *see supra*, §38], it can result in a fraudulent transfer if it occurs when the debtor is insolvent or if it renders the debtor insolvent, *and* the debtor receives less than reasonably equivalent value from the proceeds of the sale. [B.C. §548(a)(2)(A), (B)(i)]

    (a) **"Reasonably equivalent value":** [§419] The Supreme Court has held that the sale price received at a *noncollusive* foreclosure sale conclusively constitutes reasonably equivalent value, if "all the requirements of the State's foreclosure law have been complied with." [BFP v. RTC, 114 S. Ct. 1757 (1994)]

        1) **But note:** Any fraud, collusion, or other defect in the sale that would invalidate it under state law "will deprive the sale price of its conclusive force" and subject the sale to possible avoidance under section 548(a)(1) or (a)(2)(A). [BFP v. RTC, *supra*]

c. **Receipt of less than reasonably equivalent value and debtor's undercapitalization:** [§420] A transfer also is deemed fraudulent if the debtor received less than reasonably equivalent value for the transfer, after which there was unreasonably small capital remaining for the operation of the debtor's business. [B.C. §548(a)(2)(A), (B)(ii)]

(1) **Example:** Parent Corporation has defaulted on its indebtedness to Bank. In an effort to refinance, Parent arranges for its wholly owned subsidiary, Debtor, to borrow $250,000 from Bank, *secured by Debtor's assets*, with a portion of the funds going to Parent and the rest being used to repay Parent's outstanding debt to Bank. Debtor receives no benefit from the transaction and, as a result, has insufficient working capital remaining to operate its business. Eight months later, it files a voluntary bankruptcy petition. The trustee will be able to avoid the transfer (*i.e.*, the security interest in Debtor's assets), and Bank will be treated as an unsecured creditor. [Wells Fargo Bank v. Desert View Building Supplies, Inc., 475 F. Supp. 693 (D. Nev. 1978), *aff'd*, 633 F.2d 225 (9th Cir. 1980)]

(2) **Leveraged buyout:** [§421] The purchase of a target corporation sometimes is accomplished by means of a leveraged buyout (also called

"asset-based lending"), in which the purchasing company uses the assets of the target corporation as collateral for a bank loan obtained to finance the purchase price. If the transaction results in the undercapitalization or insolvency of the company acquired, the transfer might constitute a fraudulent conveyance in the event of the target corporation's bankruptcy, because the target does not receive reasonably equivalent value in exchange for the grant of a security interest in *its own assets*. Instead, value in the form of the loan proceeds is given to the purchasing company, which uses the funds to pay the seller. [United States v. Tabor Court Realty Corp., 803 F.2d 1288 (3d Cir. 1986); Wieboldt Stores, Inc. v. Schottenstein, 94 B.R. 488 (N.D. Ill. 1988); *but see* Mellon Bank, N.A. v. Metro Communications, Inc., 945 F.2d 635 (3d Cir. 1991)—indirect benefits may be evaluated (*e.g.*, debtor's ability to borrow money and creation of strong synergy by new affiliation); *and see* Moody v. Security Pacific Business Credit, Inc., 971 F.2d 1056 (3d Cir. 1992—debtor neither rendered insolvent nor left with unreasonably small capital]

d. **Receipt of less than reasonably equivalent value and debtor's intentional overextension:** [§422] Another kind of transfer that is also deemed to be fraudulent is where the debtor receives less than reasonably equivalent value for the transfer and intends to incur debts that he will be unable to repay as they mature. [B.C. §548(a)(2)(A), (B)(iii)]

e. **Compare—third-party transactions with indirect benefit to debtor:** [§423] While a transfer benefiting *only* a nondebtor third party does not yield reasonably equivalent value to the debtor, a transaction that ultimately provides consideration or economic benefit to the debtor, after passing through the hands of a third party, is not a fraudulent transfer if the consideration received indirectly by the debtor constitutes reasonably equivalent value. [Rubin v. Manufacturers Hanover Trust Co., 661 F.2d 979 (2d Cir. 1981)]

  (1) **Example:** On January 1, Third Party borrows $100,000 from Bank, with the understanding that the loan is solely for the benefit of Debtor Corporation. On the same day, Third Party loans the $100,000 to Debtor Corporation, which makes the regular monthly interest payments to Bank. On December 1, Debtor Corporation files a voluntary bankruptcy petition. Even if Debtor Corporation was insolvent when the interest payments were made, they are not fraudulent transfers since they constitute reasonably equivalent value in exchange for the consideration received indirectly by Debtor Corporation. [*See In re* Holly Hill Medical Center, Inc., 44 B.R. 253 (Bankr. M.D. Fla. 1984)]

4. **Good Faith Transferee:** [§424] A good faith transferee for value is entitled to retain, or to receive a lien on, any property conveyed to her, *to the extent of* **any value given** by the transferee to the debtor. [B.C. §548(c)] This provision applies to transfers voidable under section 548, unless the transfer also is subject to the trustee's avoiding power under section 544, 545, or 547 (*see supra*, §§351 *et seq.*).

  a. **Good faith:** [§425] "Good faith" requires the indicia of an arm's length transaction, taking into account all of the surrounding circumstances. [Bullard v. Aluminum Co. of America, 468 F.2d 11 (7th Cir. 1972)]

5. **Partnership Debtor:** [§426] Any transfer by a partnership debtor *to a general partner* within one year prior to bankruptcy is voidable if it was made at a time when the debtor was insolvent or if it caused the debtor to become insolvent. [B.C. §548(b)]

H. POST-PETITION TRANSACTIONS

1. **General Rule—Avoidance:** [§427] The trustee may avoid a transfer of estate property occurring after the filing of the bankruptcy petition, unless the transfer comes within one of the exceptions described below or is authorized under the Bankruptcy Code or approved by the court. [B.C. §549(a)]

    a. **Example:** Debtor owed $1 million in federal excise taxes at the time it filed its bankruptcy petition on January 1. All of the tax liability related directly to pre-petition sales. On February 1, Debtor paid $500,000 to the Internal Revenue Service on this liability. The trustee may avoid the post-petition transfer in its entirety. [*In re* Air Florida Systems, Inc., 50 B.R. 653 (Bankr. S.D. Fla. 1985)]

    b. **Compare:** Debtor, a widget manufacturer, files a voluntary Chapter 11 petition. A trustee is not appointed, and Debtor continues to operate the business as a debtor in possession, making numerous sales of widgets in the ordinary course of business. Since the Bankruptcy Code permits these types of transactions without court approval, they are valid post-petition transfers and are not subject to avoidance. [B.C. §363(c)(1); *see infra*, §840]

2. **Transferor Without Notice or Knowledge:** [§428] A transferor (such as a bank) that has neither actual notice nor knowledge of the bankruptcy case is protected from liability concerning a good faith post-petition transfer. [B.C. §542(c); *see supra*, §324] This occurs, for example, when a bank honors the debtor's check after the commencement of the case. Although the bank is not liable, the transferee may be subject to the trustee's avoiding power under Code section 549(a)(2)(A).

    a. **Example:** Debtor is in the retail business of selling widgets, and on June 1, it pays $10,000 by checks to its suppliers. On June 3, Debtor files a voluntary bankruptcy petition, and on June 5, all of the checks are honored by Bank, in good faith and without actual notice or knowledge of the case. No liability will be imposed on Bank since it acted in good faith and without notice or knowledge of Debtor's bankruptcy petition. [B.C. §542(c)] If the transfers are deemed to have occurred when Bank *paid* the checks, they are post-petition payments of pre-petition debts and thus are avoidable by the trustee. [B.C. §549(a)(2)(A); *see In re* Isis Foods, Inc., 37 B.R. 334 (W.D. Mo. 1984)] However, if the transfers are deemed to have occurred when the checks were *delivered* to the creditors (suppliers), they are pre-petition payments and thus are not subject to avoidance as post-petition transfers. [Quinn Wholesale, Inc. v. Northern, 873 F.2d 77 (4th Cir. 1989)] *Note*: If the transfers are treated as pre-petition, they may be avoidable as preferences under Code section 547 (*see supra*, §§364 *et seq.*).

3. **Exceptions to Trustee's Avoidance:** [§429] The trustee's power to avoid post-petition transfers is subject to the following exceptions and limitations:

a. **Gap transferee in involuntary case:** [§430] While the debtor may continue to operate its business and dispose of property during the period between the filing of an involuntary petition and the entry of an order for relief [B.C. §303(f); *see supra*, §174], the trustee may exercise the avoiding power against a gap transferee *except to the extent of any post-petition value, including services* given by the transferee. This exception does not include the satisfaction or securing of a pre-petition debt. [B.C. §549(a)(2)(A), (b); *and see supra*, §175]

   (1) **Example:** On May 10, an involuntary Chapter 11 petition is filed against Debtor by several of its creditors. On May 20, Debtor sells yarn having a fair market value of $1,000 to Customer for the price of $750. On May 30, an order for relief is entered, and a trustee is appointed. The trustee may avoid the transfer (and recover for the benefit of the estate) only to the extent of $250, the amount by which the value of the yarn transferred exceeds the price paid by Customer. [*In re* Jorges Carpet Mills, Inc., 41 B.R. 60 (Bankr. E.D. Tenn. 1984)]

   (2) **Notice or knowledge irrelevant:** [§431] This exception applies regardless of whether the gap transferee has notice or knowledge of the bankruptcy case. [B.C. §549(b)]

b. **Bona fide purchaser of real property:** [§432] A post-petition transfer of real property to a good faith purchaser who does not know of the bankruptcy case and has paid *present fair equivalent value* cannot be avoided by the trustee if notice of the bankruptcy case has not been filed, prior to perfection of the transfer, in the office where real property transactions are recorded for the county in which the land is located. [B.C. §549(c); 4 Collier ¶549.03(3); *In re* Konowitz, 905 F.2d 55 (4th Cir. 1990)—unperfected post-petition foreclosure avoidable by trustee]

   (1) **Less than present fair equivalent value:** [§433] If notice of the bankruptcy petition has not been filed in the proper office for recording before perfection of the transfer, and a good faith purchaser without knowledge of the case has given less than present fair equivalent value, she is entitled to a lien on the property, but only to the extent of the *present value furnished*. [B.C. §549(c)]

I. LIMITATIONS ON TRUSTEE'S AVOIDING POWERS

1. **Statute of Limitations:** [§434] Most of the trustee's avoiding powers are subject to a statute of limitations requiring that the trustee file an action to avoid a transfer before the *earlier* of (i) the later of *two years* after the entry of the order for relief, or *one year* after the appointment or election of the first trustee if the appointment or election occurs before the expiration of the two-year period, or (ii) *the time of the closing or dismissal* of the case. [B.C. §546(a)] This section resolves an issue that had divided the courts concerning the statute of limitations for avoiding powers in Chapter 11 cases where a trustee was appointed.

   a. **Transfers affected:** [§435] This period of limitations applies to a trustee's action to avoid a setoff [B.C. §553], a statutory lien [B.C. §545], a transfer avoidable under the strongarm clause [B.C. §544(a)], a transfer avoidable by the trustee as successor to certain actual creditors [B.C. §544(b)], a preference [B.C. §547], or a fraudulent transfer [B.C. §548].

 b. **Compare—statute of limitations for avoidance of post-petition transactions:** [§436] To avoid a post-petition transfer, the trustee must file an action before the *earlier* of (i) two years after the *transfer* was made, or (ii) the time of the closing or dismissal of the case. [B.C. §549(d)]

 c. **Equitable tolling:** [§437] Case law has consistently held that limitation periods may be equitably tolled because of wrongful conduct that was not discovered by the trustee, "without any fault or want of diligence or care on his part." [*In re* Olsen, 36 F.3d 71 (9th Cir. 1994)—limitation period under section 549(d) tolled; *In re* United Insurance Management, Inc., 14 F.3d 1380 (9th Cir. 1994)—equitable tolling may apply to section 546(a)(1), but not here, due to trustee's lack of diligence]

2. **Retroactive Perfection:** [§438] The trustee's avoiding powers under Code sections 544(a) (strongarm clause), 544(b) (successor to certain actual creditors), 545 (certain statutory liens), and 549 (post-petition transactions) are subject to any applicable nonbankruptcy law that permits retroactive perfection of a security interest. Such laws usually are state statutes, such as U.C.C. section 9-301(2), which provides a 10 (or 20)-day grace period in which to perfect a purchase money security interest that will have priority over an intervening lien creditor. Thus, when such a statute applies, the Bankruptcy Code allows a creditor to perfect its security interest *post-petition* with retroactive effect, provided that such perfection occurs within the time permitted under the applicable nonbankruptcy law. [B.C. §546(b)(1)(A); *In re* Griggs, 965 F.2d 54 (6th Cir. 1992)]

 a. **Example:** Debtor borrows $10,000 from Bank and grants Bank a purchase money security interest in a new business computer that Debtor purchases with the loan proceeds on April 1 and takes into his possession on the same day. On April 5, Debtor files a voluntary bankruptcy petition, and on April 6, Bank files a U.C.C. financing statement to perfect its security interest in the computer. Applicable state law provides a 10-day grace period, after the debtor acquires possession of the collateral, within which the secured party may perfect a purchase money security interest and still have priority over an intervening lien creditor. Therefore, the trustee, having the rights of a hypothetical judicial lien creditor on the date of bankruptcy, is subject to Bank's retroactive perfection, and will be unable to avoid Bank's purchase money security interest. [B.C. §546(b); U.C.C. §9-301(2)]

 b. **Continuation statements:** [§439] The trustee's rights and avoiding powers under sections 544(a) (strongarm clause), 544(b) (successor to certain actual creditors), 545 (certain statutory liens), and 549 (post-petition transfers) also are subject to any applicable law permitting secured creditors to maintain or continue perfection of an interest in property, such as by filing a continuation statement under U.C.C. section 9-403(3). [B.C. §546(b)(1)(B)]

 c. **Exception to automatic stay:** [§440] The post-petition perfection described above (*see supra*, §438), and the filing of a continuation statement (*see supra*, §439) *are excepted* from the statutory injunction of the automatic stay. [B.C. §362(b)(3)]

3. **Seller's Reclamation of Goods:** [§441] The Bankruptcy Code provides for a seller's statutory or common law right to reclaim goods from an insolvent buyer (such as under U.C.C. section 2-702(2)) to prevail over the trustee's power to avoid (i) a transfer under the strongarm clause [B.C. §544(a)], (ii) a statutory lien [B.C. §545], (iii) a preference [B.C. §547], or (iv) a post-petition transfer [B.C. §549]. [*See* B.C. §546(c)]

   a. **Elements required for reclamation:** [§442] The following elements must be present for a *seller* to reclaim goods from the debtor [B.C. §546(c)]:

      (1) **Goods:** [§443] The property sought to be reclaimed must be goods. The overwhelming weight of authority refuses to allow reclamation of proceeds [*In re* Coast Trading Co., 744 F.2d 686 (9th Cir. 1984)], although, in one nonbankruptcy case, the court ruled (by analogy to Bankruptcy Code section 546(c)) that a reclaiming seller could be granted a priority claim in proceeds that were traced to the goods [United States v. Westside Bank, 732 F.2d 1258 (5th Cir. 1984)].

      (2) **Sale in ordinary course of seller's business:** [§444] For the seller to reclaim the goods, the seller must have sold the goods to the debtor in the ordinary course of the seller's business. [B.C. §546(c)]

      (3) **Debtor insolvent:** [§445] The debtor must have received the goods while insolvent under the bankruptcy ("balance sheet") definition of insolvency. [B.C. §101(32), *see supra*, §37; *In re* Storage Technology Corp., 48 B.R. 862 (D. Colo. 1985)]

         (a) **"Receipt":** [§446] The debtor is deemed to have received the goods when it has taken *physical possession* of them. For example, gasoline was considered to have been received when it was pumped by the common carrier into the storage tanks of the debtor. [U.C.C. §2-103(1)(c); *In re* Marin Motor Oil, Inc., 740 F.2d 220 (3d Cir. 1984)]

      (4) **Written demand for reclamation:** [§447] The seller must have made a written demand for reclamation no later than *10 days* after the debtor received the goods. However, if the 10-day period expires after the commencement of the bankruptcy case, the demand must be made no later than *20 days* after the goods were received. [B.C. §546(c)(1)]

         (a) **Demand must specify reclamation:** [§448] The seller's demand must indicate clearly that the seller seeks reclamation; a demand for the payment of damages is not sufficient. [*In re* Marin Motor Oil, Inc., *supra*]

         (b) **Compare—U.C.C. demand:** [§449] While the demand required of the seller under U.C.C. section 2-702(2) may be oral or written, the demand under the Bankruptcy Code must be *in writing*. [B.C. §546(c)(1)] Also, the exception to the 10-day rule found in U.C.C. section 2-702(2) concerning the debtor's written misrepresentation to the seller does not apply in bankruptcy. [*In re* Charter Co., 52 B.R. 263 (Bankr. M.D. Fla. 1985)]

(c) **Dispatch rule:** [§450]   For the purpose of determining whether the seller's demand has been made timely, some courts consider the demand effective upon dispatch (rather than upon receipt), provided that the method of communication is commercially reasonable. For example, in one case, the demand was held to be timely where it was telexed on the evening of the tenth day, with the debtor receiving the message on the morning of the eleventh day. [*In re* Marin Motor Oil, Inc., *supra*]

b. **Denial of reclamation:** [§451]   Reclamation is not a mandatory remedy, and thus where all the essential elements for reclamation (including the seller's demand) have been satisfied, the court nonetheless may deny the seller's reclamation of goods from the debtor. In such case, the court is required to grant the seller either a lien securing his claim or an administrative expense priority. [B.C. §§546(c)(2), 503(b); *see infra*, §537]

c. **Seller's right to stop goods in transit:** [§452]   Relevant judicial interpretation also has construed the Code's reclamation provision as subjecting the specified avoiding powers of the trustee (*see supra*, §441) to the seller's state-law right to stop goods in transit upon learning of the debtor's insolvency. [U.C.C. §§2-702(1), 2-705(1); *In re* National Sugar Refining Co., 27 B.R. 565 (S.D.N.Y 1983)]

d. **Grain farmers and United States fishermen:** [§453]   The Code contains a similar provision allowing the reclamation of grain or fish sold by a grain farmer or a United States fisherman, respectively, to a grain storage facility or a fish processing facility that is owned or operated by the debtor, and that has received such goods while insolvent. [B.C. §546(d)]

4. **Return of Goods:** [§454]   A Chapter 11 debtor may, with the creditor's consent, return goods shipped by the creditor before bankruptcy, and the creditor may offset the purchase price against any pre-petition claim. This action requires a motion by the trustee within 120 days after the order for relief, notice and a hearing, and a determination by the court that a return is in the estate's best interests. [B.C. §546(g)—but should be lettered (h)]

J. TRANSFEREE'S LIABILITY TO ESTATE FOR AVOIDED TRANSFER

1. **Automatic Preservation for Benefit of Estate:** [§455]   Any transfer that has been avoided or any lien that is void under Bankruptcy Code section 506(d) (*see infra*, §533) is automatically preserved for the estate's benefit. [B.C. §551]

2. **What Trustee May Recover:** [§456]   By avoiding a transfer, the trustee is entitled to recover *either the property transferred* or, if ordered by the court, *its value*. [B.C. §550(a)]

3. **From Whom Trustee May Recover:** [§457]   The trustee may seek recovery from: (i) the initial transferee, (ii) the entity whom the initial transfer was designed to benefit, or (iii) any future transferee after the first transfer. [B.C. §550(a); *In re* Bullion Reserve of North America, 922 F.2d 544 (9th Cir. 1991)]

a. **Initial transferee:** [§458]   Where a transfer is made directly from the debtor to another entity, that entity will be deemed the initial transferee only if he has "dominion or control over the funds," *i.e.*, "the right to put the money to one's own use." [*In re* Coutee, 984 F.2d 138 (5th Cir. 1993)—bank, rather than law firm, held to be initial transferee concerning funds deposited in firm's trust account and then paid to bank in repayment of client's loan from bank]

(1) **Example:** Debtor owes Creditor $7,000, and Creditor assigns the claim to Collection Agency. On May 20, Collection Agency obtains a judgment against Debtor, and on July 9, it executes on Debtor's bank account and collects approximately $5,300. On July 10, Debtor files a Chapter 11 bankruptcy petition. On July 14, Collection Agency pays Creditor $3,700, but retains approximately $1,600 as its fee. The July 9 transfer can be *avoided* as a preference. Hence, $3,700 can be *recovered* from Creditor, and $1,600 can be *recovered* from Collection Agency, the initial transferee. [B.C. §550(a); *In re* Mill Street, Inc., 96 B.R. 268 (Bankr. 9th Cir. 1989)]

b. **Exception—good faith future transferees:** [§459] The trustee may not recover from a *future transferee* who (i) did not know that the transfer was voidable, (ii) took the transfer in good faith, and (iii) gave value in exchange. Furthermore, all subsequent good faith transferees of such a future transferee are protected. [B.C. §550(b)]

(1) **Value:** [§460] For purposes of this exception, value includes the "satisfaction or securing of a present or antecedent debt." [B.C. §550(b)(1)]

c. **"DePrizio" problem fixed:** [§461] Prior to the Bankruptcy Reform Act of 1994, the authorities were divided as to whether a transfer to a non-insider creditor, made between 90 days and a year before bankruptcy and benefiting an insider-guarantor, if avoided as a preference, could be *recovered* from the outside creditor. The Code was amended to disallow recovery from a non-insider transferee under those circumstances. [B.C. §550(c)]

(1) **Example:** On January 1, Debtor Corporation, while insolvent, paid $100,000 to Bank in full satisfaction of an unsecured antecedent loan, which had been guaranteed by Officer of Debtor Corporation. Still insolvent on June 1, Debtor Corporation filed a voluntary bankruptcy petition. The trustee will succeed in *avoiding* the January 1 transfer as a preference (even though it occurred more than 90 days before bankruptcy) because the transfer benefited Officer, an insider-guarantor, and was made within one year before the bankruptcy petition was filed. [B.C. §547(b)(4)(B); *and see supra*, §374] However, the trustee cannot *recover* the $100,000 from Bank, a non-insider, and any recovery will have to come from Officer, the insider-guarantor. [B.C. §550(c)]

(2) **Comment:** The amendment to section 550 did not cure the problem entirely, such as where a payment to a fully secured creditor (*e.g.*, first mortgagee) benefits an undersecured creditor (*e.g.*, second mortgagee). Under the literal language of section 550(a)(1), the payment still is recoverable from the first mortgagee—the initial transferee, and the amendment does not alter this result.

4. **Single Satisfaction:** [§462]   A trustee who has avoided a transfer is permitted only one satisfaction in the case. [B.C. §550(d)]

5. **Good Faith Transferee's Lien:** [§463]   If the trustee recovers from a good faith transferee under Bankruptcy Code section 550(a), the transferee receives a lien on the property recovered, for the purpose of securing the cost of any improvements he made after the transfer (less any profits from the property), or the amount by which such improvements enhanced the property's value, whichever figure is smaller. [B.C. §550(e)]

6. **Statute of Limitations:** [§464]   To recover property or its value under section 550, the trustee must institute an action before the earlier of (i) *one year* after the corresponding transfer was avoided, or (ii) the *time of the closing or dismissal* of the case. [B.C. §550(f)]

K. POST-PETITION EFFECT OF SECURITY INTEREST

1. **General Rule for After-Acquired Property Clauses:** [§465]   An after-acquired property clause in a pre-petition security agreement is *not* effective to create a security interest in property acquired by the debtor or the estate *after* the filing of the bankruptcy petition. [B.C. §552(a); *In re* Transportation Design & Technology, Inc., 48 B.R. 635 (Bankr. S.D. Cal. 1985)] *Note:* This provision applies only to *consensual liens*, and thus it does not apply to federal tax liens, since they are statutory. [B.C. §101(50), (51); *In re* May Reporting Services, Inc., 115 B.R. 652 (Bankr. D.S.D. 1990)]

2. **Exception—Certain Post-Petition Proceeds:** [§466]   If the security interest created by a pre-petition security agreement includes collateral that the debtor *acquired prior to bankruptcy* and also the proceeds, profits, product, or offspring of such collateral, then the security interest is deemed valid and operative as to any such proceeds and similar property that the estate obtains post-petition. [B.C. §552(b)(1); United Virginia Bank v. Slab Fork Coal Co., 784 F.2d 1188 (4th Cir. 1986); *and see In re* Bumper Sales, Inc., 907 F.2d 1430 (4th Cir. 1990)—second generation traceable proceeds (post-petition inventory, accounts, and identifiable cash) covered by exception]

    a. **Note—judicial discretion allowed:** [§467]   The court has the authority not to apply this exception, depending on the equities. For example, in a case where the trustee or the debtor in possession has used or invested other property of the estate to effect an appreciation in the value of the secured party's collateral (*e.g.*, by converting raw materials into finished products), thereby producing post-petition proceeds that exceed the collateral's original value, the court may refuse to extend the security interest to the proceeds. Notice and a hearing are required. [B.C. §552(b)(1); J. Catton Farms v. First National Bank of Chicago, 779 F.2d 1242 (7th Cir. 1985)]

3. **Exception—Certain Post-Petition Rents and Room Revenues:** [§468]   One of the amendments in the Bankruptcy Reform Act of 1994 benefits secured creditors whose pre-petition security interest in real property extends to the rents or hotel/motel room revenues from that property. Prior to this amendment, post-petition rents would have been covered only if the security interest in them had been fully perfected under state law before bankruptcy (which may have required some action

not taken by the creditor, such as actual possession of the real property), and whether post-petition hotel/motel room revenues were covered was highly questionable. Now, if the assignment of rents or hotel/motel *room* revenues (which do not include, for example, restaurant and bar revenues) is specified in the mortgage, they will be treated as secured, and as cash collateral, unless the court orders otherwise based on the equities of the case. [B.C. §§552(b)(2); 363(a); *see infra*, §845]

L. ABANDONMENT OF ESTATE PROPERTY

1. **Inconsequential or Burdensome Property:** [§469] The trustee may abandon property that is burdensome or of inconsequential value to the estate. Notice and the opportunity for a hearing are required; however, the court is not likely to conduct a hearing unless an objection to the abandonment is filed. [B.C. §554(a); Bankruptcy Rule 6007; *see supra*, §14] Generally, when abandonment occurs, the property is considered to be abandoned to the debtor, although abandonment does not affect the continuing validity of a secured creditor's lien on the property. Thus, following abandonment of property subject to a lien, the debtor might reaffirm the debt (if agreeable to the creditor) or, under appropriate circumstances, redeem the collateral (*see infra*, §§733-755). Otherwise, the secured party usually will seek relief from the automatic stay to obtain possession of the property under applicable nonbankruptcy law.

   a. **Example:** Debtor files a voluntary Chapter 7 petition. Included in the property of the estate is Debtor's car, which has a fair market value of $5,000. Debtor still owes $8,000 of the original purchase price to Finance Company, which holds a perfected security interest in the vehicle. Since there is no equity in the property, the trustee abandons the automobile to Debtor.

   b. **Exception—violation of environmental laws:** [§470] The trustee is prohibited from abandoning estate property that is in violation of state or federal environmental laws if the consequence will be to threaten the health or safety of the public with "imminent and identifiable harm" (*e.g.*, "risks of explosion, fire, contamination of water supplies, destruction of natural resources, and injury, genetic damage, or death through personal contact"). [Midlantic National Bank v. New Jersey Department of Environmental Protection, 474 U.S. 494 (1986)] This exception to the trustee's power of abandonment is narrow and appears to apply "only where there is an imminent danger to public health and safety." [*In re* Smith-Douglass, Inc., 856 F.2d 12 (4th Cir. 1988)] The effect of this restriction on abandonment could result in the trustee's expenditure of "all the unencumbered assets of the estate in remedying the situation." [*See In re* Peerless Plating Co., 70 B.R. 943 (Bankr. S.D. Cal. 1987)]

      (1) **Example:** Debtor operates a waste oil processing facility. Debtor violates a state environmental law by accepting oil contaminated with certain prohibited toxic chemicals, which are extremely dangerous both to the natural environment and to the public. Debtor files a voluntary Chapter 11 petition and subsequently is ordered by the state environmental protection agency to clean up the site. There is no equity in the property, and the expected cost of cleanup is $2.5 million. The case is converted to Chapter 7, and the trustee seeks to abandon the property as burdensome to the estate. Such abandonment will not be permitted because it would violate the state environmental law and would constitute an imminent

threat to the health and safety of the community. [Midlantic National Bank v. New Jersey Department of Environmental Protection, *supra*]

    (2) **Automatic stay:** [§471] An environmental protection agency's cleanup order does not violate the automatic stay, since one of the exceptions permits a state or federal regulatory unit to initiate or continue an action to enforce its regulatory power even after a bankruptcy petition has been filed. [B.C. §362(b)(4); *see infra*, §796]

2. **Request to Abandon Burdensome Property:** [§472] A party in interest may make a motion for abandonment, and the court, after notice and the opportunity for a hearing, may order the trustee to abandon property that is burdensome or of inconsequential value to the estate. [B.C. §554(b)]

3. **Unadministered Property:** [§473] Any property that the debtor has listed in his schedules [B.C. §521(1); *see supra*, §153] that has not been administered before the case is closed is deemed to be abandoned to the debtor unless the court rules differently. [B.C. §554(c)]

M. SOVEREIGN IMMUNITY

1. **Waiver:** [§474] Bankruptcy Code section 106 waives the sovereign immunity of governmental units with respect to a number of bankruptcy issues. [*See* B.C. §106(a)(1)—listing sections] This waiver is intended to apply to monetary recoveries (other than punitive damages award) as well as to declaratory or injunctive relief. [B.C. §106(a)(3)] *But note:* In a recent nonbankruptcy case, the United States Supreme Court has seriously challenged the validity of section 106's waiver of states' sovereign immunity. [*See* Seminole Tribe of Florida v. Florida, 116 S. Ct. 1114, 1131-1132, and footnote 16 (1996); *and see* Ohio Agricultural Commodity Depositors Fund v. Mahern, 116 S. Ct. 1411 (1996)—vacating Seventh Circuit decision that upheld constitutionality of B.C. §106's waiver of sovereign immunity]

2. **Application:** [§475] A governmental unit's sovereign immunity is waived with respect to the automatic stay, preferences, fraudulent transfers, and turnovers, because Code sections 362, 547, 548, and 542 (respectively) are included in the list in Code section 106(a)(1).

    a. **Compare:** It is significant that Code section 541 (*see supra*, §§294 *et seq.*) is excluded from the sections specified in Code section 106(a)(1), the effect of which is that the trustee has no greater rights than the debtor concerning causes of action under section 541. Therefore, if property of the estate includes a debtor's cause of action against a governmental unit that is barred by sovereign immunity, the trustee cannot pursue the action. However, if the property of the estate includes a matured debt (or one payable on demand or order) that would be barred by sovereign immunity, the trustee can sue for the amount of the debt under Code section 542(b) (*see supra*, §320), which is one of the sections with respect to which sovereign immunity is waived.

3. **Offset Against Governmental Claims Permitted:** [§476] Where property of the estate includes a claim against a governmental unit that would be barred by

sovereign immunity, the trustee can offset that claim against a claim of the governmental unit (for example, an unrelated tax claim), but only up to the amount of the government's claim, *regardless of whether a claim of the governmental unit has been filed or allowed*. [B.C. §106(c)]

4. **Compulsory Counterclaims—Sovereign Immunity Waived:** [§477] Where property of the estate includes a claim (otherwise barred by sovereign immunity) that constitutes a compulsory counterclaim to a governmental unit's claim *that has been filed*, the trustee can seek affirmative recovery for the claim (where applicable) in excess of the amount of the claim filed by the governmental unit. [B.C. §106(b)]

[§478]

VI. CLAIMS OF CREDITORS

chapter approach

This chapter discusses (i) who the various claimants are in a bankruptcy case; (ii) how they may qualify to participate in the distribution of the assets of the estate; and (iii) which kinds of claims are paid ahead of others. You must thoroughly understand the following issues to answer exam questions on these topics. Use the following general approach:

1. Ordinarily, the *filing of a proof of claim* (by a creditor) or a *proof of interest* (by an equity security holder) is the first step taken by an entity seeking payment in the case—although it is not required in all instances. Remember that if a creditor does not file a proof of claim, the debtor, trustee, or a co-debtor or surety may file one on the creditor's behalf.

2. Next ascertain *whether a claim is allowable* under Bankruptcy Code section 502. Allowance is the basis for the distribution of assets of the estate, whether in a Chapter 7 liquidation or pursuant to a repayment plan under Chapter 11, 12, or 13. If a claim is not allowed, the creditor will not receive a distributive share of the estate.

3. If an exam question requires you to evaluate a *secured claim*, be sure to determine the value of the property that secures it, since the claim is deemed secured only *up to the value of the collateral*. Therefore, if the claim is undersecured, it will be necessary to bifurcate the claim into two claims: one secured and the other unsecured.

4. When considering *unsecured claims*, determine whether a particular claim fits into any of the *nine priority categories*, which are paid ahead of the rest of the general unsecured claims. The first priority claims are the administrative expenses, followed (in order) by involuntary case gap claims, wages and commissions, employee benefit contributions, claims of grain farmers or United States fishermen, consumer "layaway" claims, alimony and spousal or child support, taxes, and claims of certain federal regulators for the debtor's failure to maintain the capital requirements of an insured depository institution.

5. Check the facts of the question for a *claim of a co-debtor or surety* who has paid the principal creditor. Note that the co-debtor or surety must elect between a claim for reimbursement or contribution, on one hand, or a claim for subrogation (to the rights of the principal creditor) on the other.

6. Finally, keep in mind that sometimes, certain claims or interests are *subordinated* in bankruptcy, such as a claim governed by an enforceable subordination agreement, a claim for rescission or damages arising from the purchase or sale of a security of the debtor, or a claim (usually) involving some misconduct on the part of the claimant that triggers the doctrine of equitable subordination.

A. **FILING PROOFS OF CLAIMS**

1. **Claim:** [§478] The Code defines a claim as a *"right to payment*, whether or not such right is reduced to judgment, liquidated, unliquidated, fixed, contingent, ma-

tured, unmatured, disputed, undisputed, legal, equitable, secured, or unsecured." [B.C. §101(5)(A); *see supra*, §34]

a. **Examples:** The outstanding balance owed to a bank on a promissory note constitutes a claim, even if the remaining installments have not matured as of the date of bankruptcy. [*See also In re* Stewart Foods, Inc., 64 F.3d 141 (4th Cir. 1995)—unmatured payments under nonexecutory contract held to be a claim]

   (1) **Compare:** A shareholder's right to vote for the corporate board of directors is *not* a claim because it does not give rise to a right to payment.

b. **Equitable remedy:** [§479] The right to an equitable remedy for breach of performance is considered a claim if the breach gives rise to a right to payment. [B.C. §101(5)(B); Ohio v. Kovacs, *supra*, §34—a state's right to the payment of a money judgment to enforce a state court's environmental cleanup order against the debtor is a claim; *see also In re* Chateaugay Corp., 944 F.2d 997 (2d Cir. 1991)—an environmental cleanup order is a claim only if it imposes an obligation "entirely as an alternative to a payment right," such as where the governmental unit ordering the cleanup has the option of cleaning up the site itself and suing for the costs (*but see* dicta stating that most environmental injunctions will not constitute claims); *compare In re* Udell, 18 F.3d 403 (7th Cir. 1994)—right to injunction to enforce noncompete covenant held not to be a claim]

c. **Claims against property:** [§480] A claim against property of the debtor is also considered to be a claim against the debtor. [B.C. §102(2)]

d. **Broad interpretation of "claim":** [§481] The majority of courts, recognizing Congress's intent to give "claim" an expansive definition in the bankruptcy context (*see supra*, §34), have held that pre-petition claims may include causes of action arising from pre-bankruptcy conduct and pre-petition legal relationships, but which under state or other applicable nonbankruptcy law would not have accrued until after the petition had been filed. [*In re* Johns-Manville Corp., *supra*, §42; *see also In re* Jensen, 127 B.R. 27 (Bankr. 9th Cir. 1991), *aff'd*, 995 F.2d 925 (9th Cir. 1993); *and see In re* National Gypsum Co., 139 B.R. 397 (N.D. Tex. 1992)—future environmental damages (based on pre-petition conduct) *"fairly contemplated"* at time of bankruptcy are claims]

   (1) **Example:** Victim was a user of an intrauterine device ("IUD") manufactured and sold by Debtor Corporation. The device caused serious bodily harm to Victim before Debtor Corporation filed a Chapter 11 petition, although Victim did not discover the cause of her injury until shortly after the bankruptcy case was filed. Victim has a pre-petition claim since it arose "when the acts giving rise to the alleged liability were performed." [*In re* A.H. Robins Co., 63 B.R. 986 (Bankr. E.D. Va. 1986), *aff'd*, 839 F.2d 198 (4th Cir. 1988); *compare* Lemelle v. Universal Manufacturing Corp., 18 F.3d 1268 (5th Cir. 1994)—pre-petition defects in manufacture of mobile homes causing deaths more than two years after confirmation of Chapter 11 plan did not result in dischargeable claims where decedents had no pre-petition contact, privity, or other relationship with debtor]

(2) **Example:** Debtor operated a restaurant that incurred substantial damage as the result of a fire intentionally caused by Debtor or his agent. More than two years after the fire, Debtor filed a Chapter 11 petition and obtained permission from the bankruptcy court to proceed in a pending state court action against his insurer. Six months after the filing of the petition, the insurance company paid $136,000 in proceeds to certain lessors and mortgagees as loss payees under Debtor's insurance policy, and also filed a counterclaim against Debtor in the state court litigation for the same amount, based on subrogation. The insurance company prevailed in the state court and was awarded a judgment of $136,000. Its subrogation claim against Debtor in his Chapter 11 bankruptcy is treated as a pre-petition claim because all of the operative acts (the leases, mortgages, insurance policy, and the fire) happened prior to bankruptcy. [*In re* Yanks, 49 B.R. 56 (Bankr. S.D. Fla. 1985)]

(3) **Minority view:** [§482] On the other hand, it has been held that a cause of action for indemnity based on the debtor's pre-petition negligence is *not* a pre-petition claim if the third party's suit against the claimant (who, in turn, seeks indemnification from the debtor) was brought *after* the filing of the debtor's bankruptcy petition. The rationale is that the claim for indemnification accrues when the judgment arising from the debtor's negligence is paid, not when the negligent conduct occurred. [*In re* M. Frenville Co., 744 F.2d 332 (3d Cir. 1984), *cert. denied*, 469 U.S. 1160 (1985)] *But note:* The holding in this case has been rejected by many authorities.

e. **Future tort claims:** [§483] Recently, courts have grappled with the issue of whether a tort victim has a claim in the Chapter 11 bankruptcy case of the tortfeasor where the latent pre-petition tort has not yet been discovered by the victim. This question is best illustrated by the asbestos tort claims of victims who have been exposed to asbestos but *whose injuries have not yet become apparent*. These circumstances possibly are covered by the broad definition of "claim." Significantly, courts have held that these potential tort claimants are parties in interest and are entitled to the appointment of a legal representative. [B.C. §1109(b); *In re* Amatex Corp., *supra*, §115; *and see infra*, §1019] Moreover, at least one court has confirmed a Chapter 11 plan that provides for future asbestos tort claimants, even though these claimants were not accorded creditor status. [Kane v. Johns-Manville Corp., 843 F.2d 636 (2d Cir. 1988); *compare* Epstein v. Official Committee of Unsecured Creditors, 58 F.3d 1573 (11th Cir. 1995)—class of future claimants did not hold claims because there was "no preconfirmation exposure to a specific identifiable defective product [here, aircraft or parts] or other preconfirmation relationship"] *Note:* The Bankruptcy Code now provides for the type of trust/injunction used in the *Johns-Manville* case (*supra*) in Chapter 11 cases involving *asbestos-related liabilities*. [B.C. §524(g); *see infra*, §§1134-1137]

2. **Claimants**

a. **Who must file:** [§484] Generally, for his claim or interest to be allowed, an *unsecured creditor* must file a proof of claim and an *equity security holder* must file a proof of interest. [Bankruptcy Rule 3002; *but see infra*, §§490-491, 495, 500]

b. **Who may file:** [§485] A *proof of claim* may be filed by a secured creditor, an unsecured creditor, or an indenture trustee; a *proof of interest* may be filed by an equity security holder. [B.C. §501(a)] If a creditor fails to file a proof of claim, one may be filed for the creditor by a co-debtor, surety, or guarantor; by the debtor; or by the trustee. [B.C. §501(b), (c); *see infra*, §§490-491]

   (1) **Creditor:** [§486] A creditor is an entity holding a claim against the debtor that arose or is deemed to have arisen *at or prior to the order of relief*. A creditor may also be an entity possessing a community claim. [B.C. §101(10)]

   (2) **Indenture trustee:** [§487] An indenture trustee is a trustee under a mortgage, deed of trust, or indenture contract relating to an outstanding security of the debtor. For example, if the debtor issues $10 million of debentures, the indenture is the bond contract, and the indenture trustee is the representative of the bondholders. [B.C. §101(28), (29)]

   (3) **Equity security holder:** [§488] An equity security holder is one in possession of a share in a corporation, an interest in a limited partnership, or a warrant (other than a right to convert) to buy or sell an equity security. [B.C. §101(16), (17)]

   (4) **Class of creditors:** [§489] There is a split of authority concerning whether a proof of claim may be filed for a class of creditors who are similarly situated, but the trend at the appellate level appears to allow this practice. [*In re* American Reserve Corp., 840 F.2d 487 (7th Cir. 1988)—yes; *In re* Charter Co., 876 F.2d 866 (11th Cir. 1989)—yes; Reid v. White Motor Corp., 886 F.2d 1462 (6th Cir. 1989)—yes; *In re* Standard Metals Corp., 817 F.2d 625 (10th Cir. 1987)—no]

   (5) **Co-debtor, surety, or guarantor:** [§490] A co-debtor, surety, or guarantor of the debtor may file a proof of claim *for a creditor* if the creditor has not timely filed a proof of claim in her own behalf. [B.C. §501(b); 3 Collier ¶501.02] The purpose of this filing is to decrease the surety's ultimate liability to the extent of a distribution to the principal creditor from the estate. [Bankruptcy Rule 3005(a)]

   (6) **Debtor or trustee:** [§491] If a creditor does not file a proof of claim on or before the first date set for the section 341 meeting of creditors (*see supra*, §§191-203), the debtor or the trustee may file a proof of claim *in the creditor's name.* [B.C. §501(c); Bankruptcy Rule 3004] This course of action could be advantageous to the debtor, especially if the debt owed to the creditor is nondischargeable (*see infra*, §§675 *et seq.*), since any distribution in the bankruptcy case would reduce the debtor's post-bankruptcy liability for a debt that is not discharged. [*In re* Johnson, 95 B.R. 197 (Bankr. D. Colo. 1989)]

3. **Time to File:** [§492] The time within which to file a proof of claim or interest depends on the chapter of the Bankruptcy Code governing the particular case.

   a. **Chapters 7, 12, and 13:** [§493] In a Chapter 7, 12, or 13 case, a proof of claim ordinarily must be filed within *90 days* after the first date set for the section 341 meeting. [Bankruptcy Rule 3002(c)]

b. **Chapter 11:** [§494] In a Chapter 11 case, the court fixes (and sends notice of) a ***bar date***, which operates as a deadline for the filing of proofs of claims or interests. [Bankruptcy Rules 3003(c)(3), 2002(a)(7); for exceptions, *see* Bankruptcy Rules 3003(c)(3), 3002(c)(2), (3), (4)]

   (1) **Scheduled claims—automatic filing:** [§495] Any claim or interest listed in the schedules filed by the debtor or the trustee (*see supra*, §153) is ***deemed filed automatically*** (for the scheduled amount) unless the claim or interest is scheduled as contingent, unliquidated, or disputed. [B.C. §1111(a); Bankruptcy Rule 3003(b)] *Note:* This exemption from filing applies only under Chapter 11.

   (2) **Late filing:** [§496] The filing of a proof of claim or interest is permitted after the bar date in the following circumstances:

   (a) **Excusable neglect:** [§497] If, for example, a creditor does not receive notice of the bar date set by the court and, therefore, fails to timely file her proof of claim, it has been held that a late filing would be permitted on the basis of excusable neglect. [*In re* Yoder Co., 758 F.2d 1114 (6th Cir. 1985); *and see* Bankruptcy Rule 9006(b)(1)] The Supreme Court has held that whether there exists excusable neglect to permit a late filing **in a Chapter 11 case** should be determined by considering all relevant circumstances, including (i) any ***prejudice to the debtor***, (ii) the ***length of the delay*** and its effect on judicial proceedings, (iii) the ***reason for the delay***, and whether it was within the reasonable control of the party and her attorney, and (iv) whether the party and counsel acted in ***good faith***. The Court ruled that the issue is whether the neglect of the party ***and the attorney*** is excusable and held that clients will "be held accountable for the acts and omissions of their chosen counsel." [Pioneer Investment Services Co. v. Brunswick Associates Limited Partnership, 507 U.S. 380 (1993)—neglect found to be excusable because of unusual and inconspicuous placement of bar date notice; for application of these criteria, *see In re* Eagle Bus Manufacturing, Inc., 62 F.3d 730 (5th Cir. 1995)]

   (b) **Filing by debtor:** [§498] If a creditor does not file a proof of claim by the bar date, the debtor is entitled to a reasonable period of time within which to file a claim on behalf of the creditor. [B.C. §501(c); *In re* Middle Plantation of Williamsburg, Inc., 48 B.R. 789 (E.D. Va. 1985)]

   (3) **Amendments after the bar date:** [§499] Generally, a post-bar-date amendment will be permitted for the purpose of: curing a defect in the original claim, describing the claim with greater particularity, or pleading a new theory of recovery on the facts stated in the original claim. Courts usually scrutinize such amendments "to assure that there was no attempt to file a new claim under the guise of an amendment." [*In re* International Horizons, Inc., 751 F.2d 1213 (11th Cir. 1985)]

c. **Conversion to Chapter 7:** [§500] In a case that has been converted from Chapter 11, 12, or 13 to Chapter 7, all claims ***actually*** filed in the superseded case are considered automatically filed in the Chapter 7 case. Thus, a second filing is not required. [Bankruptcy Rule 1019(3)] However, a claim must be filed if it was only deemed filed in a case converted from Chapter 11 (*see supra*, §495).

d. **Governmental claims:** [§501] Claims of a governmental unit may be filed up to 180 days after the order for relief unless a later time is permitted by the Federal Rules of Bankruptcy Procedure. [B.C. §502(b)(9)]

4. **Claims Deemed Pre-Petition:** [§502] The following post-petition claims are treated as pre-petition claims for the ***purpose of filing*** [B.C. §501(d)]:

   a. *A co-debtor's or surety's claim for reimbursement or contribution* that becomes fixed after the bankruptcy petition has been filed [B.C. §502(e)(2)];

   b. *A claim arising in the ordinary course of the debtor's business* or financial affairs after the filing of an *involuntary petition* but before the earlier of the order for relief or the appointment of a trustee [B.C. §502(f)];

   c. *A claim arising from the rejection of an executory contract or an unexpired lease* that the trustee or the debtor in possession has not assumed [B.C. §502(g)];

   d. *A claim arising from the recovery of property* by the trustee or the debtor [B.C. §502(h)];

   e. *A post-petition tax claim entitled to eighth priority* [B.C. §§502(i), 507(a)(8); *see infra*, §§564 *et seq.*] (since eighth priority tax claims usually are pre-petition, section 502(i) covers the occasional situation where a tax claim arises post-petition as a result of pre-petition activities of the debtor); and

   f. *A claim*, other than one for administrative expenses [B.C. §503(b); *see infra*, §§537-553], *arising after the order for relief* in a Chapter 11, 12, or 13 case, but *before the case is converted to another chapter* [B.C. §348(d); *and see supra*, §214].

5. **Secured Claims:** [§503] A secured creditor may file a proof of claim; but if she does not, her lien on the collateral securing the claim ordinarily remains intact. [B.C. §506(d)(2); *and see infra*, §533] Nevertheless, a cautious creditor may prefer to file a claim. (*See infra*, §§1118, 1212.)

B. ALLOWANCE OF CLAIMS

1. **General Rule—Allowance:** [§504] Unless a party in interest objects, a claim or interest that has been filed will be allowed by the court and will serve as the basis for distribution. [B.C. §502(a)]

   a. **Partnership debtor:** [§505] If the debtor is a partnership in a Chapter 7 case, a creditor of any of the general partners of the partnership is deemed to be a party in interest for the purpose of objecting to allowance of a claim. [B.C. §502(a)]

   b. **Objection:** [§506] Ordinarily, if an objection to a claim is raised, the court (after notice and a hearing) determines the amount of the claim *as of the date* *of the filing of the bankruptcy petition*, and allows the claim unless it falls within one of the following recognized exceptions.

2. **Exceptions to Allowance:** [§507]   A claim for any of the following items is not allowable in a bankruptcy case. [B.C. §502(b)]

   a. **Claim unenforceable due to valid defense:** [§508]   A claim that is unenforceable against the debtor and his property because the debtor has a *valid defense* under any applicable law or agreement (*e.g.*, the statute of limitations or failure of consideration) is not allowable. However, this exception does not include a claim that is unenforceable solely because it is unmatured or contingent. [B.C. §502(b)(1); *In re* Dunn, 50 B.R. 664 (Bankr. W.D.N.Y. 1985); *see infra*, §518 concerning estimation of contingent claims]

   b. **Claim for post-petition interest:** [§509]   Post-petition (or unmatured) interest on an *unsecured claim* is generally not allowable. [B.C. §502(b)(2); *In re* Healis, 49 B.R. 939 (Bankr. M.D. Pa. 1985)] However, if the estate is *solvent*, unsecured creditors are entitled to post-petition interest. [B.C. §726(a)(5); *In re* Manville Forest Products Corp., 43 B.R. 293 (Bankr. S.D.N.Y. 1984)]

   c. **Claim for unsecured property tax in excess of debtor's equity:** [§510]   An unsecured property tax is allowable but only up to the debtor's equity in the property. Amounts claimed above the debtor's equity are not allowed. [B.C. §502(b)(3)]

   d. **Unreasonable claim for insider's or attorney's services:** [§511]   The services of an insider (*see supra*, §§30-33) or an attorney of the debtor are allowable, but only up to a reasonable value. Amounts claimed above a reasonable value are not allowed. [B.C. §502(b)(4)]

   e. **Unmatured claim for alimony or child support:** [§512]   Nondischargeable alimony, maintenance, or spousal or child support that is unmatured as of the date of bankruptcy is not allowable. [B.C. §§502(b)(5), 523(a)(5); United States v. Sutton, 786 F.2d 1305 (5th Cir. 1986)]

   f. **Excessive claim for damages for terminated lease:** [§513]   A lessor's damages for termination of a lease of real property are allowable, but only up to the greater of the rent under the lease (without acceleration) for one year or 15% of the rent for the balance of the lease (up to a maximum of three years' rent) after the earlier of the date of bankruptcy or the date the property was repossessed or relinquished, *plus* any unpaid rent due (without acceleration) as of the earlier of the two dates. Claims for damages above that amount are not allowed. [B.C. §502(b)(6); *In re* Watkins Management Group, Inc., 120 B.R. 586 (Bankr. S.D. Ala. 1990)]

   g. **Excessive claim for employer's breach of contract:** [§514]   An employee's damages for breach of an employment contract are allowable, but only up to one year's compensation under the contract (after the earlier of the date of the bankruptcy petition or the date the employee's performance was terminated), plus any unpaid wages on the earlier of the two dates. Claims for damages above that amount are not allowed. [B.C. §502(b)(7)]

h. **Claim for disallowance of employment tax credit:** [§515] A claim for disallowance of a federal employment tax credit caused by late payment of state unemployment insurance taxes is not allowable. [B.C. §502(b)(8)]

i. **Claim by possessor of estate property or transferee of avoidable transfer:** [§516] Any claim of an entity that is in possession of property recoverable by the estate or that is a transferee of an avoidable transfer is not allowable *unless* the entity returns the property or pays its value. [B.C. §502(d)]

j. **Tardy claim:** [§517] A tardily filed claim will be disallowed unless and to the extent permitted by the Federal Rules of Bankruptcy Procedure [B.C. §502(b)(9); Bankruptcy Rule 3002(c)(1)], or unless one of the following exceptions applies:

(1) For late *nonpriority* unsecured claims: (i) the creditor did not have notice or actual knowledge of the bankruptcy case to be able to file his claim timely, but the claim was filed in time for distribution, or (ii) there is a surplus in the estate sufficient to pay claims beyond those specified in section 726(a)(1) and (a)(2) (*see infra*, §§948-949) [B.C. §§502(b)(9); 726(a)(2)(C),(a)(3); *see infra*, §§950, 951];

(2) For late *priority* claims, filing was made before the trustee began distribution under section 726 [B.C. §§502(b)(9); 726(a)(1); *see infra*, §948], except that late administrative expense claims have the additional requirement of court approval of tardy filing, for cause. [B.C. §503(a)];

(3) *Governmental* claims may be timely filed up to 180 days after the order for relief (unless the Federal Rules of Bankruptcy Procedure provide for a longer time) [B.C. §502(b)(9); Bankruptcy Rule 3002(c)(1)].

3. **Estimation of Claims:** [§518] If a claim is *contingent or unliquidated*, and the fixing or liquidation of it would cause undue delay in the administration of the bankruptcy case, the court must estimate the claim. This estimate is solely *for the purpose of allowance*. [B.C. §502(c)(1); *In re* Patrick Cudahy, Inc., 97 B.R. 489 (Bankr. E.D. Wis. 1989)]

a. **Example:** Debtor Corporation, a manufacturer of asbestos-containing products that have seriously harmed the health of thousands of individuals, files a Chapter 11 petition. At a time when the bankruptcy court has not yet confirmed a plan of reorganization, Victim files a motion to withdraw a proceeding to the district court for trial of his personal injury claim. To avoid undue delay in the administration of the case, Victim's motion probably will be denied, after which the bankruptcy judge can proceed to estimate the tort claim. The bankruptcy court's estimation of Victim's claim will be solely for the purpose of allowing the claim, and not for the purpose of distribution, since any trial of the latter issue must occur in the district court (*see supra*, §62). [See *In re* Johns-Manville Corp., 45 B.R. 823 (S.D.N.Y. 1984)]

b. **Equitable remedy:** [§519] Similarly, if a right to an equitable remedy for breach of performance gives rise to a right to payment, the court must estimate the claim for the purpose of allowance. [B.C. §502(c)(2)]

4. **Claim for Reimbursement or Contribution:** [§520] The claim of a co-debtor, surety, or guarantor for reimbursement or contribution *will be disallowed* if (i) the claim is *contingent* (*i.e.,* if the surety has not paid the principal creditor) at the time of allowance or disallowance; (ii) the *principal creditor's claim* is disallowed; *or* (iii) the *surety elects subrogation* to the principal creditor's rights [B.C. §509; *see infra,* §§591-598] instead of reimbursement or contribution. [B.C. §502(e)(1); *In re* Baldwin-United Corp., 55 B.R. 885 (Bankr. S.D. Ohio 1985); *In re* Charter Co., 862 F.2d 1500 (11th Cir. 1989)]

   a. **Rationale:** This provision ensures that a co-debtor or surety will not participate in the distribution of estate property until she pays the principal creditor. At such time, the co-debtor or surety has the option of seeking either reimbursement or contribution, on one hand, or subrogation to the rights of the creditor, on the other, whichever is more beneficial. This decision may depend on whether the debtor has provided collateral to secure the claim of the surety for reimbursement or contribution, or to secure the claim of the principal creditor. [3 Collier ¶502.05(1)]

   b. **Payment by surety:** [§521] If the co-debtor or surety pays the principal creditor after the petition has been filed, her claim for reimbursement or contribution then becomes fixed and will be allowed or disallowed as a *pre-petition claim.* [B.C. §502(e)(2)]

5. **Claims Deemed Pre-Petition:** [§522] The following types of claims are considered pre-petition claims for the purpose of allowance:

   a. *Claims arising in the ordinary course of the debtor's business* or financial affairs after the commencement of an *involuntary* case but before the earlier of the appointment of a trustee or the order for relief [B.C. §502(f)];

   b. *Claims arising from the trustee's* (or debtor in possession's) *rejection of executory contracts or unexpired leases* that have not been assumed [B.C. §502(g)];

   c. *Claims arising from the recovery of property* by the trustee or the debtor [B.C. §§502(h), 522(i), 550, 553];

   d. *Post-petition tax claims entitled to eighth priority* [B.C. §§502(i), 507(a)(8); *see infra,* §564] (while eighth priority tax claims generally are pre-petition, section 502(i) covers the situation where a priority tax claim arises post-petition as a result of pre-petition activities of the debtor); and

   e. *Claims,* other than administrative expenses, arising after the order for relief in a Chapter 11, 12, or 13 case but *prior to conversion to another chapter* [B.C. §348(d); *and see supra,* §214].

C. SECURED CLAIMS

1. **Definition:** [§523] In bankruptcy, a secured claim is one that has been allowed (*see supra,* §§504 *et seq.*) and is either *secured by a lien* on property of the estate or is subject to *setoff* (*see supra,* §§334 *et seq.*). [B.C. §506(a)] The Bankruptcy Code treats a claim as secured *only to the extent of the value of the creditor's collateral* or up to the amount subject to setoff.

2. **Undersecured Claims—Bifurcation:** [§524] A claim is totally secured where the value of the collateral equals or is greater than the amount of the claim. However, if the amount of the creditor's claim exceeds the value of the collateral, the claim is undersecured and is divided into two separate claims: (i) a *secured claim* equal to the value of the collateral, and (ii) an *unsecured claim* equal to the amount by which the claim exceeds the value of the collateral. [B.C. §506(a)]

   a. **Example:** Bank has an allowed claim against Debtor in the amount of $200,000 arising from a loan agreement secured by a first mortgage on Debtor's house. If the value of Debtor's house is $200,000 or more, Bank's claim is fully secured. However, if Debtor's house is valued at $160,000, Bank is considered to be undersecured, and its $200,000 claim will be bifurcated into a secured claim for $160,000 and an unsecured claim for $40,000.

3. **Valuation of Collateral:** [§525] The value of the collateral securing a creditor's claim is a question of fact under the particular circumstances. The court's determination must take into account both the *purpose of the valuation* and the *intended disposition or use* of the collateral. [B.C. §506(a)]

   a. **Purpose of the valuation:** [§526] There are various occasions when a bankruptcy judge is required to value property securing a creditor's claim. For example, a judge may value property for the purpose of providing adequate protection to the creditor [B.C. §361; *see infra*, §§761 *et seq.*]; for distribution in a Chapter 7 case [B.C. §§725-726; *see infra*, §§945 *et seq.*]; for redemption of collateral [B.C. §722; *see infra*, §§752 *et seq.*]; for confirmation of a repayment plan under Chapter 11, 12, or 13 [B.C. §§1129, 1225, 1325; *see infra*, §§1100, 1271-1272, 1201]; or for ascertaining the amount of the debtor's exemptions [B.C. §522; *see infra*, §§609 *et seq.*]. [3 Collier ¶506.04(2)]

   b. **Proposed use or disposition:** [§527] By requiring that the court also consider the intended use or disposition of the collateral, the law contemplates that the collateral may have a different value depending on its use or disposition—*e.g.*, whether the secured party is permitted to foreclose on it (liquidation value), or whether the debtor plans to keep the property and continue to use it in his business (going concern value). [Fortang and Mayer, *Valuation in Bankruptcy*, 32 U.C.L.A. L. Rev. 1061 (1985)]

   c. **Time of valuation:** [§528] The time as of which collateral is valued should depend primarily on the purpose of the valuation. [3 Collier ¶506.04(2)]

4. **Oversecured Claims:** [§529] To the extent that the value of the collateral exceeds the amount of the creditor's claim that it secures (plus any surcharges under Code section 506(c); *see infra*, §532), the creditor is entitled to the allowance of *post-petition interest*, regardless of whether the creditor's lien is consensual (*e.g.*, a mortgage or a U.C.C. security interest) or nonconsensual (*e.g.*, a tax lien). Also, any reasonable fees (*e.g.*, attorney's fees), costs, or other charges *specified in the agreement* can be recovered to the extent that the claim is oversecured. [B.C. §506(b): United States v. Ron Pair Enterprises, Inc., 489 U.S. 235 (1989)] Nonconsensual lienholders cannot recover statutory claims for *post-petition* penalties,

costs, or attorney's fees. [*In re* Brentwood Outpatient Ltd., 43 F.3d 256 (6th Cir. 1994)]

- a. **Accrual of interest and fees:** [§530] Any post-petition interest, and any fees, costs, or charges that are allowed to the holder of an oversecured claim, usually are *accrued* until the time of distribution in a Chapter 7 case, or until the effective date of a Chapter 11, 12, or 13 plan. Present payments are not required by the statute. [B.C. §506(b); see *In re* Delta Resources, Inc., 54 F.3d 722 (11th Cir. 1995), *cert. denied*, 116 S. Ct. 488 (1995); *but see In re* Revco D.S. Inc., 901 F.2d 1359 (6th Cir. 1990)—allowing interim payments; 3 Collier ¶506.05]

- b. **Interest rate:** [§531] In the case of an oversecured consensual lien, the authorities are split on the rate of interest to be applied, but the better rule uses the rate established in the contract with the debtor. [*In re* Laymon, 958 F.2d 72 (5th Cir. 1992)] Whether a contractual post-default interest rate will be applied depends on the facts and equities of the particular case. [*In re* Terry Limited Partnership, 27 F.3d 241 (7th Cir. 1994)—default rate allowed; *In re* Consolidated Properties Limited Partnership, 152 B.R. 452 (Bankr. D. Md. 1993)—unreasonable default rate not allowed]

5. **Surcharge Against Collateral:** [§532] To the extent that a secured creditor *benefits directly* from the preservation or disposition of the collateral, the trustee or the debtor in possession may be *reimbursed* from the collateral for the necessary and reasonable costs of preserving or disposing of the collateral. This surcharge is paid ahead of an award of post-petition interest or fees to an oversecured creditor. [B.C. §506(c); *In re* Flagstaff Foodservice Corp., 762 F.2d 10 (2d Cir. 1985)] The prevailing view in the appellate courts holds that third parties may have standing to recover the surcharge if the trustee or debtor in possession refuses to bring an action. [*In re* Parque Forestal, Inc., 949 F.2d 504 (1st Cir. 1991); *but see In re* JFK Chevrolet, Inc., 26 F.3d 481 (4th Cir. 1994)—standing limited to trustees and debtors in possession]

6. **Liens Deemed Void:** [§533] The general rule is that a valid lien securing a creditor's claim passes through and survives bankruptcy, even if the secured creditor does not file a proof of claim. [B.C. §506(d)(2); *In re* Tarnow, 749 F.2d 464 (7th Cir. 1984); *but see infra*, §§1118, 1212, 1242] However, for a reason *other than* the secured creditor's failure to file a proof of claim, or the disallowance of the claim under Bankruptcy Code section 502(b)(5) (for nondischargeable alimony, maintenance, or spousal or child support that is unmatured as of the date of bankruptcy; *see supra*, §512) or the disallowance of a claim for reimbursement or contribution on any of the grounds set forth in section 502(e) (*see supra*, §520), a lien is *void* to the extent that it secures a claim that is *not an allowed secured claim*.

    - a. **Real property:** [§534] In a Chapter 7 case, where the collateral is real property worth less than the amount of the claim it secures, the debtor may not use Code section 506(d) to strip down the creditor's lien on the real property to the value of the collateral. [Dewsnup v. Timm, 502 U.S. 410 (1992)]

        - (1) **Example:** Debtor owns a home subject to Bank's properly recorded mortgage of $80,000. When Debtor files a voluntary Chapter 7 petition, the present market value of the home is $50,000. Debtor seeks to avoid

Bank's lien on his residence to the extent of $30,000. Under the rule above, Debtor may not strip down Bank's lien to the value of the collateral.

7. **Treatment of Secured Claims:** [§535] Prior to final distribution to the unsecured creditors in a Chapter 7 case, a secured creditor usually receives cash equal to the total amount of her allowed secured claim or, in the alternative, a return of the property that secures that claim. [B.C. §725] For example, the trustee may sell collateral that has equity and use the net proceeds to pay the corresponding secured claim, with any excess being remitted to the estate. In Chapters 11, 12, and 13, there are special provisions concerning the treatment of secured claims that must be satisfied for the court to confirm a plan (*see infra*, §§1100, 1271, 1201).

8. **Adequate Protection:** [§536] A secured creditor has the right to receive adequate protection of her interest in the collateral [B.C. §361], and the failure to provide it constitutes sufficient cause for granting the creditor relief from the automatic stay. [B.C. §362(d)(1); *see infra*, §813] Also, the secured creditor is entitled to adequate protection if her collateral is used, sold, or leased by the trustee or the debtor in possession [B.C. §363(e); *see infra*, §849], or if the creditor's lien on the collateral is primed by a senior or equal lien authorized by the court for the purpose of enabling the trustee or the debtor in possession to obtain credit. [B.C. §364(d)(1)(B); *see infra*, §871]

D. **ADMINISTRATIVE EXPENSES**

1. **Priority:** [§537] After the payment of secured claims from property constituting collateral, entities holding claims for administrative expenses ordinarily are entitled to the highest priority in the distribution of the assets of the estate. [B.C. §§503, 507(a)(1); *see infra*, §556]

   a. **Note:** A request for administrative expenses must be *timely filed* or receive court approval, for cause, to be filed late. [B.C. §503(a)]

2. **Allowable Administrative Expenses:** [§538] The following items are allowable as administrative expenses, after notice and a hearing [B.C. §503(b)]:

   a. **Post-petition costs of preserving estate:** [§539] The actual and necessary post-petition costs of preserving the bankruptcy estate are administrative expenses. For example, these costs could include compensation for services performed after the filing of the petition (*e.g.*, attorney's fees), rent, and the reasonable costs incurred by an environmental agency to clean up hazardous wastes that violate environmental laws. [B.C. §503(b)(1)(A); Commissioner of Pennsylvania Department of Environmental Resources v. Conroy, 24 F.3d 568 (3d Cir. 1994)] Generally, the normal post-petition operating costs of running a Chapter 11 business are allowable as administrative expenses.

   b. **Post-petition taxes:** [§540] Post-petition taxes incurred by the estate (*e.g.*, taxes arising from the management of the debtor's business by the debtor in possession or a trustee in a Chapter 11 case) are administrative expenses. [B.C. §503(b)(1)(B)(i); United States v. Friendship College, Inc., 737 F.2d 430 (4th Cir. 1984)]

(1) **Note:** A *fine or penalty* relating to a post-petition tax of the estate also is allowable as an administrative expense. [B.C. §503(b)(1)(C); *In re* St. Louis Freight Lines, Inc., 45 B.R. 546 (Bankr. E.D. Mich. 1984)] Although the courts are not in total agreement on the issue of whether *interest* on an unsecured post-petition tax claim is to be accorded administrative expense status, the overwhelming weight of appellate authority is that such interest constitutes an administrative expense. [*In re* Mark Anthony Construction, Inc., 886 F.2d 1101 (9th Cir. 1989); *In re* Flo-Lizer, Inc., 916 F.2d 363 (6th Cir. 1990)]

c. **Compensation and reimbursement:** [§541] Compensation and reimbursement awarded to a trustee, an examiner, a Chapter 12 or 13 individual, debtor's attorney, or a professional person employed by a trustee, debtor in possession, or creditors' committee, are administrative expenses. [B.C. §§503(b)(2), 330(a); *and see supra,* §§269 *et seq.*]

d. **Expenses of involuntary petition:** [§542] The actual and necessary expenses of a creditor who files an involuntary petition against the debtor are administrative expenses. [B.C. §503(b)(3)(A)]

e. **Expenses of recovery of concealed or transferred property:** [§543] The actual and necessary expenses of a creditor who, with court approval, recovers for the benefit of the estate property that the debtor has either concealed or transferred are administrative expenses. [B.C. §503(b)(3)(B)]

f. **Expenses of criminal prosecution:** [§544] The actual and necessary expenses incurred by a creditor in a criminal prosecution related to the bankruptcy case or to the debtor's property or business are administrative expenses. [B.C. §503(b)(3)(C)]

g. **Expenses of substantial contributor:** [§545] The actual and necessary expenses of a creditor, an indenture trustee, an equity security holder, or an *unofficial* creditors' or equity security holders' committee (*i.e.,* one not appointed by the United States trustee under Code section 1102) that makes a *substantial contribution* in a Chapter 11 or Chapter 9 case are administrative expenses. [B.C. §503(b)(3)(D); Lebron v. Mechem Financial, Inc., 27 F.3d 937 (3d Cir. 1994)]

h. **Expenses and compensation of pre-petition custodian:** [§546] The actual and necessary expenses, as well as compensation, for the services of a pre-petition custodian who has been superseded under Bankruptcy Code section 543 are administrative expenses. [B.C. §503(b)(3)(E); *and see supra,* §328]

(1) **Compare:** A creditor who acts only in her *own self-interest* to attach and sell the debtor's property prior to bankruptcy is not a custodian and is not entitled to administrative expenses. [B.C. §101(11); *In re* Meyers, Inc., 15 B.R. 390 (Bankr. S.D. Cal. 1981); *see supra,* §328]

i. **Expenses of official Chapter 11 creditors' committee:** [§547] The actual and necessary expenses incurred by the members of an official Chapter 11 creditors' or equity security holders' committee (appointed under section 1102; *see infra,* §§995 *et seq.*) in performing the duties of the committee are treated as administrative expenses. [B.C. §503(b)(3)(F)] Such expenses would include, for example, travel and lodging, but not compensation for services rendered.

j. **Attorney's or accountant's fees and expenses:** [§548] Administrative expenses include *reasonable* compensation for services, as well as *reimbursement* of actual and necessary expenses, of an attorney or an accountant of an entity entitled to administrative expenses under Bankruptcy Code section 503(b)(3)(A)-(F). [B.C. §503(b)(4); *In re* North Port Development Co., 36 B.R. 19 (Bankr. E.D. Mo. 1983); *see supra*, §§542-547]

k. **Compensation of indenture trustee:** [§549] Reasonable compensation for the services of an indenture trustee who has made a *substantial contribution* in a Chapter 11 or Chapter 9 case is an administrative expense. [B.C. §§503(b)(5), 101(29)]

l. **Pre-confirmation retiree benefits:** [§550] In a Chapter 11 case, retiree benefit payments that must be made prior to the effective date of a confirmed plan are administrative expenses. [B.C. §1114(e)(2)]

m. **Witnesses' fees:** [§551] Finally, witnesses' fees and mileage expenses are administrative expenses. [B.C. §503(b)(6); 28 U.S.C. §1821]

3. **Exception—Gap Creditors' Claims:** [§552] In an *involuntary* case, post-petition claims that arise "in the ordinary course of the debtor's business or financial affairs ... before the earlier of the appointment of a trustee [or] the order for relief" [B.C. §502(f); *see supra*, §522] are *not* treated as administrative expense claims, but rather are given *second priority* in the order of distribution. [B.C. §§503(b), 507(a)(2); *see infra*, §557]

4. **Exempt Property:** [§553] As a general rule, administrative expenses are not payable out of property that the debtor exempts. [B.C. §522(k)] However, property exempted by the debtor is liable for administrative expenses representing the debtor's fractional share of the cost of avoiding a transfer of such property or the cost of its recovery by the trustee or the debtor. [B.C. §522(k)(1), (2)]

E. **PRIORITY CLAIMS**

1. **In General:** [§554] Priority claims generally are the first *unsecured claims* to be paid in a bankruptcy case following distribution to secured creditors. There are nine tiers of priority claims [B.C. §507(a)] which, in a Chapter 7 case, are entitled to payment in the order of their priority ranking (*i.e.*, all of the claims in a priority level must be paid in full before moving down to the next priority level) before any distribution is made to the general (nonpriority) unsecured creditors. [B.C. §726(a)(1)]

2. **Order of Priority:** [§555] Priority claims that have been *allowed* are paid in the following order [B.C. §507(a)]:

a. **First priority—administrative expenses:** [§556] The first priority includes administrative expenses [B.C. §503(b); *see supra*, §§537-553], the filing fee for the particular case, and certain quarterly fees required in Chapter 11 cases. [B.C. §507(a)(1); 28 U.S.C. §1930]

b. **Second priority—involuntary case gap claims:** [§557] The second priority includes those claims in an involuntary case that arise "in the ordinary course of the debtor's business or financial affairs after the commencement of the case but before the earlier of the appointment of a trustee [or] the order for relief"—*i.e.*, in the gap period. [B.C. §§507(a)(2), 502(f); *and see supra*, §522]

c. **Third priority—wages and commissions:** [§558] The third priority includes wages, salaries, or commissions earned by an *individual* within *90 days* before bankruptcy or "the cessation of the debtor's business," whichever is earlier. This provision applies regardless of the individual's position of employment and includes vacation pay, severance pay, and sick leave pay, as well as the employee's portion of any withholding tax (*i.e.*, income tax or social security tax) attributable to a third priority item. [B.C. §507(a)(3)(A); 3 Collier ¶507.04(3)(f)] The third priority also includes commissions earned by certain independent sales representatives who are individuals, or corporations with only one employee. [B.C. §507(a)(3)(B)]

   (1) **Limitation:** Each third priority claim is limited to $4,000. [B.C. §507(a)(3)]

   (2) **Example:** Patty Parker and Sam Smith are president and secretary, respectively, of Debtor Corporation. Debtor Corporation files a voluntary bankruptcy petition on May 1 and stops doing business on the same day. From February 1 until May 1, Parker and Smith each earned, in the employ of Debtor Corporation, $5,000 in salaries, which remained unpaid as of May 1. Since any individual employee is entitled to a priority for wages or salaries earned within the 90-day period, both Parker and Smith will receive third priority treatment of their salary claims against Debtor Corporation to the extent of $4,000 each. In addition, they will each hold a $1,000 general unsecured claim, which is not entitled to priority but which will share equally with the other general unsecured claims. [B.C. §507(a)(3)(A)]

   (3) **"Cessation of business":** [§559] The courts have construed the language "cessation of the debtor's business" to mean the *end of the debtor's principal business operations*. Thus, in one case, the cessation of the debtor's business occurred on the last day on which the debtor maintained facilities to produce clothing, and, in another case, on the day the debtor (a common carrier) terminated its general freight division. [B.C. §507(a)(3); *In re* Bodin Apparel, Inc., 56 B.R. 728 (S.D.N.Y. 1985); *In re* Davidson Transfer & Storage Co., 41 B.R. 805 (Bankr. D. Md. 1984)]

d. **Fourth priority—employee benefit plans:** [§560] The fourth priority is for contributions to an employee benefit plan for services rendered within *180 days* before either bankruptcy or "the cessation of the debtor's business," whichever is earlier. [B.C. §507(a)(4); *In re* Columbia Packing Co., 47 B.R. 126 (Bankr. D. Mass. 1985)]

   (1) **Limitation:** This priority is limited to the number of employees covered by the plan multiplied by $4,000, minus the total amount paid to such employees as third priority wage claims. [B.C. §507(a)(4)(B); *see supra*, §§558-559]

(2) **Examples:** Employee pension plans, life insurance plans, and health insurance plans are the most common examples of fourth priority claims. (*Note:* Whether claims for unpaid workers' compensation insurance premiums are entitled to fourth priority status is not a settled issue. [Employers Insurance of Wausau v. Plaid Pantries, Inc., 10 F.3d 605 (9th Cir. 1993)—yes; *In re* HLM Corp., 62 F.3d 224 (8th Cir. 1995)—no])

e. **Fifth priority—grain farmers and United States fishermen:** [§561] The fifth priority is for claims of grain producers or United States fishermen against a debtor who operates or owns a grain storage facility or against a debtor who operates a fish produce storage or processing facility, respectively. [B.C. §507(a)(5); *In re* Esbon Grain Co., 55 B.R. 308 (Bankr. D. Kan. 1985)]

(1) **Limitation:** Each farmer or fisherman is limited to $4,000 for a fifth priority claim. [B.C. §507(a)(5)]

f. **Sixth priority—consumer claims:** [§562] The sixth priority, which also is known as the "layaway" priority, is for claims of individuals arising from the pre-petition deposit of money with the debtor for the purchase, lease, or rental of property, *or* the purchase of services, that have not been delivered or provided. The property or services must have been intended for the personal, family, or household use of the claimant. [B.C. §507(a)(6); *In re* Carolina Sales Corp., 43 B.R. 596 (Bankr. E.D.N.C. 1984)]

(1) **Limitation:** Each individual is limited to $1,800 for a sixth priority claim. [B.C. §507(a)(6)]

(2) **Example:** Buyer deposited "earnest money" in the amount of $3,000 with Debtor, a residential builder, according to a contract to purchase a new home. Debtor never completed the home and subsequently filed a voluntary bankruptcy petition. Buyer has a sixth priority claim against Debtor for $1,800 arising from the pre-petition deposit. The balance of Buyer's deposit, $1,200, is treated as a general unsecured claim, which is not entitled to priority. [B.C. §507(a)(6)]

g. **Seventh priority—alimony and support:** [§563] The seventh priority includes claims for alimony, or spousal or child support, unless the debt has been assigned to another entity or is not actually intended to constitute alimony or support. [B.C. §507(a)(7)]

h. **Eighth priority—taxes:** [§564] The eighth priority includes the following unsecured pre-petition tax claims of governmental units. [B.C. §507(a)(8)]

(1) **Income taxes:** [§565] The following claims for income tax are eighth priority claims:

(a) An income tax for a taxable year ending on or before bankruptcy for which a *return was last due* (including extensions) *within three years* prior to the date of the bankruptcy petition [B.C. §507(a)(8)(A)(i)];

(b) An income tax that has been *assessed within 240 days* before the date of the petition [B.C. §507(a)(8)(A)(ii)]; and

(c) An income tax that was not assessed pre-petition but which is *assessable post-petition*, *other than* a tax that is nondischargeable because a return was not filed, a return was filed late within two years prior to bankruptcy, or the debtor filed a fraudulent return or intentionally tried to evade the tax. [B.C.§§507(a)(8)(A)(iii); 523(a)(1)(B),(C); *see infra*, §679]

(2) **Property tax:** [§566] A property tax assessed prior to bankruptcy that was last payable without a penalty *within one year* before the date of the petition is an eighth priority claim. [B.C. §507(a)(8)(B)]

(3) **Trust fund tax:** [§567] Any trust fund tax that the debtor was *obligated to collect or withhold* from a third party and for which the debtor is liable in any capacity is an eighth priority claim. [B.C. §507(a)(8)(C)] Under this provision, the debtor could be either an employer or a responsible person or officer liable for the trust fund tax under the Internal Revenue Code's 100% penalty. [26 U.S.C. §6672(a)]

   (a) **Example—employee's withholding taxes:** Any amount of income tax or social security tax that should have been withheld from an employee, and which is not a third priority item (*see supra*, §558), is treated as an eighth priority claim. [3 Collier ¶507.04(8)(d)]

   (b) **Example—certain excise taxes:** The majority rule includes, as a trust fund tax, an excise tax or a sales tax that "a seller of goods or services is required to collect from a buyer and pay over to a taxing authority." [S. Rep. No. 989, 95th Cong., 2d Sess. 71 (1978); DeChiaro v. New York State Tax Commission, 760 F.2d 432 (2d Cir. 1985)]

   (c) **Note—no time limit:** [§568] A claim for a trust fund tax qualifies as an eighth priority item regardless of how old the tax liability is. [3 Collier ¶507.04(8)(d)]

(4) **Employment tax:** [§569] An employment tax (on the employer) concerning wages, salaries, or commissions paid before bankruptcy and for which a return was last due *within three years* before the date of the petition, as well as the employer's share of the taxes relating to third priority claims for wages, salaries, or commissions earned from the debtor are eighth priority claims. [B.C. §507(a)(8)(D)]

(5) **Excise tax:** [§570] An excise tax concerning a transaction that occurred or for which a return was last due *within three years* before bankruptcy is an eighth priority claim. [B.C. §507(a)(8)(E)]

(6) **Customs duties:** [§571] Certain customs duties relating to the importation of merchandise and arising *within one or four years* (depending on the circumstances) before bankruptcy are eighth priority claims. [B.C. §507(a)(8)(F)]

(7) **Penalty on eighth priority tax claim:** [§572] A penalty attributable to an eighth priority tax claim is also an eighth priority claim, but only if

the penalty constitutes *compensation for actual pecuniary loss*. [B.C. §507(a)(8)(G); *In re* Coleman, 19 B.R. 529 (Bankr. D. Kan. 1982)—*e.g.*, the 100% penalty imposed, under 26 U.S.C. section 6672(a), on a responsible person or officer who intentionally fails to remit a withholding tax]

    i. **Ninth priority—failure to maintain capital requirements of an insured depository institution:** [§573]   The ninth priority is for unsecured claims of a federal depository institutions regulatory agency (such as the FDIC or RTC) for the amount of any deficiency under the debtor's agreement to maintain the capital of an insured depository institution. [B.C. §§507(a)(9), 101(21B), 101(35)]

3. **Special Rules for Priority Tax Claims:** [§574]   The following principles relate to the treatment of priority tax claims:

   a. **Erroneous refund:** [§575]   A claim for an erroneous refund or credit of a tax is entitled to the *same priority* as the tax to which it pertains. [B.C. §507(c)]

      (1) **Note:** While Bankruptcy Code section 507(a)(8)(A)-(G) (*see* above) accords eighth priority status to most pre-petition taxes, other tax claims may be entitled to first priority as (post-petition) administrative expenses, second priority as involuntary case gap claims, or third priority as trust fund taxes related to pre-petition wages. [B.C. §§503(b)(1)(B), 507(a)(1)-(3)]

   b. **Pre-petition interest:** [§576]   Almost all courts view pre-petition interest as part of an eighth priority tax claim, and thus an equivalent priority status is given to any interest accrued on the tax before bankruptcy. [*In re* Treister, 52 B.R. 735 (Bankr. S.D.N.Y. (1985); *In re* Garcia, 955 F.2d 16 (5th Cir. 1992)]

4. **Insufficient Funds—Pro Rata Distribution Within Priority:** [§577]   In a Chapter 7 case, if the estate is unable to pay all claims of a particular priority, then distribution on such claims must be made on a pro rata basis. There is no exception for eighth priority tax claims, which also share pro rata, and not in any priority among themselves. [B.C. §726(b); *In re* Penn-Mahoning Mining, Inc., 45 B.R. 51 (Bankr. M.D. Pa. 1984)]

   a. **Note:** The law is unclear as to whether ninth priority claims must be prorated. [4 Collier ¶726.03; *see supra*, §573]

   b. **Exception—conversion to Chapter 7:** [§578]   If a case is converted from Chapter 11, 12, or 13 to a case under Chapter 7, the administrative expense claims in the Chapter 7 case *after conversion* have priority over the administrative expenses incurred prior to conversion. [B.C. §726(b)]

5. **Superpriority—Inadequately Protected Secured Creditor:** [§579]   If adequate protection is furnished under Bankruptcy Code section 362, 363, or 364 (*see infra*, §§761 *et seq.*) to a creditor whose claim is secured by a lien on the debtor's property, but the adequate protection ultimately proves to be deficient, the creditor will receive an administrative expense claim with *priority over all other administrative*

expenses allowed against the debtor's estate. [B.C. §507(b); *In re* Mutschler, 45 B.R. 494 (Bankr. D.N.D. 1984)]

    a. **Example:** Debtor files a voluntary Chapter 11 petition. Creditor, whose claim is fully secured by a lien on several items of Debtor's equipment, seeks relief from the automatic stay based on lack of adequate protection. [B.C. §362(d)(1)] The parties enter into a court-approved stipulation, providing for substantial adequate protection payments from Debtor during the next year, but after a few payments, Debtor is unable to comply and thus defaults on the agreement. Creditor obtains relief from the automatic stay and repossesses the collateral, which has declined greatly in value, leaving Creditor undersecured to the extent of $11,000. In compensation for the loss caused by the failure of the adequate protection provided, Creditor's $11,000 unsecured claim will be given a superpriority administrative expense status, thereby ranking ahead of all other administrative expense claims in the case, including Debtor's attorneys' fees. [B.C. §507(b); *In re* Becker, 51 B.R. 975 (Bankr. D. Minn. 1985)]

6. **Super-Superpriority—Post-Petition Credit:** [§580] If the trustee or the debtor in possession is unable to obtain unsecured post-petition credit by means of an administrative expense priority, the court may approve new credit or debt with priority over all administrative expense claims, *including* any superpriority claims arising from the failure of adequate protection. [B.C. §364(c)(1); *In re* Flagstaff Foodservice Corp., 739 F.2d 73 (2d Cir. 1984); *see infra*, §§867-868]

7. **Subrogation:** [§581] A third party, such as a co-debtor or a surety, who becomes subrogated to the rights of a holder of a claim entitled to a third through ninth priority does *not* become subrogated to the holder's right to priority. Therefore, the subrogated claim would be treated as a nonpriority claim. [B.C. §507(d); *In re* Dubose, 22 B.R. 780 (Bankr. N.D. Ohio 1982)]

    a. **Compare—assignment:** [§582] Subrogation needs to be contrasted with an assignment, whereby the assignee should acquire the rights of—*including the same priority* as—the assignor. [3 Collier ¶507.07] Thus, where a supermarket cashed payroll checks of employees who would have been entitled to third priority wage claims in the ensuing bankruptcy of their employer, the supermarket succeeded by assignment to the third priority claims when the checks subsequently were dishonored and the employer filed a Chapter 11 petition. [*In re* Missionary Baptist Foundation of America, Inc., 667 F.2d 1244 (5th Cir. 1982)]

    b. **Administrative expenses and involuntary case gap claims:** [§583] Subrogees to administrative expense claims and gap claims in involuntary cases [B.C. §507(a)(1), (2); *see supra*, §§556-557] become subrogated to the respective priorities of such claims. [3 Collier ¶507.07]

F. TAX CLAIMS

1. **Determination of Tax Liability:** [§584] The bankruptcy court has jurisdiction to determine the amount or legality of any tax, fine, penalty, or addition to tax that has not been contested in and adjudicated by an appropriate judicial or administrative court *prior to bankruptcy*. The court may exercise its power to determine tax liability regardless of whether the tax has been assessed or paid. [B.C. §505(a)(1), (2)(A)]

a. **Example:** Debtor is a landowner in X County. The taxing authority for X County assesses Debtor's real property at $10 million and asserts a tax liability of $180,000. Debtor does not contest the assessment and, several months later, files a voluntary bankruptcy petition. The bankruptcy court may redetermine Debtor's real property tax liability. [*In re* Palm Beach Resort Properties, Inc., 51 B.R. 363 (Bankr. S.D. Fla. 1985)]

b. **Criteria:** [§585] Although there is limited case law concerning when the bankruptcy court should exercise its jurisdiction under Bankruptcy Code section 505 or when it should defer the matter to the Tax Court, one court has considered the following factors [*In re* Hunt, 95 B.R. 442 (Bankr. N.D. Tex. 1989)]:

   (1) *The complexity of the tax issues* and whether they are especially technical or esoteric;

   (2) *"The asset and liability structure of the debtor"*;

   (3) *The need to determine* the amount of the tax claim *"in a timely manner* to ensure a prompt resolution of the bankruptcy case";

   (4) *The likelihood of a more expeditious resolution* of the tax liability *in the bankruptcy court* as opposed to the Tax Court;

   (5) *The burden that would be imposed on the bankruptcy court's docket*; and

   (6) *Any apparent whipsaw effect*, *i.e.*, "when two different taxpayers take positions with respect to a particular transaction which are so inconsistent with each other that only one should logically succeed and yet, because of jurisdictional or procedural reasons, first one and then the other prevails against the government."

2. **Tax Refund:** [§586] The bankruptcy court also may determine the *estate's* right to a tax refund, but only after the earlier of 120 days after a proper request by the trustee for the refund from the appropriate governmental unit, *or* an actual determination by that governmental unit of the trustee's request. [B.C. §505(a)(2)(B)]

3. **Tax Liability of Estate:** [§587] A trustee may request that the appropriate taxing authority determine any unpaid tax liability *of the estate* incurred during the administration of the case. The trustee does this by tendering to the governmental unit a tax return accompanied by a request for a determination of the tax. [B.C. §505(b)]

   a. **Discharge—payment:** [§588] Once the trustee has requested a determination of the estate's liability for taxes incurred during the case, a discharge from any liability for the tax on the part of the trustee, the debtor, or a successor to the debtor will occur when there is payment of:

      (1) *The tax indicated on the return* if the taxing authority either fails to notify the trustee within 60 days that the return has been chosen for audit, or fails to complete an audit and notify the trustee of any tax owing within 180 days after the trustee's request for determination (unless extended, for cause, by the court) [B.C. §505(b)(1)];

(2) *The tax determined by the taxing authority* [B.C. §505(b)(3)]; or

(3) *The tax determined by the court*, after the taxing authority has finished its audit. [B.C. §505(b)(2)].

    b. **Exception—fraud:** [§589] The trustee, the debtor, or any successor to the debtor will not be discharged from tax liability incurred by the estate during the case if the return tendered by the trustee to the taxing authority is fraudulent or contains a material misrepresentation. [B.C. §505(b)]

4. **Assessment:** [§590] After the court makes a determination of a tax liability under section 505, the appropriate taxing authority may assess the amount of the tax against the estate, the debtor, or a successor to the debtor notwithstanding the automatic stay provisions of the Bankruptcy Code. [B.C. §505(c), 362; *see infra*, §§778-831]

G. SUBROGATION CLAIMS

1. **Subrogee:** [§591] A subrogee is an entity that *has paid* a creditor's claim against the debtor because the entity either had secured the claim or was liable with the debtor on the claim as a co-debtor, co-maker, surety, or guarantor. [B.C. §509(a); 3 Collier ¶509.01]

2. **Subrogee Receives Creditor's Rights:** [§592] Generally, a subrogee succeeds to the rights of the creditor whose claim it paid to the extent of the amount paid. [B.C. §509(a); *but see supra*, §581]

3. **Exceptions:** [§593] Subrogation to the rights of a creditor is not allowed in the following situations [B.C. §509(b)]:

    a. **Reimbursement or contribution claim allowed:** [§594] To the extent that a corresponding claim of the co-debtor for reimbursement or contribution has been allowed under Bankruptcy Code section 502 (*see supra*, §§504 *et seq.*), subrogation is not allowed. [B.C. §509(b)(1)(A)]

        (1) **Rationale:** A co-debtor who has paid the principal creditor's claim is entitled to only one claim in the case and must choose between filing a claim for reimbursement or contribution, on one hand, or subrogation to the principal creditor's claim, on the other. This election could depend on whether the debtor has provided collateral to secure either the co-debtor's claim for reimbursement or contribution, or the claim of the principal creditor. [B.C. §§502(e)(2), 509(a); 3 Collier ¶509.03(1)]

    b. **Reimbursement or contribution claim disallowed:** [§595] To the extent that a corresponding claim of the co-debtor for reimbursement or contribution has been disallowed on a ground *other than* Bankruptcy Code section 502(e) (*see supra*, §520), such as for one of the reasons specified in Code section 502(b) (*see supra*, §§507-517), subrogation is not allowed. [B.C. §509(b)(1)(B)]

    c. **Reimbursement or contribution claim subordinated:** [§596] To the extent that a corresponding claim of the co-debtor for reimbursement or contribution has been subordinated under Bankruptcy Code section 510 (*see infra*, §§599 *et seq.*), subrogation is not allowed. [B.C. §509(b)(1)(C)]

d. **Co-debtor received consideration:** [§597]   To the extent that the co-debtor, rather than the debtor, was the party who actually received the consideration for the claim held by the principal creditor, subrogation is not allowed. [B.C. §509(b)(2)]

4. **Subordination to Principal Creditor's Claim:** [§598]   A co-debtor's claim, either by way of subrogation or for reimbursement or contribution, will be subordinated to the principal creditor's claim until that claim is satisfied fully, either through distribution under the Bankruptcy Code or by other means. [B.C. §509(c)]

H. SUBORDINATION OF CLAIMS

1. **Subordination Agreement:** [§599]   A claim in a bankruptcy case may be subordinated to the payment of other claims by a subordination contract enforceable under applicable nonbankruptcy law. [B.C. §510(a)]

2. **Defrauded Security Holders:** [§600]   A claim for damages, rescission, or contribution or reimbursement arising from the purchase or sale of a security of the debtor or its affiliate *must be subordinated* to all claims or interests *senior or equal* to that which the security represents. [B.C. §510(b); *In re* Amarex, Inc., 78 B.R. 605 (W.D. Okla. 1985)]

   a. **Exception—common stock:** [§601]   If the security is common stock, then the claim will be subordinated to the *same priority as common stock*, not to a lower priority. [B.C. §510(b)]

   b. **Examples**

      (1) Debtor Corporation files a voluntary Chapter 7 petition, and Security Holder files a claim for rescission of certain purchases of *preferred stock*, based on alleged violations by Debtor Corporation of section 10(b) of the Securities Exchange Act of 1934 [15 U.S.C. §78j(b)]. For purposes of distribution, Security Holder's claim for rescission will be subordinated to a position *below* the interests of the preferred shareholders but *above* the interests of the common shareholders.

      (2) Assume the same facts as above, except that Security Holder's claim, instead, is for rescission of certain purchases of Debtor Corporation's *debentures*. In this instance, Security Holder's claim will be subordinated to a level below the claims of the general unsecured creditors but above the interests of the preferred shareholders.

      (3) Assume that one of the claimants in Debtor Corporation's bankruptcy case is Accountant, who has been held liable, in federal district court, to certain common shareholders for damages arising from the sale of Debtor Corporation's securities in violation of the federal securities laws. Accountant has paid the judgment and now seeks reimbursement or contribution from Debtor Corporation. Accountant's claim will be subordinated to the same extent that the claims of the common shareholders would have been subordinated if they had elected to file claims for damages or rescission in the bankruptcy case—*i.e.*, to the same level of distribution as the other holders of common stock.

3. **Equitable Subordination:** [§602]   The court also has the equitable power to subordinate all or part of an allowed secured or unsecured claim to another allowed claim, or to subordinate all or part of an allowed interest to another allowed interest. [B.C. §510(c); *In re* N & D Properties, Inc., 799 F.2d 726 (11th Cir. 1986)]

   a. **Proof of fault:** [§603]   Generally, an essential element in the equitable subordination of a claim or interest is the showing of some fault on the claimant's part. Usually, such misconduct falls into one of the following categories: (i) fraud, illegality, or breach of fiduciary duties; (ii) undercapitalization; or (iii) the claimant's use of the debtor as a mere instrumentality or alter ego. [*In re* Missionary Baptist Foundation of America, Inc., 712 F.2d 206 (5th Cir. 1983)] (*Note:* While some courts did not require proof of fault for subordination of nonpecuniary loss tax penalties, the Supreme Court has held that bankruptcy courts may not categorically subordinate these claims but must decide on a case-by-case basis. [United States v. Noland, 116 S. Ct. 1254 (1996); *and see* United States v. Reorganized CF&I Fabricators of Utah, Inc., 116 S. Ct. 2106 (1996)] However, the Supreme Court left open the issue whether a finding of misconduct is required before a claim may be equitably subordinated. [United States v. Noland, *supra*])

   b. **Test:** [§604]   The recognized standard for establishing fault requires proof of the following elements:

   (i) *Inequitable conduct* on the claimant's part;

   (ii) *Injury to the creditors* of the debtor, or an *unfair advantage* to the claimant, due to the misconduct; and

   (iii) Equitable subordination of the claim is *consistent with the provisions of the Bankruptcy Code*.

   [*In re* Clark Pipe & Supply Co., 893 F.2d 693 (5th Cir. 1990)]

   c. **Causation:** [§605]   When equitable subordination is used, the claim or interest is subordinated only to the extent necessary to offset the harm caused to the debtor and his creditors by the claimant's conduct. [*In re* Lemco Gypsum, Inc., 911 F.2d 1553 (11th Cir. 1990)]

   d. **Insiders and fiduciaries:** [§606]   While a claimant's status as an insider [B.C. §101(31); *see supra*, §§30-33] or as a fiduciary generally should not, in the absence of inequitable conduct, result in subordination of his claim, courts usually examine with strict scrutiny the dealings of insiders and fiduciaries for *good faith and fairness*. [Pepper v. Litton, 308 U.S. 295 (1939); *In re* Multiponics, Inc., 622 F.2d 709 (5th Cir. 1980)] Consequently, equitable subordination, when invoked, generally will affect claims of insiders or fiduciaries, or those considered to be insiders because they control the debtor. [*In re* Fabricators, 926 F.2d 1458 (5th Cir. 1991); *and see In re* American Lumber Co., 5 B.R. 470 (D. Minn. 1980)—bank's inequitable exercise of control over debtor] However, the doctrine also may be applied to non-insiders where the claimant's misconduct was of *moral turpitude*, causing damage to other creditors [*see* W.T. Grant, 4 B.R. 53 (Bankr. S.D.N.Y. 1980)], or was "gross and egregious" and "tantamount to fraud, misrepresentation, overreaching or spoliation" [*see In re* 80 Nassau Associates, 169 B.R. 832 (Bankr. S.D.N.Y. 1994)].

I. DISTRIBUTION OUTSIDE OF BANKRUPTCY CODE

1. **Foreign Proceeding:** [§607] A creditor who holds an allowed claim in a case under the Bankruptcy Code and who receives distribution on that claim in a foreign proceeding is prohibited from receiving any payment (on the claim) in the domestic case until all of the creditors in the domestic case with whom she would have shared equally have received payment equal to her distribution in the foreign proceeding. [B.C. §508(a)]

2. **Creditors of Partnership:** [§608] The same principle applies to a creditor of a partnership debtor who receives payment on an allowed claim against the partnership from a general partner who is not a debtor in a Chapter 7 case and who has not secured the creditor's claim with a lien on the general partner's own property. [B.C. §508(b)]

VII. DEBTOR'S EXEMPTIONS AND DISCHARGE OF INDEBTEDNESS

chapter approach

This chapter covers the areas of bankruptcy law that give the debtor a "fresh start." The most important of these topics are considered below.

First of all, recall that an individual debtor is entitled to certain *property exemptions*, which generally allow the debtor to come through the bankruptcy with some assets. The debtor may elect either the exemptions provided for by the Bankruptcy Code (if the debtor's domiciliary state has not opted out) or those permitted under applicable state exemption law. Furthermore, note that judicial liens and certain nonpossessory nonpurchase-money security interests *may be avoided* to the extent that they impair an exemption of the debtor.

The main source of the debtor's fresh start is the *discharge* of indebtedness. The key things to remember are that a discharge *relieves the debtor of personal liability* on all debts that are discharged and also *permanently enjoins* creditors from attempting to collect or recover such claims from the debtor personally. However, a discharge does not necessarily wipe the slate totally clean, since a discharge granted to an individual debtor (other than a standard Chapter 13 discharge which has different criteria for nondischargeability of debts) does not include any of the 16 kinds of *nondischargeable debts* described in Bankruptcy Code section 523(a): debts involving taxes; fraud; unscheduled debts; defalcation or fraud while acting in a fiduciary capacity, or embezzlement, or larceny; alimony or support; property settlements in a separation agreement or divorce decree; willful and malicious injury; certain fines and penalties; student loans; drunk or drugged driving; fiduciary fraud or defalcation of officers and directors of financial institutions; failure to maintain capital commitment concerning insured depository institutions; federal criminal restitution; debts incurred to pay federal taxes; certain condominium or cooperative housing fees; and a prior bankruptcy in which the debtor either waived discharge or was denied a discharge (under section 727(a)) for a reason other than the six-year prohibition against a subsequent discharge.

Also, in some instances, the debtor may desire to enter into a *reaffirmation agreement*, such as where the debt is secured by a nonavoidable lien on collateral that the debtor wishes to retain. Keep in mind that a reaffirmation agreement is enforceable only if it complies with the Code's requirements. In other instances, an individual debtor may choose to *redeem* tangible personal property from a lien by paying the secured party the market value of the collateral. Note that redemption is available in only a Chapter 7 case and only for dischargeable consumer debts.

Finally, remember that the law *prohibits discrimination* by a governmental unit, by a private employer, or by a lender engaged in a guaranteed student loan program, against one who has been a debtor in a bankruptcy case.

A. EXEMPTIONS

1. **Fresh Start—Exempt Property:** [§609] Usually, an individual debtor does not come out of bankruptcy completely dispossessed of all assets, because she is

entitled to certain exemptions from property of the estate, either under the Bankruptcy Code (*see infra,* §613) or pursuant to applicable state law and nonbankruptcy federal law (*see infra,* §§631-638). These exemptions apply only to individual debtors—not to partnerships or corporations—in cases under Chapters 7, 11, 12, and 13, and exemptions cannot be waived in favor of an unsecured creditor. [B.C. §§103(a), 522(e)]

    a. **States opting out:** [§610] Thirty-five states have rejected the federal bankruptcy exemption scheme, thereby restricting their domiciliaries to the exemptions allowable under state law and federal nonbankruptcy law. The states' power to opt out is authorized by Bankruptcy Code section 522(b)(1) and has been held to be constitutional. [*In re* Sullivan, 680 F.2d 1131 (7th Cir. 1982)]

    b. **States not opting out:** [§611] In states that have not opted out, the debtor is free to choose *either* the federal bankruptcy exemptions or those permitted under applicable state (and federal nonbankruptcy) law. [B.C. §522(b)(1), (2)]

        (1) **Joint case:** [§612] In a case filed or administered jointly (*see supra,* §§147-150), both spouses must elect the same exemption plan, either state or federal. If the debtors are not able to agree, they will be deemed to have chosen the federal bankruptcy exemptions. [B.C. §522(b)]

2. **Federal Bankruptcy Exemptions:** [§613] In states that have not opted out, the maximum exemptions of a debtor's interests in property permitted under the Code are as follows [B.C. §522(d)]:

    a. **Homestead:** [§614] The debtor may exempt up to $15,000 in real or personal property used by the debtor or a dependent as a *residence.* [B.C. §522(d)(1)]

    b. **Motor vehicle:** [§615] There is a maximum exemption of $2,400 allowed for *one* motor vehicle. [B.C. §522(d)(2)]

    c. **Household goods, crops, animals:** [§616] There is an exemption of up to $400 in any item of household furnishings, household goods, clothing, appliances, books, musical instruments, crops, or animals, whose primary purpose is for the *personal, family, or household use* of the debtor or a dependent. *But note:* This exemption may not exceed $8,000 in total value. [B.C. §522(d)(3)]

    d. **Jewelry:** [§617] There is an exemption of up to $1,000 in jewelry held principally for the personal, family, or household use of the debtor or a dependent. [B.C. §522(d)(4)]

    e. **Wildcard exemption:** [§618] There is an exemption of up to $800, plus up to $7,500 of any unused portion of the homestead exemption, *in any property.* [B.C. §522(d)(5), (1)] This exemption, with a ceiling of $8,300, is designed primarily for the benefit of nonhomeowner debtors.

    f. **Tools of the trade:** [§619] The debtor may exempt $1,500 in her professional books or tools of the trade or those of a dependent. [B.C. §522(d)(6)]

    g. **Life insurance:** [§620] Any *unmatured* life insurance contract owned by the debtor, except a credit life insurance contract, may be exempted. [B.C. §522(d)(7)]

h. **Loan value or accrued interest of life insurance:** [§621]   There is an exemption of up to $8,000 in the loan value or in accrued interest or dividends of any unmatured life insurance contract that the debtor owns. [B.C. §522(d)(8)]

   (1) **Insured:** [§622]   For purposes of this exemption, the insured must be either the debtor or an individual with respect to whom the debtor is a dependent. [B.C. §522(d)(8)] A dependent, as used in this section, includes (but is not limited to) a spouse, regardless of whether the spouse is, in fact, dependent. [B.C. §522(a)(1)]

i. **Health aids:** [§623]   There is an exemption for health aids prescribed by a professional for the debtor or a dependent. [B.C. §522(d)(9)]

j. **Government benefits:** [§624]   There is an exemption for the debtor's right to receive social security benefits, veterans' benefits, local public assistance, unemployment benefits or compensation, or disability or illness benefits. [B.C. §522(d)(10)(A)-(C)]

k. **Alimony, support, or maintenance:** [§625]   The debtor's right to receive alimony, support, or maintenance, to the extent that it is reasonably necessary to support the debtor and any dependent, is exempted. [B.C. §522(d)(10)(D)]

l. **Pension plan:** [§626]   The debtor's right to receive payments under an eligible pension plan, or similar contract based on length of service, age, illness, disability, or death, to the extent that such payment is reasonably necessary to support the debtor and any dependent, is exempted. [B.C. §522(d)(10)(E)]

m. **Crime victim award:** [§627]   The debtor's right to receive property or payment pursuant to an award under a law for a crime victim's reparation is exempted. [B.C. §522(d)(11)(A)]

n. **Wrongful death award:** [§628]   There is an exemption for the debtor's right to receive payment arising from the wrongful death of, or a life insurance policy on, an individual with respect to whom the debtor was a dependent, to the extent that such payment is reasonably necessary to support the debtor and any of her dependents. [B.C. §522(d)(11)(B), (C)]

o. **Personal injury award:** [§629]   The debtor's right to receive payment, up to a maximum of $15,000, arising from personal bodily injury of the debtor or an individual with respect to whom the debtor is a dependent, is exempted. [B.C. §522(d)(11)(D); *In re* Harris, 50 B.R. 157 (Bankr. E.D. Wis. 1985)]

   (1) **But note:** This exemption does not include compensation for pain and suffering or compensation for actual pecuniary loss, such as medical expenses. [B.C. §522(d)(11)(D); 3 Collier ¶522.20]

p. **Loss of future earnings:** [§630]   The debtor's right to receive compensation for the loss of future earnings of either the debtor or an individual with respect to whom the debtor was or is a dependent, to the extent that such payment is reasonably necessary to support the debtor and any of her dependents, is exempted. [B.C. §522(d)(11)(E); *In re* Harris, *supra*]

3. **State Exemptions and Nonbankruptcy Federal Exemptions:** [§631] If the debtor does not elect the federal bankruptcy exemptions, or if the debtor's domiciliary state has opted out (*see supra*, §610), then the exemptions available to the debtor are those allowable under applicable state law and nonbankruptcy federal law. [B.C. §522(b)(2)]

   a. **State law exemptions:** [§632] The exemptions allowable under state law are those in effect as of the date of the filing of the bankruptcy petition in the state where the debtor has been domiciled for the ***180 days*** prior to bankruptcy or for the longest part of such period. State law exemptions vary widely from state to state. [B.C. §522(b)(2)(A)]

   b. **Nonbankruptcy federal law:** [§633] Federal statutes other than the Bankruptcy Code sometimes provide exemptions that may be claimed under Bankruptcy Code section 522(b)(2)(A), such as social security payments [42 U.S.C. §407], veterans' benefits [38 U.S.C. §5301], or civil service retirement benefits [5 U.S.C. §8346(a)].

   c. **Tenancy by the entirety and joint tenancy:** [§634] A debtor who uses the state exemption alternative also may exempt any interest in property she held, immediately prior to bankruptcy, as a tenant by the entirety or as a joint tenant, to the extent that applicable nonbankruptcy law (usually state property law) exempts such interest from process. [B.C. §522(b)(2)(B)]

      (1) **Filing by both tenants:** [§635] Where both tenants are debtors in the bankruptcy case, property held in joint tenancy or in tenancy by the entirety passes to the trustee and may not be exempted under section 522(b)(2)(B). [Reid v. Richardson, 304 F.2d 351 (4th Cir. 1962)]

      (2) **Filing by one tenant:** [§636] Where only one of the tenants is a debtor in the case, her entitlement to exempt property under section 522(b)(2)(B) may depend not only on any protection from process afforded by applicable nonbankruptcy law, but also on the absence of any joint creditors.

         (a) **Tenancy by the entirety:** [§637] Where a bankruptcy petition is filed by one spouse holding property in tenancy by the entirety with her nonfiling husband, such property is exempt in most jurisdictions if there are no joint creditors. [B.C. §522(b)(2)(B); *In re* Lausch, 16 B.R. 162 (M.D. Fla. 1981); *but see In re* Persky, 893 F.2d 15 (2d Cir. 1989)—debtor's interest not exempt under New York law (which is not typical entireties law)] However, to the extent of any claims in the case by creditors to whom the debtor and her spouse are ***indebted jointly***, property held by the entirety is not exempt (in most jurisdictions) under section 522(b)(2)(B) [*In re* Garner, 952 F.2d 232 (8th Cir. 1991)] and should be available to satisfy joint creditors, either through administration by the trustee [B.C. §363(h); Sumy v. Schlossberg, 777 F.2d 921 (4th Cir. 1985)]; through proceedings against the property in the bankruptcy court by the joint creditors [*In re* Grosslight, 757 F.2d 773 (6th Cir. 1985)]; or by such creditors' obtaining relief from the automatic stay and a delay of the debtor's discharge in order to seek judgment and execution against the property in a state court. [Chippenham Hospital, Inc. v.

Bondurant, 716 F.2d 1057 (4th Cir. 1983); *but see In re* Hunter, 122 B.R. 349 (Bankr. N.D. Ind. 1990), *aff'd*, 970 F.2d 299 (7th Cir. 1992)—entirety property held exempt, under Indiana statute, from reach of joint creditors]

- (b) **Joint tenancy:** [§638] Where a bankruptcy petition is filed by a debtor holding property in joint tenancy with a nonfiling tenant, the result differs, because a joint tenant's interest in the property may be reached by her individual creditors during her lifetime. [Burby on Real Property 3d ed. 1965 (West) p. 221] Thus, the filing of the petition *severs the joint tenancy*, the bankruptcy trustee and the nonfiling tenant become tenants in common, and the trustee may seek to partition and sell the property. [*In re* Lambert, 34 B.R. 41 (Bankr. D. Colo. 1983)] Consequently, any claim of exemption in the property must be grounded on state exemption law [B.C. §522(b)(2)(A)], rather than on Bankruptcy Code section 522(b)(2)(B).

- (3) **Compare—federal bankruptcy exemptions:** [§639] If the debtor elects the exemptions under the Bankruptcy Code [B.C. §522(d); *see supra*, §§613 *et seq.*], the trustee can sever the tenancy by the entirety (or joint tenancy) and sell the property, provided that the conditions set forth in Bankruptcy Code section 363(h) are met (*see infra*, §855).

4. **Joint Case:** [§640] In a joint case (*see supra*, §147), *each debtor* is entitled to a separate claim of any allowable exemptions. [B.C. §522(m)]

   a. **Federal exemptions:** [§641] The law is clear that joint debtors who elect the federal exemptions may stack their exemptions to claim, for example, up to $30,000 in a homestead, $4,800 in automobiles, an aggregate of $16,000 in certain items intended for the personal, family, or household use of the debtors, $2,000 in personal jewelry, etc. [B.C. 522(m); *In re* Gallo, 49 B.R. 28 (Bankr. N.D. Tex. 1985)]

      - (1) **But recall:** In a joint case, *both debtors* must choose either the federal exemptions or the state exemptions, since the Code prohibits the stacking of federal and state exemptions. Thus, one spouse may not elect the federal exemptions while the other spouse elects the state exemptions. [B.C. §522(b)]

   b. **State exemptions:** [§642] The courts are split on the issue of whether Bankruptcy Code section 522(m) (allowing each joint debtor separate exemptions) applies to states that have opted out of the federal bankruptcy exemption scheme. One line of authority holds that section 522(m) applies only to the federal exemptions and does not bind states that have opted out. Under this view, such states may provide one set of exemptions to be shared by both debtors in a joint case. [*In re* Granger, 754 F.2d 1490 (9th Cir. 1985)] On the other hand, at least one circuit court has ruled that section 522(m) requires that each debtor in a joint case be entitled "to take some exemptions, whether the amount is determined by state or federal law." [Cheeseman v. Nachman, 656 F.2d 60 (4th Cir. 1981)] Thus, under this view, a state opting out of the federal exemptions nevertheless must permit each debtor in a joint case to claim separate exemptions.

(1) **Example:** Husband and Wife, domiciliaries of Nevada, file a joint bankruptcy petition. Nevada has opted out of the federal bankruptcy exemptions and provides one homestead exemption of $90,000 which, for a married couple, may be claimed by either spouse or shared by both spouses. Under the *Granger* view, Husband and Wife are entitled to a total homestead exemption of only $90,000, not $180,000. [*In re* Lenox, 58 B.R. 104 (Bankr. D. Nev. 1986)]

5. **List of Exemptions:** [§643] On the schedule of assets filed by the debtor (*see supra*, §153), she also must list the property claimed as exempt. However, if the debtor fails to file a list of exemptions, it may be filed by a dependent of the debtor. [B.C. §522(1); Bankruptcy Rule 4003(a)]

   a. **Amendments:** [§644] The courts are liberal in granting the debtor an opportunity to amend her claim of exemptions, provided that no adverse rights have intervened. [*In re* Maxwell, 5 B.R. 58 (Bankr. N.D. Ga. 1980); *but see In re* Yonikus, 996 F.2d 866 (7th Cir. 1993)—amendment denied where debtor intentionally concealed asset]

   b. **Objections:** [§645] Any creditor or the trustee may object to the debtor's claim of exemptions within 30 days after either the conclusion of the section 341 meeting or the filing of an amendment to the list or supplemental schedules (unless, within that period the court grants an extension). Objections must be served on the trustee, the debtor (or the dependent who filed the list), and the debtor's attorney. [Bankruptcy Rule 4003(b); *In re* Hilmoe, 56 B.R. 262 (Bankr. D.S.D. 1985)]

      (1) **Failure to object:** [§646] If no objection is filed by the trustee or a creditor, the property described on the debtor's list of exemptions is deemed as exempt. [B.C. §522(1)] A late objection will not be allowed even if the debtor has no colorable basis for claiming the exemption. [Taylor v. Freeland & Kronz, 503 U.S. 638 (1992)]

6. **Effect of Exemptions—Not Liable for Debts:** [§647] The general rule is that, unless the case is dismissed, property exempted by the debtor is not liable ***during or after the case*** for any pre-petition debt or any debt deemed to have arisen before bankruptcy. [B.C. §522(c)]

   a. **Exceptions:** [§648] There are certain kinds of debts which may, however, be satisfied from the debtor's exempt property; they are:

      (i) *Nondischargeable taxes* [B.C. §§522(c)(1), 523(a)(1); *see infra*, §679];

      (ii) *Nondischargeable alimony, maintenance, or spousal or child support* [B.C. §§522(c)(1), 523(a)(5); *see infra*, §691];

      (iii) *A debt secured by a lien* that is not void under B.C. section 506(d) (*see supra*, §533) and that has not been avoided under another provision of the Code [B.C. §522(c)(2)(A)];

      (iv) *A debt secured by a tax lien* if notice of the lien has been filed properly [B.C. §522(c)(2)(B)]; and

[§§649-651]

- (v) *A debt, owed by an institution-affiliated party of an insured financial institution* (to a federal depository institutions regulatory agency), for fraud or defalcation while acting in a fiduciary capacity or embezzlement or larceny, *or* for willful and malicious injury to another entity or its property. [B.C. §§522(c)(3), 523(a)(4), 523(a)(6); *see infra* §§689, 695]

    (1) **Note:** Taxes, alimony, and spousal or child support, if large enough, could consume most or all of the debtor's exempt assets.

7. **Avoidance of Liens that Impair Exemption:** [§649] Most judicial liens and certain nonpossessory, nonpurchase-money security interests may be avoided by the debtor when they *impair an exemption* that the debtor could otherwise claim. [B.C. §522(f)(1)] To avoid such a lien, the debtor must have had an interest in the property *before* the lien attached, since technically it is the *fixing of the lien* that may be avoided. [Farrey v. Sanderfoot, 500 U.S. 291 (1991)] The debtor may bring a proceeding to avoid such a lien by filing a motion. [Bankruptcy Rule 4003(d)]

    a. **"Impair an exemption":** [§650] The phrase "impair an exemption," is defined in terms of the following statutorily prescribed mathematical computation: *add* (i) the judicial lien (or nonpossessory nonpurchase-money security interest), (ii) all the other liens on the property, and (iii) the amount of the exemption available in the absence of any liens, and *subtract* the value of the debtor's interest in the property without any liens. If the value of the property is less than the total of the liens and the exemption, then the exemption is impaired to the extent of the difference. If the property is subject to more than one lien, the calculation should not include a lien that has been avoided. This formula does not apply to a mortgage foreclosure judgment. [B.C. §522(f)(2)]

        (1) **Example:** If there is a judicial lien in the amount of $10,000, a mortgage in the amount of $25,000, a homestead exemption of $7,500 (thereby making a total of $42,500 for purposes of the computation), and the value of the property in the absence of any liens is $30,000, then the lien can be avoided in its entirety because the difference of $12,500 (*i.e.*, the extent of impairment) exceeds the amount of the lien ($10,000). However, if the property is worth $42,500 or more, the exemption is not impaired and the lien cannot be avoided at all. If the property is worth $40,000, then the lien can be avoided to the extent of $2,500. [B.C. §522(f)(2)(A)]

    b. **Judicial lien:** [§651] A judicial lien is avoidable to the extent that it impairs an exemption of the debtor. [B.C. §522(f)(1)(A)] Under the Code, a judicial lien is a "lien obtained by judgment, levy, sequestration, or other legal or equitable process or proceeding." [B.C. §101(36)] For example, where a creditor obtains and records a judgment, which by state law constitutes a lien on the debtor's home, that lien is called a judicial lien which can be avoided to the extent that it impairs an exemption. (*See supra*, §650.)

        (1) **Compare:** State court judgment grants a divorce to Debtor and Spouse and divides their property, awarding to Debtor sole title to the family home (which had been owned by them jointly) and requiring Debtor to pay Spouse a dollar sum, secured by a lien on the home. The amount secured by the lien is approximately equal to the value of Spouse's previous interest in the home. Debtor fails to pay, files a voluntary Chapter 7

petition, and seeks to avoid the lien on the ground that it impairs his homestead exemption under state law. The lien *cannot be avoided*. The parties held the home in joint tenancy before their divorce, but under state law that interest was destroyed by the divorce judgment and a new interest was created—Debtor's fee simple interest. The lien attached to the fee simple interest *at the same time* the interest was created. Therefore, Debtor did not have the interest to which the lien attached before it attached. [Farrey v. Sanderfoot, *supra*]

(2) **Exception—alimony and child support:** [§652] A judicial lien securing a debt for alimony, or spousal or child support, is *not avoidable* unless the debt has been assigned to another entity or is not actually intended to constitute alimony or support. The legislative history to this provision explains that it was intended to supplement the holding in *Farrey v. Sanderfoot, supra*. [B.C. §522(f)(1)(A)(i), (ii)]

c. **Security interest:** [§653] The debtor may avoid a *nonpossessory, nonpurchase-money* security interest in any of the following items, to the extent that it "impairs an exemption to which the debtor would have been entitled." [B.C. §522(f)(1)(B)]:

(i) *Household goods* or furnishings, clothing, jewelry, appliances, books, musical instruments, crops, or animals that are held primarily for the debtor's (or a dependent's) *personal, family, or household use* [B.C. §522(f)(1)(B)(i)];

(ii) *Professional books or tools of the trade* of the debtor or a dependent [B.C. §522(f)(1)(B)(ii)]; or

(iii) *Health aids* prescribed by a professional for the debtor or a dependent [B.C. §522(f)(1)(B)(iii)].

(1) **Nonpossessory:** [§654] The security interest is avoidable by the debtor only if it is nonpossessory. [B.C. §522(f)(1)(B)] Thus, the security interest is not avoidable if the creditor has perfected by taking possession of the collateral, such is in the case of a pledge.

(2) **Nonpurchase-money:** [§655] The security interest is avoidable by the debtor only if it is *not* purchase-money in nature. [B.C. §522(f)(1)(B)] A purchase money security interest arises where money or credit is advanced by the creditor to enable the debtor to purchase the collateral, and the debtor uses that money or credit to do so. [*See* U.C.C. §9-107]

(a) **Example:** On February 1, Debtor purchased from Seller on credit a 42-foot utility flatbed trailer and granted to Seller a security interest in the trailer and, in lieu of a down payment, a security interest in a certain old cab-tractor owned by Debtor. Both the utility trailer and the cab-tractor were used by Debtor in his trucking business. After experiencing financial difficulties, Debtor filed a Chapter 7 petition on November 1, electing the federal exemptions and seeking to avoid, under section 522(f)(1)(B) the liens on both the utility trailer and the cab-tractor. The lien on the utility trailer may not be avoided since it constitutes a purchase-money security interest. However, the lien on the cab-tractor is a nonpossessory, *nonpurchase-money* security interest in a tool of the trade of Debtor and thus is avoidable to the extent that it impairs an exemption to which Debtor is entitled. [B.C. §522(f)(1)(B)(ii); *In re* Dillon, 18 B.R. 252 (Bankr. E.D. Cal. 1982)]

(b) **Refinancing:** [§656] There is a split of authority concerning whether the refinancing of a debt secured by a purchase-money security interest extinguishes the purchase-money quality of the security interest.

   1) **Transformation rule:** [§657] Some courts have held that such refinancing automatically "extinguishes the purchase-money character of the original loan because the proceeds of the new loan [which are used to satisfy the original indebtedness] are not used to acquire rights in the collateral." [*In re* Matthews, 724 F.2d 798 (9th Cir. 1984)]

   2) **Dual status rule:** [§658] Other courts have held that refinancing does not automatically extinguish the purchase-money nature of the security interest, but that the answer depends on whether the parties intended the "new note to extinguish the original debt and security interest." [*In re* Billings, 838 F.2d 405 (10th Cir. 1988)]

(c) **After-acquired property clauses and future advances:** [§659] Similarly, case law has produced two views concerning the use of a future advances clause or an after-acquired property clause to consolidate a debt secured by a purchase-money security interest with subsequent purchases. (*Note:* An after-acquired property clause in a security agreement grants a creditor a security interest in property acquired by the debtor in the future. A future advances clause in a security agreement retains a security interest in the debtor's property for advances made by the creditor to the debtor in the future.)

   1) **Transformation rule:** [§660] Some authorities have held that such use of a future advances clause or an after-acquired property clause destroys the purchase-money character of the original debt, such as in the instance of a floating lien on inventory, where the lender has not established a formula for ascertaining the allocation of payments to specific items of collateral. [Southtrust Bank of Alabama v. Borg-Warner Acceptance Corp., 760 F.2d 1240 (11th Cir. 1985)]

   2) **Dual status rule:** [§661] Other courts have sustained a purchase money security interest where either state law or the contract between the parties provided a method to allocate payments (such as "first-in first-out"). Thus, a purchase-money security interest in goods has been upheld to the extent that, under a specific rule of apportionment, the goods secured the unpaid portion of their own purchase price, even though they also secured subsequent purchases of other items. [Pristas v. Landaus of Plymouth, Inc., 742 F.2d 797 (3d Cir. 1984)]

(3) **Consumer goods:** [§662] A nonpossessory, nonpurchase-money security interest in any of the consumer or household items described in Bankruptcy Code section 522(f)(1)(B)(i) (*see supra*, §653) may be avoided only if the goods are held principally for the personal, family, or household use of the debtor or a defendant.

   (a) **Example:** Debtors, who were engaged in farming, were not permitted to void a lien on 210 pigs, even though it was argued that some of the pigs would have been consumed by the Debtors personally. The court ruled that the pigs constituted "a capital venture" and were not household or consumer goods under Bankruptcy Code section 522(f)(1)(B)(i). [*In re* Thompson, 750 F.2d 628 (8th Cir. 1984)]

   (b) **Automobiles:** [§663] An automobile is not a household good, and a security interest in a car may not be avoided under section 522(f)(1)(B)(i). [*In re* Ramey, 45 B.R. 562 (Bankr. W.D. Va. 1984)] However, some cases have held that a motor vehicle needed and used by the debtor to carry on an occupation, such as insurance or real estate sales (as opposed to merely commuting from home to a job), may qualify for lien avoidance as a tool of the trade under section 522(f)(1)(B)(ii). [*In re* Weinstein, 44 B.R. 987 (Bankr. E.D. Pa. 1984); *see* below]

(4) **Tools of the trade:** [§664] Courts differ about what may constitute tools or implements of the trade. In one case, an agricultural debtor was allowed to avoid a bank's lien on expensive farm equipment (including a tractor and a trailer), where the bankruptcy court ruled that such collateral constituted tools or implements of his trade under a broad interpretation adopted by the district court [B.C. §522(f)(1)(B)(ii); Middleton v. Farmers State Bank of Fosston, 45 B.R. 744 (Bankr. D. Minn. 1985) *on remand from* 41 B.R. 953 (D. Minn. 1984)] Conversely, the Seventh Circuit has held that, under the *federal exemptions*, neither an expensive tractor used in dairy farming nor the debtor's cows constituted tools of the trade, but that rakes and other hand tools of modest value did. Hence, a lien on the proceeds resulting from sale of the tractor and cows was not avoidable. [*In re* Patterson, 825 F.2d 1140 (7th Cir. 1987)] Interestingly, though, the same court held that under the relevant *state* exemption for tools of the trade, a lien on a combine, tractors, and other equipment used in farming could be avoided under section 522(f)(1)(B)(ii). [*In re* Thompson, 867 F.2d 416 (7th Cir. 1989); *see also In re* Heape, 886 F.2d 280 (10th Cir. 1989)—"modest herd of breeding cattle" constituted necessary tool of the trade for farmer under state exemption]

   (a) **Note—federal wildcard exemption:** [§665] Remember that a nonpossessory, nonpurchase-money security interest in tools of the trade is avoidable only to the extent that it impairs an exemption to which the debtor would have been entitled (*supra,* §653). Although the maximum federal exemption for tools of the trade is $1,500 [B.C. §522(d)(6); *see supra,* §619], the exemption may be supplemented by an amount equal to $800 plus up to $7,500 of any unused part of the debtor's homestead exemption, or, in a joint case, $1,600 plus up to $15,000 of any unused part of the homestead exemptions.

[B.C. §522(d)(5); *see supra*, §618] Thus, if such a lien is secured by tools of the trade exceeding $1,500 in value, the amount of the lien that is avoidable under Bankruptcy Code section 522(f)(1)(B)(ii) potentially may be augmented to the extent permitted by the wildcard exemption. [Augustine v. United States, 675 F.2d 582 (3d Cir. 1982)] However, in a jurisdiction that narrowly defines tools of the trade as being limited to items of modest value, a debtor having, for example, expensive farming equipment might not be able to avoid a lien securing the equipment at all if she chooses the federal exemptions, but may be able to do so by electing the applicable state exemptions if the state definition of tools of the trade is more comprehensive. [*In re* Thompson, *supra*, §664]

(5) **Pre-Bankruptcy Code security interests—noretroactivity:** [§666] A nonpossessory nonpurchase-money security interest created prior to the *enactment* of the Bankruptcy Code (November 6, 1978) may not be avoided under section 522(f)(1)(B). [United States v. Security Industrial Bank, 459 U.S. 70 (1982); *see supra,* §653]

d. ***Owen v. Owen* substantially overruled:** [§667] Prior to the Bankruptcy Reform Act of 1994, a problem arising under section 522(f) concerned the avoidance of a lien on personal property such as tools of the trade, where applicable state law defined its exemptions in a way that denied the exemption when the property was subject to a consensual lien. In 1991, the United States Supreme Court held that a state law definition of exemptions that excludes property encumbered by a lien could not prevent the debtor from avoiding a lien, under section 522(f), that "impairs an exemption to which he *would have been* entitled but for the lien itself." [Owen v. Owen, 500 U.S. 305 (1991)] This decision was substantially overturned by a statutory provision setting a *ceiling of $5,000* on the avoidance of a nonpossessory nonpurchase-money security interest in *implements, professional books, tools of the trade, farm animals, or crops* of the debtor or a dependent, where (i) a state has opted out of the federal exemptions or the debtor has chosen the state exemptions, and (ii) applicable state law allows the debtor unlimited exemptions except where the property is subject to a consensual lien, or prohibits the avoidance of a consensual lien on property that otherwise would be exempt. [B.C. §522(f)(3)]

(1) **Applicability:** [§668] Section 522(f)(3), *supra*, is limited to the specific types of property described (*i.e.*, it does not cover household goods, clothing, etc.), is limited to nonpossessory nonpurchase-money security interests (*i.e.*, it does not extend to judicial liens), and does not apply if the debtor chooses the federal exemptions. [B.C. §522(f)(3)]

e. **Chapter 13:** [§669] The vast majority of courts recognize that the lien avoidance provisions of section 522(f) apply not only in Chapter 7 cases, but also in cases under Chapter 13. [B.C. §103(a); *In re* Hall, 752 F.2d 582 (11th Cir. 1985); *and see supra*, §8] In addition, section 522(f) is applicable in a case under Chapter 11 or Chapter 12, provided that the debtor is an individual (or an individual and her spouse). [B.C. §§103(a), 522(b)]

8. **Property Recovered by Trustee:** [§670] The debtor may *exempt* property that had been transferred, which (absent the transfer) could have been exempted under

applicable federal or state law, and which has been recovered and brought into the estate by the trustee, if (i) the debtor *did not voluntarily* transfer the property or conceal it [B.C. §522(g)(1)]; or (ii) the transfer *could have been avoided* under Bankruptcy Code section 522(f)(1)(B) by the debtor [B.C. §522(g)(2); *see supra*, §§649 *et seq.*].

    a. **Examples:** Where the debtor voluntarily transferred funds into a bank account that he erroneously thought had been closed, he was not entitled to exempt such property when it subsequently was recovered by the trustee. [Redmond v. Tuttle, 698 F.2d 414 (10th Cir. 1983)] However, where a debtor paid money to a creditor as the consequence of continuous harassment by a collection agency and the threat of a sheriff's sale of his home, the transfer was deemed to have been involuntary, and the debtor was permitted to exempt the funds that the trustee recovered. [B.C. §522(g)(1)A); *In re* Taylor, 8 B.R. 578 (Bankr. E.D. Pa. 1981)]

    b. **Limitation:** [§671] This provision may be used to exempt property only to the extent that the debtor has not already claimed the maximum amount allowable for the relevant category of exemption. [B.C. §522(j)]

9. **Avoidance by Debtor:** [§672] If the trustee can avoid a transfer of property or recover a setoff but does not attempt to pursue it, the debtor may *avoid* the transfer or may *recover* the setoff to the extent that she could have exempted the property under section 522(g)(1) (*see supra*, §§670-671) if the trustee had used his avoiding powers. [B.C. §522(h); Deel Rent-A-Car, Inc. v. Levine & Freehling, 721 F.2d 750 (11th Cir. 1983)]

    a. **Example:** Where a nonjudicial foreclosure sale of the debtor's property constituted a fraudulent conveyance that the trustee did not attempt to avoid and that could have been exempted to the extent of the debtor's equity in the property, the debtor was permitted to avoid the transfer, since the debtor had not voluntarily conveyed the property and had not concealed it. [B.C. §522(h); *In re* Willis, 48 B.R. 295 (S.D. Tex. 1985]

    b. **Compare:** Where the debtor *voluntarily* granted a security interest in property to a creditor who failed to perfect the security interest, the debtor was not permitted to avoid the transfer when it was not pursued by the trustee. [B.C. §522(h), (g)(1)(A); *In re* Evingham, 27 B.R. 128 (Bankr. W.D. N.Y. 1983)]

10. **Debtor's Recovery and Exemption:** [§673] A debtor who avoids a transfer of property or recovers a setoff pursuant to section 522(f) or 522(h) may *recover* the property or the setoff in accordance with Bankruptcy Code section 550 (*see supra*, §§456-464) and may *exempt* it to the extent permitted under the applicable exemption scheme. [B.C. §522(i), (b)]

    a. **But note:** Section 522(i) may be used to exempt property only to the extent that the debtor already has not claimed the maximum amount allowable for the relevant category of exemption. [B.C. §522(j)]

11. **Administrative Expenses:** [§674] Subject to certain exceptions, exempt property usually is not liable for the payment of administrative expenses. [B.C. §522(k); *see supra*, §553]

B. NONDISCHARGEABLE DEBTS

1. **Exceptions to Discharge:** [§675] Certain debts of an *individual debtor* are nondischargeable and, therefore, survive the bankruptcy of an individual who has been granted a discharge under Chapter 7, 11, or 12, or who has received a hardship discharge under Chapter 13. [B.C. §523(a)]

    a. **Effect of nondischargeability:** [§676] Unlike the creditors whose claims against the debtor are expunged by the discharge and who thus are enjoined permanently from attempting to collect or recover such debts personally from the debtor [B.C. §524(a)(2); *see infra*, §729], a creditor who obtains a judicial determination that a particular debt is nondischargeable will be free to pursue the debtor and to attempt to recover that debt subsequent to the debtor's discharge.

    b. **Compare—denial of debtor's discharge:** [§677] A determination of nondischargeability under Bankruptcy Code section 523(a) excepts *a specific debt* from the debtor's discharge. On the other hand, the complete denial of a debtor's discharge allows *all of the debts* to survive bankruptcy, and all claimants may thereafter compete for satisfaction of their claims. [B.C. §727(a): *see infra*, §§969 *et seq.*]

    c. **Chapter 13:** [§678] Many of the provisions of section 523(a) do not apply to a standard discharge under Chapter 13. Under that chapter, all debts provided for in the debtor's plan of repayment are discharged except alimony, maintenance, and spousal or child support, student loans, liability for drunk or drugged driving, criminal restitution or a criminal fine, and certain kinds of long-term indebtedness. [B.C. §1328(a); *see infra*, §1215]

2. **Taxes:** [§679] The following taxes are nondischargeable [B.C. §523(a)(1)]:

    a. *Taxes entitled to second or eighth priority* under Bankruptcy Code section 507(a)(2) or 507(a)(8). [B.C. §523(a)(1)A); *In re* Shank, 792 F.2d 829 (9th Cir. 1986)] Second priority taxes (*see supra*, §557) are the unsecured tax claims arising during the gap period in an involuntary case in the ordinary course of the debtor's business. Eighth priority taxes (*see supra*, §§564-572) include various unsecured pre-petition tax claims (*e.g.*, an income tax for which a return was due within three years prior to bankruptcy);

    b. *Taxes for which a return either has not been filed*, or was filed late and within two years of bankruptcy [B.C. §523(a)(1)(B)]; and

    c. *Taxes concerning which the debtor filed a fraudulent return* or intentionally tried to evade the tax. [B.C. §523(a)(1)(C); *In re* Dube, 169 B.R. 886 (Bankr. N.D. Ill. 1994), *aff'd*, 1995 W.L. 238674 (N.D. Ill. 1995)] The appellate courts have split on whether this basis for nondischargeability covers a debtor's failure to pay taxes. [*In re* Bruner, 55 F.3d 195 (5th Cir. 1995)—yes, where there was a pattern of nonpayment and concealment of income; *In re* Haas, 48 F.3d 1153 (11th Cir. 1995)—no, where debtor used income to pay personal and business debts instead of taxes, which were accurately reported (*i.e.*, "mere" nonpayment)];

d. *Note:* Although the courts are split, the prevailing view at the appellate level is that *post-petition interest* on a nondischargeable tax is also nondischargeable. [*In re* Burns, 887 F.2d 1541 (11th Cir. 1989)] It has been consistently held that *pre-petition interest* on a nondischargeable tax is nondischargeable, with most courts treating the interest as included in the pre-petition claim. [*In re* Larson, 862 F.2d 112 (7th Cir. 1988)]

3. **Fraud:** [§680] Debts for money, property, services, or credit obtained by false representation or fraud (other than a statement about the financial condition of the debtor or an insider) are nondischargeable if the creditor justifiably relies on the fraudulent representation. [B.C. 523(a)(2)(A); Field v. Mans, 116 S. Ct. 437 (1995)]

   a. **Example—credit card spree:** Where Debtor, who is unemployed and has no other source of income, purchases numerous items on a credit card account shortly before bankruptcy with the intent not to pay for them, the ensuing indebtedness is nondischargeable. [B.C. §523(a)(2)(A); *In re* Deloian, 60 B.R. 169 (Bankr. N.D. Ill. 1986)]

   b. **Statutory presumptions:** [§681] *Consumer debts* totaling more than $1,000 for *luxury goods or services* owed to a single creditor and incurred by an individual debtor within 60 days before the order for relief are presumed to be nondischargeable. Similarly, *cash advances* totaling more than $1,000 that are extensions of consumer credit pursuant to an open-end credit plan received by an individual debtor within 60 days before the order for relief are presumed to be nondischargeable. [B.C. §523(a)(2)(C)]

      (1) **"Luxury goods or services":** [§682] Goods or services that a debtor or a dependent reasonably needs for maintenance or support are not considered to be luxury items. [B.C. §523(a)(2)(C)]

   c. **Punitive damages:** [§683] The courts are split on the issue of whether punitive damages are nondischargeable under Code section 523(a)(2)(A). [*In re* Levy, 951 F.2d 196 (9th Cir. 1991)—dischargeable (majority view); *In re* St. Laurent, 991 F.2d 672 (11th Cir. 1993)—nondischargeable (minority view)]

   d. **False financial statements:** [§684] A debt for money, property, services, or credit obtained by the use of a false statement about the financial condition of the debtor or an insider is nondischargeable *only* if the following elements are present:

      (i) The statement was in *writing;*

      (ii) It was *materially* false;

      (iii) The debtor made the statement with the *intent to deceive*;

      (iv) The statement related to the *financial condition* of the debtor or an insider [B.C. §101(31); *see supra*, §30]; and

      (v) It was *reasonably relied upon* by the creditor to whom the debt is owed.

      [B.C. §523(a)(2)(B); *In re* Coston, 991 F.2d 257 (5th Cir. 1993)]

(1) **Example:** In applying for welfare benefits from State X, Debtor intentionally makes materially false representations in writing concerning her financial condition. State X reasonably relies on the misrepresentations and awards Debtor $10,000 in welfare benefits. In a criminal trial, Debtor is convicted of fraud on three counts: Aid to Families with Dependent Children, Food Stamps, and Medicaid. After serving time in the state penitentiary, Debtor files a Chapter 7 petition, and State X seeks to have the $10,000 debt declared nondischargeable. State X should prevail, and the debt will survive Debtor's bankruptcy. [B.C. §523(a)(2)(B)]

e. **Costs and attorney's fees:** [§685] A creditor who unsuccessfully brings a proceeding to have a *consumer debt* declared nondischargeable under section 523(a)(2) is liable to the debtor for costs and reasonable attorney's fees if the court finds that the creditor's complaint was not substantially justified. [B.C. §523(d); *In re* Wiencek, 58 B.R. 485 (Bankr. E.D. Va. 1986)] However, costs and attorney's fees will not be imposed on the creditor if an award would be *unjust* due to special circumstances. [B.C. §523(d)]

4. **Failure to Schedule Debts:** [§686] A debt that the debtor fails to list or schedule as the Code requires [B.C. §521(1); *see supra*, §153] is nondischargeable under the following circumstances [B.C. §523(a)(3)]:

   a. **Section 523(a)(2), (a)(4), or (a)(6) debts:** [§687] For a debt that is included in Bankruptcy Code section 523(a)(2), (a)(4), or (a)(6) (*i.e.*, fraud, misrepresentation, or use of a false financial statement; larceny, embezzlement, fiduciary fraud or defalcation; or willful and malicious injury), the debt is nondischargeable if the failure to list or schedule it precludes a creditor without notice or actual knowledge of the bankruptcy case from timely filing both a proof of claim *and* a complaint to determine the dischargeability of the debt (*see infra*, §723) [B.C. §523(a)(3)(B)] *Note:* Congress seems to have inadvertently failed to include Code section 523(a)(15) debts (property settlements and "hold harmless" agreements, *infra*, §694) in section 523(a)(3)(A), (B) (*see infra*, §688). This oversight is inconsistent with inclusion of these debts in Code section 523(c)(1) (*infra*, §723). [3 Collier ¶523.13(5)(b) at note 30a]

   b. **Other debts:** [§688] For any debt other than those described in Bankruptcy Code section 523(a)(2), (a)(4), or (a)(6), the debt is nondischargeable if the failure to list or schedule it precludes a creditor who has no notice or actual knowledge of the bankruptcy case from timely filing a proof of claim. [B.C. §523(a)(3)(A)]

5. **Fiduciary Fraud or Defalcation:** [§689] Debts for fraud or defalcation *while acting in a fiduciary capacity* are nondischargeable. Also, debts for embezzlement or larceny are nondischargeable, but there is no requirement that the wrongdoing occur in a fiduciary context. [B.C. §523(a)(4); *see also In re* Bugna, 33 F.3d 1054 (9th Cir. 1994—punitive damages for fiduciary fraud held to be nondischargeable]

   a. **Technical express trust required:** [§690] For nondischargeability to be based on fiduciary fraud or defalcation, there must be a technical or express trust (*i.e.*, this exception to discharge does not cover implied, constructive, or resulting trusts). The modern trend is to construe this requirement as covering (breaches of) trust-type fiduciary duties arising by statute or common law, without a formal trust agreement. [Quaif v. Johnson, 4 F.3d 950 (11th Cir. 1993)—Georgia insurance statute requiring segregation of insurance premiums; *In re* Bennett, 989 F.2d 779 (5th Cir. 1993), *as amended* 1993 WL 268299 (1993)—managing partner's debt for breach of fiduciary duty imposed under Texas case law]

(1) **Example:** Contractor agreed to build a house for Owner at a price of $21,000. Contractor then purchased lumber costing $6,000 from Materialman and used it in the construction of the house. Owner paid $21,000 to Contractor; however, Contractor failed to pay the $6,000 to Materialman, who filed a lien on the house. Owner brought an action in state court and was granted a $6,000 judgment against Contractor, who subsequently filed a Chapter 7 petition. Owner then filed a complaint in the bankruptcy court to determine the dischargeability of the debt. Since, under relevant law, contractors are charged with an express statutory trust as well as fiduciary duties to the property owner, Contractor's defalcation in failing to pay Materialman for the lumber used in the construction of Owner's house resulted in a debt that is nondischargeable. [B.C. §523(a)(4); *In re* Weedman, 65 B.R. 288 (Bankr. W.D. Ky. 1986)]

6. **Alimony, Maintenance, and Support:** [§691]   Debts owed for alimony, maintenance, or spousal or child support, arising out of a separation agreement, property settlement agreement, divorce decree, other court order, or a governmental unit's determination based on state or territorial law, are nondischargeable. [B.C. §523(a)(5)]

   a. **Assignment:** [§692]   A debt for alimony, maintenance, or spousal or child support remains nondischargeable if it is assigned to the federal government or to a state or municipality (*e.g.*, support assigned under the Social Security Act as a condition for receiving certain welfare benefits), but the debt is dischargeable if it is assigned to any other entity. [B.C. §523(a)(5)(A)] A debt for support owed under state law to a state or municipality is nonchargeable if it is enforceable under the Social Security Act. [B.C. §523(a)(18)]

   b. **Child support creditors—appearance:** [§693]   Child support creditors or their representatives may appear and intervene in a bankruptcy case without charge if they file a form containing information that describes the child support debt and its status. [Bankruptcy Reform Act of 1994, §304(g), 108 Stat. at 4134]

7. **Property Settlements and "Hold Harmless" Obligations:** [§694]   Property settlements and "hold harmless" obligations arising out of a separation agreement, divorce decree, other court order, or a governmental unit's determination based on state or territorial law, are nondischargeable. [B.C. §523(a)(15)]

   a. **Rationale:** In a divorce, the custodial parent sometimes accepts a low amount of child support in exchange for the other parent's assuming the couple's marital debts. If the noncustodial parent could be discharged from these debts by declaring bankruptcy, the marital debts would unfairly fall on the custodial parent.

   b. **Exceptions:** There are two exceptions to the nondischargeability of property settlements and hold harmless agreements: (i) where the debtor does not have the ability to pay the debt, or (ii) where discharging the debt would produce a benefit to the debtor that outweighs the harm to the spouse, ex-spouse, or child. [B.C. §523(a)(15)(A), (B)]

8. **Willful and Malicious Injury:** [§695] Debts for willful and malicious injury caused by the debtor to another entity or its property are nondischargeable. [B.C. §523(a)(6); Piccicuto v. Dwyer, 39 F.3d 37 (1st Cir. 1994)—"intentional interference with an advantageous business relationship and unfair trade practices in a commercial context"] Recent cases have construed this provision to require "a deliberate and intentional [wrongful] act which necessarily leads to injury." However, under this view, it is not necessary to prove spite, hatred, or a specific (subjective) intent to cause harm where the harm was "substantially certain to result." [*In re* Hartley, 100 Bankr. 477 (W.D. Mo. 1988), *aff'd*, 874 F.2d 1254 (8th Cir. 1989)—debtor threw a lighted firecracker into a room knowing that it was filled with gasoline fumes and that employee was working there, and causing "psychological and permanent physical impairments and disfiguration"; *In re* Cecchini, 780 F.2d 1440 (9th Cir. 1986)]

   a. **"Willful":** [§696] The element of willfulness is judged by a strict standard, which requires "deliberate or intentional" conduct on the part of the debtor, not merely a reckless disregard. [*In re* Conte, 33 F.3d 303 (3d Cir. 1994); 3 Collier ¶523.16(1)]

   b. **"Malicious":** [§697] The predominant view is that the debtor's malice may be implied by her conduct under the circumstances. [*In re* Yanks, 931 F.2d 42 (11th Cir. 1991)] Thus, where a debtor wrongfully sells or disposes of a secured creditor's collateral with the knowledge or expectation that the action is "certain or substantially certain" to harm the creditor's economic interests, malice exists; however, an innocent or technical conversion is not automatically malicious. [*In re* Long, 774 F.2d 875 (8th Cir. 1985); United Bank of Southgate v. Nelson, 35 B.R. 766 (N.D. Ill. 1983)]

      (1) **Example:** Debtor, a potato farmer, borrowed large sums from Bank and granted Bank a security interest in all crops growing or to be grown on Debtor's farm and in all accounts arising from the sale or disposition of the collateral. Debtor knew that the security agreement conditioned any disposition of the potato crop collateral upon (i) the naming of Bank as the payee on the purchaser's check and (ii) the remittance of any such payments to Bank. However, in intentional violation of this provision, Debtor sold a portion of the potato crop collateral and converted approximately $129,000 of the proceeds to pay expenses incurred in Debtor's farming business. Furthermore, nearly $29,000 of the proceeds were entirely unaccounted for. Subsequently, Debtor filed a Chapter 11 petition, and Bank requested that the indebtedness of approximately $158,000 be ruled nondischargeable. Bank prevailed. [B.C. §523(a)(6); *In re* Clark, 50 B.R. 122 (Bankr. D.N.D. 1985)]

      (2) **Compare:** Where Debtors sold a trailer in violation of a security agreement with Finance Company, but the court found that Debtors were "relatively inexperienced in business matters, that they had difficulty in understanding business concepts, and that they had not read the security agreement," the sale was held to constitute at most a technical conversion, which was not excepted from Debtors' discharge under Bankruptcy

Code section 523(a)(6). The element of malice was not present. [*In re* Posta, 866 F.2d 364 (10th Cir. 1989)]

    c. **Damages:** [§698] The overwhelming view at the appellate level is that both the compensatory as well as any punitive portion of a debt for willful and malicious injury are nondischargeable. [*In re* Miera, 926 F.2d 741 (8th Cir. 1991)]

9. **Fines and Penalties; Court Costs:** [§699] A fine, penalty, or forfeiture owed to and for the benefit of a governmental unit is nondischargeable unless it is in compensation for actual pecuniary loss. [B.C. §523(a)(7)] (Also, fees for filing any case, appeal, complaint, or motion, as well as any other costs assessed in connection with the filing are nondischargeable even if the debtor files *in forma pauperis* or has the status of a prisoner. [B.C. §523(a)(17)])

    a. **Tax penalties:** [§700] A noncompensatory tax penalty is nondischargeable if the underlying tax to which it relates is nondischargeable and the penalty does not concern an event or transaction that happened more than three years before bankruptcy. [B.C. §523(a)(7)(A), (B); *see In re* Roberts, 906 F.2d 1440 (10th Cir. 1990); *contra*, Cassidy v. Commissioner of Internal Revenue, 814 F.2d 477 (7th Cir. 1987)]

    b. **State criminal restitution:** [§701] Court-ordered state criminal restitution payments imposed as part of a defendant's sentence and as a condition for probation are penal in nature and thus nondischargeable. [B.C. §523(a)(7); Kelly v. Robinson, 479 U.S. 36 (1986); for *federal* criminal restitution, *see infra,* §712; *see also In re* Thompson, 16 F.3d 576 (4th Cir. 1994)—costs of prosecution in criminal conviction held nondischargeable]

        (1) **Note:** In *Kelly v. Robinson, supra,* the Supreme Court stated: "Because criminal proceedings focus on the State's interest in rehabilitation and punishment, we conclude that restitution orders imposed in such proceedings operate 'for the benefit of' the State . . . [and] are not assessed 'for . . . compensation' of the victim."

    c. **Hazardous waste disposal:** [§702] Criminal fines and civil penalties for illegal disposal of hazardous wastes are nondischargeable. [B.C. §523(a)(7); *In re* Tinkham, 59 B.R. 209 (Bankr. D.N.H. 1986)]

        (1) **Compare:** Civil damages awarded to a governmental unit ***in compensation for*** the harm caused by violations of environmental laws (*e.g.*, the costs of clean up) are dischargeable under Bankruptcy Code section 523(a)(7); however, they may be nondischargeable under Code section 523(a)(6) if the violator's actions are considered to be willful and malicious under the circumstances. [*In re* Tinkham, *supra*; and *see supra,* §§695-698]

10. **Student Loans:** [§703] An educational loan made, insured, or guaranteed by a governmental unit, or extended under a program funded by a governmental unit or a nonprofit institution, is nondischargeable unless (i) the loan first became due more than ***seven years*** before the filing of the bankruptcy petition, or (ii) there will be an ***undue hardship*** on the debtor and her dependents if the debt is not discharged. [B.C. §523(a)(8)]

a. **"First became due":** [§704] The majority of courts measure the seven-year period from the date that the *first payment on the loan* was due, not from the date that each installment was due. [B.C. §523(a)(8)(A); *see In re* Nunn, 788 F.2d 617 (9th Cir. 1986)]

   (1) **Example:** To attend college, Debtor obtained a student loan guaranteed by the State of Washington. The first installment on the loan was due on March 1, 1984, and Debtor made several payments from that time until May 1987, after which she defaulted on all payments. In December 1991, she filed a Chapter 7 petition. The balance of the loan is dischargeable since the first installment came due on March 1, 1984, a date more than seven years before the filing of Debtor's bankruptcy petition. [B.C. §523(a)(8)(A); *see In re* Nunn, *supra*]

b. **Undue hardship:** [§705] The "undue hardship" exception to the nondischargeability of student loans is strictly construed and applies only in exceptional circumstances, which are likely to involve the presence of many dependents, the occurrence of a serious disease or illness, and/or the absence of occupational skills. Thus, for a debtor to obtain a discharge of a student loan that first became due within seven years before bankruptcy, the following elements should exist:

   (i) *The debtor and her dependents will be deprived of a "minimal standard of living"* if repayment is required under the debtor's present financial circumstances;

   (ii) *The financial condition of the debtor and her dependents probably will not improve sufficiently* during the time remaining for repayment of the debt; and

   (iii) *The debtor has made a bona fide attempt to repay the student loan.*

   [B.C. §523(a)(8)(B); *In re* Brunner, 46 B.R. 752 (S.D.N.Y. 1985), *aff'd*, 831 F.2d 395 (2d Cir. 1987); *see also In re* Cheesman, 25 F.3d 356 (6th Cir. 1994)]

c. **HEAL loans:** [§706] A Health Education Assistance Loan ("HEAL") is a loan extended for educational purposes to a health professional (*e.g.*, a medical student) by a private lender (*e.g.*, a bank), which is guaranteed by the United States Department of Health and Human Services. The dischargeability of this type of debt must satisfy the requirements of the applicable nonbankruptcy federal statute. [42 U.S.C. §292f(g)] A HEAL loan is not dischargeable unless three conditions are met, one of which is a finding by the court that the failure to discharge the debt would be *unconscionable.* [*In re* Johnson, 787 F.2d 1179 (7th Cir. 1986)]

   (1) **Unconscionability:** [§707] To determine whether the failure to discharge the debt is unconscionable under 42 U.S.C. section 292f(g), the court applies a higher standard than the "undue hardship" test of Bankruptcy Code section 523(a)(8)(B), above. It has been held that the court must find shockingly unreasonable terms, with particular importance being placed on the presence or absence of an excessive disparity of bargaining power, and that the court should also consider the extent to which

the debtor understood the terms of the loan agreement. Determinations of unconscionability are made on a case by case basis. [*In re* Hines, 63 B.R. 731 (Bankr. D.S.D. 1986); *and see* Matthews v. Pineo, 19 F.3d 121 (3d Cir. 1994)—nondischarge was not unconscionable under National Health Service Corps Scholarship Program (which uses same test as HEAL for unconscionability), where debtor breached agreement to provide service in the "health professional shortage area" (South Dakota) to which she was assigned by the National Health Service Corps]

(2) **Other elements:** [§708] In addition to unconscionability, the discharge of a HEAL loan requires proof that *seven years* have expired from the date that repayment was required to begin, and that the Secretary of Health and Human Services *has not waived* statutory rights to set off the balance of the debt against any federal payments or reimbursements for health services to HEAL borrowers who are carrying on their professions and have failed to repay such loans. [42 U.S.C. §292f(g), (f)]

11. **Liability for Drunk or Drugged Driving:** [§709] Any debt for death or personal injury resulting from the debtor's use of a motor vehicle while intoxicated or drugged is nondischargeable. [B.C. §523(a)(9)]

12. **Fiduciary Fraud of Officers and Directors of Financial Institutions:** [§710] Any debt arising from a judgment, consent decree, or settlement agreement, caused by the debtor's fraud or defalcation while acting in a fiduciary capacity (*see infra*, §725) with respect to any depository institution or insured credit union is nondischargeable. [B.C. §§523(a)(11), 101(34)]

13. **Failure to Maintain Capital Commitment of Insured Depository Institutions:** [§711] Any debt for *malicious or reckless* failure to maintain the capital of an insured depository institution (in breach of an agreement with a federal depository institutions regulatory agency) is nondischargeable. [B.C. §§523(a)(12), 101(35), 101(21B)]

14. **Federal Criminal Restitution:** [§712] The payment of an order of restitution under title 18 of the United States Code, for most *federal* crimes, is nondischargeable. [B.C. §523(a)(13)] In addition, fines or restitution ordered in connection with certain federal crimes (*e.g.*, sexual abuse, sexual exploitation and other abuse of children, domestic violence, telemarketing fraud) are nondischargeable under *all chapters* of the Code, and liens securing them filed in favor of the United States are *not avoided* in bankruptcy. [18 U.S.C. §3613(e)]

   a. **Note:** Payment of *state* court orders of criminal restitution imposed as part of the defendant's sentence and as a condition for probation are nondischargeable under Code section 523(a)(7), following the Supreme Court's ruling in *Kelly v. Robinson*, supra, §701.

15. **Debts Incurred to Pay Federal Taxes:** [§713] Debts incurred to pay federal taxes that would be nondischargeable under section 523(a)(1) (*see supra*, §679) are nondischargeable. [B.C. §523(a)(14)] This provision should facilitate the use of credit cards to pay such taxes.

16. **Condominium Fees:** [§714] Condominium or cooperative housing fees that become due and payable *after the order for relief* are nondischargeable if they are for a period during which the debtor either physically occupied the unit or received rental payments from a tenant. [B.C. §523(a)(16)]

17. **Prior Bankruptcy:** [§715] A debt is nondischargeable if it was or could have been listed by the debtor in a prior bankruptcy case in which the debtor either waived discharge or was denied a discharge under Bankruptcy Code section 727(a) (*see infra* §§972 *et seq.*) for any reason except the prohibition against receiving a discharge in a subsequent bankruptcy case filed within six years. [B.C. §523(a)(10)]

    a. **Reaffirmation:** [§716] A debtor's reaffirmation of indebtedness in an earlier case (*see infra,* §§733 *et seq.*) does ***not constitute a waiver*** for purposes of section 523(a)(10), and therefore such a debt is dischargeable in a subsequent bankruptcy of the debtor unless there is some other basis for its nondischargeability. [*In re* Lones, 50 B.R. 801 (Bankr. W.D. Ky. 1985)]

18. **Proof:** [§717] The Supreme Court has held that the ***preponderance-of-the-evidence*** standard of proof applies to the exceptions to discharge contained in section 523(a). [Grogan v. Garner, 498 U.S. 279 (1991)]

19. **Prior State Court Judgments:** [§718] In determining whether a particular debt is dischargeable, the bankruptcy court is not bound by a prior state court judgment, since the doctrine of res judicata (which would foreclose all issues that could have been tried in the earlier case) does not apply. Thus, the bankruptcy court independently adjudicates issues of dischargeability, considering both the record in the state court action as well as any new evidence admitted in the bankruptcy proceeding. [Brown v. Felsen, 442 U.S. 127 (1979)]

    a. **Collateral estoppel:** [§719] The Supreme Court has ruled that the doctrine of collateral estoppel does apply in discharge exception proceedings under Code section 523(a) to preclude the retrial of issues of fact which have been "actually litigated and determined" in an earlier action in a nonbankruptcy court. [Grogan v. Garner, *see supra,* §717]

        (1) **Elements:** [§720] The following elements are required for collateral estoppel:

            (i) "The issue at stake must be ***identical*** to the one involved in the prior litigation";

            (ii) "The issue must have been ***actually litigated*** in the prior litigation"; and

            (iii) "The determination of the issue in the prior litigation must have been a ***critical and necessary part*** of the judgment in that earlier action."

        [*In re* Halpern, 810 F.2d 1061 (11th Cir. 1987); Recoveredge L.P. v. Pentecost, 44 F.3d 1284 (5th Cir. 1995)]

        (2) **Consent judgment:** [§721] Where the prior state court action was settled by a consent judgment, the bankruptcy court also must find that the parties understood that the agreement would conclusively determine the issue of dischargeability in the event of bankruptcy. Thus, the consent judgment usually includes a stipulation that the debt will be nondischargeable in any future bankruptcy case. Furthermore, the court must

find that the stipulation included specific findings of fact supporting nondischargeability. [*See* Klingman v. Levinson, 831 F.2d 1292 (7th Cir. 1987); *In re* Graham, 973 F.2d 1089 (3d Cir. 1992)]

20. **Special Rules**

   a. **Debts under Bankruptcy Code section 523(a)(1), (a)(3), and (a)(8):** [§722] Debts for *taxes* [B.C. §523(a)(1)], *unscheduled liabilities* [B.C. §523(a)(3)] or *educational loans* (including HEAL loans) [B.C. §523(a)(8)] that were held to be nondischargeable in a prior bankruptcy case concerning the debtor are dischargeable in a subsequent bankruptcy case unless they *independently* are found to be nondischargeable under section 523(a) (or, for HEAL loans, under 42 U.S.C. §292f(g)) in the later case. [B.C. §523(b)]

   (1) **Example:** Debtor files a Chapter 7 petition on May 1, 1985, and receives a discharge of all her pre-petition debts, except a student loan that first became due on May 1, 1982, a date within seven years of the bankruptcy petition. [B.C. §523(a)(8)(A); *see supra*, §§703-704] On May 1, 1993, Debtor files another Chapter 7 petition. The student loan is dischargeable in the later case unless, for example, the court finds that the loan had been procured by the use of a false financial statement satisfying all the elements of Code section 523(a)(2)(B). [B.C. §523(b)]

   b. **Debt under Bankruptcy Code section 523(a)(2), (a)(4), (a)(6), and (a)(15):** [§723] The bankruptcy court has exclusive jurisdiction to determine the dischargeability of the following types of debts. A *complaint* requesting such determination *must be filed by the creditor within 60 days* after the first date set for the section 341 meeting (unless the deadline is extended by the court for cause); otherwise, the debts are discharged. [B.C. §523(c)(1); Bankruptcy Rule 4007(c); *In re* Gordon, 988 F.2d 1000 (9th Cir. 1993); *but see* §523(a)(3)(B), *supra*, §687—exception for unscheduled debts; *and see* §§523(c)(2), 101(21B)—exception for federal depository institutions regulatory agencies; *and see In re* Benedict, 90 F.3d 50 (2d Cir. 1996)—time period under Rule 4007(c) not jurisdictional and thus "subject to waiver, estoppel, and equitable tolling"]

   (1) *Debts for fraudulently obtaining money, property, services, or credit* [B.C. §523(a)(2); *see supra*, §§680-685];

   (2) *Debts for fraud or defalcation by a fiduciary,* for embezzlement, or for larceny [B.C. §523(a)(4); *see supra*, §§689-690];

   (3) *Debts for willful and malicious injury* [B.C. §523(a)(6); *see supra*, §§695-698]; and

   (4) *Property settlements and "hold harmless" obligations* [B.C. §523(a)(15); *see supra*, §694]

   c. **Other dischargeability proceedings:** [§724] A complaint requesting a determination of the dischargeability of a debt, *other than* one under section 523(a)(2), (a)(4), (a)(6), or (a)(15), may be filed at any time, even if it requires reopening the case. [Bankruptcy Rule 4007(b)]

   d. **"Fiduciary capacity":** [§725] For purposes of Code sections 523(a)(4) and (a)(11), (*see supra*, §§689, 710), any institution-affiliated party of an insured depository institution is deemed to be acting in a fiduciary capacity. [B.C. §§523(e), 101(33), (35)] *Note:* The legislative intent was to cover "only those persons who personally were involved in wrongful acts that jeopardized the financial health of financial institutions. There was no intention to affect the discharge of innocent persons." [Bankruptcy Counsellor, vol. 3, number 23, page 4, November 19, 1990]

C. EFFECTS OF DISCHARGE

1. **Relief from Personal Liability:** [§726]   A debtor is relieved of *personal* liability for all debts that are discharged. [B.C. §524(a)(1), (a)(2)] Thus, while a valid lien that has not been avoided in the bankruptcy case survives in rem and ultimately may be enforced against the property securing the debt, no action is permitted against the debtor personally for a deficiency if the debt has been discharged. [*In re* Landmark, 48 B.R. 626 (Bankr. D. Minn. 1985)]

    a. **"Debt" defined:** [§727]   The bankruptcy definition of a debt is "liability on a claim." [B.C. §101(12); Ohio v. Kovacs, *supra* §479; *and see supra*, §35]

    b. **Judgments:** [§728]   A discharge automatically voids any judgment against the debtor for personal liability on a debt that is included in the discharge. [B.C. §524(a)(1)]

    c. **Injunction:** [§729]   A discharge also constitutes a permanent statutory injunction prohibiting creditors from taking any action, or filing or continuing a law suit, designed to recover or collect a discharged debt from the debtor personally. [B.C. §524(a)(2)]

    (1) **Example:** Debtor files a Chapter 7 petition on August 3, 1983, and is granted a discharge on January 31, 1984. One of the claims in the case is for Debtor's 1977 federal income tax liability, which, due to its age, is not entitled to priority and therefore is dischargeable. On June 6, 1984, the IRS sends Debtor a past due notice demanding payment of the tax within seven days and threatening enforcement proceedings unless Debtor complies. The IRS notice constitutes an attempt to collect the discharged debt as a personal liability of Debtor and, consequently, violates the injunction of Bankruptcy Code section 524(a)(2). Therefore, the IRS will be held in civil contempt, will be enjoined from any future acts to collect or recover the tax, and may be required to compensate Debtor for attorney's fees. [*In re* Conti, 50 B.R. 142 (Bankr. E.D. Va. 1985); *see also In re* Abernathy, 150 B.R. 688 (Bankr. N.D. Ill. 1993)—IRS violated permanent injunction of Code section 524(a)(2)]

    (2) **Example:** Debtor files a Chapter 7 petition and obtains a discharge of all his pre-petition debts, including a student loan owed to University. Subsequently, Debtor requests his academic transcript, and University refuses to release it until debtor makes full repayment of the discharged student loan. University is in violation of the injunction of section 524(a)(2) and will be directed to deliver official copies of Debtor's transcript to him. [Parraway v. Andrews University, 50 B.R. 316 (W.D. Mich. (1984)]

d. **Community property:** [§730] In community property states, a discharge also enjoins any act by a creditor to collect or recover an allowable community claim [B.C. §101(7)] from community property acquired by the debtor *after* the filing of the bankruptcy petition unless (i) the community claim is nondischargeable under section 523(a) (*see supra,* §§675 *et seq.*) or (for certain long-term debts) under section 1228(a)(1) or 1328(a)(1) in the debtor's case or in a hypothetical bankruptcy case concerning the debtor's spouse, *or* (ii) the debtor's spouse has been denied a discharge in a case filed within six years of the debtor's petition or would be denied a discharge in a Chapter 7 case filed on the date of the debtor's petition. [B.C. §524(a)(3), (b); *In re* LeSueur, 53 B.R. 414 (Bankr. D. Ariz. 1985)]

2. **Co-Debtor or Surety—No Discharge:** [§731] The discharge of a debt does *not* affect the liability of any entity other than the debtor (such as a co-debtor, surety, or guarantor) or of the property of another entity. [B.C. §524(e); Union Carbide Corp. v. Newboles, 686 F.2d 593 (7th Cir. 1982); *In re* Edgeworth, 993 F.2d 51 (5th Cir. 1993)—liability of debtor's insurer for medical malpractice; *but see In re* Specialty Equipment Companies, Inc., 3 F.3d 1043 (7th Cir. 1993)—third party nondebtors released under consensual Chapter 11 plan; Republic Supply Co. v. Shoaf, 815 F.2d 1046 (5th Cir. 1987)—third-party guarantor released under Chapter 11 plan; *and see In re* A.H. Robins, Inc., 880 F.2d 694 (4th Cir.), *cert. denied,* 493 U.S. 959 (1989)—Chapter 11 plan enjoined suits against debtor's directors, insurance company, and attorneys as joint tortfeasors. (For use of Manville-type injunction/trust in Chapter 11 asbestos cases, *see* B.C. §524(g), *infra,* §§1134-1137] An exception exists, under certain circumstances, for community property acquired post-petition. [B.C. §524(a)(3); *see* above]

3. **Voluntary Repayment:** [§732] The Code expressly permits the debtor to voluntarily repay any debt. [B.C. §524(f)] However, in the absence of an enforceable reaffirmation agreement with a creditor [B.C. §524(c)], the debtor has no personal *legal* obligation to repay a debt that has been discharged.

D. REAFFIRMATION AGREEMENTS

1. **Definition:** [§733] A reaffirmation agreement is a voluntary contract between the debtor and the holder of a dischargeable claim whereby the debtor promises to repay all or part of the debt after bankruptcy. [B.C. §524(c)]

2. **Requirements for Enforceability:** [§734] A reaffirmation agreement is enforceable only if all of the following conditions are satisfied [B.C. §524(c)]:

   a. **Enforceable contract:** [§735] The reaffirmation agreement must be enforceable under nonbankruptcy law.

   b. **Made before discharge:** [§736] The agreement must have been executed prior to the granting of the debtor's discharge. [B.C. §524(c)(1); *In re* Jackson, 49 B.R. 298 (Bankr. D. Kan. 1985)]

   c. **Advice to debtor:** [§737] The agreement must include a clear and conspicuous statement advising the debtor that she *lawfully may rescind the reaffirmation* at any time before discharge or within 60 days after the reaffirmation agreement has been filed, whichever happens later. [B.C. §524(c)(2)(A)] The agreement also must contain a clear and conspicuous statement advising the debtor that a *reaffirmation is not mandatory* under the Bankruptcy Code or under state law. [B.C. §524(c)(2)(B)]

    d. **Filing with court and attorney's declaration:** [§738] The agreement must be filed with the court along with an affidavit or a declaration by the debtor's attorney (if debtor has one) stating that the debtor has been fully informed and has entered into the agreement voluntarily, that the reaffirmation "does not impose an undue hardship on the debtor or a dependent of the debtor," and that the attorney has fully advised the debtor of the legal effect and consequences of the reaffirmation and of any subsequent default. [B.C. §524(c)(3)]

    e. **Unrepresented debtor:** [§739] Where the debtor is an individual who was *not represented by an attorney when the agreement was negotiated*, the reaffirmation agreement, to be enforceable, must be approved by the court based on a finding that it is in the debtor's best interest and does not cause an undue hardship for the debtor or a dependent. [B.C. §524(c)(6)(A); *In re* Reidenbach, 59 B.R. 248 (Bankr. N.D. Ohio 1986)]

        (1) **Exception—consumer debt secured by real property:** [§740] Judicial sanction is not required if the agreement relates to a consumer debt secured by real property of the debtor. [B.C. §524(c)(6)(B)]

        (2) **"Best interest of the debtor":** [§741] While the issue of whether a reaffirmation agreement is in the debtor's best interest depends on the particular circumstances, some courts, when required to make this determination, will find that it generally is not in the debtor's best interest to reaffirm unsecured debts or undersecured debts that greatly exceed the value of the collateral, especially where the collateral is a luxury item. The rationale is that the debtor's fresh start should not be overburdened with unnecessary debts, especially since the debtor voluntarily may repay any debts after bankruptcy without being legally bound by a reaffirmation agreement. [B.C. §524(f); *see supra*, §732] Examples of reaffirmation agreements that are likely to be considered as being in the best interest of the debtor often concern debts secured by collateral such as (i) an automobile necessary for the debtor's transportation to work, the value of which is not substantially less than the amount of the debt, or (ii) essential household goods that are subject to a purchase-money security interest (*e.g.*, a washer or dryer, or an infant's playpen or stroller).

    f. **No rescission:** [§742] The debtor must not have rescinded the reaffirmation agreement by notifying the holder of the claim within the time permitted. [B.C. §524(c)(4)]

    g. **Discharge hearing:** [§743] The requirements concerning a discharge hearing must have been fulfilled. [B.C. §524(c)(5),(d); *see infra*, §§745-750]

3. **Creditor Pressure Forbidden:** [§744] The automatic stay prohibits creditors from attempting to coerce the debtor to reaffirm any pre-petition indebtedness. [B.C. §362(a)(6)]

4. **Discharge Hearing:** [§745] A discharge hearing is a judicial hearing at which the court informs an *individual debtor* whether her discharge has been granted or

denied under Chapter 7, 11, 12, or 13. If the discharge has been denied, the court explains the grounds for denial. [B.C. §524(d)]

    a. **Permissive:** [§746] If the debtor either does not reaffirm any debts, or does reaffirm and was *represented by an attorney* when the agreement was negotiated, a discharge hearing is discretionary with the court. However, if the judge schedules a hearing, the debtor must attend. [B.C. §§524(d), 521(5); *see supra* §208]

    b. **Mandatory:** [§747] Where a debtor who receives a discharge desires to enter into one or more reaffirmation agreements negotiated without attorney representation, the court must hold a discharge hearing and the debtor must attend in person. [B.C. §§524(d), 521(5)] At that time, the court must advise the debtor that a reaffirmation agreement is completely voluntary and is not required either by the Bankruptcy Code or by state law. The judge must also inform the debtor that the legal effect of the agreement is to bind the debtor contractually to repay a debt that could have been discharged and thus expose the debtor to personal liability should the debtor default on the agreement in the future. [B.C. §524(d)(1)]

        (1) **Failure to advise:** [§748] If, when required, the court does not convey these warnings to the debtor, there is a risk that any reaffirmation agreements executed by the debtor will be unenforceable. [B.C. §524(c)(5), (d)(1); *see* Arnhold v. Kyrus, 851 F.2d 738 (4th Cir. 1988)—decided prior to 1994 Bankruptcy Reform Act, which amended Code section 524(d) to require warnings only where debtor negotiated the reaffirmation agreement without attorney representation]

        (2) **Court approval:** [§749] If the debtor was without an attorney during the negotiation of an agreement reaffirming a *consumer debt not secured by real property* of the debtor, the court also must ascertain whether the reaffirmation agreement is in the debtor's best interest and whether it imposes an undue hardship on the debtor or a dependent. [B.C. §524(d)(2), (c)(6)(A); *see supra*, §§739-741]

    c. **Failure to attend discharge hearing:** [§750] If the court schedules a discharge hearing, the debtor is required to appear in person. [B.C. §§524(d); 521(5)] Failure to attend, unless excused, could constitute sufficient cause for revocation of the discharge. [*In re* Flowers, 55 B.R. 661 (Bankr. M.D. Ala. 1985)]

5. **No Absolute Right to Reaffirm:** [§751] Since a reaffirmation agreement is a voluntary contract from the perspective of both the debtor and the creditor, a secured creditor is not obligated to agree to a debtor's proposed reaffirmation. In many instances, the creditor may prefer the return of the collateral. [*In re* Whatley, 16 B.R. 394 (Bankr. N.D. Ohio 1982); *In re* Nikokyrakis, 109 B.R. 260 (Bankr. N.D. Ohio 1989)—bank could have refused to reaffirm, but was equitably estopped from denying existence of reaffirmation]

E. REDEMPTION—CHAPTER 7 CASES ONLY

1. **Tangible Personal Property:** [§752] In a Chapter 7 case, an *individual debtor* has the right to redeem tangible personal property from a lien that secures a

dischargeable consumer debt if the property is held mainly for personal, family, or household use, and it either has been exempted by the debtor (*see supra*, §§609 *et seq.*) or has been abandoned by the trustee (*see supra*, §§469 *et seq.*). The debtor may retain such collateral by paying the secured party the ***amount of the allowed secured claim***, which is determined by the collateral's market value. [B.C. §§722, 506(a); *see supra*, §§523-524]

    a. **Example:** Debtor, an individual, files a Chapter 7 petition and lists among her assets the family car, which currently is valued at $7,000, is subject to a purchase money security interest in favor of Bank, and is used solely for personal driving. The outstanding balance on the car loan is $10,000. Since Debtor has no equity in the vehicle, it is abandoned by the trustee. Debtor may redeem the automobile by paying a lump sum of $7,000 to Bank.

    b. **Lump sum:** [§753] To redeem collateral, the debtor must make payment in a lump sum and not by installment payments. [*In re* Bell, 700 F.2d 1053 (6th Cir. 1983)] Although there is some disagreement among the authorities, the better view holds that, in a Chapter 7 case, redemption and reaffirmation are the exclusive means of retaining possession of tangible personal property securing a dischargeable consumer debt, even where the debtor has remained current in her payments and has not defaulted on any installment. [*In re* Taylor, 3 F.3d 1512 (11th Cir. 1993); B.C. §521(2)] However, there are appellate cases holding that a debtor not in default can retain the collateral, without redeeming or reaffirming, by continuing to make payments pursuant to the contract. [*In re* Belanger, 962 F.2d 345 (4th Cir. 1992); *and see* B.C. §521(2)(C)]

2. **Changed Intention:** [§754] A debtor who has filed a statement of intention to reaffirm a secured consumer debt [B.C. §521(2)(A); *see supra*, §205] is not bound irrevocably by the decision and still may redeem the collateral, irrespective of her original intention. [B.C. §521(2)(C); *In re* Eagle, 51 B.R. 959 (Bankr. N.D. Ohio 1985)]

3. **No Waiver:** [§755] A debtor's right of redemption under the Bankruptcy Code cannot be waived. [B.C. §722]

F. PROTECTION AGAINST DISCRIMINATION [§756]

In addition to relieving the debtor of personal liability for any debts discharged, the law enhances her fresh start by providing express prohibitions against discriminatory treatment of one who has been a debtor under the Bankruptcy Code or a bankrupt under the Bankruptcy Act. [B.C. §525]

1. **Governmental Discrimination:** [§757] A governmental unit may not discriminate against a ***person*** (*see supra*, §28) solely because that person (i) is or was a debtor (or a bankrupt) in a bankruptcy case, (ii) was insolvent before or during such a case, or (iii) has not paid a debt that was discharged or is dischargeable in the case. This prohibition prevents a governmental unit from terminating an employee; from discriminating with respect to employment; or from denying, revoking, suspending, or declining to renew a license, franchise, or similar privilege for any of these reasons. [B.C. §525(a); Perez v. Campbell, 402 U.S. 637 (1971)]

    a. **Example:** State Industrial Commission prohibits Chapter 13 Debtor from continuing to operate a business solely because of Debtor's pre-petition default in payment of premiums to a certain workers' compensation fund. The governmental action is discriminatory and will be enjoined by the court. [B.C. §525(a); *In re* Geffken, 43 B.R. 697 (Bankr. N.D. Ohio 1984)]

    b. **Compare—post-bankruptcy credit:** [§758] The evaluation of a post-discharge credit application may consider the applicant's *future* financial responsibility, provided that such consideration [does] not discriminate against bankruptcy debtors. [3 Collier ¶525.02(2)]

2. **Private Employer:** [§759] A private employer may not discriminate with respect to employment against an *individual* who has been a debtor (or a bankrupt) in a bankruptcy case nor terminate the individual's employment, if such treatment is based solely upon any of the three reasons described above in connection with the statutory ban on governmental discrimination. [B.C. §525(b); Comeaux v. Brown & Williamson Tobacco Co., 915 F.2d 1264 (9th Cir. 1990); *see supra*, §757]

    a. **Example:** Debtor, a bank teller with an excellent employment record at Local Bank, files a Chapter 7 petition. The next morning, City Newspaper prints an article publicizing the bankruptcy case, disclosing Debtor's total assets and liabilities, and pointing out her outstanding indebtedness of $189,000 to Local Bank. After learning of the newspaper article, Local Bank immediately transfers Debtor from her job as a teller to a noncontact position in the bank's bookkeeping department. Debtor's supervisor admits that the sole reason for the transfer is Debtor's involvement in the bankruptcy case. Local Bank's conduct is unlawfully discriminatory in violation of section 525(b). Therefore, Local Bank will be directed to restore Debtor to her preferred position as a teller. [*In re* Hicks, 65 B.R. 980 (Bankr. W.D. Ark. 1986; *compare* Laracuente v. Chase Manhattan Bank, 891 F.2d 17 (1st Cir. 1989)—Code provision was not violated where termination of Debtor (bank employee) was not *solely* because of her bankruptcy status, but resulted from Debtor's abuse of position of trust by participating in loans to family members and husband's employees]

3. **Student Loans:** [§760] Any governmental unit or lender engaged in a guaranteed student loan program is prohibited from discriminating against a student loan applicant because the applicant (i) is or was a debtor in a bankruptcy case, (ii) was insolvent before or during such a case, or (iii) failed to pay a debt that was discharged or is dischargeable in the case. [B.C. §525(c)]

    a. **But note:** As drafted, however, Code section 525(c) appears to cover any loan (*i.e.,* not only student loans) made by a lender that is engaged in a guaranteed student loan program.

VIII. ADMINISTRATIVE POWERS

chapter approach

It is very likely that your bankruptcy exam will include questions requiring you to apply the law concerning adequate protection, the automatic stay, and the administrative powers of the trustee or debtor in possession. The following questions should help you to focus on the important points for discussion of the topics:

1. **Automatic Stay:** Does a particular act come within any of the types of conduct *prohibited* by the automatic stay provisions of Bankruptcy Code section 362(a)? Remember that the automatic stay protects the debtor, the estate property, and the debtor's property from the moment the bankruptcy petition is filed. On the other hand, be sure to check to see whether the act is *excepted from the stay* under Code section 362(b). Finally, if the act is subject to the automatic stay, is there a basis for granting *relief from the stay*?

2. **Adequate Protection:** Is an entity's interest in property adequately protected by periodic cash payments, by an additional or replacement lien, by an equity cushion, or in some other manner constituting the indubitable equivalent of the entity's interest? Adequate protection of an entity's interest in property is required for property subject to the *automatic stay*; for property *used, sold, or leased* by the trustee or debtor in possession; or when the court authorizes the trustee or debtor in possession to incur debt or obtain credit secured by an *equal or senior lien* on property of the estate that is already subject to the entity's lien.

3. **Administrative Powers of Trustee or Debtor in Possession**

   a. If the trustee or debtor in possession wants to *use, sell, or lease property* of the estate, will the transaction occur in or out of the ordinary course of the debtor's business? Such transactions that are out of the ordinary course of business require notice and a hearing (*see supra*, §14). Also remember that if the property constitutes *cash collateral*, court authorization (after notice and hearing) or the consent of all entities having an interest in the property is required.

   b. If *post-petition financing* is needed, will it be in or out of the ordinary course of business, and on what basis can financing be obtained? Possibilities include: (i) as an *administrative expense*, (ii) by the grant of a *super-superpriority* that is ahead of all administrative expenses, or (iii) by the grant of a *lien*.

   c. If the debtor is a party to an *executory contract or unexpired lease*, be sure to discuss: (i) whether the trustee or debtor in possession wants to assume, assign, or reject it; (ii) if and how this may be accomplished (don't forget court approval); and (iii) what the legal consequences of the assumption, assignment, or rejection are.

   d. Finally, has the debtor been *denied utility service* because of the bankruptcy case? Has the debtor provided the utility with adequate assurance of payment for services rendered after the order for relief?

A. ADEQUATE PROTECTION

1. **Interest in Property:** [§761] In certain instances, the Bankruptcy Code mandates that a party's interest in property be protected. Thus, adequate protection of an entity's interest in property is required in the following circumstances [B.C. §361]:

    a. **Property subject to automatic stay:** [§762] Where the entity's interest in property is subject to the automatic stay, and the court has not granted relief from the stay, adequate protection is required. [B.C. §362(d)(1); *see infra*, §813]

    b. **Property used, sold, or leased:** [§763] Where the entity has an interest in property that is used, sold, or leased by the trustee or the debtor in possession, adequate protection is required. [B.C. §363(e); *see infra*, §849]

    c. **Equal or senior lien on property:** [§764] Where the court authorizes the trustee or the debtor in possession to incur debt or to obtain credit secured by a lien on property of the estate that is equal or senior to a lien held by the entity on the same property, adequate protection of the entity's interest is required. [B.C. §364(d)(1)(B); *see infra*, §871]

2. **Methods of Providing Adequate Protection:** [§765] An entity's interest in property may be adequately protected in a variety of ways; the Bankruptcy Code sets forth three nonexclusive methods [B.C. §361]:

    a. **Periodic cash payments:** [§766] The trustee or debtor in possession may provide adequate protection by making periodic cash payments to the extent that an entity's interest in the property has decreased in value due to the automatic stay; as a result of the use, sale, or lease of the property; or because of the grant of a lien of equal or higher priority on the property. [B.C. §361(1)]

    b. **Additional or replacement lien:** [§767] The trustee or debtor in possession may provide adequate protection by furnishing an additional or replacement lien to the extent of any decrease in value of the entity's interest in the property caused by the automatic stay; the use, sale, or lease of the property; or the grant of a senior or equal lien on the property. [B.C. §361(2)]

    c. **Indubitable equivalent:** [§768] The Code contains a catchall provision for furnishing adequate protection by means of relief constituting the indubitable equivalent of the entity's interest in the property. [B.C. §361(3)] Any relief granted under this provision must be "completely compensatory." [*In re* Murel Holding Corp., 75 F.2d 941 (2d Cir. 1935)] While the court is afforded great flexibility in fashioning adequate protection appropriate in a particular instance, usually protection against depreciation and the payment of taxes, insurance, and maintenance expenses concerning the property are important considerations.

        (1) **Example—third-party guarantee:** Under certain circumstances, an entity might be provided with adequate protection by the guarantee of a third person who agrees to compensate the entity for any decrease in the value of the entity's interest.

(2) **Restriction:** [§769] An entity's entitlement to adequate protection may not be satisfied by giving the entity an administrative expense. [B.C. §§361(3), 503(b)(1); *see supra*, §§537 *et seq.*]

3. **Equity Cushion:** [§770] Often, an *oversecured* creditor is adequately protected by an equity cushion—the amount by which the value of the collateral exceeds the debt owed to the creditor. A substantial equity cushion may adequately protect a secured creditor's interest from depreciation of the collateral that might occur while the property is being used, sold, or leased by the trustee or the debtor in possession, or while the automatic stay precludes the secured party from taking possession. [*In re* Mellor, 734 F.2d 1396 (9th Cir. 1984)]

   a. **Example:** Debtor, the owner of certain land valued at $100,000, files a Chapter 11 petition. First Mortgagee is owed $50,000, secured by a mortgage on the realty. Second Mortgagee holds a junior lien on the same property in the amount of $80,000. First Mortgagee files a motion to lift the automatic stay, under Bankruptcy Code section 362(d)(1), on the ground of lack of adequate protection. Unless the land is expected to depreciate rapidly, the equity cushion of $50,000 appears to be sufficient to adequately protect First Mortgagee's interest. Therefore, First Mortgagee's motion for relief from the stay probably will be denied.

      (1) **Note:** In determining whether the equity cushion adequately protects First Mortgagee's interest in the property, the court compares the value of the property to the amount of the secured claim plus all senior secured claims. Therefore, the court does not take into consideration Second Mortgagee's junior lien of $80,000. However, it would be relevant to a determination, under Bankruptcy Code section 362(d)(2)(A), that Debtor has no equity in the property. [*In re* Liona Corp., N.V., 68 B.R. 761 (Bankr. E.D. Pa. 1987)]

   b. **Compare—equity:** [§771] Equity is the amount by which the value of collateral exceeds the aggregate value of *all secured claims* against that property. [La Jolla Mortgage Fund v. Rancho El Cajon Associates, 18 B.R. 283 (Bankr. S.D. Cal. 1982)]

   c. **Accrual of post-petition interest:** [§772] While an oversecured creditor is entitled to the *accrual* of post-petition interest, this allowance does not entitle the oversecured creditor to *present payments* of post-petition interest. [B.C. §506(b); *In re* Delta Resources, Inc., *supra*, §530; 3 Collier ¶506.05; *but see In re* Revco D.S., Inc., *supra*, §530—allowing interim payments; *and see supra*, §§530-531] Recently, a few cases have held that after *Timbers* (*see infra*, §774) an oversecured creditor is not entitled to protection of its equity cushion to cover the accrual of post-petition interest where the value of collateral is not declining. [*In re* Westchase I Associates, L.P., 126 B.R. 692 (W.D.N.C. 1991); *see also In re* Delta Resources, Inc., *supra*]

4. *American Mariner* **Rule—Lost Opportunity Cost:** [§773] In the past, some courts had held that adequate protection of an *undersecured* creditor's interest in property required compensation for the delay caused by the automatic stay in exercising the creditor's right to repossess and sell the collateral and to reinvest the proceeds. [B.C. §§362(d)(1), 361; *In re* American Mariner Industries, Inc., *supra*, §118]

This rule was designed to preserve the present value of the secured party's interest as well as the benefit of his bargain. Consequently, in jurisdictions where this doctrine was applied, post-petition interest payments to undersecured creditors were approved as one method of furnishing adequate protection that was completely compensatory, *i.e.*, that not only sufficiently safeguarded the principal, but that also assured present value.

    a. **Rejection of *American Mariner*:** [§774] The United States Supreme Court rejected the *American Mariner* approach and held that the requirement of adequate protection does *not* entitle an undersecured creditor to receive compensation (*i.e.*, interest) for the delay caused by the automatic stay in foreclosing on the creditor's collateral and reinvesting the proceeds. This decision construes adequate protection to mean protection against ***depreciation in "the value of the collateral,"*** and not protection of "a secured party's right to immediate foreclosure." [United Savings Association of Texas v. Timbers of Inwood Forest Associates Ltd., 484 U.S. 365 (1988)] As pointed out by the Fifth Circuit, secured creditors are provided with other remedies to safeguard against unreasonable delay. These include seeking relief from the automatic stay for the purpose of foreclosure when the debtor has no equity in the collateral and there is no reasonable possibility of a successful reorganization [B.C. §362(d)(2)], requesting conversion or dismissal of the case [B.C. §1112(b)], or proposing a Chapter 11 plan of reorganization or liquidation after the debtor's period of exclusivity has expired [B.C. §1121(c)]. [*In re* Timbers of Inwood Forest Associates, Ltd., 808 F.2d 363 (5th Cir. 1987), *aff'd*, 484 U.S. 365 (1988)]

5. **Valuation of Collateral:** [§775] To determine what constitutes adequate protection in any particular case, it is necessary to ascertain the value of the collateral as accurately as possible. As indicated earlier, the valuation will differ depending on whether the court applies a liquidation standard or a going concern approach (*see supra*, §§525-528). Therefore, the question of valuation should remain flexible and ultimately will depend on the specific circumstances surrounding the intended use or disposition of the collateral, as well as the probability of an effective reorganization. [B.C. §506(a); 2 Collier ¶361.02]

6. **Failure of Adequate Protection:** [§776] If adequate protection is provided to a creditor whose claim is secured by a lien on property of the debtor, but the "adequate protection" eventually is shown to have been deficient, the secured creditor will receive an administrative expense claim with priority over all other administrative expenses allowed in the case. [B.C. §507(b); *see supra*, §579]

7. **Chapter 12 Cases:** [§777] The adequate protection provisions of Bankruptcy Code section 361 are *not* applicable in a case under Chapter 12 concerning a family farmer. The Code contains special rules for adequate protection in a case under that chapter. [B.C. §1205; *see infra*, §1249]

B. AUTOMATIC STAY [§778]

The automatic stay is a statutory injunction that takes effect ***when a bankruptcy petition is filed*** and protects the debtor, the property of the estate, and the property of the debtor from certain actions by creditors. It is designed to provide a respite for the debtor and promote an orderly administration of the bankruptcy case. The stay applies to ***all entities***. [B.C. §§362, 101(15); *see supra*, §29]

1. **Acts Enjoined:** [§779] Once the bankruptcy petition has been filed, the following acts are prohibited by the automatic stay [B.C. §362(a)]:

    a. **Proceedings against debtor:** [§780] The commencement or continuation (including the issuance or service of process) of a judicial, administrative, or other action against the debtor is stayed if the action is intended to recover a *pre-petition claim* against the debtor, or if the action was commenced or could have been commenced before the bankruptcy petition was filed. [B.C. §362(a)(1); Ellis v. Consolidated Diesel Electric Corp., 894 F.2d 371 (l0th Cir. 1990)]

        (1) **Claim:** [§781] Since the concept of a bankruptcy claim is viewed expansively by most courts, pre-petition claims may include causes of action that have resulted from pre-bankruptcy conduct and pre-petition legal relationships which, under state law, are not cognizable until after the filing of the bankruptcy petition. [B.C. §101(5); *In re* Johns-Manville Corp., *supra*, §481]

            (a) **Compare—post-petition claims:** [§782] Causes of action *against the debtor* that are purely post-petition in nature, such as fraud committed by the debtor after the filing of the bankruptcy petition, are not barred by the automatic stay. [*In re* Vacuum Cleaner Corp. of America, 58 B.R. 101 (Bankr. E.D. Pa. 1986)]

    b. **Pre-petition judgments:** [§783] The enforcement against the debtor or against property of the estate of a pre-petition judgment is enjoined. [B.C. §362(a)(2)]

    c. **Acts against estate property:** [§784] Any act to obtain possession of estate property or property in the possession of the estate, or to exert control over estate property, is prohibited regardless of whether the underlying claim arose before or after the filing of the bankruptcy petition. [B.C. §362(a)(3)]

        (1) **Example:** On March 1, Debtor contracted to lease certain real property from Lessor for a period of one year, with rent to be paid monthly. Debtor took possession immediately and paid the first month's rent in full, but thereafter defaulted on all payments. On September 1, Debtor filed a Chapter 11 bankruptcy petition, while remaining in possession of the property. Since Debtor's interest in the lease constitutes estate property [B.C. §541(a)(1); *see supra*, §§295-296], the automatic stay prevents Lessor from terminating the lease and retaking the property. [B.C. §362(a)(3)] Under these circumstances, Lessor must file a motion requesting relief from the automatic stay to retake possession of the property. [B.C. §362(d); *see infra*, §§809 *et seq.*, 825]

        (2) **Example:** Insurance Company issued a "prepaid excess officers and directors liability" policy to Debtor, who shortly thereafter filed a voluntary Chapter 11 bankruptcy petition. Insurance Company then canceled the policy and sent notice to Debtor. Cancellation of the policy violated the automatic stay since the insurance policy constituted property of the estate. [B.C. §362(a)(3); *In re* Minoco Group of Companies, Ltd., 799 F.2d 517 (9th Cir. 1986)]

d. **Liens against estate property:** [§785] Any act designed to create, perfect, or enforce a lien against estate property is enjoined. [B.C. §362(a)(4)]

   (1) **Example—foreclosure:** A mortgagee may not foreclose on property of the estate without first obtaining relief from the automatic stay. [B.C. §362(a)(4); *In re* Lewis, 63 B.R. 90 (Bankr. E.D. Pa. 1986)]

   (2) **Example—perfection:** Likewise, a mortgagee is precluded from recording a mortgage on estate property, and a secured creditor is barred from filing a financing statement, under Article 9 of the Uniform Commercial Code, to perfect a security interest in property of the estate. [B.C. §362(a)(4)]

      (a) **Note:** There is a limited exception to the stay that authorizes post-petition perfection in certain circumstances. [B.C. §362(b)(3); *see infra*, §795]

e. **Liens against debtor's property:** [§786] Any act intended to create, perfect, or enforce a lien against property of the debtor is prohibited *to the extent that the lien secures a pre-petition claim*. [B.C. §362(a)(5)]

   (1) **Examples:** Property that has been *abandoned* by the trustee under Bankruptcy Code section 554 (*see supra*, §469) reverts to the debtor and is protected by the automatic stay from any lien securing a pre-bankruptcy claim. [*In re* Motley, 10 B.R. 141 (Bankr. M.D. Ga. 1981)] The stay also shields the debtor's *exempt property* and property *acquired post-petition*. [B.C. §362(a)(5); 2 Collier ¶362.04(5)]

f. **Collection efforts:** [§787] Any act to collect, recover, or assess a claim against the debtor that arose prior to the bankruptcy petition is forbidden. Thus, creditors may not bother or intimidate the debtor about repayment of pre-petition obligations. [B.C. §362(a)(6)]

   (1) **Example:** On March 1, Debtor, owing $2,000 to Credit Union, filed a Chapter 7 petition, and notice of the case was sent to Credit Union. Between March 2 and April 1, Credit Union's agent telephoned Debtor on 10 different occasions, demanding repayment of its claim. These acts are in clear violation of the automatic stay and are likely to subject Credit Union to contempt proceedings as well as liability for damages. [B.C. §362(a)(6), (h); *see infra*, §831]

   (2) **Example:** A creditor's *garnishment* of the debtor's wages to recover a pre-petition debt similarly would contravene the automatic stay. [B.C. §362(a)(6); *In re* O'Connor, 42 B.R. 390 (Bankr. E.D. Ark. 1984)]

g. **Tax Court proceedings:** [§788] The commencement or continuation of a case in the United States Tax Court concerning the debtor is specifically stayed, since the jurisdiction of the bankruptcy court includes the power to adjudicate relevant tax liability issues. [B.C. §§362(a)(8), 505; 2 Collier ¶362.04(8)]

h. **Setoffs:** [§789] The automatic stay also enjoins the post-petition setoff of mutual debts. Thus, the setoff of a pre-petition debt owing to the debtor against a claim asserted against the debtor is prohibited unless the court grants relief from the stay. [B.C. §§362(a)(7), 553; *see supra*, §§334 *et seq.*]

(1) **Compare—bank's administrative freeze:** [§790] The United States Supreme Court has held that a bank's *temporary hold* on a debtor's deposit account (up to the amount allegedly subject to setoff), while the bank seeks relief from the automatic stay and the court's determination of its right to a setoff, does not violate the automatic stay. [Citizens Bank of Maryland v. Strumpf, *supra*, §§346-349]

2. **Exceptions to Automatic Stay:** [§791] The filing of a bankruptcy petition does not operate as a stay of the following actions [B.C. §362(b)]:

   a. **Criminal proceedings:** [§792] The commencement or continuation of a criminal action against the debtor is not enjoined by the automatic stay. [B.C. §362(b)(1); United States v. Troxler Hosiery Co., 41 B.R. 457 (M.D.N.C. 1984); *aff'd*, 796 F.2d 723 (4th Cir. 1986); *and see In re* Fussell, 928 F.2d 712 (5th Cir. 1991)—discussion of bankruptcy court's authority **under Code section 105** (*see supra*, §42) to enjoin a state criminal proceeding]

   b. **Alimony or support:** [§793] The collection of alimony, maintenance, or spousal or child support is not forbidden if it is obtained from assets that are not property of the estate, such as property that is exempt or is acquired post-petition by the debtor. [B.C. §362(b)(2)(B); United States v. Sutton, *supra*, §512; 2 Collier ¶362.05(2)]

   c. **Modification orders and paternity suits:** [§794] The commencement or continuation of a paternity suit or of an action seeking modification of an order for alimony, maintenance, or support is excepted from the automatic stay. [B.C. §362(b)(2)(A)]

   d. **Certain acts of perfection:** [§795] The perfection of an interest in property is not prohibited by the automatic stay if it occurs within the 10- (or 20-, for purchase-money transactions) day grace period allowed by Bankruptcy Code section 547(e)(2)(A) (*see supra*, §400), or if it would prevail over the trustee's avoiding powers pursuant to section 546(b) (*see supra*, §§438-440), such as in the case of retroactive perfection of a purchase-money security interest under U.C.C. section 9-301(2). Also, the filing of a *continuation statement* is excepted from the automatic stay. [B.C. §362(b)(3); *see also In re* Lionel Corp., 29 F.3d 88 (2d Cir. 1994)—post-petition perfection of mechanic's lien (under New York Lien Law) did not violate automatic stay]

   e. **Police or regulatory actions:** [§796] The commencement or continuation of a proceeding by a governmental unit to enforce its police or regulatory power is not stayed. [B.C. §362(b)(4); Board of Governors of the Federal Reserve System v. MCorp Financial, Inc., 502 U.S. 32 (1991)—administrative proceedings against bank holding company not enjoined] Courts usually look to see if the primary purpose of the governmental proceeding is to effectuate public policy (excepted), rather than to protect its pecuniary interest in the debtor's property or advance private rights (not excepted). [Eddleman v. United States Department of Labor, 923 F.2d 782 (10th Cir. 1991); *see also* City of New York v. Exxon Corp., 932 F.2d 1020 (2d Cir. 1991)—governmental actions under CERCLA to recover costs expended in response to completed environmental violations are not stayed]

(1) **Example:** The commencement or continuation of an action by the Equal Employment Opportunity Commission to enjoin violations of Title VII of the 1964 Civil Rights Act, to reinstate victims of alleged unlawful discrimination, *and* to recover back pay for the victims "is not subject to the automatic stay until its monetary claims are reduced to judgment." [EEOC v. McLean Trucking Co., 834 F.2d 398 (4th Cir. 1988); *see also* N.L.R.B. v. Edward Cooper Painting, Inc., 804 F.2d 934 (6th Cir. 1986)—unfair labor practice proceeding resulting in *entry, but not enforcement*, of money judgment for backpay to employees was excepted from the automatic stay]

(2) **Example:** Debtor owns 33 acres of land on which he operates a truck salvage business in violation of Town's zoning ordinance. Town brings an action in state court seeking to enjoin Debtor's activities, and Debtor unsuccessfully attempts to obtain a zoning variance to use part of his property as a junkyard. Subsequently, Debtor files a Chapter 11 bankruptcy petition, while remaining in possession of his property and continuing to violate the ordinance. Town then files contempt charges against Debtor in the state court, which orders Town to clear the land by removing and selling Debtor's inventory of used truck parts, and to remit the proceeds in excess of the cleanup costs to the Debtor's estate. Town's continuation of the proceeding to enforce its zoning ordinance is not a violation of the automatic stay, and it may proceed to implement the state court's judgment. [B.C. §362(b)(4), (5); Cournoyer v. Town of Lincoln, 790 F.2d 971 (1st Cir. 1986)]

f. **Enforcement of judgments by governmental units:** [§797] The enforcement of a judgment obtained by a governmental unit in implementing its police or regulatory power is not subject to the automatic stay if the judgment is one *other than a money judgment*. [B.C. §362(b)(5)]

(1) **Example:** Debtor operates coal mines in violation of certain environmental protection laws and enters into an agreement with the Department of Environmental Resources to correct the infractions. Debtor fails to comply, stops all operations, and files a Chapter 7 bankruptcy petition. The Department of Environmental Resources then obtains a state-court mandatory injunction directing Debtor to correct the infractions. Debtor files an action for contempt in the bankruptcy court, alleging violation of the automatic stay. According to the Third Circuit, the action comes within the State's police and regulatory powers, and the automatic stay will not prevent the Department from enforcing the injunction by compelling Debtor to restore the environment. The injunction is not a compensatory monetary judgment capable of being reduced to a sum certain, but rather constitutes equitable relief to avert future damage to the environment. [B.C. §362(b)(4), (5); Penn Terra Limited v. Department of Environmental Resources, 733 F.2d 267 (3d Cir. 1984)]

(a) **Note:** A contrary interpretation is possible if the court finds that Debtor's only obligation in performing the court's order is the payment of money. Thus, in the preceding example, assume that, prior to bankruptcy, the state court had dispossessed Debtor from his property (for failure to comply with a cleanup order) by appointing a receiver to clear the land, and that the Department now seeks a post-petition order from the state court directing that the costs of cleanup be defrayed by payments from Debtor's current income. In essence, the relief requested is equivalent to the enforcement of a *money judgment* against Debtor, and such action is enjoined by the stay. [B.C. §362(b)(5); *see In re* Kovacs, 681 F.2d 454 (6th Cir. 1982), *vacated and remanded*, 459 U.S. 1167 (1983), *dismissed as moot*, 755 F.2d 484 (6th Cir. 1985)]

g. **Securities, repo, and swap setoffs:** [§798]   The setoff of a claim against the debtor for a margin or settlement payment [§101(38), (51A)] in connection with a securities contract, commodity contract, forward contract, or repurchase agreement is not stayed with respect to a mutual debt. The setoff must be one made by a stockbroker, commodity broker, forward contract merchant, repo participant, securities clearing agency, or financial institution. [B.C. §362(b)(6), (7)] Also excepted from the automatic stay is the setoff of a claim against the debtor by a swap participant, with respect to a mutual debt, and in connection with any swap agreement. [B.C. §§362(b)(17), 101(53 B, C)]

h. **HUD mortgage foreclosures:** [§799]   The *commencement* of certain mortgage or deed of trust foreclosure actions by the Secretary of Housing and Urban Development is excepted from the automatic stay. [B.C. §362(b)(8)]

i. **Tax audits and assessments:** [§800]   A tax audit, an issuance of a notice of tax deficiency, a demand for tax returns, and an assessment of any tax and issuance of a notice and demand for payment of the assessed tax are excepted from the automatic stay. [B.C. §362(b)(9)]

   (1) **Tax lien:** [§801]   Any tax lien that otherwise would attach to property of the estate as a result of the assessment will *not be effective*, unless the tax debt is nondischargeable and the property or its proceeds are transferred out of the estate to the debtor or otherwise revest in the debtor (apparently referring to abandoned or exempt property, or revesting of property under Code sections 1141(b), 1227(b), or 1327(b)) (*see infra*, §§1118, 1242, 1211). [B.C. §362(b)(9)(D)]

j. **Recovery of property by certain lessors:** [§802]   Also not prohibited by the automatic stay is any act by a debtor's lessor to obtain possession of nonresidential real property when the lease has terminated *by the expiration of its stated term* prior to the filing of the bankruptcy petition or during the case. [B.C. §362(b)(10); *In re* Northeastern International Airways, Inc., 56 B.R. 247 (S.D. Fla. 1986); *In re* Neville, *supra*, §311]

   (1) **Note:** A debtor's leasehold interest in nonresidential realty for which the lease has terminated at the expiration of its stated term, before or during the case, is not included in property of the estate. [B.C. §541(b)(2); *see supra*, §311]

k. **Presentment of negotiable instruments:** [§803]   The presentment of a negotiable instrument, sending notice of dishonor, and protesting dishonor are not barred by the stay. [B.C. §362(b)(11); Morgan Guaranty Trust Co. of New York v. American Savings & Loan Association, 804 F.2d 1487 (9th Cir. 1986)]

l. **Certain actions against educational institutions:** [§804] Any action by an accrediting agency or state licensing body concerning the accreditation status or licensure of the debtor as an educational institution is not enjoined by the stay, nor is any action by a guaranty agency or the Secretary of Education concerning the debtor's eligibility to participate in programs under the Higher Education Act of 1965. [B.C. §362(b)(14), (15), (16)]

m. **Repossession of aircrafts and vessels:** [§805] In a *Chapter 11 case* concerning a debtor that is a certified air or water carrier, the Code provides lessors, conditional vendors, and secured parties (whether or not their security interest is purchase money) with qualified protection from the automatic stay in connection with their repossession of certain aircrafts, aircraft equipment, or vessels. [B.C. §1110]

n. **Ad valorem property tax liens:** [§806] The creation or perfection of a statutory lien for ad valorem property taxes that *become due post-petition* are excepted from the automatic stay. [B.C. §362(b)(18)]

3. **Expiration of Stay:** [§807] Unless the court grants relief from the automatic stay (*see* below), it remains operative from the time that the bankruptcy petition is filed until it statutorily terminates as follows:

(i) The stay of an *act against estate property* is effective until the property no longer constitutes property of the estate [B.C. §362(c)(1)]; and

(ii) The stay of *any other act* enjoined under Bankruptcy Code section 362(a) (*see supra*, §§779 *et seq.*) continues until a discharge is granted or denied, the case is dismissed, or the case is closed, whichever occurs first [B.C. §362(c)(2)].

a. **Example:** Trustee, in compliance with Bankruptcy Code section 363, sells an asset of the estate to Third Party. The automatic stay is terminated with respect to the asset at the time that it ceases to be property of the estate. [B.C. §362(c)(1)]

b. **Compare:** Trustee abandons an overencumbered asset of the estate. Debtor has not been granted or denied a discharge, and the case has neither been closed nor dismissed. Although the asset is no longer property of the estate, it becomes Debtor's property (*see supra*, §469) and continues to be protected by the automatic stay. [B.C. §362(a)(5), (c)(2); *In re* Motley, *supra*, §786]

(1) **Note:** If, in this example, Debtor had been granted a discharge by the court, the automatic stay would terminate at the time of the discharge, and the secured party may then proceed to foreclose her lien on the property. [B.C. §362(c)(2)(C); *In re* Cornist, 71 B.R. 118 (Bankr. S.D. Cal. 1980)]

(2) **Comment:** In the two paragraphs above, the results would not change if the asset constitutes exempt property of Debtor, instead of property abandoned by Trustee.

c. **Chapter 11 case:** [§808] Usually, confirmation of a Chapter 11 plan vests all of the property of the estate in the debtor, and also discharges the debtor from pre-confirmation debts. [B.C. §1141(b), (d)(l)(A); *see infra*, §§1118-1125] Thus, another effect of the confirmation is to terminate the automatic stay. [B.C. §362(c)(1), (2)(C); *In re* Paradise Valley Country Club, 31 B.R. 613 (D. Colo. 1983)]

4. **Relief from Stay:** [§809] Upon request, relief from the automatic stay may be granted to a party in interest, after notice and a hearing. [B.C. §§362(d), 102(1); *and see supra*, §14]

   a. **Nature of relief:** [§810] The kinds of relief that may be provided include termination, annulment, modification, or conditioning of the stay. [B.C. §362(d)]

   (1) **Example:** Where Debtor made no payments to Secured Creditor for more than one year, was unable to provide adequate protection, and could not prove that the collateral was essential to an effective reorganization, the stay was *terminated* to allow Secured Creditor to foreclose on the property. [*In re* Park West Hotel Corp., 64 B.R. 1013 (Bankr. D. Mass. 1986)]

   (2) **Example:** Where the bankruptcy petition is not filed in good faith, the court may *annul* the stay and thereby retroactively validate acts that occurred during its pendency. [*In re* Albany Partners, Ltd., 749 F.2d 670 (11th Cir. 1984)]

   b. **Grounds for relief:** [§811] *For cause*, the court will grant relief from the stay of *any act* enjoined under Bankruptcy Code section 362(a) (*see supra*, §§779 *et seq.*). In the case of a stay of *an act against property*, an alternative basis for lifting the stay also exists where the debtor lacks equity in the property and it is not needed for an effective reorganization. [B.C. §362(d)(1), (2)]

   (1) **"Cause":** [§812] The bankruptcy court, as a court of equity, enjoys broad discretion to determine what constitutes cause for granting relief from the automatic stay in the particular circumstances of each case. The Code offers one nonexclusive example, which is the lack of adequate protection. [B.C. §362(d)(1)]

   (a) **Lack of adequate protection:** [§813] The debtor's failure to provide adequate protection of an entity's interest in property (*see supra*, §§761 *et seq.*) is sufficient cause for the court to order relief from the stay. [B.C. §362(d)(1)]

   1) **Example:** Chapter 11 Debtor owes $1.8 million to Bank, secured by assets worth $1.5 million. Although payments of $16,000 are due monthly, Debtor has made only one payment of $1,000 during a period of approximately two years, and interest is accruing at the rate of $650 per day. The court finds that Debtor's prospects of successfully reorganizing are highly speculative. Debtor fails to offer any substitute or additional collateral to Bank and proposes periodic payments that are not sufficient to satisfy accruing interest charges. Bank files a motion for relief from the automatic stay, based on lack of adequate protection, and the motion is granted. [*In re* Day Resource & Development Co., 21 B.R. 176 (Bankr. D. Idaho 1982)]

2) ***American Mariner* doctrine rejected:** [§814]   The United States Supreme Court has held that an undersecured creditor's right to adequate protection does not entitle him to receive post-petition interest payments on the collateral to compensate for the delay in foreclosure during the period that the automatic stay remains in effect. Rather, adequate protection is required to protect the secured party against depreciation in the *value of the collateral* securing his claim. [B.C. §362(d)(1); United Savings Association of Texas v. Timbers of Inwood Forest Associates, Ltd., 484 U.S. 365 (1988); *and see supra*, §§773-774]

(b) **Lack of good faith:** [§815]   The debtor's lack of good faith in filing the bankruptcy petition can constitute cause for granting relief from the automatic stay. [B.C. §362(d)(1); *In re* Victory Construction Co., 9 B.R. 549 (Bankr. C.D. Cal. 1981), *vacated and remanded for mootness*, 37 B.R. 222 (Bankr. 9th Cir. 1984); *see also In re* Laguna Associates Ltd. Partnership, 30 F.3d 734 (6th Cir. 1994)] In determining whether the debtor intended "to abuse the judicial process," the court usually will consider the timing of the bankruptcy filing, the debtor's financial condition, and the reasons for filing (*e.g.*, whether the petition was filed solely to circumvent pending litigation or to reject an unprofitable contract). [*In re* Dixie Broadcasting, Inc., 871 F.2d 1023 (11th Cir. 1989)] Often, some or all of the following facts will be present in bad faith cases [*In re* Little Creek Development Co., 779 F.2d 1068 (5th Cir. 1986)]:

1) The debtor has *only one asset* (such as land), which is subject to the liens of secured creditors;

2) Other than principals, there are *no employees*;

3) Cash flow is *minimal or nonexistent*;

4) There are *no sources of income* from which to fund either adequate protection payments or a Chapter 11 plan of reorganization;

5) There are *not many unsecured creditors*, and those who exist hold fairly small claims;

6) The *secured creditors are attempting to foreclose* on the debtor's sole asset; and

7) The debtor may have been *guilty of some wrongdoing*.

(c) **Certain nonbankruptcy matters:** [§816]   Sometimes, the suitability of adjudicating an action outside of the bankruptcy court may be cause for granting relief from the automatic stay, especially where the bankruptcy court's expertise is not required. Thus, for example, relief from the stay would be appropriate to permit the debtor's ex-wife to bring an action in a state court for modification of her spousal support. [B.C. §362(d)(1); *In re* MacDonald, 755 F.2d 715 (9th Cir. 1985)]

(d) **Recovery from the debtor's insurer:** [§817] Another situation in which there may be cause for granting relief from the stay is where a tort victim desires to proceed in a different forum against the debtor, *to the extent of the debtor's insurance coverage*. Neither the debtor's property nor that of the estate will be jeopardized if the insurance company must defend the action and the tort victim seeks recovery from the insurer. Of course, the tort victim would be prohibited from attempting to collect any judgment from the debtor personally. [*In re* Honosky, 6 B.R. 667 (Bankr. S.D. W. Va. 1980)]

    1) **Comment:** The equities in favor of granting relief from the stay are especially compelling in jurisdictions where the plaintiff cannot sue the insurance company directly. [*In re* Honosky, *supra*]

(e) **Enforcement of "drop-dead" agreement:** [§818] There may be cause for granting relief from the stay when the debtor defaults in connection with a binding stipulation between the parties, known as a "drop-dead" agreement. Sometimes, where a secured party has requested relief from the stay, the debtor and the secured party stipulate jointly to a court order or judgment that fixes a date by which the debtor must do certain acts (*e.g.*, conclude a sale of real property and pay the mortgagee a set amount). Usually, the order or judgment stipulates that if the debtor fails to comply by the time that the moratorium expires, the stay will be *modified or terminated automatically*, and the secured party will be allowed to foreclose. [*In re* B.O.S.S. Partners I, 37 B.R. 348 (Bankr. M.D. Fla. 1984)]

(f) **Judicial discretion:** [§819] The above examples of what constitutes cause for granting relief from the automatic stay are not exhaustive. Since "cause" is not defined, the courts follow a case-by-case approach. [B.C. §362(d)(1); *In re* MacDonald, *supra*]

(2) **Acts against property:** [§820] Relief from the stay of an act against property will be granted (other than for cause) if (i) the debtor has no equity in the property and (ii) the property is not necessary for an effective reorganization. [B.C. §362(d)(2)]

  (a) **No equity:** [§821] Most courts view equity as the "difference between the value of the property and all encumbrances upon it." [B.C. §362(d)(2)(A); Stewart v. Gurley, 745 F.2d 1194 (9th Cir. 1984)]

    1) **Example:** Debtor owns certain land encumbered by a $100,000 first mortgage in favor of Bank A, and a $50,000 second mortgage in favor of Bank B. The property has a fair market value of $130,000. Under the definition above, the debtor has no equity in the property since the *total* of all encumbrances ($150,000) exceeds the value of the property.

  (b) **Not necessary for an effective reorganization:** [§822] Property will be deemed not necessary for an effective reorganization upon a finding that the debtor does not have a reasonable possibility of successfully reorganizing within a reasonable time. [B.C. §362(d)(2)(B); United Savings Association of Texas v. Timbers of Inwood Forest Associates, Ltd., *supra*, §814]

1) **Example:** Debtor, who operates a farming business at his residence in Iowa, purchases a second farm in Missouri, 200 miles away, for the purpose of conducting a livestock operation. Following a drought and a substantial decline in the cattle market, Debtor sells his herd and begins growing corn and soybeans. The Missouri farm suffers great losses and becomes a financial drain on the combined Missouri-Iowa farming operations. Debtor files a voluntary Chapter 11 petition, and Mortgagee seeks relief from the automatic stay to proceed against the Missouri farm, in which Debtor has no equity. Since little or no profit can reasonably be anticipated from the intended use of the property, and since the expenses of commuting and maintaining equipment at both farms will merely make debtor's financial plight worse, the Missouri farm is not necessary for an effective reorganization. Thus, both elements are satisfied, and relief from the stay will be granted. [B.C. §362(d)(2); *In re Greiman*, 45 B.R. 574 (Bankr. N.D. Iowa 1984)]

2) **Comment:** During the first 120 days of a Chapter 11 case, the court generally requires less detailed proof of the likelihood of a successful reorganization, and, therefore, as a practical matter, it is probably more difficult in the early stages of the case to obtain relief from the stay on this ground [B.C. §362(d)(2)] than it is for cause [B.C. §362(d)(1)]. However, even within the first 120 days, "lack of any realistic prospect of effective reorganization will require section 362(d)(2) relief." [United Savings Association of Texas v. Timbers of Inwood Forest Associates, Ltd., *supra*]

(3) **Single asset real estate:** [§823] The Code provides an additional ground for relief from the automatic stay of an act against single asset real estate not exceeding $4 million in value, where, within 90 days after entry of the order for relief, the debtor has neither filed a reorganization plan that has a reasonable possibility of being confirmed within a reasonable time, nor commenced monthly interest payments, at a current fair market rate, to each creditor secured by the real estate (other than creditors with a judgment lien or an unmatured statutory lien). For cause, the court may extend the 90-day period by an order entered within the 90 days. [B.C. §362(d)(3)]

(a) **Single asset real estate defined:** Single asset real estate is defined as follows: "real property constituting a single property or project, other than residential real property with fewer than four residential units, which generates substantially all of the gross income of a debtor and on which no substantial business is being conducted by a debtor other than the business of operating the real property and

(4) **Lessors:** [§824] While Code section 363(e) requires adequate protection of an entity's interest in property that is leased by the trustee or debtor in possession, it also precludes a lessor of *personal property* from seeking relief from the automatic stay under section 362 (*see infra*, §§849, 851). Whether a lessor of *real property* may seek relief from the stay under section 362 (as an alternative to relief under section 365) is not clear.

c. **Procedure for requesting relief:** [§825] To initiate stay litigation, a party in interest files a motion for relief from the stay. [Bankruptcy Rule 4001(a)(1)]

   (1) **Acts against estate property—hearing:** [§826] When the relief sought is from the stay of an act against *property of the estate*, the stay terminates (by operation of law) 30 days after the motion is filed unless, after notice and a hearing, the court orders that the stay remain operative until a final hearing is concluded. The general rule is that "if there is a reasonable likelihood that the party opposing relief from the stay will prevail at the conclusion of such final hearing," the court will order that the stay continue in effect until such time. [B.C. §362(e)]

   (a) **Preliminary hearing:** [§827] Where the court directs that the stay will remain in effect until a final hearing has been concluded, the initial hearing is called a preliminary hearing. The final hearing must *conclude* within 30 days after the conclusion of the preliminary hearing, unless the period is extended by consent of the parties or by the court, for a specific time, due to compelling circumstances. The parties may agree, or the court may direct, that the preliminary and final hearings be consolidated. [B.C. §362(e)]

   (2) **Burden of proof:** [§828] In litigation concerning relief from the stay of *any act* enjoined under section 362(a) (*see supra*, §§779 *et seq.*), the party seeking relief has the burden of proof regarding the debtor's equity in property; the party opposing relief must bear the burden of proof on all other issues. [B.C. §362(g)]

   (3) **Ex parte relief:** [§829] In the exceptional case where irreparable harm to an entity's interest in property will occur before there is time for notice and a hearing, the court may grant ex parte relief from the stay to prevent the threatened loss. It should be a measure of last resort, and the court will examine closely the efforts made to notify the adverse party. [B.C. §362(f); Bankruptcy Rule 4001(a)(2)]

   (4) **Appeal:** [§830] A decision to grant or deny relief from the stay is a final order, which may be appealed. [*In re* American Mariner Industries, Inc., *supra*, §773]

5. **Willful Violation of Stay:** [§831] An individual who is injured by a *willful* violation of the automatic stay may recover actual damages, costs, attorney's fees, and, when warranted, punitive damages. [B.C. §362(h); *In re* Bloom, 875 F.2d 224 (9th

Cir. 1989)] In some jurisdictions, this provision is not limited to individuals, but is also available to other entities (*e.g.*, corporations and partnerships) that are harmed by willful violations of the stay. [Budget Service Co. v. Better Homes of Virginia, Inc., 804 F.2d 289 (4th Cir. 1986)] In other jurisdictions, the provision applies only to natural persons. Corporations and partnerships may seek contempt proceedings. [*In re* Chateaugay Corporation, 920 F.2d 183 (2d Cir. 1990)]

    a. **Example:** Debtor Corporation files a Chapter 11 bankruptcy petition while in possession of an automobile leased from Lessor. After having been informed of the bankruptcy filing by Debtor Corporation's attorney, Lessor's president deliberately causes the automobile to be repossessed in violation of the automatic stay. Debtor Corporation incurs $1,250 in actual damages for its employees' time consumed in trying to recover the vehicle, $250 in costs, and $9,080 in legal fees. The court (applying the broader interpretation) grants Debtor Corporation a judgment against Lessor for the aggregate amount, as well as $1,000 in punitive damages. [B.C. §362(h); *In re* Tel-A-Communications Consultants, Inc., *supra* §296]

C. USE, SALE, OR LEASE OF PROPERTY

1. **In General:** [§832]   The use, sale, or lease of estate property, both in and out of the ordinary course of the debtor's business, is an integral part of the bankruptcy process, such as when the trustee liquidates a Chapter 7 debtor's estate, or when a debtor in possession or trustee is authorized to operate the debtor's business or farm in a case under Chapter 11 or Chapter 12. [B.C. §363]

    a. **Debtor in possession:** [§833]   Ordinarily, a Chapter 11 or 12 debtor in possession has nearly all of the rights, powers, functions, and duties of a Chapter 11 trustee, including the right to use, sell, and lease property of the estate. [B.C. §§1107(a); 1203]

    b. **Chapter 13:** [§834]   There are also special provisions authorizing a debtor (or a debtor engaged in business) to use, sell, or lease property in a case under Chapter 13. [B.C. §§1303, 1304; *see infra*, §§1152-1153]

2. **Out of Ordinary Course of Business:** [§835]   After *notice and a hearing*, a trustee or a debtor in possession may use, sell, or lease property of the estate out of the ordinary course of the debtor's business. Whether any individual sale, use, or lease of property is deemed to be outside the ordinary course of business is a question of fact under the circumstances. [B.C. §363(b)(1); *and see infra*, §§841-842]

    a. **"Notice and a hearing":** [§836]   The statutory rule of construction authorizes the doing of an act *without* an actual hearing if appropriate notice is provided and no party in interest timely requests a hearing. [B.C. §102(1)] Thus, for example, following proper notice to creditors in a Chapter 7 case, if no objection is made to a trustee's proposed liquidation of certain assets, the trustee may proceed to sell the property without obtaining approval from the bankruptcy court. [B.C. §363(b)(1)]

    b. **Purchaser's good faith:** [§837]   When a party objects to a proposed use, sale, or lease of property, a hearing is conducted, at which the judge determines whether the prospective purchaser is acting in good faith and is paying value. [B.C. §363(b)(1); *In re* Abbotts Dairies, Inc., 788 F.2d 143 (3d Cir. 1986)]

    c. **Chapter 11 case:** [§838] A post-petition, pre-confirmation use, sale, or lease of property out of the ordinary course of business may not be used in lieu of the Chapter 11 reorganization process or in a manner that circumvents the protective requirements of a reorganization plan (such as disclosure, voting, or confirmation). [*In re* Continental Air Lines, Inc., 780 F.2d 1223 (5th Cir. 1986)]

       (1) **Example:** Debtor files a Chapter 11 bankruptcy petition and continues to operate its business as a debtor in possession. To appease creditors, and for no other stated reason, Debtor desires to sell its principal asset, an 82% stock holding in a large electronics company. Upon objection by Debtor's equity security holders, the court will deny permission to sell the stock unless Debtor can prove that there is either an emergency or a good business reason justifying aborting the normal reorganization process by a sale of property out of the ordinary course of business. [B.C. §363(b)(1); *In re* Lionel Corp., 722 F. 2d 1063 (2d Cir. 1983); *see also* Stephens Industries, Inc. v. McClung, 789 F.2d 386 (6th Cir. 1986)—valid business reason justified sale of debtor's radio station]

    d. **Secured creditor's right to bid:** [§839] Ordinarily, a secured creditor whose lien secures an allowed claim will be permitted to bid and buy property sold *outside the ordinary course of business* and to offset her claim against the purchase price. [B.C. §363(k)]

3. **In Ordinary Course of Business:** [§840] A trustee or a debtor in possession who is authorized to operate the debtor's business may use, sell, or lease property of the estate in the ordinary course of business *without notice or a hearing*, unless the court orders otherwise. [B.C. §363(c)(1)]

    a. **Creditor's expectation test:** [§841] In determining whether a particular transaction is in or out of the ordinary course of business, courts use the creditor's expectation test (also known as the *vertical dimension test*) to ascertain whether, given the debtor's normal business practices, the transaction subjects creditors to risks of a different character than the risks present when credit was extended. [*In re* James A. Phillips, Inc., 29 B.R. 391 (S.D.N.Y. 1983)]

    b. **Industry-wide test:** [§842] To determine ordinariness, some courts also apply the *horizontal dimension test*, which compares the debtor's business to other similar businesses. "Thus raising a crop would not be in the ordinary course of business for a widget manufacturer because that is not a widget manufacturer's ordinary business." [*In re* Waterfront Companies, Inc., 56 B.R. 31 (Bankr. D. Minn. 1985)]

    c. **Application of tests:** [§843] Debtor, a "Fortune 500" company that mines and manufactures asbestos-containing products and that has been named as a defendant in thousands of asbestos-related personal injury tort actions, files a Chapter 11 bankruptcy petition. Debtor continues to operate its business as a debtor in possession, during which time Debtor maintains its long-standing, pre-petition business practice of employing nonlawyer lobbyists to assert Debtor's views concerning various areas of legislation, including asbestos compensation. Other asbestos producers, "Fortune 500" companies, and Chapter 11 debtors also hire lobbyists on a regular basis. Therefore, under both the vertical and horizontal dimension tests, Debtor's employment of lobbyists is an activity within the ordinary course of its business and may be continued without the need for notice or a hearing. [B.C. §363(c)(1); *In re* Johns-Manville Corp., 60 B.R. 612 (Bankr. S.D.N.Y. 1986)] However, it is important to note that the court found, under these particular circumstances, that the lobbyists were not "professional persons" (whose employment would require court approval under Bankruptcy Code section 327).

  d. **Exception—cash collateral:** [§844] The trustee or the debtor in possession may use, sell, or lease cash collateral in the ordinary course of business only if she obtains either ***court authorization***, after notice and a hearing, or the ***consent*** of all entities having an interest in the cash collateral. [B.C. §363(c)(2)]

    (1) **Definition:** [§845] "Cash collateral" includes cash, negotiable instruments, documents of title, securities, deposit accounts, and other cash equivalents in which both the debtor's estate and a third party have an interest. Also included are proceeds, rents, profits, products, offspring, and hotel or motel room revenues covered by a security interest under Bankruptcy Code section 552(b). [B.C. §363(a); United Virginia Bank v. Slab Fork Coal Co., *supra*, §466]

    (2) **Hearing:** [§846] When a request is made for authorization to use cash collateral, usually time is of the essence, and thus the court will act promptly to schedule a hearing ***based on the needs of the debtor***. The hearing may be a preliminary hearing or may be consolidated with a hearing on adequate protection (*see infra*, §§849-851). If it is a preliminary hearing, the court may authorize the use, sale, or lease of cash collateral only if there is a reasonable probability that the trustee or the debtor in possession will prevail at the final hearing on adequate protection. [B.C. §363(c)(3), (e)]

    (3) **Duty to segregate:** [§847] The trustee or the debtor in possession has a mandatory duty to segregate and account for any cash collateral in her possession, custody, or control, except to the extent that the cash collateral has been used, sold, or leased pursuant to proper authorization. [B.C. §363(c)(4); *In re* Anchorage Boat Sales, Inc., 4 B.R. 635 (Bankr. E.D.N.Y. 1980)]

 4. **Automatic Stay:** [§848] Any use, sale, or lease of property by the trustee or the debtor in possession must not be in conflict with any relief granted from the automatic stay. [B.C. §§363(d), 362(c)-(f)]

 5. **Adequate Protection:** [§849] Upon the motion of an entity having an interest in property that is (or is proposed to be) used, sold, or leased by the trustee or the debtor in possession, the court will ***prohibit or condition*** the use, sale, or lease in a manner that provides adequate protection of the entity's interest. [B.C. §363(e); Bankruptcy Rule 4001(a)(1)] In deciding the question of adequate protection, the following factors have been considered:

(i) The *value* of the secured party's interest;

(ii) The *risks* to that value that ensue from the use, sale, or lease of the property; and

(iii) Whether the adequate protection offered by the debtor protects the value against the risks, under the *"indubitable equivalent"* standard (*see supra*, §768).

[*In re* Martin, 761 F.2d 472 (8th Cir. 1985)]

    a. **Example:** Debtor, a farmer, files a voluntary Chapter 11 petition and requests authorization to use the cash proceeds from the sale of certain crops to finance next year's farming operations. Both the crops and the proceeds are subject to Bank's security interest, which Debtor proposes to adequately protect by providing a replacement lien in *next year's* grain harvest, for which there has been no planting. Debtor does not have crop insurance. Given the uncertainties of weather and prices, unless Debtor can demonstrate how a replacement lien in the nonexistent crops will adequately protect the value of Bank's security interest in the presently existing crops and proceeds, the court will deny Debtor's request and will prohibit use of the cash collateral. [B.C. §363(e); First Bank of Miller v. Wieseler, 45 B.R. 871 (D.S.D. 1985)]

    b. **Insurance:** [§850] Frequently, the use, sale, or lease of property may be *conditioned* on the procurement of insurance as one of the elements of adequate protection. [B.C. §363(e)]

    c. **Unexpired leases of personal property:** [§851] While the Code requires adequate protection of a lessor's interest in personal property that is subject to an unexpired lease, this remedy is to the exclusion of relief from the automatic stay under section 362(d) (*see supra*, §§809 *et seq.*). [B.C. §363(e)]

6. **Ipso Facto or "Bankruptcy" Clauses:** [§852] The right of a trustee or a debtor in possession to use, sell, or lease property in or out of the ordinary course of business, or under a Chapter 11, 12, or 13 plan, is unaffected by any provision in a contract, lease, or nonbankruptcy law that otherwise would cause a forfeiture, modification, or termination of the debtor's interest in the property as a result of any of the following occurrences:

(i) *The insolvency or inadequate financial condition* of the debtor;

(ii) *The commencement of a case* under the Bankruptcy Code concerning the debtor;

(iii) *The appointment of a bankruptcy trustee or a nonbankruptcy custodian*; or

(iv) *The seizure of property* by a bankruptcy trustee or a nonbankruptcy custodian.

[B.C. §363(l)]

7. **Sale Free and Clear:** [§853] When the trustee or the debtor in possession sells property of the estate, either in or out of the ordinary course of business, the sale

may be transacted free and clear of any lien or other interest in the property if one or more of the following prerequisites is present:

(i) *Applicable state or other nonbankruptcy law allows* a free and clear sale of the property;

(ii) *There is consent* by the entity holding the interest;

(iii) *If the interest is a lien*, the *selling price is greater than the total value of all liens* on the property [*In re* Perroncello, 170 B.R. 189 (Bankr. D. Mass. 1994—face value; *In re* Beker Industries Corp., 63 B.R. 474 (Bankr. S.D.N.Y. 1986)—fair market value];

(iv) *There exists a bona fide dispute* concerning the entity's interest in the property; or

(v) *The entity holding the interest could be required to accept a money satisfaction* in a legal or equitable action.

[B.C. §363(f)]

8. **Sale Affecting Dower, Curtesy, or Co-Ownership Interests**

   a. **Dower or curtesy:** [§854] Notwithstanding the conditions above for a free and clear sale, the trustee or the debtor in possession may sell property free and clear of an entity's vested or contingent right of dower or curtesy. [B.C. §363(g)]

   b. **Co-owner's interest:** [§855] When property of the estate is held in co-ownership with another entity, the trustee or the debtor in possession may sell the interests of both the estate *and* a tenant in common, a joint tenant, or a tenant by the entirety if all of the following elements are satisfied:

   (i) *It is impracticable to partition* the property between the estate and the co-owner;

   (ii) *The amount that would be realized* for the estate from a sale of its undivided interest in the property is *substantially less* than from a sale of the asset free of the co-owner's interest;

   (iii) *The benefit to the estate* from a sale free of the co-owner's interest *outweighs any harm to the co-owner*; and

   (iv) *The property is not used in producing, transmitting, or distributing,* for the purpose of sale, *electric energy or gas* for heat, light, or power.

   [B.C §363(h)]

   c. **Right of first refusal:** [§856] Before the completion of (i) a sale of property free and clear of dower or curtesy rights, (ii) a sale of a co-owner's interest in property, or (iii) a sale of community property, an opportunity must be provided to the debtor's spouse or to the co-owner to purchase the property at the same price for which it is about to be sold. [B.C. §363(i)]

d. **Distribution of proceeds:** [§857]   After a sale of property free and clear of dower or curtesy rights, or a sale of a co-owner's interest in property, the trustee or the debtor in possession must pay the appropriate portion of the net proceeds to the debtor's spouse or the co-owner, without any deduction for compensation earned by the trustee. [B.C. §363(j)]

9. **Burden of Proof:** [§858]   In any hearing concerning the use, sale, or lease of property, the trustee or debtor in possession has the burden of proof regarding the question of adequate protection, while the entity claiming an interest in property bears the burden of showing the validity, priority, or extent of that interest. [B.C. §363(o)]

10. **Appeal—Mootness:** [§859]   Absent a stay pending appeal, the validity of an authorization to sell or lease property, in or outside the ordinary course of business, is not affected by a reversal or modification on appeal if the purchaser (or lessee) acted in *good faith*, regardless of the purchaser's (or lessee's) knowledge of the appeal. [B.C. §363(m); *In re* Stadium Management Corp., 895 F.2d 845 (1st Cir. 1990); *see also In re* CGI Industries, Inc., 27 F.3d 296 (7th Cir. 1994)—appeal moot where stay not obtained before sale was completed]

    a. **Exceptions to mootness doctrine:** [§860]   Even if a stay pending appeal has not been obtained, the appeal will not be moot where: (i) real property has been sold to a creditor (involved in the appeal) subject to a statutory right of redemption, or (ii) the transaction, otherwise, could be set aside under state law. [*In re* Mann, 907 F.2d 923 (9th Cir. 1990)]

11. **Collusive Sale:** [§861]   If the sale price of the estate property is controlled by an agreement among bidders, the trustee or debtor in possession may avoid the sale, or may recover from any of the conspirators damages equal to the value of the property minus the price paid, plus any costs, attorney's fees, or expenses of obtaining relief. Moreover, in instances of willfulness, the recovery also may include punitive damages. [B.C. §363(n)]

12. **Sales and Use Taxes Permitted:** [§862]   The United States Supreme Court has held that a bankruptcy liquidation sale is not immune from a nondiscriminatory state sales or use tax. [California State Board of Equalization v. Sierra Summit, Inc., 490 U.S. 844 (1989)]

D. **OBTAINING CREDIT**

1. **In General:** [§863]   A trustee, debtor in possession under Chapter 11 or 12, or debtor engaged in business under Chapter 13 often needs to obtain credit or incur debt. The Code provides for the acquisition of both unsecured and secured credit or debt under varying circumstances. [B.C. §364]

    a. **Chapter 13:** [§864]   A debtor engaged in business in a case under Chapter 13 ordinarily is permitted to operate the business and will be treated, for purposes of her entitlement to obtain credit, as having the rights of a trustee under Code section 364. [B.C. §1304(b)]

2. **In Ordinary Course of Business:** [§865]   A trustee or debtor in possession authorized to operate the debtor's business may procure *unsecured credit* (such as trade credit) and incur *unsecured debt* in the ordinary course of business without

notice or a hearing, unless the court orders otherwise. Such credit or debt is allowable as an *administrative expense*. [B.C. §§364(a), 503(b)(1); *see supra*, §§537 *et seq.*]

3. **Out of Ordinary Course of Business:** [§866]   After *notice and a hearing*, the court may approve the request of a trustee or debtor in possession to obtain unsecured credit or to incur unsecured debt out of the ordinary course of business as an allowable expense of administration. A creditor who does not have court approval before lending money or extending credit out of the ordinary course of the debtor's business may be denied an administrative expense priority and will instead be treated as a general unsecured creditor. [B.C. §364(b); 2 Collier ¶364.03]

   a. **Example:** Debtor files a voluntary Chapter 11 petition and continues to operate the business as a debtor in possession. Fully aware of the bankruptcy case, and in expectation of buying Debtor's business, Creditor makes a $5,000 unsecured loan to finance Debtor's purchase of inventory. Notice of the transaction is not given, there is no opportunity for a hearing, and court authorization to incur the debt is not obtained. Subsequently, the parties fail to consummate the sale of the business, Debtor stops operations, and the case is converted to Chapter 7. Since the loan from Creditor was made out of the ordinary course of business and without prior court approval, Creditor will be denied an administrative expense and will be treated as a general unsecured creditor. [*In re John Deskins Pic Pac, Inc.*, 59 B.R. 809 (Bankr. W.D. Va. 1986)]

4. **Priority or Security:** [§867]   Prospective post-petition lenders may not be satisfied with an administrative expense priority even though it is the first category of unsecured claims to be paid (*see supra*, §556). Thus, when the trustee or debtor in possession is *unable* to obtain unsecured credit without offering more than an administrative expense, the court, after notice and a hearing, may authorize credit to be acquired or debt to be incurred as follows. (Note that the trustee or debtor in possession must show "that it has reasonably attempted, but failed, to obtain unsecured credit under sections 364(a) or (b)." [*In re* Ames Department Stores, Inc., 115 B.R. 34 (Bankr. S.D.N.Y. 1990)]):

   a. **Super-superpriority:** [§868]   The court may authorize a super-superpriority that is ahead of all administrative expense claims and also of any superpriority administrative expense claims resulting from the failure of adequate protection. [B.C. §364(c)(1); *see supra*, §§579-580]

   b. **Lien on unencumbered property:** [§869]   The court may authorize secured credit or debt by granting a lien on unencumbered property of the estate. [B.C. §364(c)(2)]

   c. **Junior lien on encumbered property:** [§870]   The court may authorize secured credit or debt by granting a junior lien on property of the estate that already is encumbered. [B.C. §364(c)(3)]

5. **Priming Lien:** [§871]   If the trustee or the debtor in possession cannot obtain credit on any basis other than by the grant of a senior (or equal) lien on property that already is encumbered, the court, after notice and a hearing, may approve new credit or debt to be secured by a lien on estate property that will be *senior or equal* to any lien held by another entity on the same property. Adequate protection must

be provided to the original lienholder, and the trustee or debtor in possession bears the burden of proof on this issue. [B.C. §364(d); Anchor Savings Bank F.S.B. v. Sky Valley, Inc., 99 B.R. 117 (N.D. Ga. 1989)]

6. **Cross-Collateralization:** [§872]   When providing post-petition financing, sometimes a creditor will seek, as part of the transaction, authorization to use the debtor's collateral as security for both the post-petition debt and pre-petition indebtedness. This arrangement, known as cross-collateralization, is prohibited by many courts. [*In re* Saybrook Manufacturing Co., 963 F.2d 1490 (11th Cir. 1992)] However, some courts, after notice and a hearing, have permitted cross-collateralization as a last resort where (i) the debtor's business would not survive without the financing offered; (ii) other credit or debt is unavailable on reasonable terms; (iii) the lender will not grant the financing without cross-collateralization; and (iv) "the best interests of the general creditor body" will be served if the financing is approved. [*In re* Vanguard Diversified, Inc., 31 B.R. 364 (Bankr. E.D. N.Y. 1983)]

7. **Notice:** [§873]   Although a hearing concerning the approval of prospective financing for a debtor in possession often is needed without delay, sufficient notice must be provided or else the validity of the financing order obtained at the hearing could be challenged later. [*In re* Center Wholesale, Inc., 759 F.2d 1440 (9th Cir. 1985)] The appropriateness of a hearing on short notice depends on the exigencies of the particular circumstances. [B.C. §102(1)(A)]

8. **Appeal:** [§874]   Absent a stay pending appeal, the validity of authorization to obtain credit or incur debt, or the validity of any lien or priority granted by the court under section 364 (*see supra*, §§863 *et seq.*), is not affected by a reversal or modification on appeal if the lender acted in ***good faith***—even if the lender knew of the appeal. [B.C. §364(e); *In re* Ellingsen MacLean Oil Co., 65 B.R. 358 (W.D. Mich. 1986), *aff'd*, 834 F.2d 599 (6th Cir. 1987); *but see In re* Swedeland Development Group, Inc., 16 F.3d 552 (3d Cir. 1994)—lender not protected concerning money not yet disbursed]

E. EXECUTORY CONTRACTS AND UNEXPIRED LEASES

1. **Definitions:** [§875]   Neither an executory contract nor an unexpired lease is defined in the Bankruptcy Code. Thus, the courts have attempted to construe these terms in the bankruptcy context in applying the provisions of Code section 365, concerning assumption or rejection.

   a. **Executory contract:** [§876]   In determining whether a contract is executory, many courts look to see if there is substantial performance left to be done by **both the debtor and the nondebtor party**. [Gloria Manufacturing Corp. v. International Ladies' Garment Workers' Union, 734 F.2d 1020 (4th Cir. 1984)] However, there also is authority that a contract could be executory if there is substantial performance, other than the mere payment of money, remaining on ***either*** side. [*In re* Norquist, 43 B.R. 224 (Bankr. E.D. Wash. 1984); *see also* Texaco, Inc. v. Louisiana Land and Exploration Co., 136 B.R. 658 (M.D. La. 1992)—Louisiana's unique mineral lease, obligating the lessee to develop the property, explore for minerals, and pay royalties, held to be executory contract (analogizing to an attorney's contingent fee contract, where "performance is imposed almost exclusively upon one party")] A third view applies a functional approach, deemphasizing the definition of "executory" and emphasizing the benefit to the estate "from performance or breach." [*In re* Drexel Burnham Lambert Group, Inc., 138 B.R. 687 (Bankr. S.D.N.Y. 1992)]

b. **Unexpired lease:** [§877] Under section 365, an unexpired lease must be a true lease, rather than one intended as a secured transaction. The bankruptcy court should use applicable state law in making this determination. [*In re* Holywell Corp., 51 B.R. 56 (Bankr. S.D. Fla. 1985)] To distinguish between a true lease and a security agreement, courts often consider the following factors [American Standard Credit, Inc. v. National Cement Co., 643 F.2d 248 (5th Cir. 1981)]:

(1) *Reserving title* in a lease or including an *option to purchase* does not necessarily make the lease a security agreement.

(2) However, if the lease permits the *lessee to become the owner* of the property at the end of the lease for *little or no additional consideration*, the lease is deemed to be a security agreement as a matter of law.

(3) *A true lease* is indicated by:

(a) A lease provision setting the purchase option price at the *approximate market value* at the time of the exercise of the option;

(b) A provision for rental charges that indicates an intent to *compensate the lessor for loss of value* during the lease due to aging, wear, and obsolescence;

(c) A provision calling for *reasonable rental* (not excessive) *and option purchase price* (not too low); and

(d) Other facts indicating that the lessee is *not acquiring equity* in the property during the term of the lease.

2. **Assumption or Rejection:** [§878] An executory contract or an unexpired lease of the debtor may be assumed or rejected by the trustee or debtor in possession with the approval of the court. [B.C. §365(a)] A motion is required, as are reasonable notice and an opportunity for a hearing. [Bankruptcy Rules 6006, 9014]

Note: Another way that assumption or rejection can occur is by a permissive provision in a confirmed plan under Chapter 11, 12, or 13. [B.C. §§1123(b)(2), 1222(b)(6), 1322(b)(7); *see infra*, §§1059, 1239, 1185; *see In re* Aneiro, 72 B.R. 424 (Bankr. S.D. Cal. 1987)—lease assumption under Chapter 13 plan]

a. **Court approval mandatory:** [§879] Assumption or rejection by conduct alone is not valid since express judicial authorization is required (except when rejection occurs automatically upon the expiration of certain statutory time limits placed on the power to assume or reject). [B.C. §365(a); *In re* Harris Management Co., 791 F.2d 1412 (9th Cir. 1986)]

(1) **Example:** Debtor, operating its business as a debtor in possession, makes post-petition premium payments to Insurance Agent, pursuant to certain insurance policies. The payments represent both post-petition and pre-petition insurance coverage; no court approval is obtained to assume the

agreements. Several months later, Debtor decides to reject the contracts, but Insurance Agent asserts that they have already been assumed by Debtor's post-petition conduct. The court will not grant retroactive validation of the alleged assumption and, therefore, Insurance Agent will be required to repay the amounts received in payment of the pre-petition portion of the indebtedness. [*In re* A. H. Robins Co., 68 B.R. 705 (Bankr. E.D. Va. 1986)]

b. **Business judgment rule:** [§880] When considering a request to assume or reject an executory contract or an unexpired lease, courts generally apply the *business judgment rule* and approve the decision of the trustee or debtor in possession unless there is bad faith or a gross abuse of discretion. [Lubrizol Enterprises, Inc. v. Richmond Metal Finishers, Inc., 756 F.2d 1043 (4th Cir. 1985)] (*Note:* For circumstances concerning rejection of an executory contract involving a license to intellectual property, *see* B.C. section 365(n) (*infra*, §§933-935), which was enacted subsequent to *Lubrizol*.)

(1) **Minority rule:** [§881] A very few courts have refused to apply the business judgment rule and, instead, have adopted a *balancing of the equities test*, under which the court ascertains whether rejection would *disproportionately harm the nondebtor party* in comparison with any benefit that might accrue to the general unsecured creditors of the debtor. [Infosystems Technology, Inc. v. Logical Software, Inc., Bankr. L. Rep. ¶71,899 (D. Mass. 1987); *In re* Monarch Tool & Manufacturing Co., 114 B.R. 134 (Bankr. S.D. Ohio 1990)]

(2) **Exception—collective bargaining agreements:** [§882] In a Chapter 11 case, the rejection of a collective bargaining agreement is governed by the standards set forth in Bankruptcy Code section 1113 (*see infra*, §§1039 *et seq*.).

c. **Election:** [§883] The trustee or debtor in possession may not assume the benefits and reject the burdens of an executory contract or an unexpired lease. The contract or lease must be either assumed or rejected in its entirety. [Richmond Leasing Co. v. Capital Bank, N.A., 762 F.2d 1303 (5th Cir. 1985)]

d. **Pre-bankruptcy termination:** [§884] The trustee or debtor in possession cannot assume a contract or a lease that has been legally terminated prior to the commencement of the bankruptcy case, with no right to cure. [Moody v. Amoco Oil Co., *supra*, §59]

3. **Assumption of Contracts and Leases in Default:** [§885] The trustee or debtor in possession may assume an executory contract or an unexpired lease that is in default only if the following three requirements are met at the time of assumption [B.C. §365(b)(1)]:

a. **Cure:** [§886] The trustee or debtor in possession must cure the default or provide adequate assurance that the default will be cured promptly [B.C. §365(b)(1)(A); *In re* R/P International Technologies, Inc., 57 B.R. 869 (Bankr. S.D. Ohio 1985)];

(1) **Nondefault rate:** [§887]   The debtor may cure a default at the nondefault rate and without having to perform nonmonetary obligations under the contract or lease. [B.C. §365(b)(2)(D)]

b. **Compensation:** [§888]   The trustee or debtor in possession must either compensate or provide adequate assurance of prompt redress to the nondebtor party for any monetary loss caused by the default [B.C. §365(b)(1)(B)]; and

c. **Adequate assurance of future performance:** [§889]   The trustee or debtor in possession must furnish adequate assurance of future performance of the executory contract or the unexpired lease [B.C. §365(b)(1)(C)].

(1) **Criteria:** [§890]   Ordinarily, the issue of adequate assurance of future performance is determined on the basis of (i) the debtor's capability of paying future debts from her expected income; (ii) the overall economic prognosis for the debtor's industry; and (iii) the existence of a guaranty. [Richmond Leasing Co. v. Capital Bank, N.A., *supra*, §883]

(2) **Shopping center leases:** [§891]   The Bankruptcy Code is more specific with respect to the elements of "adequate assurance of future performance of a lease of real property in a shopping center." [B.C. §365(b)(3)]

(a) **"Shopping center":** [§892]   Although the term is not defined in the statute, a "shopping center" usually is evidenced by factors such as a master lease, the presence of common areas of the property (especially parking), contiguity of stores, fixed times when every store is open, and joint advertising. [*In re* Goldblatt Bros., Inc., 766 F.2d 1136 (7th Cir. 1985); *In re* Joshua Slocum, Ltd., 922 F.2d 1081 (3d Cir. 1990)]

(b) **"Adequate assurance":** [§893]   In the context of a shopping center lease, adequate assurance of future performance includes:

1) *The source of rent*, and when applicable, the financial condition and operating performance of an expected assignee and its surety [B.C. §365(b)(3)(A)];

2) *The continuation*, without a significant decrease, *of any percentage rent* required by the lease [B.C. §365(b)(3)(B)];

3) *In an assumption or assignment*, the inclusion of *all lease provisions*, such as any terms concerning location, use, radius, or exclusivity [B.C. §365(b)(3)(C)]; and

4) *In an assumption or assignment*, the *maintenance of any tenant mix* in the shopping center [B.C. §365(b)(3)(D)].

d. **Exceptions:** [§894]   A default triggering the operation of section 365(b)(1) (*see supra*, §885) is one *other than* a default constituting a breach of a contractual term regarding: (i) the insolvency or financial state of the debtor [B.C. §365(b)(2)(A)]; (ii) the commencement of a case under the Bankruptcy Code concerning the debtor [B.C. §365(b)(2)(B)]; (iii) the appointment of a bankruptcy trustee or a nonbankruptcy custodian [B.C. §365(b)(2)(C)]; (iv) the seizure of property by a bankruptcy trustee or a nonbankruptcy custodian [B.C. §365(b)(2)(C)]; or (v) the satisfaction of a penalty rate, or the failure of the debtor to perform nonmonetary obligations under the contract or lease [B.C. §365(b)(2)(D)].

    e. **Incidental services and supplies:** [§895] Prior to the assumption of an unexpired lease in default (other than because of a default specified in section 894, *supra*), the lessor is not obligated to provide incidental services or supplies unless the trustee or debtor in possession pays, according to the terms of the lease, for any services or supplies furnished before assumption. [B.C. §365(b)(4)]

4. **Agreements Not Assumable or Assignable:** [§896] Certain kinds of executory contracts and unexpired leases may not be assumed or assigned by the trustee or debtor in possession. [B.C. §365(c)]

    a. **Personal service contracts and government contracts:** [§897] Where *applicable nonbankruptcy law* excuses the nondebtor party from accepting performance from, or furnishing performance to, an entity other than the debtor or the debtor in possession, the contract or lease may not be assumed or assigned by the trustee unless the nondebtor party consents. [B.C. §365(c)(1)] Likewise, a debtor in possession is prohibited from assigning such a contract or lease without the other party's consent, although the law is not settled as to whether a debtor in possession may assume and perform a contract of this kind. [B.C. §1107(a); *In re* West Electronics, Inc., 852 F.2d 79 (3d Cir. 1988)—no (government contract); *In re* Catron, 158 B.R. 629 (E.D. Va. 1993), *aff'd*, 25 F.3d 1038 (4th Cir. 1994)—no (partnership agreement); *In re* Cardinal Industries, Inc., 116 B.R. 964 (Bankr. S.D. Ohio 1990)—yes, if performance will be the same as if no bankruptcy petition had been filed (partnership agreement); *see also In re* James Cable Partners, L.P., 27 F.3d 534 (11th Cir. 1994)]

        (1) **Example:** Absent consent, the trustee could not assume or assign an executory contract of the debtor to play professional football.

        (2) **Example:** The prohibition against assumption and assignment is not limited solely to personal service contracts, as the following example illustrates: Airline #1 files a voluntary Chapter 11 petition and remains in control of its business as a debtor in possession. Airline #1 then seeks court approval to assign to Airline #2 its rights to certain landing slots under an unexpired lease with Airport, which opposes the assignment. The applicable nonbankruptcy law requires Federal Aviation Administration ("FAA") approval before any entity can operate at Airport. Airline #2 has not been approved by the FAA to operate at Airport, and, therefore, Airline #1 may not assign its rights under the lease to Airline #2. [B.C. §365(c)(1); *In re* Braniff Airways, Inc., 700 F.2d 935 (5th Cir. 1983); *see also In re* Magness, 972 F.2d 689 (6th Cir. 1992)—Chapter 7 trustee barred from assuming and assigning debtor's golf membership in country club]

    b. **Contracts to loan money or to issue securities:** [§898] The trustee or debtor in possession may not assume or assign an executory contract to make a loan or to grant other debt financing or financial accommodations (*e.g.,* surety or guaranty contracts) to the debtor, or to issue a security of the debtor. [B.C. §365(c)(2)] For example, an option to purchase real property for a cash deposit and a note secured by a first priority trust deed was held to be nonassumable. [*In re* Easebe Enterprises, Inc., 900 F.2d 1417 (9th Cir. 1990); *and see In re* Sun Runner Marine, Inc., 945 F.2d 1089 (9th Cir. 1991)—financial accommodations contract was nonassumable despite lender's consent] This prohibition, however, does not apply to ordinary contracts for the sale or lease of goods or services that provide for "incidental financial accommodations or extensions of credit." [2 Collier ¶365.05(1)] Recently, it was held that a credit card merchant agreement between a bank and a merchant does not constitute a financial accommodations contract. [*In re* Thomas B. Hamilton Co., 969 F.2d 1013 (11th Cir. 1992)—good discussion of financial accommodations]

c. **Nonresidential leases terminated before bankruptcy:** [§899] The trustee or debtor in possession may not assume or assign a lease of nonresidential real property that has been terminated under nonbankruptcy law prior to the order for relief. [B.C. §365(c)(3)] Thus, it is necessary to determine whether the lease was validly terminated under applicable nonbankruptcy law [*In re* Mimi's of Atlanta, Inc., 5 B.R. 623 (Bankr. N.D. Ga. 1980) *aff'd*, 11 B.R. 710 (N.D. Ga. 1981)], and, in some instances, whether the termination would have been reversible under a state antiforfeiture law [*In re* Waterkist Corp., 775 F.2d 1089 (9th Cir. 1985)].

5. **Time Limitations for Assumption or Rejection:** [§900] The period within which the trustee or debtor in possession may assume or reject an executory contract or an unexpired lease depends on the chapter under which the case is filed and the nature of the property that is the subject matter of the contract or lease. [B.C. §365(d)]

   a. **Chapter 7 cases:** [§901] The trustee, in a case under Chapter 7, has 60 days after the order for relief within which to assume or reject an executory contract or an unexpired lease of *personal property or residential real property*. Otherwise, the contract or the lease is deemed rejected. The court may extend the period for cause. [B.C. §365(d)(1)]

      (1) **Administrative expense:** [§902] If, during the 60 days following the order for relief, the Chapter 7 trustee retains the subject matter of an executory contract, or personal property or residential real property under an unexpired lease, the nondebtor party is entitled to an administrative expense, but only to the extent of any *actual benefit to the estate*. Thus, where a Chapter 7 trustee retained the right to use a scrambled television signal (under an executory contract) for 60 days until the contract automatically was deemed rejected under section 365(d)(1), but the trustee used the signal for only 17 days, the creditor received an administrative expense claim only for the 17-day period that the estate actually benefited from its use. [B.C. §365(d)(1); *In re* Subscription Television of Greater Atlanta, 789 F.2d 1530 (11th Cir. 1986)]

   b. **Chapter 11, 12, and 13 cases:** [§903] Assumption or rejection of an executory contract or unexpired lease of *personal property or residential real property* may occur at any time prior to the confirmation of a plan under Chapter 11, 12, or 13. [B.C. §365(d)(2)]

(1) **Expedited decision:** [§904] In a case under Chapter 11, 12, or 13, the nondebtor party may request that the court direct the trustee or debtor in possession to elect either to assume or reject an executory contract or an unexpired lease of personalty or residential realty within a fixed period of time. [B.C. §365(d)(2)] (This provision may be especially helpful in a prolonged Chapter 11 case in which confirmation of a plan of reorganization is not expected in the near future. However, bankruptcy courts often are reluctant to order the debtor to decide in a short period of time, and thus, the nondebtor party may want to ask the court to fashion a remedy during the limbo period regarding payments for what is being supplied to the debtor.)

(2) **Leases of personal property in Chapter 11 cases:** [§905] In a Chapter 11 case, the trustee or debtor in possession must timely perform all obligations (except those required under Code section 365(b)(2), *supra*, §894) in a lease of *nonconsumer personal property*, including payment of the amount of rent specified, first arising from 60 days after the order for relief until the lease is assumed or rejected, regardless of the extent of the property's use or the benefit to the estate. An exception could arise where the court, after notice and a hearing and based on the equities, orders otherwise. [B.C. §365(d)(10)] Most often, unexpired leases of personal property are *equipment leases*.

  (a) **Adequate protection:** [§906] Adequate protection of the lessor's interest in the personal property is required, both during and after the 60-day period, but the lessor may not seek relief from the automatic stay under section 362(d) (*see supra*, §§809 *et seq.*). [B.C. §363(e); *see supra*, §§849-851]

c. **Leases of nonresidential real property:** [§907] If the debtor is the lessee, a trustee in a case under *any chapter* (or the debtor in possession, where applicable) has 60 days after the order for relief within which to assume or reject an unexpired lease of nonresidential real property, or else the lease is deemed to be rejected and the property must be immediately surrendered to the lessor. [B.C. §365(d)(4); *In re* Longua, 58 B.R. 503 (Bankr. W.D. Wis. 1986)] However, for cause arising during the 60-day period, some courts may grant an extension of time for the trustee or debtor in possession to decide whether to assume or reject if *a motion to extend is filed within the 60-day period*, also. [*In re* Southwest Aircraft Services, Inc., 831 F.2d 848 (9th Cir. 1987)] Other cases have held that, under the plain meaning of Bankruptcy Code section 365(d)(4), the *court's order* granting the extension must also be entered within the 60-day period. [*In re* Horowitz, 167 B.R. 237 (Bankr. W.D. Okla. 1994)] The difficulty with this approach, however, is that the hearing date, which is scheduled by the court, is beyond the movant's control. Several appellate courts have held that an additional extension of time may be granted for cause, where the motion to extend is filed and granted before the end of the period as previously extended. [*In re* Channel Home Centers, Inc., 989 F.2d 682 (3d Cir. 1993)—without ruling on whether a timely motion could be granted after the expiration of the extended period]

(1) **Trustee's obligations:** [§908] The trustee or debtor in possession must timely perform all duties arising under an unexpired lease of nonresidential

realty after the order for relief and until assumption or rejection. The only duties excluded are those described in Bankruptcy Code section 365(b)(2) (*see supra*, §894). [B.C. §365(d)(3)] Therefore, all rents due under such a lease during this period must be *timely paid at the rate specified in the lease*, without the necessity of notice or a hearing. [B.C. §365(d)(3); *In re* Coastal Dry Dock & Repair Corp., 62 B.R. 879 (Bankr. E.D.N.Y. 1986)]

   (a) **Administrative expense:** [§909]   Where a lease of nonresidential real property is *rejected or deemed rejected* for failure to assume the lease within the 60-day period, and rents due after the order for relief and during the pre-rejection period have not been paid, the *majority view* treats the accrued rent as an administrative expense equal to the total amount of rent due under the lease during this period, regardless of the extent of use by the trustee or debtor in possession, and independent of the usual requirement of proving the reasonableness of an administrative expense claim under Bankruptcy Code section 503(b)(1). [*In re* Pacific-Atlantic Trading Co., 27 F.3d 401 (9th Cir. 1994)] However, a *minority* of cases have held that administrative status of a claim for accrued rent must be determined under the test of Bankruptcy Code section 503(b)(1), taking into account the benefit to the estate (actual and necessary use) and the reasonableness of the rent. [*In re* Tammey Jewels, Inc., 116 B.R. 292 (Bankr. M.D. Fl. 1990); *see also In re* Mr. Gatti's, Inc., 164 B.R. 929 (Bankr. W.D. Tex. 1994)—thoroughly analyzing relevant case law, and allowing administrative expense claim for only four days' actual use at contract rate where reasonableness was not contested]

   (b) **Failure to perform:** [§910]   Where the trustee or debtor in possession fails to perform the duties arising under a lease of nonresidential realty during the 60 days following the order for relief, the outcome under the Bankruptcy Code is not specified. At least one case has held that such a failure does not terminate the lease automatically, and that the result will depend on the particular circumstances. [*In re* Westview 74th Street Drug Corp., 59 B.R. 747 (Bankr. S.D.N.Y. 1986)]

(2) **Assumption—court approval required:** [§911]   Court approval must be obtained in order to assume a lease, and thus conduct by the trustee or debtor in possession during the section 365(d)(4) 60-day period following the order for relief is not sufficient. [B.C. §365(a); *In re* Treat Fitness Center, Inc., 60 B.R. 878 (Bankr. 9th Cir. 1986)] A motion is required (unless the assumption is part of a plan), as are reasonable notice and an opportunity for a hearing. [Bankruptcy Rules 6006, 9014; Sea Harvest Corp. v. Riviera Land Co., 868 F.2d 1077 (9th Cir. 1989)] Most courts have held that the time limit established by section 365(d)(4) within which to assume or reject an unexpired lease of nonresidential property is satisfied if the trustee's or the debtor in possession's motion to assume is filed within the 60-day period (even where the hearing is held after the 60 days), although the assumption itself is not effective unless and until it is approved by the court. [*In re* By-Rite Distributing, Inc., 55 B.R. 740 (D. Utah 1985)]

6. **Ipso Facto Provisions:** [§912] An executory contract or unexpired lease may not be terminated or modified *after* the filing of a bankruptcy petition solely on account of an ipso facto clause in the contract or lease relating to: (i) the insolvency or financial state of the debtor [B.C. §365(e)(1)(A)]; (ii) the commencement of a case under the Bankruptcy Code concerning the debtor [B.C. §365(e)(1)(B)]; (iii) the appointment of a bankruptcy trustee or a nonbankruptcy custodian [B.C. §365(e)(1)(C)]; or (iv) the seizure of property by a bankruptcy trustee or a nonbankruptcy custodian [B.C. §365(e)(1)(C)].

   a. **Example:** The post-petition cancellation of Debtor's insurance policy under an "at will" clause of the contract, solely because of the filing of an involuntary petition against Debtor, is ineffective, and thus the policy continues in force. [B.C. §365(e)(1)(B); *In re* B. Siegel Co., 51 B.R. 159 (Bankr. E.D. Mich. 1985)]

   b. **Compare—pre-petition termination:** [§913] A pre-bankruptcy termination of an executory contract under an ipso facto clause, for example, solely because of the debtor's insolvency, would not be prohibited. [*In re* LJP, Inc., 22 B.R. 556 (Bankr. S.D. Fla. 1982)]

   c. **Other exceptions:** [§914] A post-petition termination or modification under an ipso facto clause can be effective with respect to a personal service agreement, or a contract to make a loan or grant other debt financing to the debtor or to issue a security of the debtor. [B.C. §365(e)(2)(A), (B); *and see supra*, §§897-898]

7. **Assignment:** [§915] An executory contract or an unexpired lease may be assigned by the trustee or debtor in possession only if it has been properly assumed and if adequate assurance of the assignee's future performance is provided, regardless of whether there has been a default. [B.C. §365(f)(2); *In re* Kinglore Farms, Inc., 64 B.R. 260 (Bankr. N.D. Ill. 1986)] A motion is required (unless the assignment is part of a plan), as are reasonable notice and an opportunity for a hearing. [Bankruptcy Rules 6006, 9014]

   a. **Ineffectiveness of restrictions on assignment:** [§916] Except as indicated below, an assignment that complies with the requirements of section 365(f)(2) is valid despite any provision in the contract or lease or in applicable nonbankruptcy law that prohibits, restricts, or conditions the assignment, or that terminates or modifies the contract or lease because of the assignment. [B.C. §365(f)(1), (3); *In re* U.L. Radio Corp., 19 B.R. 537 (Bankr. S.D.N.Y. 1982)]

      (1) **Exceptions:** [§917] Certain kinds of contracts and leases are not assignable, such as (i) a personal service contract or a government contract, without consent (both usually are nondelegable under nonbankruptcy law); (ii) a contract to make a loan to the debtor or to issue a security of the debtor; or (iii) a lease of nonresidential real property that was terminated under nonbankruptcy law before the order for relief. [B.C. §365(f)(1), (c); 41 U.S.C. §15; *and see supra*, §§896 *et seq.*]

   b. **Liability of trustee:** [§918] The assignment of an executory contract or an unexpired lease has the effect of relieving the trustee and the estate from any liability resulting from a breach occurring after the assignment. [B.C. §365(k)]

c. **Landlord's deposit:** [§919] The assignment of an unexpired lease under which the debtor is the lessee entitles the lessor to demand substantially the same deposit or other security that she would have received under the original lease from a comparable tenant. [B.C. §365(l)]

8. **Rejection Constitutes Breach:** [§920] Generally, a rejection by the trustee or debtor in possession statutorily operates as a breach of the executory contract or the unexpired lease. The time that the breach is deemed to have occurred is prescribed by Bankruptcy Code section 365(g) and will determine the nature of the nonbreacher's claim.

   a. **Where there has been no assumption:** [§921] If the trustee or debtor in possession has not assumed the contract or the lease at any time prior to rejecting it, then the breach caused by the rejection is deemed to have occurred *pre-petition* and, therefore, the nonbreacher's claim is subject to any limitations that normally apply to the kind of pre-petition claim he holds. [B.C. §§365(g)(1), 502(g); *see In re* Aslan, 909 F.2d 367 (9th Cir. 1990)—date of breach is the day immediately before bankruptcy petition was filed] Thus, for example, a lessor's claim that ensues from the rejection of a lease of property is limited to the amount fixed by section 502(b)(6) (*see supra*, §513), and an employee's claim for damages caused by the rejection of an employment contract is limited to the amount allowable under section 502(b)(7) (*see supra*, §514). [*In re* Steiner, 50 B.R. 181 (Bankr. N.D. Ohio 1985)]

      (1) **Compare—post-petition use of property:** [§922] Any post-petition use by the trustee or debtor in possession of property that is the subject matter of a lease ultimately rejected is treated as an administrative expense. It is measured by the fair and reasonable market value, and is not subject to the limitations on pre-petition claims discussed above. While the rent specified in the lease is presumptive evidence of the fair market value, it is not conclusive. [*In re* Thompson, 788 F.2d 560 (9th Cir. 1986)]

   b. **Where there has been an assumption:** [§923] Administrative expense status is also accorded where the contract or lease first was assumed by the trustee or debtor in possession, but later was rejected. In this instance, the breach is deemed to have occurred *at the time of the rejection* if the case has not been converted to Chapter 7 prior to the rejection. [B.C. §365(g)(2)(A); *In re* Frontier Properties, Inc., 979 F.2d 1358 (9th Cir. 1992)]

      (1) **Conversion to Chapter 7:** [§924] Where the case has been converted to Chapter 7 *before the rejection*, the following rules apply: if the contract or lease was assumed before the conversion, the breach is deemed to have occurred *immediately prior to the date of conversion* [B.C. §365(g)(2)(B)(i)]; but if the assumption took place after the conversion, the breach is deemed to have occurred *at the time of the rejection* [B.C. §365(g)(2)(B)(ii)].

         (a) **Priority of administrative expenses in converted cases:** [§925] When a case has been converted to Chapter 7, the administrative expenses of the Chapter 7 case have priority over the administrative expenses of the superseded case. [B.C. §726(b)]

1) **Example:** On May 1, Debtor (lessee) files a voluntary Chapter 11 petition and, on June 1, obtains court approval to assume an unexpired lease of certain real property. On July 1, Debtor rejects the lease and, on August 1, converts the case to Chapter 7. The rejection of the lease constitutes a breach deemed to have occurred on July 1, and for which Lessor is entitled to an administrative expense. [B.C. §365(g)(2)(A); *see supra*, §923] However, any administrative expenses arising *after conversion* in the Chapter 7 case will have priority over Lessor's administrative expense claim, which was incurred prior to conversion. [B.C. §726(b); *In re* Multech Corp., 47 B.R. 747 (Bankr. N.D. Iowa 1985)]

9. **Debtor as Lessor:** [§926] Where the debtor is the lessor under an unexpired lease of real property, and the lease has been rejected by the trustee or debtor in possession, the lessee either may consider the lease terminated or, *if the term of the lease has commenced*, retain rights under the lease for the balance of the current term and for any period of renewal or extension enforceable under nonbankruptcy law. These rights include, for example, the amount and timing of rental payments; use; possession; quiet enjoyment; subletting; assignment; hypothecation; and (in the context of a shopping center lease) enforceability of any lease provisions concerning radius, location, use, exclusivity, or tenant mix or balance. [B.C. §365(h)(1)]

    a. **Timeshares:** [§927] Similarly, a nondebtor timeshare interest purchaser has the choice of treating a rejected timeshare plan as terminated or, if the term of the timeshare interest has commenced, retaining rights in the timeshare interest for the balance of the term and for any period of renewal or extension enforceable under nonbankruptcy law. [B.C. §§365(h)(2)(A), 101(53D)]

    b. **Continued possession:** [§928] If the lessee or timeshare interest purchaser elects to retain her rights, she may offset against her post-rejection rent (or monies due for the timeshare interest) any damages occurring after the date of rejection from the failure of the trustee or debtor in possession to perform its obligations under the lease (or under the timeshare plan). The right of setoff is the exclusive remedy against the estate or the debtor for post-rejection damages. [B.C. §365(h)(1)(B), (2)(B)]

10. **Debtor as Vendor:** [§929] Where the debtor is the vendor under an executory contract to sell real property, and the contract has been rejected by the trustee or debtor in possession, the purchaser, *if she is in possession*, may consider the contract as terminated or may stay in possession of the property. [B.C. §365(i)(1)]

    a. **Continued possession:** [§930] If the purchaser chooses to remain in possession of the property, she is obligated to make all payments required by the contract, but she may offset against the payments any damages occurring after the date of rejection from nonperformance by the trustee or debtor in possession. The right of setoff is the exclusive remedy against the estate for post-rejection damages. [B.C. §365(i)(2)(A)]

        (1) **Title:** [§931] The trustee or debtor in possession is required to deliver the title to the purchaser after all payments have been made (or as other-

wise provided for in the contract of sale), but is not obligated to perform any other duties under the contract. [B.C. §365(i)(2)(B)]

    b. **Termination of contract:** [§932] Where the trustee or debtor in possession has rejected an executory contract to sell real property, and the vendee either elects to consider the contract terminated or is not in possession of the property, the vendee is granted a *lien* on the property to the extent of any payments made toward the purchase price. [B.C. §365(j)]

11. **Intellectual Property:** [§933] Where the debtor is the licensor of a right to intellectual property, and the trustee or debtor in possession rejects an executory contract under which the license has been granted, the licensee may consider the contract terminated or may retain its contractual rights to the intellectual property (including any right to exclusivity, but excluding any other right to specific performance of the contract) and use the property for the remaining period of the contract and any rightful extension. [B.C. §365(n)]

    a. **Retention of rights:** [§934] Where the licensee elects to retain its contractual rights to the property, it continues to be responsible for all royalty payments under the contract (or any extension thereof) but waives any right of setoff concerning the contract and any claim for administrative expenses resulting from performance of the contract. Following rejection, the trustee or debtor in possession is relieved of future obligations under the contract, other than: (i) the duty to allow the licensee to exercise its rights to the intellectual property under the contract; (ii) any contractual duty to provide to the licensee the intellectual property (held by the trustee or debtor in possession); and (iii) the duty not to interfere with the licensee's rights to the property under the contract. [B.C. §365(n); *In re* Prize Frize, Inc., 32 F.3d 426 (9th Cir. 1994)—"license fees" for use of patents, technology, and proprietary rights in french fry vending machine held to constitute royalties]

    b. **"Intellectual property" defined:** [§935] Intellectual property includes trade secrets; inventions, processes, designs, or plants protected under United States Code title 35; patent applications; plant varieties; works of authorship protected under title 17; and mask work (relating to semiconductor chip production) protected under chapter 9 of title 17. [B.C. §101(35A)]

12. **Capital Commitment of a Financial Institution:** [§936] In a Chapter 11 case, the trustee or debtor in possession is deemed to have assumed (and must immediately cure any deficiency under) any commitment by the debtor to a federal depository institutions regulatory agency (such as the FDIC or RTC) to maintain the capital of an insured depository institution. [B.C. §§365(o), 101(21B), 101(35); *In re* Firstcorp, Inc., 973 F.2d 243 (4th Cir. 1992)] Any subsequent breach will result in a claim entitled to ninth priority. [B.C. §§365(o), 507(a)(9); *see supra*, §573]

F. UTILITY SERVICE

1. **Protection for Debtor:** [§937] The utility services of the trustee or debtor may not be discontinued, altered, or refused; nor may a utility discriminate against the trustee or debtor solely because of the filing of a bankruptcy case or because of failure to timely pay a debt owed by the debtor for utility services furnished prior to the order for relief. [B.C. §366(a); *In re* Whittaker, 882 F.2d 791 (3d Cir. 1989)—

utility, having terminated service pre-petition, required to restore service during 20-day period and prior to securing payment of adequate assurance; *see infra*, §938]

2. **Exception—Insufficient Security:** [§938] Utility services, however, may be discontinued, altered, or refused if, within *20 days* after the order for relief, neither the debtor nor the trustee provides a deposit or other security constituting adequate assurance that the utility will be paid for services rendered after the order for relief. A hearing may be requested by a party in interest on the issue of adequate assurance. [B.C. §366(b); *In re* Hanratty, 907 F.2d 1418 (3d Cir. 1990)]

IX. CHAPTER 7—LIQUIDATION

chapter approach

In a Chapter 7 case, the trustee collects the property of the estate, reduces it to cash, and pays claimants in a prescribed order. A likely exam question will ask you to discuss the *order and amount of distribution* to each creditor. Some key things for you to consider in answering this type of question are:

(1) Ordinarily, *secured* creditors are paid out of their collateral.

(2) *Unsecured priority* claimants receive distribution ahead of the general unsecured creditors.

(3) If there is not enough money to pay all claims at a particular level, claimants within that level take a *pro rata share*.

(4) Liens for certain kinds of penalties *can be avoided* by the trustee, and *tax liens* are subject to subordination.

(5) If your question concerns a *partnership* debtor, remember that special rules apply when there are insufficient assets to pay all the claims against the partnership.

You probably will also be asked to determine whether the debtor should receive a *discharge* under Chapter 7. Look for any of the 10 grounds for denial of a discharge (*e.g.*, the debtor is not an individual, or she transferred property with the intent to hinder, delay, or defraud a creditor). If the facts do not show any of the grounds for denial, a discharge *must* be granted, although under appropriate circumstances, a discharge may be *revoked*.

Finally, keep in mind that the debtor may *convert* a Chapter 7 case to Chapter 11, 12, or 13 if the case has not been converted earlier and the debtor is eligible under the other chapter. Also, the court may *dismiss* a case for cause or if a consumer debtor has substantially abused Chapter 7 relief.

A. INTRODUCTION

1. **Eligibility for Relief:** [§939] A person (individual, partnership, or corporation) that resides or has a domicile, a place of business, or property in the United States may be a debtor under Chapter 7, unless specifically excepted. [B.C. §109(a), (b); *and see supra*, §120]

   a. **Exceptions:** [§940] The following persons are not eligible to be debtors under Chapter 7 [B.C. §109(b); *and see supra*, §124]:

      (1) *Railroads* [B.C. §109(b)(1)];

      (2) *Domestic banks, insurance companies,* credit unions, savings and loan associations, building and loan associations, homestead associations, cooperative banks, and other similar institutions [B.C. §109(b)(2)];

(3) *Foreign banks, insurance companies,* and other similar financial institutions, that are engaged in business in the United States [B.C. §109(b)(3)]; and

(4) *An individual or a family farmer* who was a debtor in a case that was *dismissed in the preceding 180 days* because of the debtor's intentional failure to obey court orders or to appear before the court, or because of the debtor's request for a voluntary dismissal of the case following a party's request for relief from the automatic stay [B.C. §109(g)].

2. **Chapter 7 Trustee:** [§941]   Immediately after the order for relief, the United States trustee appoints a disinterested member of the panel of private trustees to serve as the interim trustee in a Chapter 7 case. [B.C. §701(a)(1)] Then, either a trustee is elected at the section 341 meeting of creditors or (as usually occurs) the interim trustee automatically becomes the permanent trustee in the case. [B.C. §702]

   a. **Duties of trustee:** [§942]   In a Chapter 7 case, the trustee's primary responsibilities are to locate and collect property of the estate; to convert the property to cash; to make distributions to claimants in the order established by the Bankruptcy Code; and to close the estate expeditiously. [B.C. §§704(1), 725-726] Additional administrative duties of the Chapter 7 trustee are described in Bankruptcy Code section 704 (*see supra*, §241).

3. **Authority to Operate Debtor's Business:** [§943]   Occasionally, the trustee may receive authorization from the court to operate the debtor's business temporarily, under circumstances where continuing the business for a while is in the best interest of the estate and will assist in its orderly liquidation. Such a situation may arise where an attempt is being made to sell the debtor's business as a going concern or where completing the manufacture of unfinished commodities is likely to result in a substantially greater liquidation price. [B.C. §721; 4 Collier ¶721.02]

4. **Meeting of Creditors:** [§944]   Within 20 to 40 days after the order for relief, the United States trustee convenes and presides at the section 341 meeting, where creditors often participate in many of the following matters [B.C. §341(a)]:

   a. *Examination of the debtor*, under oath, by creditors, the trustee or an examiner in the case, or the United States trustee [B.C. §343; *see supra*, §197]

   b. *The election of a trustee*, when requested by a sufficient number of unsecured creditors [B.C. §702];

   c. *Election of a creditors' committee*, when desired, consisting of between three and eleven unsecured creditors, to act in an advisory role in consultation with the trustee in the case or with the United States trustee [B.C. §705];

   d. *Discussion about the trustee's abandonment* of property that is burdensome or of inconsequential value to the estate [B.C. §554, *see supra*, §§469 *et seq.*];

   e. *Discussion about an individual debtor's redemption* of tangible personal property intended primarily for consumer use [B.C. §722; *see supra*, §§752 *et seq.*]; and

f. *Discussion about the debtor's reaffirmation* of particular debts [B.C. §524(c); *see supra*, §§733 *et seq.*].

B. DISTRIBUTION OF PROPERTY OF ESTATE

1. **Order of Payment:** [§945] Claimants in a Chapter 7 case receive distribution according to the order prescribed by Bankruptcy Code sections 725 and 726.

    a. **Secured creditors:** [§946] Claims that have been allowed as secured are paid first. They are paid from the collateral securing their claims. [B.C. §725] Remember that in bankruptcy a claim is deemed secured only to the extent of the value of the creditor's collateral. [B.C. §506(a); *see supra*, §§523-524]

        (1) **Oversecured creditors:** [§947] Recall that, to the extent that the value of a *secured* party's collateral exceeds his allowed secured claim, any allowed post-petition interest, and any fees, costs, or charges (under the agreement) that are allowed generally accrue until the time of distribution in a Chapter 7 case. [B.C. §506(b); *see supra*, §§529-531]

    b. **Priority claims:** [§948] Next, unsecured claims entitled to priority under section 507 (*see supra*, §§554 *et seq.*) (that are timely filed, or tardily filed before the trustee begins distribution) are paid in the following order [B.C. §726(a)(1)]:

        (1) *Administrative expenses* [B.C. §507(a)(1)] (note that a tardy claim for administrative expenses requires **court approval**, for cause, to be filed [B.C. §503(a)]);

        (2) *Involuntary case gap claims* [B.C. §507(a)(2)];

        (3) *Wages, salaries, or commissions* [B.C. §507(a)(3)];

        (4) *Contributions to employee benefit plans* [B.C. §507(a)(4)];

        (5) *Claims of grain farmers and United States fishermen* [B.C. §507(a)(5)];

        (6) *Consumer layaway claims* [B.C. §507(a)(6)];

        (7) *Alimony, or spousal or child support* [B.C. §507(a)(7)];

        (8) *Unsecured pre-petition taxes* [B.C. §507(a)(8)]; and

        (9) *Capital requirements of insured depository institutions* [B.C. §507(a)(9)].

    c. **General unsecured claims:** [§949] After the priority claims have been satisfied, the general unsecured claims that have been filed timely and have been allowed are paid. [B.C. §726(a)(2)(A), (B)]

        (1) **Justifiably tardy claims:** [§950] Also included in this category are claims that have been filed late due to the creditor's lack of notice or actual knowledge of the case—as long as the claims were filed in time for distribution. [B.C. §726(a)(2)(C); *In re* Columbia Ribbon & Carbon Manufacturing Co., 54 B.R. 714 (Bankr. S.D.N.Y. 1985)]

d. **Unexcused tardy claims:** [§951]   Unsecured claims that were filed late, without legal justification (*see* above), are paid after the other general unsecured claims. [B.C. §726(a)(3)]

e. **Penalty claims:** [§952]   Next in the order of distribution are unsecured or secured claims for punitive, exemplary, or multiple damages, or for fines, penalties, or forfeitures that do not constitute compensation for actual pecuniary loss. [B.C. §726(a)(4)]

f. **Interest:** [§953]   If the estate is solvent, after all of the claims above have been satisfied, post-petition interest at the legal rate is paid on claims under section 726(a)(1)-(4) from the date that the bankruptcy petition was filed. [B.C. §726(a)(5)]

g. **Payment to debtor:** [§954]   If there is any property of the estate left after payment of post-petition interest on the unsecured claims, it is distributed to the debtor. [B.C. §726(a)(6)]

2. **Pro Rata Payment:** [§955]   Claims within any tier of priority under section 507(a), or within any level of distribution under section 726(a), share pro rata in the property distributed to that particular category of claims. [B.C. §726(b); *In re* IML Freight, Inc., 52 B.R. 124 (Bankr. D. Utah 1985)]

   a. **Example:** Debtor Corporation files a voluntary Chapter 7 petition. There are no secured creditors, and the general unsecured claims total $30,000. Administrative expenses are $5,000, and each of 10 employees of Debtor Corporation holds a third priority wage claim in the amount of $1,000. Unsecured pre-petition tax claims, with eighth priority status, total $20,000. If the amount available for distribution is $10,000, the administrative expenses will be paid in full ($5,000), and the 10 employees will receive $500 each. The holders of the priority tax claims and the general unsecured claims will receive nothing. [B.C. §726(b)]

   b. **Note:** The law is unclear as to whether ninth priority claims must be prorated. [4 Collier ¶726.03; *see supra*, §573]

   c. **Exception—converted case:** [§956]   In a case that has been converted to Chapter 7 from Chapter 11, 12, or 13, the administrative expenses allowed in the Chapter 7 case *after conversion* have priority over any administrative expenses incurred prior to conversion. [B.C. §726(b); *In re* Tandem Group, Inc., 61 B.R. 738 (Bankr. C.D. Cal. 1986)]

3. **Community Property:** [§957]   If any property of the estate constitutes community property [B.C. §541(a)(2)], it must be segregated from other property of the estate. Special rules for distribution apply, including the payment of administrative expenses, either from the community property or from the other property of the estate, as justice requires. [B.C. §726(c); *In re* Merlino, 62 B.R. 836 (Bankr. W.D. Wash. 1986)]

4. **Exception—Subordination of Claims:** [§958]   While the claims in a Chapter 7 case ordinarily are paid in the order described above, some claims could be subordinated to a lower rank in the distribution, such as when there is a subordination

agreement, there are claims of defrauded security holders, or the principles of equitable subordination apply. [B.C. §§726(a), 510; *see supra*, §§599 *et seq.*]

5. **Tax Debt—Allocation of Payments:** [§959] In Chapter 7 cases, the courts consistently have refused to order that tax payments be allocated first to trust fund taxes before being applied to non-trust fund tax liabilities [U.S. v. Pepperman, 976 F.2d 123 (3d Cir. 1992)]; but, where necessary for a successful Chapter 11 reorganization, such allocation has been allowed, *see infra*, §1059]

C. TREATMENT OF CERTAIN LIENS IN CHAPTER 7 CASE

1. **Avoidance of Liens Securing Penalties:** [§960] The trustee may avoid a lien securing the type of claim described in Bankruptcy Code section 726(a)(4) for a fine, penalty, or forfeiture, or for punitive, multiple, or exemplary damages that do not constitute compensation for actual pecuniary loss. [B.C. §724(a); *and see supra*, §952]

2. **Subordination of Tax Liens:** [§961] Where an allowed tax claim is secured by a nonavoidable lien (*e.g.*, a perfected tax lien) on estate property, distribution of the property or its proceeds is made in the following order:

    (i) *To any lienholder* possessing an allowed claim secured by a nonavoidable lien on the collateral that is *senior to the tax lien* [B.C. §724(b)(1)];

    (ii) *To the holders of any priority claims* under section 507(a)(1)-(7), with the aggregate of such distributions not to exceed the amount of the allowed secured tax claim [B.C. §724(b)(2); *see supra*, §§554 *et seq.*] (*But note:* The priority claimants entitled to distribution under section 724(b)(2) do not include eighth priority unsecured tax claims [B.C. §507(a)(8)]);

    (iii) *To the tax lienholder* to the extent that the allowed secured tax claim is *greater* than the total of all distributions made under section 724(b)(2) to priority claimants [B.C. §724(b)(3)];

    (iv) *To any lienholder* possessing an allowed claim secured by a nonavoidable lien on the collateral that is *junior to the tax lien* [B.C. §724(b)(4)];

    (v) *To the tax lienholder* to the extent that the allowed secured tax claim is *not satisfied* under section 724(b)(3) [B.C. §724(b)(5)]; and

    (vi) *To the Chapter 7 estate* [B.C. §724(b)(6)].

    [B.C. §724(b)]

    a. **Example:** Debtor Corporation files a voluntary Chapter 7 petition, and the only property available for distribution is a building that is worth $20,000. The Internal Revenue Service holds an allowed claim for $7,000, secured by a perfected tax lien on the building. Bank A holds a $10,000 claim secured by a nonavoidable lien on the building that is senior to the tax lien. Bank B holds a $2,000 claim secured by a nonavoidable lien on the building that is junior to the tax lien. Administrative expenses in the case total $4,000, and there also are priority claims in the amount of $1,000 for pre-petition wages owed to employees of Debtor Corporation. If the building is sold for a price of $20,000, distribution in the case will be as follows: (i) to Bank A in the amount of $10,000; (ii) to the priority claimants for the expenses of administration ($4,000) and for the employees' wages ($1,000); (iii) to the IRS in the amount of $2,000, which is the extent that its allowed secured tax claim ($7,000) exceeds the total payments to the priority claimants ($5,000); (iv) to Bank B in the amount of $2,000; and (v) to the IRS in the amount of $1,000, which are the only funds remaining. Thus, as a result of the subordination of its tax lien in the Chapter 7 case, the IRS receives a total distribution of only $3,000 on its allowed secured claim. [B.C. §724(b)]

3. **Multiple Claimants:** [§962] Payment to more than one claimant within any particular level of distribution under section 724(b) (above) is made in the order that would have been required under the Code outside of the provisions for the treatment of tax liens. [B.C. §724(c)]

4. **Similar Statutory Liens:** [§963] Any statutory lien (such as an ERISA lien) whose priority is determined by the same method as that prescribed under 26 U.S.C. section 6323 for the priority of a tax lien, is treated under Bankruptcy Code section 724(b) exactly like a tax lien, and is subordinated accordingly. [B.C. §724(d)]

D. PARTNERSHIP TRUSTEE'S CLAIM AGAINST GENERAL PARTNERS

1. **Deficiency of Partnership Property:** [§964] Where the estate of a Chapter 7 partnership debtor lacks sufficient property to fully satisfy all claims against the partnership, the *trustee* is entitled to a claim for the *deficiency* against any general partner who is personally liable, but only to the extent that the general partner is personally liable under applicable nonbankruptcy law. [B.C. §723(a)]

   a. **Nondebtor general partners:** [§965] In attempting to recover the deficiency, the trustee, where practicable, must first pursue any general partner who is not a debtor in a bankruptcy case. Under these circumstances, the court may require the partner to supply indemnity or other assurance of payment, or may enjoin the partner from disposing of property, until the amount of the deficiency is determined. [B.C. §723(b)]

   b. **General partners who are debtors:** [§966] The trustee's claim against the estate of each general partner who is a debtor in a bankruptcy case equals the total of allowed creditors' claims in the partnership's bankruptcy case. The trustee receives distribution on a parity with the general partner's individual unsecured creditors. [B.C. §723(c); 4 Collier ¶723.04(3)]

      (1) **Disallowance of claims of partnership creditors:** [§967] A creditor's claim for which both the partnership debtor and a general partner are responsible will be *disallowed in the bankruptcy case of the general partner*, except to the extent that the claim is secured solely by the general partner's property and not by the partnership's assets. [B.C. §723(c)]

2. **Excess Recovery by Trustee:** [§968] If the trustee in the partnership's bankruptcy case recovers from the debtor general partners an amount that exceeds a deficiency remaining after payment by the nondebtor general partners, the surplus will be returned to the debtor general partners' estates in an equitable manner. [B.C. §723(d)]

E. CHAPTER 7 DISCHARGE

1. **In General:** [§969] An individual Chapter 7 debtor must be granted a discharge, unless one of the 10 independent statutory grounds for denial of a Chapter 7 discharge applies. [B.C. §727(a); *see* below] The effect of the discharge is to discharge the debtor from all debts that arose prior to the order for relief under Chapter 7, as well as from all debts that, under Bankruptcy Code section 502, are treated as prepetition debts (*see supra*, §522). [B.C. §727(b)]

    a. **Exception—nondischargeable debts:** [§970] The discharge does not include particular debts that are nondischargeable under section 523 (*see supra*, §§675 *et seq.*). [B.C. §727(b)] It is important to distinguish between a *denial of the entire discharge* under section 727, and a determination under section 523 that a *specific debt is nondischargeable*. A denial of the entire discharge allows *all* creditors to pursue their claims post-bankruptcy; whereas if a discharge is granted, only those creditors who are owed debts found to be nondischargeable under section 523 will be free to collect their claims post-bankruptcy.

2. **Objection to Discharge:** [§971] An objection to the debtor's discharge may be filed by a creditor, by the trustee in the case, or by the United States trustee. Also, when a party in interest requests, the court may order the trustee to investigate the debtor's conduct to determine whether there is a basis for denying the discharge. [B.C. §727(c)(1), (2)]

3. **Grounds for Denial of Discharge:** [§972] A Chapter 7 discharge may be denied for any of the reasons described below, in which case all of the debtor's debts will survive bankruptcy. [B.C. §727(a)(1)-(10)]

    a. **Debtor not an individual:** [§973] Under Chapter 7, only an individual may receive a discharge. Therefore, other persons (*e.g.*, corporations and partnerships) will not be granted a discharge, even though they may qualify to be debtors under Chapter 7 and may achieve an orderly liquidation of their estate while under the Bankruptcy Code's protection, including that provided by the automatic stay. [B.C. §727(a)(1)]

    b. **Transfer of property with intent to hinder, delay, or defraud creditors:** [§974] The debtor will be denied a discharge if she transferred, removed, concealed, mutilated, or destroyed *property of the debtor*, within one year before the petition was filed, or *property of the estate*, after the petition was filed, with the intent to hinder, delay, or defraud a creditor or an officer of the estate entitled to possession of the property. [B.C. §727(a)(2); *In re* Chastant, 873 F.2d 89 (5th Cir. 1989)]

        (1) **Example:** On May 1, Creditor obtains a judgment of $200,000 against Debtor, who is insolvent and whose only major asset is property known as Blackacre. On May 21, before Creditor has time to record the judgment as a lien against Blackacre, Debtor sells Blackacre to Friend for $110,000. The property is valued on Debtor's books at $250,000 and by Creditor's appraiser at $450,000. On May 22, Debtor executes a Chapter 7 petition, which she files on May 28. Creditor files a timely objection to Debtor's discharge. Since Debtor's transfer of Blackacre to Friend was

made with the intent to hinder, delay, or defraud Creditor and occurred within one year before bankruptcy, the court will deny Debtor a discharge under Chapter 7. [B.C. §727(a)(2); *see In re* Marcus, 45 B.R. 338 (S.D.N.Y. 1984)]

(2) **Conversion of nonexempt to exempt property on eve of bankruptcy:** [§975] While converting nonexempt property to exempt property prior to bankruptcy *"without more"* is permissible, the debtor will be denied a discharge if the court finds that the conversion was done with the intent to hinder, delay, or defraud creditors. [*In re* Carey, 938 F.2d 1073 (10th Cir. 1991)—no fraud; Norwest Bank Nebraska, N.A. v. Tveten, 848 F.2d 871 (8th Cir. 1988)—discharge denied because of debtor's intent to hinder, delay, and defraud creditors] Courts will examine the facts on a case-by-case basis to distinguish between astute pre-bankruptcy planning and bankruptcy fraud.

c. **Destruction or concealment of books or records:** [§976] Another ground for denying a discharge to the debtor is her destruction, concealment, mutilation, falsification of, or failure to keep books, records, documents, or other recorded information from which her business transactions or financial state might be determined. [B.C. §727(a)(3); Meridian Bank v. Alten, 958 F.2d 1226 (3d Cir. 1992)—debtors' failure to keep records not justified)]

(1) **But note:** If the debtor's conduct with respect to her books and records was *justified* in light of all of the circumstances, her discharge will not be denied. [B.C. §727(a)(3); *In re* Cox, 41 F.3d 1294 (9th Cir. 1994)—debtor's reliance on husband to keep records was justifiable under the circumstances]

(2) **Comment:** Authority exists that, when appropriate, the bankruptcy court should allow the debtor (at her own expense) a reasonable time to "present all records in an orderly manner, completely organized with an appropriate accountant's explanation." [*In re* Hughes, 873 F.2d 262 (11th Cir. 1989)]

d. **Perjury, bribery, extortion, and other fraudulent acts:** [§977] The debtor also will be denied a Chapter 7 discharge if she *knowingly and fraudulently* (i) made a false oath or account about a material issue; (ii) submitted a false claim; (iii) paid, offered, obtained, or tried to procure money, property, or advantage, for the commission of or forbearance from any action (*i.e.*, extortion or bribery, or an attempt of such); or (iv) withheld any books, records, or other recorded information concerning the debtor's property or finances from an officer of the estate entitled to possession. [B.C. §727(a)(4); Swicegood v. Ginn, 924 F.2d 230 (11th Cir. 1991); 4 Collier ¶727.06]

e. **Failure to account for loss of assets:** [§978] Another basis for denial of the debtor's discharge is her failure to adequately explain any loss of assets or deficiency of assets to meet her liabilities. [B.C. §727(a)(5); *In re* Hendren, 51 B.R. 781 (Bankr. E.D. Tenn. 1985)]

(1) **Example:** Debtor, who is in the business of breeding livestock, files a voluntary Chapter 7 petition. Shortly thereafter, Debtor makes repeated

sales of what constitutes all of her breeding stock, in violation of both her security agreement with Creditor and a cease and desist order from the bankruptcy court. In addition, Debtor fails to return a garden tractor in which Creditor has a security interest, claiming that the tractor merely vanished when Debtor was away for a short time. Debtor's discharge will be denied on two grounds: (i) her failure to satisfactorily explain the disappearance of the garden tractor and (ii) her transfer of the breeding stock (property of the estate) with the intent to defraud Creditor. [B.C. §727(a)(5), (2)(B); *In re* Devers, 759 F.2d 751 (9th Cir. 1985)]

f. **Violation of court order or refusal to respond to material question:** [§979] The debtor also will be denied a discharge if she (i) refuses to obey a valid judicial order (other than one directing the debtor to testify or to answer a material question); (ii) refuses, for a reason other than the appropriate use of the Fifth Amendment privilege against self-incrimination, to testify or to answer a material question that has been approved by the judge; or (iii) refuses, on the basis of the privilege against self-incrimination, to testify or to answer a judicially approved material question *after she has been granted immunity* regarding the privileged matter. [B.C. §727(a)(6)]

g. **Acts committed in insider case:** [§980] Another ground for denial of the discharge is the debtor's commission, within one year before the petition was filed, or during the case, of an act described in Bankruptcy Code section 727(a)(2)-(6) (*see* above) in connection with a separate bankruptcy case regarding an insider. [B.C. §§727(a)(7), 101(31); *see supra*, §§30-33; *In re* Morris, 51 B.R. 462 (Bankr. E.D. Tenn. 1985), *aff'd,* 822 F.2d 1088 (6th Cir. 1987)]

h. **Prior discharge obtained under Chapter 7 or Chapter 11:** [§981] The debtor will be denied a discharge if she previously received a discharge in a Chapter 7 or a Chapter 11 case that was *commenced within six years* before the date that the petition was filed in the present case. [B.C. §727(a)(8); *In re* Blanchette, 54 B.R. 890 (Bankr. D.R.I. 1985)]

i. **Prior discharge obtained under Chapter 12 or Chapter 13:** [§982] Similarly, the debtor will be denied a Chapter 7 discharge if she previously was granted a discharge in a Chapter 12 or a Chapter 13 case that was *commenced within six years* before the date of the filing of the petition in the current case, *unless*:

(i) All of the allowed unsecured claims in the earlier case were *paid in full* [B.C. §727(a)(9)(A)]; or

(ii) Payments under the plan in the earlier case totaled *at least 70%* of the allowed unsecured claims, and the debtor's plan was *proposed in good faith and represented her best effort* [B.C. §727(a)(9)(B)].

[B.C. §727(a)(9)]

j. **Waiver:** [§983] If the debtor has executed a court-approved written waiver of discharge after the Chapter 7 order for relief, a discharge will not be granted. [B.C. §727(a)(10)]

4. **Revocation of Discharge:** [§984] A creditor, the trustee in the case, or the United States trustee may request that the court, after notice and a hearing, revoke the debtor's discharge on the grounds that:

   a. *The debtor obtained the discharge fraudulently*, and the party seeking revocation did not discover the fraud until after the discharge was granted [B.C. §727(d)(1)];

   b. *The debtor acquired or became entitled to acquire property* that would constitute property of the estate, and she *knowingly and fraudulently* failed to disclose this fact or turn over the property to the trustee [B.C. §727(d)(2); *In re* Yonikus, 974 F.2d 901 (7th Cir. 1992)]; or

   c. *The debtor committed one of the acts of impropriety* described in Bankruptcy Code section 727(a)(6) (*see supra*, §979) [B.C. §727(d)(3)].

5. **Statute of Limitations for Discharge Revocation:** [§985] A request to revoke the debtor's discharge under section 727(d)(1) may be filed within one year after the granting of the discharge. A request under section 727(d)(2) or (d)(3) may be filed within that time or prior to the date that the case is closed, whichever is later. [B.C. §727(e)]

F. CONVERSION

1. **Voluntary Conversion:** [§986] If a Chapter 7 case has not been converted from Chapter 11, 12, or 13, the debtor has an *absolute nonwaivable right* to convert the case from Chapter 7 to any of such other chapters at any time. [B.C. §706(a); *In re* Martin, 880 F.2d 857 (5th Cir. 1989)]

   a. **Example:** Debtor files a voluntary Chapter 7 petition. Creditor, who is owed $30,000, seeks a determination that the debt is nondischargeable because of Debtor's fraud while acting in a fiduciary capacity. [B.C. §523(a)(4); *see supra*, §689] The court rules in Creditor's favor. Debtor then decides to convert the case to Chapter 13, where the discharge provisions appear to be more favorable under the circumstances. [B.C. §1328(a)] Since the case has not been converted to Chapter 7 previously, Debtor may convert the case to Chapter 13 and file a proposed plan of repayment, which will be subject to the usual requirements for confirmation. [B.C. §706(a); *In re* Street, 55 B.R. 763 (Bankr. 9th Cir. 1985); *but see In re* Caldwell, 895 F.2d 1123 (6th Cir. 1990)—conversion to Chapter 13 denied for lack of good faith]

2. **Involuntary Conversion:** [§987] Absent a request by the debtor, the court may *not* convert a Chapter 7 case to one under Chapter 12 or 13. [B.C. §706(c)] However, the court may convert a Chapter 7 case to one under Chapter 11, upon a request by a party in interest, after notice and a hearing. [B.C. §706(b)]

3. **Eligibility:** [§988] Conversion of a Chapter 7 case to another chapter of the Code requires that the debtor be eligible for relief under the particular chapter to which the case is being converted. [B.C. §706(d)]

G. DISMISSAL

1. **For Cause:** [§989] After notice and a hearing, the court may dismiss a Chapter 7 case for cause [B.C. §707(a)], such as where:

a. ***The debtor is guilty of an unreasonable delay that is prejudicial to creditors*** [B.C. §707(a)(1)];

b. ***The debtor has not paid fees or charges*** prescribed by chapter 123 of title 28 [B.C. §707(a)(2)];

c. ***The debtor in a voluntary case has not filed a list of creditors and all schedules and statements*** required under section 521(1) within 15 days (or any extension granted by the court) after the petition was filed. [B.C. §707(a)(3); *see supra*, §153] (*Note:* A dismissal under section 707(a)(3) may be ordered only upon a motion filed by the United States trustee); or

d. ***Other appropriate cause*** warrants dismissal [B.C. §707(a); *In re* Huckfeldt, 39 F.3d 829 (8th Cir. 1994)—case dismissed where Chapter 7 petition was filed in bad faith, for purposes of frustrating divorce decree and pushing ex-wife into bankruptcy].

2. **Substantial Abuse of Chapter 7:** [§990]   A case also may be dismissed, after notice and a hearing, if the bankruptcy petition was filed by an individual debtor ***with primarily consumer debts*** under circumstances constituting a substantial abuse of relief under Chapter 7. [B.C. §707(b); *In re* Kelly, 841 F.2d 908 (9th Cir. 1988)—principal factor is debtor's ability to repay debts; *see also In re* Green, 934 F.2d 568 (4th Cir. 1991)—totality of circumstances analysis] The motion to dismiss must be filed by the United States trustee or must be made sua sponte by the court; a dismissal under this provision cannot be initiated by a motion or suggestion of a party in interest. [B.C. §707(b); *but see In re* Clark, 927 F.2d 793 (4th Cir. 1991)—motion can be filed by United States trustee even though initially suggested by a creditor]

    a. **Criteria:** [§991]   The following factors have been considered in deciding whether to dismiss a Chapter 7 case on the ground of substantial abuse [B.C. §707(b); *In re* Newsom, 69 B.R. 801 (Bankr. D.N.D. 1987)]:

        (1) ***The probability that the debtor's future expected income will be sufficient*** to pay a significant percentage of the unsecured claims under a Chapter 13 plan;

        (2) ***The debtor's reason for filing the Chapter 7 petition***, *e.g.*, because of unemployment, medical expenses, disability, or other misfortune;

        (3) ***The extent to which the debtor obtained cash advances and made consumer purchases beyond her ability to repay***;

        (4) ***The excessiveness or extravagance of the debtor's anticipated family budget***; and

        (5) ***The extent to which the debtor's income statement misrepresents*** her actual financial condition.

    b. **Presumption:** [§992]   There is a statutory presumption *in the debtor's favor* regarding the question of whether granting relief would be a substantial abuse of Chapter 7. [B.C. §707(b)]

X. CHAPTER 11—REORGANIZATION

chapter approach

A Chapter 11 reorganization sometimes is the means by which a troubled business may continue to operate and revitalize itself while also paying creditors and keeping workers employed. In recent years, it also has been used as a vehicle for sustaining large companies that are defendants in multitudinous tort actions throughout the country, and for providing *in one forum* a method by which the tort victims may be compensated. In short, it may be a favorable alternative to a Chapter 7 liquidation. Note that individuals not engaged in business can also be eligible.

In answering an exam question about Chapter 11, keep in mind that the Code provides for the debtor to continue to manage the business as a *debtor in possession* unless the conduct of current management or the interests of creditors, equity security holders, and the estate necessitate the appointment of a *trustee*. However, if a trustee is appointed, note that the debtor then loses the exclusive right to file a plan even if the 120-day period of exclusivity has not expired. If a trustee has not been appointed, sometimes an *examiner* is appointed to investigate the debtor's operations and financial condition, and to advise whether the business should be continued.

If you are asked to prepare a *reorganization plan*, pay careful attention to the manner in which *claims are classified*, and to the kinds of plan provisions that the Code either requires or permits. While all *mandatory provisions* must be included as part of the plan, those that are *discretionary* generally are left to the ingenuity of the plan's proponent.

Remember that a unique feature of Chapter 11 is the right of a partially secured creditor *to elect to have her entire claim treated as secured*, under Bankruptcy Code section 1111(b), but at the cost of forfeiting an unsecured claim for a deficiency. Be prepared to consider the advisability of this election in light of factors such as (i) how much the *unsecured creditors are being offered* under the plan, (ii) whether the plan proposes to *cash out* the secured creditor at the value of her collateral, (iii) whether confirmation will involve application of the Code's *cram down* provisions with respect to the secured creditor, and (iv) whether her *collateral is likely to appreciate or depreciate* in value.

Of great importance too is the adequacy of the information contained in the *disclosure statement*, which must be approved by the court prior to the *post-petition solicitation of acceptances or rejections* from creditors and equity security holders. You may be asked to consider the plan from the perspective of various classes in the case and to determine whether the plan can be confirmed. Your answer will require an understanding of the Code's *requirements for confirmation* (*see infra*, §§1079-1116), including application of the *absolute priority rule* and the use of the *cram down* provisions concerning any dissenting classes that are impaired.

A. ELIGIBILITY FOR RELIEF

1. **In General:** [§993] Relief under Chapter 11 is available to any person (individual, corporation, or partnership) who qualifies to be a debtor under Chapter 7 (*see supra*, §§939-940), except for a stockbroker or a commodity broker. In

addition, railroads *are* eligible for relief under special provisions of Chapter 11 (a topic beyond the scope of this book). [B.C. §109(d)]

2. **Business or Consumer Debtors:** [§994] Chapter 11 is designed primarily for ***business reorganizations***. However, the Supreme Court has held that a consumer debtor (*i.e.*, an individual not engaged in business) also may qualify for relief under this chapter. [Toibb v. Radloff, *supra*, §11]

B. **ADMINISTRATION OF CHAPTER 11 CASE**

1. **Creditors' Committees:** [§995] Shortly after the order for relief, the United States trustee appoints a committee of unsecured creditors, usually consisting of those willing ***persons*** (*see supra*, §28) holding the ***seven largest unsecured claims*** against the debtor. [B.C §1102(a)(1), (b)(1); *but see* "small business" debtor, *infra*, §§1131-1133]

   a. **List of creditors:** [§996] The debtor is required to file a list of the creditors holding the 20 largest unsecured claims, excluding insiders. In a voluntary case, the list must be filed with the petition; in an involuntary case, it must be filed within two days after the entry of the order for relief. [Bankruptcy Rule 1007(d)]

   b. **Membership on creditors' committee:** [§997] Membership on a creditors' committee is not limited to individuals; other persons holding large unsecured claims may be appointed. [*See In re* Altair Airlines, Inc., 727 F.2d 88 (3d Cir. 1984)—airline pilots' labor union appointed to committee of unsecured creditors; unpaid wages and benefits owed to its members constituted second largest unsecured claim against debtor]

      (1) **Certain governmental units:** [§998] Generally, governmental units are excluded from the definition of the term *person*. However, for purposes of eligibility to serve on a Chapter 11 creditors' committee, "person" includes a governmental unit that (i) acquires an asset as a result of a loan guarantee agreement, or as a receiver or liquidating agent of a person (such as the FDIC), (ii) is a guarantor of pension benefits payable by or for the debtor or an affiliate (such as the Pension Benefit Guaranty Corporation), or (iii) is the legal or beneficial owner of an asset of a certain type of pension plan (such as a state employee pension fund). [B.C. §101(41)] These kinds of governmental units are eligible to serve on a Chapter 11 creditors' committee.

      (2) **Pre-petition committee:** [§999] A creditors' committee may consist of the members of a committee created before the petition was filed if the members were selected fairly and exemplify the types of claims to be represented. [B.C. §1102(b)(1); Bankruptcy Rule 2007]

   c. **Additional committees:** [§1000] Additional committees of creditors or equity security holders may be appointed by the United States trustee, either in his own discretion or as ordered by the court at the request of a party in interest to assure adequate representation. [B.C. §1102(a)(1), (2)]

      (1) **Equity security holders:** [§1001] If a committee of equity security holders is appointed, it usually will consist of the seven largest holders

(in amount) of the type of equity securities represented by the committee. [B.C. §1102(b)(2)] (Note that the debtor must file a list of equity security holders of each class within 15 days after the entry of the order for relief. [Bankruptcy Rule 1007(a)(3)])

d. **Powers and duties:** [§1002]   A creditors' committee or an equity security holders' committee may engage in any of the following activities during a Chapter 11 case [B.C. §1103(c)]:

   (1) *Consultation with the debtor in possession* or with the trustee if one has been appointed [B.C. §1103(c)(1)];

   (2) *Investigation of the debtor's conduct, finances, and business operations*, and the *propriety of continuing* the debtor's business [B.C. §1103(c)(2)];

   (3) *Participation in the preparation of a plan of reorganization* [B.C. §1103(c)(3)];

   (4) *Advising the creditors or equity security holders* it represents of the committee's judgment or conclusions concerning any plan formulated [B.C. §1103(c)(3)];

   (5) *Collection and filing of acceptances or rejections of a plan* [B.C. §1103(c)(3)];

   (6) *When appropriate, requesting the appointment of a trustee or an examiner* in the case [B.C. §1103(c)(4)]; and

   (7) *Rendering other services* for the benefit of the creditors or equity security holders represented by the committee [B.C. §1103(c)(5)].

e. **Employment of attorneys or accountants:** [§1003]   A creditors' committee or an equity security holders' committee may hire attorneys, accountants, or other professionals if such employment is authorized at a scheduled meeting attended by a majority of the committee members and *court approval* is obtained. [B.C. §1103(a); for compensation, *see supra*, §§269 *et seq.*]

   (1) **Limitation—no adverse interest:** [§1004]   An attorney or an accountant hired by a creditors' committee or an equity security holders' committee is prohibited from representing, during the period of her employment, any entity possessing an adverse interest. However, the representation of a creditor of the same class as the committee represents is not automatically deemed representation of an adverse interest. [B.C. §1103(b)]

   (2) **Prior approval:** [§1005]   It is important that a lawyer or an accountant employed by a creditors' committee or an equity security holders' committee make certain that court approval is obtained *before* rendering services, since, in many jurisdictions, a retroactive order approving employment is granted only in extraordinary circumstances. [*In re* Arkansas

Co., *supra*, §259; *and see supra*, §258; *but see In re* Singson, *supra*, §258—excusable neglect standard]

2. **Debtor in Possession:** [§1006] Unless a trustee is appointed in the case *(see below)*, the debtor remains in possession of the property of the estate and continues to operate the business unless the court orders otherwise. The debtor in possession has all of the rights, powers, and duties of a trustee, *except* the right to compensation and the duty to investigate the debtor. [B.C. §§1101(1), 1107(a), 1108]

   a. **Business judgment rule:** [§1007] In operating the business, the debtor in possession has the authority to make reasonable business judgments concerning the ordinary affairs of the debtor, and generally the court will not disturb these decisions absent "allegations of, and a real potential for, abuse by corporate insiders." [*In re* Simasko Production Co., 47 B.R. 444 (D. Colo. 1985)]

   b. **Employment of professionals:** [§1008] Any attorney, accountant, or other professional employed by the debtor in possession must be a disinterested person [B.C. §101(14)] and cannot hold or represent any interest that is adverse to the estate [B.C. §327(a)]. However, a professional person is not disqualified for employment *solely* because she was employed by or represented the debtor prior to the commencement of the bankruptcy case. [B.C. §1107(b)]

3. **Appointment of Trustee:** [§1009] Since the debtor in possession usually is considered to be the most appropriate person to operate the particular business, it is viewed as "the exception, rather than the rule" for a trustee to be appointed in a Chapter 11 case. [*In re* Sharon Steel Corp., 871 F.2d 1217 (3d Cir. 1989)] In fact, there is a presumption that the debtor should be allowed to remain in possession unless the need for a trustee is shown. [*In re* Macon Prestressed Concrete Co., 61 B.R. 432 (Bankr. M.D. Ga. 1986)] However, after the filing of the petition and prior to confirmation of a plan, a party in interest or the United States trustee may request the appointment of a trustee, either *for cause* or in the interest of creditors, equity security holders, and the estate. [B.C. §1104(a)(1), (2)] Courts generally require a showing of more than simple mismanagement. Some courts have used a cost-benefit analysis, taking into account the administrative expenses that are likely to ensue from the appointment of a trustee. [*In re* Parker Grande Development, Inc., 64 B.R. 557 (Bankr. S.D. Ind. 1986); *In re* Anchorage Boat Sales, Inc., *supra*, §847]

   a. **Cause for appointment:** [§1010] There is cause for the appointment of a Chapter 11 trustee if the *current management* (either before or after the filing of the bankruptcy petition) commits acts showing fraud, dishonesty, incompetence, gross mismanagement, or the like. [B.C. §1104(a)(1)]

      (1) **Example:** Where Debtor (i) used employees' funds (withheld for taxes, union dues, and contributions), (ii) issued checks knowing that there were inadequate funds in the bank, and (iii) failed to keep accurate financial records, a Chapter 11 trustee was appointed to replace Debtor's current management. [B.C. §1104(a)(1); *In re* St. Louis Globe-Democrat, Inc., 63 B.R. 131 (Bankr. E.D. Mo. 1985)]

   b. **Burden of proof:** [§1011] The party requesting appointment of a Chapter 11 trustee must prove that sufficient cause exists, and the standard applied is that of "clear and convincing evidence." [*In re* Sharon Steel Corp., *supra*]

c. **Choosing a trustee:** [§1012] If the court orders the appointment of a trustee, generally the United States trustee consults with parties in interest and then *appoints* a disinterested person, other than himself, subject to the court's approval. [B.C. §1104(d)] Alternatively (in cases other than railroad reorganizations) the Code provides for *election* of the trustee *if* a party in interest requests an election within 30 days after the court orders appointment of a trustee. The election is held at a meeting of creditors convened by the United States trustee and is conducted in the same manner as the election of a trustee under Chapter 7. [B.C. §§1104(b), 702; *see supra*, §§229-233]

d. **Duties of trustee:** [§1013] The duties of a trustee in a Chapter 11 case include the following (note that the duties in paragraphs (1) through (5) below are also duties of a Chapter 7 trustee):

(1) *To account for all property received* [B.C. §§1106(a)(1), 704(2)];

(2) *To examine proofs of claims* and object to the allowance of any improper ones [B.C. §§1106(a)(1), 704(5)];

(3) *To provide information requested by parties in interest* about the estate and the administration of the estate [B.C. §§1106(a)(1), 704(7)];

(4) *If the court authorizes the operation of the debtor's business, to file periodic financial reports*, including a statement of receipts and disbursements, with the court, the United States trustee, and the appropriate taxing authorities [B.C. §§1106(a)(1), 704(8)];

(5) *To prepare and file* with the court and with the United States trustee *a final report and account* concerning the case [B.C. §§1106(a)(1), 704(9)];

(6) *To file any document required* under Bankruptcy Code section 521(1) (*e.g.*, list of creditors, schedule of assets and liabilities) that has not been filed by the debtor [B.C. §§1106(a)(2), 521(1); *see supra*, §153];

(7) *To investigate the debtor's conduct, financial condition, and business operations*, as well as *the advisability of continuing the debtor's business* [B.C. §1106(a)(3)];

(8) *To file a report of the investigation*, relating any facts evidencing fraud, dishonesty, incompetence, misconduct, or mismanagement, and to send a copy of the findings to any creditors' committee or equity security holders' committee [B.C. §1106(a)(4)];

(9) *To file a Chapter 11 plan* as soon as feasible, or recommend conversion of the case to another chapter [B.C. §1106(a)(5)];

(10) *To provide available information to the taxing authorities* concerning any year for which the debtor failed to file a return [B.C. §1106(a)(6); and

(11) *After a plan has been confirmed, to file any required reports* [B.C. §1106(a)(7)].

e. **Authority to operate business:** [§1014] A trustee who is appointed in a Chapter 11 case is authorized to manage the business of the debtor, unless the court rules otherwise. [B.C. §1108] As a consequence, the trustee replaces the debtor's directors, and they must surrender the corporation's property to the trustee. [Commodity Futures Trading Commission v. Weintraub, *supra*, §332]

f. **Termination of trustee's appointment:** [§1015] The trustee's appointment may be terminated by the court at any time before a plan is confirmed. Such a request may be made by a party in interest or by the United States trustee, after which, upon proper notice, the court conducts a hearing (*see supra*, §14) to determine the advisability of (i) terminating the trustee's appointment and (ii) restoring the estate property and the operation of the business to the debtor. [B.C §1105]

4. **Appointment of Examiner:** [§1016] In a Chapter 11 case in which the court has not ordered the appointment of a trustee, the court sometimes will order the appointment of an examiner, prior to confirmation of a plan, *to investigate* any charges of fraud, dishonesty, incompetence, or mismanagement on the part of the debtor's present or former management. The appointment is made by the United States trustee, who selects a disinterested person other than himself. The debtor in possession, however, retains the estate property and continues to operate the business. [B.C. §1104(c), (d)]

   a. **Reasons for appointment:** [§1017] When the appointment of an examiner is requested by a party in interest or the United States trustee, the court (after notice and a hearing) *must order* that an examiner be appointed if the debtor's fixed, liquidated, unsecured debts exceed $5 million, excluding debts for goods, services, or taxes, and any debts owed to an insider. [B.C. §1104(c)(2); *In re* Revco D.S., Inc., 898 F.2d 498 (6th Cir. 1990)] The existence of *large debenture debt* is a good example of such a circumstance. The court will also order the appointment of an examiner if the appointment is in the best interests of creditors, equity security holders, and the estate. [B.C. §1104(c)(1)]

   b. **Duties of examiner:** [§1018] An examiner's duties include the following:

      (1) *To investigate the debtor's conduct, financial condition, and business operations*, as well as the *advisability of continuing the debtor's business* [B.C. §1106(b), (a)(3)];

      (2) *To file a report of the investigation*, relating any facts evidencing fraud, dishonesty, incompetence, misconduct, or mismanagement, and to send a copy of the findings to any creditors' committee or equity security holders' committee [B.C. §1106(b), (a)(4)]; and

      (3) *Any other responsibilities of a trustee* that the judge directs the debtor in possession not to perform [B.C. §1106(b)].

5. **Party in Interest's Right to be Heard:** [§1019] A party in interest may appear and be heard on any issue in a Chapter 11 case. A party in interest includes but is not limited to: the debtor, the trustee, a creditors' committee, an equity security holders' committee, or an indenture trustee. Others asserting the status of a party in interest are determined on a case-by-case basis. [B.C. §§1109(b), 102(3)]

a. **Example:** Debtor, an industrial textile manufacturer and a defendant in thousands of asbestos tort actions, files a voluntary Chapter 11 petition. Future claimants, who have been exposed to the asbestos contained in Debtor's products but whose injuries have not yet become apparent, are entitled to be heard. Therefore, the appointment of a legal representative in their behalf is appropriate. [B.C. §1109(b); *In re* Amatex Corp., *supra*, §483]

b. **Intervention in adversary proceeding by creditors' committee:** [§1020] The courts are split on the issue of whether a creditors' committee has an absolute statutory right to intervene in an adversary proceeding in a Chapter 11 case. [B.C. §1109(b); *In re* Marin Motor Oil, Inc., 689 F.2d 445 (3d Cir. 1982), *cert. denied*, 459 U.S. 1207 (1983)—yes; Fuel Oil Supply & Terminaling v. Gulf Oil Corp., 762 F.2d 1283 (5th Cir. 1985)—no, because intervention must be under Bankruptcy Rule 7024 and Fed. R. Civ. P. 24; for thorough discussion, *see In re* Allegheny International, Inc., 107 B.R. 518 (W.D. Pa. 1989); *see also* Phar-Mor, Inc., 22 F.3d 1228 (3d Cir. 1994)—creditors' committee has "an unconditional right to intervene in a non-core, 'related-to' proceeding before a federal district court"]

c. **Securities and Exchange Commission:** [§1021] The Securities and Exchange Commission also is entitled to appear and be heard on any issue in a Chapter 11 case, but it may not appeal from any order or judgment entered by the court. [B.C. §1109(a)]

6. **Claims and Interests:** [§1022] The filing of proofs of claims or interests and the allowance of secured claims are accorded special treatment in a Chapter 11 case. [B.C. §1111]

    a. **Proofs of claims or interests:** [§1023] In a Chapter 11 case, the court fixes (and sends notice of) a ***bar date***, which operates as a deadline for filing proofs of claims or interests (*see supra*, §494). However, a claim or interest that is listed in the schedules filed by the debtor is deemed filed (for the scheduled amount), unless it is scheduled as disputed, contingent, or unliquidated. Therefore, in a Chapter 11 case, the holder of a correctly scheduled, undisputed, noncontingent, liquidated claim or interest is not required to file a proof of claim or a proof of interest. [B.C. §1111(a)]

    b. **Secured claims:** [§1024] In a Chapter 11 case, both recourse and nonrecourse secured claims are treated as recourse claims for the purpose of allowance. [B.C. §1111(b)(1)(A)] (Outside of bankruptcy, if a claim is recourse, the creditor has a right to seek a personal judgment against the debtor for any deficiency; if a claim is nonrecourse, there is no such right.) Thus, while an undersecured creditor holding a nonrecourse claim, either under an agreement or under applicable nonbankruptcy law, ordinarily cannot assert a deficiency claim for the portion of her claim exceeding the value of the collateral, the creditor is given recourse status under Chapter 11, with the effect being that the unsecured part of the claim will not be disallowed under Bankruptcy Code section 502(b)(1) (*see supra*, §508).

        (1) **Example:** Creditor holds a $500,000 claim secured by a first mortgage on Blackacre, which is valued at $400,000. The agreement between Creditor and Debtor provides that Creditor's claim is nonrecourse. Debtor files a Chapter 11 bankruptcy petition. Under section 1111(b)(1)(A),

Creditor's claim will be treated as if it were a recourse claim, and thus the $100,000 deficiency will be allowed as a general unsecured claim. (Note that absent this provision, the unsecured portion of Creditor's claim would not be allowable under section 502(b)(1) because of its nonrecourse character.) Of course, Creditor also holds an allowed secured claim in the amount of $400,000 [B.C. §506(a)]. [*In re* Greenland Vistas, Inc., 33 B.R. 366 (Bankr. E.D. Mich. 1983)]

(2) **Exceptions:** [§1025] There are a few situations in which a claim is not treated as if the holder has recourse, thus barring any unsecured claim for a deficiency:

  (a) *If the creditor does not have recourse* and the *property is sold* either under Bankruptcy Code section 363 (*see supra*, §§832 *et seq.*) or under the plan of reorganization [B.C. §1111(b)(1)(A)(ii)];

  (b) *If the creditor does not have recourse* and, during the case (i) the *collateral is abandoned or is returned* to the secured creditor, or (ii) the *secured party forecloses* on the property after having been granted relief from the automatic stay [*In re* DRW Property Co. 82, 57 B.R. 987 (Bankr. N.D. Tex. 1986); *In re* Tampa Bay Associates, Ltd., 864 F.2d 47 (5th Cir. 1989)]; or

  (c) *If the class to which the claim belongs makes the section 1111(b) election* by at least two-thirds in amount and more than half in number (*see* below) [B.C. §1111(b)(1)(A)(i)]. (*Note:* Usually, each secured claim is placed alone in a separate class. [*In re* Hallum, 29 B.R. 343 (Bankr. E.D. Tenn. 1983); *see infra*, §1053])

c. **Section 1111(b) election:** [§1026] A partially secured creditor may elect to have her claim in a Chapter 11 case treated as *secured to the full extent that the claim is allowed*, even though under section 506(a) it otherwise would be considered secured only up to the value of the collateral. [B.C. §1111(b)(2)]

  (1) **Example:** Debtor owes $500,000 to Creditor pursuant to a nonrecourse loan secured by a first mortgage on Blackacre, which has a fair market value of $400,000. Creditor's claim is classified in a separate class from the other claims in the case, and Creditor makes the election, under section 1111(b), to have her entire $500,000 claim treated as secured. Subsequently, Debtor defaults on payments to Creditor under the confirmed reorganization plan at a time when Blackacre has *appreciated in value* to $500,000. In this instance, the effect of the election will be to enable Creditor to recover the full amount of her claim.

   (a) **Compare:** Assume the same facts as above, except that Creditor does *not* make the section 1111(b) election. Following Debtor's default, a third-party bidder pays $500,000 for Blackacre at the foreclosure sale. Since Creditor's allowed secured claim was $400,000, the surplus of $100,000 will go to Debtor's estate. Creditor's recovery will be limited to $400,000, plus whatever percentage she is entitled to under the plan on her unsecured claim for a deficiency.

(2) **Exceptions:** [§1027] The section 1111(b) election cannot be made under either of the following circumstances:

   (a) *If the creditor's interest in the property is of inconsequential value*, as in the case of a low priority junior lien that would bring minimal or zero recovery at foreclosure [B.C. §1111(b)(1)(B)(i)]; or

   (b) *If the creditor has recourse and the collateral is sold* under section 363 or under the plan [B.C. §1111(b)(1)(B)(ii)].

(3) **Waiver of deficiency claim:** [§1028] If the section 1111(b) election is made, the secured party forfeits her unsecured claim for any deficiency and also loses the opportunity to affect the decision of the unsecured class to accept or reject the reorganization plan. [B.C. §1111(b)(2); Bankruptcy Rule 3018(d); *In re* Southern Missouri Towing Service, Inc., 35 B.R. 313 (Bankr. W.D. Mo. 1983)]

   (a) **Example:** Assume the same facts as in the first example above, except that the value of Blackacre has *depreciated* to $300,000 at the time of Debtor's default after confirmation. Because Creditor made the section 1111(b) election, she loses her unsecured claim for a deficiency, and her recovery will be only $300,000.

(4) **Preventing a cash out:** [§1029] The section 1111(b) election sometimes is invoked where the plan proposes no payment to the unsecured creditors and the electing creditor desires to avert a cash out for the value of her collateral. [B.C. §1111(b)(2); *In re* Griffiths, 27 B.R. 873 (Bankr. D. Kan. 1983)]

(5) **Cram down:** [§1030] Where a secured creditor making the section 1111(b) election rejects the proposed Chapter 11 plan, confirmation can be obtained under the Code's "cram down" provisions if the plan (in addition to providing for the creditor's retention of her lien) proposes to pay the electing creditor deferred cash payments that (i) equal at least the *full dollar amount* of her allowed claim (without interest) and (ii) have a *present value*, as of the effective date of the plan, of at least the value of the collateral. [B.C. §1129(b)(2)(A)(i); *In re* Webster, 66 B.R. 46 (Bankr. D.N.D. 1986)]

   (a) **Example:** Creditor loans Debtor $500,000, secured by a first mortgage on Blackacre, which has a value of $600,000. Debtor defaults and then files a Chapter 11 petition. Blackacre has depreciated and is worth $400,000, and Creditor makes the section 1111(b) election. The proposed plan provides for Creditor to retain her lien on Blackacre and to receive deferred cash payments on her claim. Creditor rejects the plan. For the plan to be confirmed over Creditor's rejection, the proposed payments must total at least $500,000 and must have a present value, as of the effective date of the plan, of at least $400,000. [B.C. §1129(b)(2)(A)(i); *In re* Southern Missouri Towing Service, Inc., *supra*, §1028]

(6) **Time of election:** [§1031] The section 1111(b) election may be exercised at any time before the end of the hearing on the disclosure

statement (*see infra*, §1066) or within a later time set by the court. [Bankruptcy Rule 3014]

7. **Conversion or Dismissal:** [§1032] In appropriate circumstances, a Chapter 11 case may be dismissed or may be converted to another chapter of the Bankruptcy Code under which the debtor is eligible. The rules vary depending on (i) whether the conversion or dismissal is voluntary or involuntary, (ii) the chapter to which the case is being converted, (iii) the kind of debtor that the case concerns, and (iv) the particular circumstances giving rise to the conversion or the dismissal. [B.C. §1112]

   a. **Voluntary conversion to Chapter 7:** [§1033] The debtor may convert the case to Chapter 7 provided that (i) a trustee has not been appointed under Chapter 11, (ii) the case was not originally commenced by the filing of an involuntary Chapter 11 petition, and (iii) the case was not involuntarily converted to Chapter 11 (*i.e.*, on the request of an entity other than the debtor). No notice or hearing is required. [B.C. §1112(a); 5 Collier ¶1112.03(1)]

   b. **Discretionary conversion to Chapter 7 or dismissal:** [§1034] On request by the United States trustee, the bankruptcy administrator, or a party in interest (including the debtor), the court *for cause* may dismiss the case or convert it to Chapter 7, whichever is better for creditors and the estate. Notice and a hearing are required. [B.C. §1112(b)]

      (1) **Sua sponte dismissal:** [§1035] When cause exists, the court, on its own motion, may convert the case to Chapter 7 or dismiss it. However, the court should sparingly exercise its sua sponte powers to dismiss or convert. [B.C. §105(a); *In re* Daily Corp., *supra*, §43]

      (2) **"Cause":** [§1036] A Chapter 11 case may be dismissed or converted to Chapter 7 for any of the following reasons or for other sufficient cause [B.C. §1112(b)]:

         (a) *Lack of good faith* in filing the Chapter 11 petition [*In re* Natural Land Corp., 825 F.2d 296 (11th Cir. 1987); *In re* Marsch, 36 F.3d 825 (9th Cir. 1994)—case filed solely to prevent entry of state court judgment and avoid posting appeal bond];

         (b) *Continuing loss to the estate* and *no reasonable probability of rehabilitation* [B.C. §1112(b)(1); *In re* Albany Partners, Ltd., *supra*, §810];

         (c) *Inability to effectuate a Chapter 11 plan* [B.C. §1112(b)(2)];

         (d) *Unreasonable and prejudicial delay* by the debtor [B.C. §1112(b)(3)];

         (e) *Failure to file a Chapter 11 plan on or before a deadline* set by the court [B.C. §1112(b)(4)];

         (f) *Denial of confirmation of every plan* that has been filed, and denial of a request for an extension of time to file another plan or to modify a plan [B.C. §1112(b)(5)];

(g) *Revocation of a confirmation order* and denial of confirmation of a different or a modified plan [B.C. §1112(b)(6)];

(h) *Inability to substantially consummate a plan* that has been confirmed [B.C. §1112(b)(7)];

(i) *A material default by the debtor* concerning a plan that has been confirmed [B.C. §1112(b)(8)];

(j) *Termination of a plan by the happening of a condition* contained in the plan [B.C. §1112(b)(9)];

(k) *Failure to pay any necessary fees or charges* imposed under chapter 123 of title 28 [B.C. §1112(b)(10)]; or

(l) *Failure to file the information* required by Bankruptcy Code section 521(1) and a list of the creditors holding the 20 largest unsecured claims with their amounts within 15 days after the filing of the Chapter 11 petition (note that this ground applies only in a voluntary case, upon a request made by the United States trustee) [B.C. §1112(e)].

c. **Exceptions—farmers and nonbusiness corporations:** [§1037] If the debtor is a farmer or a nonbusiness corporation, conversion of the case to Chapter 7 is prohibited unless the debtor requests the conversion. [B.C. §1112(c)]

d. **Conversion to Chapter 12 or 13:** [§1038] The court may convert a Chapter 11 case to a Chapter 12 or 13 case only if the following elements are present [B.C. §1112(d)]:

(1) *The debtor requests the conversion* [B.C. §1112(d)(1)];

(2) *The debtor has not received a Chapter 11 discharge* [B.C. §§1112(d)(2), 1141(d); *and see infra*, §§1119 *et seq.*]; and

(3) *If the conversion sought by the debtor is to Chapter 12*, the court finds that the conversion is *equitable* [B.C. §1112(d)(3)].

C. REJECTION OF COLLECTIVE BARGAINING AGREEMENTS [§1039]

The rejection of a collective bargaining agreement may be an important consideration in the debtor's effort to reorganize [National Labor Relations Board v. Bildisco & Bildisco, 465 U.S. 513 (1984)], and it is governed by a different standard than other kinds of executory contracts in a Chapter 11 case. [B.C. §1113]

1. **Prerequisites for Rejection:** [§1040] Court approval of an application to reject a collective bargaining agreement requires that the debtor in possession (or the trustee, if one has been appointed) prove the following nine elements:

(i) "The debtor in possession must make a *proposal to the Union to modify* the collective bargaining agreement." [B.C. §1113(b)(1)(A)]

(ii) "The proposal must be *based on the most complete and reliable information* available at the time of the proposal." [B.C. §1113(b)(1)(A)]

(iii) "The proposed *modifications must be necessary* to permit the reorganization of the debtor." [B.C. § 1113(b)(1)(A)]

(iv) "The proposed modifications must assure that *all creditors, the debtor, and all of the affected parties are treated fairly and equitably.*" [B.C. §1113(b)(1)(A)]

(v) "The debtor must *provide to the Union such relevant information as is necessary to evaluate* the proposal." [B.C. §1113(b)(1)(B)]

Note: These first five elements must occur after the filing of the Chapter 11 petition and before the filing of the application to reject. [B.C. §1113(b)(1)]

(vi) "Between the time of the making of the proposal and the time of the hearing on approval of the rejection of the existing collective bargaining agreement, the *debtor must meet at reasonable times with the Union.*" [B.C. §1113(b)(2)]

(vii) "At the meetings the debtor must *confer in good faith* in attempting to reach mutually satisfactory modifications of the collective bargaining agreement." [B.C. §1113(b)(2)]

(viii) "The Union must have *refused to accept the proposal without good cause.*" [B.C. §1113(c)(2); *In re* Maxwell Newspapers, Inc., 981 F.2d 85 (2d Cir. 1992)]

(ix) "The balance of the equities must *clearly favor rejection* of the collective bargaining agreement." [B.C. §1113(c)(3)]

[B.C. §1113; *In re* American Provision Co., 44 B.R. 907 (Bankr. D. Minn. 1984)]

2. **Hearing:** [§1041] A hearing on an application to reject a collective bargaining agreement must be scheduled to occur within 14 days after the application is filed, and the court must rule on the issue within 30 days after the commencement of the hearing. [B.C. §1113(d)]

3. **Interim Changes:** [§1042] The court may permit the debtor in possession or trustee to make temporary interim modifications in the terms of a collective bargaining agreement when such changes are necessary to continue the debtor's business or to avoid irreparable harm to the estate. Notice and a hearing are required. [B.C. §1113(e); *In re* Evans Products Co., 55 B.R. 231 (Bankr. S.D. Fla. 1985)]

4. **Unilateral Action Prohibited:** [§1043] The debtor in possession or trustee may not unilaterally terminate or modify any terms of a collective bargaining agreement before compliance with the provisions set forth in section 1113. [B.C. §1113(f)]

D. CHAPTER 11 PLAN

1. **Filing a Plan:** [§1044] In a voluntary case, the debtor may file a plan of reorganization with the Chapter 11 petition or at any other time. In an involuntary case, the debtor may file a plan at any time. [B.C. §1121(a)]

a. **Exclusivity period:** [§1045] Unless a trustee has been appointed in the case, the ***debtor*** has the exclusive right to file a plan for the first ***120 days*** after the order for relief. [B.C. §1121(b)]

b. **Other proponents:** [§1046] A plan may be filed ***by any party in interest*** (but not by the United States trustee [B.C. §307]), including the debtor, the trustee, a creditor, a creditors' committee, an equity security holder, an equity security holders' committee, or an indenture trustee, under any of the following circumstances [B.C. §1121(c)]:

   (1) ***Where a Chapter 11 trustee has been appointed*** [B.C. §1121(c)(1)];

   (2) ***Where the debtor has not filed a plan within 120 days*** after the order for relief [B.C. §1121(c)(2)]; or

   (3) ***Where the debtor has not filed a plan and obtained the acceptances*** of every impaired class of claims or interests within ***180 days*** after the order for relief [B.C. §1121(c)(3)].

c. **Extension or reduction of time:** [§1047] For cause shown by a party in interest, and after notice and a hearing, the court may shorten or lengthen the 120-day period or the 180-day period referred to above. [B.C. §1121(d); *In re Public Service Co. of New Hampshire*, 88 B.R. 521 (Bankr. D.N.H. 1988)]

2. **Classification of Claims or Interests:** [§1048] The Bankruptcy Code requires that a Chapter 11 plan classify the claims as well as the equity interests in the case. [B.C. §1123(a)(1)] However, the statutory provisions regarding the manner of classification are relatively brief, and much case law has developed in this area. [B.C. §1122]

   a. **"Substantially similar" claims or interests:** [§1049] A claim or interest ***may*** be placed in a particular class only if it is substantially similar to the other claims or interests included in that class. [B.C. §1122(a); *In re* AOV Industries, Inc., 792 F.2d 1140 (D.C. Cir. 1986)] This provision has been construed by two discordant lines of cases.

      (1) **Majority view:** [§1050] The interpretation by most courts is that Bankruptcy Code section 1122(a) does not compel the classification of all substantially similar claims together in one class, and thus, separate classes of claims may be designated where the classification is for a reasonable and bona fide purpose (*i.e.*, a legitimate business reason) and where each class is homogeneous. [*In re* AG Consultants Grain Division, Inc., 77 B.R. 665 (Bankr. N.D. Ind. 1987); *In re* U.S. Truck Co., 800 F.2d 581 (6th Cir. 1986)]

         (a) **Example:** Debtor Corporation files a voluntary Chapter 11 petition and a plan of reorganization that proposes the designation of the following classes: Class I, consisting of National Bank, whose claim is fully secured by Blackacre; Class II, consisting of unsecured pre-petition wage claims entitled to priority; Class III, consisting of all general unsecured claims that do not exceed $100; ***Class IV, consisting of all unsecured claims of tort victims in excess of $100***; Class V, consisting of all the other general unsecured claims in excess of

$100. Under the rule discussed above, the proposed classification scheme should be permissible if the court finds the existence of a valid reason for separately grouping the unsecured claims of the tort victims.

(2) **Minority view:** [§1051] A more restrictive interpretation adopted by some courts is that, except for certain small claims (*see infra*, §1055), similar claims *must* be classified together; separate classes of unsecured claims are permitted only where the claims are of differing legal status. Thus, for example, under this view, an unsecured pension fund claim would have to be placed in the same class with the other unsecured claims in the case. [B.C. §1122(a); Granada Wines, Inc. v. New England Teamsters & Trucking Industry Pension Fund, 748 F.2d 42 (1st Cir. 1984)]

(3) **Gerrymandering:** [§1052] Separate classification should be denied where the purpose for designating multiple classes of unsecured claims is to achieve confirmation by the creation of a class of impaired claims that will vote for the plan. [B.C. §§1122(a), 1129(a)(10); *In re* Greystone III Joint Venture, 995 F.2d 1274 (5th Cir. 1991); *and see infra*, §1088] This purpose is likely to be considered an improper basis for classification because of its manipulative nature. The issue has arisen recently in cases concerning separate classification of an unsecured mortgage deficiency claim (frequently involving a single-asset partnership). [*See In re* Boston Post Road Limited Partnership, 21 F.3d 477 (2d Cir. 1994)—classification of unsecured mortgage deficiency claim separately from unsecured claims of trade creditors denied absent legitimate business reason; *but see In re* Woodbrook Associates, 19 F.3d 312 (7th Cir. 1994)—separate classification of section 1111(b) (*see supra*, §1024) unsecured deficiency claim required where debtor is fully encumbered single-asset partnership; *In re* ZRM-Oklahoma Partnership, 156 B.R. 67 (Bankr. W.D. Okl. 1993)—gerrymandering allowed (flexible classification); for a thorough discussion, *see In re* Bloomingdale Partners, 170 B.R. 984 (Bankr. N.D. Ill. 1994)]

b. **Specific types of claims or interests**

(1) **Secured claims:** [§1053] Usually, where secured creditors' liens are in different property or are entitled to different priorities in the same property, each secured claim should be placed alone in a separate class. [*In re* Commercial Western Finance Corp., 761 F.2d 1329 (9th Cir. 1985); *In re* Holthoff, 58 B.R. 216 (Bankr. E.D. Ark. 1985)]

(2) **Priority claims:** [§1054] Administrative expenses, involuntary case gap claims, and eighth priority (*i.e.*, unsecured, pre-petition) tax claims are excepted from the requirement of classification since the standards for confirmation require that the plan provide for such claims on an individual basis. [B.C. §§1123(a)(1), 1129(a)(9)(A), (C)] However, third, fourth, fifth, sixth, seventh, and ninth priority claims (*i.e.*, wages and commissions, contributions to employee benefit plans, claims of grain farmers and United States fishermen, consumer layaways, alimony and child or spousal support, capital requirements of an insured depository

institution) should be placed in separate classes together with claims of equal priority. [B.C. §§1123(a)(1), 507(a)(3)-(a)(7), (a)(9)]

(3) **Administrative convenience class:** [§1055] The Code permits the plan to designate a separate class of small claims comprised of all unsecured claims that are less than, or by consent decreased to, an amount approved by the court as *reasonable and necessary*. Generally, such claims are paid in full (in cash), and the estate benefits by the reduction of administrative expenses. [B.C. §1122(b); *In re* Jartran, Inc., 44 B.R. 331 (Bankr. N.D. Ill. 1984); 5 Collier ¶1122.03(2)]

(4) **Interests:** [§1056] Equity interests in a sole proprietorship, a partnership, or a corporation must be classified separately from creditors' claims. Furthermore, common stock and preferred stock interests ought to be placed in different classes. [B.C. §1122(a); 5 Collier ¶1122.03(3)]

3. **Contents of Plan:** [§1057] The Code specifies several provisions that must be included in a Chapter 11 plan, and, in addition, indicates other terms that may be part of a plan. [B.C. §1123]

   a. **Mandatory provisions:** [§1058] A Chapter 11 plan must do the following:

   (1) *Classify all claims and interests*, other than priority claims for administrative expenses, involuntary case gap claims, or eighth priority taxes. [B.C. §§1123(a)(1), 507(a)(1), (2), (8)];

   (2) *Specify any class that is not impaired* [B.C. §1123(a)(2); *In re* Polytherm Industries, Inc., 33 B.R. 823 (W.D. Wis. 1983); *see infra*, §§1062 *et seq.*];

   (3) *Describe the treatment to be accorded any impaired class* [B.C. §1123 (a)(3)];

   (4) *Treat every claim or interest within a particular class identically*, unless a holder consents to less favorable treatment [B.C. §1123(a)(4); *In re* Weiss-Wolf, Inc., 59 B.R. 653 (Bankr. S.D.N.Y. 1986)—Debtor's Chapter 11 plan, which proposes to pay **undisputed claims** in a class a specified percentage on the effective date of confirmation and to pay **disputed claims** in that class pro rata from Debtor's remaining assets at a future time after all contested issues have been resolved, is defective since it does not provide the same treatment for each claim in the class];

   (5) *Establish adequate ways to implement the plan*, such as by [B.C. §1123(a)(5)(A)-(J)]:

   (a) *The debtor's retention* of estate property;

   (b) *The transfer of estate property* to another entity (note that the Supreme Court has held that a trustee appointed to liquidate and distribute property pursuant to a Chapter 11 plan is an assignee of the property and is required to file federal income tax returns and to pay the income taxes [Holywell Corporation v. Smith, 503 U.S. 47 (1992)]);

   (c) *Merger or consolidation*;

(d) ***The sale of estate property free and clear of liens***, or the ***distribution of estate property to the holders*** of any interests in the property;

(e) ***The satisfaction or modification of a lien***;

(f) ***The cancellation or modification of an indenture***;

(g) ***Curing or waiving a default***;

(h) ***Extending the maturity date***, or altering the interest rate or other terms of outstanding securities;

(i) ***Amending the debtor's charter***; or

(j) ***Issuing securities of the debtor*** or a successor to the debtor, or of an entity with whom the debtor has merged or has been consolidated;

(6) ***Include, in the charter of a corporate debtor, a provision prohibiting the issuance of nonvoting stock***, and complying with certain other requirements concerning voting powers [B.C. §1123(a)(6)]; and

(7) ***Provide for the selection of officers and directors*** in a manner (i) consistent with the interests of creditors and equity security holders and (ii) that does not violate public policy [B.C. §1123(a)(7)].

b. **Permissive provisions:** [§1059] In addition to the mandatory items described above, a plan *may* provide for:

(1) ***Any class of claims or interests to be impaired or unimpaired*** [B.C. §1123(b)(1); *see infra*, §§1062 *et seq.*];

(2) ***The assumption, rejection, or assignment of executory contracts or unexpired leases*** [B.C. §1123(b)(2)];

(3) ***The settlement of any claim or interest*** held by the debtor or the estate, or the retention and enforcement of such action by the debtor, trustee, or an appointed representative of the estate [B.C. §1123(b)(3); *In re* Sweetwater, 884 F.2d 1323 (10th Cir. 1989)];

(4) ***The liquidation of all or substantially all of the estate property***, and distribution of the proceeds [B.C. §1123(b)(4)];

(5) ***The modification of the rights of secured creditors or unsecured creditors, except*** where the creditor's claim is secured *solely* by a security interest in real property constituting the debtor's principal residence [B.C. §1123(b)(5)] (note that this prohibition against modification of home mortgages applies only to an individual Chapter 11 debtor, and that, due to a decision by the United States Supreme Court construing the identical language in Chapter 13, the effect of this provision will be to prevent a Chapter 11 debtor from *stripping down* an undersecured mortgage on his principal residence to the fair market value of the residence [Nobelman v. American Savings Bank, 113 S. Ct. 2106 (1993)]; and

(6) *Any other appropriate measure* that is consistent with the provisions of the Bankruptcy Code [B.C. §1123(b)(6)]. For example, the Supreme Court has upheld a plan's provision requiring the IRS to allocate a Chapter 11 debtor's tax payments first to *trust fund taxes*, before being applied to non-trust fund tax liabilities, where *necessary for the success of the debtor's reorganization*. [United States v. Energy Resources Co., 495 U.S. 545 (1990)]

c. **Exempt property:** [§1060] If the debtor is an individual, any plan proposed by another entity may not include a provision to use, sell, or lease exempt property without the consent of the debtor. [B.C. §1123(c)]

d. **Interest on arrearages:** [§1061] Where the plan proposes to cure a default, the Code addresses the issue of interest on interest (for example, interest on mortgage arrearages that include interest). The amount necessary to cure the default is determined by looking to the underlying contract and applicable nonbankruptcy law. [B.C. §1123(d)] Therefore, a creditor will be entitled to interest on interest only if it was agreed to by the parties and is permissible under state law, or alternatively if it is required by state law.

4. **Impairment of Classes:** [§1062] Whether a class of claims or interests is impaired under a plan is of great significance in a Chapter 11 case, because if a particular class is *not* impaired, there is a *conclusive presumption* that the plan has been accepted by the class and by the holder of each claim or interest in the class. Consequently, it is unnecessary for the proponent of the plan to solicit their acceptances. [B.C. §1126(f); 5 Collier ¶1124.03] A class is *deemed impaired unless* the plan provides for all claims or interests of that class to be treated in accordance with either of the two methods set forth below [B.C. §1124]:

    a. **Rights unmodified:** [§1063] A class is considered unimpaired if the plan does *not alter* the legal, equitable, or contractual rights of the holders of the claims or interests. Any change in a holder's rights, even a favorable change, will cause the class to be impaired. [B.C. §1124(1); *see In re* L & J Anaheim Associates, 995 F.2d 940 (9th Cir. 1993)]

        (1) **Example:** Debtor Corporation files a voluntary Chapter 11 petition and is current on its payments to the unsecured bondholders, at a contractual rate of 6%. Under Debtor's plan, the bondholders will be paid, when due, at a rate of 7%. The class is impaired because its rights have been altered. [B.C. §1124(1)]

    b. **Cure and deacceleration:** [§1064] A class is deemed unimpaired if, regardless of any contractual or other legal right to accelerate payment upon default, the plan proposes: (i) to *cure any default* (other than one under Bankruptcy Code section 365(b)(2); *see supra*, §894); (ii) to *reinstate the original maturity date*; (iii) to *pay for any damages* caused by the claimant's or the interest holder's *reasonable reliance* on the right to accelerate; and (iv) *not to otherwise alter* the legal, equitable, or contractual rights of the holder of the claim or interest. [B.C. §1124(2); *In re* Southeast Co., 868 F.2d 335 (9th Cir. 1989)]

        (1) **Example:** Debtor owes Bank $100,000, secured by a first mortgage on Blackacre. Debtor defaults, and Bank, relying on an acceleration clause

in the contract, accelerates the debt and obtains a state court foreclosure judgment against Blackacre. Subsequently, Debtor files a Chapter 11 petition, and Bank unsuccessfully seeks relief from the automatic stay as the court permits Debtor, pursuant to its plan, to cure the default and reinstate the original maturity of the obligation on the same terms. For Bank (which has been placed alone, in a separate class) to be unimpaired, Debtor must not only cure the default and deaccelerate the debt, but also compensate Bank for the damages, including attorney's fees, incurred in accelerating the debt and instituting the foreclosure proceedings. [B.C. §1124(2)(C); *In re* Hewitt, 16 B.R. 973 (Bankr. D. Alaska 1982)] However, the damages will not include the attorney's fees incurred in seeking relief from the automatic stay, since those costs did not arise as a result of Bank's reliance on its right to accelerate the debt. [*In re* Masnorth Corp., 36 B.R. 335 (Bankr. N.D. Ga. 1984)]

(2) **Cure period:** [§1065] Usually, the debtor is permitted to cure the default and reinstate the obligation at any time ***prior to a foreclosure sale***. [*In re* Madison Hotel Associates, 749 F.2d 410 (7th Cir. 1984)] However, in states where the mortgage merges into the foreclosure judgment, some courts have held that there is nothing to cure and reinstate. [*In re* Celeste Court Apartments, Inc., 47 B.R. 470 (D. Del. 1985)] Other cases suggest that merger is irrelevant because section 1124(2) evidences Congress's intent to permit deacceleration. [5 Collier ¶1124.03(5)]

5. **Solicitation and Disclosure:** [§1066] Post-petition solicitation for acceptances or rejections of a plan may be conducted only at or after the time that the plan (or a summary of it) and a ***written court-approved disclosure statement*** have been sent to the holders of the claims or interests whose acceptances or rejections are sought. If there is an objection to a proposed disclosure statement, the court conducts a hearing to determine whether the disclosure statement contains adequate information. [B.C. §1125(b); 5 Collier ¶1125.03(2)]

   a. **Adequate information:** [§1067] Since the purpose of the disclosure statement is to provide information to creditors and equity security holders adequate to evaluate the plan, the Code requires that the disclosure statement contain sufficient information, under the circumstances, to "enable a hypothetical reasonable investor typical of holders of claims or interests of the relevant class to make an informed" decision to accept or reject the plan. [B.C. §1125(a)(1); *In re* Monnier Brothers, 755 F.2d 1336 (8th Cir. 1985)] The most important factors generally considered in approving or disapproving the adequacy of a disclosure statement are derived from several bankruptcy court opinions, and, while they may vary from case to case, these factors have been consolidated into one list by the court in *In re Metrocraft Publishing Services, Inc.*, 39 B.R. 567 (Bankr. N.D. Ga. 1984):

   (1) *The events leading to the filing* of the bankruptcy petition;

   (2) *A description of the available assets and their value*;

   (3) *The anticipated future of the company*;

   (4) *The source of the information* stated in the disclosure statement;

(5) *A disclaimer*;

(6) *The present condition of the debtor* while in Chapter 11;

(7) *The scheduled claims*;

(8) *The estimated return to creditors* under a Chapter 7 liquidation;

(9) *The accounting method* used to produce financial information and the *names of the accountants* responsible for such information;

(10) *The future management* of the debtor;

(11) *The Chapter 11 plan* or a summary thereof;

(12) *The estimated administrative expenses*, including attorney's and accountant's fees;

(13) *The collectibility of accounts receivable*;

(14) *Financial information, data, valuations, or projections* relevant to the creditors' decision to accept or reject the Chapter 11 plan;

(15) *Information relevant to the risks* posed to creditors under the plan;

(16) *The actual or projected realizable value from recovery of preferential or otherwise voidable transfers*;

(17) *Litigation likely to arise* in a nonbankruptcy context;

(18) *Tax attributes* of the debtor; and

(19) *The relationship of the debtor with affiliates*.

b. **Distribution of disclosure statement:** [§1068] Since the information needed by separate classes of claims or interests may vary in kind and detail, different disclosure statements may be sent to different classes. However, the holders of the claims or interests of any particular class must receive the identical disclosure statement. [B.C. §1125(c)]

c. **Nonbankruptcy securities laws, rules, and regulations:** [§1069] The adequacy of the information contained in a post-petition disclosure statement is determined without regard to any nonbankruptcy securities law, rule, or regulation that otherwise would apply, although the Securities and Exchange Commission may appear and be heard on the issue of the adequacy of the disclosure statement. [B.C. §1125(d)] Also, Chapter 11 includes a *safe harbor provision*, insulating from liability for violation of any applicable securities law, rule, or regulation, a person who in good faith and in compliance with the provisions of the Bankruptcy Code solicits acceptances or rejections of a plan, or participates in the offer, issuance, purchase, or sale of a security under a plan. [B.C. §1125(e)]

d. **Compare—pre-petition solicitation:** [§1070] Acceptances or rejections of a plan may be solicited before the filing of a Chapter 11 petition only if the solicitation meets the disclosure requirements of any applicable securities or other nonbankruptcy law or regulation, or in the absence of any such law or regulation, is preceded by the disclosure of adequate information, as defined in Bankruptcy Code section 1125(a). [B.C. §1126(b); *see supra*, §1067] Adherence to this rule could be of great significance when an attempted extrajudicial "workout" fails, and a Chapter 11 petition subsequently is filed.

6. **Acceptance of Plan:** [§1071] Any creditor or equity security holder whose claim or interest has been allowed may accept or reject a Chapter 11 plan by a signed writing identifying the plan and conforming to the appropriate Official Form. [B.C. §1126(a); Bankruptcy Rule 3018(c)] If the acceptance or rejection occurs before the commencement of the case, it is valid only if it was solicited in accordance with the Code's requirements for pre-petition solicitation (above) and if the plan was sent to substantially all creditors and equity security holders of the same class within a reasonable time to accept or reject the plan. Also, for a pre-petition acceptance or rejection to be valid, if the claim of the creditor or equity security holder was based on a security of record, the creditor or equity security holder must have been the holder of record on the date specified in the solicitation. [B.C. §1126(b); Bankruptcy Rule 3018(b); *but see In re* Southland Corporation, 124 B.R. 211 (Bankr. N.D. Texas 1991)—questioning validity of Bankruptcy Rule 3018(b)]

   a. **Classes of claims:** [§1072] Acceptance of a plan by a class of claims requires acceptance by creditors holding at least *two-thirds in amount and more than half in number* of the allowed claims actually being voted. [B.C. §1126(c); *In re* White Farm Equipment Co., 38 B.R. 718 (N.D. Ohio 1984)]

   b. **Classes of interests:** [§1073] Acceptance of a plan by a class of interests requires acceptance by equity security holders having at least *two-thirds in amount* of the allowed interests actually being voted. [B.C. §1126(d)]

   c. **Bad faith votes:** [§1074] The court, after notice and a hearing, may discount any acceptance or rejection not made in good faith or that was not solicited in good faith or in compliance with the provisions of the Code. [B.C. §1126(e); *In re* MacLeod Co., 63 B.R. 654 (Bankr. S.D. Ohio 1986); *In re* Allegheny International, Inc., 118 B.R. 282 (Bankr. W.D. Pa. 1990)—votes disqualified because claims acquired in bad faith for stated purpose of taking over debtor, which would require blocking confirmation of debtor's reorganization plan; *but see In re* Marin Town Center, 142 B.R. 374 (N.D. Cal. 1992)—vote of holder of purchased claim not disqualified merely because purpose was to block confirmation of reorganization plan]

   d. **Unimpaired classes:** [§1075] If a particular class is not impaired under a plan, there is a conclusive presumption that the plan has been accepted by the class and by the holder of each claim or interest in the class. Consequently, it will be unnecessary for the proponent of the plan to solicit their acceptances. [B.C. §1126(f); *and see supra*, §1062]

   e. **Classes receiving no property:** [§1076] A class that receives or retains no property under a plan is deemed to have rejected the plan. [B.C. §1126(g)]

7. **Modifying a Plan:** [§1077] Prior to confirmation, a plan may be modified only by its proponent. After confirmation and before substantial consummation of a

plan, it may be modified, if warranted, by the proponent *or* by the reorganized debtor. Any modification must satisfy the statutory requirements concerning classification of claims or interests [B.C. §1122], contents of the plan [B.C. §1123], and disclosure [B.C. §1125]. An acceptance or a rejection of a plan before modification will be deemed to apply to the plan as modified unless the vote is changed within the deadline set by the court. [B.C. §1127]

E. CONFIRMATION OF PLAN

1. **Confirmation Hearing:** [§1078] After proper notice, the court conducts a hearing to determine whether a proposed plan satisfies the elements necessary for confirmation. An objection to confirmation may be filed by any party in interest. [B.C. §1128; Bankruptcy Rule 3020(b)]

2. **Requirements for Confirmation:** [§1079] A plan will be confirmed only if it satisfies the following statutory requirements [B.C. §1129(a); *In re* Johns-Manville Corp., 68 B.R. 618 (Bankr. S.D.N.Y. 1986)—detailed discussion of elements of confirmation, *aff'd*, 78 B.R. 407 (S.D.N.Y. 1987), *aff'd*, 843 F.2d 636 (2d Cir. 1988)]:

    a. **Plan complies with Code provisions:** [§1080] The plan must comply with the applicable provisions of the Bankruptcy Code, such as the requirements for classification of claims and the mandatory contents of a Chapter 11 plan. [B.C. §1129(a)(1); *see supra*, §§1048-1058]

    b. **Proponent complies with Code provisions:** [§1081] The proponent of the plan must comply with the applicable provisions of the Code, such as those concerning disclosure and solicitation of acceptances. [B.C. §1129(a)(2); *see supra*, §§1066 et seq.]

    c. **Plan in good faith:** [§1082] The plan must be proposed in good faith. [B.C. §1129(a)(3); *In re* Coastal Cable T.V., Inc., 709 F.2d 762 (1st Cir. 1983)]

    d. **Payment for services or expenses approved:** [§1083] All payments for services or expenses related to the plan (*e.g.*, attorney's fees) must be approved by the court as reasonable, where the payments are made by the proponent of the plan, the debtor, or a person issuing securities or receiving property under the plan. [B.C. §1129(a)(4)]

    e. **Officers, directors, insiders disclosed:** [§1084] The plan must disclose the names and affiliations of all individuals who will be officers, directors, or voting trustees of the debtor or a successor to the debtor after confirmation (consistent with the interests of creditors, equity security holders, and public policy), and the names and proposed compensation of all insiders who will be employed or retained by the reorganized debtor. [B.C. §1129(a)(5)]

    f. **Rate change approved:** [§1085] Where the debtor's rates are regulated by a governmental commission, any rate change proposed by the plan must be approved by the commission. [B.C. §1129(a)(6)]

    g. **"Best interests of creditors test" met:** [§1086] Each *holder* of a claim or interest of an impaired class either must (i) have accepted the plan *or* (ii) receive under the plan property having a present value, as of the effective date of the plan, of not less than the amount that the holder would receive in a Chapter 7 liquidation. (This element of confirmation usually is called the "best interests of creditors test.") [B.C. §1129(a)(7)(A)]

    (1) **Exception:** Where a holder has made the *election under section 1111(b)*, the plan must provide that she receive property having a present value, as of the effective date of the plan, of at least the value of the collateral securing her claim. [B.C. §1129(a)(7)(B); *and see supra*, §§1026 *et seq.*]

h. **All impaired classes accept plan:** [§1087] Each class of claims or interests must have accepted the plan *or be unimpaired* under the plan. [B.C. §1129(a)(8); *see supra*, §§1062 *et seq.*]

    (1) **Note:** If this element (section 1129(a)(8)) is the *only element not satisfied* for confirmation of a proposed plan under section 1129(a), the plan might still be confirmed by a cram down under section 1129(b) (*see infra*, §1097).

i. **At least one impaired class of creditors accepts plan:** [§1088] If the plan impairs any class of *claims*, then the plan must be accepted by at least one class of claims that is impaired, excluding any acceptances by insiders of the consenting class. [B.C. §1129(a)(10)] This element has the effect of preventing a cram down (*i.e.*, confirmation under Bankruptcy Code section 1129(b); *see infra*, §1097) under circumstances where none of the impaired classes of claims has accepted the plan.

    (1) **Artificial impairment:** [§1089] There is authority holding that a class of claims is not deemed impaired for purposes of section 1129(a)(10) when the plan marginally alters the creditors' rights (*e.g.*, by delaying payment to the class for a short period) for the sole purpose of impairing a class that agrees to vote for the plan. [*In re* Windsor on the River Associates, Ltd., 7 F.3d 127 (8th Cir. 1993); *but see In re* Hotel Associates of Tuscon, 165 B.R. 470 (Bankr. 9th Cir. 1994)]

j. **Administrative expenses and involuntary gap claims provided for:** [§1090] Each claim that is entitled to priority as an administrative expense or as an involuntary case gap claim must be paid completely in cash on the effective date of the plan, unless the holder of the claim consents to different treatment. [B.C. §§1129(a)(9)(A), 507(a)(1), (2)]

k. **Third, fourth, fifth, sixth, and seventh priority claims provided for:** [§1091] Each class of claims entitled to priority for wages or commissions, contributions to an employee benefit plan, grain farmers or United States fishermen, consumer layaways, or alimony or spousal or child support must be dealt with as follows, unless the holder of a particular claim consents to different treatment [B.C. §§1129(a)(9)(B), 507(a)(3)-(a)(7)]:

    (1) *If the class has accepted the plan*, each claimant is entitled to receive deferred cash payments having a present value, as of the effective date of the plan, equal to the allowed amount of her claim. [B.C. §1129(a)(9)(B)(i)]

(2) *If the class has rejected the plan*, each claimant must receive total payment of her claim, in cash, on the effective date of the plan. [B.C. §1129(a)(9)(B)(ii)]

l. **Eighth priority tax claims provided for:** [§1092]   Unless it consents to different treatment, each tax claimant that is entitled to eighth priority must receive deferred cash payments having a present value, as of the effective date of the plan, equal to the allowed amount of the claim. The payout period may not extend beyond *six years* following the date that the tax was assessed. While the cases vary on the question of what interest rate to apply, it has been held that the prevailing market rate for a loan of similar duration and risk is appropriate. (*Note:* Although the interest rate prescribed by 26 U.S.C. section 6621 for delinquent tax claims is relevant to ascertaining the prevailing market rate, it should not be conclusive, since it usually lags behind the current market rate and fails to account for factors such as risk and the length of time allowed for payment under the plan.) [B.C. §§1129(a)(9)(C), 507(a)(8); United States v. Neal Pharmacal Co., 789 F.2d 1283 (8th Cir. 1986)]

m. **Ninth priority claims:** [§1093]   The Code is silent concerning treatment of ninth priority claims. [B.C. §507(a)(9)]

n. **Plan is feasible:** [§1094]   The plan must be feasible, which means that it has a reasonable probability of being successful and that it is unlikely that, following confirmation, there will be a need for a liquidation or any further reorganization not proposed in the plan. [B.C. §1129(a)(11); *In re* Acequia, Inc., 787 F.2d 1352 (9th Cir. 1986)]

o. **Bankruptcy fees paid:** [§1095]   All bankruptcy fees required under 28 U.S.C. section 1930 must be paid or will be paid on or before the effective date of the plan. [B.C. §1129(a)(12)]

p. **Retiree insurance benefits protected:** [§1096]   The plan must provide for the continued payment of all retiree benefits at the level established before bankruptcy unless (i) a modification is agreed to by the trustee (or debtor in possession) and the authorized representative of the recipients or (ii) the court orders the payments to be modified in accordance with Bankruptcy Code section 1114. [B.C. §1129(a)(13)]

3. **Cram Down:** [§1097]   A plan can be confirmed where all of the above requirements have been satisfied *except* section 1129(a)(8), which requires every class of claims or interests to accept the plan or be unimpaired under the plan. Thus, upon request by the proponent of a plan, the court will confirm the plan, despite the rejection by one or more impaired classes, if the plan is *not unfairly discriminatory* and *is fair and equitable* with respect to any dissenting impaired classes. [B.C. §1129(b)(1)]

   a. **Unfair discrimination:** [§1098]   To determine whether discriminatory treatment of a dissenting class is fair, the courts consider the following factors:

      (i) Whether there is a *reasonable basis* for the discriminatory treatment;

      (ii) Whether the plan could be implemented *without the discrimination*;

(iii) The presence or absence of *good faith*; and

(iv) The *manner in which the class is treated* under the plan.

[*In re* Ratledge, 31 B.R. 897 (Bankr. E.D. Tenn. 1983)]

(1) **Example:** Debtor Corporation files a Chapter 11 plan, designating seven classes of claims. Class III consists of a disputed and unliquidated tort claim for $35 million. Class IV consists of undisputed, general unsecured claims held by trade creditors and attorneys, totaling $171,000. The plan proposes to pay the Class IV creditors 50¢ on the dollar, without interest, over 36 months, and to pay the Class III claimant $50,000 in cash, from guaranteed funds of Debtor Corporation's president, within 180 days after confirmation. Under the above standard, the plan does not discriminate unfairly against the Class III creditor, whose disputed and unliquidated claim will be paid regardless of the future success or failure of Debtor Corporation. [B.C. §1129(b)(1); *In re* Rochem, Ltd., 58 B.R. 641 (Bankr. D.N.J. 1985)]

b. **Fair and equitable:** [§1099] The Code provides specific guidelines for determining whether a plan is fair and equitable with respect to a particular class. These tests differ according to whether the class is comprised of secured claims, unsecured claims, or equity interests. [B.C. §1129(b)(2)]

(1) **Secured claims:** [§1100] For secured claims, the plan must propose one of the following three methods of treatment if it is to be considered fair and equitable:

(a) **Secured party retains lien and receives deferred cash payments:** [§1101] The plan may allow the creditor to retain her lien on the collateral for the allowed amount of the claim and also receive payment in deferred *cash* installments that total at least the allowed amount of the secured claim and that have a present value, as of the effective date of the plan, of at least the value of the collateral. [B.C. §1129(b)(2)(A)(i)]

1) **Interest rate:** [§1102] In determining present value, many courts require the debtor to pay the interest rate "charged by institutional lenders for similar commercial transactions" as the prevailing market rate. [*In re* Memphis Partners, L.P., 99 B.R. 385 (Bankr. M.D. Tenn. 1989); *In re* Southern States Motor Inns, Inc., 709 F.2d 647 (11th Cir. 1983); *see also*, General Motors Acceptance Corp. v. Jones, 999 F.2d 63 (3d Cir. 1993)—interest rate was that "charged by the creditor in the regular course of its business for loans similar in character, amount, and duration"; United Carolina Bank v. Hall, 993 F.2d 1126 (4th Cir. 1993)—rate of return creditor would obtain in its lending market for new loans (considering both the interest rates it receives and the expenses in obtaining the loans), but capped at the contract rate]

2) **Section 1111(b) election:** [§1103] Recall that if a partially secured creditor elects, under Code section 1111(b), to have her

entire claim treated as secured, then the deferred cash payments in a cram down must equal the full dollar amount of her allowed claim (without interest) and must have a present value of at least the value of the collateral (*see supra*, §1026).

    3) **Negative amortization:** [§1104] Where a plan proposes to defer all or part of the interest on a secured claim, "with the accrued interest added to the principal and paid when income is higher," most courts have refused to hold that the provision is, *per se*, not fair and equitable, but rather have evaluated the provision with reservations and suspicion on a case-by-case basis. [Great Western Bank v. Sierra Woods Group, 953 F.2d 1174 (9th Cir. 1992)—listing 10 non-exclusive factors that might be considered; *In re* Bouy, Hall and Howard and Associates, 141 B.R. 784 (Bankr. S.D. Ga. 1992)—negative amortization allowed; *In re* Apple Tree Partners, L.P., 131 B.R. 380 (Bankr. W.D. Tenn. 1991)—negative amortization not allowed] Confirmation of a plan providing for negative amortization appears to be "the unusual case." [*In re* Club Associates, 107 B.R. 385 (Bankr. N.D. Ga. 1989)—negative amortization allowed]

(b) **Secured party receives indubitable equivalent:** [§1105] The second method of treating secured claims provides that the creditor realize the indubitable equivalent of her secured claim. [B.C. §1129(b)(2)(A)(iii)]

    1) **Example:** Creditor's receipt of 21 individual buyers' notes secured by 21 separate pieces of real property was held to constitute the indubitable equivalent of Creditor's first mortgage on 200 acres of land where the present value of the notes was $153,777, the total debt was $153,521, and the value of the 21 lots was $287,500. [*In re* Sun Country Development, Inc., 764 F.2d 406 (5th Cir. 1985)]

    2) **Example:** An undersecured creditor's receipt of the actual property securing its claim constituted indubitable equivalence of its secured claim. [*In re* Sandy Ridge Development Corp., 881 F.2d 1346 (5th Cir. 1989); *see supra*, §524]

(c) **Collateral sold and lien attaching to proceeds treated as above:** [§1106] The third method of treating secured claims provides for the collateral to be sold free and clear of the creditor's lien, with the lien to attach to the proceeds of the sale and to be treated in a manner described in (a) or (b) above (*supra*, §§1101, 1105). Note that the sale is subject to the creditor's right, under section 363(k), to bid at the sale, purchase the property, and offset her claim against the purchase price. [B.C. §1129(b)(2)(A)(ii)]

(2) **Unsecured claims:** [§1107] For a class of unsecured claims, the plan must propose one of the two following methods of treatment if it is to be considered fair and equitable:

(a) **Each creditor receives property equal to allowed claim:** [§1108] Each creditor of the class receives property (although not necessarily cash—*e.g.*, notes, stock, or other property of the debtor) having a present value, as of the effective date of the plan, equal to the allowed amount of her claim. [B.C. §1129(b)(2)(B)(i); *In re* Perez, 30 F.3d 1209 (9th Cir. 1994)—plan proposing to pay face amount of debt over period of 67 months with no interest was defective]

(b) **Senior classes fully paid before junior classes:** [§1109] No creditor or holder of an interest that is junior to the class receives or retains any property at all. This principle is known as the *absolute priority rule*, and it requires full payment to senior classes before any distribution can be made to junior classes. [B.C. §1129(b)(2)(B)(ii)]

1) **Example:** Where a debtor corporation is insolvent, the absolute priority rule prevents shareholders from retaining their interest in the business, absent the consent of all classes of unsecured creditors whose claims are not fully paid. [*In re* W. E. Parks Lumber Co., 19 B.R. 285 (Bankr. W.D. La. 1982)]

2) **"New value exception":** [§1110] The courts are split concerning the continuing validity of a pre-Code, judicially created exception allowing equity security holders to retain an interest where they invest (i) *new capital*, (ii) *in money or money's worth*, that is (iii) *a substantial contribution*, (iv) *reasonably equivalent to the interest received or retained*, and (v) *necessary for a successful reorganization*. [*See* Case v. Los Angeles Lumber Products Co., 308 U.S. 106 (1939); *In re* Bonner Mall Partnership, 2 F.3d 899 (9th Cir. 1993)—"new value exception, with its stringent requirements, survives" but must be applied on a case-by-case basis (majority view); Kham & Nate's Shoes No. 2, Inc. v. First Bank of Whiting, 908 F.2d 1351 (7th Cir. 1990)—questions validity of exception (here, guarantees of new loans insufficient); 5 Collier ¶1129.03(4)(e)(i)—"there was neither the intention nor the language in the Code to carry over any new value exception"]

a) **Note:** The Supreme Court has held (in a Chapter 11 case concerning a family farm) that even if the exception has survived, the requirement of a substantial new investment cannot be satisfied by a promise of future labor (*i.e.*, "sweat equity"). [Norwest Bank Worthington v. Ahlers, 485 U.S. 197 (1988)]

(3) **Equity interests:** [§1111] For a class of interests, the plan must propose one of the two following methods of treatment if it is to be considered fair and equitable:

(a) **Holder receives or retains property equal to fixed liquidation preference, fixed redemption price, or equity interest:** [§1112] Each interest holder receives or retains property having a present value, as of the effective date of the plan, equal to any applicable fixed liquidation preference, any applicable fixed redemption price, or the value of her equity interest, *whichever is the greatest*. [B.C. §1129(b)(2)(C)(i)]

    (b) **Senior classes fully paid before junior classes:** [§1113] No interest holder that is junior to the class receives or retains any property at all. [B.C. §1129(b)(2)(C)(ii)]

  (4) **Valuation:** [§1114] To determine whether a plan is fair and equitable with respect to a dissenting class of unsecured claims or equity interests, it may be necessary for the court to value the reorganized debtor as a going concern. This process could involve the capitalization of the future expected average yearly earnings of the reorganized corporation, based on an appropriate capitalization rate over the estimated future life of the entity or the discounting of future expected earnings. [5 Collier ¶1129.03(4)(f)(ii)]

 c. **Exception—repossession of certain aircrafts and vessels:** [§1115] In a Chapter 11 case concerning a debtor that is a certified air or water carrier, the Code provides lessors, conditional vendors, and secured parties (whether or not their security interest is purchase money) with qualified protection from cram down in connection with their repossession of certain aircrafts, aircraft equipment, or vessels. [B.C. §1110]

4. **Denial of Confirmation:** [§1116] On the request of a governmental unit that is a party in interest, the court must deny confirmation of a plan if it finds that the plan's principal purpose is to avoid taxes or registration under section 5 of the Securities Act of 1933. [B.C. §1129(d)]

F. POST-CONFIRMATION MATTERS

1. **Effects of Confirmation:** [§1117] The provisions of a confirmed Chapter 11 plan are binding on all creditors and equity security holders, the debtor, any general partner in the debtor, and any entity that issues securities or acquires property under the plan—regardless of whether or not they have accepted the plan or are impaired under the plan. [B.C. §1141(a)]

 a. **On property:** [§1118] Unless the plan or the confirmation order provides otherwise, confirmation causes all property of the estate to vest in the debtor, and all property that is dealt with by the plan to be free and clear of all claims and interests (*but see infra*, §§1120-1122). [B.C. §1141(b), (c)]

  (1) **But note:** There is authority holding that a secured creditor who fails to file a proof of claim in a Chapter 11 case does not lose his pre-petition lien if no action has been brought to avoid the lien. Under this view, the secured party may disregard the bankruptcy case and rely on his lien to satisfy the debt. [B.C. §§506(d), 1141(c); Relihan v. Exchange Bank, 69 B.R. 122 (S.D. Ga. 1985)] However, conflicting authority requires a secured creditor to file a proof of claim or object to the plan in order to prevent the property from vesting in the debtor free and clear of the creditor's pre-petition lien. [*In re* Pennsylvania Iron & Coal Co., 56 B.R.

492 (Bankr. S.D. Ohio 1985); 5 Collier ¶1141.01(3)] Moreover, an appellate case has held that where a proof of claim has been filed by a secured creditor, and the reorganization plan provides for payment of the claim but is silent concerning the lien, confirmation extinguishes the lien, because the creditor participated in the case. [*In re* Penrod, 50 F.3d 459 (7th Cir. 1995)] Thus, in a jurisdiction following the *Penrod* interpretation of section 1141(c), it appears that a secured creditor could more effectively protect his lien by requiring the plan to expressly preserve the lien.

b. **Discharge of debts:** [§1119]   Generally, unless the plan or the confirmation order provides otherwise, confirmation discharges the debtor from *all preconfirmation debts*, as well as from debts arising from (i) the rejection of executory contracts or unexpired leases not assumed by the trustee or debtor in possession; (ii) the recovery of property by the trustee or the debtor under section 522, 550, or 553; and (iii) eighth priority tax claims that occasionally arise post-petition. [B.C. §§1141(d)(1)(A), 502(g),(h),(i)] These debts are discharged regardless of whether (i) a proof of claim was filed, (ii) the claim was allowed, or (iii) the holder accepted the plan.

(1) **Note:**   A Chapter 11 discharge is not restricted to individual debtors (as in Chapter 7); thus, *corporations and partnerships* may be discharged as well. Also, confirmation terminates all rights and interests of general partners and equity security holders who are dealt with by the plan. [B.C. §1141(d)(1)(B)]

(2) **Exceptions to discharge:** [§1120]   Confirmation does not discharge the following:

(a) **Individual's nondischargeable debts:** [§1121]   If the debtor is an individual, a Chapter 11 discharge does not include any debts that are nondischargeable under Bankruptcy Code section 523 (*e.g.*, certain taxes, alimony, and child support). [B.C. §1141(d)(2); *In re* Grynberg, 986 F.2d 367 (10th Cir. 1993)—gift taxes); *see supra*, §§675 *et seq.*]

(b) **Liquidating plan:** [§1122]   The debtor will not receive a discharge if (i) the confirmed plan provides for the *liquidation of all or substantially all of the estate property*; (ii) the debtor does *not continue in business* after the plan is consummated; and (iii) the debtor *would not be granted a discharge in a Chapter 7 case* under section 727(a) (*see supra*, §§972 *et seq.*). Thus, for example, a corporation or a partnership will not receive a discharge where a Chapter 11 liquidating plan is confirmed and the debtor's business is discontinued. [B.C. §1141(d)(3)]

(c) **Officers and directors:** [§1123]   Since confirmation of a Chapter 11 plan discharges only the debtor, it should be understood that officers and directors of a debtor corporation are *not* discharged from any liabilities incurred *personally* while associated with the debtor (*e.g.*, claims for tortious conduct brought by former shareholders). [*In re* Inforex, Inc., 9 Bankr. Ct. Dec. 1373 (Bankr. D. Mass. 1983)]

(d) **Failure to give notice:** [§1124] Where the debtor knows of a creditor's claim but fails to schedule it, and the creditor does not receive notice of the bankruptcy proceedings, the principle of due process should prevail over the Code's discharge provisions, and so the debt should not be discharged. [*See* Broomall Industries v. Data Design Logic Systems, 786 F.2d 401 (Fed. Cir. 1986); 5 Collier ¶1141.01(4)(b); *see also In re* Unioil, 948 F.2d 678 (10th Cir. 1991)—formal notice of bar date and confirmation hearing required, despite post-petition creditor's actual knowledge of debtor's bankruptcy; *but see In re* Christopher, 28 F.3d 512 (5th Cir. 1994)—formal notice not required where creditor had actual notice of debtor's bankruptcy]

c. **Termination of automatic stay:** [§1125] Generally, confirmation of a Chapter 11 plan terminates the automatic stay, since property that vests in the debtor is no longer property of the estate and confirmation of a reorganization plan usually discharges the debtor. [B.C. §362(c)(1), (2)(C); *In re* Draggoo Electric Co., 57 B.R. 916 (Bankr. N.D. Ind. 1986)]

2. **Implementation of Plan:** [§1126] Notwithstanding any nonbankruptcy law concerning financial condition, the Bankruptcy Code requires that the debtor and any successor implement the plan and comply with all court orders. Furthermore, the court is authorized to order the debtor and any other necessary party to execute or deliver any instrument required for the transfer of property under the plan and to perform whatever else is needed to consummate the plan. [B.C. §1142; *In re* Johns-Manville Corp., 97 B.R. 174 (Bankr. S.D.N.Y. 1989)]

3. **Distribution:** [§1127] Where the plan provides that an entity's participation in distribution is contingent on the entity's surrender or presentment of a security or on the doing of some other act, the entity must perform accordingly within five years after the date of the *entry* of the confirmation order or it will forfeit the right to share in distribution under the plan. [B.C. §1143]

4. **Revocation of Confirmation Order:** [§1128] Within 180 days after the entry of the order confirming the Chapter 11 plan, a party in interest may request that the order be revoked, but only on the ground that it was procured by fraud. If after notice and a hearing, the confirmation order is revoked, the court must provide protection for any rights that have been acquired by an entity's good faith reliance on the confirmation order, and it also must revoke any discharge received by the debtor. [B.C. §1144]

5. **Exemption from Securities Laws:** [§1129] Generally, securities offered or sold by the debtor or its successor under a Chapter 11 plan in exchange for claims against or interests in the debtor or for administrative expense claims are exempt from the registration requirements of section 5 of the 1933 Securities Act and from registration requirements in any state or local securities law. [B.C. §1145(a); *In re* Amarex, Inc., 53 B.R. 12 (Bankr. W.D. Okla. 1985)] Furthermore, such an issuance is deemed to be a public offering, hereby escaping the restrictions imposed by rule 144 of the Securities and Exchange Commission concerning the resale of securities that are part of a private placement [B.C. §1145(c)]

a. **Underwriter:** [§1130] Usually, a creditor or an equity security holder receiving securities under a Chapter 11 plan may resell them unless he is an "underwriter," a term which the Code defines in great detail. [B.C. §1145(b)] An underwriter includes, for example, an entity that purchases a claim against or an interest in the debtor, or an administrative expense claim, with the intention of distributing securities that it will acquire under a Chapter 11 plan in exchange for the claim or interest. Similarly, it includes an entity that offers to sell securities on behalf of those receiving securities under a plan, or that offers to buy such securities from them for the purpose of resale pursuant to an agreement related to the plan. While the bankruptcy definition of an underwriter also covers an issuer, as used in section 2(11) of the Securities Act of 1933, this obviously does not mean the debtor or its successor. However, it appears that an issuer does include a controlling person, *i.e.*, a creditor holding 10% or more of the debtor's securities. [5 Collier ¶1145.02(2)] Any party considered to be an underwriter must comply with the registration requirements and any resale restrictions of the securities laws.

G. SMALL BUSINESSES [§1131]

The Bankruptcy Reform Act of 1994 amended several sections of Chapter 11 to expedite the reorganization of a small business.

1. **Definition: "Small Business":** [§1132] A "'small business' means a person engaged in commercial or business activities (but does not include a person whose primary activity is the business of owning or operating real property and activities incidental thereto) whose aggregate noncontingent liquidated secured and unsecured debts as of the date of the petition do not exceed $2,000,000." [B.C. §101(51C)]

2. **Effects of Election:** [§1133] In a Chapter 11 case where a debtor elects to be treated as a small business [B.C. §1121(e)], the court, on the request of a party in interest and for cause, may order that a creditors' committee not be appointed. [B.C. §1102(a)(3)] Also, the electing small business debtor is provided an exclusivity period of 100 days after the order for relief during which only the debtor may file a plan. [B.C. §1121(e)(1)] All other plans must be filed within 160 days after the order for relief. [B.C. §1121(e)(2)] However, upon a timely request by a party in interest, and after notice and a hearing, the court may reduce the 100-day period or the 160-day period for cause, or increase the 100-day period due to circumstances for which the debtor should not be held accountable. [B.C. §1121(e)(3)] In addition, the court is authorized to approve a conditional disclosure statement, which can be used to solicit acceptances and rejections (if the debtor provides adequate information to creditors and interest holders, and the statement is mailed at least 10 days before the confirmation hearing), and the court may conduct a combined hearing on the disclosure statement and confirmation of the plan. [B.C. §1125(f)]

H. *MANVILLE*-TYPE TRUST/INJUNCTION [§1134]

The Bankruptcy Code contains a provision [B.C. §524(g)] authorizing the court to order the type of trust/injunction used in the *Johns-Manville* case. [Kane v. Johns-Manville Corp., 843 F.2d 636 (2d Cir. 1988)] It applies only to cases in Chapter 11 involving *asbestos-related liabilities* of the debtor when an indeterminable number of substantial future demands for payment necessitate use of the trust in order to deal equitably with claims and future demands. [B.C. §524(g)]

1. **Actions Against Debtor Enjoined:** [§1135]   This provision permits the court, after notice and a hearing, to enjoin suits against (i) the debtor; (ii) officers, directors, affiliates, and insurance companies of the debtor; (iii) successors to the debtor; and (iv) any other entity directly or indirectly liable for claims or demands against the debtor. Instead of suits being brought against the debtor (or such other entities), ***present and future claims and demands will be brought against the trust***, that will be established under the plan of reorganization and will be funded by securities of the debtor and future payments to be made by the debtor. [B.C. §524(g)]

2. **Elements of the Trust/Injunction:** [§1136]   The requirements for the trust/injunction include the following: (i) at least 75% of those voting in each class of present claims must approve the plan; (ii) the trust must own or have the right to become the owner of a majority of the stock of the reorganized debtor; (iii) a legal representative must be appointed for persons who might assert future demands; and (iv) the trust must provide reasonable assurance that it will value, and be able to pay, present claims and future demands (that are similar in kind) in substantially the same manner. [B.C. §524(g)]

3. **Note—Rule of Construction:** [§1137]   The Bankruptcy Reform Act of 1994, which amended the Code to authorize use of the *Manville*-type trust/injunction, also contains the following rule of construction: "Nothing in [Code section 524(g)] shall be construed to modify, impair, or supersede any other authority the court has to issue injunctions in connection with an order confirming a plan of reorganization." [Bankruptcy Reform Act of 1994, §111(b), 108 Stat. at 4117]

XI. CHAPTER 13—INDIVIDUAL WITH REGULAR INCOME

chapter approach

Chapter 13 is designed for an ***individual debtor***, including a debtor engaged in business, who has a regular source of income and who desires to repay all or a percentage of her debts pursuant to a plan, which she has the ***exclusive right*** to propose. Keep in mind that a case under Chapter 13 is very different from a Chapter 7 liquidation, inasmuch as the Chapter 13 debtor usually remains in possession of the property of the estate and makes payments to creditors, through the Chapter 13 trustee, based on her ***anticipated income*** over the life of the plan. Also, note that property of the Chapter 13 estate includes, in addition to "all section 541 property," the debtor's ***post-petition property and earnings***.

If you see an exam question concerning Chapter 13, you probably will need to determine first whether the debtor satisfies the ***eligibility requirements*** of Chapter 13. Be sure to consider the ***stability and regularity*** of the debtor's expected income, and make sure that her unsecured and secured debts meet the specific dollar limitations (under $250,000 and $750,000, respectively). Remember that only ***voluntary*** cases are permitted.

You may next have to consider the ***co-debtor stay***. Remember that under Chapter 13, the debtor is protected by the automatic stay provision [B.C. §362] and the special co-debtor stay generally protects an individual who is liable on a ***consumer debt*** with the debtor.

Finally, you should be prepared to apply the Chapter 13 principles relating to (i) the mandatory and permissive ***plan provisions***, (ii) the requirements for ***confirmation*** of a plan, and (iii) the ***discharge*** of debts. Note carefully which debts cannot be discharged in a Chapter 13 case.

A. ELIGIBILITY FOR RELIEF

1. **In General:** [§1138] Chapter 13 relief is available to an individual (i) who has *regular income*, (ii) whose *unsecured debts* total less than $250,000, and (iii) whose *secured debts* total less than $750,000. The indebtedness used in these calculations must be noncontingent and liquidated liabilities, determined as of the date of the filing of the petition. [B.C. §109(e); *In re* Pearson, *supra*, §136] In determining eligibility where at least one of the debts is undersecured, most courts apply the general rule that a claim is secured only up to the value of the collateral, with the balance constituting an unsecured claim. [Miller v. United States Through Farmers Home Administration, 907 F.2d 80 (8th Cir. 1990); *see supra*, §524]

   a. **Individual with regular income:** [§1139] An individual with regular income is defined as an "individual whose income is sufficiently stable and regular to enable such individual to make payments under a plan under Chapter 13." [B.C. §101(30)] In most cases, a Chapter 13 debtor's regular income is generated from her wages or salary, but it may be derived from almost any legitimate source, such as interest income, rental income, a business, a pension, a trust, social security, or even welfare, if it is regular enough to fund the debtor's plan of repayment. [*In re* Hammonds, *supra*, §138]

b. **Voluntary petition only:** [§1140] A Chapter 13 case may be commenced only by the filing of a voluntary petition. [B.C. §§301, 303(a)]

c. **Joint case:** [§1141] An individual with regular income and her spouse may file a joint petition, in which case the debt limitations of $250,000 and $750,000 (above) apply to their *aggregate* indebtedness. [B.C. §§302(a), 109(e)]

2. **Individuals Ineligible for Chapter 13 Relief:** [§1142] Stockbrokers and commodity brokers are not eligible for relief under Chapter 13. [B.C. §109(e)] Also, an individual debtor in a case that was dismissed in the preceding 180 days is not eligible if the dismissal was due to the debtor's intentional failure to obey court orders or appear before the court, or was a result of the debtor's request for a voluntary dismissal of the case following a party's request for relief from the automatic stay. [B.C. §109(g)]

B. **CO-DEBTOR STAY** [§1143]

The filing of a Chapter 13 petition invokes not only the automatic stay of Bankruptcy Code section 362 (*see supra*, §§778 *et seq*.), but also a stay against any civil action or other act by a creditor to collect a *consumer debt from an individual who has guaranteed or secured a liability* of the debtor or who is otherwise *liable on a debt with the debtor*. [B.C. §1301 (a)]

1. **Consumer Debt:** [§1144] The Code defines a consumer debt as one "incurred by an individual primarily for a personal, family, or household purpose." [B.C. §101(8)]

2. **Exceptions to Co-Debtor Stay:** [§1145] The co-debtor stay does not apply where the Chapter 13 case has been closed, dismissed, converted to Chapter 7 or 11, or in circumstances where the co-debtor's liability was incurred in the ordinary course of *his* business. [B.C. §1301(a)(1), (2)]

3. **Grounds for Relief from Stay:** [§1146] A creditor may be granted relief from the co-debtor stay under any of the following circumstances [B.C. §1301(c)]:

    a. **Co-debtor received consideration:** [§1147] To the extent that the co-debtor was the actual recipient of the consideration for the claim, the creditor may be granted relief from the stay. [B.C. §1301(c)(1)]

        (1) **Example:** Debtor and Son co-sign a promissory note payable to the order of Bank, which has agreed to finance Son's purchase of new furniture for his home. Son takes possession of the furniture and makes six monthly payments. Debtor then files a Chapter 13 petition. Bank may seek relief from the co-debtor stay to continue to collect the debt from Son, since Son was the one who actually received the consideration. [B.C. §1301(c)(1)]

    b. **Creditor's claim unpaid under plan:** [§1148] To the extent that the creditor's claim will not be paid under the debtor's proposed Chapter 13 plan, the creditor may receive relief from the stay. [B.C. §1301(c)(2)]

(1) **Example:** Debtor borrows $3,000 from Credit Union and executes a consumer promissory note, which Friend co-signs as a favor. Subsequently, Debtor files a Chapter 13 petition with a plan proposing to pay Credit Union 70% of its claim. Credit Union may seek relief from the co-debtor stay to pursue Friend for the other 30% of its claim. [B.C. §1301(c)(2)]

(2) **Note:** If a motion for relief from the co-debtor stay is filed on this basis [B.C. §1301(c)(2)], the stay automatically terminates with respect to the movant 20 days later if a written objection has not been filed by the debtor or the co-debtor. [B.C. §1301(d)]

c. **Irreparable harm to creditor:** [§1149] Where the creditor will be irreparably harmed if the stay remains in effect, relief from the stay will also be granted. [B.C. §1301(c)(3)]

(1) **Example:** Debtor borrows $3,000 from Credit Union and executes a consumer promissory note, which Friend co-signs as a favor. Subsequently, Debtor files a Chapter 13 petition and a proposed plan. Friend purchases a one-way ticket to Switzerland with the stated intention of permanently residing there beginning next week. Credit Union should be justified in making a prompt request for relief from the co-debtor stay under section 1301(c)(3).

C. ADMINISTRATION OF CHAPTER 13 CASE

1. **Appointment of Chapter 13 Trustee:** [§1150] In regions where many Chapter 13 cases are filed, the United States trustee ordinarily appoints a qualified individual to serve as a *standing trustee*. Otherwise, the United States trustee appoints a disinterested person as the trustee for a particular case, or the United States trustee may serve as the trustee in the case himself. [B.C. §1302(a); 28 U.S.C. §586(b)]

   a. **Duties of trustee:** [§1151] The duties of a Chapter 13 trustee include the following (note that duties (1) through (7) described below are also duties of a Chapter 7 trustee):

   (1) *To account for all property received* [B.C. §§1302(b)(1), 704(2)];

   (2) *To monitor the debtor's performance* of her intentions regarding collateral securing consumer debts (although this duty usually applies only to a Chapter 7 trustee) [B.C. §§1302(b)(1), 704(3), 521(2)(B); 5 Collier ¶1302.01(3)(A)(ii)];

   (3) *To investigate* the debtor's financial affairs [B.C. §§1302(b)(1), 704(4)];

   (4) *To examine proofs of claims* and object to the allowance of any improper ones [B.C. §§1302(b)(1), 704(5)];

   (5) *If circumstances warrant*, to *object* to the debtor's discharge [B.C. §§1302(b)(1), 704(6)];

   (6) *To provide information requested by parties in interest* about the estate and the administration of the estate [B.C. §§1302(b)(1), 704(7)];

(7) *To prepare and file* with the court and with the United States trustee a *final report and account* concerning the case [B.C. §§1302(b)(1), 704(9)];

(8) *To appear and be heard at any hearing* regarding (i) valuation of property on which there is a lien, (ii) confirmation of a Chapter 13 plan, or (iii) post-confirmation modification of a plan [B.C. §1302(b)(2)];

(9) *To furnish nonlegal advice* to the debtor, and to assist the debtor in implementing the plan [B.C. §1302(b)(4)];

(10) *To ensure that the debtor begins making the payments* proposed by the plan within 30 days after the filing of the plan [B.C. §§1302(b)(5), 1326(a)(1)];

(11) *If the debtor is engaged in business* (*see* below):

   (a) *To investigate* the debtor's conduct, financial condition, and business operations, as well as the *advisability of continuing* the debtor's business [B.C. §§1302(c), 1106(a)(3)]; and

   (b) *To file a report* of the investigation, relating any facts evidencing fraud, dishonesty, incompetence, misconduct, or mismanagement [B.C. §§1302(c), 1106(a)(4)]; and

(12) *Ordinarily, to disburse the payments* to creditors under a confirmed plan. [B.C. §1326(c); *see infra*, §1208]

2. **Rights and Powers of Debtor:** [§1152] In a Chapter 13 case, the *debtor has the exclusive right* to use, sell, or lease estate property under Bankruptcy Code section 363(b), (d), (e), (f), or (1) (*see supra*, §§832 *et seq.*). Thus, for example, a debtor may use, sell, or lease property out of the ordinary course of business, in accordance with section 363(b) (*see supra*, §§835 *et seq.*). [B.C. §1303]

   a. **Debtor engaged in business:** [§1153] A debtor engaged in business is a self-employed individual who incurs trade credit in producing income from her business, which she is *entitled to operate unless the court orders otherwise*. Usually, a Chapter 13 debtor engaged in business has, in addition to the rights described in the preceding paragraph (§1152), the exclusive right to use, sell, or lease property in the ordinary course of business [B.C. §363(c)] and to obtain credit [B.C. §364]. However, these rights are subject to any limitations specified in those sections, as well as to any restrictions or conditions imposed by the court. [B.C. §1304(a), (b)]

      (1) **Duties:** [§1154] A debtor engaged in business must file periodic financial reports (including a statement of receipts and disbursements) with the court, the United States trustee, and the appropriate taxing authorities. [B.C. §§1304(c), 704(8)]

3. **Post-Petition Claims:** [§1155] Certain kinds of post-petition claims may be filed in a Chapter 13 case. One is for *taxes* that become due during the pendency of the case, and another is for *consumer debts* incurred by the debtor after the order for relief for property or services that the debtor needs to carry out the plan. [B.C. §1305(a)]

a. **Allowance:** [§1156] Post-petition claims for such taxes and necessary consumer debts are treated as pre-petition claims for the purpose of allowance, but they are determined as of the date that they arise. [B.C. §1305(b)]

b. **Exception—failure to obtain approval:** [§1157] A post-petition claim for necessary consumer debts will be disallowed if the claimant knew or should have known that prior approval of the debt by the trustee was practicable and was not procured. [B.C. §1305(c)]

4. **Property of Estate:** [§1158] The Chapter 13 estate consists of (i) all "section 541 property" (*see supra*, §§294 *et seq.*); (ii) all "section 541 property" acquired by the debtor post-petition, but before the earliest of the closing, dismissal, or conversion of the case; and (iii) all of the debtor's earnings from services performed post-petition, but before the earliest of the closing, dismissal, or conversion of the case. [B.C. §1306(a)] The *debtor retains possession* of all property of the Chapter 13 estate *unless a confirmed plan or confirmation order provides otherwise*. [B.C. §1306(b)]

5. **Conversion or Dismissal:** [§1159] In appropriate circumstances, a Chapter 13 case may be dismissed or converted to another chapter of the Bankruptcy Code under which the debtor is eligible. [B.C. §1307]

    a. **Voluntary conversion to Chapter 7:** [§1160] The debtor has an absolute right to convert the case to Chapter 7, and this right cannot be waived. [B.C. §1307(a)]

    b. **Voluntary dismissal:** [§1161] The debtor also has the nonwaivable right to dismiss the case if it has not been converted earlier from Chapter 7, 11, or 12. [B.C. §1307(b); *In re* Nash, 765 F.2d 1410 (9th Cir. 1985)]

    c. **Discretionary dismissal or conversion to Chapter 7:** [§1162] Upon a request by a party in interest or the United States trustee, the court, *for cause*, may dismiss the case or convert it to Chapter 7, whichever is better for creditors and the estate. While the Code specifies numerous examples of cause, conversion or dismissal of the case is discretionary and not a matter of right, even where one or more grounds exist. Notice and a hearing are required. [B.C. §1307(c); *In re* Green, 64 B.R. 530 (Bankr. 9th Cir. 1986)]

        (1) **"Cause":** [§1163] Reasons for dismissal of the case or conversion to Chapter 7 include the following [B.C. §1307(c)]:

            (a) *Unreasonable and prejudicial delay* on the part of the debtor [B.C. §1307(c)(1)];

            (b) *Failure to pay any necessary fees or charges* imposed under chapter 123 of title 28 [B.C. §1307(c)(2)];

            (c) *Failure to file a plan* within 15 days after the filing of the petition (or within 15 days after conversion to Chapter 13), unless an extension is granted for cause [B.C. §1307(c)(3); Bankruptcy Rule 3015(b); *see infra*, §1167];

            (d) *Failure to begin making payments* under the proposed plan within 30 days after the plan is filed [B.C. §§1307(c)(4), 1326(a)(1)];

(e) *Denial of confirmation of the debtor's plan*, and denial of a request for an extension of time to file another plan or to modify the plan [B.C. §1307(c)(5)];

(f) *A material default* by the debtor concerning a provision of a plan that has been confirmed [B.C. §1307(c)(6)];

(g) *Revocation of a confirmation order procured by fraud*, and the court's refusal to confirm a modified plan [B.C. §§1307(c)(7), 1330];

(h) *Termination of a confirmed plan because of the happening of a condition contained in the plan* (other than completing all payments) [B.C. §1307(c)(8)];

(i) *Failure to file* within 15 days (or any extension) after the filing of the petition a list of creditors, a schedule of assets and liabilities, a schedule of current income and current expenditures, and a statement of the debtor's financial affairs. *But note:* This ground applies only upon a request for conversion or dismissal made by the United States trustee [B.C. §§1307(c)(9), 521(1)]. (Another basis set forth in the Code for conversion or dismissal, when requested by the United States trustee, is the debtor's failure to timely file the information required by Bankruptcy Code section 521(2). However, that section applies only to Chapter 7 cases, and, therefore, it should not constitute a ground for conversion or dismissal of a Chapter 13 case. [B.C. §1307(c)(10); 5 Collier ¶1307.01(4)(ix); and *see supra*, §205]); or

(j) *Lack of good faith* in filing the Chapter 13 petition [*In re* Love, 957 F.2d 1350 (7th Cir. 1992)].

d. **Conversion to Chapter 11 or 12:** [§1164] Before a Chapter 13 plan is confirmed, the court may convert the case to Chapter 11 or 12 upon a request by a party in interest (including the debtor) or the United States trustee. Notice and a hearing are required to determine if the alternative chapter would be more suitable, and the court also must find that the debtor is eligible for relief under that chapter. [B.C. 1307(d)]

e. **Exception—farmers:** [§1165] If the debtor is a farmer, a Chapter 13 case cannot be converted to Chapter 7, 11, or 12 *unless* the request for conversion is made by the debtor. [B.C. §1307(e)]

f. **Property of estate in converted case:** [§1166] If a case is converted from Chapter 13 to another chapter of the Code, property of the estate in the converted case consists of property of the estate on the date of the Chapter 13 filing that remains in the possession or control of the debtor on the date of conversion. If payments have been made to secured creditors under the Chapter 13 plan, their allowed secured claims will be reduced, commensurately. If the debtor converts the case in bad faith, however, property of the estate in the converted case will consist of the estate property on the date of conversion. [B.C. §348(f); for example, *see supra*, §216]

D. CHAPTER 13 PLAN

1. **Filing a Plan:** [§1167] Only the *debtor* may file a Chapter 13 plan, and it must be filed with the petition or within 15 days thereafter (or within 15 days after conversion to Chapter 13), unless the court grants an extension for cause. [B.C. §1321; Bankruptcy Rule 3015(b)]

2. **Mandatory Provisions:** [§1168] A Chapter 13 plan must include the following provisions [B.C. §1322(a)]:

   a. **Sufficient income to be turned over to trustee:** [§1169] The plan must provide that such amount of the debtor's future earnings or other future income as is required for the implementation of the plan will be turned over to the Chapter 13 trustee. [B.C. §1322(a)(1)]

   b. **Full payment of priority claims:** [§1170] The plan must provide that all priority claims will be paid fully in deferred cash payments, unless a particular creditor consents to different treatment. [B.C. §1322(a)(2); *In re* Escobedo, 28 F.3d 34 (7th Cir. 1994)]

      (1) **Note:** While priority claimants in a Chapter 13 case are entitled to receive payments totaling the full amount of their claims, the payments need not equal the *present value* of their claims. [*In re* Young, 61 B.R. 150 (Bankr. S.D. Ind. 1986)]

   c. **Same treatment for claims of a class:** [§1171] If the plan designates classes of claims, it must provide identical treatment for all claims within any one class. [B.C. §1322(a)(3)]

3. **Permissive Provisions:** [§1172] A Chapter 13 plan may include any of the following provisions [B.C. §1322(b)]:

   a. **Classification of claims:** [§1173] The plan may specify various classes of *unsecured claims* in accordance with Bankruptcy Code section 1122 (*see supra*, §§1048 *et seq.*), provided that it does not discriminate unfairly against any particular class. However, the Code expressly permits a Chapter 13 plan to provide different treatment for a consumer debt on which an individual co-debtor is also liable than for other unsecured claims. [B.C. §1322(b)(1)]

      (1) **"Unfair discrimination":** [§1174] Most courts apply the following criteria in determining whether discrimination against a class is fair:

         (i) Whether there is a *reasonable basis* for the discriminatory treatment;

         (ii) Whether the plan could be implemented *without* the discrimination;

         (iii) The presence or absence of *good faith*; and

         (iv) The *manner* in which the class is treated under the plan.

      [*In re* Storberg, 94 B.R. 144 (Bankr. D. Minn. 1988); *see also In Re* Leser, 939 F.2d 669 (8th Cir. 1991)—describing the fourth factor (above)

(a) **Example:** Debtor files a Chapter 13 petition and a plan designating two classes of unsecured claims. Class I consists of debts incurred in a business that Debtor has closed, and Class II consists of consumer debts. Debtor's plan proposes to pay nothing to the claimants in Class I, and to pay 100% to the claimants in Class II. The plan is unfairly discriminatory under the four criteria above, and thus the court denies confirmation. [B.C. §1322(b)(1); *In re* Harris, 62 B.R. 391 (Bankr. E. D. Mich. 1986)]

(b) **Example:** Debtor files a Chapter 13 petition and a plan proposing to pay in full a class consisting of an unsecured nondischargeable student loan, and proposing to pay 40% to a class consisting of the other unsecured claims. The plan is unfairly discriminatory, as the nondischargeability of student loans does not justify separate classification and "substantial discrimination against other, dischargeable unsecured claims." Confirmation is denied. [*In re* Groves, 39 F.3d 212 (8th Cir. 1994)]

(c) **Compare:** Debtor files a Chapter 13 petition accompanied by a plan proposing the following: Class I—all priority claims, to be paid in full; Class II—child support claims, to be paid in full; Class III—unsecured claims of $100 or less, to be paid in full; and Class IV—all other unsecured claims, to be paid 18%. The trustee objects to confirmation of the plan because of the difference in treatment between Classes II and IV. However, "in light of the overwhelming public policy in favor of providing support for children" and the virtual impossibility of a successful Chapter 13 plan not providing full payment of child support, Debtor's plan is not unfairly discriminatory and therefore is confirmed by the court. [B.C. §1322(b)(1); *and see In re* Storberg, 94 B.R. 144 (Bankr. D. Minn. 1988)]

b. **Modification of creditors' rights:** [§1175] The plan may modify the rights of secured creditors or unsecured creditors (such as by "changing the size and timing of installment payments"), *except* where the creditor's claim is secured *solely* by a security interest in real property constituting the debtor's principal residence. [B.C. §1322(b)(2)] Note that the Code defines a security interest as a *lien created by an agreement*. [B.C. §101(51)] Of course, any such modification must be consistent with the pertinent requirements for confirmation of a Chapter 13 plan. [B.C. §1325(a)(4), (5); *see infra*, §§1200-1201]

(1) **Example:** Debtor owes Bank $10,000 with an interest rate of 23% and secured solely by a first mortgage on real property constituting Debtor's principal residence. Debtor files a Chapter 13 plan proposing to repay Bank at a rate of 14%. The modification will not be permitted since it falls squarely within the exception. [B.C. §1322(b)(2); *In re* Rorie, 58 B.R. 162 (Bankr. S.D. Ohio 1985)]

(2) **Compare:** Finance Company is the holder of a claim secured by a mortgage on real property on which Debtor resides and on which there also

exist two rental units that generate 46% of Debtor's income. The rate of interest on the mortgage note is 18%. Debtor's proposed Chapter 13 plan *may* modify Finance Company's rights by reducing the interest rate on the mortgage note since the claim is not secured *solely* by real property that is the principal residence of debtor. [B.C. §1322(b)(2); *In re* Ramirez, 62 B.R. 688 (Bankr. S.D. Cal. 1986)] Confirmation, however, will depend on whether the plan satisfies Bankruptcy Code section 1325(a)(5). Similarly, modification of a secured creditor's rights would be permitted where the creditor's security interest also includes *personal property*, where the security interest is in real property that is not the debtor's *principal* home, or where the creditor's lien is one that was *not created by agreement* (*e.g.*, in the case of a judicial lien or a statutory lien). [5 Collier ¶1322.06(1)(a)]

(3) **Bifurcation of home mortgage:** [§1176] Bankruptcy Code section 1322(b)(2) *prohibits* a Chapter 13 debtor from *stripping down* an undersecured mortgage on the debtor's principal residence to the fair market value of the home, notwithstanding section 506(a). [Nobelman v. American Savings Bank, 113 S. Ct. 2106 (1993); *but see In re* Hammond 27 F.3d 52 (3d Cir. 1994)—allowing bifurcation of a home mortgage that also created security interests in *personal property*]

(4) **Permissible modification of home mortgage payments:** [§1177] Where the final payment on a debt secured solely by a security interest in real property constituting the debtor's principal residence is due *before* the last payment under the plan, it is permissible for the plan to modify payment of the debt in accordance with Code section 1325(a)(5) (*see infra*, §1201) [B.C. §1322(c)(2)]

c. **Cure or waiver of default:** [§1178] The plan may cure or waive any default. [B.C. §1322(b)(3); Grubbs v. Houston First American Savings Association, 730 F.2d 236 (5th Cir. 1984)]

d. **Order of payments:** [§1179] The plan may provide for any general unsecured claim to be paid concurrently with any secured claim or with any unsecured priority claim. [B.C. §1322(b)(4); 5 Collier ¶1322.08]

e. **Long-term debts:** [§1180] The plan may provide for the *curing of any default* within a reasonable time and the *maintenance of payments*, during the period that the case is pending, on any long-term secured or unsecured debt for which the final payment is due *after* the final payment required by the Chapter 13 plan. [B.C. §1322(b)(5)] This section, by specific statutory authorization, frequently is applied with respect to claims secured solely by the principal residence of the debtor, notwithstanding the exception contained in Code section 1322(b)(2) concerning nonmodification of such home mortgages.

(1) **Cure:** [§1181] Where the debtor seeks to cure a default with respect to a lien on his principal residence, cure is permitted until a properly conducted foreclosure sale has occurred [B.C. §1322(c)(1)], unless (according to the legislative history) applicable nonbankruptcy law provides a longer redemption period. [140 Cong. Rec. H10,769 (daily ed. Oct. 4, 1994)]

(2) **"Reasonable time":** [§1182] What constitutes a reasonable time to cure a default depends on the circumstances of the particular case, but two or three years is not uncommon. Some of the factors that the court is likely to take into account include: (i) the amount and reason for the arrearage; (ii) the availability of the debtor's discretionary income to cure the default; (iii) whether the debtor is putting forth her best effort to cure the default; and (iv) the debtor's ability to meet the obligations of the plan and to continue current payments on the installment obligations. [*In re* Hickson, 52 B.R. 11 (Bankr. S.D. Fla. 1985)]

(3) **Interest on arrearages:** [§1183] Where the plan proposes to cure a default (for example, interest on mortgage arrearages including interest), the amount necessary to cure the default is determined by looking to the underlying contract and applicable nonbankruptcy law. [B.C. §1322(e)] Therefore, a creditor will be entitled to interest on interest only if it was agreed to by the parties and is permissible under state law, or alternatively if it is required by state law.

f. **Post-petition tax claims or necessary consumer debts:** [§1184] The plan may provide for the payment of any allowed post-petition claims for taxes that become due during the pendency of the case, or for necessary consumer debts incurred after the order for relief. [B.C. §§1322(b)(6), 1305; *see supra*, §1155]

g. **Assumption or rejection of executory contracts or unexpired leases:** [§1185] The plan may provide for any previously unrejected executory contract or unexpired lease to be assumed, rejected, or assigned in accordance with section 365. [B.C. §1322(b)(7); *and see supra*, §§875 *et seq.*; *In re* Aneiro, *supra*, §878]

h. **Property used to pay claims:** [§1186] The plan may provide for particular claims to be paid from property of the estate or from the debtor's property. [B.C. §1322(b)(8); *see supra*, §1158]

i. **Vesting of property:** [§1187] The plan may provide for property of the estate to vest in the debtor or in another entity when the plan is confirmed or at a subsequent time. [B.C. §1322(b)(9)]

j. **Miscellaneous provisions:** [§1188] The plan also may contain any other provisions that are appropriate and consistent with the Bankruptcy Code. [B.C. §1322(b)(10)]

(1) **Exception—lien avoidance:** [§1189] Where the debtor seeks to avoid a lien under Bankruptcy Code section 522(f), the proper procedure is to *file a motion* to avoid the lien, and not to include it as a provision of the plan. [Bankruptcy Rule 4003(d); *In re* McKay, 732 F.2d 44 (3d Cir. 1984); *see supra*, §§649 *et seq.*]

(2) **Example—mortgage lien securing discharged obligation:** [§1190] The Supreme Court has held that, in light of the broad definition of *"claim"* (*see supra*, §§15, 34) it is permissible to provide for a mortgage lien in a Chapter 13 plan, even though the underlying personal debt that the mortgaged property secures has been discharged in an earlier Chapter 7 case. [Johnson v. Home State Bank, 501 U.S. 78 (1991)]

4. **Duration of Plan:** [§1191] The payments under a Chapter 13 plan may not extend beyond *three years* unless, for cause, the court approves a longer payback period, up to a maximum of *five years*. [B.C. §1322(d); *In re* Greer, 60 B.R. 547 (Bankr. C.D. Cal. 1986)]

5. **Modification of Plan:** [§1192] The debtor has the exclusive right to modify a plan *prior to confirmation*. The modified plan must meet the specifications set forth in section 1322 (*see supra*, §§1168-1191). [B.C. §1323]

E. CONFIRMATION OF PLAN

1. **Confirmation Hearing:** [§1193] After proper notice, the court conducts a hearing to determine whether a proposed plan satisfies the elements necessary for confirmation. An objection to confirmation may be filed by any party in interest. [B.C. §1324; Bankruptcy Rule 3015]

2. **Requirements for Confirmation:** [§1194] A plan will be confirmed only if it satisfies the following statutory elements [B.C. §1325(a)]:

   a. **Plan complies with Code provisions:** [§1195] The plan must comply with the provisions of Chapter 13, as well as with the other applicable provisions of the Code. [B.C. §1325(a)(1)] For example, a plan that classifies claims but provides dissimilar treatment for various claims within a particular class cannot be confirmed. [B.C. §1322(a)(3); *see supra*, §1171] Similarly, a plan filed by an individual who was a debtor in a case that was dismissed in the preceding 180 days because of the debtor's intentional failure to obey court orders cannot be confirmed. [B.C. §109(g); *see supra*, §143]

   b. **Fees paid:** [§1196] All fees (*e.g.*, the filing fee), charges, or amounts required to be paid prior to confirmation by chapter 123 of title 28, or by the plan, must have been paid. [B.C. §1325(a)(2)]

   c. **Plan filed in good faith:** [§1197] The plan must be proposed in good faith. [B.C. §1325(a)(3)] Factors that are considered to be important in determining whether there is good faith include:

   (i) "Whether the debtor has *stated his debts and expenses accurately*;"

   (ii) "Whether he has made *any fraudulent misrepresentation* to mislead the bankruptcy court;" and

   (iii) "Whether he has *unfairly manipulated* the Bankruptcy Code."

   [Education Assistance Corp. v. Zellner, 827 F.2d 1222 (8th Cir. 1987); *see also In re* Smith, 848 F.2d 813 (7th Cir. 1988)—"totality of the circumstances" test; for an example of bad faith, *see* Noreen v. Slattengren, 974 F.2d 75 (8th Cir. 1992)]

   (1) **Amount of debtor's payment:** [§1198] Since the Code provides a *best efforts requirement* for application of the debtor's expected disposable income over a three-year period [B.C. §1325(b); *see infra*, §§1203-1204] "there is no longer any reason for the amount of a debtor's payments to be considered as even part of the good faith standard." [5 Collier ¶1325.04(3)]

(2) **When no objection filed:** [§1199]   If no objection to confirmation has been filed, the court may determine that the plan was proposed in good faith without receiving evidence on this issue. [Bankruptcy Rule 3015(f)]

d. **Unsecured creditors—"best interests of creditors" test met:** [§1200]   The plan must provide that *each unsecured creditor* holding an allowed claim will receive property having a present value, as of the effective date of the plan, of not less than the amount he would receive for his claim in a Chapter 7 liquidation on that date, taking into account the exemptions that would be available to the debtor. This element of confirmation usually is referred to as the "best interests of creditors test." [B.C. §1325(a)(4); *In re* Morris, 48 B.R. 313 (W.D. Va. 1985)]

e. **Secured creditors accept plan or receive collateral or amount of secured claim:** [§1201]   Each allowed secured claim provided for by the plan must be treated by one of the following three methods [B.C. §1325(a)(5)]:

(1) *The secured creditor accepts the plan* [B.C. §1325(a)(5)(A)];

(2) *The debtor surrenders the collateral* to the secured creditor [B.C. §1325(a)(5)(C)]; or

(3) *The plan preserves the creditor's lien* on the collateral and provides him with a distribution of *cash installments or other property* having a present value, on the effective date of the plan, of at least the amount of his allowed secured claim. [B.C. §1325(a)(5)(B)] As discussed earlier, a claim is treated as secured only up to the value of the creditor's collateral [B.C. §506(a); *see supra*, §523], and for an oversecured creditor, the secured claim includes (as allowed by the court) any attorney's fees, costs, or other charges agreed upon in the contract, as well as post-petition interest. [B.C. §506(b); *In re* Colvin, 57 B.R. 299 (Bankr. D. Utah 1986); *see supra*, §§529-531]

(a) *In determining present value*, many courts require the debtor to pay interest at the "rate charged by institutional lenders for similar commercial transactions" as the prevailing market rate. [*In re* Memphis Partners, L. P., *supra*, §1102; *In re* Southern States Motor Inns, Inc., *supra*, §1102; *see also* General Motors Acceptance Corp. v. Jones, *supra*, §1102—interest rate was that "charged by the creditor in the regular course of its business for loans similar in character, amount, and duration"; United Carolina Bank v. Hall, *supra*, §1102—rate of return creditor would obtain in its lending market for new loans (considering both the interest rates it receives and the expenses in obtaining the loans), but capped at the contract rate]

f. **Plan is feasible:** [§1202]   The plan must be feasible. Thus, the court must find that the debtor will be able to carry out the plan, taking into consideration her budget as well as dependents. [B.C. §1325(a)(6)]

3. **Best Efforts of Debtor:** [§1203]   Where an objection to confirmation is filed by an unsecured creditor or the Chapter 13 trustee, the court may not confirm the plan *unless*: (i) the plan proposes to pay the objecting creditor the *total amount*, although (according to Collier) not necessarily the present value, of his allowed

claim (or, if the objection is made by the trustee, the plan proposes to fully satisfy all the allowed unsecured claims), or (ii) all of the debtor's *"projected disposable income" for three years* from the due date of the first payment under the plan will be used to make payments in accordance with the plan. [B.C. §1325(b)(1); 5 Collier ¶1325.08(3); *see also In re* Anderson, 21 F.3d 355 (9th Cir. 1994)—projected disposable income is calculated at time of confirmation (plan need not provide for "*actual* disposable income"; *but see* Rowley v. Yarnall, 22 F.3d 190 (8th Cir. 1994)—Chapter 12 case holding that "projected disposable income" means "actual net disposable income received during the plan period"]

    a. **Disposable income:** [§1204] The Code defines disposable income as that portion of the debtor's income which is "not reasonably necessary" to maintain or support the debtor or her dependents, and (in applicable cases) to pay the expenses required for the continuation, operation, and preservation of the business of a debtor engaged in business. [B.C. §1325(b)(2); *In re* Tracey, 66 B.R. 63 (Bankr. D. Md. 1986)]

        (1) **Example:** Debtor files a Chapter 13 plan proposing to repay unsecured creditors 14% of their claims. Debtor's budget includes excessive expenses for Debtor's children's tuition at college and private secondary school and excessive expenses for food and housing. The proposed payments under the plan total $132 per month. An unsecured creditor objects to confirmation, and the court finds that the debtor's disposable income is $510 per month. Since the creditor will not receive the total amount of his claim and not all of debtor's disposable income is being used to make payments, confirmation will be denied. [B.C. §1325(b)(1); *In re* Jones, 55 B.R. 462 (Bankr. D. Minn. 1985)]

  4. **Payment Orders:** [§1205] After a plan has been confirmed, the court may order the debtor's employer, or any other entity providing income to the debtor, to make direct payments to the Chapter 13 trustee. The Social Security Administration, however, is not subject to such income deduction orders concerning the debtor's social security benefits. [B.C. §1325(c); *In re* Buren, 725 F.2d 1080 (6th Cir. 1984)]

F. PAYMENTS

1. **Commencement of Payments:** [§1206] The debtor's payments under a proposed plan must begin within *30 days* after the plan is filed, unless the court rules otherwise. [B.C. §1326(a)(1)]

    a. **Pre-confirmation payments:** [§1207] Any payment made before confirmation of a plan must be held by the trustee until the confirmation hearing. If the plan is confirmed, then the trustee makes distribution as provided for by the plan as soon as practicable. However, if confirmation is denied, the money must be returned to the debtor, less any unpaid administrative expenses that have been allowed. [B.C. §1326(a)(2)]

    b. **Distribution:** [§1208] Ordinarily, the payments under a confirmed plan are sent to creditors *by the trustee* unless the plan or the confirmation order provides otherwise, such as where a debtor engaged in business is allowed to perform this function. [B.C. §1326(c); *see In re* Aberegg, 961 F.2d 1307 (7th Cir. 1992)—plan confirmed allowing debtor to pay residential mortgagee directly]

2. **Administrative Expenses:** [§1209]   Prior to or concurrent with each payment to creditors under a Chapter 13 plan, the trustee is required to pay any unpaid administrative expenses or bankruptcy fees or charges, as well as the percentage fee set for a standing trustee (where one has been appointed). [B.C. §1326(b)] The deadline for paying the entire filing fee for the Chapter 13 petition is the time of the first payment to creditors. [5 Collier ¶1326.01(3)(a)]

G. POST-CONFIRMATION MATTERS

1. **Effects of Confirmation:** [§1210]   A confirmed plan binds the debtor *and every creditor*, regardless of whether a creditor has accepted or rejected the plan or has objected to confirmation of the plan, or whether his claim is provided for by the plan. [B.C. §1327(a)]

    a. **Property:** [§1211]   Unless the Chapter 13 plan or the confirmation order provides otherwise, confirmation causes all property of the estate to vest in the debtor "free and clear of any claim or interest of any creditor provided for by the plan." [B.C. §1327(b),(c)]

    (1) **Liens:** [§1212]   There is authority holding that a creditor's lien not provided for by the plan passes through bankruptcy undisturbed if the secured party fails to file a proof of claim and the claim is not provided for in the plan. [B.C. §§1327(c), 506(d); *In re* Thomas, 883 F.2d 991 (11th Cir. 1989)] However, if the *claim* is provided for by the plan, the secured party may more effectively protect his lien (in light of the language of section 1327(c)), by filing a proof of claim and requiring that the plan specifically provide for his retention of the lien. [5 Collier ¶1327.01(3)]

    b. **Debts:** [§1213]   In a Chapter 13 case, confirmation does *not* operate as a discharge of the debtor's debts. [B.C. §1328]

2. **Chapter 13 Discharge:** [§1214]   The debtor will be granted a discharge under Chapter 13 after she has made all payments under the plan, unless subsequent to the order for relief, she has executed a court-approved written waiver of discharge. [B.C. §1328(a)]

    a. **Debts discharged:** [§1215]   A standard Chapter 13 discharge includes all debts that are provided for by the plan or that have been disallowed by the court under section 502, *except* for [B.C. §1328(a)]:

    (1) *Long-term debts* for which the plan has provided for the curing of a default within a reasonable time and the maintenance of payments during the case, with the final payment being due after the last payment required by the Chapter 13 plan [B.C. §§1328(a)(1), 1322(b)(5); *see supra*, §1180];

    (2) *Alimony, maintenance, and spousal or child support* [B.C. §§1328(a)(2), 523(a)(5); *see supra*, §691];

    (3) *Student loans*, unless (i) the loan first became due more than *seven years* before the filing of the bankruptcy petition or (ii) there will be an *undue hardship* on the debtor and her dependents if the debt is not discharged. [B.C. §§1328(a)(2), 523(a)(8); *see supra*, §§703-705];

(4) *Health Education Assistance Loans* ("HEAL"), where the three conditions for discharge required by the applicable federal nonbankruptcy statute have not been satisfied [42 U.S.C. §292f(g); *In re* Johnson, *supra*, §706, *and see supra*, §§706-708];

(5) *Liability for drunk or drugged driving* that caused death or personal injury [B.C. §§1328(a)(2), 523(a)(9); *see supra*, §709];

(6) *Criminal restitution*, or a criminal fine, that is included in the debtor's sentence [B.C. §1328(a)(3)]; and

(7) *Allowed post-petition claims for necessary consumer debts* which were not approved in advance by the trustee, under circumstances where procuring his prior approval was practicable [B.C. §1328(d); §1305(a)(2); *see supra*, §1155-1157].

b. **Note—nonapplicability of section 523(a):** [§1216]   In a chapter 13 case, only the debts described above (*see supra*, §1215) are nondischargeable, and any other debts that would be nondischargeable under the general dischargeability provisions of section 523(a) (*see supra*, §§675 et seq.) *are discharged* by a standard Chapter 13 discharge.

c. **Hardship discharge:** [§1217]   If the debtor has not made all payments under the plan, the court, after notice and a hearing, may award a hardship discharge where the following three conditions exist:

(i) *The reason for the debtor's failure* to complete the payments under the plan is not one for which, in fairness, she should be held accountable [B.C. §1328(b)(1)];

(ii) *Each unsecured creditor holding an allowed claim has received property* under the plan, having a present value as of the effective date of the plan, of not less than the amount that he would have received for his claim in a case under Chapter 7 if the estate had been liquidated (*i.e.*, the "best interests of creditors test") [B.C. §1328(b)(2)]; and

(iii) *Modification of the plan is not practicable* [B.C. §1328(b)(3)].

[B.C. §1328(b)]

(1) **Example:** Debtor files a Chapter 13 plan, proposing to pay 40 monthly installments of $140 each. The plan is confirmed, and Debtor makes the payments, as scheduled, for 37 months, before dying. All of the unsecured creditors have received more than they would have received on their claims if the estate had been liquidated under Chapter 7. Under these circumstances, a hardship discharge is appropriate. [B.C. §1328(b); *In re* Graham, 63 B.R. 95 (Bankr. E.D. Pa. 1986)]

(2) **Debts discharged in hardship case:** [§1218]   A Chapter 13 hardship discharge includes the unsecured debts that would be discharged under a standard Chapter 13 discharge (*see supra*, §1215), except that it does not discharge *any* debts that would be nondischargeable under section 523(a) (*see supra*, §§675 et seq.). Any long-term debts provided for under the

cure provision of Code section 1322(b)(5) also are nondischargeable. [B.C. §1328(c); *see supra*, §1180]

- d. **Revocation of discharge:** [§1219] The court may revoke a Chapter 13 discharge that was *obtained by the debtor's fraud* if the party in interest seeking the revocation did not discover the fraud until after the discharge was awarded. The statute of limitations for requesting revocation of a discharge is one year from the date the discharge was granted, and notice and a hearing are required. [B.C. §1328(e); *and see In re* Cisneros, 994 F.2d 1462 (9th Cir. 1993)—discharge vacated because of mistake of fact]

3. **Post-Confirmation Modification:** [§1220] The debtor, the trustee, or an unsecured creditor may request a modification of a plan at any time after it has been confirmed but before all payments have been made. Modification may result in larger or smaller payments to a particular class, a longer or shorter payout period, or a change in the amount to be paid to a creditor to adjust for any payment obtained from a third party or from property outside of the plan. Generally, a request for post-confirmation modification of a plan occurs under circumstances where the income or expenses of the debtor have changed materially and unexpectedly. [B.C. §1329(a); 5 Collier ¶1329.01(1)(b)] For example, where the debtor's annual income (which at the time of confirmation had been approximately $80,000) had risen to almost $200,000, the court granted an unsecured creditor's motion (i) to increase the debtor's monthly payments under the plan from $800 to $1,500, and (ii) to extend the payment period from three years to five years. [*In re* Arnold, 869 F.2d 240 (4th Cir. 1989)] In another case, the debtor was permitted to increase payments to a secured creditor to cure post-petition arrearages that had accrued during a period when the debtor was unemployed for health reasons and was not receiving wages. However, the modification had to satisfy the requirements for confirmation, and, more specifically, the cram down provisions of Bankruptcy Code section 1325(a)(5). [*In re* Mannings, 47 B.R. 318 (Bankr. N.D. Ill. 1985); *see also In re* Hoggle, 12 F.3d 1008 (11th Cir. 1994)—plan modified to allow cure of post-confirmation default on secured claim]

4. **Revocation of Confirmation Order:** [§1221] Within 180 days after an order confirming a Chapter 13 plan has been entered, a party in interest may request that the order be revoked on the ground that it was procured by fraud. Revocation is discretionary. If after notice and a hearing the confirmation order is revoked, the court may grant the debtor time to propose and obtain confirmation of a modified plan. Otherwise, the court must convert or dismiss the case under section 1307. [B.C. §1330; 5 Collier ¶1330.01(2)]

5. **Debtor's Failure to Make Payments:** [§1222] If the debtor fails to make all payments under the plan, a party in interest or the United States trustee may move for dismissal of the case or conversion to Chapter 7 (*see supra*, §1162). Alternatively, the debtor might request a hardship discharge if the circumstances warrant (*see supra*, §1217).

XII. CHAPTER 12—FAMILY FARMER WITH REGULAR ANNUAL INCOME

chapter approach

In response to the economic crisis in the agricultural community, Congress amended the Bankruptcy Code to include a new chapter designed to provide relief for family farmers with regular annual income, while allowing these debtors to continue to operate their farms. Chapter 12 became effective on November 26, 1986, and it will be repealed automatically on October 1, 1998, unless extended.

If your exam question involves a farming operation, consider whether Chapter 12 will apply, and if so, its advantages for the debtor. Study carefully the Bankruptcy Code's definition of a *family farmer* [B.C. §101(18)], and note that corporations and partnerships, as well as individuals (and their spouses) may qualify for Chapter 12 relief. Recall that Chapter 12 gives the family farmer access to the bankruptcy court through a speedier, simpler, and less expensive procedure than under Chapter 11, and with higher debt limitations than those of Chapter 13. Also, in situations where farmland has depreciated greatly in value, Chapter 12 may constitute a favorable alternative for the family farmer debtor.

Although many of the provisions of Chapter 12 are very similar (or identical) to their counterparts found in Chapter 13, there are some important differences. Thus, for example, on an exam, it is important to note that Code section 361 does not apply in a Chapter 12 case, and that the issue of *adequate protection* must be resolved under section 1205 instead.

Finally, as to secured creditors, remember that the section 1111(b) election applies only in Chapter 11 cases (*see supra*, §§1026 *et seq.*) and, thus, is *not* available in Chapter 12.

A. ELIGIBILITY FOR RELIEF

1. **In General:** [§1223] Chapter 12 relief is available only to a family farmer with regular annual income. [B.C. §109(f)]

2. **Definitions**

   a. **"Family farmer with regular annual income":** [§1224] The Bankruptcy Code defines a family farmer with regular annual income as a "family farmer whose annual income is sufficiently stable and regular to enable such family farmer to make payments under a plan under Chapter 12 of this title." [B.C. §101(19)]

   b. **"Farming operation":** [§1225] The Code's definition of a farming operation "includes farming, tillage of the soil, dairy farming, ranching, production or raising of crops, poultry, or livestock, and production of poultry or livestock products in an unmanufactured state." [B.C. §101(21)]

      (1) **Compare—receiving rent from farmland:** [§1226] Receiving rental income from farmland leased to a tenant farmer might not, alone, constitute a farming operation, such as where rent is received upfront, in cash,

and *without any of the risks of farming*. [B.C. §101(20), (21); *In re* Armstrong, 812 F.2d 1024 (7th Cir. 1987)] However, many courts will consider whether, under the *totality of the circumstances*, the debtor intends to continue to engage in a farming operation even though he was not engaged in the physical activity of farming at the time the petition was filed. [*In re* Watford, 898 F.2d 1525 (11th Cir. 1990); *but see In re* Easton, 883 F.2d 630 (8th Cir. 1989—rejecting both tests]

c. **"Family farmer":** [§1227] The Code's definition of a family farmer includes (i) certain individuals, or individuals and their spouses, and (ii) certain corporations or partnerships. The definition varies depending on the nature of the entity. [B.C. §101(18)]

  (1) **Individuals:** [§1228] An individual (or an individual and spouse) is considered to be a family farmer if [B.C. §101(18)(A)]:

  (a) The individual (or individual and spouse) is *engaged in a farming operation*;

  (b) The individual's (or individual and spouse's) *total debts are not more than $1.5 million* [*In re* Stedman, 72 B.R. 49 (Bankr. D.N.D. 1987)];

  (c) As of the date of the bankruptcy petition, at least *80% of their total noncontingent, liquidated debts come from a farming operation* owned or operated by the individual (or individual and spouse), excluding any debt relating to their principal residence, unless the debt arises from a farming operation; and

  (d) *More than 50% of their gross income* for the taxable year before the taxable year in which the bankruptcy case is commenced was *derived from the farming operation*.

  (2) **Corporations and partnerships:** [§1229] A corporation or a partnership is considered to be a family farmer where [B.C. §101(18)(B)]:

  (a) If the entity is a corporation, its *stock is not traded publicly*;

  (b) *One family* (or one family and their relatives) *holds more than 50% of the outstanding stock or equity* in the corporation or the partnership;

  (c) The *family or the relatives conduct the farming operation* (*i.e.*, "some member of the family plays an active role in farming the land") [*In re* Tim Wargo & Sons, Inc., 869 F.2d 1128 (8th Cir. 1989); *and see supra*, §§1225-1226];

  (d) *More than 80% of the value of the corporate or partnership assets concerns the farming operation*;

  (e) The *total debts* of the corporation or the partnership are *not greater than $1.5 million*; and

(f) On the date that the Chapter 12 bankruptcy petition is filed, *at least 80% of the total noncontingent, liquidated debts* of the corporation or the partnership *come from a farming operation* that it owns or operates, excluding any debt relating to a home that it owns and that constitutes the principal residence of a shareholder or a partner, unless the debt arises from a farming operation. [*In re* Henderson Ranches, 75 B.R. 225 (Bankr. D. Idaho 1987)]

3. **Voluntary Petition:** [§1230] A case under Chapter 12 may be commenced only by the filing of a voluntary bankruptcy petition. [B.C. §§301, 303(a)]

4. **Multiple Petitions:** [§1231] A family farmer is *ineligible* for relief under Chapter 12 if the family farmer was a debtor in a case that was dismissed in the preceding 180 days (i) because of the family farmer's intentional failure to obey court orders or to appear before the court, or (ii) as a result of the family farmer's request for a voluntary dismissal of the case following a party's request for relief from the automatic stay. [B.C. §109(g)]

B. SIMILARITIES TO CHAPTER 13

Many of the elements of a Chapter 12 case bear a great resemblance to their counterparts in Chapter 13.

1. **Filing Petition:** [§1232] As mentioned, the Chapter 12 case may be commenced only by the filing of a *voluntary* petition. This is also true of a Chapter 13 case. [B.C. §§301, 303(a); *see supra*, §1140]

2. **Co-Debtor Stay:** [§1233] As in the Chapter 13 case, in addition to the automatic stay of Code section 362(a), there is a stay against individuals who are liable with the debtor on consumer debts or who have secured consumer debts of the debtor. [B.C. §§1201, 1301; *see supra*, §§1143 *et seq.*]

3. **Trustee:** [§1234] The appointment of a trustee (either a standing trustee or one for the particular case) is mandatory, and the trustee's duties in Chapter 12 and Chapter 13 are very similar as long as the debtor continues to be a debtor in possession. [B.C. §§1202(a),(b)(1)-(4), 1302; *and see supra*, §§1150-1151] However, if a Chapter 12 debtor is removed from possession (*see infra*, §1236) the trustee is charged with several of the duties of a Chapter 11 trustee and also with operation of the debtor's farm. [B.C. §§1202(b)(5), 1203]

4. **Property of Estate:** [§1235] Estate property is the same in a Chapter 12 case as in a Chapter 13 case. [B.C. §§1207(a), 1306(a); *see supra*, §1158] Ordinarily, a Chapter 12 debtor remains in possession of property of the estate unless otherwise directed by (i) a court order removing the debtor from possession, (ii) a provision in a confirmed plan, or (iii) the confirmation order. [B.C. §§1207(b), 1306(b); *see supra*, §1158] Furthermore, the Code expressly provides for a *Chapter 12 debtor in possession to continue to operate the farm*. [B.C. §§1203, 1304(b); *and see supra*, §1153]

   a. **Removal:** [§1236] The causes for removal of a debtor in possession parallel those in a Chapter 11 case, *i.e.*, for "fraud, dishonesty, incompetence, or gross mismanagement . . ." [B.C. §§1204(a), 1104(a)(1); *see supra*, §1010]

5. **The Plan:** [§1237]   The debtor has the *exclusive right* to file a plan, even if he is not a debtor in possession. [B.C. §§1221, 1321; *and see supra*, §1167]

6. **Duration of Plan:** [§1238]   Payments under the plan may not extend beyond *three years* unless, for cause, the court approves a longer period not exceeding *five years*. [B.C. §§1222(c), 1322(d); *and see supra*, §1191] However, the repayment of certain long-term debts is not subject to these limitations in a Chapter 12 case. [B.C. §1222(b)(5), (9)]

7. **Mandatory Provisions:** [§1239]   The mandatory provisions of a Chapter 12 plan are essentially the same as those under Chapter 13, including the treatment of priority claims, except that, in a Chapter 12 case, the holder of a particular claim or interest may consent to less favorable treatment than others of the same class. [B.C. §§1222(a), 1322(a); *and see supra*, §§1168-1171]

    a. **Note:** The *permissive* provisions of a Chapter 12 plan generally parallel those under Chapter 13; however, there are a few significant differences (*see infra*, §§1251-1254). [B.C. §§1222(b), 1322(b); *and see supra*, §§1172-1190]

8. **Confirmation:** [§1240]   The requirements for confirmation are the same as in Chapter 13 [B.C. §1225, 1325], except for one difference in the "best efforts" test (*see infra*, §1256). Objections to confirmation are governed by the same rule of procedure as in Chapter 13. [Bankruptcy Rule 3015(f)]

9. **Payments:** [§1241]   The Chapter 12 trustee's disbursement of payments to creditors under a confirmed plan parallels the procedure under Chapter 13. However, the Code does not provide a specific period within which a Chapter 12 debtor must begin to make payments (30 days for Chapter 13 debtor). [B.C. §§1226, 1326; *see supra*, §§1206-1209]

10. **Effects of Confirmation:** [§1242]   The Chapter 12 provisions concerning the binding nature of a confirmed plan and the vesting of property of the estate in the debtor "free and clear" are similar to those under Chapter 13, except to the extent that they are altered by the Chapter 12 discharge provisions (*see infra*, §1257). Also, as in Chapter 13, confirmation does not operate as a discharge. [B.C. §§1227, 1327; *see supra*, §§1210-1213]

11. **Modification of Plan:** [§1243]   The provisions for pre-confirmation and post-confirmation modification of a Chapter 12 plan parallel the respective provisions of Chapter 13. [B.C. §§1223, 1229, 1323, 1329; *see supra*, §§1192, 1220]

12. **Revocation of Confirmation Order:** [§1244]   The provisions for revocation of a Chapter 12 confirmation order procured by fraud parallel the corresponding provisions of Chapter 13. [B.C. §§1230, 1330; *see supra*, §1221]

C. DIFFERENCES FROM CHAPTER 13

Chapter 12 differs from Chapter 13 in the ways described below.

1. **Eligibility for Relief:** [§1245]   The debt ceiling for eligibility under Chapter 12 is $1.5 million, which is significantly higher than under Chapter 13 (unsecured debts less than $250,000, and secured debts less than $750,000). [B.C. §§101(18), 109(e); *see supra*, §1138]

2. **Filing of Plan:** [§1246]   A Chapter 12 debtor must file a plan *within 90 days* after the order for relief, unless an extension is granted for cause for which the debtor should not justly be held accountable. Under Chapter 13, the debtor ordinarily must file a plan within 15 days after the filing of the petition (or within 15 days after a case is converted to Chapter 13). [B.C. §1221; Bankruptcy Rule 3015(a), (b)]

3. **Commencement of Payments:** [§1247]   In Chapter 12, the debtor does *not* have to begin making payments within 30 days after the filing of the plan, as must be done under Chapter 13. As mentioned *supra*, §1241, there is no specific period in which a Chapter 12 debtor must begin making payments. [B.C. §§1226, 1326(a)(1)]

4. **Debtor's Rights and Duties:** [§1248]   In addition to permitting the debtor to continue to operate his farm, Chapter 12 confers on a debtor in possession *all of the rights and duties of a Chapter 11 trustee*, except the right to compensation and the duty to investigate the debtor. [B.C. §§1203, 1303, 1304]

5. **Adequate Protection:** [§1249]   The Code expressly states that *section 361* (regarding adequate protection; *see supra*, §§761 et seq.) *is inapplicable in Chapter 12 cases*, and, thus, a separate section has been enacted to deal exclusively with this issue under Chapter 12. [B.C. §1205] This provision specifies that adequate protection is designed to protect against a decline in the value of the *property* securing a claim, rather than against a decrease in the value of an entity's interest in the property. The statute sets forth the following nonexclusive methods of providing adequate protection in a Chapter 12 case:

   (i) *A cash payment or periodic cash payments* [B.C. §1205(b)(1)];

   (ii) *An additional or replacement lien* [B.C. §1205(b)(2)];

   (iii) *If the collateral is farmland, the reasonable rent* prevailing in that locality, taking into account "the rental value, net income, and earning capacity of the property" [B.C. §1205(b)(3); *In re* Kocher, 78 B.R. 844 (Bankr. S.D. Ohio 1987)]; or

   (iv) *Other relief* that will protect the value of the collateral, other than by granting the creditor an administrative expense claim [B.C. §1205(b)(4)].

   Note: The concept of "indubitable equivalence" is absent from the Chapter 12 provisions concerning adequate protection. [B.C. §§1205, 361(3)]

6. **Sales Free and Clear:** [§1250]   To reduce the level of farming operations, a *Chapter 12 trustee* may sell farmland or farm equipment free and clear of liens or other interests, on the condition that the proceeds received from the sale become subject to the secured creditor's interest. Notice and a hearing are required. [B.C. §1206; *but see In re* Brileya, 108 B.R. 444 (Bankr. D. Vt. 1989)—debtor-in-possession (*i.e.*, the family farmer) authorized to sell farmland under this provision]

7. **Permissive Provisions of Chapter 12 Plan:** [§1251]   The provisions that may be included in a plan under Chapter 12 differ from those allowable in a Chapter 13 plan, as follows:

a. **Modifying rights:** [§1252] The power of a Chapter 12 debtor to modify the rights of secured or unsecured creditors is not subject to the exception found in Chapter 13 regarding a claim secured solely by a security interest in real property constituting the principal residence of the debtor (*see supra*, §1175). [B.C. §§1222(b)(2), 1322(b)(2)]

b. **Sale or distribution of property:** [§1253] A Chapter 12 plan may propose to sell estate property or distribute it among entities having an interest in the property. [B.C. §1222(b)(8)]

c. **Payment of secured claims:** [§1254] A Chapter 12 plan also may provide for secured creditors to be paid over a longer period than the three or five years referred to in Bankruptcy Code section 1222(c) (*see supra*, §1238). However, any such provision must be in conformity with the requirement for confirmation contained in section 1225(a)(5) (*see infra*, §1271). [B.C. §1222(b)(9); Travelers Insurance Co. v. Bullington, 878 F.2d 354 (11th Cir. 1989)—plan's 30-year mortgage upheld]

8. **Confirmation Hearing:** [§1255] In a Chapter 12 case, the court must conclude the confirmation hearing within **45 days** after the plan is filed, "except for cause." This requirement does not exist in Chapter 13. [B.C. §§1224, 1324]

9. **Best Efforts:** [§1256] If an unsecured creditor or the trustee objects to confirmation of a Chapter 12 plan that does not propose full repayment of the respective allowed claims(s), confirmation will be denied unless the debtor commits to payments under the plan all of his expected disposable income for three years ***or for any longer plan period*** approved by the court, ***not exceeding five years*** (such as where debtor needs a "reserve" to finance the next year's farming operations). [5 Collier ¶1225.04] The corresponding requirement under Chapter 13, however, is limited to ***three years***. [B.C. §§1225(b)(1), 1325(b)(1); *see supra*, §1203]

10. **Discharge:** [§1257] A standard discharge under Chapter 12 differs significantly from a standard Chapter 13 discharge, in that ***all debts that are nondischargeable under section 523*** (*see supra*, §675) are not discharged in a Chapter 12 case. [B.C. §§1228(a)(2), 1328(a)]

D. DIFFERENCES FROM CHAPTER 11

Some of the more important distinctions between Chapter 12 and Chapter 11 are set forth below.

1. **Voluntary Petition Only:** [§1258] The Chapter 12 case can be commenced only by the filing of a voluntary petition, unlike the Chapter 11 case. [B.C. §§301, 303(a)]

2. **Trustee:** [§1259] A Chapter 12 trustee (either a standing trustee or one appointed for the particular case) serves in the case even though the family farmer remains a debtor in possession unless removed by the court. [B.C. §1202]

3. **Co-Debtor Stay:** [§1260] In a Chapter 12 case, the co-debtor stay applies, while it does not in a case under Chapter 11. [B.C. §1201]

4. **Adequate Protection:** [§1261] Under Chapter 12, adequate protection is determined by Code section 1205 (*see supra*, §1249), rather than under section 361 as in the Chapter 11 case.

5. **No Creditors' Committees:** [§1262] There is no provision in Chapter 12 for the appointment of creditors' committees or equity security holders' committees, as occurs in Chapter 11 cases. [B.C. §1102]

6. **Filing Plan—By Debtor Only:** [§1263] In a Chapter 12 case, no party other than the debtor may file a plan.

7. **No Impairment of Classes:** [§1264] The concept of impairment of classes of claims or interests does not apply in a Chapter 12 case, since it is unique to Chapter 11. [B.C. §1124; *see supra*, §§1062 *et seq.*]

8. **No Solicitation of Acceptance or Rejection:** [§1265] Under Chapter 12, creditors and equity security holders do not vote to accept or reject the plan, and, thus, the debtor is not burdened by the necessities of preparing and obtaining court approval of a disclosure statement or of soliciting acceptances from the various classes. [B.C. §§1125-1126]

9. **Earlier Confirmation:** [§1266] The Chapter 12 confirmation hearing is ordinarily concluded much earlier (within 45 days after the plan is filed) than it would be under Chapter 11. [B.C. §§1224, 1128]

10. **No Absolute Priority:** [§1267] The absolute priority rule does not apply in a Chapter 12 case, and therefore, the debtor is not barred from keeping his property where the plan fails to provide for full satisfaction of the claims of nonconsenting unsecured creditors. [B.C. §1129(b)(2)(B)(ii); *see supra*, §1109]

11. **Confirmation of Plan Not a Discharge:** [§1268] Confirmation of the debtor's plan does not constitute a discharge under Chapter 12 as it generally does in Chapter 11 cases. [B.C. §§1228, 1141(d)]

12. **No Election by Partially Secured Creditors:** [§1269] Partially secured creditors cannot elect to have their claims treated as fully secured under Chapter 12. This election is a unique feature of Chapter 11. [B.C. §1111(b); *see supra*, §§1026 *et seq.*]

13. **Trustee Pays Creditors:** [§1270] Ordinarily, the trustee disburses the payments to creditors under the Chapter 12 plan. [B.C. §1226(c)]

E. SECURED CREDITORS

1. **Requirement for Confirmation:** [§1271] Each allowed secured claim provided for by the plan must be treated by one of the following three methods:

   (i) *The secured creditor accepts the plan* [B.C. §1225(a)(5)(A)];

   (ii) *The debtor surrenders the collateral* to the secured creditor [B.C. §1225(a)(5)(C); *see In re* Kerwin, 996 F.2d 552 (2d Cir. 1993)—debtor surrendered to oversecured creditor portion of collateral (farmland) valued at amount equal to the debt, and debtor retained rest of collateral for farming, without creditor's lien]; or

(iii) *The plan preserves the creditor's lien* on the collateral and provides him with distribution of *cash installments or other property* having a present value, on the effective date of the plan, of at least the amount of his allowed secured claim [B.C. §1225(a)(5)(B)].

[B.C. §1225(a)(5)]

2. **Permissive Plan Provisions:** [§1272] Where there has been a large decline in the value of the debtor's farm, Chapter 12 may be used to "write down" a creditor's secured claim to the market value of the collateral, and to provide for payments to be made over a longer period of time and at a lower (but reasonable) rate of interest. [B.C. §1222(b)(2), (9)]

   a. **Example:** Debtor borrows $1.7 million from Bank, at 13% interest, secured by a 25-year first mortgage on Debtor's farm, which is valued at $2 million. Several years later, Debtor files a Chapter 12 bankruptcy petition. The market value of the farm has decreased to $1 million. Debtor's plan provides for Bank to retain its lien on the farm, and for Bank's claim to be modified by reducing the principal of its allowed secured claim to $1 million (the value of the collateral), and proposing payments, having a present value of $1 million, over 30 years at a discount rate of 10%. The provision should be permissible if the terms are found to be reasonable. It also satisfies the applicable requirement for confirmation. [B.C. §§1222(b), 1225(a)(5)(B)] Note that Bank's total claim of $1.7 million has been bifurcated, and that it now holds an unsecured claim in the amount of $700,000. [B.C. §506(a)]

F. **UNSECURED CREDITORS**

1. **"Best Interests of Creditors Test":** [1273] As in a Chapter 13 case, the plan must provide that *each unsecured creditor* holding an allowed claim will receive property having a present value, as of the effective date of the plan, that is not less than the amount he would receive for his claim in a case under Chapter 7 if the estate were liquidated on that date, taking into account the exemptions that would be available to the debtor. [B.C. §1225(a)(4)]

2. **Best Efforts:** [§1274] If an unsecured creditor or the Chapter 12 trustee objects to confirmation of a plan that does not propose full repayment (but, according to Collier, not necessarily the present value) of the creditor's allowed claim (or, for an objecting trustee, full repayment of all allowed unsecured claims), the court may not confirm the plan unless the debtor commits to payments under the plan all of his *"projected disposable income"* for three years or for any longer plan period approved by the court not exceeding five years. [B.C. §1222(c)] [B.C. §1225(b)(1); 5 Collier ¶1225.04; *see also In re* Anderson, *supra*, §1203—Chapter 13 case holding that projected disposable income is calculated at the time of confirmation (plan need not provide for *"actual* disposable income"); *but see* Rowley v. Yarnall, *supra*, §1203—Chapter 12 case holding that "projected disposable income" means "actual net disposable income received during the plan period."]

   a. **Disposable income:** [§1275] The Code defines disposable income as that portion of the debtor's income "which is not reasonably necessary" to maintain or support the debtor or his dependents, or to pay the expenses required for the continuation, operation, and preservation of the debtor's business (which may include minor nonfarming businesses). [B.C. §1225(b)(2); 5 Collier ¶1225.04]

G. CONVERSION OR DISMISSAL

1. **Voluntary Conversion to Chapter 7:** [§1276] The debtor has an absolute right to convert the case to Chapter 7, and this right cannot be waived. [B.C. §1208(a)]

2. **Voluntary Dismissal:** [§1277] The debtor also has the nonwaivable right to dismiss the case if it has not been converted earlier from Chapter 7 or Chapter 11. [B.C. §1208(b)] [*In re* Cotton, 992 F.2d 311 (11th Cir. 1993)]

3. **Discretionary Conversion to Chapter 7:** [§1278] The court may convert the case to Chapter 7, on the request of a party in interest, where the debtor has committed *fraud* concerning the case. Notice and a hearing are required. [B.C. §1208(d); *In re* Graven, 936 F.2d 378 (8th Cir. 1991)—conversion to Chapter 7 despite debtor's motion to dismiss]

4. **Discretionary Dismissal:** [§1279] On the request of a party in interest, the court may dismiss the case for cause. Notice and a hearing are required. [B.C. §1208(c)]

    a. **"Cause":** [§1280] Reasons for which a Chapter 12 case may be dismissed include:

    (1) *Gross mismanagement or unreasonable delay by the debtor* that is detrimental to creditors [B.C. §1208(c)(1)];

    (2) *Failure to pay any necessary fees* or charges imposed under chapter 123 of title 28 [B.C. §1208(c)(2)];

    (3) *Failure to file a plan within 90 days* after the order for relief, or within any period of extension granted by the court [B.C. §§1208(c)(3), 1221];

    (4) *Failure to begin making timely payments* under a plan that has been confirmed [B.C. §1208(c)(4)];

    (5) *Denial of confirmation* of the debtor's plan, and denial of a request for an extension of time to file another plan or to modify the plan [B.C. §1208(c)(5)];

    (6) *A material default by the debtor* concerning a provision of a plan that has been confirmed [B.C. §1208(c)(6)];

    (7) *Revocation of a confirmation order that was procured by fraud*, and the court's refusal to confirm a modified plan [B.C. §§1208(c)(7), 1230];

    (8) *Termination of a confirmed plan because of the happening of a condition* contained in the plan [B.C. §1208(c)(8)];

    (9) *Continuing loss* to the Chapter 12 estate, and the *absence of a reasonable probability of rehabilitation* [B.C. §1208(c)(9)];

(10) ***Lack of good faith*** in filing the Chapter 12 petition [*In re* Turner, 71 B.R. 120 (Bankr. D. Mont. 1987)]; or

(11) ***The debtor's fraud*** in the case [B.C. §1208(d)].

H. SUNSET PROVISION [§1281]

On October 1, 1998, Chapter 12 will automatically be repealed (unless extended). However, the provisions of Chapter 12 will remain in effect for all cases filed before the deadline, and thus all matters and proceedings in pending cases will be adjudicated as if the Chapter had not expired. [Family Farmer Bankruptcy Act of 1986, Pub. L. No. 99-554, §302(f); P. L. No. 103-65, §1]

REVIEW QUESTIONS

FILL IN ANSWER

JURISDICTION AND PROCEDURE

1. Several months before bankruptcy, Debtor was involved in an automobile accident in which the driver of the other car (Victim) was seriously injured when Debtor failed to stop at a red light. Victim files a claim for personal injury in Debtor's bankruptcy case. Will Victim's claim be tried in the bankruptcy court? _____

2. Debtor files a Chapter 7 petition, and Trustee brings two actions in the bankruptcy court: one to avoid and recover a fraudulent transfer made by Debtor within a year before bankruptcy, and the other to recover a large pre-petition account receivable owed to Debtor.

   a. Is Trustee's action to avoid and recover the fraudulent transfer a core proceeding? _____

   b. Is Trustee's action to recover the pre-petition account receivable a core proceeding? _____

3. Debtor files a Chapter 7 petition, and Shareholders file claims for damages, under section 10(b) of the Securities Exchange Act of 1934, arising out of purchases of Debtor's preferred stock. Intricate questions of law are presented to the court concerning both Debtor's liability under the Securities Exchange Act of 1934, as well as the extent to which the Bankruptcy Code requires shareholders' claims to be subordinated for the purpose of distribution. If a motion for withdrawal is filed timely, must the proceeding be withdrawn by the district court? _____

4. Debtor and Uncle are residents of State X. Debtor brings an action in state court under Grandfather's will to recover certain real property from Uncle. The outcome hinges on the interpretation of an obscure state statute, enacted in 1935, which modified the common law Rule Against Perpetuities. The trial in state court begins on the day before the filing of Debtor's bankruptcy petition, and it is expected to last for three days. Debtor removes the action from state court to the bankruptcy court. Uncle files a motion in the bankruptcy court requesting that the bankruptcy court abstain from hearing the proceeding and that it be remanded to state court. Is abstention appropriate? _____

5. Debtor is in default on an installment note, and Creditor files a motion requesting relief from the automatic stay in order to foreclose on certain collateral securing the note. The bankruptcy court denies relief from the stay. Can Creditor appeal the decision? _____

COMMENCEMENT AND ADMINISTRATION OF THE CASE

6. Debtor, a solvent individual residing in Maryland, is undergoing financial difficulties and is thinking about filing a voluntary bankruptcy petition. Will the fact that she is not insolvent preclude Debtor from being eligible for relief under the Bankruptcy Code? _____

7. In January, Debtor (an individual) files a Chapter 13 petition, which is dismissed in March because of Debtor's intentional failure to obey certain orders of the bankruptcy court. In June, Debtor seeks to file another Chapter 13 petition. Is she eligible?

8. Debtor Corporation desires to file a voluntary Chapter 11 petition. Is a resolution by its board of directors necessary?

9. Debtor is engaged in a multistate manufacturing business and is indebted to hundreds of creditors. Since Debtor very consistently is not paying its debts as they become due, three creditors holding unsecured claims totaling $3,000 file an involuntary petition against Debtor. Will an order for relief be entered?

10. Assume the same facts as in Question 9, above, except that the unsecured claims of the petitioning creditors total $12,000. Debtor defends on the basis that the court, in determining whether Debtor is "generally not paying its debts as they become due," should consider only the amount of the unpaid liabilities and not the number of unpaid creditors. Is this a valid defense?

11. Debtor owes Creditor $11,000 pursuant to an unsecured promissory note. The note has been in default for 10 months, although, as Creditor is well aware, Debtor has been paying all of his other debts (which range from $50,000 to $100,000) as they mature. Creditor is upset and files an involuntary bankruptcy petition against Debtor to harass Debtor and collect the debt. The court dismisses the petition. Will the court award any damages to Debtor?

OFFICERS OF THE ESTATE

12. An involuntary Chapter 11 petition is filed against Debtor Corporation, a nationwide marketing firm, and an order for relief is entered in the case. Because of the incompetence of current management, Trustee is appointed under Bankruptcy Code section 1104. Does Trustee have the authority to operate the Debtor's business?

13. Assume the same facts as in Question 12, above. Does Trustee have the authority to waive Debtor Corporation's attorney-client privilege concerning communications made by the former officers and directors to Debtor Corporation's attorney prior to bankruptcy?

14. Debtor files a voluntary Chapter 11 petition, and allegations of fraud and dishonesty are made against Debtor's management. If the court does not order the appointment of a trustee, are there any means by which the charges against Debtor's management can be investigated appropriately?

15. Debtor files a voluntary Chapter 7 petition, and a trustee is appointed. Because of the complicated financial and legal issues in the case, the trustee wants to hire an attorney and an accountant. Should court approval of their employment be obtained before any professional services are rendered?

THE BANKRUPTCY ESTATE AND THE TRUSTEE'S AVOIDING POWERS

16. Debtor, an individual, files a Chapter 7 petition. Are the wages that Debtor earns post-petition included in property of the estate?

17. Lessee leases 10 computers from Lessor, with the term of the lease beginning on January 1 and ending on December 31. The lease contains a provision that causes a termination of the lease and a forfeiture of Lessee's interest in the computers if and when Lessee becomes a debtor in a case under the Bankruptcy Code. On June 1, Lessee files a voluntary Chapter 11 petition. Is Lessee's leasehold interest in the computers included in property of the estate? _____

18. Debtor, who owes $10,000 to Bank, files a Chapter 7 petition, and Bank receives notice of the filing. Can Bank temporarily freeze the $5,000 remaining in Debtor's checking account without being considered in violation of the automatic stay? _____

19. Debtor owes $25,000 in federal income tax. On September 1, the tax is assessed, thereby fixing a lien on Debtor's property. On November 1, Debtor files a Chapter 7 petition and the IRS has not yet filed notice of the tax lien. Is the government's tax lien voidable by the bankruptcy trustee? _____

20. Debtor purchases office equipment on credit, granting Seller a security interest in the equipment. Six months later, Debtor files a Chapter 7 petition and Seller has failed to perfect his security interest. Can Trustee avoid Seller's security interest in the equipment? _____

21. Every month for the past 10 years, Debtor has bought goods on credit from Supplier, always remitting full payment within 30 days after receipt of the goods, in accordance with the agreement between the parties and consistent with the norm in Supplier's industry. If Debtor receives goods from Supplier on June 1, pays for them in full on July 1 in the ordinary course of business, and files a Chapter 7 petition on August 1, can the bankruptcy trustee avoid the payment to Supplier as a preferential transfer? _____

22. Debtor, an individual, has suffered numerous financial reverses and decides to file a voluntary Chapter 7 petition. Ten days before filing, Debtor forms a corporation solely for the purpose of sheltering assets that otherwise would be used to satisfy creditors. On the day before bankruptcy, Debtor transfers her $250,000 house to the corporation for no consideration. Is the transfer voidable by the bankruptcy trustee? _____

23. Debtor is in default to Creditor on a $40,000 debt, and Creditor forecloses on its collateral, a building. The foreclosure sale occurs on February 1, when Debtor is insolvent. The sale has been advertised appropriately and is conducted regularly and in compliance with "all the requirements of the State's foreclosure law," proper notice has been given, and there is no evidence of any collusion. Creditor purchases the building for a price of $40,000. The fair market value of the building is $90,000. On July 1, Debtor files a Chapter 7 petition. Is the transfer voidable by the bankruptcy trustee? _____

24. On March 1, Debtor buys and takes possession of new office furniture, while granting Seller a purchase-money security interest in the furniture. On March 5, Debtor files a voluntary Chapter 7 petition. Applicable state law provides that a purchase-money security interest perfected within 10 days after the debtor receives possession of the collateral has priority over an intervening lien creditor. [U.C.C. §9-301(2)] On March 8, Seller perfects its security interest.

a. Will Seller's security interest have priority over the bankruptcy trustee's rights and avoiding powers under the strongarm clause?

b. Does Seller's post-petition perfection of its security interest violate the automatic stay?

25. Debtor purchases goods on credit from Seller and is insolvent when she receives the merchandise on June 1. On June 2, Debtor files a voluntary bankruptcy petition. Can Seller reclaim the goods from Debtor?

CLAIMS OF CREDITORS

26. Debtor, an insolvent corporation, files a Chapter 7 petition. Creditor holds an unsecured claim evidenced by a promissory note bearing an interest rate of 14%. Is Creditor entitled to post-petition interest on his claim?

27. Debtor files a Chapter 11 petition, and thousands of tort victims file unliquidated personal injury claims arising from certain defective products sold by Debtor. May the bankruptcy court estimate the claims for the purpose of allowance?

28. Debtor files a Chapter 7 petition. She owes Bank $100,000 pursuant to an 11% mortgage note secured by land that has a fair market value of $90,000. Is Bank's claim fully secured?

29. Assume the same facts as in Question 28, above, except that the value of the land is $120,000. Is Bank entitled to post-petition interest on its claim?

30. Debtor files a Chapter 11 petition in an attempt to reorganize its business. Will the wages to be paid to its employees for post-petition services be classified as administrative expenses in the case?

31. Debtor files a Chapter 7 petition and owes $50,000 in unsecured pre-petition federal income taxes for the taxable year preceding bankruptcy. Will the tax claim be treated as a general unsecured claim?

32. Debtor files a Chapter 11 petition. Creditor's claim is fully secured by a lien on Debtor's equipment, which is depreciating rapidly. Creditor requests and is denied relief from the automatic stay, but the court orders Debtor to provide Creditor with an additional lien on other property as adequate protection. If the additional lien ultimately proves to be deficient, causing Creditor to be undersecured to the extent of $20,000, will the undersecured portion of Creditor's claim be treated as a general unsecured claim?

33. Debtor files a Chapter 7 petition. One of the unsecured claims in the case is held by Debtor's President, who personally had loaned Debtor $100,000. Will President's claim be subordinated to the claims of the other unsecured creditors?

DEBTOR'S EXEMPTIONS AND DISCHARGE OF INDEBTEDNESS

34. Husband and Wife file a joint Chapter 7 petition. If the applicable state law has not opted out of the federal exemption scheme, may Husband elect the federal exemptions while Wife elects the state exemptions?

35. Debtor files a Chapter 7 petition. Prior to bankruptcy, Debtor had bought household goods on credit, granting to Seller a purchase-money security interest in all of the items purchased. Can Debtor avoid Seller's security interest, under Bankruptcy Code section 522(f), to the extent that it impairs an exemption? _____

36. Debtor, an individual, files a *Chapter 7* petition. Would the following debts be dischargeable in his case?

    a. A judgment for $1,500 arising from Debtor's fraudulent sale of an automobile to his neighbor. _____

    b. A debt for $5,000, which Debtor borrowed from Creditor six months prior to bankruptcy. Debtor fails to list or schedule the debt, and Creditor has neither notice nor actual knowledge of the bankruptcy case and thus is unable to timely file a proof of claim. _____

    c. A debt owed for misappropriation of $50,000 in Debtor's capacity as a bank officer. (Assume that the act did not constitute larceny or embezzlement.) _____

    d. A debt for $25,000 that was intended to constitute a property settlement arising out of a separation agreement with Debtor's first spouse. _____

    e. A debt in the amount of $10,000 for alimony owed to Debtor's second spouse, arising out of a separation and property settlement agreement. _____

37. Debtor owes Creditor $5,000 and files a Chapter 7 petition. All of her debts are discharged (including the debt owed to Creditor), and she does not reaffirm any debts. May Debtor voluntarily repay the debt owed to Creditor following her discharge in bankruptcy? _____

38. Debtor, an individual, desires to reaffirm a consumer debt secured by personal property. All of the elements of an enforceable reaffirmation agreement are satisfied, and Debtor is represented by an attorney during the negotiation of the agreement. Is it necessary to obtain independent court approval of the agreement? _____

39. Debtor files a Chapter 7 petition and does not desire to reaffirm any of his debts. Is the court required to hold a discharge hearing? _____

40. Debtor files a Chapter 7 petition and desires to retain possession of her car, which has a fair market value of $5,000. The car was financed by Bank, which holds a purchase-money security interest in the car. The debt owed to Bank is $7,000, the trustee has abandoned any interest in the car, and Debtor wants to reaffirm the debt. However, Bank has a policy of "no reaffirmations" and insists that Debtor may keep the car only if she redeems it by paying $5,000 in a lump-sum payment. If Debtor is current in her car payments to Bank and has not defaulted on any installment, will she be able to retain possession of the car other than by redemption? _____

ADMINISTRATIVE POWERS

41. Debtor owes Creditor $100,000 pursuant to a mortgage note secured by a building that has a fair market value of $90,000. Creditor seeks relief from the automatic stay, under Code section 362(d)(1), alleging that his interest in the building is not adequately protected unless he receives interest payments for the delay caused by the automatic stay in exercising his right to foreclose on the building and reinvest the proceeds. Is Creditor entitled to interest payments on his collateral as adequate protection? _____

42. Debtor files a voluntary Chapter 7 petition. Would the following post-petition actions be enjoined by the automatic stay? In each instance, assume that the nondebtor party has received notice of Debtor's bankruptcy filing.

    a. Creditor's commencement of a lawsuit against Debtor in a state court to recover a pre-petition claim. _____

    b. Bank's repossession of Debtor's automobile, which constitutes collateral securing a pre-petition claim. _____

    c. Telephone calls and letters from Appliance Store's credit department demanding payment of a pre-petition claim. _____

    d. Continuation of an administrative proceeding by the National Labor Relations Board to determine whether Debtor's pre-petition termination of a collective bargaining agreement constituted an unfair labor practice. _____

43. Debtor files a *Chapter 7* petition. Creditor requests relief from the automatic stay, under Code section 362(d)(2), to foreclose on certain real property securing a pre-petition debt that is in default. The debt is $50,000, and the collateral has a fair market value of $25,000. Will the court grant relief from the stay? _____

44. Debtor Corporation files a Chapter 7 petition and Trustee seeks to sell the company's factory building to a willing buyer. Is a hearing concerning the proposed sale *required*? _____

45. Debtor files a Chapter 11 petition and has $100,000 on deposit in a checking account at Bank, which serves as collateral for a debt owed to Secured Creditor. May Debtor use the money in the account in the ordinary course of business? _____

46. Debtor files a Chapter 11 petition and is unable to obtain unsecured post-petition financing without offering more than an administrative expense priority. May the court authorize an unsecured loan from Bank that will have priority over all administrative expense claims in the case, as well as over any superpriority administrative expense claims that might result from the failure of adequate protection? _____

47. Debtor leases industrial equipment pursuant to a lease that begins on January 1 and ends on December 31. After defaulting on the payments due under the lease for June, July, and August, Debtor files a Chapter 11 petition on August 15. May Debtor assume the lease? _____

48. On October 1, Debtor, a professional singer, enters into a binding agreement with Variety, Inc. to perform in a series of concerts to be held the following summer. Her compensation will be $25,000. On March 1, Debtor files a voluntary

Chapter 11 petition and a trustee is appointed for cause. May the trustee assume the contract? _____

49. Debtor is the tenant of certain nonresidential real property and has defaulted on the monthly rental payments for six consecutive months, as the result of which Landlord unilaterally terminates the lease in accordance with terms of the agreement and notifies Debtor in writing. Under applicable state law, all steps necessary to terminate the lease have occurred, and there is no state anti-forfeiture law under which the termination could be reversed. Debtor then files a Chapter 11 petition while still in possession of the premises. Can Debtor assume the lease? _____

50. Debtor is the lessee under an unexpired lease of residential real property, and she files a voluntary Chapter 11 petition. May she assume the lease three months after the order for relief if the court has not yet confirmed a Chapter 11 plan? _____

CHAPTER 7—LIQUIDATION

51. An involuntary Chapter 7 petition is filed against Debtor. Certain trade creditors hold unsecured claims that arose in the ordinary course of Debtor's business after the commencement of the case but prior to the entry of the order for relief and the appointment of the trustee. If the nonexempt assets available for distribution are sufficient to pay all administrative expenses but not all of the involuntary gap claims, will the trade creditors be entitled to receive any distribution? _____

52. Debtor files a voluntary Chapter 7 petition and refuses to testify at a hearing in the case. She does not assert the constitutional privilege against self-incrimination as an excuse. Will Debtor be denied a discharge? _____

53. Debtor files a voluntary Chapter 7 petition. Shortly thereafter, she decides that Chapter 13 would be more appropriate and seeks to convert the case to one under that chapter. Creditor objects. May Debtor convert the case to Chapter 13? _____

54. Debtor, an individual with primarily consumer debts, files a voluntary Chapter 7 petition, substantially misrepresenting his financial condition in his schedules and statement of financial affairs. His future expected income is sufficient to pay all of his unsecured debts in full under a Chapter 13 plan, and his anticipated family budget is grossly extravagant. If the United States trustee files a motion to dismiss the case, under Bankruptcy Code section 707(b), will the motion be granted? _____

CHAPTER 11—REORGANIZATION

55. Debtor files a Chapter 11 petition, and a committee of unsecured creditors is appointed. Can Attorney be hired by the creditors' committee if Attorney also represents an unsecured creditor in the case? _____

56. Debtor files a Chapter 11 petition. Although the company shows a loss for the past two years, it hopes to reorganize under the Bankruptcy Code. Will a trustee automatically be appointed in the case? _____

57. Debtor files a Chapter 11 petition. Creditor holds an allowed claim in the amount of $100,000, secured by collateral having a fair market value of $75,000. Can Creditor elect to have his claim treated as secured to the extent of $100,000? _____

58. On February 1, Debtor files a voluntary Chapter 11 petition and continues to operate the business as a debtor in possession. Under normal circumstances, may Creditor file a proposed plan on April 1? _____

59. Debtor files a Chapter 11 petition and subsequently files a proposed plan designating a separate class for all unsecured claims that are less than $100. Is this classification permissible? _____

60. Debtor files a Chapter 11 petition and subsequently files a proposed plan. May Debtor begin to solicit acceptances from the various classes even though his disclosure statement has not yet been approved by the court? _____

61. An involuntary Chapter 11 petition is filed against Debtor Corporation, and an order for relief is entered in the case. Debtor Corporation files a proposed plan of reorganization that is accepted by all classes and confirmed by the court. Does confirmation operate as a discharge with respect to Debtor Corporation? _____

CHAPTER 13—INDIVIDUAL WITH REGULAR INCOME

62. Debtor is employed and earns $2,000 per week. She owes $300,000 in unsecured debts and $600,000 in secured debts. Is she eligible for relief under Chapter 13? _____

63. Debtor owes $90,000 in unsecured debts, owes no secured debts, and earns a salary of $1,000 per week. Three creditors file an involuntary Chapter 13 petition against Debtor. If Debtor is generally not paying his debts as they become due, will an order for relief be entered? _____

64. Debtor files a Chapter 13 petition accompanied by a plan proposing to pay all unsecured creditors in full over a period of three years. One of his liabilities is an unsecured consumer loan (from Bank) that was co-signed by Fellow Employee. Can Bank sue Fellow Employee while the Chapter 13 case is pending? _____

65. Debtor files a Chapter 13 petition. She operates her own business as a sole proprietor, she has regular income from the business, and her debts do not exceed the limitations for eligibility established under Code section 109(e). Is she considered to be a "debtor engaged in business?" _____

66. Debtor files a Chapter 13 petition.

    a. May Debtor retain possession of property of the estate? _____

    b. Will Debtor's wages from post-petition services be included in property of the estate? _____

67. Debtor files a Chapter 13 petition. She owes $10,000 in unsecured federal income taxes for the taxable year prior to bankruptcy. May her Chapter 13 plan provide for the IRS to be paid 70% of its claim over a period of three years if the IRS does not consent to such treatment? _____

68. Debtor files a Chapter 13 petition accompanied by a proposed plan that is confirmed by the court. Does confirmation operate as a discharge of Debtor's debts? _____

69. Debtor's Chapter 13 plan is confirmed and after making all payments under the plan, she is granted a standard Chapter 13 discharge. Will a pre-petition debt for Debtor's fraud while acting in a fiduciary capacity be discharged if it was provided for in Debtor's plan? _____

CHAPTER 12—FAMILY FARMER WITH REGULAR ANNUAL INCOME

70. Farmer, who meets the eligibility requirements, files a Chapter 12 petition. The standing Chapter 12 trustee proceeds to serve in the case. May Farmer continue to operate his farm? _____

71. Farmer files a Chapter 12 petition. Creditor holds a mortgage on the farm. Can the requirement of adequate protection be satisfied by reasonable rental payments even if they are substantially less than the normal interest payments under the farm mortgage? _____

ANSWERS TO REVIEW QUESTIONS

1. **NO** — Personal injury tort and wrongful death claims must be tried in the district court. [§62]

2.a. **YES** — Trustee's action to avoid and recover the fraudulent transfer is one of the types of core proceedings set forth in 28 U.S.C. section 157(b)(2). [§63]

b. **PROBABLY NOT** — Under the majority view, Trustee's action to recover the pre-petition account receivable is a non-core proceeding (also known as a "related matter") and is the kind of state-law cause of action for which the *Marathon* case requires final adjudication in an Article III court. However, some courts might treat the action as a core proceeding on the ground that it concerns the administration of the estate, involves turnover of property of the estate, or affects the liquidation of the estate's assets or the adjustment of the debtor-creditor relationship. [§§65-67]

3. **YES** — Under the majority view, withdrawal by the district court is mandatory (if a timely motion has been filed) because "the proceeding requires consideration of bankruptcy law and the substantial and material consideration of [a] non-bankruptcy federal statute" regulating organizations involved in interstate commerce (here, the federal securities law). Even under the minority view, withdrawal is mandatory since the facts indicate that the resolution of the proceeding requires "substantial and material consideration" of *both* the federal securities law (a nonbankruptcy federal statute) and the Bankruptcy Code. [§§82-84]

4. **PROBABLY YES** — Consider *permissive abstention:* It appears that respect for state law and comity with state courts would favor resolution of this proceeding in the state court, especially in light of the obscurity of the state property law involved. Thus, abstention probably would be appropriate. [28 U.S.C. §1334(c)(1)] [§86]

   Also consider *mandatory abstention:* The action is a proceeding based on a state-law cause of action related to the bankruptcy case that (i) could not have been brought in a federal court without bankruptcy jurisdiction, (ii) already has been filed in an appropriate state court, and (iii) is expected to be adjudicated expeditiously in that forum. The issue is whether the proceeding is one that did *not* arise in the bankruptcy case or under the Code. Under a narrow interpretation of such language, mandatory abstention would be appropriate. [*See* 28 U.S.C. §1334(c)(2)] [§87] (*Note:* Under the majority view, the proceeding would be considered non-core. [§§65-67]).

5. **YES** — Rulings that grant or deny relief from the automatic stay are final decisions and, therefore, can be appealed. [§118]

6. **NO** — Insolvency is not a prerequisite for relief under the Bankruptcy Code. If Debtor is eligible under Chapter 7, 11, 12, or 13, she will not be denied relief merely because she is solvent. [§121]

7. **NO** — Debtor is ineligible for relief because she was a debtor in a case that was dismissed in the preceding 180 days due to her willful failure to obey the court's orders. [§143]

8. **YES** — Generally, before a corporation files a voluntary bankruptcy petition, its board of directors must authorize the filing by an appropriate resolution. [§151]

9.	**NO**	Since Debtor has more than 12 creditors, the filing of an involuntary petition against Debtor requires at least three petitioning entities holding noncontingent, undisputed claims, at least $10,000 of which, in the aggregate, are unsecured. Here, the combined unsecured claims of the petitioning creditors total only $3,000. Therefore, the petition will be dismissed. [§163]
10.	**NO**	In determining whether Debtor is generally not paying his debts as they become due, the court considers both the amount of the unpaid liabilities as well as the number of unpaid creditors. Therefore, Debtor's defense is not valid, and, under these facts, an order for relief probably will be entered. [§172]
11.	**PROBABLY YES**	If Creditor has filed the involuntary petition against Debtor in bad faith, the court may award any damages proximately caused by the filing and/or punitive damages. Even if the court does not find that the petition was filed in bad faith, it may award Debtor costs and/or reasonable attorney's fees. [§§178-179]
12.	**YES**	When a trustee is appointed in a Chapter 11 case, she has the authority to operate the debtor's business unless the court orders otherwise. [§247]
13.	**YES**	On appointment, Trustee effectively becomes Debtor Corporation's new management and, therefore, the corporate attorney-client privilege passes from former management to Trustee. Thus, Trustee has the power to waive Debtor Corporation's attorney-client privilege concerning communications made by former officers and directors to Debtor Corporation's attorney before bankruptcy. [§247]
14.	**YES**	In a Chapter 11 case in which appointment of a trustee has not been ordered, the court sometimes will order the appointment of an examiner to investigate any charges of fraud, dishonesty, incompetence, or mismanagement on the part of the debtor's present or former management. The appointment is made by the United States trustee, who selects a disinterested person other than himself. The debtor in possession, however, retains possession of his property and continues to operate the business. [§§251-253]
15.	**YES**	It is important that court approval of employment of the attorney and accountant be obtained prior to their rendering professional services. Otherwise, their applications for compensation may be denied since many courts will not grant approval retroactively in the absence of extraordinary circumstances. Also, they must be disinterested persons who do not have an interest adverse to the estate. [§§256-259]
16.	**NO**	An individual debtor's earnings from services performed post-petition are specifically excluded from "section 541 property" and thus are not part of the bankruptcy estate. *But note:* This example is in the context of a Chapter 7 case, and the answer would differ if it were a case under Chapter 12 or 13. [§304]
17.	**YES**	The forfeiture clause in the lease is an example of an ipso facto or "bankruptcy" clause, which is not enforceable under Code section 541(c)(1). Consequently, Lessee's leasehold interest in the computers is included in property of the estate notwithstanding the termination provision in the agreement. [§306] With respect to assumption or rejection of the unexpired lease, Code section 365 will control. [§§875 *et seq.*]

18.	**YES**	The Supreme Court has held that a bank's temporary administrative freeze of a Debtor's checking account is not in violation of the automatic stay, but Bank also should promptly request relief from the stay and a determination of its right of setoff. [§§345-349]
19.	**YES**	A statutory lien that is not perfected or enforceable against a bona fide purchaser at the time that the bankruptcy petition is filed may be avoided by the trustee. Here, the tax lien is not enforceable against a bona fide purchaser because notice of it has not been filed by the IRS. Therefore, it can be avoided by the trustee. [§354]
20.	**YES**	As a hypothetical judicial lien creditor at the time the bankruptcy case is commenced, Trustee has the power to avoid Seller's unperfected security interest in the office equipment. [§§357-358] (Under U.C.C. section 9-301(1)(b), a judicial lien has priority over an unperfected security interest.)
21.	**NO**	Even if all of the elements of a voidable preference under Bankruptcy Code section 547(b) are present, this case comes within the "ordinary course of business" exception. [B.C. §547(c)(2)] Therefore, the transfer cannot be avoided by the trustee. [§383]
22.	**YES**	The conveyance constitutes a fraudulent transfer made with the actual intent to hinder, delay, or defraud creditors. Since it occurred within one year before bankruptcy, it is voidable by the trustee. [§413]
23.	**NO**	A transfer is any *voluntary or involuntary* disposition of property, including a foreclosure sale of collateral. [§410] Here, the foreclosure sale occurred (within one year before bankruptcy) at a time when Debtor was insolvent. However, under these facts, the proceeds derived from the sale should constitute *reasonably equivalent value*. The Supreme Court has held that the sale price received at a *noncollusive* foreclosure sale conclusively establishes reasonably equivalent value if state foreclosure laws are followed. Therefore, the trustee should not be able to avoid the transfer. [§§416-419]
24.a.	**YES**	The trustee's avoiding powers under the strongarm clause are subject to any applicable nonbankruptcy law that permits retroactive perfection of a security interest. Thus, Seller's post-petition perfection within the 10-day period allowed under state law will relate back and will prevail over the bankruptcy trustee's intervening rights as a hypothetical judicial lien creditor. [§438]
b.	**NO**	Seller's post-petition perfection under these circumstances comes within an exception to the automatic stay. [§440]
25.	**DEPENDS**	Generally, Seller can reclaim the *goods* from Debtor if: (i) the sale was in the ordinary course of Seller's business; (ii) Debtor received the goods while insolvent; and (iii) Seller made a written demand for reclamation within 10 days after Debtor received the goods, or (as applicable here) within 20 days after Debtor's receipt if the 10-day period expired after the commencement of the bankruptcy case. [§§441-451]
26.	**NO**	Unless the estate is solvent, holders of unsecured claims are not entitled to post-petition interest. [§509]

27.	**YES**	While personal injury tort claims must be tried in the district court for the purpose of distribution, if the fixing or liquidation of a contingent or unliquidated claim would cause undue delay in the administration of the case, the bankruptcy court is required to estimate the claim for the purpose of allowance. [§518]
28.	**NO**	Bank's claim is secured only to the extent of the value of its collateral ($90,000), and the balance of its claim ($10,000) is treated as an unsecured claim. (*Note:* The Supreme Court has ruled, however, that Debtor may not strip down Bank's lien to the value of the land.) [§§523-524, 534]
29.	**YES**	To the extent that Bank is oversecured, it is entitled to the allowance of post-petition interest, and also to any reasonable fees, costs, or other charges agreed to in the mortgage contract. The authorities are split on the rate of interest to be applied, but the better rule uses the contract rate. [§§529-531]
30.	**YES**	Actual and necessary post-petition costs of preserving the estate, including wages and salaries for post-petition services, are allowable as administrative expenses. [§539]
31.	**NO**	An unsecured pre-petition tax claim of this kind is accorded eighth priority status. In a Chapter 7 case, the priority claims are paid in full before any distribution is made to the general unsecured creditors. [§§564-565]
32.	**NO**	Since the adequate protection furnished to Creditor proved to be deficient, Creditor will receive an administrative expense claim ($20,000) with ***priority*** over all other administrative expenses allowed in the case. [§579] *But note:* Creditor's superpriority claim will not prevail over a priority approved under section 364(c)(1) for post-petition credit. [§580]
33.	**DEPENDS**	Under these facts, there does not appear to be a subordination agreement. Furthermore, President's status as an insider generally should not result in the equitable subordination of his claim in the absence of any misconduct. However, courts usually examine the dealings of insiders and fiduciaries with strict scrutiny for good faith and fairness. [§§599, 602-606]
34.	**NO**	In a case filed or administered jointly, both spouses must elect the same exemption plan, either state or federal. If the debtors are unable to agree, they will be deemed to have chosen the federal exemptions. [§612]
35.	**NO**	The security interest must be nonpossessory and ***nonpurchase-money*** for Debtor to be able to avoid it. Here, the Seller's security interest is purchase-money and, therefore, cannot be avoided by Debtor. [§§653-655]
36.a.	**NO**	Debts for money, property, services, or credit obtained by false representation or fraud are nondischargeable. [§680]
b.	**NO**	Debtor's failure to list or schedule the debt makes it nondischargeable since Creditor, lacking notice or actual knowledge of the bankruptcy case, was precluded from timely filing a proof of claim. [§§686, 688]
c.	**NO**	Since the debt arose from Debtor's defalcation while acting in a fiduciary capacity, it is nondischargeable. [§§689-690]

d. **PROBABLY NOT** — Generally, a debt intended to constitute a property settlement arising out of a separation agreement, divorce decree, or other court order is nondischargeable unless the debtor doesn't have the ability to pay the debt, or discharging the debt would produce a benefit to the debtor that outweighs the harm to the ex-spouse. Therefore, unless one of these exceptions applies, the $25,000 debt owed to Debtor's first spouse is nondischargeable. [§694]

e. **NO** — Debts owed for alimony, maintenance, or spousal or child support, arising out of a separation agreement, a property settlement agreement, a divorce decree, or other court order are nondischargeable. Therefore, the $10,000 debt owed to Debtor's second spouse is nondischargeable. [§691]

37. **YES** — While Debtor has no personal obligation to repay the discharged debt that was owed to Creditor, the Code expressly permits Debtor to voluntarily repay any debt if she so desires. [§732]

38. **NO** — If Debtor had not been represented by an attorney during the negotiation of the reaffirmation agreement, it would be necessary to obtain court approval, which requires a finding that the agreement is in Debtor's best interest and it does not impose an undue hardship on Debtor or any of his dependents. However, here, Debtor was represented by an attorney, and, according to the facts, all of the elements of an enforceable reaffirmation agreement were met, one of which is the attorney's filing of an affidavit or a declaration stating that: (i) Debtor has been fully informed; (ii) Debtor has entered into the agreement voluntarily; (iii) the reaffirmation does not impose an undue hardship on Debtor or any of his dependents; and (iv) the attorney has fully advised Debtor of the legal effects of the reaffirmation and of any subsequent default. Therefore, independent court approval is not necessary in this case. [§§734 *et seq.*]

39. **NO** — If Debtor does not reaffirm any debts, the holding of a discharge hearing is within the court's discretion. On the other hand, if Debtor desires to reaffirm one or more debts negotiated without attorney representation, the court must conduct a discharge hearing, at which time the judge explains to Debtor the legal effect of a reaffirmation agreement and advises him that such an agreement is completely voluntary. [§§745-747]

40. **SPLIT** — Although there is a split of appellate authority, the better rule is that in a Chapter 7 case, redemption and reaffirmation are the exclusive means of retaining possession of tangible personal property that is subject to a lien, even if the debtor has not defaulted on any installment. Moreover, there is no absolute right to reaffirm, since a reaffirmation agreement is a voluntary contract on the part of both the debtor and the creditor. However, some appellate courts have allowed a nondefaulting debtor to retain the collateral, without redeeming or reaffirming, by continuing to make payments pursuant to the contract. [§§751, 753]

41. **NO** — Adequate protection does not entitle an undersecured creditor to compensation (*i.e.*, interest) for the delay in foreclosure on his collateral and reinvestment of the proceeds. In the *Timbers* case, the United States Supreme Court ruled that adequate protection means protection against depreciation in "the value of the collateral," and not protection of "a secured party's right to immediate foreclosure." [§774]

42.a. **YES** — The commencement or continuation of a judicial, administrative, or other action against Debtor to recover a pre-petition claim is enjoined by the automatic stay. [§780]

b. **YES** — Any act to obtain possession of property of the estate, or property in the possession of the estate, is prohibited by the automatic stay. Also enjoined is any act to enforce a lien against property of the estate. (Note that even if the vehicle has been abandoned by the trustee, thus becoming property of Debtor, the stay would enjoin Bank's repossession since its lien secures a pre-petition claim.) [§§784-786]

c. **YES** — Any act to collect, recover, or assess a pre-petition claim against Debtor is enjoined. Here, Appliance Store's telephone calls and letters are clearly in violation of the automatic stay. [§787]

d. **NO** — The commencement or continuation of a proceeding by a governmental unit (here, the NLRB) to enforce its police or regulatory power is excepted from the automatic stay. [§796]

43. **YES** — Under Bankruptcy Code section 362(d)(2), Creditor is entitled to relief from the stay of an act against the property since there is no equity in the property and it is not necessary for an effective reorganization. [§§820-822]

44. **DEPENDS** — The sale of the factory building is out of the ordinary course of Debtor's business, and therefore requires proper notice and the *opportunity* for a hearing. However, if no party in interest timely objects, the building may be sold without a hearing. [§§835-836]

45. **DEPENDS** — The checking account constitutes cash collateral, which the Debtor may not use in the ordinary course of business without either Secured Creditor's consent or (after notice and a hearing) court approval. [§844]

46. **YES** — If Debtor is unable to obtain unsecured post-petition financing as an administrative expense, one of the permissible alternatives is for the court to authorize the obtaining of credit or the incurring of debt that will have priority over all administrative expense claims in the case, and also over any superpriority administrative expense claims arising from the failure of adequate protection. Notice and a hearing are required. [§§867-868]

47. **DEPENDS** — For Debtor to assume the unexpired lease of the equipment, she must at the time of assumption: (i) cure the default for June, July, and August or provide adequate assurance that it will be cured promptly; (ii) compensate the lessor for any monetary loss caused by the default (or provide adequate assurance of prompt compensation); and (iii) furnish adequate assurance of future performance of the lease. [§§885 *et seq.*] Court approval is required. [§879]

48. **NO** — The question concerns the assumption of a personal service contract. Unless Variety, Inc. consents (an event that is highly unlikely), the trustee may not assume or assign the executory contract to sing since, as a general rule, applicable nonbankruptcy law would excuse Variety, Inc. from accepting performance from, or furnishing performance to, an entity other than Debtor (or the debtor in

possession). (Note that had a trustee not been appointed, there is a split of authority as to whether the debtor in possession could assume and perform the contract.) [§§896-897]

49. **NO**   A trustee or a debtor in possession may not assume or assign a lease of nonresidential real property that has been terminated under applicable nonbankruptcy law prior to the order for relief. [§899]

50. **YES**   In a Chapter 11 case, assumption or rejection of an executory contract or an unexpired lease of personal property or residential real property may occur at any time prior to the confirmation of a plan. However, the nondebtor party may request that the court, in its discretion, direct the trustee or the debtor in possession to assume or reject within a fixed period of time. [§§903-904]

51. **YES**   Claims within any tier of priority under Code section 507(a) share pro rata in the property distributed to that particular category of claims. Thus, the trade creditors who are holding second priority involuntary gap claims will share pro rata in the property available for distribution after the administrative expenses have been paid in full. [§955]

52. **YES**   In a Chapter 7 case, the refusal (for a reason other than the appropriate use of the Fifth Amendment privilege against self-incrimination) to testify, or to answer a material question that has been approved by the judge, is a ground for denial of Debtor's discharge. [§979]

53. **YES**   Since the Chapter 7 case has not been converted previously from Chapter 11, 12, or 13, Debtor has an absolute nonwaivable right to convert the case from Chapter 7 to any of the other chapters at any time (provided that Debtor meets the eligibility requirements for the chapter). [§986]

54. **PROBABLY YES**   Upon the court's own motion or one filed by the United States trustee, the court may dismiss a Chapter 7 case involving an individual debtor with primarily consumer debts under circumstances that the court finds to constitute a substantial abuse of relief under Chapter 7. Even though there is a statutory presumption in Debtor's favor, the facts of this case appear to justify dismissal. [§§990-992]

55. **DEPENDS**   Attorney may be hired by the creditors' committee if he does not "represent any other entity having an *adverse interest* in connection with the case" during his employment. [B.C. §1103(b)] Representation of a creditor of the same class as the committee represents is not automatically deemed representation of an adverse interest. [§§1003-1005]

56. **NO**   Since the debtor in possession usually is considered to be the most appropriate one to conduct the operations of the business, it is viewed as an exception for a trustee to be appointed in a Chapter 11 case, and (unless shown otherwise) there is a presumption that the debtor should be allowed to remain in possession. However, after the filing of the petition and prior to confirmation of a plan, a party in interest or the United States trustee may request the appointment of a trustee, either *for cause* or in the interest of creditors, equity security holders, and the estate. The court generally requires evidence showing more than simple

mismanagement, and some courts have used a cost-benefit analysis, taking into account the administrative expenses that are likely to ensue from the appointment of a trustee. [§§1009-1011]

57.	**YES**	By making the election under Code section 1111(b), Creditor can have his claim treated as secured to the full extent that the claim is allowed ($100,000), even though ordinarily it would be deemed secured only up to the value of the collateral ($75,000). However, by making the election (which is available only in a Chapter 11 case), Creditor forfeits his unsecured claim for any deficiency. [§§1026-1028]
58.	**NO**	As long as a trustee has not been appointed in the case, Debtor has the exclusive right to file a plan for the first 120 days after the order for relief. [§1045]
59.	**PROBABLY YES**	The Code permits the plan to designate a separate class of small claims comprised of all unsecured claims that are less than, or by consent are decreased to, an amount approved by the court as reasonable and necessary. Generally, such claims are paid in full (in cash), and the estate benefits by the reduction of administrative expenses. [§1055]
60.	**NO**	Debtor may solicit post-petition acceptances only at or after the time the plan (or a summary of it) and a written court-approved disclosure statement have been sent to the holders of the claims or interests whose acceptances are sought. [§§1066 *et seq.*] *But note:* If debtor has elected to be treated as a small business, the court may conditionally approve a disclosure statement that can be used to solicit acceptances if it contains adequate information and is mailed at least 10 days before the confirmation hearing. [§§1131-1133]
61.	**YES**	In a Chapter 11 case, a discharge is not limited to an individual debtor as it is in Chapter 7. Unless the plan or the confirmation order provides otherwise, *confirmation* discharges Debtor Corporation from all pre-confirmation debts, as well as from certain other debts specified in Code section 1141(d)(1)(A). [§§1119 *et seq.*] (*Note:* The result would be different if the confirmed plan were a liquidating plan and Debtor Corporation—which would be denied a discharge under Chapter 7—did not engage in business after consummation of the plan. [§1122])
62.	**NO**	Chapter 13 relief is available only to an individual who has regular income, whose unsecured debts total less than $250,000, and whose secured debts total less than $750,000. Here, Debtor's unsecured debts of $300,000 exceed the statutory limitation and thus make her ineligible for Chapter 13 relief. [§1138]
63.	**NO**	A Chapter 13 case may be commenced only by the filing of a voluntary petition. Therefore, the involuntary petition against Debtor will be dismissed. [§1140]
64.	**NO**	Fellow Employee is protected by the Chapter 13 co-debtor stay, which became effective when Debtor filed his Chapter 13 petition, and which enjoins the commencement or continuation of any civil action or other act by a creditor to collect a consumer debt from an individual who has guaranteed or secured a liability of Debtor, or who is otherwise liable on a debt with Debtor. [§§1143-1149]
65.	**DEPENDS**	If Debtor, as a *self-employed* individual, *incurs trade credit* in producing income from her business, then she will be treated as a "debtor engaged in

		business." As such, Debtor will be permitted to continue to operate her business unless the court directs otherwise. [§1153]
66.a.	YES	In a Chapter 13 case, ordinarily the debtor retains possession of all property of the estate unless a confirmed plan or confirmation order provides otherwise. [§1158]
b.	YES	The Chapter 13 estate consists not only of all "section 541 property," but also of all "section 541 property" acquired by Debtor post-petition and all of Debtor's earnings from post-petition services performed prior to the earliest of the closing, dismissal, or conversion of the case. [§1158]
67.	NO	One of the mandatory provisions of a Chapter 13 plan is that all priority claims must be paid fully in deferred cash payments, unless a particular creditor consents to different treatment. Since the claim of the IRS is an eighth priority claim, Debtor's plan must provide for full repayment of the federal tax claim. [§1170]
68.	NO	In a Chapter 13 case, confirmation does not operate as a discharge as it generally does in a case under Chapter 11. A standard Chapter 13 discharge occurs only after the debtor has made all payments under the plan. [§§1213-1214]
69.	YES	A standard Chapter 13 discharge includes all debts that are provided for by the plan or that have been disallowed by the court under Bankruptcy Code section 502, *except* alimony, maintenance, and spousal or child support; certain long-term debts that have been provided for under Code section 1322(b)(5); student loans (with two possible exceptions); HEAL loans with respect to which the three conditions of 42 U.S.C. section 292f(g) have not been satisfied; debts for drunk or drugged driving that caused personal injury or death; criminal restitution or a criminal fine; and certain post-petition consumer debts. Thus, the debt arising from Debtor's pre-petition fiduciary fraud is dischargeable in the Chapter 13 case, even though it otherwise would be nondischargeable under Code section 523(a)(4). [§§1215-1216]
70.	YES	Bankruptcy Code section 1203 authorizes Farmer to continue to operate his farm unless he is removed as a debtor in possession. The causes for removal of a debtor in possession parallel those in a Chapter 11 case. [§§1235-1236]
71.	YES	In a Chapter 12 case, the issue of adequate protection is governed by Code section 1205, and not by section 361. Where the creditor's collateral is farmland, one method suggested by the Code for providing adequate protection is the payment of the reasonable rent prevailing in that locality, taking into account "the rental value, net income, and earning capacity of the property." [B.C. §1205(b)(3)] [§1249]

SAMPLE EXAM QUESTION I

Debtor is married, has four children, is employed as an office manager, earns $5,000 per month, and enjoys recreational fishing. Debtor's spouse is unemployed. Debtor files a voluntary bankruptcy petition for himself at a time when he owes (i) $280,000 to various unsecured creditors, (ii) $50,000 to Bank on a note secured by a boat that has a fair market value of $35,000, and (iii) $15,000 to Finance Company on a note secured by the family car having a value of $10,000. After exemptions, there are no assets available for distribution to unsecured creditors, and Trustee abandons any interest of the estate in the boat and automobile. Debtor wants to keep the boat and, at a time when he is not represented by an attorney, he negotiates and executes a reaffirmation agreement with Bank, allowing him to retain possession of the boat under the same terms as the original consumer loan. He also desires to redeem the car, offering to pay Finance Company $10,000 in cash, which Rich Uncle will furnish as a gift for his favorite nephew.

1. Should Debtor's bankruptcy petition have been filed under Chapter 7 or Chapter 13 of the Code?

2. Is the reaffirmation agreement with Bank enforceable?

3. Can Debtor retain possession of the car by paying Finance Company only $10,000?

SAMPLE EXAM QUESTION II

Debtor, an insolvent corporation in the business of selling widgets, files a Chapter 7 petition. Claims in the case include the following: (i) administrative expenses totaling $10,000; (ii) a note in the amount of $100,000 in favor of Bank and secured by a first mortgage on Blackacre, which has a fair market value of $120,000; (iii) a note in the amount of $50,000 in favor of Trust Company and secured by a first mortgage on Whiteacre, which has a fair market value of $20,000; (iv) an unsecured note in favor of Credit Union in the amount of $40,000; (v) unsecured claims of trade creditors totaling $100,000; (vi) unsecured claims of 10 employees, each of whom is owed $7,000 in wages earned within 90 days before the filing of Debtor's petition; (vii) an unsecured note in the amount of $100,000 in favor of Debtor's President, which, pursuant to a valid agreement, is subordinated to the payment of all other claims; and (viii) an unsecured claim for federal income taxes totaling $50,000 relating to the preceding taxable year. After all estate property is liquidated, the proceeds available for final distribution total $270,000. How much will be paid to each claimant in the case?

SAMPLE EXAM QUESTION III

On completing a joint J.D./M.B.A. program of graduate studies in May 1992, Debtor owes $10,000 to Rich Aunt, and $10,000 to First National Bank pursuant to a student loan guaranteed by the United States, with the first payment for the student loan coming due in May 1993. Debtor takes the state bar examination in July 1992, and in September begins employment as an attorney for Local Bank. In late October, he receives good news of his success on the bar examination and attends a celebration party at the home of another successful candidate. After drinking champagne until 2:00 a.m., Debtor attempts to drive home but, due to his inebriated condition, hits Pedestrian, causing personal injuries in the amount of $10,000.

Although the night of the October party is a tragic date in Debtor's life, it is not a total loss, inasmuch as, at the party, he is introduced to Kathy, with whom he falls in love and then marries in June 1993. One year later, a child is born to the couple. Debtor's salary at Local Bank is relatively high, but not adequate to repay his debts, which also include his unpaid 1993 federal income tax liability of $10,000, for which a return was never filed. Debtor succumbs to the financial pressures and embezzles (but promptly squanders) $50,000 from Local Bank in July 1994. When the embezzlement is discovered, Debtor is fired by Local Bank but, shortly thereafter, is employed in Rich Aunt's business at a salary of $4,000 per month. Kathy files for a divorce which, after a trial in February 1995, results in a decree requiring Debtor to pay $1,000 per month in alimony and child support. Debtor makes the first payment in February but fails to make any payments thereafter.

In July 1995, Debtor consults with a bankruptcy attorney about seeking relief under the Bankruptcy Code. Debtor has no debts other than those described above. He has paid his 1994 taxes but still owes the full $10,000 to IRS for the 1993 taxable year. No payments have been made on (i) the loan from Rich Aunt, (ii) the loan from First National Bank, (iii) the debt owed to Pedestrian for personal injuries caused by drunk driving, or (iv) the debt owed to Local Bank for embezzlement. If you are Debtor's attorney, what will you advise him concerning the nondischargeability of each of his obligations if he files a voluntary petition under Chapter 7 or, alternatively, under Chapter 13?

SAMPLE EXAM QUESTION IV

Debtor files a voluntary Chapter 7 petition in the bankruptcy court for the Northern District of Georgia, and there are no assets available for distribution to creditors. On the last allowable day, and solely for the purpose of harassing Debtor, Creditor files an objection to Debtor's discharge in the bankruptcy court for the District of Oregon. Debtor files a motion in the Oregon bankruptcy court to dismiss the objection or, in the alternative, to transfer the proceeding to the Northern District of Georgia.

Is venue proper in the District of Oregon, and will the objection to Debtor's discharge be heard in the bankruptcy court there?

SAMPLE EXAM QUESTION V

Debtor Corporation owns two carpet mills and employs more than half of the working population of several towns located in the vicinity. Management has grossly mismanaged the company, thereby rendering it insolvent, and Debtor files a voluntary Chapter 11 petition. The prospects for successfully reorganizing are reasonable, and the mayors of the surrounding towns have testified as to the devastating effects that would be likely to ensue if the mills were to be liquidated. A trustee is appointed to replace current management.

The trustee files a Chapter 11 plan proposing to classify the claims and interests as follows:

- Class I: Administrative expenses [B.C. §507(a)(1)]

- Class II: Priority wage claims [B.C. §507(a)(3)]

- Class III: An unsecured pre-petition tax claim entitled to eighth priority [B.C. §507(a)(8)] (*Note:* The taxes owing have not been assessed.)

- Class IV: Bank's allowed secured claim, for which the collateral is comprised of Debtor's two carpet mills and related equipment [B.C. §506(a)] (*Note:* This constitutes the secured part of Bank's total claim, which is undersecured.)

Class V: All general unsecured claims, including the deficiency portion of Bank's undersecured claim

Class VI: All shareholder interests

The trustee's plan proposes to pay each class as follows:

Class I: Full payment of the allowed amount of each claim in cash on the effective date of the plan

Class II: Full payment of the allowed amount of each claim in cash on the effective date of the plan

Class III: Full payment, on a present value basis, in deferred cash installments over a period of six years

Class IV: Retention by Bank of its lien on the two carpet mills and the equipment, and the issuance of income bonds (secured by other assets of Debtor) to pay Bank 13% cumulative interest per year, with 40% of the annual net profits of the reorganized Debtor being used to amortize the bonds over a period not to exceed 10 years after the effective date of the plan, such that Bank receives deferred cash payments having a present value equal to the full amount of its allowed secured claim

Class V: All of the new common stock to be issued by the reorganized Debtor, with each creditor in the class to receive less than full payment of his claim, but more than he would have received if Debtor's assets had been liquidated under Chapter 7 (*Note:* The stock will be issued to the unsecured creditors on a pro rata basis.)

Class VI: Nothing

Can the plan be confirmed if it is rejected by Class IV, Class V, or Class VI?

SAMPLE EXAM QUESTIONS VI-X

Sample exam questions VI through X pertain to the following fact situation:

Since 1986, Debtor Corporation ("Debtor") has manufactured, distributed, and sold cosmetics throughout the United States. At all times, its principal place of business and most of its assets have been located in Williamsburg, Virginia.

Among its many products is "Sweetness," a perfume purchased and used by American women nationwide since it was first marketed in 1988. Unfortunately, "Sweetness" contains a cancer-producing agent, known as XYZ, that has resulted in the sickness or death of thousands of individual users. Before marketing "Sweetness," Debtor had tested the perfume on flocks of chickens, many of which shortly thereafter contracted avian leukosis (bird cancer), began to lose their feathers, and died. Despite this research, Debtor's experts concluded that the perfume would not be harmful to humans. Thus, after several famous actresses agreed that the fragrance of "Sweetness" was far superior to any perfume available, Debtor, while concealing the results of the experiments that had been done on the chickens, obtained permission from the Food and Drug Administration to market "Sweetness."

Beginning in 1991, Debtor has been named as the defendant in thousands of personal injury and wrongful death actions in jurisdictions throughout the country, and the judgments recovered by the tort victims have been massive. Management has taken the product off the market, and, apparently, the adverse publicity has not substantially harmed the sale of Debtor's other products, which continue to generate large profits.

On October 1, 1994, all of Debtor's officers and directors are removed internally and replaced by new management, which decides to file a Chapter 11 bankruptcy petition in an attempt to reorganize the company. On November 1, 1994, Debtor's attorney files a voluntary Chapter 11 petition in the United States Bankruptcy Court for the Eastern District of Virginia. Debtor is insolvent at the time of filing, but sales are high and new management is optimistic.

Shortly thereafter, the United States Trustee appoints a creditors' committee comprised of creditors holding the seven largest unsecured claims against Debtor. The United States Trustee also appoints a committee of the equity security holders to represent their interests.

On November 20, 1994, the creditors' committee requests the appointment of a trustee in the case. The court denies the appointment of a trustee, and, instead, orders the appointment of an examiner. On November 30, 1994, the United States Trustee, after having consulted with creditors and equity security holders, appoints a disinterested person as examiner, and court approval is obtained on the same day.

On December 1, 1994, the section 341 meeting of creditors is held, at which time both secured and unsecured creditors examine Debtor's new president under oath.

The claimants in the case include the following:

1. Bank A, which holds a note and a perfected security interest in all of Debtor's equipment (the debt is $1 million, and the value of the equipment is $2.5 million; there are no other liens on the property);

2. Bank B, which holds a note and a perfected security interest in all of Debtor's inventory and accounts receivable (the note is fully secured, and Debtor's payments are current);

3. Bank C, which holds a note and an unrecorded mortgage on an office building in Phoenix, Arizona;

4. Bank D, which holds a note and a properly recorded first mortgage on an empty, unrented warehouse that Debtor does not intend to use (the debt is $1 million, and the value of the warehouse, which is located in New York City, is $950,000);

5. Numerous unsecured trade creditors who are owed substantial sums;

6. Employees who are owed pre-petition wages;

7. The IRS, which holds an unsecured claim for income taxes for the 1993 calendar year;

8. The landlord of Debtor's current office headquarters in Williamsburg (the last rental payment made was on August 1, 1994);

9. A significant number of general unsecured creditors, who are owed varying amounts;

10. Thousands of claimants holding claims or judgments against Debtor for personal injury or wrongful death;

11. Thousands of unknown future claimants who will have personal injury or wrongful death claims arising from the victims' exposure to XYZ prior to November 1, 1994, even though the cancerous symptoms have not yet become manifest; and

12. Debtor's shareholders.

On February 1, 1991, Best Friend had loaned Debtor $100,000 on an unsecured, interest-free basis, and on September 1, 1994, Debtor repaid the loan with a lump-sum cash payment of $100,000. Debtor was insolvent at the time of the repayment.

On December 15, 1993, Debtor had conveyed resort property worth $300,000 to Hook and Crook, both of whom were directors at that time. The transfer was made for no consideration, and Debtor was insolvent at the time of the conveyance.

On November 15, 1994, Landlord files a motion requesting relief from the automatic stay, to institute state court eviction proceedings against Debtor with respect to the office headquarters in Williamsburg. The rent for September, October, and November has not been paid. Debtor wants to assume the lease.

Debtor has defaulted on pre-petition payments to Bank A and to Bank D, and on November 30, 1994, each bank files a motion requesting relief from the automatic stay for the purpose of foreclosing on its respective collateral.

On January 15, 1995, Debtor needs emergency funding to pay its employees, and Bank E is the only financial institution willing to help. Debtor proposes to grant Bank E an administrative expense priority over all other administrative expenses in the case. However, Bank E insists that it will extend post-petition financing to Debtor only if it is granted a senior lien on all of Debtor's equipment. Debtor, after exhausting all other alternatives to obtain financing, seeks court approval to borrow money on the terms offered by Bank E.

SAMPLE EXAM QUESTION VI

Will Bank A be granted relief from the automatic stay?

Will Bank D be granted relief from the automatic stay?

SAMPLE EXAM QUESTION VII

Should Landlord be granted relief from the automatic stay for the purpose of commencing state court eviction proceedings against Debtor concerning the office headquarters in Williamsburg?

Will Debtor be permitted to assume the lease?

SAMPLE EXAM QUESTION VIII

Will the court approve the proposed post-petition loan from Bank E, secured by a priming lien on Debtor's equipment that will be senior to the lien of Bank A?

SAMPLE EXAM QUESTION IX

What will happen to Bank C's unrecorded mortgage on the office building in Phoenix?

Is there any problem with the repayment of the loan to Best Friend on September 1, 1994?

Will Hook and Crook be entitled to retain the resort property currently titled in their names jointly?

SAMPLE EXAM QUESTION X

Debtor Corporation's Chapter 11 case is converted to Chapter 7, and a trustee is appointed. Debtor owns certain real property in Williamsburg that it has used as a disposal site for the remains of the XYZ cancer-producing agent contained in "Sweetness." The hazardous waste on the property has accumulated for several years, and it constitutes a violation of environmental laws of Virginia. The state environmental protection agency has directed Debtor to clean up the site because of imminent life-threatening dangers to which it exposes the surrounding community. There is no equity in the property, as its value is less than the total of all mortgages on it and the cost of cleanup would be substantial. The trustee seeks to abandon the property as burdensome to the bankruptcy estate, and the state environmental protection agency objects. Decide.

ANSWER TO SAMPLE EXAM QUESTION I

1. *Eligibility:* Debtor's petition should have been filed under Chapter 7. Although Debtor has regular income, he does not qualify for relief under Chapter 13 because the total of his unsecured debts as of the date of bankruptcy ($280,000 plus, under the majority view, $15,000 on the boat and $5,000 on the car = $300,000) exceeds the limitation found in Bankruptcy Code section 109(e). Under this provision, Chapter 13 relief is available only to an individual who has regular income; whose noncontingent, liquidated, *unsecured* debts total less than $250,000; and whose noncontingent, liquidated, *secured* debts total less than $750,000.

2. *Reaffirmation:* Under circumstances where the debtor (i) wants to reaffirm a consumer debt that is not secured by real property of the debtor and (ii) is an individual who negotiated such an agreement without being represented by an attorney, the reaffirmation agreement is enforceable only if (in addition to its satisfying all the requirements of Code section 524(c)(1)-(5)) the court approves the agreement as being in the debtor's best interest and as not imposing an undue hardship on the debtor or his dependents. [B.C. §524(c)(6), (d)(2)] Here, the reaffirmation agreement was negotiated by Debtor without representation by an attorney, and it concerns a debt that is "for a personal, family, or household purpose," thus constituting a consumer debt. [B.C. §101(8)] Consequently, the reaffirmation agreement will be enforceable only if the court finds that the Debtor's reaffirmation of the $50,000 debt secured by a boat worth $35,000 is in Debtor's best interest and does not impose an undue hardship. Given the "fresh start" purpose of the bankruptcy laws, and especially in light of the facts that (i) the debt is undersecured by $15,000, (ii) the boat is a luxury item, and (iii) Debtor has five dependents, it seems improbable that a bankruptcy judge would approve this reaffirmation agreement, since it would saddle Debtor with $50,000 of unnecessary debt following his discharge. Without court approval, the reaffirmation agreement is not enforceable.

   Note, however, that if Debtor had been represented by an attorney during the negotiation of the agreement, it would be enforceable without court approval if all the necessary elements of a reaffirmation agreement are present [B.C. §524(c)], including the attorney's affidavit or declaration stating that Debtor was fully informed and entered into the agreement voluntarily, that the reaffirmation does not impose an undue hardship on Debtor or his dependents, and that the attorney has fully advised Debtor of the legal effect and consequences of the reaffirmation and of any subsequent default.

3. *Redemption:* The automobile, which is tangible personal property used primarily for family purposes, has been abandoned by Trustee. Therefore, under Code section 722, Debtor has the right to redeem it by paying Finance Company the amount of the allowed secured claim, which is determined by the collateral's market value—in this case, $10,000. [B.C. §506(a)] Note that the redemption provision applies only in cases under Chapter 7, and only with respect to a lien that secures a dischargeable consumer debt.

ANSWER TO SAMPLE EXAM QUESTION II

Secured claims: Claims of secured creditors are deemed secured up to the market value of their collateral [B.C. §506(a)], the proceeds of which are used first to satisfy such claims before final distribution to other creditors [B.C. §725]. Thus, Bank, which is fully secured, will receive $100,000 (exclusive of any post-petition interest, or costs or fees, allowed under Code section 506(b), or any surcharges imposed under section 506(c)). Trust Company will be paid $20,000 on the portion of its claim that is deemed secured and will share pro rata with the unsecured creditors to the extent that its claim is undersecured, which means 25% (*see* below) of $30,000. Hence, a total of $27,500 will be paid to Trust Company.

Priority claims: After the payment of the allowed secured claims, distribution will be made to the holders of unsecured priority claims. [B.C. §§726(a)(1), 507(a)] The administrative expenses of $10,000 will be the first priority claims to be paid. [B.C. §507(a)(1)] Next, each employee will receive $4,000 for his third priority wage claim [B.C. §507(a)(3)] and also will share pro rata with the general unsecured creditors on the nonpriority portion of his claim, which means 25% (*see* below) of $3,000. Hence, a total of $4,750 will be paid to each of the 10 employees. The Internal Revenue Service will receive full payment of its eighth priority tax claim of $50,000. [B.C. §507(a)(8)]

General unsecured creditors: The rest of the unsecured creditors, with the exception of Debtor's President, will share pro rata in the proceeds available after distribution to creditors holding secured claims and priority claims. [B.C. §726(a)(2)] Since the total proceeds available for distribution are $270,000, and since the secured claims total $120,000 (Bank = $100,000; Trust Company = $20,000) and the priority claims total $100,000 (administrative expenses = $10,000; third priority wages = $40,000; eighth priority taxes = $50,000), the amount remaining for distribution to the general unsecured creditors is $50,000, which will be shared pro rata (25%) among creditors holding claims totaling $200,000 (nonpriority wage claims = $30,000; trade creditors = $100,000; Credit Union = $40,000; unsecured deficiency claim of Trust Company = $30,000).

Subordinated claim: Inasmuch as there are insufficient proceeds to pay all the general unsecured creditors in full, Debtor's President will receive nothing on his subordinated claim. [B.C. §§726(a), 510(a)]

Thus, as explained above, the creditors will be paid the following amounts:

Bank:	$100,000
Trust Company:	27,500
Administrative expenses:	10,000
Ten employees (aggregate):	47,500
Internal Revenue Service:	50,000
Trade creditors:	25,000
Credit Union:	10,000
Debtor's President:	0
Total:	$270,000

ANSWER TO SAMPLE EXAM QUESTION III

Chapter 7: If Debtor files a Chapter 7 petition, the debt owed to Rich Aunt will be dischargeable; however, the other debts will probably be nondischargeable under Bankruptcy Code section 523(a). More specifically, since the federally guaranteed educational loan owed to First National Bank first came due within seven years before the filing of Debtor's bankruptcy petition, it will be nondischargeable unless the court finds that it will impose an undue hardship on Debtor and his dependents (a finding that appears unlikely under the circumstances). [B.C. §523(a)(8)] Also, Debtor's 1993 federal tax liability is nondischargeable on two independent grounds: (i) because the income taxes are less than three years old and thus entitled to priority [B.C. §523(a)(1)(A)], and (ii) because a corresponding tax return was not filed (regardless of the age of the taxes) [B.C. §523(a)(1)(B)(i)]. The debt owed to Pedestrian for personal injuries caused by Debtor's driving a motor vehicle while intoxicated is also nondischargeable [B.C. §523(a)(9)], as is the debt owed to Local Bank for the money that Debtor embezzled [B.C. §523(a)(4)]. Likewise, the debt for alimony and child support constitutes a nondischargeable debt. [B.C. §523(a)(5)]

Chapter 13: The first issue is whether Debtor is eligible for Chapter 13 relief. Chapter 13 relief is available only to an individual with regular income whose secured debts are less than $750,000 and whose unsecured debts are less than $250,000. [B.C. §109(e)] Since Debtor is an individual whose salary of $4,000 per month provides regular income, who has no secured debts, and who has unsecured debts totaling $95,000 (Rich Aunt = $10,000; First National Bank = $10,000; IRS = $10,000; Pedestrian = $10,000; Local Bank = $50,000; and alimony and child support = $5,000, for March through July), he qualifies for Chapter 13 relief. The discharge provisions of Chapter 13 differ substantially from those under Chapter 7, and thus under these facts, the only debts that would be nondischargeable in a Chapter 13 case would be the alimony and child support, the student loan, and the debt to Pedestrian for personal injuries caused by drunk driving. [B.C. §1328(a)(2)] The debt owed to Rich Aunt and the debt owed to Local Bank for embezzlement would be discharged if they were provided for by a Chapter 13 plan confirmed by the court, provided that Debtor has completed all payments under the plan. (Note that if Debtor had been prosecuted and convicted of embezzlement, and Debtor's sentence had included restitution to Local Bank, the debt for restitution would have been nondischargeable. [B.C. §1328(a)(3)]) Also, one of the mandatory provisions of a Chapter 13 plan is the full satisfaction in deferred cash payments of all priority claims, which, in this example, would include Debtor's unpaid federal income taxes for 1993. [B.C. §1322(a)(2)] Another feature of Chapter 13 is that the debtor ordinarily remains in possession of his property [B.C. §1306(b)], in contrast to Chapter 7, where the trustee liquidates the debtor's nonexempt property for distribution to creditors. Therefore, under the circumstances, Debtor probably will want to give serious consideration to filing a Chapter 13 petition accompanied by a feasible plan proposing to repay creditors either the full amount of their claims or an appropriate percentage of their claims based on the application of all of Debtor's projected disposable income for the next three years. [B.C. §1325(b)(1)(B)]

ANSWER TO SAMPLE EXAM QUESTION IV

The general rule for venue of a bankruptcy proceeding is that venue lies in the district where the case is pending, which is in the Northern District of Georgia. [28 U.S.C. §1409(a)] No exception to this principle of law is applicable under these facts, and thus venue in the District of Oregon is improper. Therefore, the court probably will grant Debtor's motion to transfer the proceeding to the Northern District of Georgia, although dismissal may be appropriate under these circumstances (especially considering Creditor's wrongful purpose in choosing the Oregon forum). The Oregon bankruptcy court could not retain the case.

ANSWER TO SAMPLE EXAM QUESTION V

The proposed Chapter 11 plan may be confirmed even if it is rejected by Class IV, Class V, or Class VI, provided that the cram down provisions of Bankruptcy Code section 1129(b) are satisfied. This section requires that the proposed plan (i) *not discriminate unfairly* and (ii) *be fair and equitable* as to each impaired class of claims or interests that has not accepted the plan. [B.C. §1129(b)(1)] Under the facts presented, there does not appear to be unfair discrimination with respect to any of the classes. Thus, if the plan is rejected by Class IV, Class V, or Class VI, the principal issue will be whether the plan is fair and equitable with respect to the secured claim, the class of unsecured claims, or the class of shareholder interests, respectively.

Priority claims: For the plan to be confirmed, it must propose to pay the priority claims in accordance with Code section 1129(a)(9). The plan here satisfies this requirement with respect to the priority claims in Classes I and II, by proposing to pay each claim fully in cash on the effective date of the plan. [B.C. §1129(a)(9)(A), (B)] The treatment of the unsecured eighth priority tax claim in Class III also passes statutory muster, which requires full payment, on a present value basis, in deferred cash installments over a period that does not exceed six years from the date of assessment of the tax. [B.C. §1129(a)(9)(C)]

Secured claim: The proposed plan should be deemed fair and equitable with respect to Class IV (Bank's secured claim), since it provides for Bank to retain its lien on the collateral and to receive full payment of its allowed secured claim from the income bonds in deferred cash installments that have a present value of (at least) the value of its collateral. [B.C. §1129(b)(2)(A)(i)] Note that because Bank has not made the election under section 1111(b), the amount of its allowed secured claim is equal to the value of the collateral. [B.C. §506(a)]

General unsecured claims: The plan also is fair and equitable with respect to Class V. Although the general unsecured creditors will not be paid in full, the plan satisfies the **absolute priority rule** in that no creditor or holder of an interest junior to the class will receive or retain any property at all. [B.C. §1129(b)(2)(B)] Furthermore, each creditor of the class (which is impaired) will receive at least as much as he would have received in a Chapter 7 liquidation, thus satisfying the "best interests of creditors test." [B.C. §1129(a)(7)(A)(ii)]

Shareholder interests: Inasmuch as Debtor is insolvent, Class VI (the shareholders) will receive nothing, and the plan is considered to be fair and equitable concerning their interests. [B.C. §1129(b)(2)(C); *In re* W. E. Parks Lumber Co., 19 B.R. 285 (Bankr. W.D. La. 1982)]

Conclusion: Under these facts, the proposed plan meets the requirements for cram down under section 1129(b). Thus, if it also satisfies all of the elements of section 1129(a) except section 1129(a)(8) (*i.e.*, that each class of claims or interests either has accepted the plan or is not impaired under the plan), the plan can be confirmed. Remember, however, that if any class of *claims* is impaired under the plan, the plan must be accepted by **at least one** class of claims that is impaired. [B.C. §1129(a)(10)] Therefore, for confirmation to occur, the plan must be accepted by either Class IV or Class V, each of which is impaired under the plan. (Class VI is deemed to have rejected the plan because it will receive nothing. [B.C. §1126(g)]) Finally, one of the essential requirements for confirmation is that the plan be feasible. [B.C. §1129(a)(11)]

ANSWER TO SAMPLE EXAM QUESTION VI

Bank A: Bank A probably will not be granted relief from the automatic stay. Under Bankruptcy Code section 362(d)(2), relief will probably be denied, because Debtor has equity in the equipment and the equipment is necessary to an effective reorganization (provided that the court finds that there is a reasonable possibility of reorganization within a reasonable time). Additionally, under Code section 362(d)(1), relief probably will be denied, because there exists an equity cushion of $1.5 million (the amount by which the value of the equipment exceeds the debt owed to Bank A), which the court is likely to find adequately protects Bank A's interest in the property.

Bank D: Bank D, on the other hand, appears to be entitled to relief from the stay because (i) Debtor has no equity in the vacant warehouse located in New York and (ii) the warehouse is not necessary to an effective reorganization. [B.C. §362(d)(2)]

ANSWER TO SAMPLE EXAM QUESTION VII

Relief from the automatic stay: The law is not clear as to whether a lessor of real property may seek relief from the automatic stay under Code section 362, or whether Code section 365 is the exclusive remedy. Even if the court adopts the broader view, only two weeks into the Chapter 11 case (November 15, 1994), the court is unlikely to grant relief from the stay under Bankruptcy Code section 362(d)(2), especially since the office headquarters in Williamsburg would be necessary to an effective reorganization if the court finds that a reasonable possibility exists. However, if Debtor cannot provide Landlord with **adequate protection**, the court might grant relief under section 362(d)(1).

Assumption of the lease: If the court does not grant Landlord relief from the stay, the next issue to consider is whether Debtor can assume the unexpired lease. Since there has been a default on the lease (other than one described in Code section 365(b)(2), *supra*, §894), Debtor can assume the lease only if it satisfies the three requirements of Bankruptcy Code section 365(b)(1) at the time of assumption and if it obtains the court's approval of the proposed assumption. Bankruptcy Code section 365(b)(1) requires that:

(i) Debtor cure or provide adequate assurance that it will promptly cure the default;

(ii) Debtor compensate or provide adequate assurance of prompt compensation for any actual pecuniary loss to Landlord resulting from the default; and

(iii) Debtor provide adequate assurance of future performance under the lease.

Post-petition rent: Since the lease concerns nonresidential real property, Debtor must timely pay post-petition rent and perform all other post-petition obligations under the lease (other than those described in Code section 365(b)(2), *supra*, §894), until the lease is assumed or rejected. [B.C. §365(d)(3)]

Timing: Debtor has 60 days after the order for relief (unless an extension is granted) within which to assume or reject the unexpired lease of nonresidential real property, or else the lease will be deemed rejected and the property must be surrendered to Landlord. [B.C. §365(d)(4)]

ANSWER TO SAMPLE EXAM QUESTION VIII

Under Bankruptcy Code section 364(d)(1), the court, after notice and a hearing, **may authorize** Debtor to enter into the proposed post-petition financing agreement with Bank E, secured by a senior lien on Debtor's equipment, provided that (i) Debtor is unable to obtain such funding otherwise and (ii) Bank A's interest is **adequately protected**.

The facts show that Debtor is unable to obtain the emergency funding to pay its employees other than by incurring the proposed debt to Bank E, secured by a senior lien on the equipment (the effect of which is to "prime" Bank A's lien). Although there is an equity cushion of $1.5 million, the court's decision most likely will depend on the amount that would be secured by Bank E's lien, as well as how rapidly the equipment is depreciating. Debtor will bear the burden of proof concerning adequate protection. [B.C. §364(d)(2)]

ANSWER TO SAMPLE EXAM QUESTION IX

Bank C: Bank C's unrecorded mortgage on the office building in Phoenix can be avoided pursuant to Bankruptcy Code section 544(a)(3), which gives the trustee (or the debtor in possession, under section 1107) the power to avoid any transfer of the debtor's property voidable by a hypothetical bona fide purchaser who has perfected the transfer of real property from the debtor at the time that the bankruptcy petition is filed. Since, under state law, a bona fide purchaser of real property generally prevails over a creditor who has failed to record a mortgage on the property, Debtor should have the power to avoid Bank C's unrecorded mortgage on the office building in Phoenix and recover the building, under Code section 550(a), for the benefit of the estate.

Best Friend: The repayment of the loan to Best Friend on September 1, 1994, constitutes a voidable preference under Bankruptcy Code section 547(b). A voidable preference occurs when there is a transfer of the debtor's interest in property that is made to or for the benefit of a creditor, concerning an antecedent debt of the debtor, at a time when the debtor is insolvent, and within 90 days prior to the filing of the bankruptcy petition (or up to one year before bankruptcy if the creditor is an insider), and that results in the creditor receiving a larger share than he would have obtained under the Bankruptcy Code if the transfer had not been made and the estate had been liquidated under Chapter 7.

Under the facts presented, Debtor transferred $100,000 to Best Friend, a general creditor, in satisfaction of a debt that had been incurred on February 1, 1991. The transfer was made on September 1, 1994, two months before bankruptcy and at a time when Debtor was insolvent (which anyway is presumed during the 90 days immediately prior to the date on which the petition was filed). Since Debtor also was not solvent when it filed its bankruptcy petition, the transfer (100% repayment) provided Best Friend with more than he would have received under the Code if the transfer had not been made and the estate had been liquidated under Chapter 7 on the date of bankruptcy. Thus, all of the elements of a preference are present, and Debtor may bring an action against Best Friend to avoid the transfer and to recover the $100,000 payment for the benefit of the estate.

Hook and Crook: Hook and Crook will not be able to retain the resort property because the conveyance constitutes a fraudulent transfer that occurred within one year prior to bankruptcy. Under the facts stated, the conveyance would be voidable since Debtor was insolvent on the date of the transfer (December 15, 1993) and received less than reasonably equivalent value in exchange (here, no consideration). [B.C. §548(a)(2)] Whether the transfer also would be voidable under Code section 548(a)(1) is less clear, since it would be necessary to prove that Debtor actually intended to hinder, delay, or defraud creditors.

ANSWER TO SAMPLE EXAM QUESTION X

Ordinarily, the trustee may abandon any property that is burdensome or of inconsequential value to the estate. [B.C. §554(a)] However, the trustee may not abandon estate property that is in violation of state or federal environmental laws if the result will be to threaten the health or safety of the public with "imminent and identifiable harm." [Midlantic National Bank v. New Jersey Department of Environmental Protection, 474 U.S. 494 (1986)] The exception to the trustee's power of abandonment is narrow and appears to apply "only where there is an imminent danger to public health and safety." [*In re* Smith-Douglass, Inc., 856 F.2d 12 (4th Cir. 1988)]

Therefore, under these circumstances, the trustee probably will not be permitted to abandon the Williamsburg disposal site, because the facts show that the resulting danger to the health and safety of the community is both imminent and life-threatening.

TABLE OF CITATIONS TO BANKRUPTCY CODE

B.C. §§	Text §§
101	§4
101(5)	§§34, 781
101(5)(A)	§478
101(5)(B)	§479
101(8)	§§36, 1144
101(9)	§122
101(9)(A)(v)	§122
101(10)	§§369, 486
101(11)	§§173, 328, 546
101(12)	§§35, 372, 727
101(13)	§19
101(14)	§§222, 257, 260, 1008
101(14)(A)	§§261, 264
101(14)(D)	§262
101(15)	§§29, 318, 778
101(16)	§§26, 488
101(17)	§§26, 488
101(18)	§§142, 1227, 1245
101(18)(A)	§1228
101(18)(B)	§1229
101(19)	§§142, 1224
101(20)	§1226
101(21)	§§1225, 1226
101(21A)	§313
101(21B)	§§573, 711, 723, 936
101(23)	§§167, 182
101(24)	§167
101(28)	§487
101(29)	§§487, 549
101(30)	§§137, 1139
101(31)	§§30, 374, 606, 684, 980
101(31)(A)	§31
101(31)(B)	§32
101(31)(C)	§33
101(32)	§§37, 372, 445
101(33)	§725
101(34)	§710
101(35)	§§573, 711, 725, 936
101(35A)	§935
101(36)	§651
101(41)	§§28, 998
101(42)(A)	§314
101(45)	§31
101(50)	§465
101(51)	§§465, 1175
101(51B)	§823
101(51C)	§1132
101(53)	§§351, 927
101(53B)	§798

B.C. §§	Text §§
101(53C)	§798
101(54)	§§38, 366, 410, 417
101(56)(A)	§314
102(1)	§§14, 809, 836
102(1)(A)	§873
102(2)	§§15, 480
102(3)	§§16, 1019
102(6)	§17
103(a)	§§8, 609, 669
105(a)	§§42, 43, 46, 1035
105(b)	§42
105(d)	§44
106(a)(1)	§§474, 475
106(a)(3)	§474
106(b)	§477
106(c)	§476
109	§121
109(a)	§§120, 123, 184, 939
109(b)	§§123, 939, 940
109(b)(1)	§§125, 940
109(b)(2)	§§126, 127, 940
109(b)(3)	§§128, 184, 940
109(d)	§§133, 184, 993
109(e)	§§136, 140 141, 1138, 1141, 1142, 1245
109(f)	§§142, 1223
109(g)	§§143, 940, 1142, 1195, 1231
109(g)(1)	§143
109(g)(2)	§143
301	§§17, 144, 1140, 1230, 1232, 1258
302(a)	§§17, 1141
302(b)	§149
303(a)	§§139, 142, 161, 541, 1140, 1230, 1232, 1258
303(b)	§162
303(b)(1)	§163
303(b)(2)	§164
303(b)(3)	§166
303(b)(3)(A)	§152
303(b)(4)	§167
303(c)	§165
303(d)	§169
303(e)	§168
303(f)	§§174, 430
303(g)	§177
303(h)	§§17, 171
303(h)(1)	§172
303(h)(2)	§173
303(i)(1)	§179

Bankruptcy—281

B.C. §§	Text §§
303(i)(2)	§179
303(j)	§180
303(k)	§182
304	§185
304(a)	§184
304(b)(1)(A)	§186
304(b)(1)(B)	§186
304(b)(3)	§186
304(c)	§187
304(c)(1)	§187
304(c)(2)	§187
304(c)(3)	§187
304(c)(4)	§187
304(c)(5)	§187
304(c)(6)	§187
305(a)	§§188, 189
305(c)	§190
307	§§293, 1046
321(a)	§221
321(b)	§§223, 255
321(c)	§224
322	§225
323	§220
323(a)	§21
324	§248
326	§§279, 285
326(a)	§§280, 282
326(b)	§283
327-331	§27
327(a)	§§247, 256, 257, 262, 1008
327(b)	§263
327(c)	§§266, 276
327(d)	§267
327(e)	§§265, 276
327(f)	§255
328	§273
328(a)	§274
328(b)	§277
328(c)	§§264, 275
329	§286
330(a)	§270
330(a)(1)	§§269, 270
330(a)(3)	§272
330(a)(4)	§270
330(a)(4)(B)	§§269, 270
330(a)(5)	§284
330(b)	§278
331	§284
341	§§29, 143, 191-196, 205, 228, 229, 645, 723, 944

B.C. §§	Text §§
341(a)	§§191, 944
341(b)	§192
341(d)	§199
342(a)	§§146, 147, 194, 213
342(b)	§145
342(c)	§210
343	§§196, 197, 292, 944
344	§200
345	§§247, 292
348(a)	§212
348(b)	§213
348(c)	§213
348(d)	§§214, 502, 522
348(e)	§215
348(f)	§§216, 1166
349(a)	§218
361	§§319, 526, 536, 761, 765, 776, 777
361(1)	§§536, 766
362(2)	§767
361(3)	§§768, 769
362	§§474, 579, 778, 824
362(a)	§§160, 194, 779, 807, 811, 828
362(a)(1)	§780
362(a)(2)	§783
362(a)(3)	§§784, 785
362(a)(4)	§785
362(a)(5)	§§786, 807
362(a)(6)	§§590, 744, 787
362(a)(7)	§§326, 345, 789
362(a)(8)	§§788, 798
362(b)	§791
362(b)(1)	§§579, 792
362(b)(2)	§793
362(b)(2)(A)	§794
362(b)(3)	§§440, 795
362(b)(4)	§§471, 496, 796, 797
362(b)(5)	§§796, 797
362(b)(6)	§798
362(b)(7)	§798
362(b)(9)	§800
362(b)(10)	§802
362(b)(11)	§803
362(b)(14)	§804
362(b)(15)	§804
362(b)(16)	§804
362(b)(17)	§798
362(b)(18)	§806
362(c)-(f)	§848
362(c)(1)	§§807, 808
362(c)(2)	§807

B.C. §§	Text §§
362(c)(2)(C)	§§807, 808, 1125
362(d)	§§809, 810
362(d)(1)	§§350, 770, 773, 811, 812, 813, 814, 815, 816, 819, 824
362(d)(2)	§§762, 773, 811, 820, 822, 824
362(d)(2)(A)	§§770, 821
362(d)(2)(B)	§822
362(d)(3)	§823
362(e)	§§763, 826, 827
362(f)	§829
362(g)	§828
362(h)	§§787, 831
362(k)	§823
363	§§247, 317, 345, 579, 832, 1025
363(a)	§§349, 468, 845
363(b)	§1152
363(b)(1)	§§14, 835, 836, 837, 838
363(c)	§1153
363(c)(1)	§§427, 840, 843, 1125
363(c)(2)	§§349, 844
363(c)(3)	§846
363(c)(4)	§847
363(d)	§§848, 851, 1152
363(e)	§§319, 345, 349, 536, 846, 849, 850, 851, 906, 1152
363(f)	§§850, 1152
363(g)	§851
363(h)	§§637, 639, 855
363(i)	§856
363(j)	§857
363(k)	§§839, 1106
363(l)	§§852, 1152
363(m)	§859
363(n)	§861
363(o)	§858
364	§§247, 579, 863, 1153
364(a)	§865
364(b)	§866
364(c)(1)	§§580, 868
364(c)(2)	§869
364(c)(3)	§869
364(d)	§871
364(e)	§874
365	§§247, 824, 875, 1185
365(a)	§§879, 911
365(b)(1)	§§885, 894
365(b)(1)(A)	§886
365(b)(1)(B)	§§764, 888
365(b)(1)(C)	§889
365(b)(2)	§§905, 1064

B.C. §§	Text §§
365(b)(2)(A)	§894
365(b)(2)(B)	§894
365(b)(2)(C)	§894
365(b)(2)(D)	§§887, 894
365(b)(3)	§891
365(b)(3)(A)	§893
365(b)(3)(B)	§893
365(b)(3)(C)	§893
365(b)(3)(D)	§893
365(b)(4)	§895
365(c)	§§896, 917
365(c)(1)	§897
365(c)(2)	§898
365(c)(3)	§899
365(d)	§§213, 900, 906
365(d)(1)	§§901, 902
365(d)(2)	§§903, 908
365(d)(3)	§908
365(d)(4)	§§907, 911
365(d)(10)	§905
365(e)(1)(A)	§912
365(e)(1)(B)	§912
365(e)(1)(C)	§912
365(e)(2)(A)	§914
365(e)(2)(B)	§914
365(f)(1)	§§916, 917
365(f)(2)	§915
365(f)(3)	§916
365(g)	§920
365(g)(1)	§921
365(g)(2)(A)	§§923, 925
365(g)(2)(B)(i)	§923
365(g)(2)(B)(iii)	§923
365(h)(1)	§926
365(h)(1)(B)	§928
365(h)(2)(A)	§927
365(h)(2)(B)	§928
365(i)(1)	§929
365(i)(2)(A)	§930
365(i)(2)(B)	§931
365(j)	§932
365(k)	§918
365(l)	§919
365(n)	§§880, 933, 934
365(o)	§936
366	§247
366(a)	§937
366(b)	§938
501(a)	§§194, 485
501(b)	§§485, 490

B.C. §§	Text §§
501(c)	§§247, 485, 491, 498
501(d)	§502
502	§§594, 969
502(a)	§§504, 505
502(b)	§§507, 595
502(b)(1)	§§508, 1024
502(b)(2)	§509
502(b)(3)	§510
502(b)(4)	§511
502(b)(5)	§§512, 533
502(b)(6)	§§513, 921
502(b)(7)	§§514, 921
502(b)(8)	§515
502(b)(9)	§517
502(c)(1)	§518
502(c)(2)	§519
502(d)	§516
502(e)	§§533, 595
502(e)(1)	§520
502(e)(2)	§§502, 521, 594
502(f)	§§502, 522, 552, 557
502(g)	§§502, 522, 921, 921, 1119
502(h)	§§502, 522, 1119
502(i)	§§502, 522, 1119
503	§537
503(a)	§§517, 537
503(b)	§§214, 451, 502, 538, 552, 556
503(b)(1)	§§769, 865, 909
503(b)(1)(A)	§539
503(b)(1)(B)	§575
503(b)(1)(B)(i)	§540
503(b)(1)(C)	§540
503(b)(2)	§541
503(b)(3)(A)	§§542, 548
503(b)(3)(B)	§543
503(b)(3)(C)	§544
503(b)(3)(D)	§545
503(b)(3)(E)	§546
503(b)(4)	§548
503(b)(5)	§549
503(b)(6)	§551
504(a)	§287
504(b)(1)	§288
504(b)(2)	§289
505	§788
505(a)(1)	§584
505(a)(2)(A)	§584
505(a)(2)(B)	§586
505(b)	§§587, 589
505(b)(1)	§588

B.C. §§	Text §§
505(b)(2)	§588
505(b)(3)	§588
505(c)	§590
506(a)	§§24, 350, 524, 525, 752, 775, 946, 1024, 1026, 1201, 1272
506(b)	§§529, 530, 772, 947, 1201
506(c)	§§529, 532
506(d)	§§455, 533, 648, 1118, 1212
506(d)(2)	§503
507	§948
507(a)	§§554, 948
507(a)(1)	§§537, 556, 575, 583, 961, 1058, 1090
507(a)(2)	§§176, 552, 557, 575, 583, 679, 948, 961, 1058, 1090
507(a)(3)	§§559, 575, 948, 961, 1091
507(a)(3)(A)	§558
507(a)(3)(B)	§558
507(a)(4)	§§560, 948, 961, 1091
507(a)(4)(B)	§560
507(a)(5)	§§561, 948, 961, 1091
507(a)(6)	§§562, 948, 961, 1091
507(a)(7)	§§679, 961, 1091
507(a)(8)	§§502, 522, 564, 948, 961, 1058, 1092
507(a)(8)(A)-(G)	§575
507(a)(8)(A)(i)	§565
507(a)(8)(A)(ii)	§565
507(a)(8)(A)(iii)	§565
507(a)(8)(B)	§566
507(a)(8)(C)	§557
507(a)(8)(D)	§569
507(a)(8)(E)	§570
507(a)(8)(F)	§571
507(a)(8)(G)	§572
507(a)(9)	§§573, 936, 948, 1092
507(b)	§§579, 776
507(c)	§575
507(d)	§581
508(a)	§607
508(b)	§608
509	§520
509(a)	§§591, 592
509(b)	§593
509(b)(1)(A)	§594
509(b)(1)(B)	§595
509(b)(2)	§597
509(c)	§596
510	§§596, 958
510(a)	§599

B.C. §§	Text §§
510(b)	§600
510(c)	§602
521(1)	§§153, 242, 473, 686, 989, 1013, 1163
521(2)	§§753, 1163
521(2)(B)	§§206, 241, 1151
521(2)(C)	§§753, 754
521(3)	§207
521(4)	§207
521(5)	§§208, 746, 747, 750
522	§§194, 317, 526, 1119
522(a)(1)	§622
522(b)	§§316, 612, 641, 669, 673
522(b)(1)	§§610, 611
522(b)(2)	§§611, 631
522(b)(2)(A)	§§632, 633, 638
522(b)(2)(B)	§§634, 635, 636, 637, 638
522(c)	§647
522(c)(1)	§648
522(c)(2)(A)	§648
522(c)(2)(B)	§648
522(c)(3)	§648
522(d)	§§613, 639
522(d)(1)	§§614, 618
522(d)(2)	§615
522(d)(3)	§616
522(d)(4)	§617
522(d)(5)	§§618, 665
522(d)(6)	§§619, 665
522(d)(7)	§620
522(d)(8)	§§621, 622
522(d)(9)	§623
522(d)(10)(A)-(C)	§624
522(d)(10)(D)	§625
522(d)(10)(E)	§626
522(d)(11)(A)	§627
522(d)(11)(B)-(C)	§628
522(d)(11)(D)	§629
522(d)(11)(E)	§630
522(e)	§609
522(f)	§§667, 669, 1189
522(f)(1)	§§648, 649
522(f)(1)(A)	§651
522(f)(1)(A)(i)	§652
522(f)(1)(A)(ii)	§652
522(f)(1)(B)	§§653, 654, 655, 666, 670
522(f)(1)(B)(i)	§§653, 655, 664, 665
522(f)(1)(B)(ii)	§§653, 655, 664, 665
522(f)(1)(B)(iii)	§653
522(f)(2)	§650

B.C. §§	Text §§
522(f)(2)(A)	§650
522(f)(3)	§668
522(g)(1)	§§670, 671
522(g)(1)(A)	§§670, 672
522(g)(2)	§670
522(h)	§672
522(i)	§§522, 673
522(j)	§§671, 673
522(k)	§674
522(k)(1), (2)	§553
522(l)	§§643, 646
522(m)	§§640, 641, 642
523	§§970, 1121
523(a)	§§675, 717, 719, 722, 730, 1216
523(a)(1)	§§648, 679, 713, 722
523(a)(1)(B)	§679
523(a)(1)(C)	§679
523(a)(2)	§§676, 685, 687, 688, 723, 724
523(a)(2)(A)	§680
523(a)(2)(B)	§§684, 722
523(a)(2)(C)	§§681, 682
523(a)(3)	§§686, 722
523(a)(3)(A)	§§687, 688
523(a)(3)(B)	§687
523(a)(4)	§§648, 687, 688, 689, 690, 723, 724, 725, 986
523(a)(5)	§§512, 648, 677, 691
523(a)(5)(A)	§692
523(a)(6)	§§648, 687, 688, 697, 702, 723, 724
523(a)(7)	§§699, 701, 702, 712
523(a)(7)(A)	§700
523(a)(7)(B)	§700
523(a)(8)	§§703, 722, 1215
523(a)(8)(A)	§§704, 722
523(a)(8)(B)	§§705, 707
523(a)(9)	§§709, 1215
523(a)(10)	§§715, 716
523(a)(11)	§710
523(a)(12)	§711
523(a)(13)	§712
523(a)(14)	§713
523(a)(15)	§§687, 694, 723, 725
523(a)(15)(A)	§694
523(a)(15)(B)	§694
523(a)(16)	§714
523(a)(17)	§699
523(a)(18)	§692
523(b)	§722
523(c)	§194

B.C. §§	Text §§	B.C. §§	Text §§
523(c)(1)	§§687, 723	543(c)	§330
523(c)(2)	§723	543(d)	§329
523(d)	§685	544-551	§247
523(e)	§725	544	§§358, 424, 944
524(a)(1)	§§726, 728	544(a)	§§357, 435, 438, 441, 439
524(a)(2)	§§676, 726, 729	544(a)(1)	§358
524(a)(3)	§§730, 731	544(b)	§§99, 363, 435, 438, 439
524(b)	§730	545	§§351, 394, 424, 435, 439, 441
524(c)	§§203, 732, 733, 734, 944	545(1)(A)	§353
524(c)(1)	§736	545(1)(B)	§353
524(c)(2)(B)	§737	545(1)(C)	§353
524(c)(3)	§738	545(1)(D)	§353
524(c)(4)	§742	545(1)(E)	§353
524(c)(5)	§§743, 748	545(1)(F)	§353
524(c)(6)(A)	§§739, 749	545(2)	§§354, 360
524(c)(6)(B)	§740	545(3)	§§356, 361, 362
524(d)	§§208, 743, 746, 747, 750	545(4)	§356
524(d)(1)	§§747, 748	546(a)	§434
524(d)(2)	§749	546(a)(1)	§436
524(e)	§731	546(b)	§§355, 359, 438, 795
524(f)	§§199, 732, 741	546(b)(1)(A)	§438
524(g)	§§483, 1134, 1135, 1136	546(b)(1)(B)	§439
525	§756	546(c)	§§441, 442, 443, 444
525(a)	§757	546(c)(1)	§§447, 449
525(b)	§759	546(c)(2)	§451
525(c)	§760	546(d)	§453
541	§§99, 475, 1158	546(g)	§454
541(a)	§294	547	§§364, 375, 424, 428, 435, 441, 475
541(a)(1)	§§295, 784	547(a)(2)	§381
541(a)(2)	§§300, 957	547(a)(3)	§393
541(a)(3)	§301	547(b)	§§364, 365, 367, 380, 407
541(a)(4)	§301	547(b)(1)	§369
541(a)(5)	§§302, 308	547(b)(2)	§371
541(a)(6)	§§303, 304	547(b)(3)	§370
541(a)(7)	§305	547(b)(4)	§374
541(b)(1)	§310	547(b)(4)(B)	§461
541(b)(2)	§§311, 802	547(b)(5)	§377
541(b)(3)	§312	547(c)	§§379, 407
541(b)(4)(B)	§314	547(c)(1)	§380
541(b)(5)	§314	547(c)(2)	§383
541(c)(1)	§306	547(c)(3)	§387
541(c)(2)	§307	547(c)(3)(A)(iv)	§388
542	§475	547(c)(3)(B)	§389
542(a)	§§317, 323	547(c)(4)	§390
542(b)	§§320, 348, 475	547(c)(5)	§§391, 404
542(c)	§§324, 326, 428	547(c)(6)	§394
542(e)	§331	547(c)(7)	§395
543	§546	547(c)(8)	§§396, 406
543(a)	§327	547(e)	§§375, 397
543(b)	§327	547(e)(1)	§398

B.C. §§	Text §§
547(e)(2)	§399
547(e)(2)(A)	§§400, 795
547(e)(2)(B)	§401
547(e)(2)(C)	§402
547(e)(3)	§§399, 403
547(f)	§373
547(g)	§408
548	§§411, 417, 424, 435, 475
548(a)	§§363, 409
548(a)(1)	§§413, 419
548(a)(2)(A)	§§416, 418, 419, 420, 422
548(a)(2)(B)(i)	§416
548(a)(2)(B)(ii)	§§420, 422
548(a)(2)(B)(iii)	§423
548(b)	§426
548(c)	§424
548(d)(1)	§411
548(d)(2)(A)	§417
549	§§325, 438, 411, 439
549(a)	§427
549(a)(2)(A)	§§428, 430
549(b)	§§175, 430, 431
549(c)	§§432, 433
549(d)	§436
550	§§325, 464, 522, 1119
550(a)	§§456, 461, 463
550(a)(1)	§461
550(b)	§459
550(b)(1)	§460
550(c)	§461
550(d)	§463
550(e)	§462
550(f)	§464
551	§455
552(a)	§465
552(b)	§466
552(b)(1)	§467
552(b)(2)	§468
553	§§247, 320, 435, 522, 789, 1119
553(a)	§§334, 345
553(a)(1)	§336
553(a)(2)	§337
553(a)(3)	§339
553(b)(1)	§§340, 341
553(b)(2)	§341
553(c)	§338
554	§§203, 247
554(a)	§469
554(b)	§472
701	§9

B.C. §§	Text §§
701(a)	§228
701(a)(1)	§941
702	§§203, 941, 944
702(a)	§230
702(b)	§229
702(c)	§233
702(d)	§228
704	§239
704(1)	§§240, 942
704(2)	§§241, 242, 243, 1013, 1151
704(3)	§§206, 241, 243, 1151
704(4)	§§241, 243, 1151
704(5)	§§241, 242, 243, 944, 1013, 1151
704(6)	§§241, 243, 1151
704(7)	§§241, 242, 243, 1013, 1151
704(8)	§§241, 242, 1013, 1154
704(9)	§§241, 242, 243, 1013, 1151
705	§203
706	§211
706(a)	§§986, 989
706(b)	§§987, 990, 991, 992
706(c)	§987
706(d)	§988
707	§217
707(a)	§989
707(a)(1)	§989
707(a)(2)	§989
707(a)(3)	§989
707(b)	§279
721	§§247, 263, 943
722	§§203, 526, 752, 755, 944
723(a)	§964
723(b)	§965
723(c)	§§966, 967
723(d)	§968
724(a)	§960
724(b)	§§961, 963
724(b)(1)	§961
724(b)(2)	§961
724(b)(3)	§961
724(b)(4)	§961
724(b)(5)	§961
724(b)(6)	§961
724(c)	§962
724(d)	§963
725	§§240, 526, 535, 942, 945, 946
726	§§240, 526, 942, 945
726(a)	§§955, 958
726(a)(1)	§§517, 948, 953
726(a)(2)	§§517, 953

B.C. §§	Text §§
726(a)(2)(A)	§949
726(a)(2)(B)	§§949, 950
726(a)(2)(C)	§517
726(a)(3)	§§517, 951, 953
726(a)(4)	§§952, 953, 960
726(a)(5)	§509
726(a)(6)	§954
726(b)	§§577, 925, 955, 956
726(c)	§957
727(a)	§§194, 677, 715, 969, 1122
727(a)(1)	§§554, 972, 973
727(a)(2)	§§972, 974, 980
727(a)(2)(B)	§978
727(a)(3)	§§972, 976, 980
727(a)(4)	§§972, 977, 980
727(a)(5)	§§972, 978, 980
727(a)(6)	§§972, 979, 980, 984
727(a)(6)(B)	§202
727(a)(7)	§§972, 980
727(a)(8)	§§972, 981
727(a)(9)	§972
727(a)(9)(A)	§982
727(a)(9)(B)	§982
727(a)(10)	§§972, 983
727(b)	§§969, 970
727(c)(1)	§971
727(c)(2)	§971
727(d)(1)	§§984, 985
727(d)(2)	§§984, 985
727(d)(3)	§§984, 985
727(e)	§985
741	§129
761	§129
1101	§11
1101(1)	§§20, 1006
1102	§§25, 203, 547, 1202
1102(a)	§292
1102(a)(1)	§§995, 1000
1102(a)(2)	§1000
1102(a)(3)	§1133
1102(b)(1)	§§995, 999
1102(b)(2)	§1001
1103(a)	§§268, 1003
1103(b)	§§268, 1004
1103(c)	§§25, 1002
1103(c)(1)	§1002
1103(c)(2)	§1002
1103(c)(3)	§1002
1103(c)(4)	§1002
1103(c)(5)	§1002

B.C. §§	Text §§
1104	§177
1104(a)	§§234, 236
1104(a)(1)	§§235, 1010, 1236
1104(b)	§§237, 292, 1012
1104(c)	§§251, 292
1104(c)(1)	§§253, 1017
1104(c)(2)	§§253, 1016
1104(d)	§§224, 234, 252, 257, 292, 1012, 1016
1105	§1015
1106(a)	§§239, 242
1106(a)(1)	§§242, 1013
1106(a)(2)	§§242, 1013
1106(a)(3)	§§242, 243, 254, 1013, 1018, 1151
1106(a)(4)	§§242, 243, 254, 1013, 1018, 1151
1106(a)(5)	§§242, 1013
1106(a)(6)	§§242, 1013
1106(a)(7)	§§242, 1013
1106(b)	§§254, 1018
1107(a)	§§256, 833, 897, 1006
1107(b)	§§276, 1008
1108	§§242, 247, 1006, 1014
1109(a)	§1021
1109(b)	§§1019, 1020
1110	§§805, 1115
1111	§1022
1111(a)	§§495, 1023
1111(b)	§§1026, 1027, 1028, 1030, 1052, 1103, 1269
1111(b)(1)(A)	§1024
1111(b)(1)(A)(i)	§1025
1111(b)(1)(A)(ii)	§1025
1111(b)(1)(B)(i)	§1027
1111(b)(1)(B)(ii)	§1027
1111(b)(2)	§§1026, 1028, 1029
1112	§§211, 217, 1032
1112(a)	§1033
1112(b)	§§43, 219, 774, 1034, 1036
1112(b)(1)	§1036
1112(b)(2)	§1036
1112(b)(3)	§1036
1112(b)(4)	§1036
1112(b)(5)	§1036
1112(b)(6)	§1036
1112(b)(7)	§1036
1112(b)(8)	§1036
1112(b)(9)	§1036
1112(b)(10)	§1036

288—Bankruptcy

B.C. §§	Text §§
1112(c)	§§774, 1037
1112(d)	§1038
1112(d)(1)	§1038
1112(d)(2)	§1038
1112(d)(3)	§1038
1112(e)	§1036
1113	§§1039, 1040
1113(b)(1)	§1040
1113(b)(1)(A)	§1040
1113(b)(1)(B)	§1040
1113(b)(2)	§1040
1113(c)(2)	§1040
1113(c)(3)	§1040
1113(d)	§1041
1113(e)	§1042
1113(f)	§1043
1114	§1096
1114(e)(2)	§550
1121(a)	§1044
1121(b)	§1045
1121(c)	§1046
1121(c)(1)	§1046
1121(c)(2)	§1046
1121(c)(3)	§1046
1121(d)	§1047
1121(e)	§1133
1121(e)(2)	§1133
1121(e)(3)	§1133
1122	§§1048, 1077, 1173
1122(a)	§§1049, 1050, 1051, 1052, 1056
1122(b)	§1055
1123	§§1057, 1077
1123(a)(1)	§§1048, 1054, 1058
1123(a)(2)	§1058
1123(a)(3)	§1058
1123(a)(4)	§1058
1123(a)(5)(A)-(J)	§1058
1123(a)(6)	§1058
1123(a)(7)	§§1054, 1058
1123(a)(9)	§1054
1123(b)(1)	§1059
1123(b)(2)	§§878, 1059
1123(b)(3)	§1059
1123(b)(4)	§§135, 1059
1123(b)(5)	§1059
1123(b)(6)	§1059
1123(c)	§1060
1123(d)	§1061
1124	§§1062, 1264, 1266
1124(1)	§1063
1124(2)	§1064
1124(2)(C)	§1064
1125	§§1077, 1265
1125(a)	§1070
1125(a)(1)	§1067
1125(b)	§§1066, 1070
1125(c)	§1068
1125(d)	§1069
1125(e)	§1069
1125(f)	§1133
1126	§1265
1126(a)	§1071
1126(b)	§1071
1126(c)	§1072
1126(d)	§1073
1126(e)	§1074
1126(f)	§1075
1126(g)	§1076
1127	§1077
1128	§§1078, 1266
1129	§526
1129(a)	§§1079, 1087
1129(a)(1)	§1080
1129(a)(2)	§1081
1129(a)(3)	§1082
1129(a)(4)	§1083
1129(a)(5)	§1084
1129(a)(6)	§1085
1129(a)(7)(A)	§1086
1129(a)(7)(B)	§1087
1129(a)(8)	§1097
1129(a)(9)(A)	§§1054, 1090
1129(a)(9)(B)	§1091
1129(a)(9)(B)(i)	§1091
1129(a)(9)(B)(ii)	§1091
1129(a)(9)(C)	§§1054, 1092
1129(a)(10)	§§1052, 1088, 1089
1129(a)(11)	§1094
1129(a)(12)	§1095
1129(a)(13)	§1096
1129(b)	§§1087, 1088
1129(b)(1)	§§1097, 1098
1129(b)(2)	§1099
1129(b)(2)(A)(i)	§§1030, 1101
1129(b)(2)(A)(ii)	§1106
1129(b)(2)(A)(iii)	§1105
1129(b)(2)(B)(i)	§1108
1129(b)(2)(B)(ii)	§§1109, 1267
1129(b)(2)(C)(i)	§1112
1129(b)(2)(C)(ii)	§1113

B.C. §§	Text §§
1129(d)	§1116
1141(a)	§1117
1141(b)	§§800, 808, 1118
1141(c)	§1118
1141(d)	§1268
1141(d)(1)(A)	§§808, 1119
1141(d)(1)(B)	§1119
1141(d)(2)	§1121
1141(d)(3)	§1122
1142	§1126
1143	§1127
1144	§1128
1145(a)	§1129
1145(b)	§1130
1145(c)	§1129
1201	§§12, 1233, 1260
1202	§§263, 1259
1202(a)	§§238, 292, 1234
1202(b)	§§239, 244
1202(b)(5)	§§247, 1234
1203	§§244, 247, 833, 1234, 1248
1204(a)	§1236
1205	§§777, 1249, 1261
1205(b)(1)	§§1234, 1249
1205(b)(2)	§§1234, 1249
1205(b)(3)	§§1234, 1249
1205(b)(4)	§§1234, 1249
1206	§1250
1207(a)	§1235
1207(a)(2)	§304
1207(b)	§§207, 238, 1235
1208	§§211, 217
1208(a)	§1276
1208(b)	§1277
1208(c)	§1279
1208(c)(1)	§1280
1208(c)(2)	§1280
1208(c)(3)	§1280
1208(c)(4)	§1280
1208(c)(5)	§1280
1208(c)(6)	§1280
1208(c)(7)	§1280
1208(c)(8)	§1280
1208(c)(9)	§1280
1208(d)	§§1278, 1280
1221	§§1237, 1246, 1280
1222(a)	§1239
1222(b)	§§1239, 1272
1222(b)(2)	§§1252, 1272
1222(b)(5)	§1238

B.C. §§	Text §§
1222(b)(6)	§878
1222(b)(8)	§1253
1222(b)(9)	§§1238, 1254, 1272
1222(c)	§§1238, 1252, 1254, 1274
1223	§1243
1224	§§1255, 1266
1225	§§526, 1240
1225(a)(4)	§1273
1225(a)(5)	§§1254, 1271
1225(a)(5)(A)	§1271
1225(a)(5)(B)	§§1271, 1272
1225(a)(5)(C)	§1271
1225(b)(1)	§§1256, 1274
1225(b)(2)	§1275
1226	§§1241, 1247
1226(c)	§1270
1227	§1242
1227(b)	§801
1228	§1268
1228(a)(1)	§730
1228(a)(2)	§1257
1229	§1243
1230	§§1244, 1280
1301	§§13, 1233
1301(a)	§1143
1301(a)(1)	§1145
1301(a)(2)	§1145
1301(c)	§1146
1301(c)(1)	§1146
1301(c)(2)	§1148
1301(c)(3)	§1149
1301(d)	§1148
1302	§1234
1302(a)	§§238, 292, 1150
1302(b)	§239
1302(b)(1)	§§243, 1151
1302(b)(2)	§§243, 1151
1302(b)(4)	§§243, 1151
1302(b)(5)	§§243, 1151
1302(c)	§243
1303	§§834, 1152, 1248
1304	§§834, 1248
1304(a)	§1153
1304(b)	§§864, 1153, 1235
1304(c)	§1154
1305	§1184
1305(a)	§1155
1305(a)(2)	§1215
1305(b)	§1156
1305(c)	§§1154, 1157

B.C. §§	Text §§	B.C. §§	Text §§
1306(a)	§§1158, 1235	1325(a)(5)(C)	§1201
1306(a)(2)	§304	1325(a)(6)	§1202
1306(b)	§§207, 238, 1158	1325(b)	§1198
1307	§§211, 217, 1159, 1221	1325(b)(1)	§§1203, 1204, 1256
1307(a)	§1160	1325(b)(2)	§1204
1307(b)	§1161	1325(c)	§1205
1307(c)	§§1162, 1163	1326	§1241
1307(c)(1)	§1163	1326(a)(1)	§§1151, 1163, 1206, 1247
1307(c)(2)	§1163	1326(a)(2)	§1207
1307(c)(3)	§1163	1326(b)	§1209
1307(c)(4)	§1163	1326(c)	§§1151, 1208
1307(c)(5)	§1163	1327	§1242
1307(c)(6)	§1163	1327(a)	§1210
1307(c)(7)	§1163	1327(b)	§§801, 1211
1307(c)(8)	§1163	1327(c)	§§1211, 1212
1307(c)(9)	§1163	1328	§§986, 1213
1307(c)(10)	§1163	1328(a)	§§678, 1214, 1215, 1257
1307(d)	§1164	1328(a)(1)	§§730, 1215
1307(e)	§1165	1328(a)(2)	§1215
1321	§§156, 1167, 1237	1328(a)(3)	§1215
1322	§1192	1328(b)	§1217
1322(a)	§§1168, 1239	1328(b)(1)	§1217
1322(a)(1)	§1169	1328(b)(2)	§1217
1322(a)(2)	§§1170, 1196	1328(b)(3)	§1217
1322(a)(3)	§§1171, 1195, 1197	1328(c)	§1218
1322(b)	§§1172, 1239	1328(d)	§1215
1322(b)(1)	§§1173, 1174	1328(e)	§1219
1322(b)(2)	§§1175, 1180, 1252	1329	§1243
1322(b)(4)	§1179	1329(a)	§1220
1322(b)(5)	§§1180, 1215	1330	§§1163, 1244
1322(b)(6)	§1184		
1322(b)(7)	§§878, 1185		
1322(b)(8)	§1186		
1322(b)(9)	§1187		
1322(b)(10)	§1188		
1322(c)(1)	§1181		
1322(c)(2)	§1177		
1322(d)	§§1191 1238		
1322(e)	§1183		
1323	§1243		
1324	§§1193, 1255		
1325	§§526, 1240		
1325(a)	§1194		
1325(a)(1)	§§243, 1195		
1325(a)(2)	§§1177, 1195		
1325(a)(3)	§219		
1325(a)(4)	§1200		
1325(a)(5)	§§1175, 1201, 1220		
1325(a)(5)(A)	§1201		
1325(a)(5)(B)	§1201		

TABLE OF CITATIONS TO FEDERAL RULES OF BANKRUPTCY PROCEDURE

Rule	Text §§
1004(a)	§152
1006	§144
1007	§§159, 181
1007(a)	§153
1007(a)(3)	§§155, 1001
1007(b)(1)	§153
1007(d)	§§155, 996
1007(g)	§158
1011(b)	§171
1013(b)	§171
1014(a)(2)	§103
1015(b)	§150
1019(3)	§500
2002(a)(1)	§193
2002(a)(7)	§494
2002(d)	§193
2002(l)	§193
2003(a)	§191
2003(b)	§195
2004	§198
2007	§999
2014	§264
2016(a)	§271
2016(b)	§286
2017	§286
3002	§484
3002(c)	§§493, 517
3002(c)(1)	§517
3002(c)(2)	§494
3002(c)(3)	§494
3002(c)(4)	§494
3003(b)	§495
3003(c)(2)	§494

Rule	Text §§
3003(c)(3)	§§493, 494
3004	§491
3005(a)	§490
3014	§1031
3015	§1193
3015(a)	§§157, 1246
3015(b)	§§156, 211, 1163, 1167, 1246
3015(f)	§§1199, 1240
3018(b)	§1071
3018(c)	§1071
3018(d)	§1028
3020(b)	§1078
4001(a)(1)	§§825, 849
4001(a)(2)	§829
4002	§209
4003(a)	§643
4003(b)	§645
4003(d)	§§649, 1189
4007(b)	§724
4007(c)	§723
6006	§§878, 911, 915
6007	§469
7004	§50
7004(h)	§51
7024	§1020
8001(a)	§111
8002(a)	§111
9001(3)	§90
9006(b)(1)	§497
9011	§48
9014	§§878, 911, 915
9020	§§45, 46
9027(a)(1)	§90

TABLE OF CASES

A & J Elastic Mills, Inc., *In re* - §231
AG Consultants Grain Division, Inc., *In re* - §1050
A. H. Robins, Inc., *In re* (1989) - §731
A. H. Robins Co., *In re* (68 Bankr. 705 (1986)) - §879
A. H. Robins Co., *In re* (63 Bankr. 986 (1986)) - §481
AOV Industries, Inc., *In re* - §1049
Abbotts Dairies, Inc., *In re* - §837
Aberegg, *In re* - §1208
Abernathy, *In re* - §729
Acequia, Inc., *In re* (1994) - §363
Acequia, Inc., *In re* (1986) - §1094
Advo-System, Inc. v. Maxway Corp. - §384
Air Florida Systems, Inc., *In re* - §427
Albany Partners, Ltd., *In re* - §§810, 1036
All Media Properties, Inc., *In re* - §172
All-Brite Sign Service Co., *In re* - §334
Allegheny International, Inc., *In re* (1989) - §1020
Allegheny International, Inc., *In re* (1990) - §1074
Allison, *In re* - §680
Almarc Manufacturing, Inc., *In re* - §372
Altair Airlines, Inc., *In re* - §997
Amarex, Inc., *In re* (78 Bankr. 605 (1985)) - §600
Amarex, Inc., *In re* (53 Bankr. 12 (1985)) - §1129
Amatex Corp., *In re* - §§115, 483, 1019
American Ambulance Service, Inc., *In re* - §391
American Lumber Co., *In re* - §606
American Mariner Industries, Inc., *In re* - §§118, 773, 774, 814, 830
American Provision Co., *In re* - §1040
American Reserve Corp., *In re* - §489
American Standard Credit, Inc. v. National Cement Co. - §877
American Universal Insurance Co. v. Pugh - §75
Ames Department Stores, Inc., *In re* - §867
Anchor Savings Bank F.S.B. v. Sky Valley, Inc. - §871
Anchorage Boat Sales, Inc., *In re* - §§847, 1010
Anderson, *In re* - §§1203, 1274
Aneiro, *In re* - §§878, 1185
Anthony Tammaro, Inc., *In re* - §84
Apple Tree Partners, L.P., *In re* - §1104
Arkansas Co., *In re* - §§259, 1005
Armstrong, *In re* - §1226
Arnhold v. Kyrus - §748
Arnold, *In re* - §1220

Arnold Print Works, Inc., *In re* - §68
Aslan, *In re* - §921
Atlas Automation, Inc., *In re* - §65
Attinello, *In re* - §319
Augustine v. United States - §665
Axona International Credit Commerce Limited, *In re* - §190

B & L Oil Co., *In re* - §344
BFP v. RTC - §419
BH & P, Inc., *In re* - §250
B.O.S.S. Partners I, *In re* - §818
B. Siegel Co., *In re* - §912
Baker v. National City Bank of Cleveland - §347
Baldwin-United Corp, *In re* - §520
Barnhill v. Johnson - §407
Basin Electric Power Cooperative v. Midwest Processing Co. - §165
Becker, *In re* - §579
Begier v. IRS - §368
Beker Industries Corp., *In re* - §853
Bel-Aire Investments, Inc., *In re* - §151
Belanger, *In re* - §753
Bell, *In re* - §753
Benedict, *In re* - §723
Bennett, *In re* - §690
Benny, *In re* - §148
Bethune, *In re* - §363
Billings, *In re* - §658
Blackman, *In re* - §72
Blanchette, *In re* - §981
Bloom, *In re* - §831
Bloomingdale Partners, *In re* - §1052
Board of Governors of the Federal Reserve System v. MCorp. Financial, Inc. - §796
Bodin Apparel, Inc., *In re* - §559
Bonner Mall Partnership, *In re* - §1110
Boston Post Road Limited Partnership, *In re* - §1052
Bouy, Halland, Honard & Associates, *In re* - §1104
Bradt v. Woodlawn Auto Workers - §303
Braniff Airways, Inc., *In re* (1993) - §390
Braniff Airways, Inc., *In re* (1984) - §§334, 350
Braniff Airways, Inc., *In re* (1983) - §897
Brentwood Outpatient Ltd., *In re* - §529
Brileya, *In re* - §1250
Broomall Industries v. Data Design Logic Systems - §1124
Brown v. Felsen - §718

Bankruptcy—295

Brown v. First National Bank of Little Rock - §367
Bruner, *In re* - §679
Brunner, *In re* - §705
Bryant, *In re* - §219
Budget Service Co. v. Better Homes of Virginia, Inc. - §831
Bugna, *In re* - §689
Bullard v. Aluminum Co. of America - §425
Bullion Reserve of North America, *In re* - §457
Bumper Sales, Inc., *In re* - §466
Buren, *In re* - §1205
Burns, *In re* - §679
Busenlehner, *In re* - §398
Butcher, *In re* - §201
By-Rite Distributing, Inc., *In re* - §911

CGI Industries, Inc., *In re* - §859
Caldwell, *In re* - §986
California State Board of Equalization v. Sierra Summit, Inc. - §862
Capitol Credit Plan of Tennessee, Inc. v. Shaffer - §112
Cardinal Industries, Inc., *In re* - §897
Carey, *In re* - §975
Carolina Produce Distributors, Inc., *In re* - §83
Carolina Sales Corp., *In re* (1985) - §257
Carolina Sales Corp., *In re* (1984) - §562
Carver v. Carver - §86
Cascade Roads, Inc., *In re* - §343
Case v. Los Angeles Lumber Products Co. - §1110
Cash Currency Exchange, Inc., *In re* - §§113, 126, 328
Cassidy v. Commissioner of Internal Revenue - §700
Castlerock Properties, *In re* - §65
Catron, *In re* - §897
Cecchini, *In re* - §695
Celeste Court Apartments, Inc., *In re* - §1065
Celotex Corporation v. Edwards - §42
Center Wholesale, Inc., *In re* - §873
Central Mortgage & Trust, Inc., *In re* - §126
Challenge Air International, Inc., *In re* - §319
Channel Home Centers, Inc., *In re* - §907
Charter Co., *In re* (876 F.2d 866 (1989)) - §489
Charter Co., *In re* (862 F.2d 1500 (1989)) - §520
Charter Co., *In re* (1985) - §448
Chastant, *In re* - §974
Chateaugay Corporation, *In re* (944 F.2d 997 (1991)) - §479
Chateaugay Corporation, *In re* (920 F.2d 183 (1990)) - §831

Cheeseman v. Nachman - §642
Cheesman, *In re* - §705
Chenowath, *In re* - §302
Chippenham Hospital, Inc. v. Bondurant - §637
Christopher, *In re* - §1124
Cisneros, *In re* - §1219
Citizens Bank of Maryland v. Strumpf - §§321, 346, 347, 348, 349, 790
City of - *see* name of city
Clark, *In re* (1991) - §990
Clark, *In re* (1989) - §304
Clark, *In re* (1985) - §697
Clark Pipe & Supply Co., *In re* - §604
Club Associates, *In re* - §1104
Coast Trading Co., *In re* - §443
Coastal Cable T.V., Inc., *In re* - §1082
Coastal Dry Dock & Repair Corp., *In re* - §908
Cochise College Park, Inc., *In re* - §246
Coleman, *In re* - §572
Columbia Gas Systems, Inc., *In re* - §293
Columbia Packing Co., *In re* - §560
Columbia Ribbon & Carbon Manufacturing Co., *In re* - §950
Colvin, *In re* - §1201
Comeaux v. Brown & Williamson Tobacco Co. - §759
Commercial Heat Treating of Dayton, Inc., *In re* - §66
Commercial Western Finance Corp., *In re* - §1053
Commissioner of Pennsylvania Department of Environmental Resources v. Conroys - §539
Commodity Futures Trading Commission v. Weintraub - §§247, 332, 1014
Compton Corp., *In re* - §370
Connecticut National Bank v. Germain - §114
Consolidated Properties Limited Partnership, *In re* - §531
Conte, *In re* - §696
Conti, *In re* - §729
Continental Air Lines, Inc., *In re* (1986) - §838
Coppie, *In re* - §405
Cornist, *In re* - §807
Coston, *In re* - §684
Cotton, *In re* - §1277
Cournoyer v. Town of Lincoln - §796
Coutee, *In re* - §458
Cox, *In re* - §976

DRW Property Co., *In re* - §1025
Daily Corp., *In re* - §§43, 1035
Davidson Transfer & Storage Co., *In re* - §559

Day Resource & Development Co., *In re* - §813
Dean v. Davis - §380
DeChiaro v. New York State Tax Commission - §567
Deel Rent-A-Car, Inc. v. Levine & Freehling - §672
Deloian, *In re* - §680
Delta Resources, Inc., *In re* - §§530, 772
Denson, *In re* - §143
Destron, Inc., *In re* - §69
Devers, *In re* - §978
Dewsnup v. Timm, - §534
Diamond Mortgage Corp. of Illinois v. Sugar - §51
Dias, *In re* - §297
Dillon, *In re* - §655
Dixie Broadcasting, Inc., *In re* - §815
Dondey, *In re* - §281
Draggoo Electric Co., *In re* - §1125
Drexel Burnham Lambert Group, *In re* - §876
Dube, *In re* - §679
Dubose, *In re* - §581
Duncan, *In re* - §341
Dunn, *In re* - §508

EEOC v. McLean Trucking Co. - §796
Eagle Bus Manufacturing, Inc., *In re* - §497
Eagle-Picher Industries, Inc., *In re* - §222
Easbe Enterprises, Inc., *In re* - §898
Easton, *In re* - §1226
Eddleman v. United States Department of Labor - §796
Edgeworth, *In re* - §731
Education Assistance Corp. v. Zellner - §1197
Ellingsen MacLean Oil Co., *In re* - §874
Ellis v. Consolidated Diesel Electric Corp. - §780
Employers Insurance of Wausau v. Plaid Pantries, Inc. - §560
Esbon Grain Co., *In re* - §561
Escobedo, *In re* - §1170
Espinoza, *In re* - §372
Estate of - *see* name of party
Evans Potato Co., *In re* - §369
Evans Products Co., *In re* - §1042
Evingham, *In re* - §672
Exclusive Industries Corp., *In re* - §108

F/S AirLease II, Inc. v. Simon - §258
Fabricators, *In re* - §606
Farrey v. Sanderfoot - §§649, 651, 652
Federated Department Stores, Inc., *In re* - §260
Field v. Mans - §680

First Bank of Miller v. Wieseler - §849
First Capital Mortgage Loan Corp. *In re* - §301
Firstcorp, Inc., *In re* - §936
Flagstaff Foodservice Corp., *In re* (1985) - §532
Flagstaff Foodservice Corp., *In re* (1984) - §580
Flaten, *In re* - §§362, 378
Flo-Lizer, Inc., *In re* - §540
Flowers, *In re* - §750
Franklin Savings v. Office of Thrift Supervision - §83
Frontier Properties, Inc., *In re* - §923
Fuel Oil Supply & Terminaling v. Gulf Oil Corp. - §1020
Fulghum Construction Corp., *In re* (1989) - §383
Fulghum Construction Corp., *In re* (1983) - §390
Fussell, *In re* - §792

Gallo, *In re* - §641
Garcia, *In re* - §576
Garner, *In re* - §637
Gaslight Club v. Official Creditors Committee - §109
Gee, *In re* - §§184, 185
Geffken, *In re* - §757
General Motors Acceptance Corp. v. Jones - §§1104, 1201
Georgetown of Kettering, Ltd., *In re* - §266
Germain v. Connecticut National Bank - §78
Gerwer, *In re* - §319
Giller, *In re* - §49
Gloria Manufacturing Corp. v. International Ladies' Garment Workers' Union - §876
Godroy Wholesale Co., *In re* - §179
Goerg, *In re* - §§182, 183
Goldblatt Bros., Inc., *In re* - §892
Gonic Realty Trust, *In re* - §122
Gordon, *In re* - §722
Gorski, *In re* - §246
Graham, *In re* (1992) - §721
Graham, *In re* (1986) - §1217
Granada Wines, Inc. v. New England Teamsters & Trucking Industry Pension Fund - §1051
Granfinanciera, S.A. v. Nordberg - §§73, 74, 79
Granger, *In re* - §642
Graven, *In re* - §1278
Great Western Bank v. Sierra Woods Group - §1104
Green, *In re* - §1162
Greene County Hospital, *In re* - §117
Greenland Vistas, Inc., *In re* - §1024
Greer, *In re* - §1191
Greiman, *In re* - §822

Greystone III Joint Venture, *In re* - §1052
Griffiths, *In re* - §1029
Griggs, *In re* - §438
Grogan v. Garner - §§717, 719
Grosslight, *In re* - §637
Groves, *In re* - §1174
Grubbs v. Houston First American Savings Association - §1178
Grynberg, *In re* - §1121

HLM, *In re* - §560
Haas, *In re* - §679
Hall, *In re* - §669
Hallahan, *In re* - §79
Hallum, *In re* - §1025
Halpern, *In re* - §720
Hammond, *In re* - §1176
Hammonds, *In re* - §§138, 1139
Hanratty, *In re* - §938
Harris, *In re* (14 Bankr. Ct. Dec. 640 (1986)) - §1174
Harris, *In re* (1985) - §§629, 630
Harris Management Co., *In re* - §879
Hartley, *In re* (1989) - §695
Hartley, *In re* (1985) - §249
Healis, *In re* - §509
Heape, *In re* - §664
Heatron, Inc., *In re* - §264
Hecht, *In re* - §308
Henderson Ranches, *In re* - §1229
Hendren, *In re* - §978
Henry, *In re* - §163
Hewitt, *In re* - §1064
Hicks, *In re* - §759
Hickson, *In re* - §1182
Hilmoe, *In re* - §645
Hines, *In re* - §707
Hipp, *In re* - §47
Hoggle, *In re* - §1220
Holford, *In re* - §344
Holly Hill Medical Center, Inc., *In re* - §423
Holthoff, *In re* - §1053
Holywell Corp., *In re* - §877
Holywell Corporation v. Smith - §1058
Honosky, *In re* - §817
Horowitz, *In re* - §907
Hotel Associates of Tucson, *In re* - §1089
Huckfeldt, *In re* - §989
Huebner, *In re* - §116
Hughes, *In re* - §976
Hunt, *In re* - §585
Hunter, *In re* - §637

IML Freight, Inc., *In re* - §955
IRFM, Inc., *In re* - §390
In re - *see* name of party
Inforex, Inc., *In re* - §1123
Infosystems Technology, Inc., v. Logical Software, Inc. - §881
International Horizons, Inc., *In re* (1985) - §499
International Horizons, Inc., *In re* (1982) - §333
Isis Foods, Inc., *In re* - §428
Israel-British Bank (London) Ltd. v. Federal Deposit Insurance Corp. - §§126, 128

J. Catton Farms v. First National Bank of Chicago - §467
JFK Chevrolet, Inc., *In re* - §532
Jackson, *In re* - §736
James A. Phillips, Inc., *In re* - §841
James Cable Partners, L.P., *In re* - §897
Jartran, Inc., *In re* - §1055
Jarvis, *In re* - §258
Jensen, *In re* - §481
Jet Florida Systems, Inc., *In re* - §380
John Deskins Pic Pac, Inc., *In re* - §866
Johns-Manville Corp., *In re* (1989) - §1126
Johns-Manville Corp., *In re* (1987) - §116
Johns-Manville Corp., *In re* (68 Bankr. 618 (1986)) - §1079
Johns-Manville Corp., *In re* (60 Bankr. 612 (1986)) - §843
Johns-Manville Corp., *In re* (57 Bankr. 680 (1986)) - §§42, 481, 781
Johns-Manville Corp., *In re* (1985) - §110
Johns-Manville Corp., *In re* (45 Bankr. 833 (1984)) - §110
Johns-Manville Corp., *In re* (45 Bankr. 823 (1984)) - §518
Johns-Manville Corp., *In re* (40 Bankr. 219 (1984)) - §296
Johnson, *In re* (1989) - §491
Johnson, *In re* (1986) - §§706, 1215
Johnson v. Home State Bank - §1190
Jones, *In re* - §1204
Jorges Carpet Mills, Inc., *In re* - §430
Joshua Slocum, Ltd., *In re* - §892

Kaiser, *In re* - §414
Kane v. Johns-Manville Corp. - §§483, 1134, 1137
Kastigar v. United States - §200
Katchen v. Landy - §§73, 77
Kelly, *In re* - §990
Kelly v. Robinson - §§701, 712

Kemble, *In re* - §85
Kendavis Industries International, Inc., *In re* - §275
Kenney's Franchise Corp. v. Central Fidelity Bank NA - §349
Kerwin, *In re* - §1271
Kham & Nate's Shoes No. 2, Inc. v. First National Bank of Whiting - §1110
Kinglore Farms, Inc., *In re* - §915
Kinnemore, *In re* - §270
Kirsch, *In re* - §680
Klingman v. Levinson - §721
Kocher, *In re* - §1249
Kokoszka v. Belford - §296
Konowitz, *In re* - §432
Koreag, *In re* - §186
Koubourlis, *In re* - §372
Kovacs, *In re* - §797
Kroh Brothers Development Co., *In re* - §§390, 407

L & J Anaheim Associates, *In re* - §1063
LCO Enterprises, *In re* - §377
LJP, Inc., *In re* - §913
Lagenkamp v. Culp - §§73, 77
Laguna Associates Ltd. Partnership, *In re* - §815
LaJolla Mortgage Fund v. Rancho El Cajon Associates - §771
Lambert, *In re* - §638
Lambert Implement Co., *In re* - §282
Land, *In re* - §258
Landmark, *In re* - §726
Lane County Sheriff's Officers Association, Inc., *In re* - §122
Lang Cartage Corp., *In re* - §232
Laracuente v. Chase Manhattan Bank - §759
Larson, *In re* - §679
Lausch, *In re* - §637
Laymon, *In re* - §531
Lebron v. Mechem Financial, Inc. - §545
Lee, *In re* - §286
Lemco Gypsum, Inc., *In re* - §605
Lemelle v. Universal Manufacturing Corp. - §481
Lenox, *In re* - §642
Leser, *In re* - §1174
LeSueur, *In re* - §730
Lewis, *In re* - §785
Lion Capital Group, *In re* - §61
Liona Corp., N.V., *In re* - §770
Lionel Corp., *In re* (1994) - §795
Lionel Corp., *In re* (1983) - §838

Little Creek Development Co., *In re* - §815
Lones, *In re* - §716
Long, *In re* - §697
Longua, *In re* - §907
Love, *In re* - §1163
Lubrizol Enterprises, Inc. v. Richmond Metal Finishers, Inc. - §880

M. Frenville Co., *In re* - §482
MacDonald, *In re* - §§816, 819
MacLeod Co., *In re* - §1074
Macon Prestressed Concrete Co., *In re* - §1009
Madison Hotel Associates, *In re* - §1065
Magness, *In re* - §897
Malone, *In re* - §147
Manchester Lakes Associates, *In re* - §172
Mann, *In re* - §860
Mannings, *In re* - §1220
Manville Forest Products Corp., *In re* (1990) - §101
Manville Forest Products Corp., *In re* (1984) - §509
Marcus, *In re* - §974
Marin Motor Oil, Inc., *In re* (1984) - §§446, 448, 450
Marin Motor Oil, Inc., *In re* (1982) - §1020
Marin Town Center, *In re* - §1074
Mark Anthony Construction, Inc., *In re* - §540
Markstein v. Massey Associates, Ltd. - §119
Marsch, *In re* - §§48, 1036
Martin, *In re* (1989) - §986
Martin, *In re* (761 F.2d 472 (1985)) - §849
Martin, *In re* (51 Bankr. 490 (1985)) - §219
Martin, *In re* (1981) - §196
Martin-Trigona, *In re* - §202
Masnorth Corp., *In re* - §1064
Matthews, *In re* - §657
Matthews v. Pineo - §707
Maxwell, *In re* - §644
Maxwell Newspapers, Inc., *In re* - §1040
May Reporting Services, Inc., *In re* - §465
McCannon v. Marston - §362
McClarty v. Gudenau - §332
McKay, *In re* - §1189
Medcare HMO, *In re* Estate of - §126
Mellon Bank, N.A. v. Metro Communications, Inc. - §421
Mellor, *In re* - §770
Memphis Partners, L.P., *In re* - §§1102, 1201
Meredith Manor, Inc., *In re* - §390
Meridian Bank v. Alten - §976
Merlino, *In re* - §957

Metrocraft Publishing Services, Inc., *In re* - §1067
Meyers Inc., *In re* - §546
Middle Plantation of Williamsburg, Inc. - §498
Middleton v. Farmers State Bank of Fosston - §664
Middleton Arms Limited Partnership, *In re* (1991) - §261
Midlantic National Bank v. New Jersey Department of Environmental Protection - §470
Miera, *In re* - §698
Mill Street, Inc., *In re* - §458
Miller, *In re* - §46
Miller v. United States Through Farmers Home Administration - §1138
Mimi's of Atlanta, *In re* - §899
Minoco Group of Companies, Ltd., *In re* - §784
Missionary Baptist Foundation of America, Inc., *In re* (1983) - §603
Missionary Baptist Foundation of America, Inc., *In re* (1982) - §582
Mitchell Excavators, Inc. v. Mitchell - §296
Mohawk Industries, Inc. v. Robinson Industries, Inc. - §66
Molded Acoustical Products, Inc., *In re* - §384
Monarch Tool & Manufacturing Co., *In re* - §881
Monnier Brothers, *In re* - §1067
Montgomery, *In re* - §143
Moody v. Amoco Oil Co. - §§59, 884
Moody v. Security Pacific Business Credit, Inc. - §421
Moore v. Bay - §363
Morgan Guaranty Trust Co. of New York v. American Savings & Loan Association - §803
Morris, *In re* (51 Bankr. 462 (1985)) - §980
Morris, *In re* (48 Bankr. 313 (1985)) - §1200
Mosby, *In re* - §122
Mosser v. Darrow - §245
Motley, *In re* - §§786, 807
Mr. Gattis, Inc., *In re* - §909
Multech Corp., *In re* - §925
Multiponics, Inc., *In re* - §606
Murel Holding Corp., *In re* - §768
Mutschler, *In re* - §579

N & D Properties, Inc., *In re* - §602
N.L.R.B. v. Edward Cooper Printing, Inc. - §796
Nash, *In re* - §1161
Nassau Associates, *In re* - §606
National City Bank of New York v. Hotchkiss - §380
National Gypsum Co., *In re* - §481

National Labor Relations Board v. Bildisco & Bildisco - §1039
National Sugar Refining Co., *In re* - §452
Natural Land Corp., *In re* - §1036
Neis, *In re* - §109
Nelkovski, *In re* - §143
Neville, *In re* - §§311, 802
New York, City of v. Exxon Corp. - §796
Newell, *In re* - §406
Newsom, *In re* - §991
Nikokyrakis, *In re* - §751
Nobelman v. American Savings Bank - §§1059, 1176
Noreen v. Slattengren - §1197
Norquist, *In re* - §876
North Port Development Co., *In re* - §548
Northeastern International Airways, Inc. - §802
Northern Pipeline Construction Co. v. Marathon Pipe Line Co. - §§5, 67
Norwest Bank Nebraska, N.A. v. Tveten - §975
Norwest Bank Worthington v. Ahlers - §1110
Nunn, *In re* - §704

Oceanquest Feeder Service, Inc., *In re* - §101
O'Connor, *In re* - §787
Ohio v. Kovacs - §§34, 479, 727
Ohio Agricultural Commodity Depositors Fund v. Mahern - §474
Old Delmar Corp., *In re* - §102
Olsen, *In re* - §437
Owen v. Owen - §667

Pacific-Atlantic Trading Co., *In re* - §909
Palm Beach Resort Properties, Inc., *In re* - §584
Paradise Valley Country Club, *In re* - §808
Park West Hotel Corp., *In re* - §810
Parker Grande Development, Inc., *In re* - §1010
Parque Forestal, Inc., *In re* - §532
Parraway v. Andrews University - §729
Patrick Cudahy, Inc., *In re* - §518
Patterson v. Shumate - §307
Pearson, *In re* (1985) - §§136, 1138
Peerless Plating Co., *In re* - §470
Penn Terra Limited v. Department of Environmental Resources - §797
Penn-Mahoning Mining, Inc., *In re* - §577
Pennsylvania Department of Public Welfare v. Davenport - §34
Pennsylvania Iron & Coal Co., *In re* - §1118
Penny Saver, Inc., *In re* - §151
Penrod, *In re* - §1118
Pepper v. Litton - §606
Perez, *In re* - §1108

Perez v. Campbell - §757
Perma Pacific Properties, *In re* - §371
Perroncello, *In re* - §853
Persky, *In re* - §637
Phar-Mor, Inc., *In re* - §1020
Phillips, *In re* - §113
Piccicuto v. Dwyer - §695
Pick, *In re* - §103
Pierce, *In re* - §264
Pioneer Investment Services Co. v. Brunswick Associates Limited Partnership - §497
Polytherm Industries, Inc., *In re* - §1058
Posta, *In re* - §697
Prescott, *In re* - §370
Prince, *In re* - §275
Pristas v. Landaus of Plymouth, Inc. - §661
Prize Frize, Inc., *In re* - §934
Production Steel, Inc., *In re* - §56
Prudential Lines, Inc., *In re* - §296
Prudhomme, *In re* - §286
Public Service Co. of New Hampshire, *In re* - §1047

Quaif v. Johnson - §690
Quinn Wholesale, Inc. v. Northern - §428

R/P International Technologies, Inc., *In re* - §886
R. Eric Peterson Construction, *In re* - §178
R.S. Pinellas Motel Partnership, *In re* - §152
Rager, *In re* - §47
Ramey, *In re* - §663
Ramirez, *In re* - §1175
Ratledge, *In re* - §1098
Recoveredge L.P. v. Pentecost - §720
Redmond v. Tuttle - §670
Reid v. Richardson - §635
Reid v. White Motor Corp. - §489
Reidenbach, *In re* - §739
Reider, *In re* - §149
Relihan v. Exchange Bank - §1118
Republic Supply Co. v. Shoaf - §731
Revco D.S., Inc., *In re* - §§530, 772, 1017
Reynolds, *In re* - §296
Richmond Leasing Co. v. Capital Bank N.A. - §§883, 890
Riggsby, *In re* - §117
Roberts, *In re* (1990) - §700
Roberts, *In re* (1987) - §264
Rochem, Ltd., *In re* - §1098
Roco Corp., *In re* - §416
Rodriguez, *In re* - §416

Rorie, *In re* - §1175
Rowley v. Yarnall - §§1203, 1274
Royal Golf Products Corp., *In re* - §367
Rubin v. Manufacturers Hanover Trust Co. - §423
Ryerson, *In re* - §296

Saco Local Development Corp., *In re* - §116
St. Angelo v. Victoria Farms, Inc. - §291
St. Laurent, *In re* - §683
St. Louis Freight Lines, Inc., *In re* - §540
St. Louis Globe-Democrat, Inc., *In re* - §1010
Sanders, *In re* - §298
Sandy Ridge Development Corp., *In re* - §1105
Sapphire Investments, *In re* - §297
Saugus General Hospital, Inc., *In re* - §334
Savig, *In re* - §392
Savoia Macaroni Manufacturing Co., *In re* - §§250, 872
Saybrook Manufacturing Co., Inc., *In re* - §872
Schoenthal v. Irving Trust Co. - §76
Sea Harvest Corp. v. Riviera Land Co. - §911
Seminole Tribe of Florida v. Florida - §474
Sequoia Auto Brokers, Ltd., *In re* - §46
Shank, *In re* - §679
Sharon Steel Corp., *In re* - §§234, 1009, 1011
Silver Mill Frozen Foods, Inc., *In re* - §77
Simasko Production Co., *In re* - §1007
Sims, *In re* - §163
Singson, *In re* - §§258, 1005
Skinner, *In re* - §46
Smith, *In re* - §1197
Smith v. Dowden - §77
Smith-Douglass, Inc., *In re* - §470
Smitty's, Inc. v. Southeast National Bank of Orlando - §327
Southeast Co., *In re* - §1064
Southern Missouri Towing Service, Inc., *In re* - §§1028, 1030
Southern States Motor Inns, Inc., *In re* - §§1104, 1201
Southland Corporation, *In re* - §1071
Southtrust Bank of Alabama v. Borg-Warner Acceptance Corp. - §660
Southwest Aircraft Services, Inc., *In re* - §907
Spada, *In re* - §382
Specialty Equipment Companies, Inc., *In re* - §731
Stadium Management Corp., *In re* - §859
Standard Metals Corp., *In re* - §489
Stanton, *In re* - §113
State Airlines, Inc., *In re* - §212
State Bank of Lombard v. Chart House - §87

Bankruptcy—301

Stedman, *In re* - §1228
Steiner, *In re* - §921
Stephens Industries, Inc. v. McClung - §838
Stewart, *In re* - §196
Stewart v. Gurley - §821
Stewart Foods, Inc., *In re* - §478
Storage Technology Corp., *In re* - §445
Storberg, *In re* - §1174
Street, *In re* - §986
Subscription Television of Greater Atlanta, *In re* - §902
Sullivan, *In re* - §610
Sumy v. Schlossberg - §637
Sun Country Development, Inc., *In re* - §1105
Sun Runner Marine, Inc., *In re* - §898
Sun World Broadcasters, Inc., *In re* - §188
Swedeland Development Group, Inc., *In re* - §874
Sweetwater, *In re* (1989) - §1059
Swicegood v. Ginn - §977

Tabor Court Realty Corp., United States v. - §421
Tammey Jewels, Inc., *In re* - §909
Tampa Bay Associates, *In re* - §1025
Tandem Group, Inc., *In re* - §956
Tarnow, *In re* - §533
Taylor, *In re* (Bankr. 1993) - §405
Taylor, *In re* (11th Cir. 1993) - §753
Taylor, *In re* (1981) - §670
Taylor v. Freeland & Kronz - §646
Tel-A-Communications Consultants, Inc., *In re* - §§296, 831
Tenna Corp., *In re* - §377
Terry Limited Partnership, *In re* - §531
Texaco, Inc., *In re* - §82
Texaco, Inc. v. Louisiana Land and Exploration Co. - §876
Things Remembered, Inc. v. Petrarca - §93
Thomas, *In re* - §1212
Thompson, *In re* (1994) - §701
Thompson, *In re* (1989) - §§664, 665
Thompson, *In re* (1986) - §922
Thompson, *In re* (1984) - §662
Tignor v. Parkinson - §296
Tim Wargo & Sons, Inc., *In re* - §1229
Timbers - *see* United Savings Association of Texas v. Timbers of Inwood Forest Associates Ltd.
Time Construction, Inc., *In re* - §54
Tinkham, *In re* - §702
Toibb v. Radloff - §§134, 994
Tolona Pizza Products Corp., *In re* - §385

Tom Carter Enterprises, *In re* - §285
Tracey, *In re* - §1204
Transportation Design & Technology, Inc., *In re* - §465
Travelers Insurance Co. v. Bullington - §1254
Treat Fitness Center, Inc., *In re* - §911
Treister, *In re* - §576
Turner, *In re* - §1280

U. L. Radio Corp., *In re* - §916
UNR Industries, Inc., *In re* (725 F.2d 1111 (1984)) - §115
UNR Industries, Inc., *In re* (45 Bankr. 322 (1984)) - §70
U.S. Truck Co., *In re* - §1050
Udell, *In re* - §479
Unioil, *In re* - §1124
Union Bank v. Wolas - §386
Union Carbide Corp. v. Newboles - §731
Union Cartage Co., *In re* - §339
United Bank of Southgate v. Nelson - §697
United Carolina Bank v. Hall - §§1104, 1201
United Insurance Management, Inc., *In re* - §437
United Savings Association of Texas v. Timbers of Inwood Forest Associates Ltd. - §§772, 774, 814, 822
United States v. Energy Resources Co. - §1059
United States v. Friendship College, Inc. - §540
United States v. Michaels - §296
United States v. Neal Pharmacal Co. - §1092
United States v. Noland - §603
United States v. Pepperman - §959
United States v. Reorganized CF&I Fabricators of Utah, Inc. - §603
United States v. Ron Pair Enterprises, Inc. - §529
United States v. Security Industrial Bank - §666
United States v. Sutton - §§512, 793
United States v. Troxler Hosiery Co. - §792
United States v. Westside Bank - §443
United States v. Whiting Pools, Inc. - §319
United States *ex rel.* Kraft v. Aetna Casualty & Surety Co. - §257
United States Trustee v. Price Waterhouse - §264
United Virginia Bank v. Slab Fork Coal Co. - §§466, 845

Vacuum Cleaner Corp. of America, *In re* - §782
Vanguard Diversified, Inc., *In re* - §872
Verco Industries, *In re* - §363
Victory Construction Co., *In re* - §815

W.E. Parks Lumber Co., *In re* - §1110
W.T. Grant, *In re* - §606
Waldron, *In re* - §219
Walker, *In re* - §307
Waterfront Companies, Inc., *In re* - §842
Waterkist Corp., *In re* - §899
Watford, *In re* - §1226
Watkins Management Group, Inc., *In re* - §513
Webster, *In re* - §1030
Weedman, *In re* - §690
Weinstein, *In re* - §663
Weiss-Wolf, Inc., *In re* - §1035
West Electronics, Inc., *In re* - §897
Westchase Associates, L.P., *In re* - §772
Westview 74th Street Drug Corp., *In re* - §910
Whatley, *In re* - §751
White, *In re* - §384
White Farm Equipment Co., *In re* - §1072
White Motor Credit, *In re* - §86
Whiteside, *In re* Estate of - §122
Whittaker, *In re* - §937

Wieboldt Stores, Inc., v. Schottenstein - §421
Wiencek, *In re* - §685
Willis, *In re* - §672
Windsor Communications Group, *In re* - §257
Windsor on the River Associates, Ltd., *In re* - §1084
Woodbrook Associates, *In re* - §1052

Yadkin Valley & Trust Co. v. McGee - §246
Yanks, *In re* - §697
Yanks, *In re* (1985) - §481
Yoder Co., *In re* - §497
Yonikus, *In re* (1993) - §644
Yonikus, *In re* (1992) - §984
Young, *In re* - §1170
Younger, *In re* - §202

ZRM-Oklahoma Partnership, *In re* - §1052
Zerodec Mega Corp., *In re* - §257
Zolfo, Cooper & Co. v. Sunbeam-Oster Company, Inc. - §272

INDEX

A

ABANDONMENT OF ESTATE
   See Bankruptcy estate
ABSTENTION
   See Jurisdiction and procedure
ADEQUATE PROTECTION
   See Protection of property; Use, sale, or lease of property
ADMINISTRATIVE EXPENSES
   See Claims of creditors
AUTOMATIC STAY
   acts enjoined
     acts against estate property, §784
     bank accounts, freeze of, §§346-349
     collection efforts, §787
     liens against debtor's property, §786
     liens against estate property, §785
     pre-petition judgments, §783
     proceedings against debtor, §§780-782
     setoffs, §§345-349, 789-790. *See also* Creditor's right to setoff
     Tax Court proceedings, §778
   and use, sale, or lease of property, §848
   defined, §778
   exceptions to stay
     acts of perfection, §795
     ad valorem tax liens, §806
     alimony, support, or paternity, §§793-794
     criminal proceedings, §792
     educational institutions, actions against, §804
     enforcement of judgments by governmental units, §797
     HUD mortgage foreclosures, §799
     police or regulatory action, §796
     presentment of negotiable instruments, §803
     recovery of property by certain lessors, §802
     repossession of aircrafts and vessels, §805
     securities, repo, and swap setoffs, §798
     tax audits and assessments, §§800-801
   expiration of stay, §§807-808
   relief from stay
     grounds for relief
       acts against property, §§820-822
       "cause," §§812-819
     lessors, §824
     nature of relief, §810
     procedure for requesting relief, §§825-830
     single asset real estate, §823
   willful violation of stay, §831
AVOIDING POWERS OF TRUSTEE
   fraudulent transfers
     definition, §§410-412
     good faith transferee, §§424-425
     in general, §409
     indirect benefit to debtor, §423
     partnership debtor, §426
     types
       intent to hinder, delay or defraud, §§413-415
       receipt of less than reasonably equivalent value, §§416-423
     hypothetical creditor or purchaser, §§357-363
       actual unsecured creditor, §363
       strong arm provision, §§357-362
   leveraged buyouts, §421
   limitations on avoiding powers
     retroactive perfection of security interest, §§438-440
     return of goods, §454
     seller's reclamation of goods, §§441-453
     statute of limitations, §§434-437
   post-petition transactions
     exceptions to trustee's avoidance, §§429-433
     bona fide purchaser, §§432-433
     gap transferee, §§429-431
     general rule—avoidance, §427
     transferor without notice or knowledge, §428
   preferential transfers
     burden of proof, §408
     elements of preference, §§365-378
     exceptions to preference rule, §§379-396
       alimony and support, §395
       consumer payments under $600, §396
       in ordinary course of business, §§383-386
       inventory and receivables, security interest in, §§391-393
       purchase money security interest, §§387-389
       statutory liens, §394
       subsequent advance of new value, §390
       substantially contemporaneous exchange for value, §§380-382
     in general, §364
     perfection rules, §§397-407
     preference time periods, §§374-376
     when transfer is made
       debtor acquires rights in property, §§403-406
       debtor pays creditor by check, §407
       time of perfection, §§400-401
   security interest
     after-acquired property clauses, §465
     certain post-petition proceeds, §§466-468
     certain post-petition rents, §468
   statutory liens avoided, §§351-356
   successor to actual unsecured creditors, §361
   trustee's recovery for avoided transfer,
     "DePrizio" problem fixed, §461
     from whom recovered, §§457-459
     good faith transferee's lien, §463
     statute of limitations, §464

B

BANKRUPTCY COURT, §§39-49
   See also Jurisdiction and procedure
BANKRUPTCY ESTATE
   See also Creditor's right of setoff; Exemptions
   abandoned property, §§469-473

certain trusts, §§307-308
ipso facto clauses, §306
property excluded, §§309-315
property included, §§294-305
turnover of property to trustee
    books and records, §§331-333
    by custodian, §§327-330
    by entity other than custodian, §§317-319
    exceptions to turnover, §§322-326
    freeze of bank accounts, §321
    payment of indebtedness to estate, §§320-326

BANKRUPTCY LAWS
amendments, §§6-7
goals, §§1-2
legislative history, §§3-7
organization of Bankruptcy Code, §§8-13
participants, §§18-27
rules of construction, §§14-17
terminology, §§28-38

C

CHAPTER 7
See Liquidation
CHAPTER 11
See Reorganization
CHAPTER 12
See Family farmer with regular income
CHAPTER 13
See Individual with regular income
CLAIMS OF CREDITORS
See also Creditor's right of setoff
administrative expenses
    allowable expenses, §§538-551
    exempt property, §553
    gap creditors' claims, §552
    priority, §537
allowance of claims
    contingent or unliquidated claims, §§518-519
    exceptions to allowance, §§507-517
    general rule, §§504-506
    pre-petition claims, §522
    reimbursement or contribution claims, §§520-521
distribution outside Code
    foreign proceeding, §607
    partnership creditors, §608
priority (unsecured) claims
    in general, §554
    order of priority, §§555-573
    pro rata distribution, §577
    special rules for tax claims, §§574-576
    subrogation, §§581-583
    superpriority—secured creditors inadequately protected, §579
    super-superpriority—post-petition credit, §580
proof of claims
    claim defined, §§478-483
    claimants, §§484-491
    future tort claims, §483
    post-petition claims treated as pre-petition, §502
    time to file, §§492-501
        conversion to Chapter 7, §500
        governmental claims, §501
secured claims
    adequate protection, §536
    defined, §523
    liens deemed void, §§533-534
    oversecured claims, §§529-531
    rights of secured creditor, §535
    surcharge against collateral, §532
    undersecured claims, §524
    valuation of collateral, §§525-528
subordination of claims
    defrauded security holders, §§600-601
    equitable subordination, §§602-606
subrogation claims, §§591-598
tax claims
    assessment, §590
    tax liability of debtor, §§584-585
    tax liability of estate, §§584-589
    tax refund, §586
unsecured claims. *See* priority claims, above

CO-DEBTORS
See Claims of creditors; Discharge; Individual with regular income—Chapter 13
COLLECTIVE BARGAINING AGREEMENTS
See Reorganization—Chapter 7
COMMENCEMENT OF CASE
abstention, §§188-190
case ancillary to foreign proceeding, §§183-187
conversion of case to another chapter, §§211-216
creditors' section 341 meeting, §§191-203. *See also* Creditors
debtor's duties, §§204-210
eligibility
    Chapter 7—"liquidation," §§123-127
    Chapter 11—"reorganization," §§130-135
    Chapter 12—"family farmer," §142
    Chapter 13—"adjustment of debts of individual," §§136-141
    ineligibility—multiple petitions, §143
    "person" defined, §§120-122
involuntary case
    answer, §169
    dismissal of petition, §§178-180
    eligibility, §161
    foreign bank, §182
    gap period, §§174-177
    order for relief against debtor, §§170-173
    petition, §§162-168
    schedules, §181
voluntary case
    automatic stay, §160
    petition, §§144-152
    schedules, §§153-159

CONVERSION
See also Commencement of case; Individual with regular income; Family farmer with regular income; Liquidation; Reorganization
authorization, §211

Chapter 7, §§986-988
Chapter 11 reorganization, §§1032-1038
Chapter 12, §§1276-1278
Chapter 13—voluntary or for cause, §§1159-1165
   farmer exception, §1165
   property of estate in voluntary case, §§216, 1166
   to Chapter 11 or 12, §1164
Chapter 7, §§986-988
effects of, §§212-213
pre-conversion claims, §214
time to file, Chapter 7, §500
trustee or examiner dismissed, §215

CORE/NON-CORE PROCEEDINGS, §§63-72
  See also Jurisdiction and procedure

CRAM DOWN
  See Reorganization—Chapter 11

CREDIT, OBTAINING
appeal, §874
cross-collateralization, §872
in general, §§863-864
in ordinary course of business, §8
notice, §873
priming lien, §871
priority or security authorized, §§867-870
out of ordinary course of business, §866

CREDITOR'S RIGHT OF SETOFF
automatic stay enjoins setoff, §343
  bank account, post-petition freeze, §§346-349
  effect, §345
  secured status of claims, §350
exceptions
  bad faith of creditor, §343
  claim transferred by nondebtor party, §337
  debt created to use for setoff, §339
  disallowed claim, §336
  improved position of creditor, §§340-342
prerequisites, §334
recoupment compared, §344
secured status of claim setoff, §348

CREDITORS
  See also Claims of creditors; Creditors' committee; Creditors' right of setoff; Distribution of property; Relief
section 341 meeting
  business of meeting, §203
  debtor must attend, §196
  equity security holders' meeting, §192
  examination of debtor, §199
  notice, §§193-194
  purpose, §§197-202
  time and place, §191
  United States trustee, §194

CREDITORS' COMMITTEE
  See Reorganization—Chapter 11

D

DEBTOR IN POSSESSION
  See Reorganization—Chapter 11

DEBTS
  See Nondischargeable debts

DISCHARGE
  See also Nondischargeable debts
Chapter 7 discharge
  grounds for denial of discharge, §§972-983
    acts committed in insider case, §980
    debtor not an individual, §973
    destruction/concealment of books or records, §976
    loss of assets, failure to account for, §978
    perjury, bribery, or other fraudulent acts, §977
    prior discharge, §§981-982
    transfer for wrongful intent, §§974-975
    violation of court order, §979
    waiver, §983
  in general, §§969-970
  objection to discharge, §971
  revocation of discharge, §§984-985
    statute of limitations, §985
co-debtor or surety—no discharge, §731
relief from personal liability, §§726-730
voluntary repayment, §732

DISCRIMINATION PROHIBITED
governmental discrimination, §§757-758
private employer, §759
student loans, §760

DISMISSAL
  See also Individual with regular income; Family farmer with regular income; Liquidation; Reorganization
bad faith, §219
effect of, §218

DISTRIBUTION OF PROPERTY
  See Liquidation—Chapter 7

E

EXAMINER
  See Officers of the estate

EXECUTORY CONTRACTS AND UNEXPIRED LEASES
agreements not assumable or assignable
  contracts to finance debt or issue securities, §898
  nonresidential leases terminated before bankruptcy, §889
  personal service and government contracts, §897
assignment, §§915-919
assumption or rejection, §§878-884
  business judgment rule, §§880-882
  court approval, §875
  election, §883
  pre-bankruptcy termination, §884
contracts and leases in default assumed, §§889-895
  adequate assurance of future performance, §§889-893
  shopping center, §§891-893
  compensation, §888
  cure of default, §§886-887
  exceptions, §894
  incidental services and supplies, §895

debtor as lessor, §§926-927
debtor as vendor, §§929-932
definitions, §§875-877
intellectual property, §§933-935
ipso facto provisions, §§912-914
rejection constitutes breach, §§920-925
time limitations to assume or reject, §§900-911

EXEMPTIONS
administrative expenses, §674
application of federal or state law, §§609-612
effect of exemptions, §§647-648
federal bankruptcy exemptions, §§613-630
joint debtors, §§640-642
    federal exemptions, §641
    state exemptions, §642
liens avoided
    Code preemption of state law, §661
    "impair an exemption," §§649-650
    judicial liens, §§651-652
    security interest, §§653-669
list of exemptions, §§643-646
nonbankruptcy federal exemptions, §633
property recovered by trustee, §§670-671
recovery and exemption by debtor, §673
tenancy by entirety and joint tenancy, §§634-639
transfer avoided by debtor, §672
state law exemptions, §§631-639

FG

FAMILY FARMER WITH REGULAR INCOME—CHAPTER 12
conversion or dismissal, §§1276-1280
differences from Chapter 11, §§1258-1270
differences from Chapter 13, §§1245-1257
eligibility for relief, §§1223-1229
multiple petitions, §1231
secured creditors, §§1271-1272
similarities to Chapter 13, §§1232-1244
sunset provision, §1281
unsecured creditors, §§1273-1275
voluntary petition only, §1231

FRAUDULENT TRANSFERS
See Avoiding powers of trustee

H

HYPOTHETICAL CREDITOR OR PURCHASER
See Avoiding powers of trustee

I

INDIVIDUAL WITH REGULAR INCOME—CHAPTER 13
co-debtor stay, §§1143-1149
conversion or dismissal, §§1159-1165
debtor—rights and powers, §§1152-1154
eligibility for relief, §§1138-1142

stockbrokers and commodity brokers ineligible, §1142
payments
    administrative expenses, §1209
    commencement of payments, §§1206-1209
plan
    confirmation of plan, §§1157-1168
        best efforts of debtor, §§1203-1204
        feasible plan, §1202
        good faith requirement, §1197
        hearing, §1193
        payment orders, §1205
        secured creditors, §1201
        unsecured creditors—best interests test, §1200
    duration, §1191
    filing, §1167
    mandatory provisions, §§1168-1171
        full payment of priority claims, §1170
        same treatments for claims of a class, §1171
        sufficient income turned over, §1169
    modification, §1192
    permissive provisions, §§1172-1190
        assumption or rejection of executory contracts or unexpired leases, §1185
        classification of claims, §§1173-1174
        cure or waiver of default, §1178
        interest on arrearages, §1183
        lien avoidance exception, §1189
        long-term debt, §§1180-1183
        modification of creditors' rights, §§1175-1177
        necessary consumer debt, §1184
        order of payments, §1179
        post-petition tax claims, §1184
        property used to pay claims, §1186
post-confirmation matters
    Chapter 13 discharge, §§1214-1219
    debts not discharged, §1213
    hardship discharge, §§1217-1218
    nonpayment by debtor, §1222
    post-confirmation modification, §1220
    property vests in debtor, §§1211-1213
    revocation of confirmation order, §1221
post-petition claims, §§1155-1157
property of estate, §1158
trustee—appointment and duties, §§1150-1151

INTERIM TRUSTEE, §177

INVOLUNTARY CASE
See Commencement of case

IPSO FACTO CLAUSES
See Bankruptcy estate; Executory contracts and unexpired leases; Use, sale, or lease of property

JK

JURISDICTION AND PROCEDURE
See also Core/non-core proceedings
abstention
    bankruptcy court, §§188-190
    district court, §§86-89

appeals
    automatic stay, §§117-118
    from abstention, §89
    from bankruptcy court, §§104-111
    from district court, §§112-117
contempt, §§45-47
jury trials, §§73-80
personal jurisdiction, §§50-51
remand from federal district court, §§92-93, 117
removal to federal district court, §§90-93
sanctions, §48
subject matter jurisdiction
    bankruptcy courts, §§56-61
    district courts, §§52-55, 62
    Marathon case, §5
    personal injury and wrongful death claims, §62
substantive consolidation, §49
venue, §§94-103
withdrawal, §§81-85

LM

LIEN—CHAPTER 7
See Liquidation

LIQUIDATION—CHAPTER 7
See also Discharge
conversion
    eligibility, §988
    involuntary, §987
    voluntary, §986
dismissal, §§989-992
distribution of property
    community property, §957
    order of payment, §§945-954
    outside Bankruptcy code, §§607-608
    pro rata payment, §§955-956
    subordination of claims, §958
liens—Chapter 7
    See also Automatic stay; Claims of creditors; Exemptions
    avoidance of liens securing penalties, §960
    multiple claimants, §962
    statutory liens, §963
    subordination of tax liens, §961
partnerships. *See* Partnership trustee's claim
relief
    authority to operate debtor's business, §943
    Chapter 7 trustee, §§941-942
    eligibility for, §§939-940
    meeting of creditors, §944. *See also* Creditors

N

NONDISCHARGEABLE DEBTS
alimony, maintenance, and support, §§691-692
condominium fees, §714
debts incurred for federal taxes, §713
defalcation or fiduciary fraud, §§689-693
drunk driving liability, §709
effect of, §676
exceptions to discharge, §§675-678
failure to maintain capital commitment, §711
failure to schedule debts, §§686-688
federal criminal restitution, §712
financial institutions, fiduciary fraud, §710
fines and penalties, §§699-702
fraud, §§680-685
prior bankruptcy, §§715-716
prior state court judgments, §§718-720
proof, standard of, §717
property settlements and hold harmless obligations, §694
special rules, §§722-725
student loans, §§703-708
taxes, §679
willful and malicious injury, §§695-698

O

OFFICERS OF THE ESTATE
compensation, §§269-289
    attorney for debtor, §§270, 286
    fee application requirements, §271
    interim compensation, §§284-286
    maximum compensation, §§279-283
    no-asset cases, §278
    reasonable compensation, §§272-277
    sharing of fees prohibited, §§287-289
examiner, §§251-255
professional persons, §§256-268
trustee
    bond requirement, §225
    duties, §§239-244
    election of, §237
    eligibility, §§221-224
    liability, §§245-246
    official representative of estate, §220
    powers, §247
    removal, §§248-250
    selection, §§226-238
United States Trustee
    administrative duties, §292
    appointment and term, §§290-291
    eligibility, §224
    standing, §293

PQ

PARTNERSHIP TRUSTEE'S CLAIM
deficiency of partnership property, §§964-967
distribution outside Code, §608
excess recovery by trustee, §968

PETITION
See Commencement of case

PLAN
See Reorganization—Chapter 11

PREFERENCES
See Avoiding powers of trustee

PRIORITY CLAIMS
  See Claims of creditors
PROPERTY OF ESTATE
  See Bankruptcy estate
PROTECTION OF PROPERTY
  American Mariner (lost opportunity cost) rejected, §§773-774
  Chapter 12 cases, §777
  equity cushion, §§770-772
  failure of adequate protection, §776
  methods of providing adequate protection, §§765-769
  valuation of collateral, §775
  when protection is required, §§761-764

R

REAFFIRMATION AGREEMENTS
  creditor pressure forbidden, §744
  defined, §733
  discharge hearing, §§745-750
  no absolute right to reaffirm, §751
  requirements for enforceability, §§734-743
RECLAMATION OF GOODS
  See Avoiding powers of trustee
REDEMPTION—CHAPTER 7 ONLY
  changed intention, §754
  no waiver, §755
  tangible personal property, §§752-753
RELIEF
  See Liquidation
REORGANIZATION—CHAPTER 11
  collective bargaining agreements, §§1039-1043
  conversion or dismissal, §§1032-1038. *See also* Conversion
    discretionary for cause, §§1034-1036
    farmers and nonbusiness corporations exception, §1037
    to Chapter 12 or 13, §1038
    voluntary, to Chapter 7, §1033
  cram down, §§1030, 1097-1115
  creditors' committee, §§995-1005
    membership, §§995-1001
    powers and duties, §1002
    professionals, employment of, §§1003-1005
  debtor in possession, §§1006-1008. *See also* Use, sale, or lease of property
    business judgment rule, §1007
  eligibility for relief, §§993-994
  examiner—appointment and duties, §§1016-1021
  Manville-type trust/injunction, §§1134-1137
  party in interest's right to be heard, §§996-998
  plan
    acceptance of plan, §§1071-1076
    classification of claims or interests, §§1048-1056
      administrative convenience class, §§1055-1056
      priority claims, §1054
      secured claims, §1053
      substantially similar claims or interests, §§1049-1052
    confirmation of plan, §§1078-1096
      administrative expenses and involuntary gap claims, §1090
      all impaired classes accept, §1087
      best interests of creditors test, §1086
      good faith proposal, §1082
      retiree insurance benefits protected, §1096
    contents, §§1057-1061
    cure and deacceleration, §§1064-1065
    denial of, §1090
    fair and equitable, §§1099-1114
    filing, §§1044-1047
    impairment of classes, §§1062-1065
    interest on arrearages, §1061
    modification of creditors' rights, §1059
    modifying a plan, §1077
    solicitation and disclosure, §§1066-1070
  post-confirmation matters
    discharge of debts, §§1119-1125
    distribution, §1127
    effects of, §§1117-1118
    exemption from securities laws, §§1129-1130
    implementation of plan, §1126
    property free of liens, §1118
    revocation of confirmation order, §1128
  proof of claims or interests, §1023
  section 1111(b) election, §§1026-1031
  secured claims, §§1024-1025
  small businesses, §§1131-1133
  trustee—appointment and duties, §§1009-1115
    authority to operate business, §1014
    cause for appointment, §§1009-1011
    duties, §1013
    termination, §1015
    who chooses, §1012

S

SECURITY INTEREST
  See Avoiding powers of trustee
SETOFF
  See Creditor's right of setoff
SOVEREIGN IMMUNITY, §§474-477
STRONG ARM PROVISION
  See Avoiding powers of trustee
SUBORDINATION
  See Claims of creditors; Liquidation—Chapter 7
SUBROGATION
  See Claims of creditors
SUBSTANTIVE CONSOLIDATION
  See Jurisdiction and procedure

T

TAXES
  See also Claims of creditors; Nondischargeable debts
  erroneous refund, §575
  post-petition, §540
  pre-petition interest, §576

TERMINOLOGY
See Bankruptcy laws
TRANSFER OF PROPERTY
See also Avoiding powers of trustee
definition, §410
fraudulent, §§412-423
when transfer occurs, §411
TRUSTEE
See Avoiding powers of trustee; Officers; Partnership trustee's claim
TURNOVER OF PROPERTY
See Bankruptcy estate

U

UNEXPIRED LEASES
See Executory contracts and unexpired leases
UNITED STATES TRUSTEE
See Officers
UNSECURED CLAIMS
See Claims of creditors
USE, SALE, OR LEASE OF PROPERTY
adequate protection, §§849-851
appeal, §§859-860
automatic stay, §848
burden of proof, §858
collusive sale, §861
dower, curtesy, or co-ownership interests, §§854-857
in general, §§832-834
in ordinary course of business, §§840-847
ipso facto or "bankruptcy" clauses, §852
out of ordinary course of business, §§835-839
sale free and clear, §853
sales and use taxes permitted, §862
UTILITY SERVICE
exemption—insufficient security, §938
protection for debtor, §938

VWXYZ

VOLUNTARY CASE
See Commencement of case
WITHDRAWAL
See Jurisdiction and procedure

gilbert
LAW SUMMARIES

BANKRUPTCY

Ned W. Waxman

1999 SUPPLEMENT

HARCOURT BRACE LEGAL AND PROFESSIONAL PUBLICATIONS, INC.
EDITORIAL OFFICES: 111 W. Jackson Blvd., 7th Floor, Chicago, IL 60604

gilbert
LAW SUMMARIES

REGIONAL OFFICES: Chicago, Dallas, Los Angeles, New York, Washington, D.C.
Distributed by: **Harcourt Brace & Company** 6277 Sea Harbor Drive, Orlando, FL 32887 (800)787-8717

Copyright © 1999 by Harcourt Brace Legal and Professional Publications, Inc. All rights reserved. No part of this publication may be reproduced or transmitted in any form or by any means, electronic or mechanical, including photocopy, recording, or any information storage and retrieval system, without permission in writing from the publisher. Printed in the United States of America.

SUPPLEMENT TO GILBERT "BANKRUPTCY" SUMMARY
(Fourth Edition)

April 1999

Some important changes were made to the Bankruptcy Code in 1998, including the addition of a provision requiring that inflation adjustments be made to dollar amounts concerning debt limitations for Chapter 13 cases, the aggregate creditor claims required to file an involuntary case, priority claim limitations, property exemptions, and nondischargeable debts. These changes are summarized in the chart below.

gilbert LAW SUMMARIES — INFLATION ADJUSTMENTS

Type of Provision	Dollar Amount to be Adjusted	New Adjusted Dollar Amount	Gilbert Sections Affected
Debt limitations for Chapter 13 cases	$250,000 $750,000	$269,250 $807,750	§§136, 140, 1138, 1141, 1245 §§136, 140, 1138, 1141, 1245
Involuntary case requirements	$10,000	$10,775	§§163, 164
Priority claim limitations	$1,800 $4,000	$1,950 $4,300	§562 §§558, 560, 561
Property exemptions	$400 $800 $1,000 $1,500 $1,600 $2,400 $7,500 $8,000 $8,300 $15,000	$425 $850 $1,075 $1,625 $1,700 $2,575 $8,075 $8,625 $8,925 $16,150	§616 §§618, 665 §617 §§619, 665 §665 §615 §§618, 665 §§616, 621 §618 §§614, 629, 665
Nondischargeable debts	$1,000	$1,075	§681

Page	Revision
16	**Insert** the following at the end of para. a. [§91]: Neither may any case be removed merely because a defense of federal character is anticipated. [Rivet v. Regions Bank of Louisiana, 522 U.S. 470 (1998)]
69	**Insert** the following after para. a. of §363:

b. **Exception—certain charitable contributions:** The trustee's avoiding power under this section does not cover the transfer of a charitable contribution not deemed to be a fraudulent transfer under Code section 548(a)(2) (*see infra,* §410). Any person's claim to recover such a transferred contribution under federal or state law will be preempted by the commencement of the bankruptcy case. [B.C. §544(b)(2)]

78 **Delete** citation at end of para. 3. [§412]; substitute the following:

[B.C. §548(a)(1)]

78 **Delete** citations at end of para. a. [§413] and the example thereunder; substitute the following:

[B.C. §548(a)(1)(A)]

78 **Delete** Code citation at end of para. b. [§416]; substitute the following:

[B.C. §548(a)(1)(B)(i), (ii)(I)]

79 **Delete** citation at end of para. (3) [§418]; substitute the following:

[B.C. §548(a)(1)(B)(i), (ii)(I)]

79 **Delete** Code citations near end of para. 1) of §419; substitute the following:

section 548(a)(1)(A) or (a)(1)(B)

79 **Delete** citation at end of para. c. [§420]; substitute the following:

[B.C. §548(a)(1)(B)(i), (ii)(III)]

80 **Delete** citation at end of para. d. [§422]; substitute the following:

[B.C. §548(a)(1)(B)(i), (ii)(III)]

80 **Insert** the following after para. d. [§422]; reletter subsequent para.:

e. **Exception—certain charitable contributions:** The Code excludes certain charitable contributions from the rule that transfers for less than reasonably equivalent value are fraudulent. A transfer of cash or a financial instrument (*e.g.,* stocks or bonds) by a ***natural person*** to a qualified charitable or religious entity or organization (as defined by the Internal Revenue Code) will not be deemed fraudulent if the contribution: (i) does not exceed 15% of the debtor's gross annual income for the year of the contribution *or* (ii) is consistent with the debtor's normal practices concerning charitable contributions. [B.C. §548(a)(2), (d)(3), (4)]

100 **Insert** the following after para. b. [§527]:

(1) **Note:** In a Chapter 13 case in which the debtor desires to keep and use a secured creditor's collateral over the creditor's objection, ***replacement value*** is the standard to be applied. [Associates Commercial Corp. v. Rash, 520 U.S. 953 (1997); *and see infra,* §1201]

128 **Delete** para. c. [§683]; substitute the following:

c. **Punitive damages:** [§683]   The Supreme Court has ruled that any liability arising from fraud under Code section 523(a)(2)(A), such as punitive damages or attorneys' fees, is nondischargeable. [Cohen v. De La Cruz, 523 U.S. 213 (1998)]

131 **Delete** para. 8. [§695]; substitute the following:

8. **Willful and Malicious Injury:** [§695] Debts for willful and malicious injury caused by the debtor to another entity or its property are nondischargeable. [B.C. §523(a)(6); Piccicuto v. Dwyer, 39 F.3d 37 (1st Cir. 1994)—"intentional interference with an advantageous business relationship and unfair trade practices in a commercial context"] The Supreme Court recently held that injuries caused by negligence or recklessness are not "willful and malicious," and therefore debts for such injuries are not excepted from discharge under this Code section. The Court stated "that nondischargeability takes a deliberate or intentional *injury*, not merely a deliberate or intentional *act* that leads to injury." [Kawaauhau v. Geiger, 523 U.S. 57 (1998)] However, there is significant authority holding that "a deliberate and intentional [wrongful] act which necessarily leads to injury" is nondischargeable. Under this view, it is not necessary to prove spite, hatred, or a specific (subjective) intent to cause harm if the harm was "substantially certain to result." [*In re* Hartley, 100 B.R. 477 (W.D. Mo. 1988), *aff'd*, 874 F.2d 1254 (8th Cir. 1989)—debtor threw a lighted firecracker into a room knowing that it was filled with gasoline fumes and that employee was working there, and causing "psychological and permanent physical impairments and disfiguration"; *In re* Cecchini, 780 F.2d 1440 (9th Cir. 1986)]

132-133 **Delete** paras. 10., 10.a., and 10.b. [§§703-705]; substitute the following and reletter subsequent paras. accordingly:

10. **Student Loans:** [§703] An educational loan made, insured, or guaranteed by a governmental unit, or extended under a program funded by a governmental unit or a nonprofit institution, is nondischargeable unless there will be an *undue hardship* on the debtor and her dependents if the debt is not discharged. [B.C. §523(a)(8)]

    a. **Undue hardship:** [§704] This exception to the nondischargeability of student loans is strictly construed and applies only in exceptional circumstances, which are likely to involve: (i) the presence of many dependents, (ii) the occurrence of a serious disease or illness, and/or (iii) the absence of occupational skills. Thus, for a debtor to obtain a discharge of a student loan based on undue hardship, the following elements should exist:

        (i) *The debtor and her dependents will be deprived of a "minimal standard of living"* if repayment is required under the debtor's present financial circumstances;

        (ii) *The financial condition of the debtor and her dependents probably will not improve sufficiently* during the time remaining for repayment of the debt; and

        (iii) *The debtor has made a bona fide attempt to repay the student loan.*

        [B.C. §523(a)(8); *In re* Brunner, 46 B.R. 752 (S.D.N.Y. 1985), *aff'd*, 831 F.2d 395 (2d Cir. 1987); *and see In re* Cheesman, 25 F.3d 356 (6th Cir. 1994)]

169 **Delete** para. b. [§898]; substitute the following:

b. **Contracts to loan money or to issue securities:** [§898] The trustee or debtor in possession may not assume or assign an executory contract (i) to make a loan or to grant other debt financing or financial accommodations (*e.g.,* surety or guaranty contracts) to the debtor, or (ii) to issue a security of the debtor. [B.C. §365(c)(2); *and see In re* Sun Runner Marine, Inc., 945 F.2d 1089 (9th Cir. 1991)—financial accommodations contract was nonassumable despite lender's consent] This prohibition, however, does not apply to ordinary contracts for the sale or lease of goods or services that provide for "incidental financial accommodations or extensions of credit." [2 Collier ¶365.05(1)] Also, it has been held that a credit card merchant agreement between a bank and a merchant does not constitute a financial accommodations contract. [*In re* Thomas B. Hamilton Co., 969 F.2d 1013 (11th Cir. 1992)—good discussion of financial accommodations]

    (1) **Options to buy real property:** An issue currently dividing the courts is whether a paid-for but unexercised option to buy real property is an executory contract covered by this Code section's prohibition. [*See In re* Robert L. Helms Construction & Development Co., 139 F.3d 702 (9th Cir. 1998)—discussing various approaches to this question, and overruling, as overbroad, *In re* Easebe Enterprises, Inc., 900 F.2d 1417 (9th Cir. 1990)]

188   **Insert** the following after para. (5) of §991; reletter subsequent para.:

    b. **Charitable contributions:** The debtor's charitable contributions to any qualified religious or charitable entity or organization may not be considered in making this determination. [B.C. §§707(b), 548(d)(3), (4)]

231   **Insert** the following after para. (3) of §1201; reletter subsequent para.:

    (a) ***In determining the value of the collateral***, replacement value is the standard to be applied in a Chapter 13 case in which the debtor desires to keep and use a secured creditor's collateral over the creditor's objection. The Court described replacement value as "the cost the debtor would incur to obtain a like asset for the same proposed use," and it indicated that ascertaining such value would "depend on the type of debtor and the nature of the property." [Associates Commercial Corp. v. Rash, *supra*]

232   **Delete** para. a. [§1204]; substitute the following:

    a. **Disposable income:** [§1204] The Code defines disposable income as that portion of the debtor's income which is "not reasonably necessary" (i) to maintain or support the debtor or her dependents (including charitable contributions to a qualified religious or charitable entity or organization in an amount not exceeding 15% of the debtor's gross income for the ye.r of contribution), and (ii) to pay the expenses required for the continuation, operation, and preservation of the business of a debtor engaged in business. [B.C. §§1325(b)(2), 548(d)(3), (4); *In re* Tracey, 66 B.R. 63 (Bankr. D. Md. 1986)]

233   **Delete** para. (3) of §1215; substitute the following:

    (3) ***Student loans***, unless there will be an ***undue hardship*** on the debtor and her dependents if the debt is not discharged. [B.C. §§1328(a)(2), 523(a)(8); *see supra*, §§703-704]

236   **Delete** the first para. of the Chapter Approach.

245   **Delete** para. H. [§1281].

Notes

Notes

Notes

Notes

Notes

Notes

Publications Catalog

Publishers of America's Most Popular Legal Study Aids!

All Titles Available At Your Law School Bookstore.

gilbert LAW SUMMARIES

Gilbert Law Summaries are the best selling outlines in the country, and have set the standard for excellence since they were first introduced more than twenty-five years ago. It's Gilbert's unique combination of features that makes it the one study aid you'll turn to for all your study needs!

Accounting and Finance for Lawyers
Professor Thomas L. Evans, University of Texas
Basic Accounting Principles; Definitions of Accounting Terms; Balance Sheet; Income Statement; Statement of Changes in Financial Position; Consolidated Financial Statements; Accumulation of Financial Data; Financial Statement Analysis.
ISBN: 0-15-900382-2   Pages: 136 $19.95

Administrative Law
By Professor Michael R. Asimow, U.C.L.A.
Separation of Powers and Controls Over Agencies; (including Delegation of Power) Constitutional Right to Hearing (including Liberty and Property Interests Protected by Due Process, and Rulemaking- Adjudication Distinction); Adjudication Under Administrative Procedure Act (APA); Formal Adjudication (including Notice, Discovery, Burden of Proof, Finders of Facts and Reasons); Adjudicatory Decision Makers (including Administrative Law Judges (ALJs), Bias, Improper Influences, Ex Parte Communications, Familiarity with Record, Res Judicata); Rulemaking Procedures (including Notice, Public Participation, Publication, Impartiality of Rulemakers, Rulemaking Record); Obtaining Information (including Subpoena Power, Privilege Against Self-incrimination, Freedom of Information Act, Government in Sunshine Act, Attorneys' Fees); Scope of Judicial Review; Reviewability of Agency Decisions (including Mandamus, Injunction, Sovereign Immunity, Federal Tort Claims Act); Standing to Seek Judicial Review and Timing.
ISBN: 0-15-900000-9   Pages: 278 $20.95

Agency and Partnership
By Professor Richard J. Conviser, Chicago Kent
Agency: Rights and Liabilities Between Principal and Agent (including Agent's Fiduciary Duty, Right to Indemnification); Contractual Rights Between Principal (or Agent) and Third Persons (including Creation of Agency Relationship, Authority of Agent, Scope of Authority, Termination of Authority, Ratification, Liability on Agents, Contracts); Tort Liability (including Respondeat Superior, Master-Servant Relationship, Scope of Employment). Partnership: Property Rights of Partner; Formation of Partnership; Relations Between Partners (including Fiduciary Duty); Authority of Partner to Bind Partnership; Dissolution and Winding up of Partnership; Limited Partnerships.
ISBN: 0-15-900327-X   Pages: 149 $17.95

Antitrust
By Professor Thomas M. Jorde, U.C. Berkeley, Mark A. Lemley, University of Texas, and Professor Robert H. Mnookin, Harvard University
Common Law Restraints of Trade; Federal Antitrust Laws (including Sherman Act, Clayton Act, Federal Trade Commission Act, Interstate Commerce Requirement, Antitrust Remedies); Monopolization (including Relevant Market, Purposeful Act Requirement, Attempts and Conspiracy to Monopolize); Collaboration Among Competitors (including Horizontal Restraints, Rule of Reason vs. Per Se Violations, Price Fixing, Division of Markets, Group Boycotts); Vertical Restraints (including Tying Arrangements); Mergers and Acquisitions (including Horizontal Mergers, Brown Shoe Analysis, Vertical Mergers, Conglomerate Mergers); Price Discrimination—Robinson-Patman Act; Unfair Methods of Competition; Patent Laws and Their Antitrust Implications; Exemptions From Antitrust Laws (including Motor, Rail, and Interstate Water Carriers, Bank Mergers, Labor Unions, Professional Baseball).
ISBN: 0-15-900328-8   Pages: 210 $18.95

Bankruptcy
By Professor Ned W. Waxman, College of William and Mary
Participants in the Bankruptcy Case; Jurisdiction and Procedure; Commencement and Administration of the Case (including Eligibility, Voluntary Case, Involuntary Case, Meeting of Creditors, Debtor's Duties); Officers of the Estate (including Trustee, Examiner, United States Trustee); Bankruptcy Estate; Creditor's Right of Setoff; Trustee's Avoiding Powers; Claims of Creditors (including Priority Claims and Tax Claims); Debtor's Exemptions; Nondischargeable Debts; Effects of Discharge; Reaffirmation Agreements; Administrative Powers (including Automatic Stay, Use, Sale, or Lease of Property); Chapter 7-Liquidation; Chapter 11-Reorganization; Chapter 13-Individual With Regular Income; Chapter 12-Family Farmer With Regular Annual Income.
ISBN: 0-15-900442-X   Pages: 311 $21.95

Business Law
By Professor Robert D. Upp, Los Angeles City College
Torts and Crimes in Business; Law of Contracts (including Contract Formation, Consideration, Statute of Frauds, Contract Remedies, Third Parties); Sales (including Transfer of Title and Risk of Loss, Performance and Remedies, Products Liability, Personal Property Security Interest); Property (including Personal Property, Bailments, Real Property, Landlord and Tenant); Agency; Business Organizations (including Partnerships, Corporations); Commercial Paper; Government Regulation of Business (including Taxation, Antitrust, Environmental Protection, and Bankruptcy).
ISBN: 0-15-900005-X   Pages: 277 $17.95

California Bar Performance Test Skills
By Professor Peter J. Honigsberg, University of San Francisco
Hints to Improve Writing; How to Approach the Performance Test; Legal Analysis Documents (including Writing a Memorandum of Law, Writing a Client Letter, Writing Briefs); Fact Gathering and Fact Analysis Documents; Tactical and Ethical Considerations; Sample Interrogatories, Performance Tests, and Memoranda.
ISBN: 0-15-900152-8   Pages: 216 $18.95

Civil Procedure
By Professor Thomas D. Rowe, Jr., Duke University, and Professor Richard L. Marcus, U.C. Hastings
Territorial (Personal) Jurisdiction, including Venue and Forum Non Conveniens; Subject Matter Jurisdiction, covering Diversity Jurisdiction, Federal Question Jurisdiction; Erie Doctrine and Federal Common Law; Pleadings including Counterclaims, Cross-Claims, Supplemental Pleadings; Parties, including Joinder and Class Actions; Discovery, including Devices, Scope, Sanctions, and Discovery Conference; Summary Judgment; Pretrial Conference and Settlements; Trial, including Right to Jury Trial, Motions, Jury Instruction and Arguments, and Post-Verdict Motions; Appeals; Claim Preclusion (Res Judicata) and Issue Preclusion (Collateral Estoppel).
ISBN: 0-15-900429-2   Pages: 410 $22.95

Commercial Paper and Payment Law
By Professor Douglas J. Whaley, Ohio State University
Types of Commercial Paper; Negotiability; Negotiation; Holders in Due Course; Claims and Defenses on Negotiable Instruments (including Real Defenses and Personal Defenses); Liability of the Parties (including Merger Rule, Suits on the Instrument, Warranty Suits, Conversion); Bank Deposits and Collections; Forgery or Alteration of Negotiable Instruments; Electronic Banking.
ISBN: 0-15-900367-9   Pages: 166 $19.95

Community Property
By Professor William A. Reppy, Jr., Duke University
Classifying Property as Community or Separate; Management and Control of Property; Liability for Debts; Division of Property at Divorce; Devolution of Property at Death; Relationships Short of Valid Marriage; Conflict of Laws Problems; Constitutional Law Issues (including Equal Protection Standards, Due Process Issues).
ISBN: 0-15-900422-5   Pages: 161 $18.95

Call To Order: 1-800-787-8717 or Order On-Line at http://www.gilbertlaw.com

gilbert LAW SUMMARIES

Conflict of Laws
By Dean Herma Hill Kay, U.C. Berkeley
Domicile; Jurisdiction (including Notice and Opportunity to be Heard, Minimum Contacts, Types of Jurisdiction); Choice of Law (including Vested Rights Approach, Most Significant Relationship Approach, Governmental Interest Analysis); Choice of Law in Specific Substantive Areas; Traditional Defenses Against Application of Foreign Law; Constitutional Limitations and Overriding Federal Law (including Due Process Clause, Full Faith and Credit Clause, Conflict Between State and Federal Law); Recognition and Enforcement of Foreign Judgments.
ISBN: 0-15-900424-1   Pages: 250 $20.95

Constitutional Law
By Professor Jesse H. Choper, U.C. Berkeley
Powers of Federal Government (including Judicial Power, Powers of Congress, Presidential Power, Foreign Affairs Power); Intergovernmental Immunities, Separation of Powers; Regulation of Foreign Commerce; Regulation of Interstate Commerce; Taxation of Interstate and Foreign Commerce; Due Process, Equal Protection; "State Action" Requirements; Freedoms of Speech, Press, and Association; Freedom of Religion.
ISBN: 0-15-900375-X   Pages: 312 $21.95

Contracts
By Professor Melvin A. Eisenberg, U.C. Berkeley
Consideration (including Promissory Estoppel, Moral or Past Consideration); Mutual Assent; Defenses (including Mistake, Fraud, Duress, Unconscionability, Statute of Frauds, Illegality); Third-Party Beneficiaries; Assignment of Rights and Delegation of Duties; Conditions; Substantial Performance; Material vs. Minor Breach; Anticipatory Breach; Impossibility; Discharge; Remedies (including Damages, Specific Performance, Liquidated Damages).
ISBN: 0-15-900014-9   Pages: 278 $21.95

Corporations
By Professor Jesse H. Choper, U.C. Berkeley, and Professor Melvin A. Eisenberg, U.C. Berkeley
Formalities; "De Jure" vs. "De Facto"; Promoters; Corporate Powers; Ultra Vires Transactions; Powers, Duties, and Liabilities of Officers and Directors; Allocation of Power Between Directors and Shareholders; Conflicts of Interest in Corporate Transactions; Close Corporations; Insider Trading; Rule 10b-5 and Section 16(b); Shareholders' Voting Rights; Shareholders' Right to Inspect Records; Shareholders' Suits; Capitalization (including Classes of Shares, Preemptive Rights, Consideration for Shares); Dividends; Redemption of Shares; Fundamental Changes in Corporate Structure; Applicable Conflict of Laws Principles.
ISBN: 0-15-900342-3   Pages: 282 $21.95

Criminal Law
By Professor George E. Dix, University of Texas
Elements of Crimes (including Actus Reus, Mens Rea, Causation); Vicarious Liability; Complicity in Crime; Criminal Liability of Corporations; Defenses (including Insanity, Diminished Capacity, Intoxication, Ignorance, Self-Defense); Inchoate Crimes; Homicide; Other Crimes Against the Person; Crimes Against Habitation (including Burglary, Arson); Crimes Against Property; Offenses Against Government; Offenses Against Administration of Justice.
ISBN: 0-15-900217-6   Pages: 271 $20.95

Criminal Procedure
By Professor Paul Marcus, College of William and Mary, and Professor Charles H. Whitebread, U.S.C.
Exclusionary Rule; Arrests and Other Detentions; Search and Seizure; Privilege Against Self-Incrimination; Confessions; Preliminary Hearing; Bail; Indictment; Speedy Trial; Competency to Stand Trial; Government's Obligation to Disclose Information; Right to Jury Trial; Right to Counsel; Right to Confront Witnesses; Burden of Proof; Insanity; Entrapment; Guilty Pleas; Sentencing; Death Penalty; Ex Post Facto Issues; Appeal; Habeas Corpus; Juvenile Offenders; Prisoners' Rights; Double Jeopardy.
ISBN: 0-15-900376-8   Pages: 244 $20.95

Estate and Gift Tax
By Professor John H. McCord, University of Illinois
Gross Estate; Allowable Deductions Under Estate Tax (including Expenses, Indebtedness, and Taxes, Deductions for Losses, Charitable Deduction, Marital Deduction); Taxable Gifts; Deductions; Valuation; Computation of Tax; Returns and Payment of Tax; Tax on Generation-Skipping Transfers.
ISBN: 0-15-900425-X   Pages: 298 $20.95

Evidence
By Professor Jon R. Waltz, Northwestern University, and Roger C. Park, University of Minnesota
Direct Evidence; Circumstantial Evidence; Rulings on Admissibility; Relevancy; Materiality; Character Evidence; Hearsay and the Hearsay Exceptions; Privileges; Competency to Testify; Opinion Evidence and Expert Witnesses; Direct Examination; Cross-Examination; Impeachment; Real, Demonstrative, and Scientific Evidence; Judicial Notice; Burdens of Proof; Parol Evidence Rule.
ISBN: 0-15-900385-7   Pages: 342 $22.95

Federal Courts
By Professor William A. Fletcher, U.C. Berkeley
Article III Courts; "Case or Controversy" Requirement; Justiciability; Advisory Opinions; Political Questions; Ripeness; Mootness; Standing; Congressional Power Over Federal Court Jurisdiction; Supreme Court Jurisdiction; District Court Subject Matter Jurisdiction (including Federal Question Jurisdiction, Diversity Jurisdiction); Pendent and Ancillary Jurisdiction; Removal Jurisdiction; Venue; Forum Non Conveniens; Law Applied in the Federal Courts (including Erie Doctrine); Federal Law in the State Courts; Abstention; Habeas Corpus for State Prisoners; Federal Injunctions Against State Court Proceedings; Eleventh Amendment.
ISBN: 0-15-900232-X   Pages: 270 $21.95

Future Interests & Perpetuities
By Professor Jesse Dukeminier, U.C.L.A.
Reversions; Possibilities of Reverter; Rights of Entry; Remainders; Executory Interest; Rules Restricting Remainders and Executory Interest; Rights of Owners of Future Interests; Construction of Instruments; Powers of Appointment; Rule Against Perpetuities (including Reforms of the Rule).
ISBN: 0-15-900218-4   Pages: 162 $19.95

Income Tax I - Individual
By Professor Michael R. Asimow, U.C.L.A.
Gross Income; Exclusions; Income Splitting by Gifts, Personal Service Income, Income Earned by Children, Income of Husbands and Wives, Below-Market Interest on Loans, Taxation of Trusts; Business and Investment Deductions; Personal Deductions; Tax Rates; Credits; Computation of Basis, Gain, or Loss; Realization; Nonrecognition of Gain or Loss; Capital Gains and Losses; Alternative Minimum Tax; Tax Accounting Problems.
ISBN: 0-15-900421-7   Pages: 279 $21.95

Income Tax II - Partnerships, Corporations, Trusts
By Professor Michael R. Asimow, U.C.L.A.
Taxation of Partnerships (including Current Partnership Income, Contributions of Property to Partnership, Sale of Partnership Interest, Distributions, Liquidations); Corporate Taxation (including Corporate Distributions, Sales of Stock and Assets, Reorganizations); S Corporations; Federal Income Taxation of Trusts.
ISBN: 0-15-900384-9   Pages: 210 $19.95

Labor Law
By Professor James C. Oldham, Georgetown University, and Robert J. Gelhaus
Statutory Foundations of Present Labor Law (including National Labor Relations Act, Taft-Hartley, Norris-LaGuardia Act, Landrum-Griffin Act); Organizing Campaigns, Selection of the Bargaining Representative; Collective Bargaining (including Negotiating the Agreement, Lockouts, Administering the Agreement, Arbitration); Strikes, Boycotts, and Picketing; Concerted Activity Protected Under the NLRA; Civil Rights Legislation; Grievance; Federal Regulation of Compulsory Union Membership Arrangements; State Regulation of Compulsory Membership Agreements; "Right to Work" Laws; Discipline of Union Members; Election of Union Officers; Corruption.
ISBN: 0-15-900340-7   Pages: 221 $19.95

Legal Ethics
By Professor Thomas D. Morgan, George Washington University
Regulating Admission to Practice Law; Preventing Unauthorized Practice of Law; Contract Between Client and Lawyer (including Lawyer's Duties Regarding Accepting Employment, Spheres of Authority of Lawyer and Client, Obligation of Client to Lawyer, Terminating the Lawyer-Client Relationship); Attorney-Client Privilege; Professional Duty of Confidentiality; Conflicts of Interest; Obligations to Third Persons and the Legal System (including Counseling Illegal or Fraudulent Conduct, Threats of Criminal Prosecution); Special Obligations in Litigation (including Limitations on Advancing Money to Client, Duty to Reject Certain Actions, Lawyer as Witness); Solicitation and Advertising; Specialization; Disciplinary Process; Malpractice; Special Responsibilities of Judges.
ISBN: 0-15-900026-2   Pages: 221 $20.95

Legal Research, Writing and Analysis
By Professor Peter J. Honigsberg, University of San Francisco
Court Systems; Precedent; Case Reporting System (including Regional and State Reporters, Headnotes and the West Key Number System, Citations and Case Finding); Statutes, Constitutions, and Legislative History; Secondary Sources (including Treatises, Law Reviews, Digests, Restatements); Administrative Agencies (including Regulations, Looseleaf Services); Shepard's Citations; Computers in Legal Research; Reading and Understanding a Case (including Briefing a Case); Using Legal Sourcebooks; Basic Guidelines for Legal Writing; Organizing Your Research; Writing a Memorandum of Law; Writing a Brief; Writing an Opinion or Client Letter.
ISBN: 0-15-900436-5   Pages: 162 $17.95

Multistate Bar Examination
By Professor Richard J. Conviser, Chicago Kent
Structure of the Exam; Governing Law; Effective Use of Time; Scoring of the Exam; Jurisdictions Using the Exam; Subject Matter Outlines; Practice Tests, Answers, and Subject Matter Keys; Glossary of Legal Terms and Definitions; State Bar Examination Directory; Listing of Reference Materials for Multistate Subjects.
ISBN: 0-15-900246-X   Pages: 776 $24.95

Personal Property
Gilbert Staff
Acquisitions; Ownership Through Possession (including Wild Animals, Abandoned Chattels); Finders of Lost Property; Bailments; Possessory Liens; Pledges, Trover; Gift; Accession; Confusion (Commingling); Fixtures; Crops (Emblements); Adverse Possession; Prescriptive Rights (Acquiring Ownership of Easements or Profits by Adverse Use).
ISBN: 0-15-900360-1   Pages: 118 $14.95

Professional Responsibility
(see Legal Ethics)

Call To Order: 1-800-787-8717 or Order On-Line at http://www.gilbertlaw.com

gilbert LAW SUMMARIES

Property
By Professor Jesse Dukeminier, U.C.L.A.

Possession (including Wild Animals, Bailments, Adverse Possession); Gifts and Sales of Personal Property; Freehold Possessory Estates; Future Interests (including Reversion, Possibility of Reverter, Right of Entry, Executory Interests, Rule Against Perpetuities); Tenancy in Common; Joint Tenancy; Tenancy by the Entirety; Condominiums; Cooperatives; Marital Property; Landlord and Tenant; Easements and Covenants; Nuisance; Rights in Airspace and Water; Right to Support; Zoning; Eminent Domain; Sale of Land (including Mortgage, Deed, Warranties of Title); Methods of Title Assurance (including Recording System, Title Registration, Title Insurance).

ISBN: 0-15-900426-8   Pages: 445 $22.95

Remedies
By Professor John A. Bauman, U.C.L.A., and Professor Kenneth H. York, Pepperdine University

Damages; Equitable Remedies (including Injunctions and Specific Performance); Restitution; Injuries to Tangible Property Interests; Injuries to Business and Commercial Interests (including Business Torts, Inducing Breach of Contract, Patent Infringement, Unfair Competition, Trade Defamation); Injuries to Personal Dignity and Related Interests (including Defamation, Privacy, Religious Status, Civil and Political Rights); Personal Injury and Death; Fraud; Duress, Undue Influence, and Unconscionable Conduct; Mistake; Breach of Contract; Unenforceable Contracts (including Statute of Frauds, Impossibility, Lack of Contractual Capacity, Illegality).

ISBN: 0-15-900325-3   Pages: 349 $22.95

Sale and Lease of Goods
By Professor Douglas J. Whaley, Ohio State University

UCC Article 2; Sales Contract (including Offer and Acceptance, Parol Evidence Rule, Statute of Frauds, Assignment and Delegation, Revision of Contract Terms); Types of Sales (including Cash Sale Transactions, Auctions, "Sale or Return" and "Sale on Approval" Transactions); Warranties (including Express and Implied Warranties, Privity, Disclaimer, Consumer Protection Statutes); Passage of Title; Performance of the Contract; Anticipatory Breach; Demand for Assurance of Performance; Unforeseen Circumstances; Risk of Loss; Remedies; Documents of Title; Lease of Goods; International Sale of Goods.

ISBN: 0-15-900367-9   Pages: 196 $19.95

Secured Transactions
By Professor Douglas J. Whaley, Ohio State University

Coverage of Article 9; Creation of a Security Interest (including Attachment, Security Agreement, Value, Debtor's Rights in the Collateral); Perfection; Filing; Priorities; Bankruptcy Proceedings and Article 9; Default Proceedings; Bulk Transfers.

ISBN: 0-15-900231-1   Pages: 191 $18.95

Securities Regulation
By Professor David H. Barber, and Professor Niels B. Schaumann, William Mitchell College of Law

Jurisdiction and Interstate Commerce; Securities Act of 1933 (including Registration Requirements and Exemptions); Securities Exchange Act of 1934 (including Rule 10b-5, Tender Offers, Proxy Solicitations Regulation, Insider Transactions); Regulation of the Securities Markets; Multinational Transactions; State Regulation of Securities Transactions.

ISBN: 0-15-9000437-3   Pages: 421 $22.95

Torts
By Professor Marc A. Franklin, Stanford University

Intentional Torts; Negligence; Strict Liability; Products Liability; Nuisance; Survival of Tort Actions; Wrongful Death; Immunity; Release and Contribution; Indemnity; Workers' Compensation; No-Fault Auto Insurance; Defamation; Invasion of Privacy; Misrepresentation; Injurious Falsehood; Interference With Economic Relations; Unjustifiable Litigation.

ISBN: 0-15-900220-6   Pages: 400 $22.95

Trusts
By Professor Edward C. Halbach, Jr., U.C. Berkeley

Elements of a Trust; Trust Creation; Transfer of Beneficiary's Interest (including Spendthrift Trusts); Charitable Trusts (including Cy Pres Doctrine); Trustee's Responsibilities, Power, Duties, and Liabilities; Duties and Liabilities of Beneficiaries; Accounting for Income and Principal; Power of Settlor to Modify or Revoke; Powers of Trustee Beneficiaries or Courts to Modify or Terminate; Termination of Trusts by Operation of Law; Resulting Trusts; Purchase Money Resulting Trusts; Constructive Trusts.

ISBN: 0-15-900039-4   Pages: 238 $20.95

Wills
By Professor Stanley M. Johanson, University of Texas

Intestate Succession; Simultaneous Death; Advancements; Disclaimer; Killer of Decedent; Elective Share Statutes; Pretermitted Child Statutes; Homestead; Formal Requisites of a Will; Revocation of Wills; Incorporation by Reference; Pour-Over Gift in Inter Vivos Trust; Joint Wills; Contracts Relating to Wills; Lapsed Gifts; Ademption; Exoneration of Liens; Will Contests; Probate and Estate Administration.

ISBN: 0-15-900040-8   Pages: 262 $21.95

Gilbert Law Summaries FIRST YEAR PROGRAM

Includes Five Gilbert Outlines:

■ **Civil Procedure**
By Professor Thomas D. Rowe, Jr.
Duke University Law School, and
Professor Richard L. Marcus
U.C. Hastings School Of Law

■ **Contracts**
By Professor Melvin A. Eisenberg
U.C. Berkeley School Of Law

■ **Criminal Law**
By Professor George E. Dix
University Of Texas School Of Law

■ **Property**
By Professor Jesse Dukeminier
U.C.L.A. Law School

■ **Torts**
By Professor Marc A. Franklin
Stanford University Law School

Plus—

■ **Gilbert's Dictionary Of Legal Terms**

■ **The 8 Secrets Of Top Exam Performance In Law School**
By Professor Charles H. Whitebread
USC Law School

All titles are packaged in a convenient carrying case with handle. $130 if purchased separately. $95 if purchased as a set. Save $35.

ISBN: 0-15-900254-0   Set $95

Gilbert's Pocket Size Law Dictionary
Gilbert

A dictionary is useless if you don't have it when you need it. If the only law dictionary you own is a thick, bulky one, you'll probably leave it at home most of the time — and if you need to know a definition while you're at school, you're out of luck!

With Gilbert's Pocket Size Law Dictionary, you'll have any definition you need, when you need it. Just pop Gilbert's dictionary into your pocket or purse, and you'll have over 4,000 legal terms and phrases at your fingertips. Gilbert's dictionary also includes a section on law school shorthand, common abbreviations, Latin and French legal terms, periodical abbreviations, and governmental abbreviations.

With Gilbert's Pocket Size Law Dictionary, you'll never be caught at a loss for words!

Available in your choice of 5 colors

■ Brown   ISBN: 0-15-900252-4 $7.95
■ Blue   ISBN: 0-15-900362-8 $7.95
■ Burgundy   ISBN: 0-15-900366-0 $7.95
■ Green   ISBN: 0-15-900365-2 $7.95

Limited Edition: Simulated Alligator Skin Cover

■ Black   ISBN: 0-15-900364-4 $7.95

The Eight Secrets Of Top Exam Performance In Law School
Charles Whitebread

Wouldn't it be great to know exactly what your professor's looking for on your exam? To find out everything that's expected of you, so that you don't waste your time doing anything other than maximizing your grades?

In his easy-to-read, refreshing style, nationally recognized exam expert Professor Charles Whitebread will teach you the eight secrets that will add precious points to every exam answer you write. You'll learn the three keys to handling any essay exam question, and how to add points to your score by making time work for you, not against you. You'll learn flawless issue spotting, and discover how to organize your answer for maximum possible points. You'll find out how the hidden traps in "IRAC" trip up most students… but not you! You'll learn the techniques for digging up the exam questions your professor will ask, before your exam. You'll put your newly-learned skills to the test with sample exam questions, and you can measure your performance against model answers. And there's even a special section that helps you master the skills necessary to crush any exam, not just a typical essay exam — unusual exams like open book, take home, multiple choice, short answer, and policy questions.

"The Eight Secrets of Top Exam Performance in Law School" gives you all the tools you need to maximize your grades — quickly and easily!

ISBN: 0-15-900323-7 $9.95

Call To Order: 1-800-787-8717 or Order On-Line at http://www.gilbertlaw.com

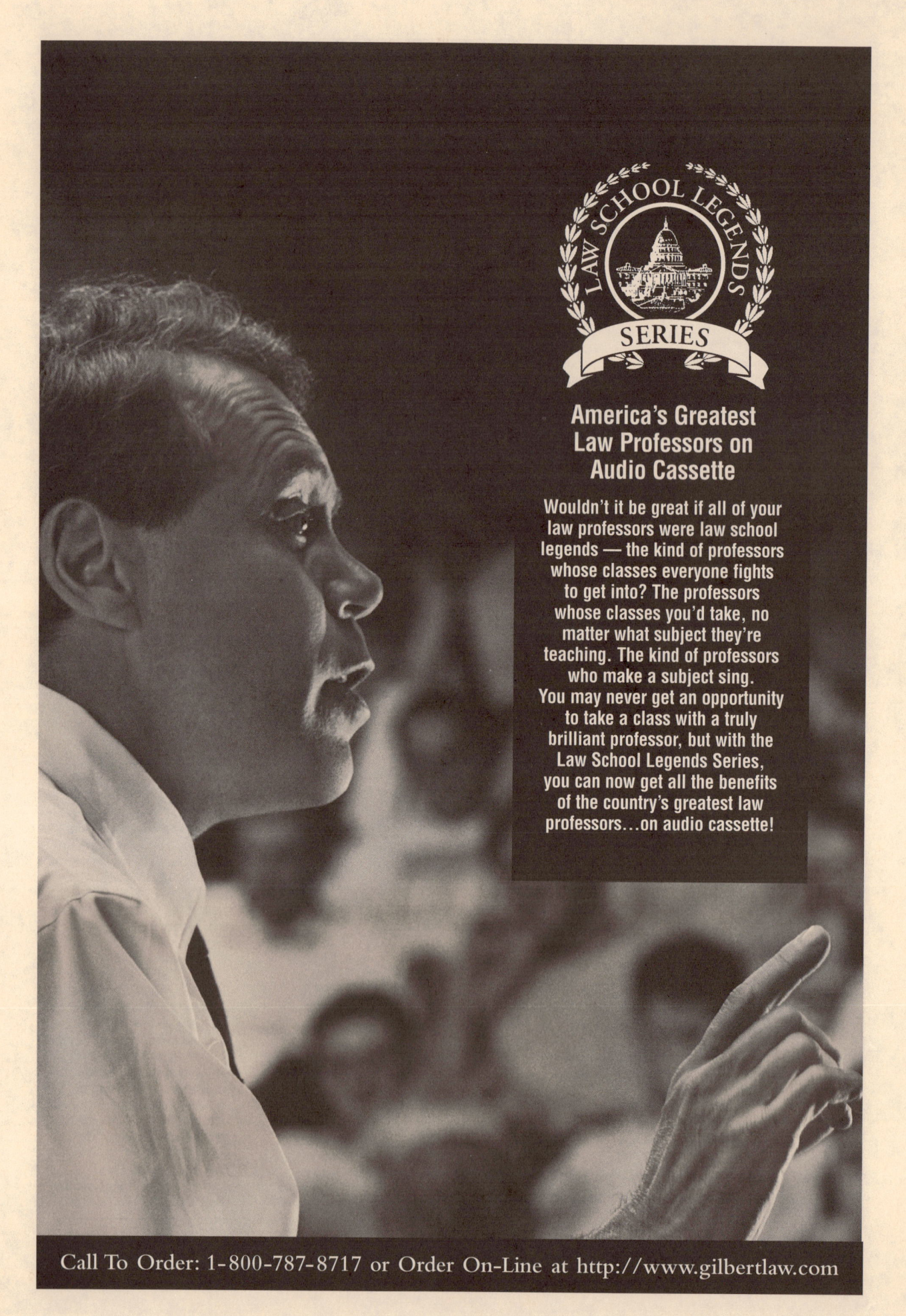

LAW SCHOOL LEGENDS SERIES

America's Greatest Law Professors on Audio Cassette

Wouldn't it be great if all of your law professors were law school legends — the kind of professors whose classes everyone fights to get into? The professors whose classes you'd take, no matter what subject they're teaching. The kind of professors who make a subject sing. You may never get an opportunity to take a class with a truly brilliant professor, but with the Law School Legends Series, you can now get all the benefits of the country's greatest law professors...on audio cassette!

Call To Order: 1-800-787-8717 or Order On-Line at http://www.gilbertlaw.com

LAW SCHOOL LEGENDS SERIES

America's Greatest Law Professors on Audio Cassette

We found the truly gifted law professors most law students can only dream about — the professors who draw rave reviews not only for their scholarship, but for their ability to make the law easy to understand. We asked these select few professors to condense their courses into a single lecture. And it's these lectures you'll find in the Law School Legends Series. With Law School Legends, you'll get a brilliant law professor explaining an entire subject to you in one simple, dynamic lecture. The Law School Legends make even the most difficult concepts crystal clear. You'll understand the big picture, and how all the concepts fit together. You'll get hundreds of examples and exam tips, honed over decades in the classroom. But best of all, you'll get insights you can only get from America's greatest law professors!

Administrative Law
Professor Patrick J. Borchers
Albany Law School of Union University
TOPICS COVERED: Classification Of Agencies; Adjudicative And Investigative Action; Rulemaking Power; Delegation Doctrine; Control By Executive; Appointment And Removal; Freedom Of Information Act; Rulemaking Procedure; Adjudicative Procedure; Trial-Type Hearings; Administrative Law Judge; Power To Stay Proceedings; Subpoena Power; Physical Inspection; Self Incrimination; Judicial Review Issues; Declaratory Judgment; Sovereign Immunity; Eleventh Amendment; Statutory Limitations; Standing; Exhaustion Of Administrative Remedies; Scope Of Judicial Review.
4 Audio Cassettes
ISBN: 0-15-900189-7 $45.95

Agency & Partnership
Professor Thomas L. Evans
University of Texas
TOPICS COVERED: Agency: Creation; Rights And Duties Of Principal And Agent; Sub-Agents; Contract Liability — Actual Authority: Express And Implied; Apparent Authority; Ratification; Liabilities Of Parties; Tort Liability — Respondeat Superior; Frolic And Detour; Intentional Torts. Partnership: Nature Of Partnership; Formation; Partnership By Estoppel; In Partnership Property; Relations Between Partners To Third Parties; Authority Of Partners; Dissolution And Termination; Limited Partnerships.
4 Audio Cassettes
ISBN: 0-15-900351-2 $45.95

Antitrust
Professor Thomas D. Morgan
George Washington University Law School
TOPICS COVERED: Antitrust Law's First Principle; Consumer Welfare Opposes Market Power; Methods of Analysis; Role of Reason, Per Se, Quick Look; Sherman Act §1: Civil & Criminal Conspiracies In Unreasonable Restraint Of Trade; Sherman Act §2: Illegal Monopolization, Attempts To Monopolize; Robinson Patman Act Price Discrimination, Related Distribution Problems; Clayton Act §7: Mengers, Joint Ventures; Antitrust & Intellectual Property; International Competitive Relationships; Exemptions & Regulated Industries; Enforcement; Price & Non-Price Restraints.
4 Audio Cassettes
ISBN: 0-15-900341-5 $39.95

Bankruptcy
Professor Elizabeth Warren
Harvard Law School
TOPICS COVERED: The Debtor/Creditor Relationship; The Commencement, Conversion, Dismissal, and Reopening Of Bankruptcy Proceedings; Property Included In The Bankruptcy Estate; Secured, Priority And Unsecured Claims; The Automatic Stay; Powers Of Avoidance; The Assumption And Rejection Of Executory Contracts; The Protection Of Exempt Property; The Bankruptcy Discharge; Chapter 13 Proceedings; Chapter 11 Proceedings; Bankruptcy Jurisdiction And Procedure.
4 Audio Cassettes
ISBN: 0-15-900273-7 $45.95

Civil Procedure
By Professor Richard D. Freer
Emory University Law School
TOPICS COVERED: Subject Matter Jurisdiction; Personal Jurisdiction; Long-Arm Statutes; Constitutional Limitations; In Rem And Quasi In Rem Jurisdiction; Service Of Process; Venue; Transfer; Forum Non Conveniens; Removal; Waiver; Governing Law; Pleadings; Joinder Of Claims; Permissive And Compulsory Joinder Of Parties; Counter-Claims And Cross-Claims; Ancillary Jurisdiction; Impleader; Class Actions; Discovery; Pretrial Adjudication; Summary Judgment; Trial; Post Trial Motions; Appeals; Res Judicata; Collateral Estoppel.
5 Audio Cassettes
ISBN: 0-15-900322-9 $59.95

Commercial Paper
By Professor Michael I. Spak
Chicago Kent College Of Law
TOPICS COVERED: Types Of Negotiable Instruments; Elements Of Negotiability; Statute Of Limitations; Payment-In-Full Checks; Negotiations Of The Instrument; Becoming A Holder-In-Due Course; Rights Of A Holder In Due Course; Real And Personal Defenses; Jus Teril; Effect Of Instrument On Underlying Obligations; Contracts Of Maker And Indorser; Suretyship; Liability Of Drawer And Drawee; Check Certification; Warranty Liability; Conversion Of Liability; Banks And Their Customers; Properly Payable Rule; Wrongful Dishonor; Stopping Payment; Death Of Customer; Bank Statement; Check Collection; Expedited Funds Availability; Forgery Of Drawer's Name; Alterations; Imposter Rule; Wire Transfers; Electronic Fund Transfers Act.
3 Audio Cassettes
ISBN: 0-15-900275-3 $39.95

Conflict Of Laws
Professor Patrick J. Borchers
Albany Law School
TOPICS COVERED: Domicile; Jurisdiction—In Personam, In Rem, Quasi In Rem; Court Competence; Forum Non Conveniens; Choice Of Law; Foreign Causes Of Action; Territorial Approach To Choice/Tort And Contract; "Escape Devices"; Most Significant Relationship; Governmental Interest Analysis; Recognition Of Judgments; Foreign Country Judgments; Domestic Judgments/Full Faith And Credit; Review Of Judgments; Modifiable Judgments; Defenses To Recognition And Enforcement; Federal/State (Erie) Problems; Constitutional Limits On Choice Of Law.
4 Audio Cassettes
ISBN: 0-15-900352-0 $39.95

Constitutional Law
By Professor John C. Jeffries, Jr.
University of Virginia School of Law
TOPICS COVERED: Introduction; Exam Tactics; Legislative Power; Supremacy; Commerce; State Regulation; Privileges And Immunities; Federal Court Jurisdiction; Separation Of Powers; Civil Liberties; Due Process; Equal Protection; Privacy; Race; Alienage; Gender; Speech And Association; Prior Restraints; Religion—Free Exercise; Establishment Clause.
5 Audio Cassettes
ISBN: 0-15-900373-3 $45.95

Contracts
By Professor Michael I. Spak
Chicago Kent College Of Law
TOPICS COVERED: Offer; Revocation; Acceptance; Consideration; Defenses To Formation; Third Party Beneficiaries; Assignment; Delegation; Conditions; Excuses; Anticipatory Repudiation; Discharge Of Duty; Modifications; Rescission; Accord & Satisfaction; Novation; Breach; Damages; Remedies; UCC Remedies; Parol Evidence Rule.
4 Audio Cassettes
ISBN: 0-15-900318-0 $45.95

Copyright Law
Professor Roger E. Schechter
George Washington University Law School
TOPICS COVERED: Constitution; Patents And Property Ownership Distinguished; Subject Matter Copyright; Duration And Renewal; Ownership And Transfer; Formalities; Introduction; Notice, Registration And Deposit; Infringement; Overview; Reproduction And Derivative Works; Public Distribution; Public Performance And Display; Exemptions; Fair Use; Photocopying; Remedies; Preemption Of State Law.
3 Audio Cassettes
ISBN: 0-15-900295-8 $39.95

Corporations
By Professor Therese H. Maynard
Loyola University Law School
TOPICS COVERED: Ultra Vires Act; Corporate Formation; Piercing The Corporate Veil; Corporate Financial Structure; Stocks; Bonds; Subscription Agreements; Watered Stock; Stock Transactions; Insider Trading; 16(b) & 10b-5 Violations; Promoters; Fiduciary Duties; Shareholder Rights; Meetings; Cumulative Voting; Voting Trusts; Close Corporations; Dividends; Preemptive Rights; Shareholder Derivative Suits; Directors; Duty Of Loyalty; Corporate Opportunity Doctrine; Officers; Amendments; Mergers; Dissolution.
4 Audio Cassettes
ISBN: 0-15-900320-2 $45.95

Criminal Law
By Professor Charles H. Whitebread
USC School of Law
TOPICS COVERED: Exam Tactics; Volitional Acts; Mental States; Specific Intent; Malice; General Intent; Strict Liability; Accomplice Liability; Inchoate Crimes; Impossibility; Defenses; Insanity; Voluntary And Involuntary Intoxication; Infancy; Self-Defense; Defense Of A Dwelling; Duress; Necessity; Mistake Of Fact Or Law; Entrapment; Battery; Assault; Homicide; Common Law Murder; Voluntary And Involuntary Manslaughter; First Degree Murder; Felony Murder; Rape; Larceny; Embezzlement; False Pretenses; Robbery; Extortion; Burglary; Arson.
4 Audio Cassettes
ISBN: 0-15-900279-6 $39.95

Call To Order: 1-800-787-8717 or Order On-Line at http://www.gilbertlaw.com

Criminal Procedure
By Professor Charles H. Whitebread
USC School of Law

TOPICS COVERED: Incorporation Of The Bill Of Rights; Exclusionary Rule; Fruit Of The Poisonous Tree; Arrest; Search & Seizure; Exceptions To Warrant Requirement; Wire Tapping & Eavesdropping; Confessions (Miranda); Pretrial Identification; Bail; Preliminary Hearings; Grand Juries; Speedy Trial; Fair Trial; Jury Trials; Right To Counsel; Guilty Pleas; Sentencing; Death Penalty; Habeas Corpus; Double Jeopardy; Privilege Against Compelled Testimony.
3 Audio Cassettes
ISBN: 0-15-900281-8 $39.95

Evidence
By Professor Faust F. Rossi
Cornell Law School

TOPICS COVERED: Relevance; Insurance; Remedial Measures; Settlement Offers; Causation; State Of Mind; Rebuttal; Habit; Character Evidence; "MIMIC" Rule; Documentary Evidence; Authentication; Best Evidence Rule; Parol Evidence; Competency; Dead Man Statutes; Examination Of Witnesses; Present Recollection Revived; Past Recollection Recorded; Opinion Testimony; Lay And Expert Witness; Learned Treatises; Impeachment; Collateral Matters; Bias, Interest Or Motive; Rehabilitation; Privileges; Hearsay And Exceptions.
5 Audio Cassettes
ISBN: 0-15-900282-6 $45.95

Family Law
Professor Roger E. Schechter
George Washington University Law School

TOPICS COVERED: Marital Relationship; Formalities And Solemnization; Common Law Marriage; Impediments; Conflict Of Laws; Non-Marital Relationship; Void And Voidable Marriages; Annulment; Divorce; Separation; Full Faith And Credit; Temporary Orders; Property Division; Community Property Principles; Equitable Distribution And Reimbursement; Marital And Separate Property; Alimony; Child Support; Enforcement Of Orders; Antenuptial And Postnuptial Agreements; Separation And Settlement Agreements; Custody; Visitation Rights; Termination Of Parental Rights; Adoption; Illegitimacy; Paternity Actions.
3 Audio Cassettes
ISBN: 0-15-900283-4 $39.95

Federal Courts
Professor John C. Jeffries
University of Virginia School of Law

TOPICS COVERED: History Of The Federal Court System; "Court Or Controversy" And Justiciability; Congressional Power Over Federal Court Jurisdiction; Supreme Court Jurisdiction; District Court Subject Matter Jurisdiction—Federal Question Jurisdiction, Diversity Jurisdiction And Admiralty Jurisdiction; Pendent And Ancillary Jurisdiction; Removal Jurisdiction; Venue; Forum Non Conveniens; Law Applied In The Federal Courts; Federal Law In The State Courts; Collateral Relations Between Federal And State Courts; The Eleventh Amendment And State Sovereign Immunity.
3 Audio Cassettes
ISBN: 0-15-900372-5 $39.95

Federal Income Tax
By Professor Cheryl D. Block
George Washington University Law School

TOPICS COVERED: Administrative Reviews; Tax Formula; Gross Income; Exclusions For Gifts; Inheritances; Personal Injuries; Tax Basis Rules; Divorce Tax Rules; Assignment Of Income; Business Deductions; Investment Deductions; Passive Loss And Interest Limitation Rules; Capital Gains & Losses; Section 1031, 1034, and 121 Deferred/Non Taxable Transactions.
4 Audio Cassettes
ISBN: 0-15-900284-2 $45.95

Future Interests
By Dean Catherine L. Carpenter
Southwestern University Law School

TOPICS COVERED: Rule Against Perpetuities; Class Gifts; Estates In Land; Rule In Shelley's Case; Future Interests In Transferor and Transferee; Life Estates; Defeasible Fees; Doctrine Of Worthier Title; Doctrine Of Merger; Fee Simple Estates; Restraints On Alienation; Power Of Appointment; Rules Of Construction.
2 Audio Cassettes
ISBN: 0-15-900285-0 $24.95

Law School Exam Writing
By Professor Charles H. Whitebread
USC School of Law

TOPICS COVERED: With "Law School Exam Writing," you'll learn the secrets of law school test taking. Professor Whitebread leads you step-by-step through his innovative system, so that you know exactly how to tackle your essay exams without making point draining mistakes. You'll learn how to read questions so you don't miss important issues; how to organize your answer; how to use limited exam time to your maximum advantage; and even how to study for exams.
1 Audio Cassette
ISBN: 0-15-900287-7 $19.95

Professional Responsibility
By Professor Erwin Chemerinsky
USC School of Law

TOPICS COVERED: Regulation of Attorneys; Bar Admission; Unauthorized Practice; Competency; Discipline; Judgment; Lawyer-Client Relationship; Representation; Withdrawal; Conflicts; Disqualification; Clients; Client Interests; Successive And Effective Representation; Integrity; Candor; Confidences; Secrets; Past And Future Crimes; Perjury; Communications; Witnesses; Jurors; The Court; The Press; Trial Tactics; Prosecutors; Market; Solicitation; Advertising; Law Firms; Fees; Client Property; Conduct; Political Activity.
3 Audio Cassettes
ISBN: 0-15-900371-7 $39.95

Real Property
By Professor Paula A. Franzese
Seton Hall Law School

TOPICS COVERED: Estates—Fee Simple, Fee Tail, Life Estate; Co-Tenancy—Joint Tenancy, Tenancy In Common, Tenancy By The Entirety; Landlord-Tenant Relationship; Liability For Condition Of Premises; Assignment & Sublease; Easements; Restrictive Covenants; Adverse Possession; Recording Acts; Conveyancing; Personal Property.
4 Audio Cassettes
ISBN: 0-15-900289-3 $45.95

Remedies
By Professor William A. Fletcher
University of California at Berkeley, Boalt Hall School of Law

TOPICS COVERED: Damages; Restitution; Equitable Remedies; Tracing; Rescission and Reformation; Injury and Destruction of Personal Property; Conversion; Injury to Real Property; Trespass; Ouster; Nuisance; Defamation; Trade Libel; Inducing Breach of Contract; Contracts to Purchase Personal Property; Contracts to Purchase Real Property (including Equitable Conversion); Construction Contracts; and Personal Service Contracts.
4 Audio Cassettes
ISBN: 0-15-900353-9 $45.95

Sales & Lease of Goods
By Professor Michael I. Spak
Chicago Kent College of Law

TOPICS COVERED: Goods; Contract Formation; Firm Offers; Statute Of Frauds; Modification; Parol Evidence; Code Methodology; Tender; Payment; Identification; Risk Of Loss; Warranties; Merchantability; Fitness; Disclaimers; Consumer Protection; Remedies; Anticipatory Repudiation; Third Party Rights.
3 Audio Cassettes
ISBN: 0-15-900291-5 $39.95

Secured Transactions
By Professor Michael I. Spak
Chicago Kent College of Law

TOPICS COVERED: Collateral; Inventory; Intangibles; Proceeds; Security Agreements; Attachment; After-Acquired Property; Perfection; Filing; Priorities; Purchase Money Security Interests; Fixtures; Rights Upon Default; Self-Help; Sale; Constitutional Issues.
3 Audio Cassettes
ISBN: 0-15-900292-3 $39.95

Securities Regulation
By Professor Therese H. Maynard
Loyola University Law School   NEW
4 Audio Cassettes
ISBN: 0-15-900359-8 $39.95

Torts
By Professor Richard J. Conviser
Chicago Kent College of Law

TOPICS COVERED: Essay Exam Techniques; Intentional Torts—Assault, Battery, False Imprisonment, Intentional Infliction Of Emotional Distress, Trespass To Land, Trespass To Chattels, Conversion; Defenses. Defamation—Libel, Slander; Defenses; First Amendment Concerns; Invasion Of Right Of Privacy; Misrepresentation; Negligence—Duty, Breach, Actual And Proximate Causation, Damages; Defenses; Strict Liability, Products Liability; Nuisance; General Tort Considerations.
4 Audio Cassettes
ISBN: 0-15-900185-4 $45.95

Wills & Trusts
By Professor Stanley M. Johanson
University of Texas School of Law

TOPICS COVERED: Attested Wills; Holographic Wills; Negligence; Revocation; Changes On Face Of Will; Lapsed Gifts; Negative Bequest Rule; Nonprobate Assets; Intestate Succession; Advancements; Elective Share; Will Contests; Capacity; Undue Influence; Creditors' Rights; Creation Of Trust; Revocable Trusts; Pourover Gifts; Charitable Trusts; Resulting Trusts; Constructive Trusts; Spendthrift Trusts; Self-Dealing; Prudent Investments; Trust Accounting; Termination; Powers Of Appointment.
4 Audio Cassettes
ISBN: 0-15-900294-X $45.95

Law School Legends Series
FIRST YEAR PROGRAM

Includes Five Law School Legends Titles:

- **Civil Procedure**
  By Professor Richard D. Freer
  Emory University Law School

- **Contracts**
  By Professor Michael I. Spak
  Chicago Kent College Of Law

- **Criminal Law**
  By Professor Charles H. Whitebread
  USC School of Law

- **Real Property**
  By Professor Paula A. Franzese
  Seton Hall Law School

- **Torts**
  By Professor Richard J. Conviser
  Chicago Kent College of Law

Plus—

- **Law School Exam Writing**
  By Professor Charles H. Whitebread
  USC Law School

All titles are packaged in a convenient carry case. $250 if purchased separately. $195 if purchased as a set. Save $55.

ISBN: 0-15-900306-7   Set $195

If you accidentally damage a tape within five years from the date of purchase we'll replace it for FREE— No questions asked!

FIVE YEAR GILBERT LAW AUDIO TAPES • TAPE REPLACEMENT GUARANTEE

Call To Order: 1-800-787-8717 or Order On-Line at http://www.gilbertlaw.com

NO QUESTIONS ASKED.

We stand behind our products... even if someone stands on them!

With the Law School Legends Series you get America's Greatest Law Professors on audio cassette — plus one of the best audio tape guarantees in the business! If you accidentally damage a Law School Legends tape within 5 years from the date of purchase, we'll replace it for free — **no questions asked!**

The Law School Legends Series
America's Greatest Law Professors on Audio Cassette

Available in Many Popular Titles. All Titles Fully Indexed for Quick Reference.

Administrative Law	Constitutional Law	Family Law	Real Property
Agency & Partnership	Contracts	Federal Courts	Remedies
Antitrust Law	Copyright Law	Federal Income Tax	Sale & Lease of Goods
Bankruptcy	Corporations	First Year Program	Secured Transactions
Civil Procedure	Criminal Law	Future Interests	Securities Regulation
Commercial Paper	Criminal Procedure	Law School Exam Writing	Torts
Conflict of Laws	Evidence	Prof. Responsibility	Wills & Trusts

Call To Order: 1-800-787-8717 or Order On-Line at http://www.gilbertlaw.com

SAVE Hundreds Of HOURS On Your READING Assignments!

Legalines

Detailed Briefs of Every Major Case Plus Summaries Of The Black Letter Law!

Call To Order: 1-800-787-8717 or Order On-Line at http://www.gilbertlaw.com

Legalines

Legalines gives you authoritative, detailed briefs of every major case in your casebook. You get a clear explanation of the facts, the issues, the court's holding and reasoning, and any significant concurrences or dissents. Even more importantly, you get an authoritative explanation of the significance of each case, and how it relates to other cases in your casebook. And with Legalines' detailed table of contents and table of cases, you can quickly find any case or concept you're looking for. But your professor expects you to know more than just the cases. That's why Legalines gives you more than just case briefs. You get summaries of the black letter law, as well. That's crucial, because some of the most important information in your casebooks isn't in the cases at all … it's the black letter principles you're expected to glean from those cases. Legalines is the only series that gives you both case briefs and black letter review. With Legalines, you get everything you need to know—whether it's in a case or not!

Administrative Law
Keyed to the Breyer Casebook
ISBN: 0-15-900169-2   176 pages $19.95
Keyed to the Gellhorn Casebook
ISBN: 0-15-900170-6   186 pages $21.95
Keyed to the Schwartz Casebook
ISBN: 0-15-900171-4   145 pages $18.95

Antitrust
Keyed to the Areeda Casebook
ISBN: 0-15-900405-5   165 pages $19.95
Keyed to the Handler Casebook
ISBN: 0-15-900390-3   158 pages $18.95

Civil Procedure
Keyed to the Cound Casebook
ISBN: 0-15-900314-8   241 pages $21.95
Keyed to the Field Casebook
ISBN: 0-15-900415-2   310 pages $23.95
Keyed to the Hazard Casebook
ISBN: 0-15-900324-5   206 pages $21.95
Keyed to the Rosenberg Casebook
ISBN: 0-15-900052-1   284 pages $21.95
Keyed to the Yeazell Casebook
ISBN: 0-15-900241-9   206 pages $20.95

Commercial Law
Keyed to the Farnsworth Casebook
ISBN: 0-15-900176-5   126 pages $18.95

Conflict of Laws
Keyed to the Cramton Casebook
ISBN: 0-15-900331-8   113 pages $16.95
Keyed to the Reese (Rosenberg) Casebook
ISBN: 0-15-900057-2   247 pages $21.95

Constitutional Law
Keyed to the Brest Casebook
ISBN: 0-15-900338-5   172 pages $19.95
Keyed to the Cohen Casebook
ISBN: 0-15-900378-4   301 pages $22.95
Keyed to the Gunther Casebook
ISBN: 0-15-900060-2   367 pages $23.95
Keyed to the Lockhart Casebook
ISBN: 0-15-900242-7   322 pages $22.95

Constitutional Law (cont'd)
Keyed to the Rotunda Casebook
ISBN: 0-15-900363-6   258 pages $21.95
Keyed to the Stone Casebook
ISBN: 0-15-900236-2   281 pages $22.95

Contracts
Keyed to the Calamari Casebook
ISBN: 0-15-900065-3   234 pages $21.95
Keyed to the Dawson Casebook
ISBN: 0-15-900268-0   188 pages $21.95
Keyed to the Farnsworth Casebook
ISBN: 0-15-900332-6   219 pages $19.95
Keyed to the Fuller Casebook
ISBN: 0-15-900237-0   184 pages $19.95
Keyed to the Kessler Casebook
ISBN: 0-15-900070-X   312 pages $22.95
Keyed to the Murphy Casebook
ISBN: 0-15-900387-3   207 pages $21.95

Corporations
Keyed to the Cary Casebook
ISBN: 0-15-900172-2   383 pages $23.95
Keyed to the Choper Casebook
ISBN: 0-15-900173-0   219 pages $21.95
Keyed to the Hamilton Casebook
ISBN: 0-15-900313-X   214 pages $21.95
Keyed to the Vagts Casebook
ISBN: 0-15-900078-5   185 pages $18.95

Criminal Law
Keyed to the Boyce Casebook
ISBN: 0-15-900080-7   290 pages $21.95
Keyed to the Dix Casebook
ISBN: 0-15-900081-5   103 pages $15.95
Keyed to the Johnson Casebook
ISBN: 0-15-900175-7   149 pages $18.95
Keyed to the Kadish Casebook
ISBN: 0-15-900333-4   167 pages $18.95
Keyed to the La Fave Casebook
ISBN: 0-15-900084-X   202 pages $20.95

Criminal Procedure
Keyed to the Kamisar Casebook
ISBN: 0-15-900336-9   256 pages $21.95

Decedents' Estates & Trusts
Keyed to the Ritchie Casebook
ISBN: 0-15-900339-3   204 pages $21.95

Domestic Relations
Keyed to the Clark Casebook
ISBN: 0-15-900168-4   119 pages $16.95
Keyed to the Wadlington Casebook
ISBN: 0-15-900377-6   169 pages $18.95

Estate & Gift Taxation
Keyed to the Surrey Casebook
ISBN: 0-15-900093-9   100 pages $15.95

Evidence
Keyed to the Sutton Casebook
ISBN: 0-15-900096-3   271 pages $19.95
Keyed to the Waltz Casebook
ISBN: 0-15-900334-2   179 pages $19.95
Keyed to the Weinstein Casebook
ISBN: 0-15-900097-1   223 pages $20.95

Family Law
Keyed to the Areen Casebook
ISBN: 0-15-900263-X   262 pages $21.95

Federal Courts
Keyed to the McCormick Casebook
ISBN: 0-15-900101-3   195 pages $18.95

Income Tax
Keyed to the Freeland Casebook
ISBN: 0-15-900361-X   134 pages $18.95
Keyed to the Klein Casebook
ISBN: 0-15-900383-0   150 pages $18.95

Labor Law
Keyed to the Cox Casebook
ISBN: 0-15-900238-9   221 pages $18.95
Keyed to the Merrifield Casebook
ISBN: 0-15-900177-3   195 pages $20.95

Property
Keyed to the Browder Casebook
ISBN: 0-15-900110-2   277 pages $21.95
Keyed to the Casner Casebook
ISBN: 0-15-900111-0   261 pages $21.95
Keyed to the Cribbet Casebook
ISBN: 0-15-900239-7   328 pages $22.95
Keyed to the Dukeminier Casebook
ISBN: 0-15-900432-2   168 pages $18.95
Keyed to the Nelson Casebook
ISBN: 0-15-900228-1   288 pages $19.95

Real Property
Keyed to the Rabin Casebook
ISBN: 0-15-900262-1   180 pages $18.95

Remedies
Keyed to the Re Casebook
ISBN: 0-15-900116-1   245 pages $22.95
Keyed to the York Casebook
ISBN: 0-15-900118-8   265 pages $21.95

Sales & Secured Transactions
Keyed to the Speidel Casebook
ISBN: 0-15-900166-8   202 pages $21.95

Securities Regulation
Keyed to the Jennings Casebook
ISBN: 0-15-900253-2   324 pages $22.95

Torts
Keyed to the Epstein Casebook
ISBN: 0-15-900335-0   193 pages $20.95
Keyed to the Franklin Casebook
ISBN: 0-15-900240-0   146 pages $18.95
Keyed to the Henderson Casebook
ISBN: 0-15-900174-9   162 pages $18.95
Keyed to the Keeton Casebook
ISBN: 0-15-900406-3   252 pages $21.95
Keyed to the Prosser Casebook
ISBN: 0-15-900301-6   334 pages $22.95

Wills, Trusts & Estates
Keyed to the Dukeminier Casebook
ISBN: 0-15-900337-7   145 pages $19.95

Call To Order: 1-800-787-8717 or Order On-Line at http://www.gilbertlaw.com

Dictionary of Legal Terms

Every Legal Term You'll Ever Need To Know... Just A Keystroke Away!

You're working away on your computer. Suddenly, you come across a legal term you don't understand. Are you going to have to waste precious time searching for your dictionary? Not anymore! The definition you're looking for will be on screen in the blink of an eye — with Gilbert's new On-Screen Dictionary of Legal Terms.

With Gilbert's on-screen dictionary, you simply highlight the word you need defined, or type it in. Then your on-screen dictionary takes over, giving you the definition you're looking for, right away. You get more than 3,500 legal terms and phrases — and that means every word you'll need throughout law school, and beyond!

But what if you come across an abbreviation you don't understand? Or one of those Latin words that show up so often in legal opinions, terms like pro tanto and res gestae? That's no problem with Gilbert's on-screen dictionary! You can instantly access the meaning of any Latin legal term (and French terms too!). You get all kinds of abbreviations, including periodical and governmental ones. You even get a complete listing of law school shorthand. No matter what kind of reference help you need, you'll find it in Gilbert's! Features over 3,500 legal terms and phrases, law school shorthand, common abbreviations, Latin and French legal terms, periodical abbreviations, and governmental abbreviations.

Includes Free Pocket Size Law Dictionary!

ISBN: 0-15-900250-8
Macintosh $27.95

ISBN: 0-15-900249-4
Windows $27.95

Call To Order: 1-800-787-8717 or Order On-Line at http://www.gilbertlaw.com

CASEBRIEFS FOR WINDOWS

100% Comprehensive, 100% Authoritative, 100% of What You Need

Detailed Briefs Of Every Major Case— At Your Fingertips!

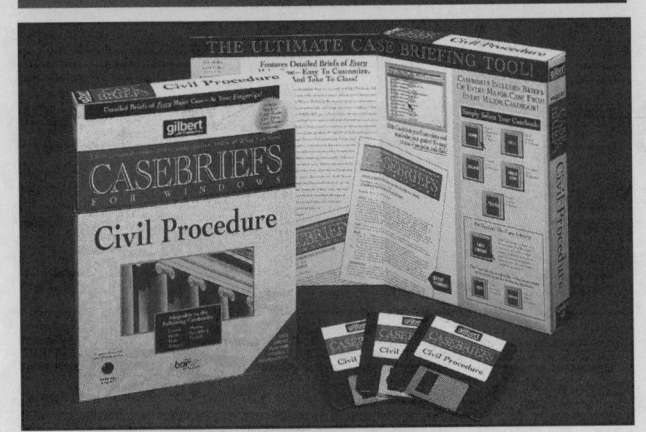

Casebriefs Interactive Software For Windows

As a law student you can't afford to waste a minute. That's why you need Casebriefs Software. With Casebriefs you simply click on the name of the case you're looking for, and you instantly have an expert brief of it at your fingertips! The facts. The issue. The holding. The rationale. Expert commentary. You'll get everything you need, whether you're preparing for class or studying for your final exam!

When you use Casebriefs, you can focus solely on the cases covered in your casebook, or you can use the Case Library, which includes briefs of all of the major cases from every major casebook. The Case Library is ideal for researching cases for writing assignments, moot court briefs, law review and other periodicals.

With Casebriefs, searching for cases is a breeze. You can search by topic. You can search alphabetically. You can search the cases in the order in which they appear in your casebook. You can even enter the date you'll cover different cases in class, and sort them by those dates. No matter how you want to look for a case, Casebriefs will help you find it instantly!

For each brief, you can add your own notes, or leave it "as is." Whether you customize the briefs or not, you can print them out and take them to class with you. You can even configure Casebriefs to access Lexis/Nexis and Westlaw directly from the Casebriefs screen (with Lexis/Nexis or Westlaw software and account). Whether you want to compare your own briefs to expert briefs, fill in gaps in your class notes, or research cases for your legal writing class, moot court, law review or other periodicals— Casebriefs is the source you'll turn to, over and over again!

Administrative Law
Includes briefs of all of the major cases from the Breyer, Gellhorn and Schwartz casebooks, many of the major cases from the Bonfield and Mashaw casebooks, plus a Case Library.
ISBN# 0-15-900190-0 $27.95

Antitrust
Includes briefs of all of the major cases from the Areeda and Handler casebooks, many of the major cases from the Sullivan casebook, plus a Case Library.
ISBN# 0-15-900400-4 $27.95

Civil Procedure
Includes briefs of all of the major cases from the Cound, Field, Hazard, Rosenberg and Yeazell casebooks, many of the major cases from the Marcus and Levin casebooks, plus a Case Library.
ISBN# 0-15-900191-9 $27.95

Commercial Law
Includes briefs of all of the major cases from the Farnsworth casebook, plus a Case Library.
ISBN# 0-15-900407-1 $27.95

Conflict Of Laws
Includes briefs of all of the major cases from the Cramton and Reese casebooks, many of the major cases from the Brilmayer casebook, plus a Case Library.
ISBN# 0-15-900192-7 $27.95

Constitutional Law
Includes briefs of all of the major cases from the Brest, Cohen, Gunther, Lockhart, Rotunda and Stone casebooks, plus a Case Library.
ISBN# 0-15-900193-5 $27.95

Contracts
Includes briefs of all of the major cases from the Calamari, Dawson, Farnsworth, Fuller, Kessler and Murphy casebooks, many of the major cases from the Burton, Crandall, Hamilton, Knapp, and Rosett casebooks, plus a Case Library.
ISBN# 0-15-900194-3 $27.95

Corporations
Includes briefs of all of the major cases from the Cary, Choper, Hamilton and Vagts casebooks, many of the major cases from the O'Kelley and Solomon casebooks, plus a Case Library.
ISBN# 0-15-900195-1 $27.95

Criminal Law
Includes briefs of all of the major cases from the Boyce, Dix, Johnson, Kadish and La Fave casebooks, many of the major cases from the Dressler, Johnson, Kaplan, Moenssens and Weinreb casebooks, plus a Case Library.
ISBN# 0-15-900196-X $27.95

Criminal Procedure
Includes briefs of all of the major cases from the Kamisar casebook, many of the major cases from the Allen, Haddad and Saltzburg casebooks, plus a Case Library.
ISBN# 0-15-900197-8 $27.95

Domestic Relations
Includes briefs of all of the major cases from the Clark and Wadlington casebooks, plus a Case Library.
ISBN# 0-15-900408-X $27.95

Estate & Gift Taxes
Includes briefs of all of the major cases from the Surrey casebook, plus a Case Library.
ISBN# 0-15-900396-2 $27.95

Evidence
Includes briefs of all of the major cases from the Sutton, Waltz, and Weinstein casebooks, many of the major cases from the Strong and Mueller casebooks, plus a Case Library.
ISBN# 0-15-900198-6 $27.95

Family Law
Includes briefs of all of the major cases from the Areen casebook, many of the major cases from the Clark, Ellman, Krause and Wadlington casebooks, plus a Case Library.
ISBN# 0-15-900199-4 $27.95

Federal Courts
Includes briefs of all of the major cases from the McCormick casebook, many of the major cases from the Bator, Currie, Low and Redish casebooks, plus a Case Library.
ISBN# 0-15-900409-8 $27.95

Income Tax
Includes briefs of all of the major cases from the Freeland and Klein casebooks, many of the major cases from the Burke and Graetz casebooks, plus a Case Library.
ISBN# 0-15-900200-1 $27.95

Labor Law
Includes briefs of all of the major cases from the Cox and Merrifield casebooks, many of the major cases from the Harper, Leslie and Meltzer casebooks, plus a Case Library.
ISBN# 0-15-900410-1 $27.95

Property
Includes briefs of all of the major cases from the Casner, Cribbet, Dukeminier and Rabin casebooks, many of the major cases from the Donahue, Johnson, Kurtz, and Singer casebooks, plus a Case Library.
ISBN# 0-15-900201-X $27.95

Remedies
Includes briefs of all of the major cases from the Re and York casebooks, many of the major cases from the Leavell and Shoben casebooks, plus a Case Library.
ISBN# 0-15-900202-8 $27.95

Securities Regulation
Includes briefs of all of the major cases from the Jennings casebook, many of the major cases from the Cox casebook, plus a Case Library.
ISBN# 0-15-900411-X $27.95

Torts
Includes briefs of all of the major cases from the Epstein, Franklin, Henderson, Keeton and Prosser casebooks, many of the major cases from the Christie, Dobbs and Shulman casebooks, plus a Case Library.
ISBN# 0-15-900203-6 $27.95

Wills, Trusts & Estates
Includes briefs of all of the major cases from the Dukeminier casebook, many of the major cases from the Wagoner casebook, plus a Case Library.
ISBN# 0-15-900204-4 $27.95

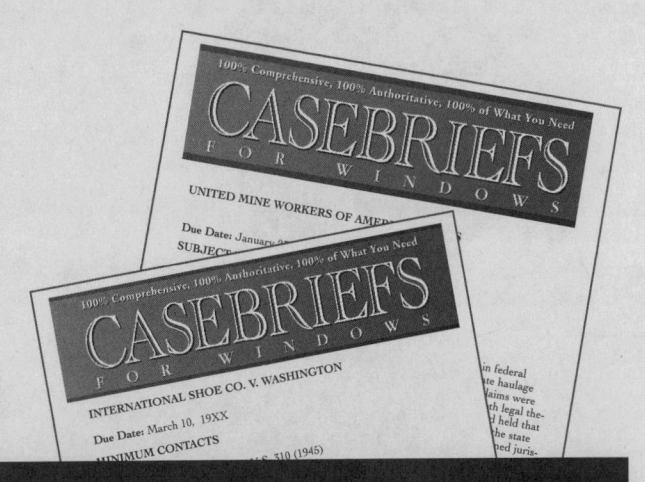

Call To Order: 1-800-787-8717 or Order On-Line at http://www.gilbertlaw.com

Check us out

www.gilbertlaw.com

America's Best-Selling Legal Employment Guides!

gilbert LAW SUMMARIES

Gilbert, Legalines, Casebriefs, Law School Legends plus Much More!

CASEBRIEFS FOR WINDOWS

Detailed Briefs of Every Major Case — Easy to Customize, Print and Take to Class!

THE JOB GODDESS

E-mail the Job Goddess with Your Job Search Questions!

100 NEW EXAMS!

Test Your Knowledge with Hundreds of Past Exams from Law Schools Nationwide!

Call To Order: 1-800-787-8717 or Order On-Line at http://www.gilbertlaw.com

on the Internet!

Order On-Line!

www.gilbertlaw.com

Pre-Law Center
Learn what law school is really like including what to expect on exams. Order your free 32-page color catalog and a free 88-page sample of Gilbert Law Summaries for Civil Procedure — the most feared first year course!

Bookstore
Review detailed information on over 200 of America's most popular legal study aids — Gilbert Law Summaries, Legalines, Casebriefs, Law School Legends audio tapes and much more. Order on-line!

gilbert LAW SUMMARIES

Past Exam Library
Browse hundreds of past exams from law schools across the country. Test your knowledge with true/false, multiple choice, short answer, essay – all of the question types (with answers!) you'll see on your midterm and final exams. Includes exams from some of the country's greatest law professors. If you can pass their exams — you can pass any exam!

100 NEW EXAMS!

Links to Law Sites
Links to hundreds of law-related sites on the web, including:
- Legal Publications
- International Law
- Legal Research
- Department of Justice
- Legal Employment
- Legal Associations

Order Products On-line!
Fast, easy and secure on-line ordering is now available 24 hours per day, 7 days per week!

Employment Center
E-mail the Job Goddess with your job search questions, and download a free copy of *The Myths of Legal Job Searches: The 9 Biggest Mistakes Law Students Make*. View content from some of America's best selling legal employment guides, including *Guerrilla Tactics For Getting The Legal Job Of Your Dreams* and *The National Directory of Legal Employers*.

THE JOB GODDESS

Wanted! Student Marketing Reps
Become a campus representative and earn hundreds of dollars of free product from Gilbert Law Summaries, Legalines, Casebriefs and more! Join our national marketing program and help promote America's most popular legal study aids at your law school!

1st Year Survival Manual
A must-read for 1L's! Learn how to prepare for class, how to handle class discussions, and the keys to successful exam performance — plus much more!

Taking the Bar Exam?
Learn how to make the transition from law school exams to the bar exam — including what to expect on the MBE, MPT, MPRE, MEE and state essay exams.

Welcome Center
Whether you're about to enter law school or you're already under way, we've created this site to help you succeed!

Call To Order: 1-800-787-8717 or Order On-Line at http://www.gilbertlaw.com

Employment Guides

A collection of best selling titles that help you identify and reach your career goals.

Guerrilla Tactics for Getting the Legal Job of Your Dreams
Kimm Alayne Walton, J.D.

Whether you're looking for a summer clerkship or your first permanent job after school, this revolutionary book is the key to getting the job of your dreams!

Guerrilla Tactics for Getting the Legal Job of Your Dreams leads you step-by-step through everything you need to do to nail down that perfect job! You'll learn hundreds of simple-to-use strategies that will get you exactly where you want to go. You'll Learn:
- The seven magic opening words in cover letters that ensure you'll get a response.
- The secret to successful interviews every time.
- Killer answers to the toughest interview questions they'll ever ask you.
- Plus Much More!

Guerrilla Tactics features the best strategies from the country's most innovative law school career advisors. The strategies in *Guerrilla Tactics* are so powerful that it even comes with a guarantee: Follow the advice in the book, and within one year of graduation you'll have the job of your dreams ... or your money back!

Pick up a copy of *Guerrilla Tactics* today ... you'll be on your way to the job of your dreams!

ISBN: 0-15-900317-2 $24.95

Proceed With Caution: A Diary Of The First Year At One Of America's Largest, Most Prestigious Law Firms
William R. Keates

Prestige. Famous clients. High-profile cases. Not to mention a starting salary approaching six figures.

In *Proceed With Caution*, the author takes you behind the scenes, to show you what it's really like to be a junior associate at a huge law firm. After graduating from an Ivy League law school, he took a job as an associate with one of New York's blue-chip law firms.

He also did something not many people do. He kept a diary, where he spelled out his day-to-day life at the firm in graphic detail.

Proceed With Caution excerpts the diary, from his first day at the firm to the day he quit. From the splashy benefits, to the nitty-gritty on the work junior associates do, to the grind of long and unpredictable hours, to the stress that eventually made him leave the firm — he tells story after story that will make you feel as though you're living the life of a new associate.

Whether you're considering a career with a large firm, or you're just curious about what life at the top firms is all about — *Proceed With Caution* is a must read!

ISBN: 0-15-900181-1 $17.95

The Official Guide To Legal Specialties
Lisa Shanholtzer

With *The Official Guide To Legal Specialties* you'll get a behind the scenes glimpse at dozens of legal specialties. Not just lists of what to expect, real life stories from top practitioners in each field. You'll learn exactly what it's like to be in some of America's most desirable professions. You'll get expert advice on what it takes to get a job in each field. How much you'll earn and what the day-to-day life is really like, the challenges you'll face, and the benefits you'll enjoy. With *The Official Guide To Legal Specialties* you'll have a wealth of information at your fingertips!

Includes the following specialties:

Banking	Intellectual Property
Communications	International
Corporate	Labor/Employment
Criminal	Litigation
Entertainment	Public Interest
Environmental	Securities
Government Practice	Sports
Health Care	Tax
Immigration	Trusts & Estates

ISBN: 0-15-900391-1 $17.95

Beyond L.A. Law: Inspiring Stories of People Who've Done Fascinating Things With A Law Degree
National Association for Law Placement

Anyone who watches television knows that being a lawyer means working your way up through a law firm — right?

Wrong!

Beyond L.A. Law gives you a fascinating glimpse into the lives of people who've broken the "lawyer" mold. They come from a variety of backgrounds — some had prior careers, others went straight through college and law school, and yet others have overcome poverty and physical handicaps. They got their degrees from all different kinds of law schools, all over the country. But they have one thing in common: they've all pursued their own, unique vision.

As you read their stories, you'll see how they beat the odds to succeed. You'll learn career tips and strategies that work, from people who've put them to the test. And you'll find fascinating insights that you can apply to your own dream, whether it's a career in law or anything else!

From Representing Baseball In Australia. To International Finance. To Children's Advocacy. To Directing a Nonprofit Organization. To Entrepreneur.

If You Think Getting A Law Degree Means Joining A Traditional Law Firm — Think Again!

ISBN: 0-15-900182-X $17.95

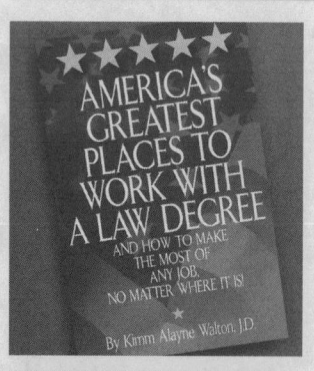

America's Greatest Places To Work With A Law Degree
Kimm Alayne Walton, J.D.

"Where do your happiest graduates work?" That's the question that author Kimm Alayne Walton asked of law school administrators around the country. Their responses revealed the hundreds of wonderful employers profiled in *America's Greatest Places To Work With A Law Degree*.

In this remarkable book, you'll get to know an incredible variety of great places to work, including:
- Glamorous sports and entertainment employers — the jobs that sound as though they would be great, and they are!
- The 250 best law firms to work for between 20 and 600 attorneys.
- Companies where law school graduates love to work and not just as in-house counsel.
- Wonderful public interest employers – the "white knight" jobs that are so incredibly satisfying.
- Court-related positions, where lawyers entertain fascinating issues, tremendous variety, and an enjoyable lifestyle.
- Outstanding government jobs, at the federal, state, and local level.

Beyond learning about incredible employers, you'll discover:
- The ten traits that define a wonderful place to work ... the sometimes surprising qualities that outstanding employers share.
- How to handle law school debt, when your dream job pays less than you think you need to make.
- How to find — and get! — great jobs at firms with fewer than 20 attorneys.

And no matter where you work, you'll learn expert tips for making the most of your job. You'll learn the specific strategies that distinguish people headed for the top ... how to position yourself for the most interesting, high-profile work ... how to handle difficult personalities ... how to negotiate for more money ... and what to do now to help you get your next great job!

ISBN: 0-15-900180-3 $24.95

About The Author

Kimm Alayne Walton is the author of numerous books and articles including two national best seller's — *America's Greatest Places To Work With A Law Degree* and *Guerrilla Tactics For Getting The Legal Job Of Your Dreams*. She is a renowned motivational speaker, lecturing at law schools and bar associations nationwide, and in her spare time, she has taken up travel writing, which has taken her swimming with crocodiles in Kakadu, and scuba diving with sharks on the Great Barrier Reef.

E-mail the Job Goddess with your own legal job search questions!
Visit www.gilbertlaw.com for details.

Call To Order: 1-800-787-8717 or Order On-Line at http://www.gilbertlaw.com

Employment Guides

A collection of best selling titles that help you identify and reach your career goals.

Company Information

1. Name, Address, and Phone Number Of Hiring Partner
2. Demographics
3. Primary Practice Areas
4. Benefits
5. Pro Bono
6. Public Interest Fellowships
7. Minority Recruitment Efforts
8. Non-Discrimination Policy
9. Narrative

Employment Information

10. Office Size
11. Total Firm Size
12. Job Opportunities
13. Summer Associate Information
14. Application Timeline For Summer Associates
15. Hiring Criteria For All Job Openings
16. Salary Information
17. Other Compensation
18. Other Data
19. Partnership Data
20. Other Offices
21. Campus Interviews

The National Directory Of Legal Employers
National Association for Law Placement

The National Directory of Legal Employers brings you a universe of vital information about 1,000 of the nation's top legal employers— *in one convenient volume!*

It includes:
- Over 22,000 job openings.
- The names, addresses and phone numbers of hiring partners.
- Listings of firms by state, size, kind and practice area.
- What starting salaries are for full time, part time, and summer associates, plus a detailed description of firm benefits.
- The number of employees by gender and race, as well as the number of employees with disabilities.
- A detailed narrative of each firm, plus much more!

The National Directory Of Legal Employers has been the best kept secret of top legal career search professionals for over a decade. Now, for the first time, it is available in a format specifically designed for law students and new graduates. *Pick up your copy of the Directory today!*

ISBN: 0-15-900434-9 $39.95

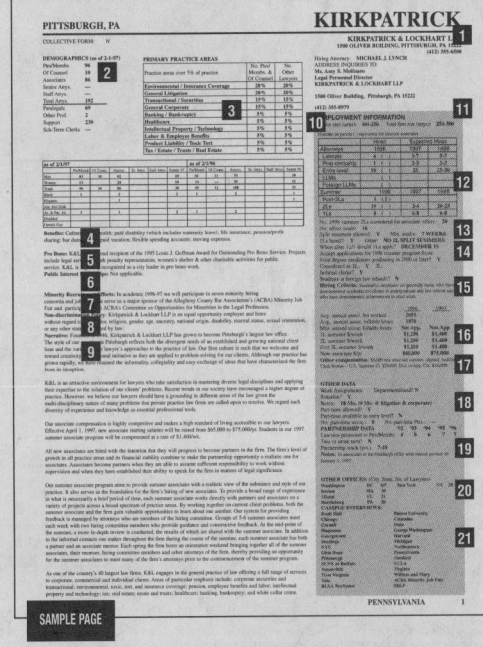

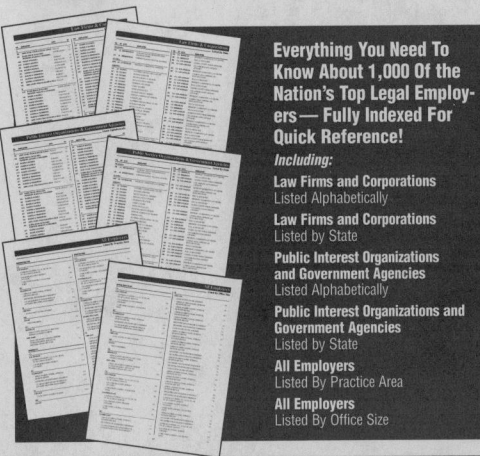

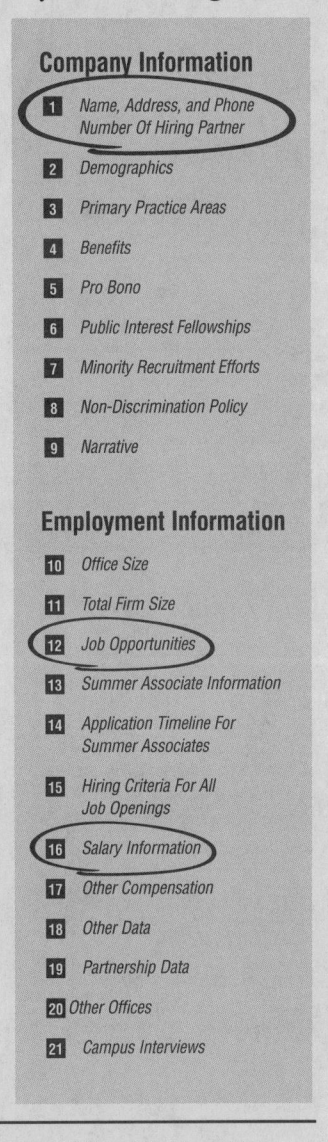

Everything You Need To Know About 1,000 Of the Nation's Top Legal Employers — Fully Indexed For Quick Reference!

Including:
- **Law Firms and Corporations** Listed Alphabetically
- **Law Firms and Corporations** Listed by State
- **Public Interest Organizations and Government Agencies** Listed Alphabetically
- **Public Interest Organizations and Government Agencies** Listed by State
- **All Employers** Listed By Practice Area
- **All Employers** Listed By Office Size

The Best Of The Job Goddess
Kimm Alayne Walton, J.D.

In her popular **Dear Job Goddess** column, legal job-search expert Kimm Alayne Walton provides the answers to even the most difficult job search dilemmas facing law students and law school graduates. Relying on career experts from around the country, the Job Goddess provides wise and witty advice for every obstacle that stands between you and your dream job!

ISBN: 0-15-900393-8 $14.95

SAMPLE COLUMN

Business Card Resumes: Good Idea, Or Not?

Dear Job Goddess,

One of my friends showed me something called a "business card resume." What he did was to have these business cards printed up, with his name and phone number on one side, and highlights from his resume on the other side. He said a bunch of people are doing this, so that when they meet potential employers they hand over these cards. Should I bother getting some for myself?

Curious in Chicago

Dear Curious,

Sigh, You know, Curious, that the Job Goddess takes a fairly dim view of resumes as a job-finding tool, even in their full-blown bond-papered, engraved 8-1/2x11" incarnation. And here you ask about a business card resume, two steps further down the resume food chain. So, no, you *shouldn't* bother with business card resumes. Here's why.

Think for a moment, Curious, about the kind of circumstance in which you'd be tempted to whip out one of these incredible shrinking resumes. You're at a social gathering. You happen to meet Will Winken, of the law firm Winken, Blinken, and Nod, and it becomes clear fairly quickly that Will is a) friendly, and b) a potential employer. The surest way to turn this chance encounter into a job is to use it as the basis for future contact. As Carolyn Bregman, Career Services Director at Emory Law School, points out, "Follow up with a phone call or note, mentioning something Winken said to you." You can say that you'd like to follow up on whatever it is he said, or that you've since read more about him and found that he's an expert on phlegm reclamation law and how that's a topic that's always fascinated you, and invite him for coffee at his convenience so you can learn more about it. What have you done? *You've taken a social encounter and* turned it into a potential job opportunity. And that makes the Job Goddess very proud.

But what happens if you, instead, whip out your business card resume, and say, "Gee, Mr. Winken, nice meeting you. Here's my business card resume, in case you ever need anybody like me." *Now* what have you done? You have, with one simple gesture, wiped out any excuse to follow up! Instead of having a phone call or a note from you that is personalized to Winken, you've got a piddling little standardized card with your vital statistics on it. Ugh. I know you're much more memorable, Curious, than anything you could possibly fit on the back of a business card.

So there you have it, Curious. Save the money you'll spend on a business card resume, and spend it later, when you have a *real* business card to print, reading, "Curious, Esq. Winken, Blinken, and Nod, Attorneys at Law."

Yours Eternally,

The Job Goddess

Call To Order: 1-800-787-8717 or Order On-Line at http://www.gilbertlaw.com

★★★★★

AMERICA'S GREATEST PLACES TO WORK WITH A LAW DEGREE

AND HOW TO MAKE THE MOST OF ANY JOB, NO MATTER WHERE IT IS!

★

By Kimm Alayne Walton, J.D.

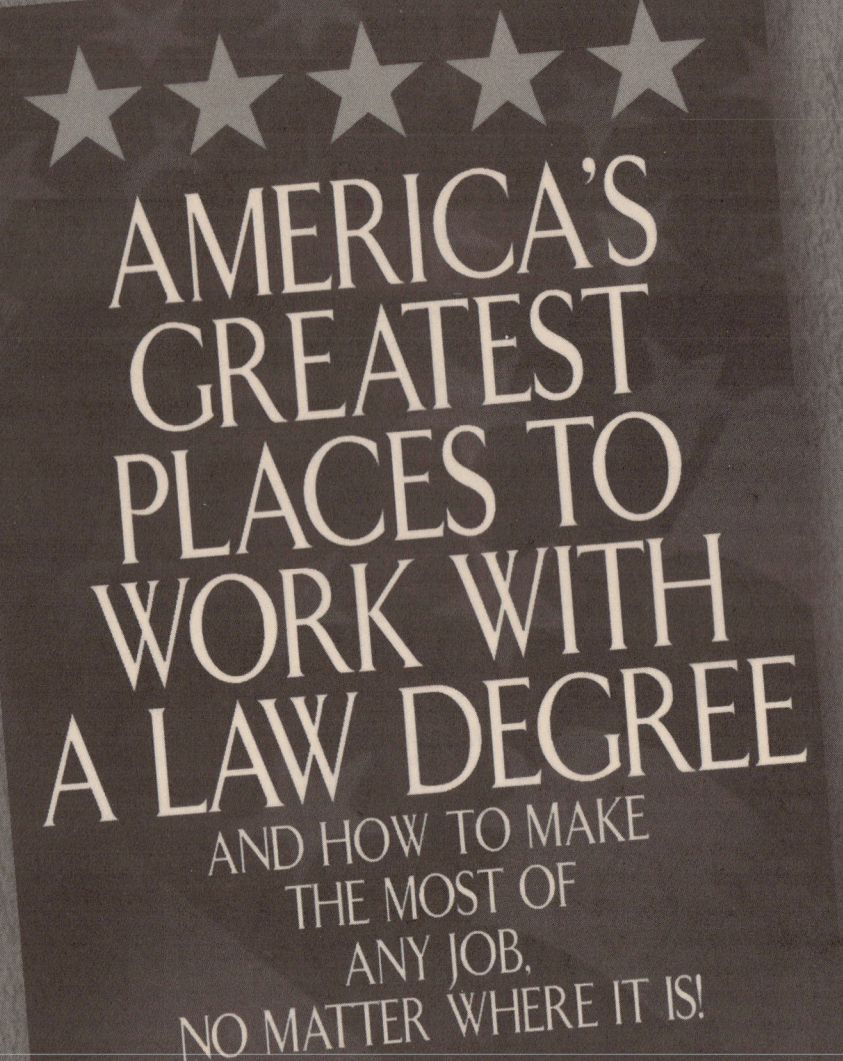

Features Hundreds Of Traditional and Non-Traditional Employers

Discover The Places Where Law School Graduates Love To Work!

Available At Your Law School Bookstore
Order Toll-Free: 1-800-787-8717
Order Online: www.gilbertlaw.com

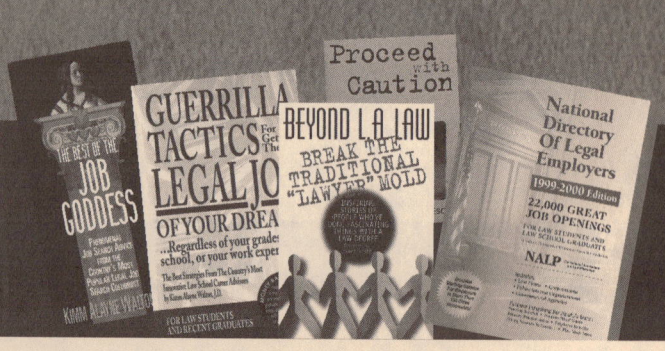